# JAPANESE BUDDHISM

# JAPANESE BUDDHISM

BY THE LATE

SIR CHARLES ELIOT
P.C., G.C.M.G., C.B.
Sometime H. M. Ambassador at Tokyo

WITH A MEMOIR OF THE AUTHOR BY

SIR HAROLD PARLETT

GYAN

*Published by*

GYAN

Gyan Publishing House
5, Ansari Road
Daryaganj, New Delhi-110002
Phone: 011-47034999, 9811692060
E-mail: books@gyanbooks.com

*Distribution Network*
gyanbooks.com
India, USA, Canada, UK, Australia, France



ISBN : 978-81-212-2921-0 (PB)
First Published, 1923

2nd Impression 2021

*Printed at:* Gyan Press, Delhi.



**Japanese Buddhism**
Author: Sir Charles Eliot

# JAPANESE BUDDHISM

BY THE LATE

SIR CHARLES ELIOT

P.C., G.C.M.G., C.B.

*Sometime H.M. Ambassador at Tokyo*

WITH A MEMOIR OF THE AUTHOR BY

SIR HAROLD PARLETT

ROUTLEDGE & KEGAN PAUL LTD

Broadway House, 68-74 Carter Lane

London, E.C.4.

# CONTENTS

## BOOK III. THE SECTS AND THEIR DOCTRINES.

## *IN PIAM MEMORIAM*

*Japanese Buddhism* is complementary to Sir Charles Eliot's earlier work, *Hinduism and Buddhism,* which appeared in 1921.[1] It may be asked what influenced him in the selection of this particular field for investigation, why his choice did not instead fall on China, Tibet, Burma, or Siam, older adherents to the faith and closer to its cradle. A partial answer is perhaps to be found in certain advantages which Japan offered for his purpose. For although in all these countries alike a vast wealth of material existed,—canonical writings, exegetical literature, and the like,—the accumulation of centuries of patient and pious toil, not in every one was it equally accessible ; and in China, in fact, it was scattered over a very wide area. In Japan, however, not only was this material available in a form both compact and complete ; but also, owing to the insular position of the country, to its entire immunity from invasion, and to a practical isolation from the rest of the world extending over more than two hundred years, the practices, ritual, documents, and iconography of Mahayanist Buddhism had been preserved in singular integrity. To quote the author's own words, the Buddhism of Japan was "the lineal and recognized descendant of the creed held by Nâgârjuna, Vasubandhu, and Śântideva". Moreover, its history offered phenomena of peculiar interest to the student of religion in Europe,—the conflict between Church and State, the growth of protestant sects "casting aside ritual to offer the common man salvation by faith" or preaching national or universal religion, the evolution of an Established Church lapsing finally into comfortable torpor,—to mention only a few examples We may conjecture that these were all material factors in shaping his choice. To them might be added a deep and abiding interest in Japan itself and its people, the unique opportunities which his position offered for the collection of the data required, and, finally, the fact that he had been obliged, for reasons beyond his control, materially to abridge the section of his work on the religions of India devoted to the discussion of the history and development of Buddhism in Japan. For when Sir Charles Eliot wrote *Hinduism and Buddhism* he was still, so to speak, a private individual, responsible to none for his opinions or their expression ; but before

[1] Published by Edward Arnold (1921). Reissued by Routledge & Kegan Paul (1954).

the moment arrived for its publication he had been appointed Ambassador in Tokyo; and, feeling that he was no longer a free lance, at liberty to write as he pleased, he decided that the chapters dealing with Japanese Buddhism must be drastically cut down and the subject treated only in the most general manner. The survey in *Hinduism and Buddhism* was therefore very brief. The material he had accumulated was nevertheless not to be lost; for he determined to make it the foundation of an entirely separate work, to be written in the distant future when his official connection with Japan should be severed.

It is on these rejected chapters, supplemented by a mass of additional information gathered during his six years' residence in the country, that *Japanese Buddhism* is based. The actual writing of it was begun in the autumn of 1926 at Nara, some months after his retirement, and, except for a brief interruption, when he turned aside to prepare two articles for the new edition of the Encyclopædia Britannica,[1] occupied most of his time till the spring of 1928. There followed a short visit to Europe; but early in 1929 he was back at work again in Nara; and by the close of the next year only the last chapter of the book, which deals with the Nichiren sect, remained unwritten. His task thus almost ended, he began to make arrangements to return to England, proposing to complete at home the final preparation of his MS. for the printer. But this was not to be. In December of 1930 he had a severe attack of influenza; and although he succeeded eventually in shaking it off, the disease had in the meantime wholly undermined a constitution never robust and already gravely impaired by another malady. He was thus really unfit to face the long and tedious voyage before him; but, despite the advice of his friends, he was determined to keep to his plans; and, accordingly, in February of 1931 he sailed from Kobe, travelling, as was his habit, via Suez in a Japanese steamer. At the start his health showed signs of improvement; but this, alas, was only momentary, and by the time the ship reached Singapore his condition had become so serious that it was clear to all that he would never live to reach his destination. Even then he insisted on continuing his journey. Two days later, on the 16th of March, he died and was buried at sea in the Straits of Malacca.

[1] He had already contributed to the 11th edition articles on Asia (History), Esthonia (in part), Hungary (language), the Tartars (in part), the Turks, etc.

It was at the close of the chapter on the Zen sect that he laid down his pen, not to take it up again. His executors have thus been faced with a dilemma. Must the book be published as it stood, incomplete, or should the missing chapter be added, written by another hand ? It was decided after careful consideration that the latter was probably what he himself would have preferred ; and thereupon Mr. G. B. Sansom,[1] of the British Embassy in Tokyo, who had read the manuscript in its draft form and had also supplied Sir Charles Eliot with a considerable amount of information on points relating to Japanese history and art, was asked to undertake the task. The last chapter is therefore his. He, too, has been responsible for the arrangement of the manuscript for the printer and, in particular, for the editing of the notes, many of which, as is indicated by marginal comments, the author meant to cut out entirely or greatly to abbreviate. The chapter headings and the index have been prepared under the superintendence of the publishers. It seems, however, almost superfluous to remark that *Japanese Buddhism* as it now leaves the printer's hands is not what it would have been had Sir Charles Eliot lived to complete it and to make those revisions he certainly contemplated; but at least it may be said that nothing has been added, nothing taken away, without careful study of all notes and other evidence which could be interpreted as showing his intention ; and, except perhaps for two-thirds of the chapter on the Nichiren sect, the book is in his own words.

In the preparation of this work its author doubtless had frequent occasion to seek advice from friends and other scholars ; but on this point our information is unfortunately incomplete. Among those, however, to whom he was certainly indebted are Professor Masaharu Anesaki and Professor Junjirō Takakusu,—those two great authorities on the religions and philosophies of the Far East,—Dr. Teitarō Suzuki, of the Ōtani University in Kyoto, the Reverend Kokai Kitagawara, of the Tōdaiji monastery at Nara, Professor Shōun Togao, of the Koyasan University, Mr. Sansom himself, as we have shown, and, last but by no means least, Mr. Shūten Inouye, of His Majesty's Consulate-General in Kobe. He must also have obtained much valuable material from the authorities of the innumerable temples and monasteries which he visited in the course of his travels in Japan ; but here we have no names to guide

[1] Author of *Japan, a Short Cultural History*, the Crpsset Press, London, 1931.

us. To all those friends, known and unknown, who helped him he would unquestionably have wished to express his indebtedness.

* * * * *

It is perhaps not unfitting that the preface of his last work should contain some account, however brief and imperfect, of the life and career of this great scholar and distinguished servant of the Empire.

He came of old and honourable stock, claiming on his father's side a distant kinship with two well-known houses of the west country,—St. Germans and Mount Edgcumbe,—and, on his mother's, descent from that Sir Thomas Wyatt, poet and courtier, who was sometime Ambassador of King Henry the Eighth at the Court of the Emperor Charles the Fifth and whose son, another Sir Thomas Wyatt, of name more familiar, died on the scaffold in the reign of Queen Mary. The family would appear to have remained through many generations closely connected with the county of its origin; but little is known of its fortunes. Towards the end of the eighteenth century, however, an Edward Eliot was Vicar of Maker, a village between Port Eliot and Mount Edgcumbe in Cornwall. His son Edward became a Fellow of Exeter College, Oxford, held for some years the post of Archdeacon of Barbados in the West Indies, then, returning to England, settled down finally as Vicar of Norton Bavant near Warminster in Wiltshire, a living in the gift of the Lord Chancellor. This Eliot in turn had a son, also named Edward, who, after a distinguished University career ending with a Fellowship at New College, decided to adopt the law as a profession, but, abandoning his intention before he had been called to the Bar, followed the family tradition and took Holy Orders instead. At Tredington in Worcestershire, where he was later curate, he fell in love with and married a very beautiful and clever girl, Elizabeth Harriet Wyatt Watling, the youngest daughter of the Rector of the parish. From Tredington the newly married pair went to live at Sibford Gower, a small independent cure in Oxfordshire; and, here, on the 8th of January, 1862, was born the subject of this memoir, Charles Norton Edgcumbe Eliot, the third, in direct descent, of a line of scholars, and destined to be by far the most distinguished. Shortly afterwards the family again moved, on this occasion to the living of Norton Bavant,—son thus succeeding father; and there the greater part of young Eliot's boyhood was passed.

At a very early age he began to show signs of mental ability quite out of the ordinary; but he was delicate and highly strung, and for this reason his education during its early stages was left almost entirely in the hands of his father. Under the latter's scholarly guidance the boy made rapid progress, and not only mastered with ease the grammar of the two great dead languages, but in his leisure devoured as well the contents of every book upon which he could lay hands; so that when he finally left home for school he was already equipped with a store of knowledge, classical and other, far beyond his years. It is told of him, for instance, among other things, that he then already knew by heart most, if not all, of the Odes of Horace.

In 1872, at the age of ten and a half, he was sent to Cheltenham College, the Headmaster of which was at that time the Reverend Herbert Snow,[1] one of the finest classical scholars of the day. Here he quickly made his mark in form, the cleverest boy, so it was said, that Cheltenham had had within its walls for many a long day; but he lacked some of those qualities which are essential for success and popularity in an English public school, where the unusual is viewed with distrust and the athlete more esteemed than the scholar. He was studious and shy, already showing signs of that aloofness which was to become so conspicuous a characteristic later, and he had neither liking nor aptitude for games. The latter disability he never overcame; and throughout life his attitude towards sport in any shape or form was one of slightly amused contempt. Readers of *Turkey in Europe* will remember his gibe at the "peculiar pleasures" of that harmless personality, the angler. "I am no sportsman myself," he writes, "and cannot conceive why anybody should try to catch a big fish with a rod when he can pay a fisherman to catch him with a net." This idiosyncrasy is the more remarkable because he was quite devoid of effeminacy and, as his subsequent wanderings in remote and barbarous regions of the earth amply demonstrated, both willing and able, when the need arose, to endure physical hardship and discomfort. But to each his limitations; and on the Honours Boards of his school, at all events, no name, not even that of the boy who was later to become Lord Chancellor and Earl Loreburn, is so conspicuous as that of Charles Eliot. Outside the classroom he lived his own life and went his own way, occupying his leisure with the study of natural history or of strange languages and religions.

[1] He later changed his name to Kynaston.

In 1879 he won an open scholarship at Balliol College; but this success was followed almost immediately by a serious nervous breakdown, and on the advice of a great specialist of the day, Sir James Crichton Browne, he was sent on a voyage to the West Indies. From this he returned speaking Spanish fluently. In 1880 he went up to Oxford, a contemporary of Sir Edward Grey,[1] the Hon. George Nathaniel Curzon,[2] Cecil Spring-Rice,[3] J. A. Hamilton,[4] W. R. Hardie,[5] F. W. Pember, Anthony Hope Hawkins,[6] Leonard Huxley,[7] Oliver Elton, D. S. MacColl, and Michael E. Sadler.[8] The last four, particularly Leonard Huxley, at whose home he was at this period a frequent visitor, were to become the most intimate of his friends, as far as intimacy was possible with one who walked so much in a world remote. He was very young, not yet nineteen, when he went into residence, but already an arresting personality. "A slim, willowy youth," so Dr. MacColl describes him, "bright-eyed ('like a hawk on its good behaviour' is Sadler's word), mobile-lipped and speaking with an anxious courtesy, punctuated with a laughing inflexion of the breath."[9] The "anxious courtesy" and the "laughing inflexion of the breath" were still noticeable forty years later. He was "full of the best jests (rather confidentially communicated)," writes Sir Michael Sadler, "but with a grave, sad look about his smile. . . . Perfectly unassuming, yet formidable, cordial but hardly ever intimate. . . . *Anima naturaliter intellectualis*, but sad, though without *accidie*; questing, critical, secretly ill at ease; cynical only when offended by pretentiousness or cocksureness; feeling his great power, but uncertain how to use it. Inwardly very old for his age; outwardly a gentle, rather diffident youth."

His career at Oxford was one of unusual brilliance, almost a triumphal progress, yet marked by no outward signs of the industry which is an expected ingredient of success. He seemed in fact to float effortless, the fortunate possessor of some magic talisman, from distinction to distinction. He took a First Class in Moderations; in 1881 he won the Hertford Scholarship, in 1883 the Boden

[1] The late Lord Grey of Fallodon.

[2] The late Lord Curzon of Kedleston.

[3] The late Sir Cecil Spring-Rice, at one time H.M. Ambassador at Washington.

[4] The late Lord Sumner.

[5] Late Professor of Humanity in the University of Edinburgh; no longer living.

[6], [7] Both died in 1933.

[8] Now Sir Michael Sadler.

[9] From an article in the *Week-End Review*, 9th May, 1931.

Sanskrit and the Ireland Scholarships, in 1884 the Craven Scholarship and the Syriac Prize, and in 1886 the Derby Scholarship. In 1884 he secured a First Class in *Literae Humaniores*, and almost immediately afterwards was made an Official Fellow of Trinity College, before he had taken his degree. There followed a year during which he took pupils in Classics; then he was nominated to a Research Fellowship, with the duty of studying Turkish or Arabic (subsequently, on his appointment to St. Petersburg, altered to Finnish); and when this expired he was elected to an "Extraordinary" Fellowship. He was thus greatly beholden to Trinity. Indeed he never severed his connection with that College, for he repeatedly revisited it on his return from his various wanderings; and finally, in 1924, it elected him to an Honorary Fellowship.

Beneath his seeming indolence, however, he was in reality ceaselessly industrious; but his brain was so acute and his memory so retentive (it has not inaptly been compared with a fly-paper) that no subject, however abstruse, held terrors for him; and what others accomplished only with heavy travail he took unconcernedly in his stride. He once said to a friend that a single thorough scanning of the page of a strange grammar was sufficient to imprint the contents on his memory. And his mind was as ready as it was keen. A story is told of him that, being on one occasion called upon by the Master of his college, the great Professor Jowett, to read an essay which had been set him but which he had neglected to prepare, he took up his note-book and without hesitation extemporized a faultless composition. Only when he was called upon to repeat a passage, and could not, was it discovered that the pages of the note-book were blank.

Many years later, on the occasion of his presentation for the Honorary Degree of Doctor of Letters at Oxford, to be described in an official oration as "*Mezzofantius alter*", he was already, while an undergraduate, an accomplished linguist, with a predilection, however, for the philological side of a language rather than the ordinary and conversational. It is uncertain how many languages he learnt in the course of his life, at least more than twenty, ranging from Finnish to Swahili, from Pali to Chinese. Before he left Oxford he was probably conversant with ten, among them Sanskrit, Pali, Hebrew, Syriac, and Russian. Arabic, Turkish, Persian, Hindustani, and others were to be acquired later. Chinese he began to study at an early stage of his travels in the Far East, and he is said to have acquired a sound knowledge of the "mandarin" dialect and of the ideographs during his residence at Hongkong; but he came too late in life to that most difficult and complicated of Oriental languages, Japanese; and although he mastered its elements, he made comparatively little further progress in it. Various anecdotes, adorned perchance at times with arabesques of legend, are told in illustration of his uncanny familiarity with strange, exotic tongues. It is said, for instance, that once, while travelling in Central Asia, he and his companions spent the night round the camp fires of a band of nomad Kurds, and were asked by their hosts to contribute to the entertainment by singing songs. Eliot replied that he could not sing, but that he would instead recite; and thereupon, to the delight of the company, he rendered into Kurdish Andrew Lang's *Mark of Cain.* Again, long afterwards, when he was High Commissioner in Siberia. he visited Ekaterinburg after the temporary expulsion of the Bolsheviks, and was taken to see the house in which the ill-fated Imperial family had a little earlier been done to death. On the walls of the rooms were scribbled in the Hebrew character scandalous lampoons in Yiddish, and, turning to his guides, he asked if they could decipher them. They shook their heads; whereupon, to their amazement, he translated the inscriptions into fluent Russian.

In 1886 he left Oxford, with inclination vacillating between an academic life and one of action, but with no clear plans for the future. At this moment of indecision he paid a visit to India, where he was the guest of Sir Mountstuart Grant Duff, then Governor of Bombay, whose son, Arthur Grant Duff, had been a close friend of his at Oxford; and while in India he met Lord Dufferin. This meeting is believed to have turned his thoughts towards diplomacy as a career; at all events when he returned to England it was with his mind definitely made up in favour of the Diplomatic Service. A nomination was obtained for him through the late Lord Rosebery; and having passed the entrance competitive examination, he was appointed an Attaché at St. Petersburg under that remarkable and inspiring personality, Sir Robert Morier. His first step on arriving at his post was to qualify for the official Language Allowance for knowledge of Russian; and from that he proceeded to the study of Finnish, producing in 1890 his *Finnish Grammar*,[1] a work which attracted considerable attention at the time among philologists both for its own merits and because it was

[1] Published by the Clarendon Press.

the first study by an Englishman of the Ugro-Finnish languages. In 1888 he was made a Third Secretary.

At St. Petersburg he lived in close contact with the Ambassador and was in fact at one time the latter's personal Secretary; but in the intervals of his official and social duties he appears to have travelled over the greater part of the Russian Empire and of Central Asia as well, even to the remote frontiers of China. When in 1891 Prince Galitzin, the Governor-General of Russian Turkestan, made an expedition to the Pamirs, a region then beginning to attract the attention of the Chanceries of Europe, Eliot was one of the party; and, once. in the depth of winter, he made a journey to Obdorsk in Eastern Siberia to meet Mr. Victor Morier,[1] a member of the Wiggins expedition, who had left his ship in the Arctic Ocean to make his way overland to Europe. But with that capacity for silence, which was one of his marked characteristics (Sir Mountstuart Grant Duff once exclaimed to him: "You are the most silent young man I have ever met"), he has left no record of his experiences in Russia or of his impressions of the country and its people.

In 1892, after a residence of nearly six years, he was transferred to Tangier to act as Chargé d'Affaires during the interregnum between the departure of Sir Charles Euan Smith and the arrival of Sir West Ridgeway, who had been appointed a Special Envoy on a temporary mission to the Sultan of Morocco. His sojourn at Tangier, however, was brief, little more than long enough to enable him to qualify for the Language Allowance for Arabic; and, in 1893, having in the meanwhile been promoted to the rank of Second Secretary, he was moved to Constantinople. In the following autumn he passed the official examination in Turkish. With intervals, during which he was in charge of the Agency at Sofia and of the Legation at Belgrade, he remained in Turkey about four years, a participant in most of the stirring events then occurring. When the Imperial Ottoman Bank at Galata in Constantinople was seized in 1896 by a band of Armenian revolutionaries, he took an active part in the work of rescuing the fugitives in the massacre which followed this rash adventure; and he was a member of the International Commission sent to Thessaly in 1897, during the war between Greece and Turkey, to investigate the accusations made by the Greek inhabitants against the Turkish

[1] A son of Sir Robert Morier.

soldiery of pillaging and atrocities. On this occasion the Turk would appear not to have lived up to his accepted reputation; for the Commission came to the conclusion that the real culprits were Albanian irregulars or the Greek troops themselves. This task accomplished, Eliot was next instructed to draw up a census of the Greeks who would come under Turkish rule when, as a result of the terms of peace, Thessaly was ceded. For these and other services he was in 1898 created a Companion of the Order of the Bath.

The same year saw him transferred to Washington as Second Secretary in charge of the Embassy Chancery there; but he had barely settled down in his new post before he was again moved, this time to Samoa in the distant South Pacific, where trouble had arisen over the succession to the "kingship". These islands had already some ten years earlier been the scene of a similar dispute between two rival chieftains named Malietoa Tanu and Mataafa, which had eventually terminated in foreign intervention and the conversion of the group into a virtual Protectorate under the joint control of Great Britain, the United States, and Germany. Malietoa Tanu was at the same time proclaimed king; and Mataafa, permanently debarred from all right to the succession, was banished to Jaluit in the Marshall Islands. But when Malietoa died in 1899, Mataafa, notwithstanding the ban, promptly returned to dispute the possession of the vacant "throne" with the rightful heir, the late king's son. Unable to compose their quarrel, both sides requested the European Chief Justice of the islands to act as arbitrator; but when he gave his verdict against Mataafa the latter refused to accept it, and, appealing to arms, succeeded in defeating his rival and seizing the reins of power. At this point the three Powers again intervened; and a Commission, of which Eliot was a member, was despatched to assume control and to make arrangements for the future. Arriving in Samoa early in 1899, the Commission decided, after investigation, that the most satisfactory solution of the difficulty would be to abolish the kingship entirely, substitute for the existing system of joint control that of a single Power, and entrust the actual work of government to an Administrator assisted by a Council and a subordinate body of native chiefs. The first of these proposals was unanimously approved by the Governments interested, and to the second Great Britain, compensated elsewhere, offered no objection; but Germany and the United States were unable to come to terms, neither being willing to yield to the other, with the result that in the end the islands were divided into two zones, one under the ægis of the United States and the other under that of Germany. For his services on this occasion Eliot was made in 1900 a Knight Commander of the Order of St. Michael and St. George.

In the autumn of 1900 was published over the *nom de plume* of "Odysseus" his *Turkey in Europe*[1]; and with its appearance he at once took his place among the foremost authorities on the Near East. It is a remarkable work, alike for its erudition, its singular freedom from prejudice, and the accuracy and shrewdness of its comment. The title hardly does it justice; for it is not merely a record of the doings of the Turks but an epitome as well of the history of the motley of peoples inhabiting that cockpit of south-eastern Europe—the Balkan Peninsula—with illuminating sidelights in the shape of brilliant little essays on the fall of the Byzantine Empire, the schisms of the Orthodox Church, Mohammedanism, and various other subjects, and punctuated at intervals with excursions into recondite problems of philology. The author is signally fair in his treatment of the Turk, who emerges from the ordeal, if not a model of all the virtues, at least as less "unspeakable" than repute had pictured him, and, indeed, as in certain respects a more refreshing character than some of his Christian victims. And with all its learning the book is easy reading, terse, graphic, and vigorous in style,—like all the author's work,—and flavoured with a number of most amusing anecdotes. Who having once read them will forget, for instance, the story of the Albanian Bey and his gargantuan entertainment which opened with a fat goose, sent by way of *hors d'œuvre* to meet the approaching guest, or the tale of the Imam Khoja Nasreddin Effendi, or the vivid thumb-nail sketch of the secretariat in the Yildiz palace, or, last and perhaps best, the inimitable interview between the bagman and the Vali, which forms the introductory chapter to the book?

But a fresh field was about to open for his energies. In the autumn of 1900 he was appointed Consul-General at Zanzibar and Commissioner for the British East Africa Protectorate; and there, occupied in laying the foundations of a new colony, he was now to spend what he afterwards described as perhaps the four "happiest and most interesting" years of his life. The task awaiting him was one completely unfamiliar and beset with difficulties; for the

[1] Published by Messrs. Edward Arnold and Co., London.

Protectorate was almost virgin territory, not even properly surveyed, the administrative service was too small for the duties it was expected to fulfil, and the funds urgently needed for development were entirely inadequate. But from the outset he found the work congenial, nay more, so absorbing that before he had been a year in Africa he declared that he wished for none but colonial appointments in future. Its charm, he wrote in one of his letters to Lady Elcho,[1] whose acquaintance he had made a little earlier and who was to prove for the rest of his life one of his staunchest friends, lay in its extreme variety :—" the law, the church, military matters, commerce, administration occupy me one after another, and I seem to become successively a judge, a clergyman, a soldier, a merchant, and a Governor."

Nor was this the sum of his activities. In the intervals of his official duties he contrived to find leisure to learn Swahili, even to write a grammar of that language,[2] and to take up again the studies of Buddhism which he had commenced at school ; while from time to time he made those extensive tours through his territory which were later to furnish most of the material for his work on the Protectorate.[3] Indeed, so deep was his interest in these comparatively unknown regions of Africa that once, when going home on leave, he even travelled overland from Mombasa into Egypt. "I started," he writes, "from Mombasa by train at the end of June, 1903, crossed Lake Victoria in the Steamer *Winifred*, then drove in a buckboard right across Uganda and Ungoro from Lake Victoria to Lake Albert. Here I took a sailing boat at Butiaba and went by river to Nimule, where began the highest rapids of the Nile. As no boat can pass through these the traveller has to march about six days from Nimule to Gondokoro, where the rapids terminate, in the hope of meeting there a small steamer to take him through the swamps of the Southern Sudan to Khartum. In all the journey to Khartum occupied about six weeks."

The years which began with such happy auspices were fated nevertheless to end disastrously in his tragic and premature retirement from the public service. A difference of opinion with the Foreign Office over certain grants of land was the immediate cause ;

[1] The present Countess of Wemyss and March.

[2] He also wrote a preface to Mr. (now Sir Claude) Hollis's *Grammar of the Masai Language*.

[3] *The East African Protectorate*, published by Messrs. Edward Arnold and Co., London.

but in the background a question of policy was at issue. Sir Charles Eliot's plans for the development of the territory committed to his charge may be summed up in the two words "white settlement". He wished to see the country thrown open to colonization by Europeans; and for the attainment of that object he laboured unceasingly from the moment of his arrival in Africa. In this he had the support of the Government at home; but there were practical difficulties in the way. The only part of the Protectorate adapted for permanent habitation by Europeans was the high plateau land in the interior; and there the region most attractive to prospective settlers, the Great Rift Valley, was already occupied by nomadic pastoral tribes of Masai, whose rights must admittedly be protected. How to secure this and yet at the same time satisfy the legitimate needs of the colonists was the problem which confronted him. Must the Rift Valley become a native Reserve, closed for ever to the white man, or was there room in it for both races? And the situation was still further complicated by the fact that the Foreign Office, under the administration of which the Protectorate then lay, had only a little earlier made a grant of five hundred square miles of land in the very heart of the country to a corporation called the East Africa Syndicate. The position of the native occupants was thus at the outset already compromised.

Sir Charles Eliot himself was opposed to the creation of a Reserve, except as a last resource, because he believed that it would only confirm the Masai in their revolting social habits and help to perpetuate a tribal organization which he wished to see broken up; and, while admitting that native rights must be safeguarded, he also maintained that the interests of the white population must always remain paramount. He considered moreover that the Masai were wasteful in their methods, occupying more land than they could properly utilize, and that even when their reasonable requirements had been satisfied a substantial balance available for other purposes would still remain. For these reasons he favoured opening the valley to white settlement. With his view the Foreign Office at first on the whole agreed; but the applications for grants, sometimes of considerable extent, in the coveted area increased so rapidly that the Government began to fear that the rights of the native occupants might be endangered; and it was accordingly suggested to him that it would be "more prudent to postpone consideration of further grants on a large scale".

Out of this arose the difference which ended in his retirement.

He had a little earlier received two separate applications for thirty-two thousand acres of land, mainly, yet not entirely, in the Masai territory; but with the immense grant to the East Africa Syndicate in his mind, he did not interpret these comparatively insignificant areas as coming within the proscribed limits set by his instructions; and he therefore allowed negotiations to proceed, practically agreeing that, subject to conditions, the applications would be granted. It happened, however, that at this moment two District Officers of the Protectorate who held views on the land question, and particularly on the Masai problem, opposed to his own, were in England on leave; and the Foreign Office, already perturbed, was so influenced by their arguments that it suddenly repudiated the policy it had hitherto countenanced, and decided not only to create a Reserve but also to refuse all further grants of land. This decision was thereupon communicated to Sir Charles Eliot, with instructions to reject the two applications just mentioned. Deeply hurt at this unexpected rebuff and resentful of the action of the Authorities in London in allowing themselves to be guided by the advice of his subordinates rather than by his own, he declined to comply. Sooner than acquiesce in such treatment or stultify himself by refusing land in one case while giving ten times as much in another,[1] he preferred, he said, to resign from the public service. His resignation was accepted; and a few weeks afterwards, in the early summer of 1904, he returned to England.

Before his departure he made a vain appeal to the Prime Minister for a public inquiry; but a little later a collection of documents bearing on the case was published in the form of a White Paper[2]; and it is from this, practically the sole source of information now available, that these facts are taken. It should, however, be added that he himself steadfastly refused to accept this official presentation of the incident, protesting that it was in some directions inaccurate and in others one-sided.[3] The whole story of this unhappy episode has never been told, probably never will be, and at that it must rest; but there is reason to believe that his original appointment

[1] The two rejected applications were for 50 square miles each; but in a dispatch to the Foreign Office on the 5th March, 1904, he said that they would probably be reduced.

[2] *Africa*, No. 8, 1904. Sir Charles Eliot's own version of the circumstances leading up to his retirement was given in a letter to *The Times* on the 4th August, 1904, and a brief statement on the same subject appears in the preface to his work on the East African Protectorate.

[3] Cf. the preface to *The East African Protectorate*.

as Commissioner was unwelcome in certain quarters at home, that he knew this and resented it, and that it was not without influence on the subsequent course of events. Be the facts as they may, it was not less than a tragedy that so brilliant an intellect should have been lost to the state at the very moment when it was approaching its fullest maturity. On the arrival of his successor preparations for the creation of a native Reserve were at once started; but it quickly became evident that the Masai could not live in proximity to Europeans without friction; and as they were willing to move elsewhere if given suitable land in exchange, two new Reserves were established for their accommodation in other parts of the Protectorate. Thither they were transferred; and the Rift Valley was then thrown open to white settlement as Sir Charles Eliot had consistently advocated.

Cut now adrift from the public service and without private fortune of his own, it was necessary for him to find other occupation. For this he had not long or far to seek. In 1905 the University of Edinburgh conferred on him the Honorary Degree of Doctor of Laws; and a little later in the year he was offered and accepted the Vice-Chancellorship of the University of Sheffield, which had just been founded by Royal Charter. The post was one of considerable responsibility, for on the wisdom with which the new institution was guided through its infancy much depended; but in Sir Charles Eliot the University Authorities had secured precisely the type of Vice-Chancellor required,—a scholar yet also a man of action, of broad vision and an open mind, and with a wide knowledge of affairs. To these qualities were added a record of brilliant achievement in the service of the Crown. He was quick to realize that on his prudence and tact depended the success of his administration, that he must ride with a loose rein, be content to deal with main issues only, and, above all, allow teachers the fullest freedom in their own departments to foster original research. On these principles accordingly he based his governance; and the steady growth in the prosperity and the repute of the young University during the seven years of his Vice-Chancellorship proved how wise and prudent was his policy.

But he was of too energetic a temperament to rest content with the direction of affairs alone. He shared in the duties of the class-room as well; and, going beyond the University walls, he played an active part in the educational work of the city outside, delivered from time to time courses of lectures for the general public on the peoples and the religions of the East, and once, in 1909, even served on a Royal Commission for Electoral Reform. His conception of hospitality was Oriental; and in Sheffield, as later in Tokyo, he kept open house for his friends and all wandering scholars. The Long Vacation he spent as a rule in India, China, or Japan, collecting material for his great life work on Hinduism and Buddhism; and it was during one of these visits, made in 1906, that he wrote, for the ephemeral purposes of a London daily paper, the series of articles which were later published in book form under the title of *Letters from the Far East*.[1] They are, alas! all too brief, covering less than two hundred pages of large type; but whatever their subject,—personal experiences on the journey, descriptions of places visited, or dissertations on the languages, religions, literature, or national characteristics of the peoples of those remote regions,—they are unfailingly entertaining and full of information of absorbing interest to the student of things Oriental. The author has no prejudices and assumes no airs of Western superiority; to him there is nothing "inscrutable and mysterious" in Eastern mentality; and he boldly avows that he would "as soon trust a Chinaman as an Englishman". Beneath the staid surface of the scholar he is full too of boyish laughter and hawk-eyed to mark the whimsical and the ludicrous, whether he is motoring in Cochin China, feasting in the Hall of Concentrated Fragrance, discoursing with the maker of images who did not worship the gods because he knew what they were made of, or watching, *spectator ab extra,* the pranks of a sudden whirlwind on the city dyke at Hankow. Among the multitude of works on the Far East this slim volume is of the small and elect number of those which are worthy to be read and re-read again and again.

Much of his leisure at Sheffield was occupied with the preparation and arrangement of the material gathered on his journeys; for relaxation he would turn to his laboratory and the study of marine zoology. Here is a notable illustration of the variety of his talent and the wide range of his intellectual curiosity. Interested from boyhood in natural history, his attention was drawn during his visit to Samoa to the shell-less molluscs found in the seas of the islands; and he became so fascinated by their unusual forms that he made a collection of specimens and wrote a monograph on them, which was published in 1899. From this he proceeded to specialize

[1] Published by Messrs. Edward Arnold and Co., London, 1907.

in one particular branch of the family, the Nudibranchiata, and during the next three years wrote seven papers on the forms found in East African waters and in the Maldive and Laccadive archipelagos. By that time he had become recognized as the leading British authority on the group. This, however, was only a beginning; and between 1903 and 1918, when his appointment as High Commissioner in Siberia forced him to put aside his studies, more than forty papers appeared over his name dealing with collections made in all parts of the world, from the Antarctic Ocean in the south through the seas of the tropics to Japan in the north. But his most important contribution to scientific literature was the monograph published by the Ray Society in 1910, a large quarto volume, admirably illustrated, in which he reviewed the whole field of research in this subject and at the same time discussed critically in the light of modern knowledge and his own investigations the work of his two most distinguished predecessors in England, Joseph Alder and Albany Hancock. It is on the results of the labours of these three students that all future research into British forms of the Nudibranchs must admittedly be based. Altogether it was a notable achievement for one who was only an amateur, without any training in natural history or marine zoology, and moreover already deeply immersed in other affairs. In scientific circles abroad the value of his work was equally recognized; and as early as 1909 his name, bracketed with that of another distinguished student of the Mollusca, had been given to a new specimen, the "Eliotia Souleyeti", discovered by the French naturalist, Vayssière, in the Gulf of Lyons.

Yet, with all these outward activities, in secret he chafed. His environment was uncongenial. After the burning suns of Africa and its great empty spaces the bleak atmosphere and the crowded ways of the grim northern manufacturing city were infinitely depressing, and his spirit wilted in his new surroundings. The work itself, too, was distasteful, not of his choice but thrust upon him by unavoidable circumstance, and his heart was not in it. Instead his thoughts reverted constantly to the service he had left, with its wider horizons and its greater opportunities for conspicuous achievement, and, confident in the justice of his case, he could not abandon the hope that a way would open for his return. Official memories, however, are long, and all the efforts of his friends, foremost among them and indomitable Lady Elcho, to procure his reinstatement were fruitless. Then unexpectedly in 1911 came a qualified release in the shape of the offer of the Vice-Chancellorship of the newly founded University of Hongkong. This was not the road of his desire, and the prospect of further indefinite confinement in an educational groove was distasteful; but at least it meant return to the East that he loved, and after a little hesitation he accepted.

In the summer of the following year he arrived in Hongkong, to find a formidable task awaiting him, with financial difficulties its dominant feature. The total revenue of the new University amounted to barely ninety thousand dollars, a sum so hopelessly inadequate that when the first session opened in the autumn of the year only two Faculties were working; and even those were practically without permanent teaching staffs. There was a Professor of Engineering and a Lecturer in Physics; but that was all. None of the Chairs in the Faculty of Medicine had been filled because funds were lacking; and for a considerable period the University Authorities were in consequence obliged to rely for instruction in this branch of knowledge on such help as could be obtained from medical practitioners in the Colony. In other directions preparations were similarly inadequate. The University was in fact still in the embryonic stage; and, as only limited assistance could be expected from the Colonial Treasury, this threatened to be protracted unless fresh sources of income were quickly discovered.

To this work accordingly the Vice-Chancellor directed his energies. His first step was to enlist the sympathy of the many wealthy Chinese living in Hongkong; and from them and their compatriots in Malaya and the Netherlands East Indies he succeeded in obtaining substantial contributions. Generous help was also given by some of the great British merchant houses interested in the China trade; but the sum total even then was far short of the University's needs. With the approval therefore of the Governor, Sir Henry May, he sent the Professor of Engineering on a special mission to England to appeal for a grant from the Boxer Indemnity Fund; but although the Government was sympathetic it professed itself unable to help, and the mission was unsuccessful. Repulsed in this direction, he turned to the Chinese in their own country. It was his custom to spend the Long Vacation in Peking, studying the language; and he now made these visits an occasion for propaganda, losing no opportunity to impress on every Chinese official he met on his wanderings the duty of supporting an institution which had been founded for the express benefit of their countrymen and which stood at their very doors. Thanks in no small measure to his personal prestige as an Oriental scholar, his efforts were not unsuccessful. A number of scholarships were founded with funds subscribed by the Chinese Government; and as the name and the reputation of the University spread, students from the most distant parts of the country were gradually attracted to it, until at last all the Eighteen Provinces were represented on its roll.

Yet, despite his utmost endeavours, he was never able to place its finances on a stable basis; and even when he left Hongkong in 1918 it was still in great difficulties. These, however, have now happily vanished. The work which Sir Charles Eliot started his successors carried on; and as the cultural value of the University became more evident, new and more substantial endowments were created, among them the vainly sought grant from the Boxer Indemnity Fund, with the result that to-day the revenues of the institution are ten times as great as they were in 1911. But although others completed what he had begun, to him still is the chief credit due; and in a memorial address shortly after his death in 1931 the present Head of the University, Sir William Hornell, confessed that he had "sometimes wondered if the institution would have survived the dangerous years of its neglected infancy, had it not been for the personality and reputation of its first Vice-Chancellor",—a doubt which is shared by others also well qualified to form an opinion.

In the class-rooms at Hongkong he was less often seen than he had been at Sheffield, and although he lectured at intervals, mainly on Chinese history, he took no part in the routine work of the University. But his eye was always watchful for the backward student who showed signs of promise. Of these there were a number, youths who had come from remote provinces of the Republic, with a knowledge of English lamentably inadequate for their needs; and for them, in their struggles with an alien tongue, he had always time and sympathy to spare, helping them individually with their studies, correcting their essays, and even on occasion, particularly in the early days, when the teaching staff was very small, stooping to give them exercises in so humble a subject as spelling. He was too remote to court or to win personal popularity; but in China learning has always been reverenced, and in the reputation of their Vice-Chancellor as a scholar the students took an intense and personal pride. An amusing exhibition of this occurred on the occasion of his presentation in 1924 for the Honorary Degree of Doctor of Laws, when, at the end of the ceremony, he was mobbed by an excited crowd of undergraduates, hustled into a motor-car, and, to his infinite discomfort and embarrassment, drawn in procession through the streets of the city.

Outside the University walls in the Vice-Chancellor's Lodge he led a detached and tranquil existence, accessible always and to his friends anxiously hospitable, but immersed as a rule in his own private studies, in which the Chinese language now took an important place. At home in the meanwhile his friends still continued their efforts on his behalf, with so little result, however, that some were beginning to despond. "I have," wrote Lord Curzon to him in the winter of 1917, "on many occasions recommended you for posts (among them Bengal). . . . I have never been successful." At that very moment hope, so long deferred, was on the eve of fulfilment.

It was then the fourth year of the war, and the Allied Powers were embarking on their ill-fated attempt to stem the tide of Bolshevism. A British Commissioner had already been installed at Archangel, the base of operations in European Russia; and His Majesty's Government were now looking for some one to fill the corresponding post of High Commissioner in Siberia, the eastern base, whither an Allied Expeditionary force was being dispatched. At this moment they bethought themselves of Sir Charles Eliot in Hongkong, and, with the acquiescence of the Authorities of the University, offered him the post. The appointment was only temporary, for the duration of the war; and it thus left the future still uncertain; but to him it meant a step in the direction of his desire, and he accepted it with alacrity. In the summer of 1918 he left for the north.

For the next twelve months he led the life of a nomad, at times in the security and comparative ease of Vladivostock or Harbin, once, for a brief period and at a hazardous moment, even as a householder at Omsk,[1] but for the most part in the cramped space of a railway carriage, and not infrequently in conditions of considerable physical discomfort. But his work kept him occupied; and he accepted everything, even the arctic rigours of the interminable Siberian winter, with pessimistic philosophy.

There is space here for no more than the most cursory survey of the events in which he played a part, or of which he was a despairing and helpless spectator. When he arrived in Siberia a Provisional

[1] He rented a house at Omsk at the moment when Admiral Kolchak's front had actually crumbled, and this courageous action helped to allay the general panic which then prevailed.

Government, the precursor, it was hoped, of something more permanent which would embrace all Russia, was already established at Omsk under the ægis of the Allies and of the Czech troops, who had marched across Asia from Europe. Even at this early stage, however, dissension was rife among the discordant elements of which it was composed or by which it was supported; and in the autumn of 1918, to prevent a *débâcle*, Admiral Kolchak, the Minister of War, was persuaded, much against his will, to assume the post of Dictator. A gallant man, able, honest, and single-hearted in his devotion to his country, he might in happier circumstances have accomplished much for Russia; but Fate had loaded the dice against him. The virus of Bolshevism was already spreading into Siberia; the Dictator himself was surrounded by a horde of dishonest and greedy place-hunters and of rabid reactionaries to whom bitter experience and adversity had taught nothing; some of his subordinate commanders, so-called, were completely beyond his control; and between him and the Czechs relations were always unhappy. Well might he exclaim in black moments of despair: "Who will deliver me from this cross?" From the outset he was doomed to disaster. "I regard myself," wrote Sir Charles Eliot to Lady Elcho in the winter of that year, "as one of a medical staff watching a patient who has a virulently infectious disease. I hope he may be prevented from infecting others and perhaps cured of Bolshevism; but I have little hope of his being restored to normal general health."

Notwithstanding, therefore, a successful offensive on the Ural front in the spring of 1919, the position of the new Government was precarious; and the suspicion and distrust with which it had from the beginning been regarded by the mass of the population was quickly turned into bitter hostility by the excesses of Ivanoff Rinoff—the commander of the Russian troops in Eastern Siberia—and of the two Cossack Atamans, Semenoff and Kalmikoff. Adherents in name of the Omsk Government, they were in reality independent freebooters and brigands, each playing his own hand, and, when occasion demanded, not hesitating to defy the authority to which he owed allegiance. For a régime which depended on such allies there could be no permanency; but it was left to the Czechs to deliver the blow which precipitated its downfall. Only indirectly interested in the cause in which they found themselves entangled, and discontented with the conditions around them, they suddenly declared that they would fight no longer, and demanded to be repatriated. The front along the Urals had already given way; but with their defection all was lost; the Bolshevik armies poured unresisted into Siberia; and the Government at Omsk collapsed like a house of cards. With its fall ended the chapter of intervention. At the beginning of 1920 the foreign Missions and troops were in full retreat towards the sea; a few weeks later the ill-starred Admiral Kolchak, deserted by his allies, was handed over by the French general Janin and the Czechs to the Bolsheviks to meet his inevitable fate[1]; and before March closed British, French, American, and Czech forces had all been withdrawn. Alone the Japanese remained behind, involved in an adventure of their own against the Reds.[2]

In the closing scenes of this ill-fated and barren enterprise Sir Charles Eliot had no part. Early in the summer of 1919 he was offered the Embassy in Tokyo; and almost immediately afterwards he sailed for England to prepare to take up his new post. The years of exile had ended.

*Hinduism and Buddhism*, on which he had spent so many years of patient labour, was now at last in the press, though it did not actually leave the hands of the publishers till the autumn of 1921. In this, his *magnum opus*, the author traces the history and development of the two great indigenous religions of India from their origin almost up to the present day, reviewing with an ample wealth of reference every important phase of each, and in the case of Buddhism carrying his investigations far beyond the confines of India to the remotest regions into which that great missionary religion has penetrated. The field covered is vast both in space and time; but to those who would object that it is "too large, that to attempt a historical sketch of the two faiths in their whole duration and extension over Eastern Asia is to choose a scene unsuited to any canvas which can be prepared at the present day", he replies that "wide surveys may sometimes be useful and are needed in the present state of Oriental studies. For the reality of Indian influence in Asia—from Japan to the frontiers of Persia, from Manchuria to Java, from Burma to Mongolia—is undoubted

[1] He died bravely,—in the words of his executioner, "straight up, like an Englishman."

[2] For most of the information here recorded the writer is indebted to Sir Bernard Pares, the Head of the School of Slavonic and East European Studies in the University of London. A detailed account of the Siberian expedition will be found in *The Far Eastern Republic of Siberia*, by H. Norton (publishers, Messrs. G. Allen and Unwin, Ltd.).

and the influence is one. You cannot separate Hinduism from Buddhism. . . . Neither is it convenient to separate the fortunes of Buddhism and Hinduism outside India from their history within it . . ."

His method of approach to the stupendous task he had set himself is worthy of his great reputation as a scholar. He is without bias, consistently cautious, dispassionate, and critical. Though himself sceptical in temperament and devoid of any ingredient of mysticism, he is never less than tolerant in his attitude towards the mysticism and occultism which are so conspicuous a feature of Indian thought or religion; and he is just even when dealing with aspects of Hinduism repellent to the Western mind. Towards Buddhism, to which he was profoundly attracted by the breadth of its conceptions, its humanity, and its almost complete freedom from dogma and sectarian spirit, he is unreservedly sympathetic. Indeed, the key-notes of his work are sympathy, tolerance, and a complete absence of spiritual or intellectual arrogance. "Religion," he writes, "depends on temperament,"[1] and "in studying Oriental religions sympathy and a desire to agree if possible are the first requisites".[2] And again:—"I cannot share the confidence in the superiority of Europeans and their ways which is prevalent in the West. . . . In fact European civilization is not satisfying, and Asia can still offer something more attractive to many who are far from Asiatic in spirit."[3]

It is difficult to determine what most compels admiration in this book,—the infinite industry, the encyclopædic knowledge, the austere accuracy, the conciseness and clarity of statement, or the unerring skill with which the author sifts the grain from the chaff in the confused mass of fact, theory, and doctrine before him. Truly it is, as the late Sir Richard Temple declared, "a mighty work of the deepest research and insight."[4]

In November of 1919 he was sworn a member of the Privy Council; and in the spring of the year following he arrived in Tokyo to take up his appointment. It was not without apprehension that some at least of those about to work under him welcomed this Ambassador who was already a legendary figure. Tall and rather heavily built, younger in appearance than his years, but walking a little uneasily,

[1] *Hinduism and Buddhism*, I, p. xcvii.
[2] Ibid., I, p. lxiv.
[3] Ibid., I, p. xcvi.
[4] *Transactions* of the Royal Asiatic Society, 1921.

the result of an injury to a kneecap during his early days in Russia, with thick dark hair growing in a level line low across his forehead, full, searching, critical eyes, and of a somewhat frosty address, he looked remote and redoubtable, a "chief" who might prove exigent in his standards of efficiency and hard to satisfy. And first experiences seemed to justify this impression.

He came to Japan at the moment when the fate of the Anglo-Japanese Alliance hung in the balance. For nearly twenty years this great stabilizing influence had been in existence, to the material benefit of both parties and to the general advantage of the world at large; now, in the changed conditions following the war, its future had suddenly become uncertain. Was it to continue or must it lapse? In England, and notably among those best acquainted with the Far East, the general feeling was in favour of its maintenance, with such modifications as altered circumstances might necessitate; and this was the course which Sir Charles Eliot himself advocated. But powerful forces were also arrayed in opposition,—public sentiment in one at least of the Dominions, American hostility, and the new internationalism working through the League of Nations at Geneva. In the end these prevailed; and at Washington in the winter of 1921 the Alliance was abrogated. It can hardly be said that the path of peace in Eastern Asia has been made smoother by its disappearance. In Japan the dissolution of a bond which had been confidently regarded as permanent was received with dismay and profound disappointment; but the Japanese are a proud people, and, deeply though their feelings were wounded, they accepted the accomplished fact, outwardly at least, with dignity and restraint. The blow was a little softened by the timely visit of His Royal Highness the Prince of Wales in 1922; but the position was nevertheless uncomfortable, and that not least for the new Ambassador, on whom now fell the duty of building up relations afresh on an entirely altered basis. With signal success he accomplished this delicate and difficult task; and to his skill, to his intimate knowledge of the East, and to the undeviating friendliness and understanding which marked all his relations with the Government and the people of the country to which he was accredited is it mainly due that the years following the abrogation of the Alliance were so smoothly traversed and so substantial a measure of the ancient friendship between the two nations preserved. Truly a "solid if not outwardly brilliant achievement".[1]

[1] Obituary notice in *The Times*, 17th March, 1931.

With more intimate acquaintance first impressions of him changed, and the earlier chill respect for his talents gradually gave place to a warmer feeling of genuine admiration and affection. The mask of aloofness which discouraged approach at the outset, and the air of cynical disillusionment hid in reality a very human personality, with an unsuspected capacity for winning the attachment of those who worked close to him. He gave his confidence very slowly, almost indeed grudgingly; but to those whom he trusted he was unswervingly loyal; he was impatient of delay, witheringly contemptuous of the slightest slovenliness in thought or expression, and often exacting; and he demanded industry unrelenting with impeccable accuracy; but he was at the same time intensely, almost pathetically, appreciative of service rendered, and he thought no effort too great if thereby he could prevent merit in a subordinate passing unregarded. And to any in trouble he was always accessible and generous. In his personal relations, too, with his staff he had habits of formal courtesy, inherited from a generation more punctilious in ceremonial than this, which were as engaging as they were unusual; and despite his great intellectual gifts and his immense learning he was completely unaffected and unassuming. His modesty indeed was one of the most attractive traits in his character.

Apart from the question of post-Alliance relations the term of Sir Charles Eliot's Ambassadorship was comparatively uneventful. Following his usual habit, he commenced immediately on his arrival in Japan to learn the language; and while his progress fell short of his hopes, the knowledge he acquired proved of material value to him in his work. In his leisure he travelled much about the country, generally in search of material for the present work; but, with the exception of isolated visits to Korea and Formosa, his journeys were within a narrow radius, rarely extending north of Tokyo or west of Kyōto; and he could never be persuaded to follow the traditional practice of migrating to the hills in the summer months. A confirmed lover of heat and sunlight, he preferred to remain in the capital even during the torrid dog-days and to make at intervals short visits to resorts like Kamakūra, Miyanoshita, or the mineral springs of Shusenji in the Idzu peninsula. His way lay often outside the beaten track with its amenities of Europeanized hotels; but this was no hardship to one of such varied experience; and although he chafed under some of its taboos and inhibitions, he took on the whole very kindly to the national mode of life, and even to the stark simplicity of some of its domestic arrangements.

His reputation for learning had long preceded him ; and with his arrival in Tokyo the Embassy became at once a centre of attraction to scholars. In 1921 the Asiatic Society of Japan, an association founded under foreign auspices in 1872 for purposes of research, elected him as its President ; and this post he retained until he left Tokyo in 1926, taking an energetic part in all the Society's activities and, except during his absence on leave, almost invariably throwing open his house for its meetings.

His conception of his duty as Ambassador, particularly towards the people of the country in which he lived, was strict, and he was at infinite pains to gain their goodwill and their confidence. In his own habits of life simple, and in secret averse from social pomps with their burdensome paraphernalia of ceremonial, he nevertheless more than worthily upheld the hospitable traditions of the Embassy, though it must also be confessed that in an atmosphere of banalities he was prone to become abstracted and to retire within himself. He could speak wittily and well when occasion or duty demanded ; but he preferred silence to speech-making ; and he was probably at his best and happiest in limited gatherings of his more intimate friends and acquaintances, when he would readily expand, to delight his listeners with the infinite variety of his information, his pungent comment, and the humour and fecundity of his anecdote.

Yet in one respect his intellectual equipment seemed curiously lacking ; he was almost completely indifferent to the appeal of the visual arts. In matters of form and colour his predilection inclined to the ornate and, perhaps, slightly barbaric,—a cause, in Tokyo, of not infrequent heartburning and mortification to a household bred in the austere simplicity of the Japanese canon ; and although so much of his life was spent in countries renowned for the achievements of their craftsmen, he would seem to have remained unmoved and completely uncovetous in the presence of the procession of beauty which passed before his eyes. Through all his Odyssean wanderings he acquired no treasures of bronze, or painted scroll, or porcelain : and a small collection of Medici reprints, regarded somewhat contemptuously as furniture, represented practically his only adventure in the realms of the artistic.

Towards the end of the spring of 1923 he left for England on leave, and while at home was made a Knight Grand Cross of the Order of St. Michael and St. George and given the Honorary Degree of Doctor of Letters by the University of Oxford. In October he returned to the East and a scene of pitiful desolation. On the

1st of September occurred one of those catastrophic disasters of earthquake and fire to which Japan seems fated to be periodically a victim; and in a few short hours a prosperous countryside was devastated, the city of Yokohama reduced to a heap of smoking ashes, and more than a third of the capital destroyed. In the Embassy itself not a building remained securely standing; two were burnt to the ground; and the Ambassador's own house narrowly escaped the same fate. Fortunately this danger was averted; and of his possessions only a few comparatively unimportant manuscripts in his valuable library were slightly damaged.[1] But he was homeless. A temporary lodging was, however, found for him close at hand while a bungalow of lath and plaster was hurriedly put up for his permanent accommodation on a lawn in the Embassy grounds; and in these confined yet not uncomfortable quarters he lived during the last two years of his official stay in Japan.

There is little more to add. The term of his Ambassadorship ended in 1925; but he remained at his post awaiting the appointment of his successor, his many friends hoping the while that his appointment might be renewed. Their hope was not realized; and in February of 1926 he bade a final farewell to the public service, though not to Japan. The rest has already been told elsewhere in this memoir.

So ended a career of great distinction and notable achievement, though perhaps, in the opinion of some, fallen short of its opening promise. Almost, if not quite, the most brilliant student of his generation at Oxford and, as he was later to prove, endowed in addition with administrative capacity of a very high order, he might reasonably have aspired, when he entered the public service, to its most coveted prizes. Certainly the augury of those earlier years was of the happiest; to be Governor of a vast territory at the age of thirty-eight is good fortune such as befalls few. Yet at the very moment when the future seemed most auspicious, disaster irremediable overtook him, and all his hopes and ambitions were shattered. "Cut is the branch that might have grown full straight . . ." Many years later he was recalled, to do useful work for his country in Siberia and Japan; but it was then too late; the ground lost could not be recovered or the days spent in exile retrieved. For him the end came not in 1926 but in 1904. It is therefore by his contributions to knowledge, and they are outstanding, that Sir Charles

[1] His library was later acquired by the Imperial University of Tokyo.

Eliot will best be remembered. This was perhaps not where his early ambitions lay; but who shall say that in *Hinduism and Buddhism* he may not have raised to himself a monument more enduring than the fame of a satrapy?

H. P.

*Note.*—To all those who have generously supplied him with material the writer of this preface wishes to offer his grateful acknowledgments,—in particular to the relatives of the late Sir Charles Eliot, to the Countess of Wemyss and March (who kindly allowed him access to a long series of letters), to Professor Oliver Elton (Honorary Fellow of Corpus Christi College, Oxford), Dr. Ponsonby Fane, Mr. W. J. Hinton, Sir William Hornell (Vice-Chancellor of the University of Hongkong), Dr. D. S. MacColl, Dr. C. H. O'Donoghue (Department of Zoology in the University of Edinburgh), Dr. F. W. Pember, Mr. J. U. Powell (Fellow and Tutor of St. John's College, Oxford), Brigadier F. S. G. Piggott, D.S.O. (a member of Cheltenham College Council), Professor C. A. Middleton Smith (University of Hongkong), and to Mr. Stephen Gaselee, C.B.E. (Librarian of the Foreign Office).

## LIST OF ABBREVIATIONS

The following are the principal abbreviations used :—

*B.E.F.E.O.* *Bulletin de l'École Française d'Extrême Orient.*

*J.A.* . *Journal Asiatique.*

*J.R.A.S.* . *Journal of the Royal Asiatic Society.*

*N.* . . *Nanjio's Catalogue of the Buddhist Tripiṭaka.*

*S.B.E.* . *Sacred Books of the East* (Clarendon Press).

*T.A.S.J.* . *Transactions of the Asiatic Society of Japan.*

# BOOK I

# A SURVEY OF BUDDHISM IN INDIA AND CHINA

# CHAPTER I

## THE CANONS

CHRISTIANS and Mohammedans are alike in acknowledging the authority of one sacred book, the Bible or Koran. Sects may differ as to its interpretation and as to the authority possessed by tradition apart from scripture, but they all appeal to the same texts which they regard as a divine revelation. But in Buddhism there are not only different sects, but they use different scriptures composed in different languages, and though some of these works are obviously later than others, they are not related to one another as are the Old and New Testaments, for in the New Testament a new teacher appears who changes and develops the old law. But in the Buddhist scriptures there is no such avowed change. All important tenets are referred back to the Buddha himself and he is represented as having preached on the same sacred mountain in India doctrines which seem to be of very different ages and provenance.

The ideas of India and Eastern Asia about scripture and revelation are more fluid than those prevalent in Europe at any period. Not that dogmatism is wanting: the four Vedas are said to be the divine word, existing before the universe came into being and from time to time revealed to human sages. The text has been most carefully preserved by memory, but it is almost universally admitted that these ancient scriptures of the golden age are not suited to the needs of degenerate modern times, and century after century Indian writers have not failed to produce new revelations and to meet with respectful acceptance. These works often take the form of discourses put into the mouth of some deity, such as Kṛishṇa or Śiva, but no historical justification is either attempted by the writer or expected by the readers. The Bhagavad Gîtâ and even the Bhâgavata Purâṇa are relatively ancient works, but the Râmâyaṇa of Tulsi Das and the Prem Sagar[1] and many others are modern. All, however, have millions of devout readers at the present day and are unhesitatingly accepted

[1] Tulsi Das lived from 1532 to 1623. The Prem Sagar is a free translation of the tenth book of the Bhâgavata Purâṇa made in 1803.

as what we call revelation.[1] Nor is it merely popular works which attain this high position. The Brahma-sûtras, a set of aphorisms containing a compendium of Upanishadic philosophy, are for most sects of unquestioned authority.

Buddhists, Indian and other, have shown a similar readiness to accept new scriptures. Even in the Pali Piṭakas we hear of new sayings claiming to be the word of the Buddha and of the standards by which they are to be judged. These standards are not always the same. Sometimes[2] the Buddha is represented as declaring that such sayings must be tested by comparing them with the Sutta and the Vinaya, which seems to imply that at the time when these passages were composed there were already collections of sayings and rules, recognized though doubtless unwritten, which could be used for reference and comparison. But in other passages[3] he is made to state emphatically that a doctrine is not to be judged by its conformity to tradition and scripture or by intellectual tests, but by the moral sense of the hearers—does it tend to remove covetousness, ill-will, and folly or to increase them?

Similarly on different occasions he is represented as taking very different attitudes as to private judgment and the questioning spirit in disciples. Once when a disciple asked an apparently reasonable though perplexing question about the soul and its deeds[4] he received no answer but brought upon himself a most violent rebuke. "Is it possible that some senseless fellow sunk in ignorance and led astray by greed may think to go beyond the Master's teaching, etc." And the Kîṭâgiri-sutta[5] insists on the necessity of absolute obedience. Yet in another discourse[6] we

[1] Thus Mallik in his book called *The Philosophy of the Vaishnava Religion* (1927) states categorically that the Bhâgavata Purâṇa possesses "supreme authoritativeness" and "if one wishes to acquire true definite knowledge of the Absolute he should look to this Purâṇa" (p. 39).

[2] Ang. Nik., iv, 180 (= vol. ii, p. 167); Dîg. Nik., xvi, 7 (= vol. ii, p. 124).

[3] Ang. Nik., iii, 65; iii, 66; iv, 193. The wording is the same but the hearers are different in these three suttas. Compare, too, the advice given to Mahâpajâpati in Cullavag., x, § 5. Whatever teachings conduce to a good life, you may say of them *Eso dhammo eso vinayo, etam satthu sâsanam*: "This is the doctrine, this the discipline, this the message of the Master".

[4] Saṃ. Nik., xxii, 82 = vol. iii, p. 103. The whole passage is extremely curious and interesting.

[5] For the faithful follower it is a principle that "the Lord is Master and I his disciple: the Lord knows and I do not know". *Satthâ Bhagavâ sâvako'ham asmi: jânâti Bhagavâ nâham jânâmi.* Maj. Nik., lxxii.

[6] Maj. Nik., xxxviii.

read: "Will you say that you affirm this out of reverence for your teacher? No, Lord. Do you affirm only what you have of yourselves known, seen and discerned? Yes, Lord. Quite right." On the whole, the view expressed in the Piṭakas is that doctrines and precepts are not to be judged too strictly by the standards of traditional orthodoxy or of reasoning but rather by their results as shown in a good life, such a life including spiritual experiences which are beyond the comprehension of ordinary men. Thus in the Sandaka-sutta Ânanda lays it down that both orthodoxy and pure rationalism are uncertain guides. They are both "partly sound and partly unsound: right here and wrong there".[1] Whereas a natural ecclesiastical instinct, common to all churches, prompts the Buddhist clergy to say like Asoka[2] that all the words of the Buddha are well said, this liberality and willingness to recognize good wherever it is found lead to the admission that everything which is well said may be considered as a word of the Buddha, a principle which is actually laid down in Mahayanist works[3] and clearly prepares the way for a very extensive canon.

At the present day Buddhists in Ceylon, Burma, Siam, and Cambodja accept the three Piṭakas in the Pali text and do not recognize or even know of the Mahayanist works venerated as scripture in the Far East. The Mahayanists are more liberal. In China and Japan large monasteries generally possess a copy of the Chinese Tripiṭaka which contains among other things translations of works similar to the first four Nikâyas, though not identical with them and originally composed in Sanskrit, not in Pali. But this Tripiṭaka, though treated with external reverence,[4] is not really equivalent to the scriptures of other religions. It is a vast collection of theological literature consisting of more than 1,600 works mostly in many volumes made by order of the Emperor of China (or to be strictly accurate it is one of many such collections), and it represents not the books approved by any section of Buddhists for purposes of devotion or doctrine but the treatises which learned Chinese thought worth preserving for any reason. Thus it often contains several translations of one Indian

[1] Maj. Nik., lxxvi.

[2] In the Bhabra Edict.

[3] Śikshâsamuccaya, p. 15 (Bendall's edition), quoting the Adhyâśayasaṃcodana-sûtra: "Everything that is well said, Maitreya, is a word of the Buddha."

[4] For instance, it is often placed in a revolving bookcase, which the devout reverently turn round, hoping to acquire the same merit as if they had read the contents.

text, and includes with wide tolerance both Hinayanist and Mahayanist writings of all schools. One considerable section consists of works composed by Chinese authors and obviously corresponding to what we should call Church history. But certain books contained in this library have a reputation and influence far greater than that enjoyed by any text known in the lands of the Hînayâna. It must be confessed that in those countries, though the Tripiṭaka is studied by the clergy and read to the laity on certain occasions, it has not the same influence as the Bible or Koran in Christian or Mohammedan countries. But in the Far East and within the limits of certain sects, some books such as the Lotus [1] and the three treatises about the Paradise of Amitâbha,[2] do enjoy a somewhat similar position. This high status is occasionally accorded to Chinese and Japanese compositions. Thus Hōnen, the founder of the Jōdo sect, expressly declares [3] that the writings of the Chinese teacher Zendō (Shan-tao, A.D. 613–681) are the direct teaching of Amitâbha and of the same value as sûtras. So, too, the Shōshinge and Wasan of Shinran are revered by millions in Japan.[4] But most Mahayanist sacred books which have influenced the Far East are Chinese translations of Indian originals. They arrived from the West claiming to be the word of the Buddha and a revelation of the truth and had been accepted as such in their native land according to the easy-going principles described above. But the Chinese have more of the critical spirit than the Hindus, and their scholars were accustomed to discuss the history and authenticity of classical texts. They could not fail to be struck by the fact that the various discourses put into the mouth of the Buddha obviously teach very different doctrines. The T'ien-t'ai sect devised an explanation of these divergences which is in substance accepted by most Buddhists in China and Japan. It is that the Buddha's teaching was progressive and that at different periods of his life he taught various

[1] The Saddharmapuṇḍarîka-sûtra commonly called Hokke-kyō in Japan, N., Nos. 134–9.

[2] The Long and Short Sukhâvatî-vyûhas and the Amitâyurdhyâna-sûtra, see N., No. 23 (5), Nos. 199, 200, and 198.

[3] In his book called Senchakushū. Compare *Hōnen the Buddhist Saint*, tr. by Coates and Ishiyuka, p. 347.

[4] The Shōshinge is written in Chinese but the Wasan or hymns are in Japanese. Rennyo, a celebrated doctor of the Shinshū, quotes in one of his Epistles (i, 2) the Sukhâvatî-vyûha and the Wasan as if they were of the same authority, and these Epistles are read in Shinshū temples as St. Paul's are in Christian churches.

doctrines, none of course erroneous, but some suited to the comprehension of simple hearers and others approximating more and more nearly to absolute truth. Five periods [1] are distinguished in the teaching of the Master and are called by the names of the sûtras in which the special doctrine revealed in each period is supposed to be preserved. The first period, extending for three weeks after he attained enlightenment, is known as 華嚴 Kegon or Avataṃsaka. In these days of ecstasy he is supposed to have preached the complete truth to nine assemblies of spirits and mortals, appearing miraculously in different places while his body remained motionless under the Bo tree. But he found that only the higher intelligencies among superhuman beings could grasp his meaning and accordingly he entirely changed his style of preaching. During the next twelve years, known as the 阿含 Agon period, he expounded the doctrine now contained in the Âgamas, that is the four treatises roughly corresponding to the Pali Nikâyas. In the third period, which lasted eight years, he preached the 方等 Hō-dō or Vaipulya-sûtras, and in the fourth, which lasted no less than twenty-two, the 般若 Hannya or Prajñâpâramitâ. In the fifth and last period, estimated as eight years, he revealed the Lotus or 法華經 Hokke-kyō, regarded as the crown and quintessence of all revelation.[2] These five phases are compared to the five forms which milk may assume, namely, ordinary milk, cream, fresh butter, clarified butter, and the ultimate essence or extract of milk.

Only a robust faith can believe that the Avataṃsaka-sûtra, which teaches a thorough-going idealism and is obviously a product of mature Mahayanism, can represent the first teaching of the Buddha. But the oldest accounts of that teaching contain two traditions which seem to be undisputed and in themselves probable. The texts which describe the Enlightenment agree in saying that at first he hesitated to preach because he thought the truth which he had learnt was too hard for mankind to grasp. It was only after an internal struggle—described in the legend as an appeal made

[1] Go-ji in Japanese. A common phrase is 五時八敎 Go-ji hak-kyō. The five periods and eight methods of teaching. The theory is explained in vols. i and x of the 妙法蓮華經玄義 Miao-fa-lien-hua-ching-hsüan-i, a commentary on the Lotus written by Chih-I (Nanjio, 1534). See also Nanjio, Nos. 1568–9 and 1551. Also the 天台四敎儀集註 T'ien-t'ai-ssŭ-chiao-i-chi-chu of Mang Jun (Nanjio, 1635).

[2] In the last day and night of his life he is said to have revealed the Mahâparinirvâna-sûtra (see Nanjio's catalogue, class v, Nos. 113 to 125). This is not the same work as No. xvi in the Pali Dīgha Nikâya.

by Brahmâ—that he resigned himself to the heavy task of making difficult truths intelligible to minds of very various capacities. Secondly, many expressions in the oldest documents imply that he knew more than he thought it wise to teach.[1] His persistent refusal to reply to several fundamental questions—such as are space and time finite or infinite and what is the condition of a Buddha after death—seems to indicate that there are subjects with which human language is inadequate to deal. Taking such passages into consideration, it is perhaps not illegitimate to imagine that after the Enlightenment he believed he had a full and complete vision of the truth, but that, when he was confronted with the practical problem of preaching, he felt that much of the vision was above and beyond all human speech and deliberately circumscribed his teaching, limiting his message to what ordinary men could make use of and understand.[2]

At first sight, too, it does not seem unreasonable to suppose that during the Buddha's long career as a teacher his views underwent some change and development or, as the orthodox would prefer to put it, that his disciples grew in wisdom and spirituality and were able to receive more and more of the truth. Certainly such a supposition would be necessary if, like Far Eastern Buddhists, we were to accept the great Mahayanist sûtras, the Lotus, the Prajñâparamitâ, and so on, as accounts of what he actually said. But the unanimous verdict of European scholars is that these works were composed many centuries after his death and that, if we desire historical information about his preaching, our only chance is to seek for it in the older parts of the Pali Piṭakas and in the Chinese translations of those Sanskrit works which cover much the same ground. It is generally agreed that these older parts are the four Nikâyas and some works (e.g. the Sutta Nipâta) included in the fifth Nikâya, as well as portions of the Vinaya. If we limit ourselves

[1] In the Saṃ. Nik., lvi, 31, it is related how he once when walking in a forest plucked a bunch of leaves. The truths, he said, which he had taught his disciples were like the leaves which he held in his hand, while those which he knew but had not taught were as many as the leaves of the forest. The parable of the blind men and the elephant (Udâna, vi, 4) seems to imply that ordinary human intelligence is incapable of grasping the Universe as a whole.

[2] The well-known passage in the Mahâparinibbâna-sûtta (ii, § 25) in which the Buddha says that there was no such thing as a closed fist in his teaching and that he had made no distinction between esoteric and exoteric may seem to contradict these ideas of gradual or partial revelation. But the saying may be fairly interpreted as applying to useful knowledge only. The Pali texts distinctly represent the Buddha as refusing to answer apparently important questions when he felt that the answer would merely perplex the questioner, e.g. Saṃ. Nik., xliv, 10.

to them, we find that they contain little which supports the idea that the later sayings of the Buddha as compared with the earlier show growth, advance, or progress. It is true that the account of the last months of his life represents him as using constantly a new formula [1] which extols the blessedness of virtue, meditation, and wisdom when found together, but except for the prominence given to paññâ or wisdom—the prajñâ which plays so prominent a part in later works—there is no approximation to Mahayanist doctrine. Nor does the discourse which he is said to have preached in the hall at Mahâvana near Vesâlî [2] and which is apparently intended as a last epitome of his teaching show any tendency towards transcendental or idealistic views. It lays stress on mindfulness, energy, and meditation: it emphasizes the idea that the spiritual life is a struggle (padhâna, vayâma) and also emphasizes wisdom (paññâ) and joy (pîti), but it cannot be said to give any revelation of the final truth which is not contained in earlier discourses.

Some passages give a picture of him in his youth as a man of boundless intellectual activity who spared neither mind nor body in the work of testing by practice as well as argument any system which seemed worthy of his attention. But when once he had made up his mind and believed that he had discovered the truth, he is represented as filled with a calm confidence in his own power and knowledge which left no room for change or development. He taught, but did not consult. There is no indication that he accepted and worked into his system ideas derived from either intelligent disciples to whom he gave explanations or opponents with whom he argued. Nor need this assurance and self-sufficiency seem strange. It is probably a gift natural to great teachers, for, like the Buddha, Christ and Mohammed do not seem to have been influenced during their ministry by either friends or opponents. They said what they felt they had to say.

But if the most ancient texts do not indicate that the Buddha changed his teaching during his lifetime, still they do not give a simple and continuous narrative. Though the varied materials of which they are composed may be all relatively old, they present obvious differences of style and date: they contain inconsistencies,[3]

[1] D.N, xvi, 1, § 12 (= ii, p. 81).

[2] D.N., xvi, iii, § 50. The same summary is also given in Maj. Nik., ciii, and Dig. Ṇik., xxviii, § 3.

[3] e.g. it is both stated and denied that women can become saints. Contrast Cullavag., xi, 1, 3, with Maj. Nik., cxv, near the end.

so that the question at once arises what part of them, if any, can be regarded as the *ipsissima verba* of the Master or even a correct statement of the original teaching.

We talk of the Mahâyâna showing growth, or perversion, but do we know the starting point? What is the original doctrine by which we test what we consider to be later developments? In order to answer this question it will be well to state briefly the little which we know about the history of the Pali Canon and our even more meagre information respecting the origin of the version now known in Chinese translations.

The Vinaya Piṭaka professes to describe the collection and composition of the Canon, for the last two chapters of the Cullavagga contain accounts of the Councils of Râjagaha and Vesâlî. The first [1] was held immediately after the Buddha's death in order to fix what was his teaching both as to the discipline to be observed by his followers and as to doctrine: the second, which met a hundred years later, considered and ultimately condemned certain innovations in discipline. This passage was obviously written some time after the second Council which it describes, but it is introduced without any intimation that it is later than the rest of the Vinaya. But we know that the Vinaya received additions. The authenticity of the work called Parivâra was disputed in Ceylon in the first century B.C., and though it was accepted by the orthodox, it was apparently composed in the island about that time. The last chapters of the Cullavagga may have a similar origin.[2]

European scholars have received the story of the Councils with much scepticism, but there is nothing improbable in its main outlines. There can be no doubt as to the respect felt for the rule of life and the doctrine enjoined by the Buddha. After his death, what more natural than to fix what that rule and doctrine were while those who had lived in the Master's company were still alive and could relate their experiences? The procedure said to have been followed by the Council was eminently reasonable. They first examined Upâli as an acknowledged expert in the Vinaya and asked him when and in what circumstances each rule had been laid down. Then in the same way they proceeded to question Ânanda "through the

[1] See especially *Le Concile de Rajagaha* by Przyluski in the series *Buddhica*.

[2] Many books of the Pali Canon, particularly some (though not all) which are included in the Khuddaka Nikâya, are undoubtedly late. e.g. the Peta-vatthu alludes to a king called Pingalaka who lived about two centuries after the Buddha's death. S. Lévi (in *Études Asiatiques*, É. F. d'Ex. Or., 1925) thinks there is proof that the Niddesa was composed "entre la fin du Ier siècle et la fin du iii[me]".

five Nikâyas", his replies about the first two suttas of the Dîgha Nikâya being quoted as an example. There is some resemblance between the style of the Buddhist suttas and of the philosophic discourses or dialogues reported in the Upanishads, but whereas these latter are interested only in the doctrines of Yâjñavalkya and others and not in those sages themselves, it is the personality of the Buddha which dominates the Pali scriptures. Did He say this and, if so, when and where? This importance attached to a personality is without parallel in Indian literature, which is singularly lacking in human detail and has preserved no portrait of kings like Asoka or philosophers like Śankara. It seems reasonable to believe that the words of the Master who made such an impression on his age have been correctly preserved, though it is also only too certain that innovators used his name to give authority to their new doctrines. Oral tradition and trained memories such as are common in India can preserve ancient texts with wonderful accuracy, but there is a universal tendency to enlarge them with later additions.

The Cullavagga itself indicates that the authority of the first Council was not undisputed. When the members had finished reciting the Dhamma and Vinaya in the form approved by them, an elder called Purâṇa arrived with a large following. They asked him to accept their version but he politely refused.[1] "The Dhamma and Vinaya have been well recited by the Theras. Nevertheless, as I heard them and received them from the very mouth of the Lord, in that form will I keep them (in my memory)." According to the Cullavagga, the first Council was concerned only with the Dhamma and Vinaya,[2] but in the account of the second Council the Mâtikâs or indexes are mentioned. They doubtless represent the beginnings of what was afterwards known as the Abhidhamma or third Piṭaka. The name Abhidhamma occurs in the Pali text of the Nikâyas,[3] but there is abundant evidence to show that this Piṭaka is later than the others and different sects included quite different works under this title.

Of the second Council one may say as of the first that the account given, though not confirmed by external evidence and though

[1] Cullavag., xi, i, ii.

[2] But the Asokâvadâna, the Vinaya of the Mûlasarvâstivâdins, and the Chia-ye-chie-ching 迦葉結經 (Nanjio, 1363) mention also the third Piṭaka which is said to have been recited by Kâśyapa.

[3] e.g. Dig. Nik., xxxiii, 10; Maj. Nik., xxxii, lxix, ciii; Ang. Nik., vi, 50. It is often in the compound form *abhidhammakathâ*, talk about the higher or more abstruse parts of the doctrine.

containing some exaggerations,[1] is in its general outlines eminently probable. It is natural that changes and relaxations of discipline should have arisen and that a meeting should have been summoned to consider them. Two points deserve notice. First the Cullavagga emphasizes the differences between the Bhikkhus of the East and the West,[2] indicating that there were already two schools with geographical limits. Secondly, Ceylonese tradition as reported in the Dîpavaṃsa[3] adds to the account given in the Vinaya the statement that the defeated party held a council of their own called the Mahâsangîti which compiled a new version of the scriptures and was the origin of the important Mahâsanghika sect, apparently the precursor of the Mahâyâna. The Chinese pilgrims Fa-Hsien and Hsüan-Tsang also know of this sect, but connect it with the first not with the second Council. Hsüan-Tsang says,[4] apparently on the strength of information received in Magadha, that the schismatic Council included laymen as well as monks and accepted as scripture additional matter including dhâraṇîs or spells. Though these traditions present inconsistencies, the substance of them is probable enough, namely, that in opposition to the strict monasticism of the Theravâda, the sect which edited the Pali Piṭakas, there was a large (Mahâsangha) and popular party, which was disposed to tolerate mythology and magic.[5]

The reign of Asoka, say about 250 B.C., is an important epoch for the history of the Buddhist scriptures. Among his inscriptions is one known as the edict of Bhabra or Bhabru in which he recommends the clergy to study seven passages, most of which have been identified with parts of the Pali Piṭakas. The passages are not quoted but are referred to by descriptive titles such as Future Dangers, the Discourse to Râhula beginning with the subject of lying and the verses about the Sage. Though some of the titles are rather vague, it is noticeable that they all suggest topics familiar

[1] e.g. the age of some of the participants.

[2] Cullavag., xii, 2, 2 ff.

[3] Dîp., 32–8. The monks of the Great Council are said to have made a Sutta Piṭaka and Vinaya Piṭaka of their own and to have rejected certain works. But these rejected works are all relatively late.

[4] Watters, *Yüan Chwang*, 2, pp. 159–161.

[5] The Mahâvastu describes itself as belonging to the Lokuttara branch of the Mahâsanghikas. It apparently corresponds to the Vinaya but, unlike the Pali text, consists chiefly of miraculous narratives, not of monastic rules. Fa-Hsien thought that the Vinaya of the Mahâsanghikas was the fullest and most complete of all the versions and he translated it into Chinese in collaboration with Buddhabhadra.

to the Pali Piṭakas as we know them. We cannot, of course, conclude that Asoka had before him the present text of the Majjhima Nikâya in which the Buddha begins his admonition to Râhula by dwelling on the dangers of untruth, but it is clear that he was acquainted with some version of such a discourse and could refer to a collection of discourses attributed to the Buddha and regarded as scripture.

According to Ceylonese tradition,[1] Asoka also summoned a Council which examined the scriptures and established the Canon. But no confirmation of this has been found in India. The Council is not mentioned in the inscriptions where Asoka records his services to religion nor in Sanskrit works[2] nor by the Chinese pilgrims. Hence many scholars regard it as a late invention.[3] But in enumerating his own good deeds Asoka also fails to mention the missions which he dispatched to foreign countries, though he speaks of them elsewhere, and the story of the Council is extremely probable. Whatever difficulties the stories about a particular council may present, it is clear that *some* councils must have been held or the tradition about them would never have arisen. Asoka, like Kanishka and Constantine in later periods, had embraced a new religion: he found that its adherents were not agreed on many important points and we know from the Bhabra inscription that he was interested in the scriptures. And if this argument, that the action attributed to him is natural, be thought insufficient, some slight confirmation is afforded by the mention of the book called Kathâvatthu in connection with the assembly. This work, which is reckoned as part of the Abhidhamma Piṭaka, is a refutation of various early heresies and its religious atmosphere seems to be that of Asoka's reign and not of later times when Mahayanism had become prominent. The commentary on it begins by stating the orthodox view that it was composed by the Buddha himself in a prophetic spirit, but subsequently it is added that Tissa Moggaliputta recited it at Asoka's Council in order to crush dissentient views. It is hard to see why this admission of human authorship was made, unless the facts connected with the Council were too well known

[1] Mahâvaṃsa, v, 228 ff. Dîpavaṃsa, vii, 40–3, 56–9, and the introduction to the Commentary (ascribed to Buddhaghosa) on the Kathâvatthu, translated in Points of Controversy, pp. 1–7.

[2] The Asokâvadâna says that Asoka summoned 300,000 monks and gave them alms, but does not speak of a council. Cf. Divyâvadâna, xxvii.

[3] But Vincent Smith and Thomas (in *Cambridge History of India*) accept it as probably historical.

to be denied. It is noteworthy that the author of the Kathâvatthu makes nearly two hundred quotations from the Pali scriptures, which he generally cites as "words spoken by the Lord" or the Suttanta. He was apparently familiar with the Vinaya, five Nikâyas, and some of the Abhidhamma.[1]

In the inscriptions of Sanchi we find the words Sutakini, one who knows a sutta, Petaki, one who knows a Piṭaka (or the Piṭakas), and Pancanekayika, one who knows the five Nikâyas. This shows that the writers were already familiar with the fivefold division, but unfortunately the date of the inscriptions is not so certain as could be wished. They may be of the second century B.C. or perhaps not earlier than the first century.[2]

The text of the Pali Piṭakas current in Ceylon, Burma, Siam, and Cambodja professes to be that which was first committed to writing in Ceylon in the time of Vattagamani, who probably reigned from 29 to 17 B.C. and summoned a council which is said to have met at the Alu Vihara near Matale. It was accepted by the great monastery called Mahâvihara but not by all the other religious establishments in the island, and for many centuries we hear of other versions of the scriptures composed by heretics, such as the Vetulyakas. Though the task of committing the whole Canon to writing was first attempted by this Council, it is obviously probable that portions of it existed in manuscript before a complete edition was contemplated, but, if so, we know nothing whatever about them. But this is no reason for suspecting the genuineness of the text, provided that there was a fixed text.[3] Probably at this time writing was not used by the Brahmans for religious purposes and the whole of the Vedic literature was still preserved in memory only. Even now that literature could be recovered if all manuscripts and printed copies were lost, for there are still many Hindus, particularly in south India, who know by heart a whole Samhitâ

[1] Points of Controversy. Index of quotations, pp. 401–4.

[2] Marshall (in *Camb. Hist. of India*, p. 682) says that the pillars bear inscriptions in early Brahmi probably of the first century B.C., but that the plinth dates back to Sunga or Maurya times. Foucher (*Le Stupa de Sanchi*) puts the inscriptions at about 150 B.C.

[3] In Maj. Nik., xxvi, the Buddha in speaking of the doctrines of Âlâra and Udaka says twice that so far as oral recital and repetition were concerned he could say off both the statement of doctrine and the elders' explanation of it (*Oṭṭhapahatamattena lapitalâpanamattena ñânavâdañca vadâmi theravâdañca jânâmi*). In Dîg. Nik., xxvii, 23, the Pali text twice contains the expression *ganthe karontâ* making books. But the corresponding passage in Chinese (Takakusu's Tripiṭaka, vol. i, p. 38, col. 3) reads 誦習爲業.

with its accessory treatises. Writing was probably regarded with more favour in Buddhist monasteries than among Brahmans, but even when the Chinese pilgrim Fa-Hsien was in India (A.D. 405–411) he found some difficulty in obtaining the manuscripts which he desired, because the various versions of the Vinaya were preserved chiefly by memory.

The text fixed in Ceylon was the canon of the school known as Theravâda or Vibhajjavâdins, but there were other ancient sects who apparently recognized other versions. Thus the Sarvâstivâdins had an Abhidhamma of their own : the Sautrântikas rejected the Abhidhamma altogether : the Sammitiyas, who held special views about the nature of the âtman, rejected texts which were unfavourable to those views.[1] There is also, as already mentioned, a very large collection of Indian scriptures extant in Chinese translations.[2] The works classed as Abhidharma in this collection are entirely different from those accepted by the Theravâda. In the section called Vinaya there are, besides numerous smaller treatises, five recensions of the whole code, one of which, the Mahîśâsaka Vinaya, appears to be similar to the Pali version, though not identical. The enormous Sûtra Piṭaka (comprising 1,081 works) contains not only several translations of the principal Mahâyâna-sûtras such as the Lotus, Lankâvatâra, and Avataṃsaka, but also a relatively short section devoted to the Hînayâna-sûtras in which are translations both complete and partial of the four Âgamas.[3] These roughly correspond to the first four of the Pali Nikâyas, the fifth being absent.[4] The Chinese translations were apparently made from Sanskrit originals[5] and various Sanskrit texts have been discovered in Central Asia which seem to be portions of a recension of the Vinaya and suttas analogous to the Pali version, though presenting differences both in arrangement and wording. These

[1] Abhidharmakośa, ix. See Poussin, vol. v, p. 251.

[2] There is also an extensive thesaurus of Tibetan translations from the Sanskrit, contained in the Kanjur. It includes the Vinaya according to the recension of the Mulasarvâstivâdins and also a section called Mdo or Sûtra. But so far as can be judged from the catalogues published, there are not in it any collections of sûtras corresponding to the Âgamas or Nikâyas, and the translations, which were mostly made in the ninth and eleventh centuries, represent the Buddhist literature studied in medieval Bengal. See my *Hinduism and Buddhism*, iii, 373.

[3] The word is found in the Pali Canon, e.g. Mahâvag., x, 1, 2, and Cullavag., xii, 2, 1. Agatâgamo, one who is well versed in the Âgama.

[4] As a collection, that is. Treatises corresponding to some of the books included in it, such as the Dhammapada, are found in other parts of the collection.

[5] But see Anesaki, "The four Buddhist Agamas in Chinese," p. 4, in *Trans. As. Soc. Japan*, 1908.

Âgamas have recently been studied by many Chinese and Japanese who are interested in modern scholarship, but they play no part in the religious life of either the clergy or laity.

We naturally think of Sanskrit and Pali as separate languages like French and Italian,[1] but it must be remembered that in Indian dramas the superior characters speak Sanskrit and the inferior Prakrit and sometimes more than one dialect[2] of Prakrit. It is assumed that they understand one another and that the reader understands them all. According to tradition the Buddha refused to let his teaching be made a series of sacred formulæ like the Vedic verses of the Brahmans and allowed all men to learn it in their own language.[3] It was, of course, laudable to record the sacred teaching in as lucid and elegant a style as possible, and at a certain period and in certain districts this meant rewriting it in Sanskrit or something like Sanskrit, for Buddhist Sanskrit is far from classical and in verse many irregular forms were allowed to remain because they could not be made correct without spoiling the metre.[4] We do not know the history of this Sanskrit recension well enough to fix the date accurately and the Chinese translations are relatively late.[5] But it is probable that renderings of the suttas into Sanskrit were

[1] Probably Modern Greek offers a parallel to the relationship of Sanskrit and Prakrit. When I was in the Levant thirty-five years ago (and probably at present) the leading articles in a Constantinople newspaper were written in a language which was almost that of Plutarch and could be understood by anyone who had learnt classical Greek in England. But a novel offered serious difficulties to such a person and a play written in the language of peasants was wholly unintelligible. But all three compositions were supposed to be Greek, though sometimes a distinction was drawn between Hellenic and Romaic.

[2] In Sanskrit plays discovered in Central Asia the Buddha is made to speak in Sanskrit and the inferior characters speak three kinds of Prakrit. See Lüders, *Bruchstücke Buddh. Dramen*, pp. 21–69.

[3] Cullavag., v, 33. I find it hard to accept Thomas's view (*Life of Buddha*, p. 254) that *sakkâya niruttiyâ* means that the word of the Buddha is to be mastered in its own grammar. The phrase occurs twice in a few lines. First it is complained that certain disciples corrupt the Buddha's words *Te sakkâya niruttiyâ buddhavacanam dûsenti*. Here the phrase is admitted to mean by the use of their own dialect or grammar. When immediately afterwards the Buddha gives permission to learn his teaching, sakkâya niruttiyâ, is he likely to be using the same phrase in an entirely different sense ? See, too, Maj. Nik., cxxix (= vol. iii, p. 233), in which it is laid down that one should neither affect provincialism in speech nor depart from recognized usage.

[4] Fragments of a Sanskrit version of the Sutta Nipâta seem to show signs of being a translation made from the vernacular. See *J.R.A.S.*, 1916, p. 719 ff.

[5] The complete translations of the Âgamas were not made till the fourth or fifth centuries A.D. and none of the earlier and fragmentary renderings are ascribed to any date earlier than the second century.

made as early as the first or second centuries B.C. The Pali text appears to represent another literary version of the Buddha's word. It is nearer to the original perhaps than Sanskrit but it can hardly be the original. For though there is no agreement among scholars as to the home of Pali, it is generally admitted that it is a literary and not very early form of some Indian dialect. It is not the same as the language of Asoka's inscriptions or, it would seem, of the scriptures as known to him. At the same time it is probable that neither Sanskrit nor Pali differed from the various Aryan vernaculars much more than standard English differs from the speech heard in Devonshire, Scotland, or Yorkshire.

The contents of the four Âgamas in the Chinese version [1] have been analysed by Professor Anesaki and more recently by Professor Akanuma. The resemblance to the Pali version is greatest in the Dîgha Nikâya.[2] The Chinese has thirty sûtras, of which twenty-eight agree more or less with the Pali. Six of the Pali sûtras are omitted, mostly for explicable reasons,[3] and three new ones are added, the principal being the last called Shiḥ-chi (Loka-dhâtu), a long account of the constitution of the Universe, which appears to be a compilation. The order in which the suttas are arranged is quite different in Pali and Chinese and this is also the case in the Majjhima Nikâya.[4] In this collection the difference of matter is more considerable. The Pali text has 152 suttas, the Chinese 221. Of the former only ninety-eight are found in the Chinese version, although thirty of those omitted are placed in other Âgamas. Of the remaining Chinese suttas, no less than seventy-five correspond to portions of the Pali Anguttara. A few are found in the Jâtaka and one in the Divyâvadâna.[5]

[1] See Anesaki, "The four Buddhist Agamas in Chinese," in *Trans. As. Soc. Japan*, 1908, and Chizen Akanuma's Comparative Catalogue of the Chinese Âgamas and Pali Nikâyas published at Nagoya in 1929.

[2] 長阿含經 Chō Agon-kyō in Japanese pronunciation.

[3] The Mahâsatipaṭṭhâna and Lakkhana-suttas, the greater part of which is found in both the Digha and Majjhima Nikâyas, are given only in the latter. The Subha-sutta is practically the same as the Sâmaññaphala-sutta. The Jâliya-sutta is merely a repetition of the Mahâli-sutta, but it is not clear why the Chinese omits both. It combines the Mahâparinibbâna and Mahâsudassana-suttas. This version is not the same as the Mahayanist account of the Buddha's last days (N., Nos. 113 and 114). The Âṭânâṭiya-sutta is perhaps omitted because it consists chiefly of a list of Indian local spirits, though the somewhat similar Mahâsamaya-sutta is included.

[4] 中阿含經 Chū Agon-kyō in Japanese pronunciation.

[5] No. 60 = Divyâv., pp. 210–226. An account of an Emperor called Mandhâta or Murdhâta.

The third or Saṃyukta-Âgama corresponding to the Saṃyutta Nikâya is called Tsa [1] in Chinese, meaning varied or miscellaneous. The division of the Pali text into chapters and sections is extremely complicated and that of the Chinese text is not less so, though the arrangement is different. Anesaki states that, though none of the divisions and sûtras can be said to be identical in the two versions, similarity and affinity are undeniable and he considers it certain that both texts are descended from one and the same source. From Akanuma's comparative tables, it appears that the greater part of the Chinese version corresponds with passages to be found in Pali, to a large extent in the Saṃyutta but also in the other Nikâyas. Quite a number of texts correspond with the Pali Itivuttaka. On the other hand, large portions of the Pali text seem not to be represented by any Chinese translation.[2]

The fourth Âgama is called in Chinese Tsêng-i,[3] which seems to represent Ekottara rather than Anguttara, though the arrangement of topics in numbered categories is not followed so strictly as in Pali. Anesaki states that the divergence from the Pali text is much more remarkable in this Âgama than in the others : that the style has the chracteristics of Mahayanist texts and that the version belonged to some school which had very different traditions from the Theravâda and perhaps was a section of the Mahâsanghikas. His analysis of the Chinese text, however, shows that parallel passages to all its sections can be found in the Pali, about half coming from the Anguttara and half from the other Nikâyas. It will be remembered that seventy-five suttas of the Pali Anguttara are included in the Chinese Majjhima.

The analogy of what happened to the compositions of later teachers warrants moderate confidence in the historical character of the Pali Nikâyas, in so far as it shows that Indians preserve the original words of a teacher, though they also make large additions to them. Thus the hymns of Nanak, the founder of the Sikhs who

[1] 雜 *Zō* in Japanese pronunciation. There are two translations of the complete text mentioned in Nanjio's catalogue, No. 544, made by Guṇabhadra about A.D. 440, and No. 546, made by unknown translators some time between 350 and 431. There is also a small selection of twenty-seven Saṃyukta sûtras, N., No. 547. See Anesaki, l.c., p. 31.

[2] Thus the whole or greater part of nineteen Saṃyuttas out of fifty-six is missing, namely, xviii, xxvi–xxxiii, xxxvii, xl, xliii, and xlv–li.

[3] 增壹 Japanese Zō-ichi. The translation was originally made by Dharmanandin, a monk of Tukhara who arrived at Chang-an in A.D. 384. Unfortunately his work was thrown into confusion by local wars, he left China, and his papers were revised and put in order by Sanghadeva, a monk from Kabul.

lived from 1469 to 1538, were preserved and apparently scholars accept the text as authentic, but no authorized collection of them seems to have been made until the time of Arjun (1581–1606), the fourth Guru or head of the Sikhs, and this collection also contains hymns by Nanak's successors, including Arjun himself, and by other writers, for the object was avowedly to collect not merely the works of Nanak but any hymns in which the true doctrine was sung. Even later some verses by Teg Bahadur (c. 1670) and a distich by Govind Singh were added and eventually Govind Singh (1675–1708) composed a supplementary scripture for his followers into which he introduced many innovations. This happened in an age when the use of writing was familiar, but in the centuries following the death of Gotama the course of events may have been slower, though not dissimilar. On the other hand, Nanak was not so great an organizer as Gotama. The constitution of the Sikh sect, as we know it, was due less to him than to the fourth Guru Ram Das. But Gotama established in his own lifetime a powerful religious order and an influential congregation of lay believers. For the existence of these bodies it was necessary to have a statement of both his rule of life and his doctrine.

He preached for some forty-five years to various audiences and in different places. It is probable that he repeated his discourses and that the Piṭakas give a correct picture when they represent particular sermons or parables as being well known even in his lifetime. We often hear that he gave them special names. "What, Lord, is the name of this exposition?" asks Ânanda. "Let it be known as the exposition of the honeyed cake." [1] So, too, he refers to the parable of the Colt which he had used long before and repeats it,[2] and Sâriputta quotes the Homily of the Saw, as if it were well-known scripture.[3] Nevertheless the Pali Piṭaka as it stands, even the Vinaya and the first four Nikâyas, cannot have been put together at the Council of Râjagaha or any meeting held about that time. Apart from obvious appendices like the description of the Councils

[1] Madhupiṇḍika, Maj. N., xviii. For other instances see Dîg. Nik., i and xxix, Maj. N., xii, xxi, xxviii, xlix, cxv, cxvii. Saṃ. Nik., xxxv, 194. Dhammapariyâya is apparently the oldest (as it is also the latest) name for the Buddha's actual words. When a discourse had been provided with an explanation of the circumstances in which it was uttered, it became a sutta.

[2] Maj. Nik., lxv.

[3] Maj. Nik., xxviii. The Kakacûpamasutta is M.N., xxi. So, too, in Maj. Nik., xxii (= Cullavagga, i, 32), ten well-known parables are mentioned by the Buddha and others, seven of which are given in detail in Maj. Nik., liv.

in the Cullavagga, it is clear that many suttas must have been composed a considerable time after that date. Some avowedly deal with events which took place after the Buddha's death,[1] and a passage in the Majjhima Nikâya speaks of the country of the Yonas where there are no castes but only masters and slaves.[2] This can hardly have been written until some time after Alexander's invasion (326 B.C.). The discussions in the Pali Nikâyas about the authenticity of words attributed to the Buddha [3] and the warnings against Suttantas remarkable for literary beauty rather than sound doctrine seem to belong to a period when several oral recensions of the scriptures had had time to grow up, and, though the Master himself is represented as giving warnings and criteria to distinguish the true and false, he is often made to do so in a prophetic spirit and with reference to the future.

Again, in the Nikâyas as we have them several strata are clearly discernible. In the first and second Nikâyas the suttas are relatively long and profess to record the discourses delivered by the Buddha on certain occasions, whether on one or more subjects. In the Saṃyutta Nikâya the discourses are shorter, deal with one matter only, and are classified according to their topics, which may be doctrinal, personal, geographical, etc. Thus one section deals with sayings about causation, others with remarks on incidents concerned with the disciple Kassapa or the kingdom of Kosala. The Anguttara is a similar collection, but the suttas are arranged not according to subjects but according to numerical categories, the three messengers of the Gods, the seven conditions of welfare, and so on. As collections, the Saṃyutta [4] and Anguttara seem to be more artificial and recent than the first two Nikâyas, but it does not follow that the sayings which they contain are recent. This is also true of the fifth or Khuddaka Nikâya, to which no corresponding Sanskrit Âgama is known. It is late as a collection and includes some very late works, but on the other hand some of its contents, such as the Sutta Nipâta, are among the most ancient Buddhist documents which we possess.

[1] e.g. Dîg. Nik., xxiii. Maj. Nik., lxxxiv, xciv, cviii. Ang. Nik., v, chap. 50, deals with a King of Pâtaliputta called Muṇḍa who began to reign about forty years after the Buddha's death.

[2] Maj. Nik., xciii.

[3] See above, pp. 10–11; Saṃ. Nik., xx, 7 (= vol. ii, p. 266). Similarly, provisions for learning suttas by heart for fear they may be forgotten (e.g. Mahâvagga, iii, 5, 9) seem to point to a period after the Buddha's death.

[4] Thus the Saṃyutta, xxii, § 4, quotes by name the Sakkapañha-sutta of the Dîgha Nikâya (No. xxi), which does not seem to be one of the oldest suttas.

Since so many long discourses are attributed to the Buddha, it is only natural to conclude that he did deliver ample homilies treating of various subjects and sometimes breaking into dialogue with his hearers. The manner of his teaching would leave its trace in tradition. But the question arises, are the long sermons which have come down to us a fairly accurate report of what he said on any one occasion, or are they a later patchwork, a not unskilful arrangement of materials found elsewhere? Take, for instance, the Alagaddûpama-sutta, the sutta of the venomous snake.[1] It is one of the most notable discourses in the Majjhima collection. Its cadences have a fervour and authority which do not ring like the words of a compiler; it passes from one deep theme to another, but the transitions, though sometimes unexpected, are not unnatural. A Bhikkhu named Ariṭṭha obstinately held that a saint can sin and and still not fall from grace, and was finally summoned by the Buddha himself and sternly reproved for his error. No one can indulge in sensuality without corrupting himself, says the Master. Those who represent me as teaching the contrary are fools. They learn the scripture and use it for dispute and argument without really understanding it. They are like a man who catches a snake and does not know how to hold it: so the snake bites him. A raft is a very useful thing when one has to cross a river, but it is foolish to carry it on one's back afterwards.[2] You must learn to discard good things and still more bad things. There are various forms of the erroneous belief in an unchanging and permanent self. You must get rid of them all and not worry about the non-existent. But can one worry about the non-existent, ask the disciples? Yes, you can, if you form fanciful ideas about the nature and destiny of the soul, for when you hear the preaching of the Buddha and learn that they are false, you will think that you have been deprived of something that you really possessed. Then follows an eloquent exposition of the true doctrine as to these matters,[3] a description of the peace of mind enjoyed by those who master it, and a most emphatic and interesting assertion that it is entirely false to say that this doctrine teaches annihilation. The Buddha is not moved by either criticism or praise, neither should you be.

[1] Maj. Nik., No. xxii.

[2] The Parable of the Raft is alluded to by name in the Mahâtaṇhâ-sankhaya-sutta (Maj. Nik., xxxviii).

[3] I am not attempting here to give an analysis of either the true doctrine or of the errors condemned, but merely to consider the literary structure of the sutta.

Put away from you all that is not yours. Here follows the celebrated parable about the sticks and leaves of the Jeta-wood, and the peroration asserts that it is beyond human power to trace the course of Saints who have finished their life-work and laid down their burden, but that those who are striving towards sanctity are sure of a happy future. It ends with the remarkable words "All who have but faith in me and love for me are destined to Paradise".

It would be most interesting to know whether these words are a genuine utterance of Gotama, for they contain in germ the emotional and popular side of later Buddhism, and many other sayings in the discourse are of historical importance. But if we turn our attention not to its literary merits but to the details of its composition, we cannot but notice that it contains an obvious interpolation. When the Buddha speaks of the scriptures, a stock phrase is put into his mouth describing them as consisting of suttas, gâthâs, jâtakas, etc., which is very much as if Christ were represented as mentioning the Gospels, Acts, and Epistles. But besides this obvious anachronism, the whole tone of the advice about the scriptures, the warnings that they may be misused, and that they have only a limited value (for that is apparently the meaning of the parable of the raft), seems natural not in the lifetime of the founder but in a rather later period when there was a danger that believers might be seduced by literary disputes and forget the great truths of religion. The first part of the sutta containing the story of Ariṭṭha is found verbatim in the Vinaya,[1] and the parable of the Jeta-wood in two passages of the Saṃyutta Nikâya.[2] It is also curious to find that in another passage of the Samyutta[3] a parable about snakes is followed immediately as here by a parable about a raft, although the details are not the same.

This sûtra is also found in the Chinese version of the Madhyama Âgama. It is called (in Japanese pronunciation) Arita-kyō and comes next to the Satei-kyō (= Maj. Nik. xxxviii) doubtless because both relate how members of the Buddha's order, Ariṭṭha and Sati, held erroneous views and were publicly reprimanded by the Master. The Chinese text is somewhat more concise than the Pali, but on the

[1] Cullavagga, i, 32, and likewise in the Sutta-Vibhanga on the 68th Pacittaya (Oldenberg, *Vinaya*, vol. iv, p. 133 ff.).

[2] Saṃ. Nik., xxii, § 33 (= vol. iii, p. 33), xxv, § 137 (= vol. iv, p. 82). It occurs twice with slight variations because it is given a place in the Khanda Saṃyutta as referring to the skandhas and in the Salayatana Saṃyutta as referring to the senses.

[3] Vol. iv, p. 172 (= xxxv, iv, 5, § 197).

whole the correspondence is close. The sequence of incidents and topics is the same, and almost all the remarkable expressions which occur in the Pali are to be found also in the Chinese. Ariṭṭha's[1] heresy is described as the doctrine that indulgence in sensual pleasures is not a hindrance to a holy life,[2] and he is duly reproved first by his colleagues and then by the Buddha. Parables are referred to, as in the Pali, but eight and not ten are mentioned.[3] It is most remarkable that the Chinese text, as well as the Pali, commits the anachronism of making the Buddha enumerate the various classes of writings which compose the canon and the enumeration is even more elaborate, for twelve categories are mentioned.[4] Then come the parables about catching a snake and the raft and the warning that one should reject good things and *a fortiori* bad things. The passage describing the six erroneous views and the subsequent discussion are somewhat difficult,[5] but the conclusion is the same. He who has true knowledge is not confined by moats or fences or bolted gates. Indra, Ishana, and Brahmâ cannot track him down. The Tathâgata does not preach annihilation and is above praise and blame. Then follow the parable of the Jeta-wood and the peroration as in the Pali. This translation was made in China between A.D. 391 and 398 by Gautama Sanghadeva, a monk from Kabul. It is probable, therefore, that he used the text current in the north-west of India. Since the translation is so late, it cannot throw any light on the date of the sûtra, but it seems to indicate that there was a very widespread tradition in the Buddhist community from Ceylon to the north-west of India, which related

[1] His epithet, which is in Pali *Gadabâdhipubba*, is not translated but treated as a proper name: "who was originally Gadabari," 本伽陀婆利.

[2] 行欲者無障礙 that those who indulge their desires have no impediment.

[3] The bone, the lump of flesh, the torch, the fire-pit, the poisonous snake, the dream, the loan, the hanging fruit.

[4] Shō-kyō 正經; Ka-ei 歌詠; Kisetsu 記說; Geta 偈他; In-en 因緣; Sen-roku 撰錄; Hon-ki 本起; Shisetsu 此說; Shō-sho 生處; Kōge 廣解; Mizō-u-hō 未曾有法; Setsu-gi 說義. In the Mahâparinirvâna-sûtra (Nanjio, 114, vol. 14) the 十二部經 Jū-ni bu-kyō, or Twelve parts of the scriptures, are mentioned. The names are all transliterations, not translations of Indian words, and correspond to Sûtra, Geya, Vyâkaraṇa, Gâthâ, Udâna, Nidâna, Avadâna, Itivuttaka, Vaipulya, Adbhûtadharma, Upadeśa.

[5] Apparently the passage *yam kiñci rûpam atîtânâgatapaccuppannam*, etc., at the bottom of p. 138, vol. i, of the Pali Text Society's edition is transferred to the description of the six views on p. 135.

without material variation how the Buddha dealt with Ariṭṭha and what comments he made.

Now assuming the story of Ariṭṭha to be historical, it is perfectly natural that it should be dealt with in both the Vinaya and the Suttas. The former is concerned with discipline and cites this case as a precedent for the penalty to be imposed on those who will not give up their errors when warned: the sutta reports a discourse of the Buddha and recounts the incident which prompted it. The parable of the Jeta-wood as it stands by itself in the Saṃyutta seems somewhat abrupt: it reads like an extract rather than a self-contained homily. But, on the other hand, its position in the sutta before us raises difficulties. Does it really support the argument which it is apparently supposed to clinch? And further, though the narrative flows on persuasively, there seems to be a difference in the mental horizon of the first part (that which recurs in the Vinaya) and of the Buddha's discourse. Ariṭṭha's sin was that he misrepresented what the Buddha had said and would not listen to wiser people who warned him that he had misunderstood it. The Buddha condemns this clearly enough but, as he continues, seems to regard it as a case of misinterpreting the scriptures.

Have we here a composite work made with good materials but tacked on in later days to a well-known ancient story, or a genuine tradition (with some later additions no doubt) of what the Buddha really did and said on this occasion? I cite this case to show the difficulties which beset our inquiries, not to offer a solution, for it is to be feared that a definite answer to such questions will never be possible and that the most that can be safely done is to indicate certain probabilities. In the first place, the Buddhist suttantas are something new in Indian literature. In spite of some resemblances to the Upanishads, they have a manner and style of their own, and the simplest and most natural explanation of this is that the new type is due to the appearance of a personality who popularized a new style of preaching. Further it seems probable that the summaries of doctrine attributed to the Buddha—such as the Noble Eight-fold Path and the discourse on Anattâ—are genuine. The great danger of Indian oral tradition is, as already mentioned, that it adds and embellishes. But the brevity of these formulæ is a guarantee that they have not been amplified, and perhaps it is not over credulous to accept in the same spirit such passages as the paragraphs on progress in the holy life which recur in the Dîgha Nikâya [1] and some of the discourses said to have been delivered during his last days and recorded in the Mahâparinibbana-sutta. But this instance reminds us of the need for caution, for if in such matters anything is certain, it is that other discourses contained in that narrative—for instance, the long reproof administered to Ânanda because he did not beg the Buddha to live on until the end of the present æon—are the products of later fancy. Probably many of the racy parables are authentic utterances, but here again we must sadly confess that many now found in the text might be the work of an imitator, and when the authenticity of a parable is a matter of real interest it is often not easy to find any criterion by which to judge it. Take for instance the striking story of the blind men who tried to describe the shape of an elephant after touching some one part, some another. It occurs in the Udâna,[2] probably a relatively late work, but a late work may contain old material. Did the Buddha really use the simile to illustrate man's efforts to understand the Universe in which he finds himself? It may be so, but his other utterances on such subjects are marked by the severest reticence and one cannot help suspecting that some clever editor may have ventured to go a little further than the master.

If we cannot be sure that any suttanta gives a correct account of what happened on a particular occasion, it may seem that everything in the life and teaching of the Buddha becomes doubtful. But we may set against this uncertainty the uniformity and on the whole the reasonableness of these ancient documents. For it is not, I think, an exaggeration to call the narrative contained in the older documents reasonable. In the East descriptions of miracles are no proof that a story is not contemporary or that the other events which it relates are untrue. Miracles were ascribed to Keshub Chunder Sen, Ramakṛishṇa, and many other recent Hindus in their lifetime [3]: to Gotama's disciples it probably seemed perfectly natural to relate how he had vanished from one place and reappeared in another. And if the composers of the Piṭakas were liberal in adding miracles to their narrative, they did not suppress incidents which showed the master as an ordinary man. Such things as his

[1] Dig. Nik., ii–xiii; Maj. Nik., xxvii, xxviii, xxxix, lxxix.

[2] Udâna, vi, 4. The parable was told to certain disciples who related to the Buddha the philosophic discussions which they had heard about such questions as the eternity and infinity of the Universe.

[3] See, for instance, Dinesh Chandra Sen, *Chaitanya and his Age*, p. 62, for an account of Prabhu Jagatbandhu of Faridpur, to whom miracles are ascribed.

doubts and troubles and mistakes in his quest for truth must surely be historical, for they would never have been invented by recorders who were obviously disposed to glorify him as an omniscient sage. It is significant that when the life of an entirely idealized Buddha is related—Vipassi[1] for instance, who is supposed to have lived ninety-one æons ago—though the general outline of Gotama's biography is followed, there is no mention of such struggles. Moreover, the repetition and monotony which are so distasteful to European students of the Nikâyas are to some extent a guarantee of historical fidelity. Passages announcing something novel and striking are comparatively rare: we become weary of the endless elaboration of well-known themes. But this iteration is what might be expected in the record of a long and wandering life.

Supposing that those who heard him preach in various places made and committed to memory an account of what he said, something like the Nikâyas would be the natural result. There is no reason to suppose that his teaching was seriously perverted in his lifetime. We read of misunderstandings like those of Ariṭṭha, Sati, and Yamaka, but they were publicly and clearly corrected. The portrait is lifelike: a teacher of wonderful energy even in extreme old age[2] continually impressing on the world certain truths which, though they might seem difficult inasmuch as they were new, were not complicated[3]: kind and in some ways liberal but in everything that concerned his teaching most definite and tolerating no variation. Clearly such a character was likely to leave in the minds of his disciples a clear recollection of what he taught.

It may be objected that no religion has undergone more changes or assimilated more foreign matter than Buddhism. This is true, but the process of transformation and admixture has been spread over wide intervals of time and space. The first great change—what we call Mahayanism—became evident about the time of the Christian era or at the earliest in the second century before that era. The irregularities condemned at Vesâlî and the heresies confuted in the Kathâvatthu may contain the germs of serious novelties but do not in themselves indicate any striking divergence from the

[1] See Digha Nikâya, sutta xiv.

[2] See the end of the Mahâsihanada-sutta. Maj. Nik., xii.

[3] Though the Buddha's doctrine is described as profound and to be understood only by the wise (*paṇḍita-vedaniya*), yet it is also said (Maj. Nik., lxxxv, near the end) that a competent pupil can master it between dawn and sunset.

standard of the Nikâyas. And the commotion which they caused indicates very clearly that there was a strictly conservative party, determined to allow no innovations in practice or doctrine and having a tradition to which they could appeal.

I think, therefore, that the earlier parts of the Pali Piṭaka—that is, the four Nikâyas with portions of the fifth Nikâya and of the Vinaya—reproduce the story of the Buddha's life and teaching as current in the generations immediately following his death and that this story is in general outline and sometimes verbally accurate. It would be unwise to attach too much importance to isolated utterances, but most statements of important doctrines are repeated many times with slight verbal differences and go back, I believe, to the recollections of the Master's disciples.

Midway between the works just mentioned and avowedly Mahayanist sûtras stand compositions like the Lalita-vistara and Mahâvastu. The language of both is somewhat irregular Sanskrit and the style exuberant. The doctrine inculcated, though it can hardly be called definite Mahayanism, shows a tendency in that direction. The Buddha is less human : he becomes a supernatural being and higher than the gods themselves.[1] His life is one long series of miracles, and exaggeration in the use of numbers is very noticeable. Nevertheless both works contain old material mixed with new, and the versions which they give of well-known legends and stanzas may be as old and worthy of attention as those found in Pali texts.[2] So far as I know, Buddhists at the present day do not read either work, but the Lalita-vistara has had great influence on art. For instance, the story of the Buddha's life as recorded in the sculptures of Borobudur in Java is clearly founded on its narrative.

The collection of Mahayanist sûtras in the Chinese Tripiṭaka is extensive and contains works of very unequal value, interest, and influence since it includes many late tantric treatises and spells. It is, however, complete—that is to say, I am not aware that any important Mahayanist sûtra is known to have existed in Sanskrit and to have disappeared entirely, though the original text has often been lost. In Japan the Hokke-kyō (Saddharmapuṇḍarîka), the

[1] Thus in chaps. viii and x the Lalita-vistara frequently calls the young Gotama Devâtideva and explicitly says that he is greater than all gods.

[2] For instance, the legend about Mâra and the temptation in Lal.-vist., chap. xviii, about Tapussa and Bhallika, chap. xxiv, and the Sanskrit versions of the lines Apârutâ tesam amatassa dvârâ (Maj. Nik., xxvi), said to have been uttered by the Buddha when he decided to preach.

sûtras about Amida's paradise, and to some extent the Vajracchedikâ are not only well-known and venerated but extracts of them serve as books of devotion. The Vimalakîrti-sûtra, commonly called Yuima-kyō, is also popular. The Avataṃsaka (Kegon), Lankâvatâra, Suvarṇaprabhâsa, Mahâparinirvâna, and Dainichi-kyō (Nanjio, No. 530) are studied by the learned but not generally known. Some of them are the textbooks of special sects.

The great Mahâyâna sûtras are concerned less with the life of the Buddha than with the doctrines which they represent him as preaching, but they generally open with some scene which recalls the narratives found in the Nikâyas and Âgamas. Thus at the beginning of the Lotus or Saddharmapuṇḍarîka we are told that he was staying on the Vulture Peak at Râjagaha, attended by a multitude of disciples among whom are figures well known in the older story such as Sâriputra and Kâśyapa but also legions of Bodhisattvas, including Mañjuśrî and Maitreya, and gods like Śakra and Sûrya with myriads of attendants. In the midst of all these hosts sits the Lord (for it hardly seems appropriate to call him the Buddha or Gotama) plunged in meditation, when suddenly from his forehead there issues a ray which illuminates the most distant worlds of the Universe and he begins to preach. The discourse which follows contains a good deal of prophecy including a prediction that all his disciples will become Buddhas, but the main doctrine is that though the truth is one and absolute, the Buddha accommodates it to human intelligence and preaches it in various forms to give all minds a chance of salvation. Then there appears in the sky a gigantic jewelled Stupa in which is the body of the former Buddha Prabhûtaratna, who attained nirvâna countless ages ago, but returns to hear the Lord and converse with him. More sermons and prophecies follow. The world bursts open on all sides and from the clefts arises a countless host of Bodhisattvas. Profound silence follows which, we are told, lasted fifty æons, though it seemed but an afternoon. The Lord explains that this innumerable multitude of beings have all been his pupils. For the good of the world he manifests himself from time to time in human form, but his existence is not limited by his apparent birth and death: it extends inconceivably far back into the past and forward into the future. After further discourses on the merit which comes from an understanding of this doctrine and the practice of piety, the two Buddhas, past and present, seat themselves on the throne within the magic stupa. Not only do the rays which issue from their persons illuminate all the universe, but they stretch out their shining tongues, which reach as far as the heaven of Brahmâ. This is said to have lasted a thousand years and probably the original version of the sûtra ended with a short epilogue (chap. xxvii). But the text which has come down to us includes several additional chapters containing stories and spells. One (chap. xxiv) dedicated to the praise of Kwannon (Avalokiteśvara) is exceedingly popular as a book of devotion in China and Japan. Another (chap. xxv) recounts the remarkable legend of an ancient Bodhisattva who burnt his body in honour of the Lord.

The Lotus declares itself to be the last and most eminent of all sûtras [1] and perhaps the author felt that he could not claim antiquity for his ideas, which show a clear resemblance to those of the Bhagavad Gîtâ. At any rate we need not speculate whether we have here an accurate report of the Buddha's words or not. The Sûtra itself treats of time and space in a manner which seems to deprive words like when and where of their ordinary meaning. But it is one of the most important and influential scriptures of Asia. Anesaki [2] even says of it that it has "played in Japanese literature a rôle nearly akin to that of the Bible in English literature".

[1] Chap. xiii, 54.

[2] *History of Japanese Religion*, p. 159.

# CHAPTER II

## THE DOCTRINES

In the last chapter I inquired whether it is possible to ascertain what Gotama really taught and came to the conclusion that the older parts of the Pali scriptures reproduce the account of his life and teaching current in the generation immediately following his death and sometimes reproduce his words. I now propose to inquire what that teaching was and in particular to notice how it sometimes leads up to the later doctrines called Mahâyâna and sometimes offers a contrast to them.

The word Mahâyâna does not admit of an exact definition, for it is not the name of a religious corporation with fixed doctrines like many Christian and Hindu sects, but is merely an honourable and descriptive title given to the new scriptures, beliefs, and practices which appear in Buddhism some time about the Christian era or perhaps rather earlier. These novelties are mainly Indian in origin, for though Mahayanism spread over all Eastern Asia, the various schools into which it is divided were as a rule evolved in India and sent abroad in a mature and developed form. Still some allowance must be made for Iranian influences in early times and when the Mahâyâna was established in China, Tibet, and Japan it acquired considerable local colour in each country. If we attempt not to define but even to describe this tangled growth of philosophy, art and literature, high aspirations and strange superstitions, we seem as we turn from one side of it to another to be dealing with different sets of ideas and institutions which have nothing in common. One obvious characteristic is elaboration of doctrine. Just as Byzantine Christianity argued about the nature of Christ and the Trinity, so the Mahayanists argued about the Buddha nature. But the analogy does not hold good in detail, for there was a strong tendency to multiply Buddhas and leave Gotama somewhat in the background, to exalt new supernatural personages or new groups of such, and at the same time to talk of one universal, pantheistic Buddha spirit. Though these speculations may seem over complicated or extravagant, still they belong to the sphere of religion. But Mahayanism has also an enormous literature about dogmas and systems (for there is more than one system) which deal with metaphysics or ontology or psychology but have nothing to do with religion as we understand it. The reader wonders how these difficult ideas, which seem like the most paradoxical parts of Einstein, can ever have found a way into the brains of ordinary men, much less have been a moral stimulus, and then he learns with amazement that Zen Buddhism was not only a great force in Japan but specially influential among the military classes.

In sharp contrast to this detached, complicated, and most unsentimental philosophy is the practical every day side of Mahayanism. The simplest human desires are its basis. We like to think that there are deities who can give health, wealth, and comfort. We are not quite sure what will happen to us when we die: we want to go to heaven and gladly believe that kindly powers will guide us on our way. From the mists of hope arise much superstition, charms and spells, and magical prayers, but there arise, too, beautiful figures like the merciful Kwannon, gracious deities whose one wish and task is to help suffering humanity. It is true that the paradoxical philosopher and the superstitious temple-goer are between them responsible for modern neglect of the original teaching and precepts —the Four Truths and the Eightfold Path. But still Mahayanist Buddhism has made one solid gift to humanity. It has proclaimed a better code of unselfish morality than any other religion and illustrated it nobly in art and literature.

These ideas—heaven and the road thither, the duty of self-sacrifice, and, since we cannot ignore the strange juxtaposition, idealist metaphysics—are all to be found in the Nikâyas, sometimes as mere seeds, sometimes as well-grown plants. But between early Buddhism and the Mahâyâna there is a great difference in emphasis. The ideals which the Buddha held up are left on one side as too difficult for ordinary humanity: aspirations which he tolerated are made the essence of religion.

The accounts of the Buddha's life agree in stating that he spent the period which elapsed between his departure from home and his attainment of Enlightenment (traditionally estimated as seven years) in investigation and inquiry. The immediate results of this quest were almost entirely negative. First he studied under two teachers[1] who appear to have taught that salvation could be obtained by entering into certain trances. He found their conclusions unsatisfactory but seems to have accepted their general scheme for leading a religious life, which was common at that period among inquirers

[1] Alâra Kâlâma and Uddaka-Râmaputta.

who did not follow Brahmanic observances, namely, membership of an order or corporation which held certain doctrines (dhamma) and obeyed a certain discipline (vinaya). Though he found their teaching insufficient, because it did not lead to peace, enlightenment, and nirvâna, yet he by no means rejected the practice of trances and meditation. On the contrary, his own enlightenment and that of ordinary saints is represented as coming after they had passed through the four jhânas.

After leaving his teachers as incompetent guides, Gotama proceeded to test the value of asceticism. He practised the severest austerities until his life was in danger. So he took nourishment and reverted to a more reasonable mode of living and then passed through an experience commonly known as the Enlightenment or Sambodhi. As it was in virtue of the truths which then became known to him that he felt competent to come forward as a teacher of mankind, these truths must clearly be of paramount importance, but the accounts of the Enlightenment present some discrepancies of detail. The simplest version, put into his own mouth in two discourses of the Majjhima Nikâya,[1] says that he sought and obtained the perfect peace of nirvâna wherein is no birth, nor decay, no disease, death, sorrow nor impurity, and there arose in him the knowledge and insight that his deliverance was assured and that he would not be born again. In two other discourses of the same Nikâya [2] he relates his experiences with more detail. In the first watch of the night he reviewed his own previous births throughout countless æons. In the second watch he beheld with the eye of the spirit (dibbena cakkhunâ) a panoramic view of the universe and saw how beings pass away and are reborn according to their deeds, In the third watch he fully understood suffering, its origin and cessation, and the road that leads to that cessation : he understood. too, the âsavas, the cankers or intoxicants—namely, the craving for pleasure, the craving for new existence, and ignorance. He saw how they arise and how they can be stopped and he knew that his task was done and that he would be reborn no more.

Other versions of the story connect the Enlightenment with the

[1] Maj. Nik., xxvi and lxxxv.

[2] Maj. Nik., iv and xxxi. In Maj. Nik., xii, these experiences are enumerated as Nos. 8–10 of the ten powers of the Tathâgata, and in Maj. Nik., lxxix ad fin., Dig. Nik., ii, § 93, and many other suttas they are described as possible for any Bhikkhu. But in Maj. Nik., xxxviii (= vol. i, p. 265), there is a remarkable passage in which the Buddha exhorts his disciples not to wonder whether or what they were in the past or will be in the future or are now.

formula known as the Chain of Causation.[1] Thus the Dîgha Nikâya in describing the Enlightenment of the ancient Buddha Vipassi (who is supposed to have discovered and preached the same doctrine as Gotama) makes him obtain it simply by thinking out the Chain of Causation, first backwards and then forwards, but only so far as consciousness, the two earlier links being omitted.[2] According to the Introduction to the commentary on the Jâtaka,[3] Gotama acquired knowledge of his own and others' previous births in the first two watches of the night and of the Chain in the third. But the narrative at the beginning of the Mahâvagga says that it was only after he had attained Enlightenment[4] that he thought out the Chain, while the Saṃyutta Nikâya[5] on the other hand says that he knew it while he was still a Bodhisattva. In spite of these discrepancies there is no real doubt as to what constitutes Enlightenment. It is the certain knowledge that the whole universe is a saṃsâra,[6] a process of birth and death which is not capricious but is regulated by a law and which can be brought to an end. Even the accounts which do not expressly mention the Chain of Causation generally imply it, for most of them say that he discovered *how* suffering and the âsavas arise and *how* they can be stopped. Of the importance attached to causal connection from the earliest times there can be no doubt. The celebrated stanza which brought about the conversion of Sâriputta[7] represents it as an epitome of Buddhism, and in a discourse of the Majjhima Nikâya[8] which appears

[1] Pali, Paticca-samuppâda. There are several versions of it. The commonest and fullest (found for example at the beginning of the Mahâvagga) is as follows: "From ignorance come the sankhâras (predispositions), from the sankhâras consciousness, from consciousness name-and-form, from name-and-form the six provinces of the senses: from these comes contact, from contact sensation, from sensation craving, from craving clinging, from clinging existence (or becoming), and from existence birth. From birth come old age and death, pain and lamentation, suffering, sorrow and despair. This is the origin of this whole mass of suffering. But by the destruction of ignorance, effected by the complete absence of lust, the sankhâras are destroyed, etc."

[2] Dig. Nik., xiv. Mahâpadâna S.

[3] Nidânakathâ: Fausböll's edition, p. 75.

[4] Mahâvag. at the beginning. Paṭhamâbhisambuddho.

[5] Saṃ. Nik., xiii, 10 (= vol. ii, p. 10).

[6] In the Sabhiya S. of the Sutta Nipâta a Buddha is defined as a Bhikkhu who has a general view of Saṃsâra.

[7] Ye dhammâ hetuppabbhavâ, etc., Mahâvag., i, 23.

[8] Maj. Nik., lxxix. So, too, in the very impressive Mahâtaṇhâsankhaya S. (Maj. Nik., xxxviii) the Buddha recites the Chain and then applies to it this formula—imasmin sati, etc. Numerous other suttas dwell on the importance of the Chain, e.g. Dîg. Nik., xv.

to be ancient the Buddha says: "I will teach you the dhamma"—that is the main doctrine or essence of my teaching. "If that is, this comes to pass: on account of the arising of that, this arises. If that is not, this does not come to pass: on account of the cessation of that, this ceases." This formula seems to treat of causation in a simple sense, perfectly intelligible to Europeans (*A* is the cause of *B*, for if *A* exists, *B* comes into existence, and if *A* does not exist, *B* does not come into existence). But the Pali name for the Chain signifies dependent origination.[1] Birth is not the cause of death in ordinary European language but the two are interdependent, for there can be no death unless there has previously been birth. Any two links of the Chain are like two bundles of reeds[2] leaning against one another, either of which must fall, if the other is removed, and the whole Universe is a system of interdependent phenomena, none of which can exist apart from the others and each of which has many causes.[3] The Chain of Causation may be applied to the Cosmos: thus the Anguttara Nikâya[4] states that the Buddha has taught how the whole world comes into being and passes away. But it bears a still closer relation to morality and the holy life. The Buddha has discovered the causes of suffering and evil and therefore he knows how to remove them.

But though Enlightenment is so intimately connected with the knowledge of causation, though its essence is to see *how* evil arises and *how* it can be brought to an end, yet it is not merely deductive logic. It has another aspect which appears alike in the early accounts of the Master's experience and in the latest developments of the Mahâyâna. Enlightenment is direct intuitive knowledge, superior to reasoning and discussion, and for those who receive it certain and incontrovertible. The Buddha had a vision in which with the eye of the spirit he beheld the world process and even now in Japan the Zen adepts suddenly obtain illumination—Satori—which gives them a new view of the Universe and makes them new men.

[1] Pali, Paticca-samuppâda; Sanskrit, Pratîtya-samutpâda.

[2] Saṃ. Nik., xii, 67 (= vol. ii, p. 114).

[3] All Buddhist Schools agree as to this though they differ in their classification of hetu and pratyaya, main and accessory causes. The Buddhist conception of cause does not seem to differ much from recent scientific views. Thus B. Russell says (*Outlines of Philosophy*, p. 123): "What we have to substitute for force is laws of correlation. Events can be collected in groups by their correlations. That is all that is true in the old notion of causality."

[4] Ang. Nik., iv, 23.

The doctrine of causation was of course accepted by the Mahâyâna and in so far as it is equivalent to the Law of Moral Retribution is still a part of popular Buddhism, but as a speculative tenet it obviously does not appeal to the emotions and even in the mouth of the Buddha was not a stirring theme for popular sermons. The philosophers, however, had to deal with it and adjusted it to their systems of idealist metaphysics. The old formula that all things are interdependent lent itself to the new theory, for if a thing exists only in virtue of its relations to other things, it is easy to show that in itself it does not exist at all. Though the Nikâyas do not teach the unreality of the external world, they contain passages which can be used to support that doctrine. Thus the Saṃyutta Nikâya [1] declares that it is wrong to say either that everything exists or that nothing exists. The correct statement is that things exist as conditioned by other things. One of the arguments advanced by the Mâdhyamakas against realism was the impossibility of understanding causation, but on the whole Mahayanist doctors were disposed to admit it as a principle regulating the phenomenal world but to deny that it applies to the absolute. The germ of this doctrine may be found in the Nikâyas, for nirvâna is declared to be asaṅkhata [2] uncompounded, that is, not produced by co-operating causes.

After the Enlightenment, Gotama was not an ordinary man but a Buddha, Jina, Tathâgata, or Arahâ,[3] words which are used as if they were well-known terms of respect needing no explanation. The idea that from time to time supermen appear in the world was common in India at this period. It appears for instance in Jainism

[1] Saṃ. Nik., xii, 15. Compare, too, Saṃ. Nik., xii, § 67 (Nalakapiyam).

[2] See especially chap. xliii of the Saṃ. Nik., called Asaṅkhata-Saṃyutta.

[3] Gotama is represented as styling himself Jina (Mahâvag., i, 6, 9, and Maj. Nik., xxvi (= vol. i, p. 171)), but the word is used sparingly in the Nikâyas, and it came to be the special title of Supermen in the Jaina sect. But in later Mahayanist works it is frequently used, especially to designate the five Buddhas Vairocana, Akshobhya, Ratnasambhava, Amitâbha, and Amoghasiddhi.

Tathâgata is a word of doubtful origin and meaning. For early explanations see Ang. Nik., iv, 23, § 3, and Dîg. Nik., xxix, §§ 28, 29, and for a late one Vajracchedikâ, xxix. In China and Japan it was understood as Tathâ-âgata and translated by 如來 Ju-lai (Nyo-rai), which apparently means He who has come as his predecessors came.

Arahâ, meaning originally honourable or worthy, is a title given in the older literature to both Buddhas and saints.

Bhagavâ or Lord seems to have been the title used by heads of religious confraternities: Maj. Nik., lxxvii, Ko nu kho imesam Bhagavatam. But it was later employed as a special divine title (e.g. Bhagavad Gîtâ) and this undoubtedly influences its use in Mahayanist works like the Lotus.

as well as in Buddhism, and according to a widespread belief the superman could be either a universal monarch or, if he rejected the things of this world, a sage and a teacher of mankind. Such a figure was probably as familiar to the imagination of ancient Indians as the Messiah to the Jews, but there is this characteristic difference between the heroes of the two nations that the Indian superman is thought of as one of a series not as an isolated and final figure. There had been Buddhas and Jinas before Gotama, and Mahâvira and others were expected in the future. The Nikâyas enumerate six previous Buddhas, but in the later parts of the Pali Canon we hear of twenty-four and, apart from precise lists, former Buddhas are often mentioned as if they were fairly numerous, as when Gotama speaks to Sâriputta about all the Buddhas of the past and future.[1] But we do not as in Mahayanist works hear of innumerable hosts of Buddhas. It is more than once laid down as a principle that there can be only one Buddha at a time in one world system,[2] which is interesting as pointing towards the later idea that there are an infinite number of world systems, each with its own Buddha. Though the tone of the suttas varies greatly, though we seem to be reading sometimes a fantastic legend and sometimes quite probable narratives of a great teacher's doings, yet the hero is always a superman. He expressly denies that he is an ordinary human being,[3] and not only in narratives that read like fairy tales but in reasoned discourses he is credited with superhuman powers.

It is not necessary to suppose that any long time elapsed before the Buddha was deified or that this deification implies any great elaboration of doctrine. In later ages Caitanya was treated as a divine being, even in his life, and Madhva was supposed to be an incarnation of Vâyu. Even so it is recorded[4] that an admirer exclaimed: "who am I that I should praise Gotama? Praise upon praise is his due, that most excellent among Gods and men." And the Greek Megasthenes who went to India about 300 B.C. says that Butta was honoured as a God.[5] In the Nikâyas we have already

[1] Maj. Nik., cxxiii ad init., Saṃ. Nik., xxxv, 83 (= vol. iv, p. 52). In Maj. Nik. we hear of 500 Pacceka Buddhas and a hundred are mentioned by name, but these beings, who do not preach to the world, are not on the same footing as real Buddhas.

[2] Maj. Nik., cxv; Dīg. Nik., xix, §§ 13, 14.

[3] Ang. Nik., iv, 36.

[4] Maj. Nik., xxvii ad init.

[5] Megasthenes, frag. 43. *Clem. Alex. Strom.*, 1, xv, 71, 6. Ed. Stahlin, Leipzig, 1905. *Εἰσι δὲ τῶν Ἰνδων οἱ τοῖς Βούττα πειθόμενοι παραγγέλμασιν ὃν δι' ὑπερβολὴν σεμνότητος εἰς θεὸν τετιμήκασιν.*

the beginnings of emotional veneration and of public worship. Gotama promises heaven to all who have but faith and love for him,[1] and in the Sutta Nipâta [2] the aged Pingiya tells of his personal devotion in moving language : "Day and night I see him with the mind and eye. I spend the night in worship (namassamâno) . . . old and feeble as I am, my body cannot go to him but in thought I go to him, for on him my mind is fixed." In the account of the Buddha's death,[3] a compilation made with materials of various dates but not very late, he gives instructions as to how the remains of a Tathâgata should be treated. Bhikkhus should not allow themselves to be distracted by honouring them : they should leave that to the pious laity. A monument (thûpa) should be erected and honoured with garlands, perfumes, paint, and salutations. Those who find calm of heart in these ceremonies will be reborn in the happy world of heaven.

Yet in spite of this disposition to make a God of the Buddha, he is not distinguished from his disciples so sharply as we might expect. The solemn words in which the tale of the Enlightenment is told make us think of it as a unique destiny, but as a matter of fact the same experiences—the vision of former births, the panorama of the cosmos, the knowledge of what evil is and how it can be cured, the assurance of peace and happiness—all this is promised to every disciple who can follow the Master's teaching. The difference is that they are merely learners. The Buddha has discovered—or rather rediscovered—the Truth and teaches it to others. But they can learn and become like him. In the Mahayanist sûtras, too, the links between the Buddha nature and humanity are not forgotten. In the Lotus Śâkyamuni is a radiant spirit clad in unearthly glory, but he tells the crowds that throng round him, "All my disciples shall become Buddhas." [4]

A Japanese priest of the Zen sect once described to me the religious instruction which he gave to his flock. He defined Enlightenment as the attainment by Gotama of the knowledge that all living things —men, animals, trees, and plants—can become Buddhas (成佛 jō-butsu). This formula illustrates the difference between the Mahâyâna and the earlier creed. It can in great part be justified from the Nikâyas, though there is probably no passage which

[1] Maj. Nik.. xxii ad fin.
[2] Sutta Nipâta (Parâyaṇavagga), 1142 ff.
[3] Dîg. Nik., xvi, v. §§ 11, 12.
[4] Saddharmap., chap. v, 44.

warrants the inclusion of the vegetable kingdom. But in the oldest documents the Buddha has a vision of the cosmos as a series of successive births: every Arhat has the same experience as a Buddha and attains to the highest stage of existence: any man can become an Arhat if he strives through successive births and an animal may be reborn as a man. Yet the formula is at best a restatement and rearrangement of ancient sayings or might be more correctly described as a deduction from them. As a summary of what the Buddha said it is doubtless unhistorical. It is presumptuous to guess what he may have thought but have kept to himself. Still, it is not impossible that he saw a vision in which all life reached the highest stage and enjoyed the knowledge which he himself had won. On the other hand, the Nikâyas hardly encourage the idea that the whole world is moving toward some happy consummation. The hope which they hold out is rather that escape from the endless saṃsâra is possible at any moment for those who really try.

The Enlightenment is not spoken of as a revelation made by any deity but rather as the discovery of a law, and in many places it is stated that former Buddhas taught the same Law.[1] Once Gotama compared himself to a man who had found the site of an ancient city in the jungle and caused it to be restored. In a remarkable passage[2] he describes how after the Enlightenment he felt the need to study under a teacher and to pay him respect, but could find no one in the world superior to himself. Then he thought, "This Dhamma in which I am supremely enlightened, what if I were to live under it paying it honour and respect?" On this Brahmâ appeared, congratulated him, and said that all previous Buddhas had done the same. This account seems to imply that the Buddha is below the Dhamma, which is an immutable Law or Truth.[3]

The results of Gotama's search for Truth up to this time are stated in a practical form in his first discourse often called the Sermon

[1] Saṃyutta Nik., xii, 65. The chapter called "The City". But in Mahâvag., i, 6, 23, Gotama speaks of "this doctrine which had formerly not been heard of", and in Maj. Nik., cviii, Ânanda says: "The Lord made a path where path there was none . . . and revealed a path until then unrevealed." Here, however, Ânanda is drawing a distinction between the Buddha and ordinary saints who have attained Enlightenment because they followed the doctrine, which he found out.

[2] It occurs Saṃ. Nik., i, v. 1, § 2 (= vol. i, p. 138), and Ang. Nik., iv, 3, 1 (= vol. ii, p. 20).

[3] For this conception of Dharma in Sanskrit see Manu, xii, 50.

at Benares.[1] Remembering no doubt his own experiences both as a prince and as an ascetic he begins by saying that those who wish to lead a religious life should abandon the two extremes of self-indulgence and self-torture, both of which are ignoble and useless. The right way is the Middle or Noble Eightfold Path defined as right views, right aims, right speech, right action, right livelihood, right effort, right mindfulness, and right rapture. Then he enumerates the Four Truths. The first declares that all clinging to existence involves suffering: the second that the cause of this suffering is taṇhâ, the craving for pleasure and rebirth. The third Truth teaches that there is a way to end suffering, for if the cause is known, it can be removed and its effects with it. Finally, the fourth Truth explains this way, which is the Eightfold Path as described above.[2]

For a European—and for the matter of that for a Chinese or Japanese—the most disputable part of this discourse is the assertion that all existence [3] involves suffering, especially as there is no hint that this suffering must be endured as a duty or in obedience to some divine will. But it is impossible to doubt that this doctrine was part of the original teaching of Gotama. He laid more emphasis on the unhappiness of ordinary life than did the Brahmans, but the men of his age accepted his views as natural and in harmony with every day experience. Though the Mahâyâna does not dwell on suffering so much as the Hînayâna, yet its philosophy, which insists on the illusory character of all phenomena, suggests the corollary that all is vanity, and the important sects which worship Amida start from even more dismal premises, since they hold that man is such a miserable creature that he can do nothing for himself, whereas the older teaching at least proclaims that he can save himself and is capable of becoming a superman.

The Japanese are a cheerful people nor can anyone criticize their

[1] Or Dhammacakkappavatana-sutta. It occurs in the Mahâvagga (i, 6, 17 ff.) and in the Saṃyutta Nikâya, where it is placed in Saṃyutta, lvi, called Sacca (= vol. v, p. 420). The Sanskrit versions in the Lalita-vistara and Mahâvastu are substantially the same.

[2] In the sutta of the Noble Quest, Maj. Nik., xxvi, in which Gotama himself gives an account of his early experiences, though there are many mentions of "the doctrine" or "this doctrine", it is not expressly defined. We are only told that his disciplies saw peril in all that is subject to rebirth, decay, death, sorrow, and impurity, and obtained the perfect peace of nirvâna in which these evils do not exist.

[3] Strictly speaking, the statement is that it is clinging to life (panc' upâdâna-kkhandâ), which is suffering.

history, as the history of India might perhaps be criticized, for being wanting in personal interest. It is one long string of romances and valiant exploits. Yet their literature from the Nara period onward is dominated by a sense of the transitoriness of human life and greatness. This feeling (called *awaré*, pathos or pity), which is always ready to see in nature, in the scattering of cherry blossoms, and the changing colours of autumn leaves an image of how all that is beautiful and splendid passes away and fades, was probably fostered in a large measure by Buddhist influence. The official handbook, called a Synopsis of the Jōdo-Shinshū Creed, [1] says that "the first question which Buddhism treats of is that of pain in life". It goes on to discuss Śûnyatâ and anattâ and mentions, though only in passing, the Noble Eightfold Path.

From such phrases as "all is evil" or "all is suffering" Europeans [2] are apt to draw the conclusion that activity must be vain, that rest and peace are the only good, that it would be well if the world process could be arrested. But such conclusions are not attributed to the Buddha and his whole life was a protest against them. When sending forth his first missionaries he bade them travel for the welfare of mankind and with his last breath he charged his disciples to strive earnestly. He is represented as a man of exceptional vigour and unselfish activity and as saying in his old age that he was still capable of wearing out his disciples and ready to go on talking and answering questions, even if he had to be carried about in a litter.[3] The really important part of his doctrine is not the insistent assertion that ordinary pleasures cannot last or satisfy but the promise of a cure and of something better. In this he does not really differ much from Christianity. No one maintains that the world is altogether happy and all Churches are allowed to dwell on its evils, provided that they also offer consolation and hope.

[1] *Synopsis of the Jōdo-Shinshū Creed*, compiled by the Education Department of the West Hongwanji, Kyōto, 1922. See pp. 1 and 7.

[2] In reading the Buddha's discourses we are apt to misplace the emphasis. Thus in well-known and eloquent words he once told his disciples that the flood of tears they had shed as they wandered through the long round of births is greater than the waters of the four seas. This makes us think of the sadness of life, but the emphasis is undoubtedly on the incalculable length of saṃsâra. The whole section is called anamatagga (Saṃ. Nik., xv), and besides the chapter on tears (§ 3) there are many others giving other illustrations of this infinity extending back into the past without beginning. The amount of mother's milk which we have drunk is greater than the waters of the four oceans. The hardships which we have experienced are innumerable (§ 11) but so are the pleasures (§ 12).

[3] Maj. Nik., xii. Mahâsihanâda S.

Probably in all the Buddhist scriptures there is no lament over the sorrows of life more strongly worded than the sentence in the English Burial Service, "We give Thee hearty thanks for that it hath pleased Thee to deliver this our brother out of the miseries of this sinful world."

The Kathâvatthu controverts the proposition that all conditioned things are dust and ashes [1]: it argues in reply that life has various pleasures and that following the teaching of the Buddha brings supreme happiness. The Dhammapada declares that the righteous are happy in this world and the next,[2] and a volume might be filled with texts which describe the happiness of the religious life. One of the most striking is the dialogue with Mahânâma [3] in which Gotama maintains that he is happier than the King of Magadha because he can remain seven days and nights without speaking or moving and yet enjoying absolute bliss. And though it is consistently maintained that monks are happier than others, yet the laity too can enjoy happiness. Gotama once told [4] the headman of a village that a good man can properly congratulate himself on being doubly lucky both here and hereafter in heaven. "At this thought gladness springs up in him. In him thus glad there arises joy and as he rejoices his body grows calm. He feels happiness and in his happiness his heart is at peace. This is the peace of mind that comes by righteousness." Buddhist art, too (when not engaged in representing hell), is often full of the joy of life. The sculptors who decorated Sanchi obviously felt real pleasure in giving cheerful and sometimes humorous pictures of the doings of men and animals.

It is remarkable that in the First sermon so little is said about saṃsâra and future lives.[5] These doctrines are indeed implied, for the cause of suffering is defined as craving which leads to rebirth and at the end the Buddha says that he knows he will not be born

[1] "Mere cinder-heaps." Kathâv., ii, 8.

[2] Dhammap., 14.

[3] Maj. Nik., xiv. For a beautiful passage about the joy of the religious life and love for others see Cûla Assapura S. (Maj. Nik., xl). In the Poṭṭhapâda S. (Dig. Nik., ix) the Buddha meets the objection that one may put away evil and become wise and yet remain sad. No, he says, if you can do that "the result will be joy, zest, peace, mindfulness, self-mastery, and a happy life". The Ang. Nik., iii, 65, § 16 (= vol. i, p. 192), states that even if there is no other world, nor any future rewards or punishments, the good life is the best here.

[4] Saṃ. Nik., xlii, 8, 13 (= vol. iv, p. 350). So, too, in the Lalita-vistâra the first four of the initiatory lights of religion are said to be *śraddhâ*, *prasâda*, *prâmodya*, and *prîti*, faith, calm, joy, and gladness.

[5] But there are many emphatic declarations of the truth of this doctrine, e.g. the beginning of Maj. Nik., cxxx. The Messengers of the Gods.

again. But the goal of the Path is simply peace, insight, enlightenment, and nirvâna, without any mention of this life or another. But shortly afterwards we are told that in instructing laymen he spoke of almsgiving, morality, and heaven.

The greater part of the Path confines itself to teaching a sound and simple morality, but the last section, samâdhi, rapture or ecstasy, seems to leave the things of this world, without however mentioning another. The first seven sections are merely preliminary and subsidiary to it, as is made plain in a discourse of the Majjhima[1] where they are described as its concomitants. But great as is the importance of samâdhi, it is not the goal. In the passage referred to and in many others it is described as leading to knowledge and deliverance, and in the account of the last days of the Buddha[2] he seems to substitute for the Eightfold Path a new formula enumerating four stages in the spiritual life, namely, morality, ecstasy, knowledge, and deliverance (sîla, samâdhi, paññâ, vimutti). This paññâ (the Sanskrit prajñâ which plays so large a part in the Mahâyâna) does not mean logically correct views but immediate, direct, intuitive knowledge. Deliverance or nirvâna is accompanied by such knowledge.[3]

The teaching of the Pali Piṭakas about nirvâna is up to a certain point clear and definite, although it does not altogether satisfy intellectual curiosity. There are two stages in nirvâna, one in this life and one after death. Nirvâna in this life means peace and perfect happiness, but it by no means excludes activity. The Buddha attained it at the beginning of his career as a teacher,[4] and though he is sometimes described as loving solitude and meditation, he is shown to us as a busy instructor and helper of mankind, still active

[1] Cattarisaka S., Maj. Nik., cxvii. In Dig. Nik., xviii. § 27, the first seven sections are called Samâdhi-parikkhârâ, the requisites for ecstasy, but Samâdhi itself is followed by knowledge and deliverance. See, too, Ang. Nik., vii, 42 (= vol. iv, p. 40), for a categorical statement that the other sections of the Path are the seven requisites of Samâdhi, and Ang. Nik., x, 121 (= vol. v, p. 236), where the Path seems to be extended to ten sections ending *sammâ, samâdhi, sammâñânam, sammâvimutti.*

[2] Several times in Dig. Nik., xvi. See especially the beginning of chap. iv. "It is through not understanding and grasping four things that we have had to wander so long in this round of Saṃsara, you and I. What are the four? Sîla. samâdhi, paññâ, and vimutti." But the same sûtra in describing the instruction which he gave to his last convert Subhadda makes him emphasize the Path as the one way to salvation.

[3] Cf. the formula Vimuttasmin vimuttam iti ñânam.

[4] See, for instance, Maj. Nik.. xxvi (the Sûtra of the Noble Quest), ajâtam anuttaram yogakkhemam nibbânam ajjhagamam.

in old age. There is therefore some ground for the Mahayanist doctrine that nirvâna and ordinary activity (saṃsâra) are the same, or two aspects of the same world. But what happens when one who has attained nirvâna dies? The question was often put to Gotama [1] and he always replied that it did not admit of an answer. It is usually mentioned in connection with other problems, classed as avyâkata, because the answer to them has not been revealed.[2] Such are (1) Is the world infinite in space or not? (2) Is the world without beginning or end in time or not? (3) Is the life (jîva) the same as the body or different from it? To none of these questions is it right to answer either (1) yes, or (2) no, or (3) both yes and no, or (4) neither yes nor no. The reason for refusing to reply is not ignorance, though it is often indicated that the questions are unprofitable, vain conundrums and philosophizings like the diṭṭhi or speculations so often condemned in the Sutta Nipâta and elsewhere.[3] It is rather that human language is not capable of framing a proper reply and also that the questions themselves are not properly put. Thus the Buddha states in one passage [4] that people hold opinions on such subjects because of their ignorance of the body, of its arising, its ceasing and the manner of its ceasing, and in another [5] it is asserted that even in this world the Tathâgata cannot be known as really and truly existing. Since then in real truth there is no such thing as a being,[6] it is a misuse of language to inquire whether in certain circumstances a Tathâgata exists or not. The idea that correct statements not merely about great mysteries but about the ordinary phenomena of existence cannot be made in human language plays a considerable part in the Mahâyâna. It is the avowed principle of the Zen school and is also implied in the negations of the Mâdhyamakas. The tradition

[1] It is usually in the form Hoti Tathâgato param maraṇâ na hoti. Does the Tathâgata pass on to another existence after death or not? The chief passages where this question is raised are Digha Nikâya, xv, 32; xxix, 30; Majjhima Nikâya, lxiii, lxxii, xxv; Saṃyutta Nikâya, chap. xliv. The Avyâkata Saṃyutta containing eleven sûtras on the subject. See, too, chaps. xvi, § 12; xxii, § 85; xxiv, §§ 15-18; xxxiii, § 1; Anguttara Nikâya, iv, chap. 38, vii, 51; x, 20; x, 93; and 95 and 96.

[2] Dîg. Nik., xv, 32 ad fin., though not very clear, seems to state that it would be inappropriate to say that an Arhat does not know the answer. Tad abhiññâ vimutto bhikkhu na jânâti na passati iti assa diṭṭhi tad akallam.

[3] See especially the Atthakavagga, suttas 3, 4, 5, 8, 9, 10, 12, and 13.

[4] Saṃ. Nik., xxxiii (= vol. iii, pp. 257-263).

[5] Saṃ. Nik., xxii, 34. See also xliv (the Avyâkata Saṃyutte), § 2, and following sections.

[6] Saṃ. Nik., xii, 62. Here is a mere heap of Sankhâras: there is no being.

which ascribes this attitude to Gotama himself must, I think, be true, for what motive can there have been to invent stories which represent the Omniscient Master as refusing to reveal the truth ?[1]

The Piṭakas consistently hold up nirvâna in this life as the goal and not the state after death. But the metaphor of blowing out a lamp must not be interpreted as implying annihilation, a doctrine which the Buddha is represented as expressly repudiating.[2] Indian ideas about the extinction of fire are not the same as ours. Thus in the Śvetâśvatara Upanishad the Supreme Spirit is extolled in theistic and devotional language but is ultimately described as "a fire which has burnt its fuel", that is apparently an unsullied flame, which is certainly not regarded as annihilated.[3] In the Sutta Nipâta[4] the Buddha states that "as a flame blown out by the force of the wind disappears and cannot be defined (attham paleti na upeti samkham), so the sage delivered from name and form disappears and cannot be defined". His questioner presses the point. "Has he disappeared or does he not exist or is he for ever free from sickness ?" The answer is : "For one who has disappeared there is no measure (attham gatassa na pamânam atthi).[5] He has nothing by which one can describe him." It is noticeable that in the Muṇḍaka Upanishad[6] almost the same words are used of absorption into the Deity. "As flowing rivers disappear in the ocean quitting name and form (astam gacchanti nâmarûpe vihâya), so the sage throwing off his name and form goes into the highest heavenly Person."

In some passages which may be suspected of being late it is expressly affirmed that the state of the Tathâgata after death cannot be described because it is infinite and unfathomable like the sands of the Ganges or the water of the ocean,[7] and the Udâna calls it

[1] Though some of these statements, particularly in the Saṃyutta Nik., are put into the mouths of disciples, the most important of them as related in the Dîgha and Majjhima are utterances of the Buddha himself. The Mâlunkyaputta S. and the Vacchagotta S. (Maj. Nik., lxiii and lxxii) are as vivid and as likely to be genuine as any discourses handed down by tradition.

[2] Maj. Nik., xxii (= vol. i, p. 141).

[3] Śvetâśv. Up., vi, 19. Cf., too, Mahâbhâr., Asvamedha par., 544 ff., where we have again the simile of the fire without fuel, and where nirvâna is identified with Brahmâ. But it must be remembered that deep sleep and the turîya, which are blissful ideals for Indians, are hardly what Europeans call conscious existence. See, too, the remarkable passage in Maj Nik., cxl (= vol. iii, pp. 245–6).

[4] Upasîvamânava puccha (No. 7 in Pârâyaṇavag).

[5] Appamâna is used for boundless. e.g., Sut. Nip., 507. Mettam cittam bhaveyam appamânam. Cultivating an all-pervading loving spirit.

[6] Muṇḍ. Up., 3, 2, 8. Cf. Praśna Up., 6, 5. Samudram prâpyâstam gacchanti.

[7] So the nun Khemâ in Saṃ. Nik., xliv, x, 1.

a state (âyatanam) which is "the end of sorrow, unborn, unoriginated, uncreated, uncompounded".[1] A whole section of the Saṃyutta Nikâya is devoted to sayings about this "uncompounded". In Mahayanist works there is a tendency to make nirvâna mean much the same as Brahman in Sanskrit. It is the prius of all things as well as that into which all things pass.[2] The Pali Nikâyas do not go so far as this: they are concerned with nirvâna as simply the goal of the holy life. But when they touch on ontology and use words like unborn and uncompounded it is clear in which way their language points.

The doctrine of the three bodies of the Buddha plays a considerable part in the Mahâyâna. They are first the Nirmâṇakâya, that is the human historical person called Gotama, second the Sambhogakâya,[3] the radiant presence to be seen in Paradise, and third the Dharmakâya, of which the other two are partial manifestations. The term seems to have meant originally body of the law, but it must be remembered that in Pali dhamma also meant phenomena and the word came to be used in the sense of the cosmical body of the Buddha, the Buddha being the ultimate reality of which the universe is the phenomenal expression, a reality to be known not by reasoning but by intuition. This ultimate reality is also called Tathatâ or suchness, and an analogous word Tathatta is occasionally used in Pali as a synonym of nirvâna.[4] No passage has been found in the Piṭakas alluding to pantheistic views about the Buddha nature, and Gotama would probably have condemned them as he condemned the fancies of people who thought that their own *attâ* was identical with the world soul.[5] Nevertheless, if it is excessive to see the germs of the doctrine of the Dharmakâya in the oldest records, we at least find there ideas and phrases which may be twisted in that direction. In the passages quoted above we are told that even in this life the Buddha is beyond the grasp of the intellect and that after death he is infinite and unfathomable. And when once nirvâna is regarded not as a goal but as corresponding to the

[1] Udâna, vii, near the beginning.

[2] See Mahâyânasûtrâlankâra, xi, 51. The dharmas are originally in peace and in parinirvâna. But the verse is missing in Sanskrit and is preserved only in Tibetan.

[3] This idea is not absent from the Nikâyas, for in the Mahâparinib. Sutta, iii, § 22, the Buddha says that when he appears among the gods his form and voice are similar to theirs.

[4] e.g. Saṃ. Nik., xli, 6. tathattâya upaneti. Cf. Kathâv., xix, 5.

[5] Maj. Nik., ii and xxii.

Brahman of the Upanishads, it does not seem illogical to regard the Buddha, who has passed into nirvâna, as being identical with ultimate reality. The word Dhammakâyo actually occurs in the Nikâyas as an epithet of the Buddha in a difficult passage.[1] Faithful disciples, we are told, are sons of the Buddha, born from his mouth, born of the Law (dhammaja), and the Buddha himself is dhammakâyo, he whose body is the Law, brahmakâyo being added as a synonym.[2] The meaning apparently is that believers are spiritual sons of the Buddha and the spirit or the doctrine which he teaches is the real essence of the Buddha. Though there is nothing pantheistic in this and the Buddha is merely regarded as what we call a world force, the point of view is becoming impersonal. The real significance and importance of the Buddha is not in his human individuality but in his teaching, which transcends the limits of personality.[3]

After enumerating the Four Truths and describing the Eightfold Path, Gotama is said to have delivered a celebrated discourse,[4] maintaining that there is nothing in the world of matter or thought to which the name of self[5] can be given. This doctrine has not found favour with some Europeans who are otherwise admirers of the Buddha, but it seems impossible to dissociate him from it or to maintain that it is a later accretion or misunderstanding of the Master's teaching. For if the doctrine is not Gotama's own, whence

[1] Dig. Nik., xxvii, § 9.

[2] *Brahmakâyo* must mean something like divine body, but doubtless not in a pantheistic sense.

[3] Compare Saṃ. Nik., xxii. 87, where a sick disciple asks the Buddha to visit him. The Buddha goes but says "He who sees the Law sees me, and he who sees me, sees the Law". Compare, too, the words of the Buddha on his deathbed. "Let the Dhamma and Vinaya which I have taught you be your teacher after my death." For Hsüan-Tsang this had come to mean "His spiritual presence abides for ever above all change" (Watters, *Yuan Chwang*, 2, p. 37). These passages clearly mean nothing more than "It is my teaching not my person which is important", but the inclination to pantheistic interpretations is very strong.

[4] Known as the Anattalakkhanasutta, Mahâvag., i, 6, 38–46.

[5] The Pali text is rûpam anattâ . . . vedanâ anattâ, etc. I do not think this should be translated "the body is not *the* self, sensation is not *the* self", as in *S.B.E.*, xiii, p. 100, for the use of "the" seems to imply that there is a self, but that it is not the body, sensation, etc. Rûpam anattâ seems to be parallel to rûpam aniccam and the meaning is that body is not permanent and is not a self: has none of the characteristics which are summed up in the word attâ but which have nothing corresponding to them in reality. "For if the body (or feeling, etc.) had the characteristics of attâ (rûpam ca h'idam attâ abhavissa) we should never be ill and should be able to be exactly what we choose." The corresponding Sanskrit words in the Mahâvastu (ed. Senart, iii, pp. 335 and 446) are rûpam anâtmâ, vedanâ anatmâ, etc.

did it come? Of its prominence in the Piṭakas there can be no doubt, and yet no other Indian sect can be cited as holding it nor can we point to any strong tendency outside Buddhism which could have influenced the early Buddhist doctors in this direction.[1] The natural inference, that anattâ, as the doctrine is compendiously termed, was part of the original teaching, is inevitable. It is equally clear that it was not easy to repudiate it. In some ways it was not congenial to Mahayanist speculations, but it was rarely denied, evidently because it was supported by overwhelmingly strong authority, and the sect which denied it has not survived. Though Mahayanist writers find some difficulty in accommodating anattâ in its technical psychological sense to their other theories and though their doctrine of the Dharmakâya differs little from the Brahmanic doctrine of the supreme Âtman, they are full of the idea that there is no real difference between self and others and the self-sacrificing Bodhisattva is their highest ideal. At the present day the doctrine is accepted (somewhat theoretically perhaps) in all Buddhist countries,[2] whether they follow the Hîna- or Mahâyâna, although it does not make the slightest difference in ordinary language or thought when such questions as salvation or life after death are discussed. And this is not unnatural, for there is no intention of denying that a human existence can be continued in another life. It is merely asserted that no existence in this world or another can rightly be called attâ, that is something permanent, unchanging, simple, and independent. All personalities human or divine are impermanent, changing, compound, and dependent on various causes. In Gotama's esteem the great importance of this doctrine seems to have been moral and practical. The Brahmans and Jains held the self or soul to be something permanent and unchangeable, but fettered and hampered by the body. They therefore strove to liberate and isolate it by mortifying the flesh. But the essence of the Buddha's doctrine is that self or soul can be changed and improved. Such a view is ethically quite reasonable and intelligible nor in the light of modern knowledge can it be

[1] The only passage cited as referring to such a theory is Kaṭhâ Up., iv, 14, which condemns those who see qualities (dharmâh) separately.

[2] e.g., the *Synopsis of the Jōdo Shinshū Creed*, published officially by the Western Hongwanji at Kyōto in 1920, says expressly (p. 7): "Buddhism denies the existence of the self and empirical world and finds the truth behind the denial of them." For a strong statement of the Anattâ doctrine in a popular Mahayanist sûtra see the answer to the question how one should conquer the mind when sick given in the Vimalakîrti (Yuima) sûtra, chap. iv.

ridiculed, for it seems to agree with the latest pronouncements of science.[1]

After hearing the first sermon, that about the Path, the five men who were the Buddha's first disciples were formally admitted as Bhikkhus or members of the religious order which he instituted; but after hearing the discourse on Anattâ, we are told, they all became Arhats or Saints. "At that time there were six Arhats in the world,"[2] no distinction being made between the Master and his pupils. The sequence of events is clearly meant to emphasize the importance of the doctrine and the great results which follow from realizing its truth. In one passage[3] it is asserted that if it were possible to find anything which can be called an attâ or self, even on the smallest scale, then the Buddha would not teach men to live the holy life. It is just because no such individuality is possible that the holy life is preached. This attâ whose existence is so emphatically denied is Self or Ego, but Self or Ego as understood by Indians, which is not quite the same as what Europeans mean by the word. When first enunciating the doctrine, the Buddha expressly stated that attâ is not subject to impermanence, change, or pain and that it can become what it pleases.[4] But we use the word self without implying such immunities and powers. It may seem that a Buddha or an Arhat has realized this Indian idea of attâ, for he is freed from all bonds, he can assume any form, and can move without heeding material obstructions, his senses (especially his sight and hearing) become cosmic in their power. Yet it would not be correct to call him attâ. It was after he had received enlightenment and all these wondrous powers that the Buddha is represented as congratulating himself on having got rid of the notion of self.[5]

[1] Bertrand Russell, *Outline of Philosophy*, p. 254: "And in psychology equally the Ego has disappeared as an ultimate conception and the unity of a personality has become a peculiar causal nexus among a series of events," and ib., p. 258: "As regards the self, he (Hume) was almost certainly right. As we have already argued a person is not a single entity but a series of events linked together by peculiar causal laws."

[2] Mahâvag., i, 6, § 47.

[3] Saṃ. Nik., xxii, §§ 96, 97.

[4] Mahâvag., i, 6, § 42.

[5] Mahâvag., i, 3, § 4. Cf. the definition of the Buddha's omniscience in the Abhidharmakośa, chap. ix, pp. 254–5 of De la Vallée Poussin's translation. "Par le mot Bouddha on désigne une certaine série: à cette série appartient cette singulière puissance que par le seul fait de l'inflexion de la pensée se produit immédiatement une connaissance exacte de l'objet relativement auquel un désir de connaissance a surgi. On appelle donc cette série du nom d'Omniscient."

Some passages suggest that the Buddha's real opinion about the attâ was not dogmatically negative. A celebrated story [1] relates how the wandering monk Vacchagotta asked him first whether a self exists (Kim nu kho bho Gotama atth'attâti) and then whether it is non-existent ( . . . natth'attâti). Both questions were received in silence. Ânanda, who was apparently astonished, subsequently inquired why no reply had been given. The Buddha said that if he had replied yes or no, he would have seemed to support the views of either the eternalists (sassatavâda) or of the annihilationists (ucchedavâda). "Yes" would have been inconsistent with the rest of his teaching: "no" would have simply bewildered Vacchagotta, who would have said "I used to have a self but now I have lost it".[2] Remarkable as this sutta is, I do not think that it should be regarded as giving us a better insight into his real view than do his other pronouncements. His own explanation of his silence is sufficient. He did not think it wise to enter into a discussion which would bewilder his untrained and inexperienced questioner. It is to be noted that in his early teaching he did not begin with the doctrine of anattâ. First he taught his five disciples the four Truths and the Path and they became Bhikkhus. Then after an interval, their minds being prepared, he preached to them anattâ and they accepted it in the right spirit. But to preach it abruptly and without preparation to a disputatious newcomer was unwise. He would mix things up and wrongly apply the new idea to the controversies of the day which filled his head. Elsewhere [3] the Buddha bids his disciples not to worry about questions like did I exist in the past or not, shall I exist in the future or not, do I exist at present or not, have I a self or not (atthi me attâ . . . n'atthi me attâ), but simply free themselves from the three bonds of individuality, doubt, and good works (sîlabbataparâmâsa). It is not, of course, meant that sîla or morality is bad: it is often declared to be indispensable, but we must not be absorbed in our own conduct and piety. So, too, we must get rid of the idea of individuality, but the proposition I have not a self (n'atthi me attâ) is a vain and confused argument because it presupposes that there is an "I" which can possess or not possess something.[4]

[1] Saṃ. Nik., xliv, 10.

[2] Cf. Maj. Nik., xxii (= vol. i, p. 137).

[3] Maj. Nik. ii. The Sabbâsavasutta.

[4] But, of course, language becomes impossible if we are to use no words implying the existence of ourselves and other selves. Attâ is frequently used in the Nikâyas in the colloquial sense. Even the end of the Anattâ-lakkhana sutta is not quite

At the same time it cannot be denied that there is an analogy between the question of the existence of a self and the question of the existence of the Tathâgata after death. The answer to the latter is expressly declared to be unrevealed. It is wrong to answer it in the negative and the later phases of Buddhism show a distinct tendency to answer it with a practical affirmative, though they may avoid unorthodox terminology. It is wrong to say that a Buddha passes on to another existence after death, but wrong only because the word existence implies limitations and weaknesses which do not affect him. It is expressly laid down in the Saṃyutta Nikâya that even in this life a Tathâgata is not intelligible as a real existence, for he cannot be defined in terms of body, feeling, perception, activities, and consciousness, as being any one of them or all of them together, nor yet can he be said to be without them.[1] Whatever be the precise meaning of the word Tathâgata in these passages, the analogy to the formulæ about anattâ is clear and we are left with the impression that though the word attâ is wrong and though no correct substitute can be found for it, yet in an enlightened mind it can be replaced by an idea which such a mind can conceive, though it cannot express it in human language. In these ideas there is the seed which bears plentiful fruit in the apparently sophistical arguments of later Mahayanist philosophy. In a series of bold negations the Vajracchedikâ [2] declares among other propositions that a Bodhisattva cannot save beings because in real truth there is no such thing as either a Bodhisattva or a being. The word śûnya or void which plays so great a part in this philosophy occurs not infrequently in the Nikâyas, especially in the expression suññam attena, void of a self or soul, and similar phrases.[3]

consistent, for it says that the disciple who understands this doctrine discards passion and acquires freedom and knowledge, whereas according to a previous statement he has abandoned the thought " I am " (Mahâv., i, 3, 4) and ought to use no personal pronouns.

[1] Yamaka and Anurâdha suttas in Saṃ. Nik., xxii, § 85 and § 86. The latter occurs again in xliv, § 2. The Pali commentator explains Tathâgata as here meaning a being, Satto.

[2] Vajracchedikâ (diamond cutter), xvii. Even in the Saṃ. Nik. (v. 10) the use of the word " being " is objected to: Nayidha sattûpalabbhati.

[3] e.g. Saṃ. Nik., xxxv, 85. Ânanda asks the meaning of the phrase suñño loka and the Buddha explains it as suññam attena va attaniyena. Cf. Saṃ. Nik., xli, § 7. Suññatâ cetovimutti, Maj. Nik., xliii (= vol. i, p. 297 ad fin.). Suññato samâdhi is mentioned in Saṃ. Nik., xliii, § 4 (= vol. iv, p. 360), and in Dîg. Nik., xxxiii. 10, 51 (= vol. iii, p. 219).

The sects known as Vajjiputtakas (Vatsiputriyas) and Sammitiyas believed in the real existence of a personality appealing to the sutta called the Burden [1] which describes human life by the metaphors of taking hold of the burden, lifting it up and laying it down. Their doctrine is condemned at the beginning of the Kathâvatthu (being no doubt considered as the most fundamental of all errors) and in the ninth chapter of the Abhidharmakośa. They were, however, numerous in India, especially in the west, and are often spoken of by Hsüan-Tsang. I-Ching mentions their presence in Champa and Sumatra. It might seem that a sect which avoided the difficult doctrine of selflessness and laid stress on the practical importance of personality was likely to succeed in missionary work among races who did not relish psychological disputes. But as a matter of fact the Sammitiyas seem to have been influential in India and in countries where Hindus settled because their doctrines were very nearly those of ordinary Hindu sects, but not in countries like China where a non-Indian population was evangelized. It does not appear that the preaching of anattâ created any difficulties for Buddhism in China or Japan.

After hearing and mastering [2] the truths enunciated in the first sermon the five disciples were admitted as members of the order with the words "Come, Bhikkhu: the doctrine is well taught: lead a holy life for making a complete end of pain". This formula suggests that the object of the Bhikkhu should be his own salvation, but the missionary and altruistic spirit was present in the very beginnings of Buddhism, and soon [3] after instituting the order of

[1] Saṃ. Nik., xxii, 22. I do not see that this sutta is inconsistent with what is said about anattâ in other passages. It treats of (1) Bhâra, the burden; (2) Bhâra-hâra, the taking hold of the burden, (3) Bhâra-âdâna, the lifting up of the burden, (4) Bhâra-nikkhepana, laying down the burden. Of these, No. 2 Bhâra-hâra is equated with puggalo—the personality, but it is not in form a noun indicating a personal agent. It is simply stated that what we call personality means taking hold of the burden which is formed of rûpa, vedanâ, saññâ, etc.

[2] The act of mastery was not immediate or simultaneous. Kondañña saw the truth first and hence was called Aññâta Kondañña; then after further instruction Vappa and Bhaddiya, and after still more Mahânâma and Assaji. The mastery is described as the Dhammacakkhu or Eye of Truth, and this is concisely defined as the knowledge that everything that has a beginning must also have an end, Yam kinci samudayadhammam, sabbam tam nirodhadhammam. The Buddha delivered a third remarkable discourse in this first part of his career known as the Fire sermon (Mahav., i, 21, and Saṃ. Nik., xxv, 38), but it does not contain any new doctrine.

[3] No date is given in terms of days and months, but the first missionaries were sent forth before the Buddha left Benares for Uruvela and at a time when there were only sixty-one Arhats in the world. Mahâvag., I, ii, 1.

Bhikkhus, the Buddha bade its members go forth and preach. "Go and wander for the gain of many, for the welfare of many, out of compassion for the world. . . . There are beings who are defiled with little dust. They are perishing through not hearing the Doctrine." This exhortation is purely altruistic. It is not even said that to serve others is the best way to find happiness for oneself, though there are many other passages which assert that those who are loving and charitable are also happy. The motive, compassion for the world (lokânukampâ), is the same which decided the Buddha to preach when he hesitated and felt discouraged by the difficulties of his task, and kindness, pity,[1] and desire to help are feelings constantly attributed to him. "All that a teacher can do for his disciples out of love and compassion, that for compassion's sake have I done for you."[2] And the disciple must imitate the master: the ideal Bhikkhu is full of kindness and compassion for everything that lives,[3] and the sutta of the Saw[4] preaches the doctrine of Love your Enemies in bold paradoxes. Should bandits carve you limb from limb with a two-handled saw, even then should you give way to anger you would not be obeying my law, says the Buddha. Even then you should be full of sympathy and goodwill and feel love even for the bandits.[5]

The sending forth of disciples to preach calls our attention to certain very important features already visible in early Buddhism, though they become much more conspicuous later. They are the missionary spirit, the idea of the Bodhisattva, the respect accorded to deities, the belief in heavens or paradises, and the position of laymen. There is a certain connection between these features, though it may not be obvious at first sight.

The society in which the Buddha was born and to which he preached had peculiarities to which it is difficult to find a parallel in any other age or country. The level of intelligence was high but religion absorbed almost the whole of intellectual life, for science, art, and literature hardly existed except as accessories to it. There was a powerful hereditary priesthood who spent their time in

[1] Karuṇâ, anukampâ. Maj. Nik., iii, near the beginning. Atthi me tumhesu anukampâ. I feel compassion for you and wish you to follow my teaching.

[2] Maj. Nik., xix ad fin. Repeated in cvi ad fin. and clii ad fin.

[3] Sabbapâṇabhûtahitânukampî viharati. Maj. Nik., xxvii.

[4] Maj. Nik., xxi. Kakacûpama-sutta.

[5] The story of Puṇṇa (Maj. Nik., xlv, and Saṃ. Nik., xxxv, § 88) is somewhat similar. It is true that according to his own statement his object was to secure his own salvation, but he made 500 converts.

theological study or in performing sacrifices on behalf of clients who seem to have been numerous and generous. But besides this priesthood there was also a large class of enquirers, some independent, some members of confraternities, who, though they were not much liked by the Brahmans, were under no sort of stigma as being heretics or dangerous radicals.[1] It was considered quite natural and proper for a man of intellectual tastes to devote himself to religion, abandon his wife, children, and profession and become a wandering student or teacher. Such a one not only incurred no odium but could count on finding food, lodging, and assistance wherever he went. If he became a teacher of any eminence, he collected round him a band of followers and a large company of lay believers who supported the Master and his disciples and to some extent adopted their doctrines and religious practices. In this way arose two important movements which became permanent religions, the Buddhists and the Jains. Others, such as the Âjîvakas, disappeared after a short existence apparently because even in India, which is very tolerant in such matters, their doctrines were considered fantastic.

In the early days of Buddhism the Bhikkhus and their supporters were not related to one another exactly as clergy and laity. The Bhikkhus were persons who devoted themselves to religion and it was meritorious to help them to live in comfort and to profit by their instruction. But it might not be possible for an ordinary family man to follow the steep and narrow path : it was recognized that less was expected of him and also that he must expect lesser blessings in future lives. And since the somewhat severe teaching of Gotama made scant provision for some things which the ordinary man expects of religion—for instance, kindly deities who will help him in the little troubles of life—he was not forbidden to supplement that teaching with beliefs and rites which strictly speaking are not Buddhist at all. These conditions led to the growth of a large confraternity, who for want of a better word may be called monks, with ample leisure and disposed to develop the psychological and philosophic sides of Gotama's teaching into elaborate systems. These systems are not inferior to European metaphysics and merit

[1] There are many warnings in the Nikâyas against becoming a monk for worldly motives. e.g. Ang. Nik., iv, 25, says that one should not lead a religious life with the object of being talked of and securing popular recognition or of obtaining gain, respect, and praise. It is remarkable that the Arthaśâstra seems to regard ascetics as the natural class to select spies from, presumably because they went everywhere and enjoyed everybody's confidence. See i, xi, and many other passages.

the attention of thinkers, but one wonders how they ever obtained a hearing outside a University. On the other hand, there were the laity, admirers of theories which they hardly understood and of aspirations which they did not presume to share, more inclined to the devotional side of religion, and more disposed to think of heaven and the help of benevolent deities than of the arduous road to nirvâna. This double outlook within the Buddhist community explains most of the developments which are collectively called Mahayanism.

Buddhism has many remarkable features but perhaps the most striking of all is its missionary spirit. From the first it preached and practised the duty of trying to convert the whole world. This was a new idea. The paganisms of the ancient world were local and national. As the Roman Empire spread, it seemed decent to erect in foreign countries temples to the deities of Imperial Rome, but the idea of converting Africans or Asiatics to the Roman religion would hardly have been intelligible in the time of Augustus. In India religion had less connection with states and cities: from the beginning there was a disposition to regard it as a search for truth and to expect revelations. Yet in practice these revelations were not regarded as divine messages to the world, and the Hindus behaved much like the Romans. In foreign countries where there were Hindu settlements there were also Hindu temples, as there are in East Africa and Singapore to-day, and the natives of Java and Cambodja adopted Hindu rites and beliefs as part of the imported civilization. But there is no record of Brahmanic missionaries. Much of the Bhagavad Gîtâ reads like an appeal to all mankind, but it insists on caste and forbids those who have learnt its doctrine to instruct unsuitable persons.[1] Even later sects such as the Lingayats or the followers of Caitanya who gave up caste in theory never sent out missionaries in the Buddhist or Christian sense. But among the non-Brahmanic confraternities of northern India about the sixth century B.C. there was a clear idea that there are such things as Truth and the Good Life which are discovered by the wise but can be understood by all: which can give salvation to all and therefore ought to be brought within the reach of all. The Jains, whose founder seems to have been a slightly older contemporary of Gotama, had this idea, and their sûtras are addressed "to Aryans and non-Aryans". Yet though they made converts

[1] Bhag. Gitâ, xviii, 67.

in India and spread in early times from the north to the extreme south it does not appear that they ever tried to evangelize foreign countries.[1] But Buddhism was from the first a message to all, "to gods and men": there is no hint that, like the doctrines of the Upanishads, it should be taught only to privileged persons. In the well-known sermon on the fruits of the Religious Life [2] the Buddha instances the case of a slave who becomes a monk and Punna [3] made 500 converts among the people of Sunaparanta who are represented as dangerous savages. A couple of centuries later, when intercourse with foreign countries had increased and Buddhists could invoke the help of the state, the extent and success of their missionary enterprises form an important chapter in the history of Asia. Asoka in his pious zeal perhaps exaggerated the efforts which he made for the conversion of Europe,[4] but there can be no doubt of his conviction that it was his duty to make the Good Law known throughout the world. Let me again emphasize the fact that before the rise of Christianity such an idea of religion was most unusual. Buddhism was preached to the Chinese and the Hellenistic kingdoms on the northern frontiers of India and accepted by them. But no Chinese or Bactrian ever dreamt of sending religious instructors to India. Chinese pilgrims went to India to obtain information: Indians went to China to teach.

The motive which inspired this missionary work, the feeling which made the Buddha face the hard task of founding a new religion, the spirit by which he bade his disciples be animated is described as anukampâ.[5] Compassion is the usual English translation, but perhaps it emphasizes the idea of superiority more than does the original, and sympathy or kindliness would be better renderings in many passages. The teacher is superior to the pupil inasmuch as he already possesses the knowledge which he wishes to impart, but otherwise he is simply "hitesin" [6]—desirous for the welfare of others. In the older writings due prominence is given to this

[1] In justice to the Jains it must be remembered that southern India was practically a foreign country both in race and language.

[2] Buddhism did not attempt to abolish caste, but it recognized merit in any caste, e.g. in Lal.-vist., xii, when there is a question of the Buddha's marriage, his father seeks for virtuous maidens in every caste on the ground that race and lineage are not important but that virtue is.

[3] Maj. Nik., cxlv.

[4] See the last Rock Edict.

[5] Etymologically the word seems to mean vibrate in sympathy with.

[6] Hitesin is an epithet of the Buddha, e.g. Maj. Nik., ciii. Saṃ. Nik., xliii, 1, 1.

motive, as I have shown, but it cannot be denied that many passages seem to hold up one's own personal private salvation as the goal of the religious life. Others[1] state that the reward is double: happiness for oneself and for others too. But in the Mahâyâna unselfishness, labour for others, and self-sacrifice are consistently held up as the ideal and this ideal is embodied in the figure of the Bodhisattva.[2]

This word occurs not infrequently in the Nikâyas and is generally used of Gotama[3] when he was a young man and had not yet obtained enlightenment or of past Buddhas in similar circumstances. More rarely it is applied to the future Buddha when in the Tusita heaven and awaiting birth.[4] The Kathâvatthu[5] discusses the career of a Bodhisattva and denies that he is reborn in purgatory or as an animal of his own free will, thus showing that such a view existed. In the Jâtakas we find fully developed the idea that the future Buddha practises through a long series of births all the virtues and more especially complete self-sacrifice or selflessness, giving up life, possessions, and everything if it will help others or even if they merely ask for it. Some centuries later such a career is not regarded as a story of what a great man did in previous births: it is humanized and made the ideal of the religious life. Manuals of devotion bid the good man be a Bodhisattva and teach him how to set about it and many saints in China and Japan have earned the title. On the other hand, the superhuman Bodhisattva, such as Avalokiteśvara (Kwannon) or Kshitigarbha (Jizō), is a new and most important figure for doctrine, art, and ritual. These great beings have no known historical origin, but they are believed to have struggled towards perfection through countless existences, like Gotama

[1] e.g. Maj. Nik., iv ad fin. Gotama says the solitary life is doubly good: "I see my own well-being here and now and I have compassion on them that come after." Also Saṃ. Nik., vii, § 2. "He who when reviled reviles not again acts for his own good as well as the good of others." The transition from one ideal to the other is illustrated in the Asokâvadâna, chap. x (Przyluski's transl., p. 423), where Yasas says to Asoka: "Votre Majesté s'est acquis des mérites exclusivement pour elle seule. C'est pourquoi ces mérites sont légers. Celui qui exhorte tout le monde à acquérir des mérites, celui-là est vraiment magnanime et la somme de ses mérites est lourde."

[2] I-Tsing long ago observed that the worship of Bodhisattvas was the chief point in which the Mahayanists differed from the Hinayanists. (See Takakusu's translation, p. 14.)

[3] Especially in the phrase which is several times put into Gotama's mouth: "such and such a thought occurred to me in the days before my Enlightenment when I was only a Bodhisattva."

[4] Maj. Nik., cxxiii, and similarly of Vipassi in Dîg. Nik., xiv.

[5] Kathâvat., xxiii, 3.

himself, and to have refused the peace of nirvâna when they had won it in order that they might continue to help suffering humanity. I shall have much to say about the development of these two aspects of the Bodhisattva in later times and will here merely point out how close is the relation of the superhuman Bodhisattvas to the deities who figure in the Nikâyas. These deities, or Devas, are not quite the same as the gods of Sanskrit literature, even when they bear the same names. They have a place in the sacred legend because they are devout, though not always very intelligent, supporters of the Buddha and his followers: they are not the governors of the world, still less teachers,[1] for they themselves need instruction and conversion. But they are an order of beings happier and stronger than men (but not than Buddhas) possessing various magic powers and living in paradises. Neither they nor their residences are eternal, though they last incalculably longer than man and his works. They owe these privileges to their meritorious conduct in previous existences[2]: they practised virtue and have obtained their reward in their own persons. They differ from future Buddhas and Bodhisattvas chiefly in not having the high unselfish resolve to save the world. But for all that they may actually be stages in the development of a Buddha. Gotama himself remembered having been Brahmâ and Sakka in previous existences.[3] When the question of the existence of Devas is raised in the Nikâyas[4] it is answered with an emphatic affirmative. Gotama declares that prosperity will come to those who support shrines and perform the proper offerings,[5] and when kindly spirits teach his disciples a spell consisting of a list of Devas and Yakkhas whose protection will secure peace and happiness, he bids them use it.[6] It will thus be seen that the modern Buddhist in China or

[1] Thus it is said in Maj. Nik., xcv, that many thousands of gods have found refuge in Gotama.

[2] In Saṃ. Nik., xi, 2, § 1–3, it is said that Sakka obtained his present high position by laying down for himself and following seven rules of conduct which include unselfishness (vigatamalamaccherena cetasâ). The idea that deities have won their present position is not unknown even in the Vedas. In *R.V.*, x, 167, 1, Indra is said to have wòn heaven by austerities (tapas).

[3] In the Itivuttaka, § 22, the Buddha says he was once Brahmâ and thirty-six times Sakka.

[4] e.g. Maj. Nik., xc, c, and cxxvii. This belief in Devas does not mean Theism or Monotheism in the European sense, that idea being unacceptable to all ordinary sects of both the Hîna- and Mahâyâna. Even Amida is not God in the Christian and Mohammedan sense, that is, he is not the creator and ruler of the world.

[5] Dig. Nik., xvi, 1, 4. Cf. the Ratana sutta of the Sutta Nipâta (223–238).

[6] Dig. Nik., xxxii. Âṭânâṭiya S.

Japan who shows respect to deities, either native or Indian, can easily justify himself from the ancient scriptures.

In this connection the devotional exercises known as Brahmavihâras or divine states are of interest. They are states of emotional meditation which lead to the companionship of Brahmâ,[1] that is to rebirth in his heaven and thus they combine the three ideas of love for all beings, a deity, and a paradise. They are fully recognized in the Nikâyas and are mentioned in the Lotus.[2] Though they are also mentioned in Brahmanic books,[3] Lord Chalmers is probably right in thinking that the emphasis laid by Buddhism on goodwill to mankind and all living creatures is " an original and independent contribution to the evolution of India's religious thought ".[4] Brahmanic sages are often represented as irritable, and the ideal of the Upanishads is not so much love and kindness as self-realization. It is in the Mahâyâna rather than in early Buddhism that an unselfish ideal receives full recognition as the mainspring and guiding spirit of religion, but it is not neglected in the Nikâyas.

The Brahmavihâras are a series of four meditations not unlike the jhânas.[5] The person who practises them is said to pervade (pharati) all living creatures in all regions with thoughts first of love[6] (mettâ), then of pity (karuṇâ), then of joy (muditâ), and finally of equanimity (upekkhâ), that is, indifference to praise and blame, kindness and unkindness. These thoughts not only bring to him who cultivates them the blessings of calm and peace, but by a species of telepathy they spread joy and love among others. And since Brahmâ himself is free from all anger and malice, the man whose

[1] The rendering " union with Brahmâ ", which is used by many translators, is liable to misunderstanding, as implying absorption into the supreme spirit as contemplated by the Upanishads. The Pali expressions (Brahmâṇam sahavyatâya maggo, Brahmuṇo saddhim samsandati sameti, Brahmuṇo sahavyûpago bhavissati) seem to mean simply associating with Brahmâ or joining his retinue. Cf. Saṃ. Nik., xlii, 2. Pahâsânam Devânam sahavyatam upapajjhati. Is reborn in the company of the Laughing Devas.

[2] Lotus, chap. v, verse 77.

[3] In the Yoga sûtras, I, 33. But many scholars assign a late date to this work. In Maj. Nik., l, it is said that the former Buddha Kakusandha taught the Brahmâvihâras.

[4] *Further Dialogues of the Buddha*. Introd., p. xxiv.

[5] Indeed they are sometimes called jhânas. See Dîg. Nik., xix, § 41 and § 43.

[6] Mettâ seems to me to be the equivalent of love or charity in the New Testament, that is Ἀγάπη not Ἔρως. It is extolled in the Nikâyas in many well-known passages. e.g. Dig. Nik., viii, § 15 ; Itivuttaka, iii, 7, and Saṃ. Nik., xx, 4, where a little love is said to be better than great gifts. For a Mahayanist definition see Śikshâsamuccaya, chap. xii, p. 212 (Bendall's edition).

thoughts are full of kindness is fit to associate with him and is reborn in his paradise after death. But it must not be supposed that heaven can be won by mere sentiment and dreamy benevolence—good conduct (sîla) and a life religious in act as well as thought are expressly required as a preliminary to the meditations.[1]

Though the Brahmavihâras are commended in the Piṭakas, they are a by-way. The main road is the path to nirvâna, wherein there is no rebirth, whereas loving thoughts lead only to the heaven of Brahmâ—sometimes called the humble world of Brahmâ.[2] This is stated emphatically in the Govinda-suttanta,[3] where the Buddha relates how in a former birth he taught the Brahmavihâras to numerous disciples, who all, even the most backward, were reborn in some paradise. But, he continues, that religious life (brahma-cariyam) did not lead to the cessation of craving and to nirvâna, but only to rebirth in Brahmâ's heaven, whereas the religious life as I now preach it—that is, the Eightfold Path—does lead to that happy consummation and to absolute passionlessness.

The followers of the Mahâyâna do not contradict such passages, though they may go so far as to say that these are counsels of perfection, good for the hero saints of old but not for the weaklings of to-day. But clearly much of the popular Buddhism now to be seen in the Far East is identical with the brahmacariyam—the religious life—to which Gotama here gives the second place. It has the same ideal, namely kindness, the same aspiration, namely heaven, and it looks for the help of approving deities or Bodhisattvas. In the Dîgha Nikâya Brahmâ himself helps Govinda to reach his heaven.[4]

The Nikâyas represent the Buddha himself as teaching the Brahmavihâras to laymen. Thus he explains them to a village headman, apparently as a sufficient method of salvation and without reference to higher things, and the headman asks to be accepted as a lay disciple.[5] It is not clear that the Eightfold Path is ever

[1] e.g. Dig. Nik., xiii, 43–75.

[2] Maj. Nik., xcvii ad fin., hîne Brahmaloke. But still the bliss of heaven is described in unstinted terms in Maj. Nik., cxxix ad fin.

[3] Dîg. Nik., xix, § 61. So, too, in Maj. Nik., vii. a Bhikkhu practises the Brahmavihâras and then he knows that there is a lower and a higher stage: deliverance lies beyond this realm of consciousness.

[4] Dîg. Nik., xix, §§ 44–6.

[5] Saṃ. Nik., xlii, § 8, called Sankha, the trumpet. See, too, Saṃ. Nik., xli, § 7, and xlii, §§ 13–44 ff. (= vol. iv, p. 351 ff.).

taught to the laity in the same way.[1] This is perhaps one reason why the Four Truths and the Path, which are fundamental formulæ for early Buddhism, are so little known in the Far East at the present day. They are not a common phrase like the Three Treasures. The Path leads to nirvâna and has nothing to do with Paradise or deities. Throughout the Pali Piṭakas it is the Bhikkhus who are regarded as the true disciples of the Buddha.[2] He forsook the world himself and advised others to do so. But for all that the good laymen had from the very first an honourable position, and clearly the success of Buddhism as a missionary creed and the place which it fills in the religious history of the world are mainly due to the appeal which it made to influential persons who were not monks or clerics. And as time went on, the ideal of becoming an Arhat (like the ideal of becoming a saint in Christianity) seemed arduous and even presumptuous, so that the more human and less austere parts of the original teaching became more and more prominent.

In the discourses which the Buddha is said to have delivered to lay believers, the chief stress is laid on morality (sîla). Morality is indispensable for Bhikkhus : indeed, six of the eight stages in the path are occupied with nothing else. But it is not sufficient for them whereas it is sufficient for the laity. And lay morality has many departments which do not concern the monk, such as the right use of riches and the proper relations between husbands and wives, parents and children. Many discourses in the Nikâyas are addressed to laymen and describe the good layman's life. One of the best known is the homily addressed to Sigala,[3] which deals with the mutual duties of (*a*) parents and children, (*b*) teachers and pupils, (*c*) husband and wife, (*d*) friends, (*e*) masters and servants, (*f*) clergy and laity. Though Buddhism has won such triumphs in China and Japan, it is noticeable that the Buddha's rules for conduct

[1] It is part of the instruction given to the headman Rasiya in Saṃ. Nik., xlii, § 12, but there, as in the Vinaya, it begins with the formula "There are two extremes which should not be followed by one who has renounced the world". Rasiya asked the Buddha whether it was true that he disapproved of ascetics (tapassî) who practise asceticism (tapas), and the Buddha replied by explaining in what respects tapas is praiseworthy or blameworthy.

[2] The inferiority of the laity is clearly indicated by such phrases as sikkham pacakkhâya hînây'âvattati (Maj. Nik., lxvii and lxxvii), he gives up his training and reverts to the lower state (of a layman). Compare the parable of the three fields (Saṃ. Nik., xlii, § 7) in which the Buddhist laity rank as the moderate field between the Bhikkhus (excellent) and the men of other creeds (poor).

[3] Dig. Nik., xxxi (the Sigâlovâda S.).

contain no reference to loyalty and political duties which hold the first place in the ethics of the Far East. But the moral code prescribed is simple, sensible, and intelligible to all nations. The principle which inspires it is the anukam pâ mentioned above, and perhaps the verb anukampati, which occurs many times in the homily, is best translated [1] by love in the Biblical sense. In one passage a man is bidden to treat his friends and companions as he treats himself.[2] He who follows these precepts wins happiness in this world and in the next. The same simple motive is approved in a discourse of the Anguttara,[3] when the Buddha enumerates four things which give happiness and good repute here—industry, carefulness, a good friend, and economy—and four which bring joy in heaven—faith, good morals, generosity, and wisdom. Wisdom in this context does not mean insight into great mysteries. It consists, we are told, in seeing the evils which come from greed, ill-will, sloth, worry, and doubt and in getting rid of them. And faith is defined as belief in the Buddha as being all-enlightened and the teacher of Gods and men. One might have expected some summary of what his teaching is, but, as a missionary appeal, the precept is simple and direct.

[1] So in the Sacred Books of the Buddhists, vol. iv, p. 181 ff.

[2] § 31, samânattayâ.

[3] Ang. Nik., viii–liv. See, too, Ang. Nik., lv, where a married couple ask the Buddha if they can meet in heaven. He replies that they can if they are samasaddhâ, samasilâ, samacâgâ, samapaññâ.

# CHAPTER III

## BUDDHISM IN INDIA

### 1

THOUGH our literary records are copious and in part ancient, it is hard to feel on firm ground when discussing the early history of the religious and philosophical systems comprised under the name of Buddhism. Books which are considered as scripture, such as the great Mahayanist sûtras, are not associated with any human name or any contemporary events, and even when works are ascribed to a simple mortal the correctness of the ascription and the period when the author lived are often matters of argument. We are not dealing with admitted facts like the date of Plato or St. Paul and, in assigning a writer to a certain period, all that we can say in the most favourable circumstances is that our conclusion harmonizes with all the available evidence. Even the history of reigns and dynasties is doubtful. The difficulties of Indian chronology are notorious and they are peculiarly acute for the period during which Buddhism underwent most change, that is from the death of the Buddha to the early centuries of the Christian era. Chinese chronology is fairly certain for events which happened in China, but unfortunately Chinese Buddhists made no attempt to study the history of India. They simply translated Indian works, and until the fifth century A.D., when Chinese pilgrims began to visit India, they have no criticisms or independent observations to offer.

In the present chapter I shall endeavour to record in chronological order such facts and dates as we know concerning the development of Buddhism in India with special reference to its connection with the Far East, and in so doing I shall deal mainly with sects and schoolmen, reserving for the next chapter an account of the Buddhas and Bodhisattvas of the Mahâyâna. Since these new figures and doctrines are of such obvious importance in the history of religion, it may seem strange to give them the second place and to treat first of relatively obscure philosophers. But it is easier to find some sort of historical setting for the philosophers. The dates of such personages as Aśvaghosha and Vasubandhu are disputable enough, but still tradition connects them with certain kings and cities and some of the works ascribed to them seem genuine. But in seeking for the origins of the worship of Amitâbha and Avalokiteśvara we have not even this modest allowance of historical detail: all is as unearthly as their own radiant Paradises. We know the dates when the Lotus and the sûtras about Amitâbha are said to have been translated into Chinese, and the style of the Sanskrit original may afford a basis for plausible theories. But that is all. Regardless of probability the texts represent themselves as the utterances of Śâkyamuni himself and no later authority is cited. Though we hear of many ancient sects distinguished by their rules of discipline and other minutiæ and though later in China and Japan sects were numerous and clearly divided, it is curious that in ancient India the Mahâyâna did not give rise to similar bodies. The worshippers of Amitâbha and Avalokiteśvara are not spoken of as if they were a corporation of any kind. In Byzantine Christianity disputes about the nature of Christ led to the formation of parties—Nestorian, Monophysite, Orthodox, and so on—but though the Mahayanist sûtras freely propound new views about the Buddha nature, these views remain singularly detached: they are not connected with the names of teachers or denominations. Hence the annals of Indian Buddhism seem peaceful. We hear less of quarrels and of persecution than in Europe, and that perhaps is creditable and civilized. But it makes it extremely difficult to trace the birth and growth of new ideas. It may be well to state briefly what is known of the political history of India in this obscure period.

In the last days of the Buddha we see Magadha emerging as the chief state of Northern India, a position which it maintained for nearly three centuries, though until the invasion of Alexander few historical events can be cited. It is important, however, to note that at this period the Persian Empire had two satrapies within the limits of modern India, in one of which, called Gandhara, was the celebrated University of Taxila,[1] near the modern Rawal Pindi. As this seat of learning was frequented by Indian students, they must have felt even in early times Persian and afterwards Hellenistic influence. There are signs of Persian influence in India in the reign of Asoka.

In 327 Alexander the Great, after overthrowing the Persian Empire, invaded India, where he remained only nineteen months. Immediately after his death in 323, Candragupta, a scion of the royal house of Magadha, put an end to Macedonian authority in

[1] This is the Greek form of the name, which is Takshaśilâ in Sanskrit and Takkasila in Pali.

India and founded the Maurya dynasty, under which Magadha became an empire comprising all northern and central India with Pataliputra as its capital. Seleucus Nicator, who had inherited the Asiatic possessions of Alexander, came into collision with Candragupta but was defeated, and about 303 B.C. had to conclude a treaty by which he ceded Kabul, Herat, and Kandahar. The grandson of Candragupta was the great Asoka, who was the first ruler of practically all India (for his dominions extended from Afghanistan almost to Madras) and an ardent Buddhist. But his empire broke up shortly after his death and we now enter on one of those chaotic periods which occur from time to time in Indian history, and there is little certain information about Magadha until the fourth century A.D. Andhra, a region comprising large parts of the districts now called Hyderabad and the Central Provinces, was the first to revolt from the Mauryas, and a dynasty of Andhra Kings ruled until A.D. 236 over varying but often extensive territories.

Alexander's invasion produced little direct effect and, strange to say, no allusion to it has been found in Indian literature. But indirectly it had a great influence on the political, artistic, and religious development of the Hindus by preparing the way for a series of later invasions from the north which brought with them a mixed culture containing Hellenistic, Persian, and other elements. Alexander had settled a considerable number of Greek soldiers in Bactria, and it was for some time ruled by kings with Greek names, who were at first vassals of the Seleucids but became independent about the same time that the dynasty of the Arsacidæ arose in Parthia (250 B.C.). A certain Demetrius seems to have conquered Kabul, the Panjab, and Sind, and somewhat later (c. 155 B.C.) Menander, celebrated in Buddhist literature as the hero of the Questions of Milinda and apparently King of the Kabul Valley, made an incursion to the east, occupied Muttra, and threatened Pataliputra itself but was repulsed. Meanwhile another set of invaders appeared on the scene, the wandering tribes known as Sakas and Yüehchih, similar to the modern Turkomans, though they probably spoke Iranian languages. After 150 B.C. western India was parcelled out among foreign princes called Sakas, Pallavas, or Yavanas, whose frontiers were constantly changing. For some time they admitted the suzerainty of the Parthians, and the most important principality, which was known as the great Satrapy and included Surashtra (Kathiawar), lasted till about A.D. 395. The

Yüehchih appear to have started from somewhere near the frontier of China about 100 B.C., and, driving the Sakas before them, settled in Bactria where they became known as Kushans from the name of one of their principal clans. They subsequently conquered the whole of North-Western India, and the empire of their great King Kanishka, whose capital was Peshawar, included Afghanistan, Bactria, Kashmir, parts of Central Asia, and perhaps extended as far as Gaya in the east. The date of this monarch, who played a part in the later history of Buddhism comparable with that of Asoka in earlier times, was long a matter of doubt and discussion,[1] but it is now generally agreed that he reigned at the end of the first century and inaugurated the era which began in A.D. 78. His successors apparently kept his empire together for some time, but early in the third century both the Andhras and Kushans collapsed for unknown reasons and the history of India is a blank until the rise of the Guptas.[2]

This dynasty, which not only restored some sort of political unity but also, roughly speaking, marked the beginning of modern Hinduism and of a reaction against Buddhism, was originally connected with Pataliputra, though subsequently Ayodhya and Kausambi became its royal residences. In 320 Candragupta I, a local Raja who bore the same name as the founder of the Mauryas and had increased his hereditary dominions, instituted the Gupta era. Samudra Gupta continued this victorious career and by 340 appears to have received the submission of nearly all the Indian peninsula, though he did not attempt to retain or administer all his conquests But his successors, beginning with his son Vikramaditya, ruled undisturbed over most of northern India, until they were overthrown by new invaders from the north, known as Hûnas,

[1] The latest researches show a tendency to put his date 40 or 50 years later. See Van Wijk in *Acta Orientalia*, v, pp. 168–170, and Sten Konow, ib., v, 28–38, and vi, 93–6, where he says: "Kanishka started from Khotan in 128, which became the initial year of his reign. The same year or in 129 we find him in Peshawar dedicating Buddhist relics in a stupa. Two years later he had established his power as far east as Benares. Later he retraced his steps . . . and settled down as King of Khotan and Suzerain of the whole Kushana Empire . . . He may be identical with the King Kien who was killed in A.D. 152." But Bachhofer (*Ostas. Ztsft*, 1927, pp. 21-43) maintains the date A.D. 78 for Kanishka's era. The Chinese annals describe the campaigns of Pan Ch'ao in Central Asia A.D. 72-103, but do not mention Kanishka. This makes it probable that he was not reigning at that time.

[2] It is remarkable that the collapse of the Andhras (A.D. 236), the death of the last Kushan King, and the rise of the Sassanian dynasty in Persia coincide very closely in date.

Ephthalites, or White Huns,[1] fierce barbarians who neither brought with them nor assimilated any form of civilization, though they held northern India from the end of the fifth to the middle of the sixth century. They were hostile to Buddhism and are said to have worshipped Śiva, but their destruction of monasteries and temples was probably due to love of pillage, not to any sectarian animosity.

Up to this time Indian princes had shown little capacity for united action, but the cruelty of these savages brought about a coalition and the Huns were driven out of India. After their expulsion all is again confusion and obscurity, until light comes with the exploits of Harsha (A.D. 606–647), a prince of Thanesar, who after thirty-five years of warfare founded a state which, though it did not outlast his life, emulated for a time the dimensions and prosperity of the Gupta Empire. Our knowledge of the intellectual and social life of this period is unusually full, for the works of Bana, Bhartrihari, and others who frequented his Court have come down to us, as well as plays attributed to Harsha himself. We have also the narrative of Hsüan-Tsang, the Chinese pilgrim who was his guest at Kanauj.

In the earlier part of Harsha's reign all forms of religion and philosophy seem to have been welcomed at his Court, but Buddhism had considerable influence. It was introduced into Tibet about 638, apparently as representing what was considered best in Indian culture, and late in life Harsha himself became a devout though not exclusive Buddhist. Nevertheless, both Hsüan-Tsang and the next pilgrim I-Ching (A.D. 671–695) regretfully report that Buddhism was decaying in India. The Guptas had been favourable to Hinduism, though not persecutors of other creeds, and though the Huns were merely destructive, yet their violence (like Mohammedan raids in later ages) did more harm to Buddhism than other religions, because so much of its strength was concentrated in monasteries which were easily demolished.

The preceding remarks refer almost exclusively to northern India. The history of the south is even more obscure in chronology and lacking in events, since the Dravidian countries were not disturbed by foreign invasions. But though remote, they were not barbarous. Apart from external influences they felt the same intellectual and religious movements as northern India, for both Buddhism and Jainism reached them considerably before our era and were possibly stronger than Brahmanism, though we hear of influential Śaivite

[1] Apparently a branch of the Huns who invaded Europe. The original name was probably something like Haptal.

and Vishnuite sects at a fairly ancient date. From early times the south was divided into three states known as the Pandya, Cera, and Cola Kingdoms, and from the sixth to the eighth century A.D. a fourth power was important, namely, the Pallavas who had their capital at Conjeevaram.

The Deccan was ruled by the Andhras from the fall of the Mauryas till A.D. 236, but for the next three centuries nothing is known of its history until the rise of the Calukyas in Bijapur. Pulakesin of this dynasty (A.D. 608–642), a contemporary of Harsha, was for some time successful in creating a rival empire which extended from Madras to Gujarat and exchanged embassies with Persia. But in 642 he was defeated and slain by the Pallavas. With the simultaneous death of Harsha, the short-lived tendency to political unification came to an end and there began what has been called the Rajput period (about A.D. 650–1000), characterized by the existence of numerous independent kingdoms ruled by dynasties nominally Hindu but often really descended from northern invaders. For our purposes it is not necessary to sketch their fortunes and contests, but the Palas, a line of Buddhist Kings who began to reign about A.D. 730, may be mentioned, for under their patronage a decadent form of Buddhism, often called Tantric, flourished in Bengal and Bihar until the Mohammedan invasions of the twelfth century. The Buddhism of Nepal and Tibet and also of Java apparently reflected the phases of religion in Bengal, and there were universities at Odontapuri and Vikramaśila at which Tibetans studied. We hear of Indian translators and teachers in China as late as the eleventh century, but the last one of any importance was Amoghavajra [1] (A.D. 719–774), who was responsible for the introduction of much Tantric literature and practices into the Far East.

The above sketch will enable the reader to understand the difficulty of tracing the evolution of Buddhism in the land of its birth. If the historian has to confess that a whole century is a blank in which nothing certain can be recorded, it is not surprising if the date of a particular doctor or doctrine remains doubtful. But one or two features are noticeable. In central and southern India Buddhism was not much affected by foreign influences, or, so far as we know, by state control. It often enjoyed or shared the favour of local potentates, but there was no institution analogous to the Roman or Chinese Empire, and the social and political ideas which spring from such an institution were also absent. The

[1] Translated as Pu-K'ung in Chinese.

weakness of Buddhism was that its adherents, especially the laity, were not sharply distinguished from other bodies, as are for instance Moslims and Parsees in modern times. They were inclined to accept and adopt prevalent ideas and practices. Not that they were merely passive and receptive. Their contribution to the religion, philosophy, and art of India was enormous, but still the net result was that Hinduism, though it was transformed, remained a religious system supervised by the Brahmans, whereas Buddhism as a separate organization ceased to exist. In the north the result was much the same, with this difference in the process that many of the warlike tribes who invaded India from Central Asia, notably the Kushans and their great King Kanishka, became converted to the faith. They gave it valuable material support: on the other hand, their mental texture was very different from that of ancient Magadha where the doctrine was first preached, and it is not surprising if they welcomed whatever mythology and ritual they found in their new faith and added more of their own. During many centuries the political frontier in the north-west was uncertain and India was not sharply distinguished from Persia, Afghanistan, Bactria, and even Central Asia either politically or in culture. In the Buddhism which grew up in this region there is no reason to doubt the presence of Hellenistic, Persian, or other foreign influences if the evidence suggests it. But we must not exaggerate the inrush of foreign ideas. Indian thought and Indian art streamed across Central Asia (and also by sea) to China and ultimately to Japan, but the process was not reciprocal. Something may have come to India from Bactria and Persia, but nothing came from China, and the converted invaders made changes not so much by introducing foreign notions as by twisting Indian ideas in their own fashion.

But we must return to the earlier stages in the development of Buddhism. As already mentioned, there are traditions of a Council held a hundred years after the death of the Buddha which, according to the Pali Vinaya, decided certain points concerning discipline rather than doctrine. Later accounts[1] add that those who did not accept the decisions of this Council organized themselves as a party called Mahâsanghikas, or the people of the Great Council,

[1] The Dîpavaṃsa and Hsüan-Tsang.

and compiled their own version of the scriptures. Though this story is not supported by any external evidence, it is highly probable that the rigid and unsentimental doctrine of the Theravâdins or orthodox party called forth some kind of popular protest. But we really know nothing about the history of Buddhism from the death of the Buddha till the reign of Asoka, who ascended the throne in 274 and became a Buddhist in 262 B.C. Later tradition gives a list of Elders or Patriarchs who are supposed to have been in some vague way heads of the Church, but only five are named for this rather long interval and the lists do not agree.[1] It is probable that many of the later works included in the Pali Piṭakas were composed in this period, though it would be very rash to assume that the Pali Abhidhamma was completed before the reign of Asoka. The growth and movement of ideas to be found in this literature is not great. It consisted chiefly of classification and elaboration and even so was concerned with psychological and quasi-metaphysical problems rather than with religion. In the absence of evidence it is useless to discuss in detail what was the doctrine and practice of Buddhism about 300 or 400 B.C., but since there is no record of any change or remarkable event we may imagine that it continued to exist as an exceptionally powerful and flourishing religious corporation of a type common in India in those days, though we have had nothing corresponding to it in Europe. It was a body of celibates, who may be called monks for want of a better word, though their mode of life involved more wandering and intercourse with the world than we associate with monkhood, occupied partly with study and contemplation, partly with preaching, and supported by a body of lay admirers who followed their teaching so far as the duties of family life allowed. Gotama's confraternity had many good points which distinguished it from others: from the first it claimed to be a message to the whole world, it advocated neither excessive mortification of the flesh like the Jains nor paradoxical doctrines like the Âjîvakas: it bade men love one another and lead good lives. Still, we may imagine that about 300 B.C. it was in some danger of becoming a philosophical system like Platonism.[2] It was Asoka who turned it into what we call a religion and a State Church.

[1] The Dîpavaṃsa gives Upali, Dasaka, Sonaka, Siggava, and Tissa Moggaliputta. The list of the Sarvâstivâdins was Mahâkasyapa, Ânanda, Sanavasa and Mâdhyantika, Upagupta, and Dhitika.

[2] Megasthenes, who was in India about 300 B.C., knew of the Buddha as a deified teacher, but does not seem to have considered Buddhism as a separate religion.

Asoka was not a theologian, philosopher, or bigot. He was in the simplest sense of the words good and kind, the friend of man and beast. In his youth he was shocked by the horrors of war as he saw them during the Kalinga campaign, and Buddhism seems to have attracted him because it taught people to live in harmony and respect animal life. Numerous inscriptions have come down to us in which he lectures his subjects on religion and morality, but though he often speaks as a professed Buddhist, in none of them does he formulate any creed or deal with such themes as Karma, Samadhi, and Nirvâna. His Buddhism was popular in the sense of avoiding dogma and metaphysics, but he shows no proclivity to mythology and ritual which were the popular side of the Mahâyâna. Also, though his didactic edicts recall the inscriptions of Darius and there is probably a real historic connection between the two, there are no other signs of Iranian influence in his utterances.

He styles the Buddha Lord and Śâkyamuni. He made a pilgrimage to his birthplace and erected an inscribed pillar there. A similar pillar records how he visited and repaired the stupa of the earlier Buddha Konâgamana, so that he clearly accepted the doctrine of a series of Buddhas. Further, he declares that all the words of the Lord Buddha are well said: he could point to some collection of scriptures regarded as the Lord's sermons and he says that they should be studied "by monks and nuns, by laymen and laywomen". I have already discussed the tradition that he summoned a Council at which the Canon was fixed. The object of most of the edicts is to exhort his subjects to follow what he calls Dhamma, that is the Law or the good life which a Buddhist layman ought to lead. He defines it [1] as obedience to parents: respect for living creatures: speaking the truth: reverence to teachers and courtesy to relations, and he extols these virtues in language which recalls the Dhammapada. His maxims resemble the edicts published in later ages by K'ang-Hsi in China and Shōtoku Taishi in Japan, but his insistence on the sanctity of animal life, to which he often recurs, goes beyond ordinary lay legislation and in one inscription he remarks that he thinks nothing of much importance except what concerns the next world. This shows that, though in such of his utterances as have survived he dwells more on the need of harmony and humanity than on the truth of any particular creed, he was inspired by real religious conviction.

This conviction filled him with missionary zeal. In the last

[1] In the Second Minor Rock Edict.

Rock Edict he expresses his horror of war and announces his intention of making conquests only by the Dhamma. He then states that he has sent missionaries, not only to the outlying parts of his own dominions and to Ceylon, but to the Kingdoms of Syria, Egypt, Macedonia, Cyrene, and Epirus. Asoka perhaps exaggerates these pious campaigns: indeed, his own language is not quite clear as to the results, and we have no confirmation of the presence of Buddhist missionaries in Europe or Africa. But he clearly enunciates the important principle that it is the duty of a good Buddhist to do all he can to spread the faith, and we know that nearer home his missionary efforts were crowned with success. Buddhism was introduced into Ceylon in his reign, and the statements of the Sinhalese chronicles as to dispatch of missionaries to the north have been confirmed by the discovery at Sanchi of urns inscribed with the names of Majjhima and others who are called teachers of the Himalaya region. The same chronicles credit him with evangelizing Suvannabhûmi or Pegu, but the statement, though quite probable, is not confirmed by any inscription. About the twenty-first year of his reign, he made a pilgrimage to the sacred sites in the district where the Buddha was born. He also visited Nepal and he erected five stupas at Lalitpur. It does not appear that he visited Kashmir personally, but by his orders Srinagar was founded and Buddhism introduced.

The tradition that he erected many stupas, temples, and monasteries is doubtless correct, though he does not mention these buildings himself. He tells us, however, that he appointed commissioners to supervise charitable institutions and the affairs of all sects, not merely Buddhists, and he orders the local authorities to hold assemblies in which the Dhamma is to be proclaimed and to arrange religious processions.[1] Later in his reign he speaks almost as Head of the Church. As we have seen, he admonishes both monks and laymen as to what are the most edifying portions of scripture, and in the Sarnath edict he prescribes the steps to be taken against those who try to provoke schism and incidentally he orders all his officials to attend the Uposatha ceremony.[2]

[1] With elephants, cars, and illuminations, he says. They must have been very like the Perahera festival still celebrated in Kandy and the processions arranged by Harsha as reported by Hsüan-Tsang.

[2] Practically equivalent to Sunday, as the ceremony was held at the new moon, full moon, and eighth day after each. He doubtless promoted good Buddhists. The Divyâvadâna (xxvii and xxix) mentions Râdhagupta and the Arhat Yasas as ministers of Asoka. The latter is also mentioned in the Sûtrâlankâra of Aśvaghosha.

### 3

It would be of great interest to know what variations in doctrine or discipline amounted to schism in Asoka's opinion, but he gives no explanation. According to tradition there existed in his reign or somewhat earlier eighteen schools or sects,[1] and to these were added a little later, but still in the same period, six others. There is nothing improbable in this acccount, but unfortunately all the narratives which give names and details are late and not quite consistent, for naturally rival sects held different views as to the origin of the various schisms. The Kathâvatthu, which tradition associates with the Council of Asoka, cites and confutes opinions only: the names of the bodies which held the opinions are given in the Commentary attributed to Buddhaghosa and more or less agreeing with the Sinhalese Chronicles.[2]

It is generally admitted that the most important differences were those which separated the Mahâsanghikas from all others and that these Mahâsanghikas were the precursors of the Mahâyâna. The celebrated Chaitya cave at Karli dating from the second century A.D. appears to have belonged to them. But we do not know to what extent there was hostility between them and the sects which called themselves Theravâdins, Sthaviras, or Vibhajjavâdins. They are not condemned or even mentioned in Asoka's inscriptions, and the probability is that all the sects were schools of thought rather than contending religious organizations like Catholics or Protestants. Nearly a thousand years later the Chinese pilgrims report that their names were still known in India and that it was a creditable thing to be versed in the scriptures of all of them. Unfortunately we cannot be sure what were the views of the Mahâsanghikas, especially

[1] According to Sinhalese authorities, the Mahâsanghikas broke away from the orthodox Theravâda after the Council of Vesâlî and split into five sects. Meanwhile, apart from this schism, the Theravâda became divided into the Vajjiputtakas and Mahimśâsakas. The former had three subdivisions including the important Sammitiyas. Most important of all were the Sarvâstivâdins, with three offshoots. They were descended from the Mahimśâsakas, as were also the Dhammaguttikas. The section of the Chinese Tripiṭaka which is devoted to the Vinaya of the Hînayâna contains translations from the literature of the following sects: Sarvâstivâdin, Mûlasarvâstivâdin, Kâśyapîya, Dharmagupta, Mahâsanghika, Mahîmśâsaka, Sammitiya.

[2] Tibetan sources furnish other accounts given by Vasumitra (see Wassilieff, *Bouddhisme*, p. 227 ff.) and Bhavya (see Rockhill, *Life of the Buddha*, p. 181). The Chinese Tripiṭaka contains three translations of a treatise on Sects by Vasumitra (Nanjio, Nos. 1284–6).

in early times. It is true that the extant work called Mahâvastu describes itself as belonging to them,[1] but it has certainly received many late interpolations (for instance, it alludes to the Hûnas and the written characters of the Chinese), and we have no safe criterion to distinguish what is old and new in matters of doctrine. The text as it stands teaches the existence of countless Buddhas and gives an account of the ten stages in a Bodhisattva's upward career. It also tells how Śâkyamuni in a previous birth took a vow to attain Buddhahood. The Kathâvatthu[2] condemns the view that Buddhas are omnipresent and the commentary says that it was held by the Mahâsanghikas. The name Lokattaravâdin refers to the doctrine that the Buddha was superhuman and doubtless the Mahâsanghikas were disposed to welcome all beliefs which fitted in with it.[3] But it is hard to say at what date any particular belief was adopted or to form any lively picture of the activities of this ancient sect.

We know more about their opponents, called Theravâdins, Sthaviras, or Vibhajjavâdins, who claimed to represent orthodox tradition, tolerating no innovations. As the old Pali literature was produced under their auspices, we have some materials for studying their history, at least from their own point of view. They are the party who triumphed at the Council of Vesâlî and also at Asoka's Council, if that meeting be historical. The Pali Abhidhamma is their work, including the Kathâvatthu, which refutes the views of which they disapproved. The names which they gave themselves mean Elders and Particularizers. They claimed to preach the doctrine as remembered by the senior disciples of the Buddha and fixed at the first Council.[4] They respected the minutiæ of tradition, and their

[1] It states that it belongs to the Lokattaravâdin branch of the Aryamahâsanghikas.

[2] Kathâvat., xxi, 6.

[3] It must be remembered that even in the P li Canon the Buddha is often represented as superhuman in our sense. For ins ance, in Sam. Nik., i, ii, 1, 10 (= vol. i, p. 50), the sun appeals to him and he prevents an eclipse. The really important change in doctrine comes when we detect a tendency to regard Buddhas as manifestations of the Universal Spirit.

[4] The word theravâda actually occurs in the Maj. Nik., xxvi, and means the accepted explanation of a teacher's doctrine as given by his senior disciples and learnt by newcomers. It is used in speaking of the Buddha's teacher, Alâra. The title Vibhajjavâdin apparently refers to sûtra xcix of the Majjhima Nikâya, where the Buddha, in reply to a question about the respective value of a householder's life and a pilgrim's, declines to generalize and says that all depends on the details of conduct. The Abhidharmakośa explains the name with special reference to their views as to the existence of the past, present, and future.

philosophy, which consisted in carefully cataloguing and analysing the moral and especially the psychological pronouncements found in the Nikâyas, was certainly free from bold generalizations and heady speculation. Indeed, it is surprising that so arid and scholastic a system can ever have been a cultural force.

The Theravâda exists at the present day in Ceylon, Burma, Siam, and Cambodja practically unchanged. This extraordinary immutability and persistence are no doubt due to the fact that at an early date it became the State religion of Ceylon, where the inhabitants welcomed civilization, art, and seemly ecclesiastical institutions but had not got the Indian love of speculation and of new ideas. There is no country in the world where an interest in religion and philosophy is so general as in India, and for this very reason, although piety and reverence may preserve much that is ancient, Indian religions are constantly changing. Those who are really interested in a subject cannot help welcoming new ideas, and in India when one appeared, as for instance Bhakti or personal devotion to a particular deity in the centuries preceding the Christian era, or again the worship of goddesses several centuries later, we can trace its influence in the most divergent sects, both Brahmanic and Buddhist. But in Ceylon currents of popular religious sentiment are relatively inconspicuous. The monasteries had their disputes and to some extent felt the influence of Mahayanism,[1] but the attitude of the laity was merely a fairly steady piety which supported Church and State, and since the monks were ultimately drawn from the laity their temperament was not fundamentally different.

The Theravâda, however, lasted some time in India. Doubtless its conservatism did not render it very popular in an age of religious ferment, but the Questions of Milinda, a Pali work apparently written about the time of the Christian era in northern India,[2] shows vitality and a certain amplification of doctrine in safe directions, such as discussions on space, time, nirvâna, and the doctrine of anattâ. Though little tendency towards Mahayanism is apparent, there is an interesting argument about the propriety of offering gifts or homage to the Buddha. Since he has attained

[1] The influence of the Mahâyâna in Ceylon was doubtless stronger than is generally supposed (see the article by S. Paravitane in *Ceylon Journal of Science*, vol. ii, part 1, Dec., 1928, pp. 35–71), but I doubt if it had ever any chance of becoming the dominant creed.

[2] Like many other works the Milinda pañha has been added to and exists in a longer and shorter version. The Chinese translation (made under the Eastern Tsin dynasty in the fourth century A.D.) omits books iv–vii.

nirvâna, such practices seem unavailing and unmeaning. Nevertheless they are defended on the ground that "acts done to the Tathâgata, though he has passed away and does not accept them, are nevertheless of value and bear fruit". If buildings are erected to contain relics, it cannot be said that the Buddha accepts the gift, but the builders obtain happiness in this or another life. The Blessed One blew over the world with the wind of his love and allayed the fever of human passion. The wind that has ceased to blow cannot be recalled, but just as fans and punkahs can produce wind, so does reverence shown to the memory of the Buddha allay the fever and distemper of the soul. The Earth knows nothing of the seeds which are put into it, yet they grow into trees and bear fruit, even so honour done to the Buddha bears fruit, though he has passed away and accepts it not. The Theravâda evidently could not forbid an almost adoring veneration of the Buddha's memory and the cult of his images. The ceremonies approved are merely commemorative and are efficacious so far as they have a good effect on the mind of the performer. But for all that, this passage sanctions much of the ritual to be seen in modern Buddhist temples. Milinda is undoubtedly Menander, the potentate with a Greek name who reigned in Kabul about 150 B.C., and it is noticeable that tradition, which can hardly be wrong, represents him as patronizing a distinctly Hinayanist type of Buddhism.

In early Buddhism one of the most prominent Hînayâna sects was that of the Sarvâstivâdins,[1] who were apparently a subdivision of the Theravâda, differing slightly from the Vibhajjavâdins. Their opinions are alluded to in the Kathâvatthu but only three questions are directed against them, which probably means that they were considered almost entirely orthodox. Their importance lies in the fact that they systematized Hinayanist philosophy and that their system became the starting point for other sects. Mahayanists appear to have accepted it in so far as it did not conflict with their special doctrines. Even the followers of Nâgârjuna had no objection to it as an analysis of the world of phenomena, though; since they held that world to be an illusion, the analysis was for them only relatively true. The Vibhajjavâdins, on the other hand, had the south for their sphere and had little direct influence on the growth of the Mahâyâna in the north or on the sects which found their way to China and ultimately to Japan.

[1] This is the Sanskrit form: the Pali equivalent is Sabbatthivâdin.

Still, translations of the Questions of Milinda and of Buddhaghosha's Commentary on the Vinaya are included in the Chinese Tripiṭaka.

The account of the Council of Vesâlî in the Cullavagga [1] indicates that there was an early difference between the schools of the East and West, and the latter seems to have been the province of the Sarvâstivâdins. In 184 B.C. what remained of the Maurya Empire was seized by Pushyamitra of the Sunga dynasty, who is described [2] as a fierce enemy of Buddhism. The persecution was probably local and not of long duration, for Buddhist inscriptions are frequent until about A.D. 100, but perhaps it accelerated the movement to the west and north. Our information is very scanty, but the names of Kausambi, Ujjayina, and Mathura (Muttra) are mentioned. The last named was a seat of Sanskrit learning and situated on a great trade route. It is probable that the Sarvâstivâdins flourished and developed there. At any rate they spread to the north and became established in Kashmir.[3] Really satisfactory evidence as to their position is not to be had until rather later, but when it comes it is decisive and interesting. King Kanishka, presumably about the end of the first century A.D., built at Peshawar a celebrated stupa to contain the relics of the Buddha which he had collected from various parts of his dominions. The edifice is described by the Chinese pilgrims, and certain remains discovered in 1908 appear to be parts of the original structure. In them was found a metal casket containing the sacred bones and bearing an inscription which states that it was made "for the acceptance of the teachers of the Sarvâstivâdin sect" and also mentions Kanishka.[4] Thus it appears that the Sarvâstivâdins were in charge of the principal religious edifice at the capital of Kanishka, who is usually associated with the beginnings of Mahayanism.

But their doctrines show little inclination that way. The one from which they took their name (which is approximately equivalent to Realists) taught that all things exist, particularly in the sense that the past and future are real as well as the present. This sounds

[1] Cullavag., xii. 2, 7.

[2] By Târanâtha (chap. xvi) and the Divyâvadâna.

[3] The Vinaya of the Mûlasarvâstivâdins and the Asokâvadâna make the Buddha visit both Mathura and Kashmir, which probably means that they considered both places sacred and important centres for their own sects.

[4] It mentions "Agisala, the overseer of works at Kanishka's Vihâra". Agisala probably represents Agesilaus, so that the building was constructed under the supervision of a foreigner with a Greek name.

like a proposition more likely to divide professors of philosophy than the leaders of religious organizations, but the account of its origin gives it a certain practical significance. The Sarvâstivâdins traced it back to a passage in the Saṃyukta Âgama [1] reporting a discussion between the Buddha and certain Âjîvakas, heretics who denied the doctrines of Karma and moral responsibility on the ground that the past does not exist and that therefore past deeds cannot affect our destinies. The Buddha in reply maintained that "everything exists" (Sabbam atthi) and defined "everything" as the senses and their objects. Of more importance for the history of dogma was the classification of the elements of existence (dharmâḥ), the Universe being regarded neither as an illusion nor as the manifestation of some one principle (both common views in India), but as an assemblage of separate though interdependent factors of whose nature and origin no further explanation was attempted. The five Skandhas of the Pali Piṭakas represent the beginning of such a classification, but the Sarvâstivâdins greatly elaborated it and made a catalogue of seventy-five elements,[2] of which nirvâna was one, its reality being thus clearly laid down. Naturally this piece of complicated dogmatism did not escape criticism. The School of the Sautrântikas objected to many items in it and not unreasonably, for the list treats as ultimate entities various forces and faculties which might easily be further analysed.[3] The School called Vijñânavâdins, on the other hand, increased the list of items to one hundred. Though the whole idea of separate ultimate elements seems unnecessary in the Mahâyâna, which was monistic in its fundamental principles, yet it was not rejected, and even in Japan at

[1] It does not occur in the Pali text of the corresponding Nikâya. See the discussion in the Abhidharmakośa, v, 24–6, translated in Stcherbatsky's *Central Conception of Buddhism*, pp. 76–91.

[2] See especially Stcherbatsky, *The Central Conception of Buddhism*, and Rosenberg, *Probleme der Buddhistischen Philosophie*, especially chaps. vii–ix. No satisfactory translation of the difficult word dharmâḥ is forthcoming, for the simple reason that the dharmâḥ as enumerated do not according to European ideas form a natural class or category of any kind. Some are mental, some physical; some are material, some are forces; some are possibly simple, others are obviously compound. The Atomic Theory was accepted by some systems of Buddhist philosophy (see Abhidharmakośa, i, 43, 44, commentary; ii, 22; iii, 85–8), the unit of matter being the paramâṇu. But it is not clear when this view was first regarded as orthodox.

[3] For instance, the forces called prâpti and aprâpti which control or prevent the collection of elements in an individual stream of life. And why should negative qualities like alobha and advesa, the absence of love or of hatred, be treated as ultimate elements?

the present day its influence may be clearly seen, not in popular religion, but in the manuals studied by the clergy.

The Sarvâstivâdins had a canon of their own. Their Sûtra Piṭaka must have had some peculiarities since it contained passages which are not in the Pali version. Their Vinaya was considered very complete and is said to be that now used in Tibet. But they attached special importance to the Abhidharma Piṭaka which, as accepted by them, was entirely different from the Pali text but of considerable antiquity, going back to at least 100 B.C. It consisted of seven books,[1] all ascribed to human authors, and still extant in Chinese translations.

King Kanishka apparently was converted to Buddhism late in life, for comparatively few of his coins, of which many specimens have been preserved, bear Buddhist figures or emblems, whereas images not only of Brahmanic but of Greek and Persian deities are frequent. The Buddhist Council held under his auspices must therefore have taken place towards the end of his reign. Common opinion connects this meeting with both the Mahayanists and Sarvâstivâdins, but the accounts which have come down to us are far from consistent, though the following conclusions seem warranted[2]:—(1) The Council is known only to Mahayanist writers. Târanâtha calls it the Third Council, thus seeming to give it a definite place in the development of what he regarded as the true doctrine. But at the present day in China and Japan only students have heard of it and it has not the same position as, for instance, the Council of Nicæa in the history of Christianity. (2) It was apparently a conference of peace and compromise. According to all accounts both parties were represented at it and Târanâtha says that it recognized all the eighteen sects and put an end to the dissensions which had distracted Buddhism for nearly a century. (3) But the literary result of the Council seems not to have been a compromise or a Mahayanist work, but the composition of a huge encyclopædic treatise which, to some extent, took the form of a commentary on the Piṭakas and especially on the

[1] The principal is the Jñânaprasthâna of Katyâyanîputra, the others being called its six feet. It was perhaps originally composed in some kind of Prakrit, but Hsüan-Tsang's translation was made from the Sanskrit.

[2] I have attempted to summarize the traditions about this Council in my *Hinduism and Buddhism* (vol. ii, pp. 77–81), published in 1921, since when no new information seems to have been obtained. The three chief sources are Hsüan-Tsang's narrative, Paramârtha's Life of Vasubandhu (Nanjio, No. 1463), and Târanâtha's history, chap. xii.

Sarvâstivâdin Abhidharma. It was called Vibhâsha [1] and hence the later Sarvâstivâdins are often called Vaibhâshikas. Târanâtha adds that all sorts of Mahayanist books appeared about this time and that the Hinayanists raised no objection, but he does not say that the Council was in any way responsible for them. Thus it remains extremely difficult to define the relations of the Sarvâstivâdins and Mahayanists. They were evidently more friendly than we might expect. The Mahâyâna was not a sect, but apparently something larger—a mode in which the special teaching of any sect might be studied. This special teaching was chiefly concerned either with discipline or with problems of ontology and psychology, whereas Mahayanist theories had quite a different range and dealt with such matters as the nature of Buddhas and Bodhisattvas. The Chinese pilgrim I-Ching ends his work by asserting that all his statements are in accordance with the Mûlasarvâstivâdin school,[2] but he was unquestionably a zealous Mahayanist. The explanation seems to be that such a one might without inconsistency accept the discipline of the Sarvâstivâdins, especially as set forth in literature, and also, to some extent at least, their Abhidharma, regarding it as an analysis of the phenomenal world to be supplemented by higher knowledge which sees ultimate reality in quite a different light.

In connection with the rise of the Mahâyâna the Sautrântikas [3] also play some part. Like the Sarvâstivâdins, they assumed special prominence but in some ways held exactly opposite views. Thus they recognized the sûtras only and entirely rejected the Abhidharma, holding it to be merely modern exegesis. As literary criticism this was sound, provided that only the ancient sûtras were accepted, but so many modern works assumed that title that the Sarvâstivâdins could justly claim a certain priority for their Abhidharma. The Sautrântikas also demurred to the assertion that the past and future can be said to exist in the same sense as the

[1] The full title is apparently Abhidharma-mahâvibhâshâ-sâstra, of which there are two translations in Chinese (Nanjio, Nos. 1263–4), one by Hsuan-Tsang in two hundred volumes.

[2] The exact difference between the Sarvâstivâdins and the Mûla (original) Sarvâstivâdins is not plain.

[3] They were apparently the same as the Sankrântikas, one of the Eighteen sects, and said to have separated from the Sarvâstivâdins. Harivarman, the author of the Satyasiddhiśâstra, is believed to have belonged to them. His name seems to be unknown in India, but his works are preserved in Chinese and Tibetan. See Yamakami Sôgen, *Systems of Buddhist Thought*, pp. 172–185.

present. They held that sensations and consciousness are merely momentary flashes, but they believed in the reality of the external world as inferred from our sensations. In more strictly religious questions, such as the nature of nirvâna and the cosmical body of the Buddha, their views approximated to the Mahâyâna.

## 4

Two other philosophical schools must be mentioned, the Mâdhyamikas[1] and the Vijñânavâdins, sometimes known as the Yogâcâra. Both drew a distinction between relative and absolute truth and regarded the ordinary world of experience as illusory. Both were strictly Mahayanist[2] and, since their doctrines influenced religion as well as philosophy, both were of practical importance, especially the Mâdhyamikas. This school appears to have been the earlier of the two and claims Nâgârjuna as its founder, though perhaps he only systematized speculations which were already prevalent, for Mâdhyamika ideas inspire the whole literature called Prajñâparamitâ. These treatises of varying but often very considerable length are an important part of the Mahayanist Canon. The best known is the Diamond Cutter (Vajracchedikâ). The Prajñâpâramitâ in ten thousand verses is said to have been translated into Chinese about A.D. 180.[3] Nâgârjuna probably lived in the second century A.D. and several works are attributed to him of which at least one, the Mûlamadhyamaka Kârikâs,[4] seems to be genuine. It consists of verses arranged in twenty-seven chapters which express with admirable terseness and lucidity—if that word can be used of such a subject—the doctrine that all things

[1] Both Mâdhyamaka and Mâdhyamika are in use.

[2] The Chinese pilgrim I-Ching, who travelled in India between A.D. 671 and 695, says that "there are only two kinds of Mahâyâna, the Mâdhyamika and the Yoga. Can one say which of the two is right? Both equally conform to truth and lead us to nirvâna". This is a remarkable statement from a religious man, who, though he was not much of a philosopher, in some ways followed the Sarvâstivâdins.

[3] Hackman, in his article on the Text of the Sûtra in forty-two sections which is said to have been translated in A.D. 67, shows that the text exists in at least three recensions, one of which (especially in §§ 18–20 and 42) indicates the influence of Mâdhyamika doctrines. But is it certain that this recension is really the earliest? The Saundarânanda of Aśvaghosha also alludes to Mâdhyamika doctrines.

[4] Edited by De la Vallée Poussin, *Bibliotheca Buddhica*, 1913.

are śûnya, void, unreal, and non-existent. None of these translations of śûnya is, however, quite satisfactory and there is much to be said for Stcherbatsky's [1] rendering—relative or contingent. Phenomena are śûnya or unreal because no phenomenon when taken by itself is thinkable: they are all interdependent and have no separate existence of their own. And ideas such as rest and motion, cause and effect, continuance and extinction, when analysed prove to be unthinkable. The arguments of Nâgârjuna have often been condemned by both Indian and European critics as sophistry and quibbles, but it must be admitted that recent science is equally destructive of our commonest notions. Thus Russell [2] in discussing "the notion of a place" says: "Is London a place? But the earth is rotating. Is the earth a place? But it is going round the sun. Is the sun a place? But it is moving relatively to the stars. At best you could talk of a place at a given time: but then it is ambiguous what is a given time, unless you confine yourself to one place. So the notion of place evaporates."

Nâgârjuna applies his destructive arguments to the most sacred subjects, such as the Buddha and nirvâna. If either is treated as part of the world of phenomena, we are landed in difficulties, for if the Buddha is a real being, he must come to an end in nirvâna. But if he is not a real being, neither can he have a real end. In the vision obtained by insight or intuition, it is seen that the Buddha, nirvâna, and saṃsâra (the world of transmigration) are not three different entities but all the same and all different aspects (if indeed that word can be used without error) of the Dharmakâya or cosmical body of the Buddha, a conception akin to pantheism. When we move among such ideas we are not breathing the atmosphere of the Pali Canon, yet many passages can be quoted from it which support them. The word suñña occurs not infrequently and the Majjhima Nikâya describes with approval how there arises in the mind "an unchanging, pure and perfect conception of emptiness".[3] It is stated,[4] too, that even in this world the nature of the Buddha is incomprehensible and that it is wrong to say either that things

[1] *The Conception of Nirvana,* 1927. He even says of the author of *Appearance and Reality*: "Bradley can be characterized as a genuine Mâdhyamika."

[2] B. Russell, *Outlines of Philosophy,* 1927, p. 114.

[3] Maj. Nik., cxxi ad fin. See, too, Maj. Nik., cxxii, xliii near end. The Sangîti Suttanta of the Dîg. Nik. recognizes concentration which interprets things as suñña.

[4] Yamaka Sut. Sam. Nik., xxii, 85, 34.

exist or that they do not.[1] And the refusal of Gotama to reply to certain questions—is the world limited in time and space or not, does the Buddha exist after death or not, is the soul the same as the body or not—can be reasonably explained in the terms of this philosophy. The questions are unanswerable because they are wrongly framed: they assume the real existence of beings and things which are merely śûnya.

Both Indian and European critics have observed that, whereas the earlier Buddhists concentrated their attention on psychological questions and denied the existence of the attâ, or self, the Mâdhyamikas applied the same destructive logic to the external world. But in the early analysis of human nature into five skandhas, matter (rûpa) is not distinguished from mind. No contrast is drawn between the material and the immaterial; but matter is one of five groups. Hence though the Piṭakas do not use idealistic language or discuss the problem of reality, they do expressly place matter and sensation on the same footing. Rûpa is expressly stated to be anattâ and it is asserted [2] that all phenomena are void of anything that can be called attâ, or self.

The Mâdhyamika system continued to be popular for some time in India, especially in the south. Âryadeva, the immediate successor of Nâgârjuna, seems to have been a native of the Dravidian countries, as was also the mysterious Bodhidharma, the reputed founder of Zen in the Far East. The two great doctors Buddhapâlita and Bhâvaviveka both flourished in the same region, apparently during the sixth century A.D., and represented two important divisions of the school. The former favoured purely negative dialectic and the method of *reductio ad absurdum*, which not only argues that the visible world has no existence but leads to the almost unthinkable conclusion that it is not even phenomenally existent, that is that our ideas have no existence. Against this Bhâvaviveka held the more reasonable view that the world of phenomena was valid phenomenally, though not real from the point of view of absolute truth. Nevertheless the views of Buddhapâlita by no means

[1] Kaccâyana Sûtra, Sam. Nik., xii, § 15. Sabbam atthîti ayam eko anto: Sabbam natthîti ayam dutiyo anto. In Saṃ. Nik., xii, § 67, it is stated that the chain of causation confutes the doctrines that dukkha, or suffering, is caused by self, by another, by both, or by neither. This is precisely the line of argument by which the Mâdhyamikas show that all our ordinary ideas, such as rest and motion, production and cessation, are untenable.

[2] Ang. Nik., 3, 134, § 3. Maj. Nik., xxxv, and especially Maj. Nik., xliii. Suññam idam attena vâ attaniyena vâti.

disappeared, for Candrakîrti, the author of a celebrated commentary on Nâgârjuna [1] who is variously assigned to the sixth or seventh century, established the system in its extreme negative form and this doctrine is also accepted by Śântideva, the author of the Bodhicaryâvatâra, one of the most beautiful books of devotion in the world. Even at the present day the Diamond Cutter [2] is read in Japan (and I believe also in Tibet) not merely by students but by ordinary religious people. It is full of paradoxes: merit is no merit and though the Buddha has delivered beings without number, yet not one has been delivered. Many members of the Zen sect, even laymen, recite every day the short sûtra called the Heart or Essence of the Prajñâpâramitâ [3] which deals chiefly with the doctrine of Emptiness, and pilgrims may often be seen wearing large hats on which are written some such lines as these: "Through ignorance the triple world seems like a castle (i.e. solid and real): through enlightenment the ten regions become empty. From the beginning there is neither East nor West. Where can be the North or South?" [4]

In fact the objections to these doctrines of non-existence and emptiness seem to have come from philosophers rather than from popular thought. Many metaphysicians did not deny that the external world is an illusion, but they felt that illusion cannot exist by itself and that it can be explained only by admitting the existence of a mind which suffers from illusion. This School of idealism is commonly known as the Yogâcâra or Vijñânavâda. Its history is complicated by a difficult question, namely, is the celebrated work called the Awakening of Faith [5] really the composition of the Aśvaghosha who flourished at the Court of Kanishka? If so, the principles of the Vijñânavâda must have been fully developed at least as early as his lifetime, for they are expounded in detail in this treatise. Tradition, however, ascribes the foundation of the

[1] It is a work of great ability but it has been plausibly suggested that in giving it the title of "Clear-worded", Prasannapadâ, the talented author, was gently ironical. See the portions translated in Stcherbatsky's *Nirvana*, pp. 81–212.

[2] Called in Japanese Kongōkyō, and translated in *S.B.E.*, vol. xlix.

[3] Called in Japanese Hannya Shin-kyō, and also translated in *S.B.E.*, vol. xlix.

[4] 迷故三界城
悟故十方空
本來無東西
何處有南北

[5] Mahâyânaśraddhotpâda 大乘起信論, N. 1249–50.

Vijñânavâda to Asanga who, at the earliest, lived from about A.D. 280 to 360 and perhaps a century later. It seems reasonable to regard the Vijñânavâda as originally a protest against the supposed extravagance of the Mâdhyamika teaching, but it would certainly be very rash to fix the date of a book by our theories as to the chronological development of ideas. Still several circumstances make the authorship of the Awakening of Faith doubtful, and I think that the evidence indicates that the writer probably lived long after Kanishka.[1]

The characteristic phrase of this school is the difficult term Âlaya-vijñâna or receptacle-intelligence.[2] I confess that I find it hard to explain this idea, because the Âlaya-vijñâna seems to be regarded as both cosmic and individual. India was accustomed from the time of the older Upanishads to the conception of an Absolute which can only be described by negatives (neti neti). To this Absolute Buddhist doctors often give the name of Tathatâ or suchness, a word which does not commit us to any attempt at definition. Tathatâ manifests itself to itself as the cosmic Âlaya-vijñâna,[3] the receptacle of all possible ideas and sensations which contains all the dharmas or elements (for the Vijñânavâda adopted but modified the Sarvâstivâdin catalogue of dharmas) and among them the important evil element of ignorance (moha or

[1] The chief points are: (*a*) The admitted works of Aśvaghosha, such as the Buddhacarita, show hardly any trace of Mahayanist doctrine. (*b*) The Buddhacarita was rendered into Chinese about A.D. 400, but the Awakening of Faith not till 550. But it is a most important and popular treatise and it is hard to say why its translation was postponed, since it is shorter than the Buddhacarita and not more difficult. (*c*) An old Chinese Catalogue does not give the name of the author. See Winternitz, *Ges. Ind. Lit.*, ii, p. 211. (*d*) The Awakening of Faith appears to quote the Lankâvatâra-sûtra, which is probably not an early work. (*e*) If Aśvaghosha really expounded the Yogâcâra doctrine some two hundred years before Asanga, why does tradition ascribe it to the latter? It is the habit of Indian schools to claim ancient celebrities as their founders and not to ignore any plausible connection. It is also noticeable that I-Ching, who mentions some of Aśvaghosha's works, does not mention the Awakening of Faith. V. P. Demiéville, "Sur l'authenticité du Ta Tch'eng K'i Sin Louen," *Bulletin de la Maison Franco-Japonaise*, ii, No. 2, Tokyo, 1929.

[2] S. Levi translates "la sensation du tréfonds".

[3] No explanation of this process is forthcoming, just as in the Vedânta there is no explanation of the association of Brahman with Mâyâ, or illusion. Since Indian religion and philosophy have a passion for ultimate problems, this inexplicability is made to appear more striking and unsatisfactory than in most European systems. But the same difficulty exists in the West. Bradley says in *Appearance and Reality*, "How there can be such a thing as appearance we do not understand?", and the familiar language of theology, God created the World, really defies further explanation or analysis.

avidyâ). Ignorance affects Suchness, much as in the Vedânta philosophy Mâyâ affects Brahman, the relation being described by the technical expression vâsanâ, perfuming or impression. Thus arises the whole external world of restless action or duḥkha. But the impression or vâsanâ is mutual, and the impression of Suchness on Ignorance produces the desire for release and, if it is successful, the attempt to lead a holy life.

This is the cosmic aspect of the Âlaya-vijñâna, but this cosmic receptacle-consciousness gives rise to an individual receptacle-consciousness in every personality. The Yogâcâra recognized eight vijñânas. The first six of these (recognized also in the Sarvâstivâdin classification) are the five senses and manas, that is mind, meaning an independent perceptive faculty which cognizes abstract objects. The seventh is the mano-vijñâna,[1] which is pure consciousness regarded not as isolated but as associated with a previous moment of consciousness and as acting sub-consciously and continuously. The eighth is the Âlaya-vijñâna, which is the sum total of consciousness and sub-consciousness, only a small portion of which can be present as personal consciousness at a particular moment. It is in a way the same as Karma, for it is not merely a receptacle in which the seeds of good and evil, enlightenment and ignorance, are stored but an ever-running stream which carries them on and recreates for each individual in successive lives the external world or saṃsâra.

The Yogâcâra School was continued by the great logician Dignâga of Orissa. He abandoned the old Abhidharma completely and based his idealistic system entirely on logic. A somewhat later logician, Dharmakîrti of the seventh century, also apparently belonged to the same school. He is interesting as having clearly stated and defined the position of insight or intuition in these half-religious, half-metaphysical matters which fill so much space in Buddhism. Intuition is frequently mentioned from the Pali Canon onwards as the source of truth, but without any clear definition of its nature. Dharmakîrti, however, states that it is one of the four forms of perception : it is without imagination and

[1] The difficulty of this exceedingly perplexing and abstruse subject is increased by the fact that the sixth and seventh vijñânas are known by the almost identical names of mano and mano-vijñâna. See for discussions of the whole matter Yamakami Sōgen, *Systems of Buddhist Thought*, chap. vi, and Rosenberg, *Die Probleme der Buddhistischen Philosophie*, chap. xiii.

consists of clear insight, produced by intense mental concentration, which sees the truth directly or immediately.

Though the Vijñânavâdins are not so open to the charge of paradox and extravagance as the Mâdhyamikas, yet their doctrine is exceedingly difficult and it is not surprising if it did not become popular. But it inspired the Lankâvatâra [1] and Avataṃsaka [2] sûtras, both of which are well known in Japan (though to the learned rather than to the devout), and also the very important treatise called Yuishiki, which is studied by all candidates for the priesthood. These philosophical systems lead up to and countenance the ideas of the cosmic body of the Buddha and the identity of the Buddha with the absolute, but they say little about the more popular beliefs which grew up together with these abstruse speculations.

5

One obvious difference between the old Buddhism and the Mahâyâna is the multiplication of Buddhas and Bodhisattvas. The new figures are not mere predecessors or attendants of Śâkyamuni. Like him they are saviours and helpers of mankind. They share his honours and sometimes (as Amitâbha) they supersede him. Yet it is extremely difficult to trace their antecedents or to date their first appearance. Neither the Edicts of Asoka, nor the sculptures and inscriptions of Bharhut and Sanchi, nor even Gandharan art, which is presumably coeval with Kanishka, nor the undoubted works of Aśvaghosha, who flourished about the same time, indicate a belief in definitely Mahayanist ideas. They depict or recount scenes taken from Gotama's life or from the Jâtakas, and the story, though embellished, is substantially the same as that in the Piṭakas. The inference is that at any rate the form of Buddhism which received royal patronage had not departed very far from the ancient lines, and this accords with the facts that the Sarvâstivâdin sect were apparently the guardians of Kanishka's stupa and that the Council which he summoned gave its authority to a Sarvâstivâdin

[1] 楞伽 Ryonga. There are three Chinese translations (Nanjio, 175-7), of which the earliest, made in A.D. 443, is shorter than the others.

[2] In the Chinese Tripitaka this is reckoned as a separate class of Sûtra 華嚴部 Kegon-bu, containing no less than twenty-five items (Nanjio, 87-112). Three of these are relatively late complete translations in 40, 60, and 80 volumes respectively. Some of the translations of extracts are ascribed to the third and even second century.

treatise. But we have seen how this school, though not Mahayanist in its teaching, was compatible with Mahayanism, and there is nothing improbable in the statement of Târanâtha (though we do not know on what it is based) that Mahayanist books began to appear at this period and that the other party raised no objections. The doctrines which these books contained were probably not novelties but had for some time been slowly growing, especially in the sect called Mahâsanghika. The belief in celestial Buddhas and merciful, helpful Bodhisattvas is doubtless connected with the development in Hinduism of the doctrine of Bhakti or faith in a special deity and personal devotion to him, and with the rise of sects worshipping Krishṇa or Śiva instead of the old Vedic gods. The new Buddhist ideas were probably not actually borrowed. A wind of feeling stirred the atmosphere and in every denomination religious minds vibrated to its influence. The resemblance between the Lotus and the Bhagavad Gîtâ is undeniable, and I think that the latter is the older.[1] There is no direct imitation, but both offer to the believer a new revelation and an apocalypse. In both a superhuman personage not only instructs the mind but amazes the eye with the blaze of his glory. In both this personage is a well-known character who in earlier documents often appears as little more than a great man, and in both (though there may be differences in the niceties of doctrine) he proclaims himself as the world spirit. Literature and epigraphy[2] indicate that the worship of Kṛishṇa and the sect called Bhâgavatas were well-known in the second century B.C., and at the same period the new phase of Buddhism was probably in the bud. It is therefore possible that by Kanishka's time Mahayanist sûtras were current and that the world was prepared to give them a good reception. The dates of the Chinese translations are not inconsistent with this. Accepting those given in Nanjio's catalogue,[3] we find that portions of the Prajñâpâramitâ,

[1] The latest editor and translator of the Gîtâ (D. P. Hill, 1918, p. 18) thinks that it appeared in its present form in the second century B.C.

[2] e.g. the inscriptions of Besnagar and Ghasundi.

[3] Mr. Conrad Ostrom of Kobe has devoted special study to the catalogues of the Chinese Tripiṭaka and has read valuable papers on the subject to the Asiatic Society at Tokyo, though to the best of my belief he has not yet published anything. He informs me that he thinks that the translations of the Sukhâvatî-vyûha ascribed to An-Shih-Kao (see Nanjio, p. 10) and to Lokaraksha (Nanjio, No. 25) are both myths, and that the first real translation is Nanjio, No. 26, made by Chih-Ch'ien A.D. 223–253. Even so, the Sanskrit original must go back at least to the second century. Stael Holstein in his edition of the Kâśyapaparivarta seems to accept Nanjio's date for the translation ascribed to Lokaraksha.

the sûtras about Amitâbha, and a few other works were translated in the second century A.D., the Lotus in the third, the Avataṃsaka, Suvarṇaprabhâ, and Lankâvatâra in the fourth. But these dates merely prove that the works were then known in China and do not show how long they had been in existence. We may argue with equal plausibility that zealous missionaries were likely to lose no time in importing literary novelties from India and Central Asia to China or that only standard works of a respectable age would be considered worthy of what was then the great labour of translation. Perhaps this second line of thought is more correct, and it is also clear that the older translators, who were nearly all natives of India or Central Asia with an imperfect knowledge of Chinese, hesitated to tackle lengthy and difficult masterpieces. The Lotus may long have been known in Sanskrit before anyone ventured to turn it into Chinese.

Aśvaghosha[1] is one of the great landmarks in the history of Indian Buddhism and it seems safe to regard him as a contemporary of Kanishka. But it is most unfortunate that there should be doubt as to his authorship of the Awakening of Faith. As already indicated, I think that on the whole the evidence is against his having written this work, and it is noticeable that according to a Chinese tradition there were no less than six Aśvaghoshas, but, so long as any doubt remains, it is hard to feel any certainty as to the chronology of Buddhist doctrine. It must be confessed that the Awakening of Faith, though known only in a Chinese translation, is a masterpiece of composition, and the author of the Sanskrit original must have been one of the literary geniuses of India. But there was certainly a tendency to ascribe well-known works to Aśvaghosha. Thus he was identified[2] with Mâtriceta, who composed hymns which are highly praised by I-Ching, and with Âryaśûra, the author of the Jâtakamâlâ, but there is no adequate reason for either identification. He seems to have been the most distinguished representative of a school to which these two writers also belonged and which endeavoured to give expression to Buddhist teaching in correct Sanskrit and classical literary form, epic, dramatic, and lyric. In their veneration for the person of the Buddha and the emphasis which they lay on the career and growth of the Bodhisattva through his long series of previous births, these works show the same emotional feeling which inspires the Mahâyâna,

[1] 馬鳴 Ma-ming, in Japanese Me-myō.

[2] By Târanâtha.

but still they cannot be said to inculcate definitely Mahayanist doctrines. Much the same is true of the compositions known as Avadânas.[1]

Aśvaghosha is also recognized as the Eleventh Patriarch, and it may be well to say a few words about this term which is frequently used in European books. It represents the Chinese Tsu-shih[2] rather than any Indian title and, though it is not a very satisfactory translation, none better is forthcoming. The Hindus have always attached great importance to spiritual lineage, and even in the Upanishads we find lists of the teachers who transmitted some special doctrine. Similar lists are given in the Sinhalese Chronicles,[3] but the persons named do not seem to have been heads of a hierarchy or to have enjoyed any ecclesiastical authority such as the word Patriarch generally implies. According to some Chinese accounts,[4] which, though they probably represent the tradition of an Indian school, are not confirmed by any known Sanskrit text, there were twenty-three or four Patriarchs, the last of whom, Simha Bhikshu, was killed by Mihirakula, the King of the Huns. But the Zen School continue the list and say that the twenty-eighth Patriarch was Bodhidharma, who arrived in China about A.D. 520. He there became the first Chinese Patriarch but only in the sense of being head of his special sect. Other sects had lists of their own, and Shinran's poem, the Shōshinge, which is daily recited by the faithful of the Shin sect in Japan, enumerates at length the doctors, beginning with Nâgârjuna, who handed down the true teaching. This shows how ingrained was the feeling that correct succession and transmission are of the utmost importance, for the Shin sect was popular and almost revolutionary in its ideas and by no means disposed to follow tradition.

[1] Przyluski thinks that the Asokâvadâna was written as early as about a century before Kanishka by a Sarvâstivâdin of Mathura. The Avadânaśataka was translated into Chinese between A.D. 223 and 253. The Divyâvadâna is apparently later in its present form, but contains material of very different ages. It opens with an invocation to all Buddhas and Bodhisattvas.

[2] 祖師. This title is to be distinguished from 國師 Kuo-shih, Instructor of the Nation, a purely official designation conferred from time to time by Emperors of China on eminent Buddhists.

[3] Mahâvaṃsa, v. 95 ff.; Dîpavaṃsa, iv, 27 ff., and v, 69.

[4] The most important is Nanjio, 1340, called Fu-fa-tsang-yin-yüan Ching, which professes to be a translation from an Indian work. The Zen views as to the succession are set forth in Tao-yüan's work, *The Transmission of the Lamp* (Nanjio, 1524), but they offer great chronological difficulties. For more on this subject see Chapter V.

After Aśvaghosha, the next great name in the history of the Mahâyâna is Nâgârjuna,[1] who in the lists of Patriarchs is generally reckoned as the second in succession from him and probably lived in the second century of our era. Though biographies of Nâgârjuna are extant, they are almost entirely fabulous and represent him as not only a theologian and philosopher but as a great magician and even as living for several centuries. Nevertheless he seems to have been an historical person,[2] and we have perhaps a fragment of truth in the tradition which says that he was a Brahman of Berar but had as teacher a sudra called Saraha (which sounds like a foreign name) or Râhulabhadra. The aphorisms of the Mâdhyamika philosophy already mentioned are unanimously ascribed to him and also the commentary on the Prajñâpâramita, an abstract of which was translated into Chinese by Kumarâjîva as early as A.D. 402–5. It quotes the Lotus and many other sûtras, so that the author must have had a considerable tradition behind him and, however prominent he may be in the history of the Mahâyâna, he cannot be regarded as its founder or even as a very early exponent. To Nâgârjuna is also ascribed an interesting work called the Suhrillekha or friendly epistle,[3] a short homily addressed to a king whose name is uncertain but who probably belonged to the Andhra dynasty. It was translated into Chinese in A.D. 434 and I-Ching devotes to it a long eulogy. It may well represent a type of Buddhism considered suitable for the laity in India in the second century. It says nothing about the Mâdhyamika philosophy but speaks of the four truths, the eightfold path, and the chain of causation almost in the language of the Pitakas. On the other hand, it mentions Amitâbha and Avalokiteśvara and commends the use of incense and images in worship.

[1] 龍樹 Lung-Shu : Ryū-jū. See Walleser's "Life of Nâgârjuna from Tibetan and Chinese Sources" in the *Hirth Anniversary Volume*, 1923, where it is admitted that we know hardly any historical facts about his life. The Sarvâstivâdins, who were strongly opposed to his doctrines, did not count him as a Patriarch.

[2] Possibly the site of Nâgârjunikonda on the lower Kistna, where there are inscriptions of the second and third centuries, has a real connection with Nâgârjuna. The *Annual Bibliography of the Kern Institute for 1929* says : "Another point of interest is the mention of Sirîpavvata corresponding to the Sanskrit Sriparvata. There is a tradition in Tibet that Nâgârjuna spent the end of his life in a monastery of that name in Southern India. If this convent is the same as the 'Vihara on the Siripavata to the East of Vijayapuri' of our inscription, it follows that his association with this locality has been preserved up to the present day in the name Nâgârjunikonda" (p. 13).

[3] Nanjio, 1440. See, too, *Jour. of Pali Text Soc.*, 1886, and Takakusu's translation of I-Ching, p. 158 ff.

Most lists make Âryadeva [1] succeed Nâgârjuna as Patriarch, and he may reasonably be supposed to have flourished about A.D. 200. The accounts of his life are fragmentary. We know that he lived in South India and that he had some knowledge of Greek astronomy, which was not impossible at the date mentioned.

His works [2] indicate a tendency towards the Vijñânavâda teaching and he also wrote refutations both of the Hînayâna and of various Brahmanic schools. The titles of these polemics in the Chinese translations seem to connect him with the Lankâvatâra-sûtra, for they say that he condemns the same heresies.

The next, and indeed the last, great names in the history of Indian Mahayanism are the brothers Asanga and Vasubandhu,[3] who are known in Japan by statues [4] as well as by their literary works. The life of Vasubandhu was written by Paramârtha,[5] and we learn from it that they were natives of Peshawar but also lived at Ayodhya at the Court of Vikramâditya. This title may have been borne by any king of the Gupta dynasty and it is most unfortunate that it should not be sufficiently precise to put the date of these important writers beyond doubt. Péri,[6] after an elaborate discussion of the question, suggested A.D. 280–360 as probable limits for the life of Vasubandhu and his conclusion has been very generally accepted, but Stcherbatsky, Takakusu, and other Japanese authorities favour a later date and assign him and his brother to the fifth century. Fa-Hsien, writing early in that century, does not mention him, but since he also fails to mention Aśvaghosha, Nâgârjuna, and Âryadeva, his silence is not conclusive. I-Ching, writing about A.D. 700, divides the Buddhist doctors of India into three classes: early, Aśvaghosha, Nâgârjuna, and Deva; middle, Vasubandhu, Asanga, Sanghabhadra, and Bhâvaviveka; late, Dharmapala, Dharmakirti, and Sthiramati. This is valuable as showing the accepted order

[1] 提婆 T'i-P'o: Daiba or 聖天 Shêng-T'ien.

[2] The best known is the Catuhsataka. For the controversial works see Nanjio, Nos. 1259 and 1260.

[3] Asanga 無著 Wu-Chao or Mujaku. Vasubandhu 天親 T'ien-Hsin, Tenjin or 世親 Shi-Hsin, Seshin. There was also a third brother called Virinci-vatsa who never became a Mahayanist.

[4] Two remarkable wooden statues of them belong to the Kōfukuji of Nara. See the excellent reproductions in Tajima's *Select Relics*, 11, x.

[5] Nanjio, No. 1463. Translated by Takakusu in *T'oung Pao*, 1904. Paramârtha is said to have made translations in China from 557 to 569.

[6] See Péri, "A Propos de la date de Vasubandhu," in *B.E.F.E.O.*, 1911.

of sequence but it is not decisive as to date. The question is too intricate for full discussion here.[1]

The best known works of Asanga are the Mahâyânasûtrâlankâra and the Bodhisattvabhûmi, both extant in Sanskrit and both describing the career of a Bodhisattva, that is to say, of a pious person who deliberately sets before himself the ideal of winning this high position by efforts maintained through a series of existences. His progress is traced through ten stages, in each of which he acquires new virtue and knowledge. The idea is not new: the stages are described in the Mahâvastu, though this proves little since, as already pointed out, that work contains both old and late material, and the Avataṃsaka-sûtra contains a similar account. The detail and dogmatic precision of the programme as defined by Asanga suggest mature development and perhaps a late rather than an early date. Asanga is also very definite in insisting on the excellence of the Mahâyâna and enumerates seven respects in which it is superior to the Hînayâna—its comprehensiveness, its universal charity, its intellectual thoroughness, its spiritual energy, its adaptability, its higher ideals, and its greater activity as manifested in Bodhisattvas. Tradition states that many of the works ascribed to him were really revelations made by Maitreya, the future Buddha, and some Oriental scholars[2] think that this story conceals the historical fact that a teacher called Maitreyanâtha was his predecessor and the founder of the Yogâcâra.

Though there are many translations from Asanga in the Chinese Tripiṭaka, he is not a great figure in Far Eastern Buddhism and his younger brother. Vasubandhu is a much more famous name. It is agreed that he followed the Sarvâstivâdin school during the greater part of his life but in a liberal spirit and not without criticism. It was only in old age that his brother succeeded in converting him

[1] Attention may be called to the following points: Péri holds that Kumârajiva, whose literary activity extended from about 402 to 412, wrote a life of Vasubandhu and that the Sata śâstra of Vasu which he translated was a work of Vasubandhu. If this can be proved, Vasubandhu was certainly anterior to the fifth century. Nanjio, 1188, ascribes this work to Deva and Vasubandhu, the latter having commented on the former, but it appears that the name of the author is given as simply Vasu K'ai-shih, the last two characters being a title. There was an earlier Vasubandhu. See Abhidbarmakośa, i, 13, and Poussin's note. On the other hand, one of the senior opponents of Vasubandhu was Sanghavarman, and if it can be proved that he was identical with the Sanghavarman who translated the Samanta-Pasidika and was at Canton in 489, Vasubandhu, who lived to be an old man, must have been alive at that time.

[2] H. P. Sastri and in Japan, Kimura and Ui.

to Mahayanism. In his earlier phase he wrote the Abhidharmakośa, consisting of 600 verses with a commentary of his own. It is a most important encyclopædic treatise which is still studied by most, if not all, sects in Japan. He was favourably disposed towards the views of the Sautrântikas, but his many-sided intellectual sympathies enabled him to write an impartial summary of doctrine which is still generally acceptable. It is not concerned with the questions which divide existing sects such as the Shinshū, Zen, and Nichiren, but with the ultimate problems of ontology, mind and matter, and the nature of the world process. Thus it deals with the theory of dharmas and dhatus, the nature of the senses and of atoms: it describes the constitution of the Universe according to the ideas of the author's time, including heavens and hells and immaterial spheres: it explains the mysteries of Karma and the anusayas: it treats of the Path and the saints who walk in it: it discusses the nature of knowledge, meditation, and rapture. A supplementary chapter refutes the doctrine of the existence of the pudgala, the Self or Soul, as affirmed by some schools. Late in life Vasubandhu is said to have written many Mahayanist works and especially a short treatise on the Sukhâvatî-vyûha, known in Japanese as the Ōjōron,[1] in virtue of which he is considered as the second Patriarch of the Amidist sects, Nâgârjuna being the first. If he was really the author of this little book, his religious horizon must have been very similar to that of Japanese priests of the Jōdo sect who study the Abhidharmakośa and worship Amida. After accepting the idealist philosophy known as Vijñânavâda, he composed two compendiums of it in twenty and thirty verses respectively called Vim'satika and Trimsika.[2] The latter is the basis of the Jōyuishikiron or Yuishiki,[3] which is still one of the principal text-books studied by the clergy in Japan. It is a collection of extracts from Dharmapala and nine other commentaries on the Trimsika, together with numerous quotations from other works, arranged by the celebrated Chinese pilgrim Hsüan-Tsang and furnished with a commentary by his disciple, K'uei-Ki.

From the first century of our era until the eleventh and even later, many foreigners went to China as teachers and translators.

[1] Nanjio, 1204, rendered as Amitâyus-sûtropadeśa or Aparimitâyus-sûtra-śâstra. Only nine leaves. Translated by Bodhiruchi A.D. 529.

[2] Both edited in Sanskrit by S. Levi in 1925.

[3] 成唯識論. See Vijnaptimatratasiddhi, *La Siddhi de Hsüan-Tsang*. Traduite et annotée par L. de La Vallée Poussin. In the series Buddhica—1928.

Of several, even in the earliest times, it is distinctly stated that they were natives of Central India, but many came from Afghanistan and Central Asia and, though they had studied Sanskrit, it is hard to say what their race may have been. Still, it is correct to describe the whole process as the conversion of Central Asia and China to Buddhism effected by Indian propaganda. Later there was also intercourse by sea with Southern India and Ceylon. Tradition says that the first Indian missionaries were invited by the Chinese, and though the desire to proselytize was not wanting, it is clear that Chinese eagerness to learn had as much to do with the spread of Buddhism in the Far East as missionary zeal.

Early in the fifth century Chinese pilgrims began to visit India and several of them have left interesting narratives of what they saw. Fa-Hsien resided in India from 405 to 411, his chief object being to collect manuscripts of the Vinaya. He speaks of the Hînayâna as prevalent in some localities, the Mahâyâna in others, but does not indicate that there was any acute rivalry between them. He mentions Maitreya but not Amitâbha, and says that offerings were made to the book Prajñâpâramitâ, to Mañjuśrî, and to Avalokiteśvara.

The two pilgrims, Sung-Yün and Hui-Shêng, visited Gandhara and Udyana in A.D. 518–521, that is during the domination of the Huns. Their evidence is important, for it shows that, whatever the barbarities of the Huns may have been, they had not destroyed Buddhism in North-Western India. The pilgrims found the local potentates devout and pious and they collected 170 volumes, all Mahayanist works.

The greatest of the Chinese pilgrims, Hsüan-Tsang,[1] spent sixteen years in India (A.D. 629–645) and left a copious narrative which has fortunately come down to us. He witnessed the religious festivities which the Emperor Harsha celebrated at Kanauj. The Buddha, Śiva, and the Sun were honoured on successive days, and though the image of the Buddha was treated with more respect than the others, the worship was evidently mixed. This was the part of India where Buddhism was most flourishing, but the pilgrim does not hide the fact that on the whole it was decaying, especially in the north-west where there were more than a thousand deserted monasteries, and in the south where Jainism was advancing at its expense. He speaks of the hostility of the Brahmans, but he does

[1] 玄奘.

not indicate that there was any serious animosity between the Mahâ- and Hînayâna, and it is remarkable that according to his statistics many more monks belonged to the latter.[1] Perhaps the strength of the Mahâyâna lay rather in its hold on the laity. He mentions statues of Târâ and Avalokiteśvara.

I-Ching,[2] who travelled in India and the Malay Archipelago from A.D. 671 to 695, gives a very similar account. He deplores the decay of the Faith even more explicitly and shows how it was possible to combine views which might be considered antagonistic, for he was a follower of the Mûlasarvâstivâdin school and yet praises both the Mâdhyamika and Yogâcâra systems. He gives an interesting description of the musical services performed in monasteries and speaks of the worship of Amitâbha with apparent approval. He specially praises the Suhrillekha of Nâgârjuna, Mâtriceta's hymns (which he tells us were learnt by all monks, both Maha- and Hinayanist), the Jâtakamâlâ, and Aśvaghosha's Sûtrâlankâra and Buddhacarita. He adds that young priests read the sûtra about Avalokiteśvara[3] and the Mahâparinibbana-sûtra, just as young laymen in Chinese study the Chinese classics.

The works of Śântideva,[4] who probably flourished about A.D. 600–650, are not deliberately descriptive but they contain much which confirms and illustrates the Chinese accounts. The worship of numerous Buddhas and Bodhisattvas is mentioned but not much emphasis is laid on Àmitâbha. Though the Mahâyâna is clearly regarded as the highest form of religion and as absolute truth, the Hînayâna is treated in a very charitable spirit. Thus in a quotation from a work called the Âkâśagarbha-sûtra, the following are counted among the "root sins" of an aspirant to the career of a Bodhisattva: preaching ideas that lead to the Hînayâna; preaching the Mahâyâna as a substitute for rules and discipline; undue disparagement of the Hînayâna. Very similar are the directions given to a teacher in the Bodhicaryâvatâra, v. 89–90. He should show the same respect to the Hînayâna and Mahâyâna. He should not teach the former to one who is worthy of the latter, but he should

[1] He gives the total number of monks as 183,000, of whom more than 96,000 belonged to the Hînayâna, 54,000 studied both systems, and only 32,000 were definitely Mahayanist.

[2] 義淨.

[3] That is, chap. xxiv of the Lotus.

[4] The Bodhicaryâvatâra and the Śikshâsamuccaya, which is a collection of extracts from various sûtras arranged according to topics.

never delude a pupil by the hope that he can succeed if he simply studies sûtras and mantras and neglects the rules of good conduct. Though the Śikshâsamuccaya quotes copious extracts recommending the life of a recluse in the forest, it also has chapters on being careful as to one's pleasures and on purity of enjoyments, and it cites the Ugraparipriccha as saying that a householder who is a Bodhisattva seeks his enjoyments rightly and not wrongly.[1] Thus no blame attaches to a life which includes innocent pleasures. Popular and attractive forms of worship are commended, such as offering flowers, incense, perfumes and banners, bathing images of the Buddhas, making, venerating, and even looking at their pictures. Such precepts and ceremonies explain the success of Buddhism among the masses in the Far East and modify the impression which its philosophical treatises are apt to produce that it is a difficult and detached system which hardly appeals to the ordinary citizens of the world.

## 6

In the sixth century and perhaps considerably earlier, for it is difficult to trace the beginnings of these wide movements, Indian religion became infected by tendencies often called Śâktism and Tantrism. It is well to distinguish the two, for though they are commonly found together, Tantrism may exist without Śâktism. It means a system of religious magic which employs such methods as spells and formulæ without meaning in ordinary language, diagrams, combinations of letters, gestures, and every kind of mystic symbolism in words and actions. The theory underlying all these practices is that there is a force pervading the Universe which can be controlled by rites, especially by sound, just as electricity can be controlled by certain processes and apparatus. A Tantric formula or dhâraṇî may be called a prayer, but it is supposed to act not as an appeal which may move a deity nor by bringing peace and comfort to the mind of him who prays but simply in virtue of the magic potency of the syllables which compose it. Śâktism means the worship of a goddess, especially of a goddess conceived as energy and as the active and creative part of a divine couple, the male deity being regarded as relatively passive and as thought rather than as action. Most Śâktist sects advocate and practise immortal rites. The

[1] Chap. vii, Bhogapunyaraksha, and chap. xv, Bhogapunyasiddhi. See Bendall, p. 267, for the quotation.

worst enemy of Buddhism could hardly maintain that even the germs of such doctrines can be found in the Piṭakas. Nevertheless they invaded late Buddhism, especially in Bengal, and passed thence to Nepal and Tibet. The various Buddhas were provided with female counterparts and such double statues may be seen in Lamaist temples in North China. But to the credit of the Far East let it be said that except in these temples Buddhism hardly shows a trace of Śâktism or phallicism in ritual or iconography.[1] Neither was there much disposition to adopt the ritual called Sâdhana, in which a devotee meditates so long and earnestly on the attributes of a Bodhisattva or Śâkti that at last the worshipper and the object worshipped become one.[2] But of tantric practices such as charms, gestures, and magic syllables, used either as aids to meditation or for their own sake, there is only too much.

The spirit which tolerated such practices is nothing new in the history of Buddhism. Our earliest records represent the Buddha as very indulgent to popular religion. The worship of Hindu deities is not condemned nor is its efficacy in a certain sphere denied, though it has nothing to do with the road to nirvâna and the really religious life. In the Dîgha Nikâya [3] friendly spirits teach the Buddha's disciples a spell by which they can protect themselves against evil spirits and the Buddha approves, although it must be remembered that the same Nikâya contains a long list of superstitious practices of which he disapproves.[4] But charms consisting of meaningless words are found in the Lotus, though only in the later supplements to it, and form a large proportion of the later sacred literature translated into Chinese by such authors as Vajrabodhi (A.D. 719–732), Amoghavajra (A.D. 719–774), and their successors. I confess that I find all this phase of decadent Buddhism, which is sometimes called Mantrayâna or Vajrayâna, most distasteful and uninteresting. Still, it is necessary to recognize its existence, for among other reasons it enables us to understand

[1] In the Shingon sect of Japan five female personages are mentioned corresponding to the five Buddhas, and are equivalent to the five Śâktis of Nepalese Buddhism. But they are not represented by statues, though their figures are found in the Taizōkai Mandara, and it is expressly denied that they are the spouses of the Buddhas. This is the only mention of the Śâktis that I have found in Japan.

[2] See for an example Benoytosh Bhattacaryya, *Buddhist Iconography*, pp. 169–175.

[3] Dîg. Nik., xxxii. See Rhys Davids's Introduction where parallel passages are quoted.

[4] The paragraphs called sîlas which are found in Dîg. Nik., i, especially 21–7, and are repeated in each one of the twelve following sûtras.

the rise in medieval Japan of vigorous and popular sects which protested against the dead formalism of the older ritual.

The word Vajra, which forms the first part of Vajrayâna and is rendered in Japanese by Kongō, means both thunderbolt and diamond, but is used to signify the real and absolute as opposed to the phenomenal world. It is often declared to be the equivalent of Śûnyatâ, but the Vajrayâna seems to have a closer connection with the Vijñânavâda than with the Mâdhyamikas, for the strict doctrine of śûnya was not altogether congenial to a school which dealt so freely in supernatural Buddhas and Bodhisattvas. Tradition connects Asanga with the introduction of Tantrism into Buddhism, but the allusions to it in his undoubted works, so far as they are known, are not numerous.[1]

[1] In the Mahâyâna-sûtrâlankâra he mentions dhâraṇîs (xviii, 71–3) and maithuna (ix, 46) without disapproval.

# CHAPTER IV

## THE PANTHEON

### 1

As already mentioned, one of the obvious differences between the older and newer forms of Buddhism is the tendency to multiply Buddhas. It is not a new idea: it is merely the growth and development of a very old one. From the very first a Buddha is one of a series, like the Avatâras of the Brahmans and the Jinas of the Jains, benevolent powers who manifest themselves from time to time in order to help and teach suffering humanity. The activity of each marks an epoch but it is not final. In the oldest scriptures we already have a procession, more or less extended, of past Buddhas, a prophecy of at least one Buddha in the future and a hint that there may be other Buddhas in other worlds. This last is the idea which grows and expands with what seems to us riotous exuberance. Unlike Europeans and Semites, Indians do not think of man and his world as constituting the universe or even as being its centre: they conceive of life as distributed throughout immeasurable time and space and it is only natural to believe that the highest forms of life—Buddhas and deities—should appear in corresponding profusion. The Lalita-vistara and Mahâvastu speak of them as innumerable, and the Lotus, which is not one of the latest Mahâyâna sûtras, makes a passing allusion to a group of thirty hundred thousand myriads of Kotis of Buddhas, a Koti being ten million. Yet, with a few noteworthy exceptions, these Buddhas have little personality, less perhaps than the Bodhisattvas: they are not a pantheon but a countless heavenly host. In the Lotus Śâkyamuni is not really one among many: Bodhisattvas wait on him and Prabhûtaratna, an ancient Buddha of the remote past, is called up to show the continuity of the true doctrine. But Śâkyamuni remains the central figure: the bewildering millions of other Buddhas and paradises are merely a background which, though gorgeous, does not impair his dignity, and their chief doctrinal importance is to prove to the faithful that the disciple can win the same position as his master and become a Buddha. Śâkyamuni is duly honoured by many Japanese sects, particularly by the

Nichiren, but in the Jōdo and Shinshū he is entirely eclipsed by Amida. In the later Mahâyâna, though it is hard to say when,[1] a group of five Buddhas was formed and is known in Japan, though specially worshipped in Tibet, Nepal, and ancient Java.[2] The names are usually given as Vairocana, Akshobhya, Amitâbha, Amoghasiddhi, and Ratnasambhava. Here Śâkyamuni seems to have disappeared, but in the fully developed form of the doctrine, accepted apparently in Tibet, he is regarded as the human reflex of Amitâbha. Vairocana seems to be regarded as the central and highest personage in the group, the other four each presiding over a point of the compass. The whole arrangement finds a parellel in Hinduism, for both Vishṇu and Siva are worshipped in five forms,[3] and the Manichæans[4] also had groups of five deities. But they may have borrowed the arrangement from the Buddhists.

In Japan the five Buddhas are known to the Shingon sect as the Go-chi-nyorai, but do not form part of popular theology. Some lists give the Indian names as above, the last two being translated as Fukūjōju and Hōshō.[5] But in this land of elastic theology they are also enumerated as Yakushi, Tahō (the Prabhûtaratna of the Lotus), Dainichi, Ashuku, and Shaka.

The germ of the idea is perhaps to be found in an exceedingly curious passage of the Lotus,[6] where Śâkyamuni states that five of his disciples (Kâśyapa, Subhûti, and others) are destined to obtain supreme enlightenment and to become "self-born Jinas". Jina is the usual title applied to Vairocana and the other members of the pentad, though they are sometimes known as Dhyâni Buddhas. The most important of the later group of five are Amitâbha and Vairocana, to whom we must now turn. Akshobhya, the Buddha of the East, must be ancient, for his paradise is described in a sûtra

[1] They are mentioned in the Dharma-sangraha, § 3. Immediately afterwards in § 4 four goddesses (catasro devyah) are mentioned—Rocanâ, Mâmaki, Pandurâ, Târâ. The silence of Śântideva is remarkable. He does not make any mention of the group of five, though it would have been natural for him to do so had he known, or at least approved, of the classification.

[2] This distribution probably implies that the idea spread from Bengal to these various countries.

[3] The Pancarâtra recognizes the highest form or Para and four Vyûhas, presiding over the points of the compass, and the worshippers of Śiva say that he has five faces, Iśâna or Sadâśiva, the highest, and four others for the four points.

[4] See Chavannes and Pelliot, in *J.A.*, 1913, i, pp. 333–8.

[5] 五智如來 Gochi-nyorai: 不空成就 Fukūjōju: 寶生 Hōshō.

[6] Lotus, chap. vi, especially verse 39, which is curious Sanskrit and perhaps corrupt, Panca mi śrâvakâ ye nirdishṭa ye te maya agrabodhaye, apparently meaning "my five disciples whom I have destined to supreme Enlightenment".

which, according to the traditional date, was one of the earliest to be translated into Chinese,[1] but it does not appear that his worship was ever popular. The Buddhas of the north and south appear to be little known except in Nepal and Java.[2] But Amitâbha, the Buddha of the West, the Lord of Measureless Light, has had a surprising destiny. Belief in him as Saviour and the Lord of Paradise has transformed Buddhism in many parts of the Far East and he is still adored by two most important sects in Japan, the Jōdo-shū and Shin-shū.

It is most difficult to explain the history and origin of this attractive and imposing figure. The legend relates that in a remote former birth he was once a man, but he does not seem to have the smallest connection with any historical personage or fact. His name is unknown in Pali literature, in the Lalita-vistara, and apparently in the Âgamas translated into Chinese. He is just mentioned in the older part of the Lotus, but without any emphasis, as one of the Buddhas of the West, and he and his paradise are spoken of more explicitly in the supplementary chapters xxii and xxiv. But in several important and fairly ancient works his worship appears fully developed. He is not merely one of the Buddhas; he is the great saviour of all mankind, and Śâkyamuni is little more than a forerunner whose mission is to preach his mercy and his merits. Of the three chief scriptures [3] which treat of him, two—the Greater and Lesser Sukhâvatî-vyûha—are extant in Sanskrit. The former is said to have been translated by An Shih-Kao (A.D. 147–170), but the translation is lost, though another of about the same date ascribed to Chih Lou Chia Ch'an is extant. Even if with some critics we reject these works as

[1] Nanjio, No. 28, ascribed to the period 147–186. Nanjio, No. 23 (6), is a later translation of the same by Bodhiruchi. It is an apocalypse very similar to the Sukhâvatî-vyûha. Śâkyamuni on the Vulture's Peak explains to Sâriputra the vow made by Akshobhya and the glories of his paradise, which is called Abhirati. Akshobhya is also mentioned in the Lotus in a list of sixteen Buddhas who preside over different directions (chap. vii) and in a similar but longer enumeration in the Lesser Sukhâvatî-vyûha. His vow is also mentioned in the Śikshâsamuccaya. The work which speaks of him most frequently appears to be the Prajñâpâramitâ.

[2] But it is remarkable that in the passage quoted above (chap. vi, prose portion soon after verse 16) Subhûti's paradise is called Ratnasambhava.

[3] The names of the three are: (1) The Greater Sukhâvatî-vyûha 無量壽經 Muryōju-kyō. See Nanjio, 23 (5) and note. (2) The Lesser Sukhâvatî-vyûha, generally called 阿彌陀經 Amida-kyō. Nanjio, Nos. 199 and 200. (3) The Amitâyurdhyâna-sûtra 觀無量壽經 Kanmuryōju-kyō or Kangyō. Nanjio, No. 198.

imaginary or spurious, a third by Ch'ih Chien (A.D. 223-253) lies under no suspicion, so that the Sanskrit original must go back to the second, and probably to the first century of our era.[1] Nine other translations attest the popularity of the work. The Lesser Sukhâvatî-vyûha was translated by Kumârajiva (402) and by Hsüan-Tsang. The third scripture is generally known as the Amitâyurdhyâna-sûtra or Meditation on Amitâyus and appears to be an undoubted translation from Sanskrit made in 424, though the original is lost, as is also the original of the little text called Ōjōron in Japanese, translated in 529 and ascribed to Vasubandhu in his old age.[2]

These texts explain clearly the personality and worship of Amitâbha which are made the centre—or rather the whole—of dogma and practice. On the other hand, it is remarkable that many other Mahayanist writings, such as the works of Nâgârjuna, Asanga, and the Awakening of Faith, treat devotion to him as something laudable but not essential. In the same spirit Hsüan-Tsang turned the Lesser Sukhâvatî-vyûha into Chinese, though his almost superhuman activity as a translator was mainly devoted to works advocating entirely different principles. One would have expected that a belief which transforms Buddhism and practically dethrones Śâkyamuni would have aroused polemics as well as enthusiasm, as in fact it did later in Japan in the days of Nichiren, but India and China were so tolerant that the new road to salvation was regarded as permissible even by authors who devoted their main attention to quite other methods. I have already pointed out [3] one reason for this. Even in the Pali Nikâyas the desire to be reborn in the heaven of Brahmâ or some other deity is admitted to be natural and proper for laymen, though it is not the quest for true happiness which is nirvâna, and this new teaching was not essentially different except that it exalted Amitâbha to a position very unlike any which the Piṭakas accord to Brahmâ. It may be, too, that another reason for the somewhat sporadic and irregular appearance of Amitâbha in Indian Buddhist literature is that his worship originally grew up somewhere in Afghanistan or the neighbouring regions under Iranian influences and only gradually spread in India proper among those to whom it was congenial. Images of him are not

[1] See above, Chap. III, p. 87.
[2] See above, Chap. III, p. 93.
[3] Chap. II, p. 47.

particularly frequent [1] and the Chinese pilgrims mention him only occasionally.[2]

The Saṃyutta Nikâya contains an exceedingly curious dialogue [3] entitled the Westerner, in which a village headman called Asibandhakaputta, or the snake charmer's son, informs the Buddha that the Brahmans of the West, who are fire-worshippers, carry out the dead, call on them by name, and send them on their way to heaven. "But the Lord," he continues, "who is an Arhat and All-Enlightened, can bring it about that the whole world, on the dissolution of the body, can be born in a happy state, in the heavenly world." Gotama condemns this view, which was evidently not approved by the Theravâda. He does not discuss what the powers of a Buddha may be in such matters, but simply says that the dead go to paradise or purgatory according as their deeds are good or bad. The praise of a great multitude with uplifted hands will not send a bad man to paradise nor can they prevent a good man from going there, just as they cannot make a rock float or oil sink. Though the doctrine is expressly condemned, the story clearly implies that there was an idea that a Buddha can enable the dead to reach heaven, and this idea is connected with the funeral customs of the West. This certainly suggests that in those regions a belief was already growing up that prayer to the Buddha is a means of obtaining heaven for oneself or others.

The main ideas of Amidism,[4] as the worship of Amitâbha is conveniently termed, are all found in the Zoroastrian scriptures.

[1] See Foucher, *Iconographie Bouddhique dans l'Inde*, and Benoytosh Bhattacaryya. *Indian Buddhist Iconography*.

[2] Fa-Hsien does not mention him at all nor does Hsüan-Tsang in his narrative, though he translated the Lesser Sukhâvatî-vyûha. I should hesitate to make such a sweeping negative statement were it not confirmed by the professors of the Ōtani University, Kyōto. I-Ching twice speaks of him with devout appreciation. Tzŭ-Ming, however, is reported to have found his worship very prevalent (see Kimura, *Hînayâna and Mahâyâna*, p. 42), but he did not arrive in India till A.D. 705.

[3] Saṃ. Nik., xlii, 6. Paccâbhumako. The western Brahmans are described as Kâmandalukâ sevâlamalikâ udakorohakâ aggiparicârikâ "carriers of water-pots, wearing garlands of sevala, bathers, tenders of the fire". The last word must not be unduly pressed to mean anything un-Brahmanic, for it might be used of priests who keep up the sacrificial fires, and udakorohakâ is used in Maj. Nik. of those who believe in ceremonial bathing.

Saññapenti seems to mean "call by name", but it is an unusual use of the word, which more commonly signifies to convince. The words about the Buddha's power are—Bhagavâ pana araham sammâsambuddho pahoti tathâ kâtum yathâ sabbo loko kâyassa bheda param maranâ sugatim saggam lokam upapajjeyâti.

[4] 阿彌陀. Amida is the shortened form of Amïtâbha in use in Japan.

The highest heaven is called Endless, or Boundless, Light,[1] a striking verbal resemblance and, like Amitâbha's paradise, it is a land of song and pleasant sounds. Prayer can win this paradise, and if anyone recites the Ahuna-vairya formula, Ahuramazda "will bring his soul to the lights of heaven". Further, it is expressly stated that Ahuramazda and his archangels will guide the dying believer on his way thither.[2] Precisely the same promise is made in the Sukhâvatî-vyûha and still consoles countless deathbeds in the Far East.

But though I think that the worship of Amitâbha first grew up in the regions to the north-west of India proper, its Iranian affinities must not be exaggerated. As presented in its earliest scriptures, it is already thoroughly Indian in its details. In strict language Amitâbha is not a benevolent deity: he is a Buddha who has followed the arduous road to Enlightenment like other Buddhas: his paradise is the result of his merits and the right to enter it is regulated by Karma, somewhat liberally interpreted, it is true. The efficacy of the deathbed prayer—that a man goes to the deity whom he remembers in his last hour—if not exactly a Buddhist doctrine, is clearly affirmed by the Bhagavad Gîtâ.[3] There is indeed a close parallel between the development of Amidism and Vishnuism. In a recent Indian work, Mallik's *Philosophy of the Vaishnava Religion*, it is stated that in this Kali age life is short and the intellect weak. Men cannot follow the Vedas. Similarly, in Japan, Hōnen and Shinran declared that modern man could not follow the Shōdōmon, or path of good works, which is practically admitted to be the original teaching of the Buddha. Secondly, Mallik states that the Purâṇas are a supplement to the Vedas: they are of the same quality, but can be read and understood by anyone. Thus relatively modern books are exalted above the ancient sacred texts, just as in Japan the average member of the Shin sect has never even heard of the Âgamas.

[1] *S.B.E.*, xxxiii, pp. 317 and 344, and iv, p. 293. The expression in the last passage "boundless light and undeserved felicity" is noticeable. In the Lesser Sukhâvatî-vyûha we are told that paradise is not the reward of merit.

[2] *S.B.E.*, xxxiii, pp. 335–7; xxxi, p. 261. The Ormazd Yasht (*S.B.E.*, xxxiii, 20–31) clearly affirms the efficacy of Ahuramazda's name as an invocation.

[3] Bhag. Gîtâ, viii, 6. A somewhat similar idea is not wholly absent in early Buddhism. In Saṃ. Nik., xli, 10, when Citta is dying the deities of the forest exhort him to aspire to be a king in his next birth. He rejects the suggestion, but it is not denied that dying aspirations can influence the next existence. See, too, Maj. Nik., xli, where it is said that a good man can be reborn a noble or a Brahman, or a god if he forms the desire.

The three Amidist scriptures all have the form of sûtras and represent Śâkyamuni as preaching the new doctrine in scenery and company familiar to the student of the Pali Piṭakas. The longer and doubtless older version of the Sukhâvatî-vyûha is a discourse delivered on the Vultures' Peak in answer to Ânanda's questions. Śâkyamuni begins by enumerating no less than eighty previous Buddhas of the remote past. After them came one called Lokeśvara-râja, in whose presence a monk called Dharmâkara, the future Amitâbha, made a series of vows. The idea that the aspirant to Buddhahood formally commences his career in this way is found even in the introduction to the Pali Jâtaka and in the Mahâvastu. In the later literature the accounts of the great Bodhisattvas, especially Avalokiteśvara [1] and Kshitigarbha, sometimes mention that they made such vows and the scene is often depicted in the frescoes found in Central Asia. Dharmâkara vowed that he would become a Buddha, but on conditions, namely, that he should be able to help others and share with them his vast store of accumulated merit. If I cannot do this, he said, then may I not obtain supreme Enlightenment. When after countless ages he obtained that Enlightenment, the conditions held good and became a law of Karma. According to the terms of the vow he is lord of a paradise called Sukhâvatî, or the Happy Land, to which those who have thought of him ten times are admitted.

The belief in the transfer of merit from one person to another (pattidâna or pariṇâmana) is hardly agreeable to the older Buddhism, which uncompromisingly asserts that we make our future by our own deeds. But it is an admitted principle in Mahayanist writings and is obviously a charitable and comforting doctrine. In practice it may be found even in Ceylon,[2] and the Amidist sects have no hesitation in saying that man is too weak and foolish to be able to save himself. Nevertheless the earliest pronouncement as found in the treatise which we are considering does not wholly reject good works: it promises paradise to those who make it the object of their thoughts and acquire merit for that purpose. It also excludes those who have committed deadly [3] sin. But the Lesser

[1] The vows made by Avalokiteśvara under innumerable Buddhas are mentioned in the Lotus, chap. xxiv, verse 3. The vows of Akshobhya, Bhaishajyaguru, and others are also described in special sûtras.

[2] For instance, prayers are still used in which the hope is expressed that merit may be transferred to departed relatives and to good spirits who protect religion.

[3] Sins which bring immediate punishment on the sinner, such as killing one's parents or provoking schism.

Sukhâvatî-vyûha, which purports to be an address delivered by Śâkyamuni to Ânanda at Śrâvastî, categorically preaches salvation by faith only. "Beings are not born in that Buddha country as a reward and result of good works done in this life. No, all men and women who hear and bear in mind for seven nights, or even only one, the name of Amitâyus,[1] when they come to die Amitâyus will stand before them in the hour of death, they will depart this life with quiet minds and will be reborn in Paradise." Both sûtras are mainly occupied with a description of the joys of this Happy Land, its gardens, flowers, rivers, music, and jewels, and much of the description recalls the account given in the Dîgha Nikâya[2] of the pleasances constructed by the Great King of Glory where there were also lotus ponds with four flights of steps surrounded by golden and jewelled trees which made music in the wind. It is noticeable that these delights, though they do not include eating, drinking, and things sexual, are mainly agreeable sights and sounds which Gotama would have pronounced vain and impermanent. But, strictly speaking, Paradise is not final bliss: it is a happy state in which believers remain "constant in absolute truth until they reach nirvâna".[3]

The third sûtra, called the Meditation on Amitâyus, presents the whole doctrine in a more advanced and developed form. It is prefaced by a historical introduction which tells how the wicked Ajâtaśatru imprisoned and wished to kill his father and mother. The latter, Queen Vaidehi, prays to Śâkyamuni, who appears miraculously in her prison, and in answer to her desire to be told of a country where there is no sorrow or trouble, gives her a vision of many radiant heavens, among which she chooses Sukhâvatî and asks how she may be born there. The scheme of salvation which Śâkyamuni unfolds is comprehensive, for a moral life, unselfishness, ceremonial observances, and meditation are all declared to be efficacious, but the method specially recommended is a series of sixteen meditations which are described in detail. Mankind are divided into many classes according to their mental and moral

[1] The names Amitâbha (Measureless Light) and Amitâyus (Measureless Life) seem to be used indifferently. The Greater Sukh.-vyûha usually employs the former, but explains Amitâyus in § 14. The two other sûtras use Amitâyus, but the Lesser Sukh.-vyûha explains Amitâbha in § 9.

[2] Dîg. Nik., xvii.

[3] Greater Sukh.-vyûha, § 24. Sarve te niyatâh samyaktve yàvan Nirvânam. Cf. Amitâyûr-Dhyâna S., § 26. But the Sukh.-vyûha also says (§ 21) that the inhabitants of paradise are as happy as a Bhikshu who has attained nirvâna.

qualities, but even the most ignorant sinner may on his deathbed meet a friend who will teach him to invoke the name of Amitâyus. Then the flames of hell will turn to heavenly flowers and he will be born in a lotus blossom which will at last unclose and leave him among the joys of Sukhâvatî. The description of the Happy Land is much the same as in the other sûtras, but the rulers of it are not one but three, the great Bodhisavattvas Avalokiteśvara and Mahâsthâma [1] being described in detail and repeatedly mentioned as aiding in the work of salvation. At the end it is even said that the sûtra should be called the Meditation on Amitâyus, Avalokiteśvara, and Mahâsthâma.

The author was evidently familiar with an extensive Mahayanist literature, for he repeatedly recommends the study of the scriptures and specially of the Vaipulya sûtras. He also knew of the doctrine of the Dharmakâya, and puts the following remarkable passage [2] into the mouth of Śâkyamuni, who, after describing the seventh meditation and the flowery throne of Amitâbha, continues :— "When you have perceived this you should think of Buddha. Why so? All Buddhas Tathâgatas are the Fa-chieh-shêng (Dharmadhâtu) which enters into the mind and thought of all sentient beings whatsoever. Therefore, when you think of the Buddha in your mind, that very mind is the thirty-two marks and eighty beautiful signs. *That mind makes Buddha : that mind is Buddha.*" This seems to be a statement that the mind makes heaven : *we obtain what we believe in.* This idea has borne fruit in the Japanese Amidist sects.

Vairocana [3] is an important figure in the Buddhism of the Far East and also of Tibet, Nepal, and Java.[4] There is even a tendency to make him the Âdi-Buddha or primal spiritual essence which is postulated by some varieties of the Mantrayâna. In Japan he is the principal object of reverence in the Shingon sect and was also

[1] They are just mentioned in the Greater Sukh.-vyûha, § 34. Avalokiteśvara is mentioned again in § 31, when he is called a son of the Buddha.

[2] Amit. Dhyâna-S., ·17. 見此事已次當想佛所以者何諸佛如來是法界身入一切衆生心想中是故汝等心想佛時是心卽是三十二想八十隨形好是心作佛是心是佛.

[3] 毗盧遮那.

[4] He is spoken of in some detail in the Javanese books Kamahayanikan and the story of Kunjarakarna. See my *Hinduism and Buddhism*, iii, 172 ff., for a further account.

at an early period identified with the Sun goddess in the conciliatory system which united Shintō and Buddhism. But though he is well-known, especially as represented by the gigantic statue in the temple at Nara,[1] he is less popular than Amitâbha. He is a pantheistic and philosophic conception rather than a saviour, and the doctrines which concern him are exceedingly abstruse. The name is a derivative of Virocana, a recognized title of the sun in Sanskrit and rendered as Tai-jih in Chinese, which in Japanese becomes Dainichi. His origin is very likely to be found outside India in Iranian countries, though it must be remembered that from Vedic times onwards there are numerous solar deities who are purely Indian. Nevertheless it is exceedingly difficult to trace his history in Sanskrit literature and his images are not numerous or early. Vairocana occurs in the Mahâvastu as the name of an otherwise unknown Buddha, and in the supplementary chapters of the Lotus (xxiii and xxv) a luminous Buddha-world called Vairocana-raśmi-pratimandita is frequently mentioned. But the chief scripture which treats of him is the important Kegon or Avataṃsaka-sûtra,[2] which appears to be identical with the Ganda-vyûha or perhaps that work is merely a portion of it. But the reports published of the Sanskrit text are not so full as could be wished. Since it was translated into Chinese in A.D. 398–421, it must be at least of moderate antiquity, and several of the partial translations are ascribed to the end of the third and even to the second century. A commentary on part of it attributed to Nâgârjuna was translated by Kumârajiva (Nan. 1180).

Locanâ [3] seems hardly distinguishable from Vairocana but is regarded as the special personification of Dharma in all its aspects,

[1] Strictly speaking, the temple and image are dedicated to Locanâ or Roshana as stated in the Shoku-Nihongi.

[2] 華嚴 Chinese Hua-yen, Japanese Kegon. The Ganda-vyûha seems to be known only by Raj. Mitra's abstract in *Nepalese Buddhist Lit.*, pp. 90 ff. For its identity with the Avataṃsaka-sûtra see Watanabe, *J.R.A.S.*, 1911, p. 663, and Pelliot, *J.A.*, 1914, ii, pp. 118–121. The translations of this sûtra, entire and partial, form a whole section of the Chinese Tripitaka, Nanjio, Nos. 87–111. The principal are (*a*) the version in sixty volumes, A.D. 317–421, (*b*) that in eighty, A.D. 695–9, (*c*) and that in forty, A.D. 796–8.

[3] 盧舍那 Japanese Roshana or Dainichi. According to the Tendai system, Vairocana is the Dharmakâya and Locanâ the Sambhogakâya. Though some authorities hold that the two forms should be distinguished, the priests of the Tōdaiji temple at Nara call the great image Birushana, although historical records call it Roshana and this is the form used in the text of the Kegon-sûtra (the edition in sixty volumes), which is specially studied in the temple.

the cosmic as well as the moral Law. In the well-known manual called Fan-Wang-Ching,[1] which in China has practically taken the place of the Vinaya as a statement of the aspirations and rules of conduct by which monks should be guided, he is presented in the introduction with peculiar emphasis as proclaiming the Law which he incarnates. Śâkyamuni, who approaches him reverently with a crowd of Bodhisattvas to receive his instructions, is but a minute portion of his essence. The throne on which he sits is surrounded by a thousand lotus petals and each petal is a universe with a Śâkya of its own. But every one of these universes contains a hundred million worlds in the human sense, all with their suns, moons, and Śâkyas. "The Buddhas of the thousand petals are transformations of myself, and the hundred million Śâkyas a thousand times repeated are transformations of them. I am the source and origin of all and my name is Locanâ."[2] In this speech we have almost a statement of the doctrine of the Âdi Buddha, or original Buddha, that is the original self-existent creative Buddha-spirit, which evolves from itself the whole world. This doctrine,[3] which is practically theism, is found among Tibetans in the Kâlacakra system and in Nepal, and apparently was prevalent in medieval Java, but it has not had much success in the Far East in spite of the passage quoted above.

The Avataṃsaka-sûtra emphasizes not so much the idea that any particular Buddha is to be regarded as the source and origin of the world as a variety of the doctrine of relativity already explained in speaking of Nâgârjuna. In the heaven of Indra there is said to be a network or pearls so arranged that if you look at one you see all the others reflected in it. In the same way each object in the world is not merely itself but involves every other object and in fact *is* everything else. "In every particle of dust there are present

[1] Nanjio, 1087, 梵網經, Bommōkyō in Japanese pronunciation. Edited and translated by De Groot under the title *Le Code du Mahayana en Chine*. The Sanskrit original is unknown but the translation professes to have been made by Kumârajiva, c. A.D. 400. It seems to have been interpolated in much later times, but there is no particular reason to suspect the introduction in which Locanâ explains his position.

[2] Very similar language is used in the Kegon-sûtra (Buddhabhadra's translation), chap. 3 and chap. 34 (fasc. 45, pp. 22–3 of the Kōkyō Shoin edition), where it is said that he emits from his body "clouds of Nirmâṇakâyas" (Keshîn-un). Compare the language of the Lotus about the Buddhas "created" by Śâkyamuni.

[3] It is also found in the metrical version of the Kâraṇḍa-vyûha, which appears to be later than the prose version, of which it is a paraphrase.

Buddhas without number" and "on the point of a single hair a whole Buddha land may be seen".[1] It is also noticeable that this sûtra, when describing Locanâ as a being manifested to mankind, speaks of him as having made vows (like Amitâbha) and as having created by their efficiency and by the good deeds which he practised through untold ages the Lotus universe of which our world is apparently a part. In Japan at the present day the Kegon-sûtra is chiefly studied by the small sect of the same name who own the great Tōdaiji temple at Nara. The far larger Shingon sect have as their principal scriptures a work commonly known as Dainichi-kyō,[2] and two other sûtras, all translated about A.D. 724. As the date indicates, this literature belongs to the Mantrayâna school made popular in China by Vajrabodhi and Amoghavajra.

The Healing Buddha[3] enjoys considerable prestige in the Far East, for like Amitâbha he makes a simple and direct appeal to humanity, but, as in the case of the Buddhas already mentioned, it is exceedingly difficult to trace his history in literature and art on Indian soil. By a natural metaphor a religious teacher is called a physician of the soul, and even in the Pali Piṭakas[4] Gotama is styled the best of healers. But the stories of his life rarely represent him as curing disease, and the powers of healing do not seem to be specially personified in any of the earlier supernatural Buddhas, or in Indian iconography.[5] Bhaishajya-râja, however, whose name must mean something like the King of Healing, is a character of importance in the Lotus.[6] He is not a Tathâgata but a Bodhisattva, and Śâkyamuni addresses him as the representative

[1] Kegon (Avataṃsaka) sûtra, chap. v.

[2] Nanjio, 530. In Chinese 大毗盧遮那成佛神變加持經 Ta-p'i-lu-chê-na-chêng-fo-shên-pien-chia-ch'ih-ching. Apparently representing Mahâvairocanâbhisambodhi in Sanskrit. The other two works are Nanjio, 534, 金剛頂經 being an abridged translation of the Vajraśekharayoga-tantra commonly called Kongōchō-kyō in Japanese, and Nanjio, 533, 蘇悉地羯羅經 Susiddhikâra-sûtra, commonly called Soshitsuji-kyō.

[3] 藥師如來 Yao-Shih-Ju-Lai: Yakushi Nyorai. The Sanskrit title is Bhaishajyaguru.

[4] Sallakattoanuttaro, Maj. Nik., xcii, and Sutta Nip., 562. Cf. Mil. Pan., iv, 5, 8, and Lotus, chap. xv, 21. Evam evâham cikitsakah sarva prajñânanathâh. In the Mahâvag., vi, 23, the Buddha cures Suppiya miraculously, but this was a very special case. As a rule sickness is regarded as the result of Karma.

[5] There seems to be no representation of a healing Buddha in the Buddhist Iconography by Benoytosh Bhattacarya.

[6] Lotus, chaps. x, xii beginning, xxi, xxii, and xxv. The name also occurs in Lal.-vist., xiii.

of that class of beings. He promises to spread the true doctrine among mankind and teaches a charm for the protection of believers. His good deeds in previous births are described at great length, and especially how he once burnt himself in honour of an ancient Buddha. This narrative, we are told, will be like medicine to those who hear it and prevent sickness, old age, and untimely death. But except in this passage Bhaishajya-râja's healing powers are not emphasized.

The Śikshâsamuccaya [1] prescribes rites for curing diseases. Forest flowers should be offered at a Caitya or to an image or to the Book of the Good Law (Sad-dharma-pustaka). A Tathâgata bearing the name of Bhaishajyaguru or some longer title is several times mentioned: we should pray that beings may be free from disease even as he is: those who invoke his name shall not fall into misery and a virtuous man is bidden to pursue the good of all creatures "like an image of Bhaishajyaguru". These passages evidently allude, though in somewhat vague language, to a popular healing Buddha. Two works in the Tripiṭaka [2] translated in the seventh century relate that like Amitâbha he made vows and asked for enlightenment on condition of being able to cure disease and drive away famine.

Śâkyamuni, Amitâbha, Vairocana, and Bhaishajyaguru are the principal and for practical purposes the only Buddhas (as distinguished from Bodhisattvas) now venerated in the Far East. Not that there is anything in the least unorthodox in showing devotion to others. As mentioned above, the Chinese Tripiṭaka contains a sûtra which extols the vows and the paradise of the Buddha Akshobhya, and statues of him may be seen occasionally in Japanese temples. It also contains a translation of a work which gives an account of the land of Padmadhâtu and its ruler, the Buddha Padmottara.[3] But such figures play no part in religious life and hardly any in art.

[1] Śikshâsamuccaya, Bendall's edition, pp. 139, 32, 174–5, 362. A work called the Bhaishajyaguru-Vaidûrya-prabhâ-sûtra is also quoted pp. 13 and 174.

[2] Nanjio, 170 and 171, called in Japanese Yakushi-hongwan-kyō. The latter was translated by Hsüan-Tsang in A.D. 650.

[3] Nanjio, No. 142, 悲華經 Pei-hua-ching, a translation (A.D. 414–421) of the Karunâpundarîka, still extant in Sanskrit.

## 2

Though in the Pali Piṭakas Gotama is more than an ordinary man, he has the outward semblance of one, but these later Buddhas, practically immortal Lords of radiant paradises, are clearly beings of quite another kind, and it is not surprising if the imagination which drew such pictures had also its philosophical side and developed new ideas of the Buddha-nature described by the formula Tri-Kâya or the three bodies.[1] I have already mentioned that this doctrine is adumbrated, though only faintly, in the Nikâyas. Still, Gotama is made to state [2] that when he frequents the assemblies of men and gods he can appear and vanish in any form he pleases without being recognized. At a comparatively early period the Mahâsanghikas held that Buddhas are supermundane (lokottara), that their rûpakâya (which appears to be a synonym of sambhogakâya) is limitless, as are also their divine power and length of life.[3] All Mahayanist sûtras, whether they make dogmatic statements or not, accept these views. The clearest and most accessible definitions are those to be found in the Awakening of Faith and in Asanga.[4] A Buddha has three bodies,[5] which are :—

(1) The Nirmâṇakâya, literally the body of transformation, that is to say, the human form which a Buddha assumes in his intercourse with mankind. Far from being the real Buddha, it is a mere magical contrivance. This recalls the ancient heresy attributed to the Vetulyakas who held that the Buddha remained in the Tusita heaven and sent a phantom to preach in the world.[6] On the other hand, the Nirmâṇakâya considered philosophically is the counterpart of the belief in the existence of the Self. The fancies of ignorant people create their own selves, their pleasures and pains, their gods and Buddhas. In reality these are all Nirmâṇakâyas.

(2) The Sambhogakâya, the body of bliss or enjoyment, is the presence of a Buddha as manifest in paradise. It is personal but

[1] 三身 Sanjin.

[2] Mahâparinib.-sutta, iii, 22.

[3] See Vasumitra's treatise translated by Masuda in *Asia Major*, ii, p. 19.

[4] Suzuki, pp. 100–1. Mahâyânasûtrâlaṇkâra, ed. Sylvain Lévi, ix, 60 ff.

[5] The three bodies are called in Japanese 應身 Ōjin or Nirmâṇakâya; 報身 Hōshin or Sambhogakâya, and 法身 Hosshin or Dharmakâya.

[6] This belief is mentioned in Kathâvatthu, xviii, 1, and the commentary says that it was held by the Vetulyakas.

above human limitations. Splendour and radiance are prominent among the qualities ascribed to it.

(3) The Dharmakâya or body of the law. This is the true Buddha. It is above personality and cannot be described as either existence or non-existence.[1] It is practically equivalent to Bhûtatathatâ, Tathâgatagarbha, Dharmadhâtu, Bodhi, and Nirvâna. It has thus obvious analogies to the Brahman or Absolute of the Upanishads, but it is only just to say that the Lankâvatâra-sûtra warns us that the two conceptions are not to be confounded.

The Suvarṇaprabhâsa-sûtra [2] shows us the doctrine in a somewhat different stage of development. It uses technical terminology in speaking of the three bodies, but still it regards them from the point of view of religion, not metaphysics, as agencies co-operating in the work of salvation, not as explanations of the mysteries of existence. The Buddha by his good deeds done in human form has acquired a spiritual power which enables him to appeal to mankind as the perfect man and to teach the first steps towards Enlightenment to those who will follow his example. This is the Nirmânakâya. But he can also appeal to Bodhisattvas, those beings who are treading the higher stages of the path: he shows them that saṃsâra and nirvâna are really the same, he destroys egoism and individuality and lays the foundation of the true Buddha nature. This is the Sambhogakâya. But both these bodies are provisional forms of his existence, assumed for special purposes. The Dharmakâya, on the other hand, is the reality: pure suchness (Tathatâ) without taint, imperfection, or emotion. Just as the light of the sun or moon reflects itself in water, without making a conscious distinction between the water and other places and without itself suffering any change, so does the Dharmakâya reflect itself in the form of the other two bodies according to the spiritual needs of believers. Some scriptures which are esteemed in Japan formulate respecting the bodies of the Buddha even more elaborate doctrines, which, however, have not become popular and are known only to the learned. Thus the Kegon or Avataṃsaka-sûtra enumerates no less than ten bodies, the theory being that the Buddha nature is present in all things animate and inanimate,

[1] Cf. the words of the Pali canon in describing the state of the Tathâgata after death. See above, pp. 43–5.

[2] I-Ching's translation, vol. ii, chap. iii, p. 5. The passage does not seem to be extant in Sanskrit.

whatever their grade of spiritual development. By a further refinement the seventh of these bodies, Nyorai-shin or Tathâgata-kâya, is again subdivided into ten Buddhas, apparently an attempt to define the various manners in which the Buddha nature may be present.[1]

The Shingon sect hold that there are four or five bodies and, moreover, give them all a title corresponding to Dharmakâya. They are: (1) Jishō-hosshin, (2) Juyō-hosshin, (3) Henge-hosshin, and (4) Tōryū-hosshin.[2] Of these the first three correspond to the three bodies of the ordinary classification. The Tōryū-hosshin is an attempt, as in the Kegon-sûtra, to explain the presence of the Buddha nature in all things. In very truth the Dharmakâya is not only in all but is all. But in virtue of the Tōryū-hosshin it may appear in the form of an animal or even of a demon. This series of four is increased to five by dividing the second body—the body of enjoyment—into two,[3] the Ji-juyō-hosshin, or body of personal enjoyment, in which a Buddha feels the bliss of enlightenment, and the Ta-juyō-hosshin in which he communicates this bliss to others who are capable of feeling it. These doctrines may be found both in translations from the Sanskrit [4] and in the works of Kōbō Daishi.[5] But the importance of such ideas does not lie in the number of bodies, not even in the relatively ancient and orthodox three, but in the Dharmakâya. Difficult as this conception is to formulate in European or even in Eastern languages and apt as it is to lead to abstruse speculations which are obviously only for the select few, yet inasmuch as it teaches that the Buddha is not to be

[1] For the Jisshin or ten bodies see the edition in 60 fasciculi Nan. No. 26. They are: (1) 衆生身 Shujō shin, (2) 國土身 Kokudo s., (3) 業報身 Gōhō s., (4) 聲聞身 Shōmon s., (5) 辟支佛身 Byakushibutsu s., (6) 菩薩身 Bosatsu s., (7) 如來身 Nyorai s., (8) 智身 Chi s., (9) 法身 Hosshin, (10) 虛空身 Kokū s. The ten Buddhas who are subdivisions of No. 7 in the above are enumerated in Nan. 42 of the same work. They are: (1) 無著佛 Mujaku Butsu, (2) 願佛 Gan Butsu, (3) 業報佛 Gōhō Butsu, (4) 持佛 Ji Butsu, (5) 涅槃佛 Nehan Butsu, (6) 法界佛 Hōkai Butsu, (7) 心佛 Shin Butsu, (8) 三昧佛 Sanmai Butsu, (9) 性佛 Shō or Sei Butsu, (10) 如意佛 Nyo-i Butsu.

[2] The Japanese characters are 自性法身, 受用法身, 變化法身, 等流法身.

[3] 自受用法身, 他受用法身.

[4] e.g. Nanjio, No. 1039 and No. 1433.

[5] Such as the Kenmitsunikyōron and Sokushin jōbutsugi.

thought of as merely a person, human or superhuman, but as a spirit present in all nature and in the human heart, it has been in the Far East a great force in religion and in art.[1]

Though triads are common enough in Hinduism, notably the three guṇas, or constituents of being, the formula of the three bodies is mainly Buddhist.[2] But the underlying idea, as so often happens in India, is characteristic of an epoch, not of any particular sect. In the Bhagavad Gîtâ Kṛishṇa is sometimes merely the charioteer of Arjuna. But he reveals himself in his divine form,[3] radiant and glorious, and besides this he is extolled as the Absolute,[4] as Being and not-Being, as the Supreme Self (paramâtma), and the Self dwelling in the heart of every creature. The resemblance here to the doctrine of the three bodies is very close, but there is a difference in tone between Buddhist and Brahmanic sentiment. Kṛishṇa, as revealed in his divine form, is splendid, but above all, terrible. But though epithets descriptive of light and glory, overwhelming and infinite, are heaped upon the Sambhogakâya of the Buddhas, there is no terror. One feels not their power and majesty, but their infinite kindness and desire to help.

The conception of the Buddha in the Lotus offers many resemblances to the Bhagavad Gîtâ. No technical dogmatic language about the three bodies is used and the description of Śâkyamuni's presence and movements, the immeasurable rays of light which issue from his countenance and so on, are so hyperbolical that there seems to be no question of a human frame. Nevertheless, this personality was "born at Kapilavastu and reached enlightenment at Gaya [5] but a short time ago" and is in that sense a nirmâṇakâya, a mere illusion. The birth and nirvâna of a Buddha are illusion: kindly devices designed to arrest attention and make men listen to the law. But He himself is beyond birth and death. He is not God in the European sense of the word, for he is not the Creator [6]

[1] Its influence on art is eloquently explained by Anesaki in his book, *Buddhist Art in its relation to Buddhist Ideals*, 1915.

[2] But Hinduism also ascribes three bodies to all living creatures: the Kâraṇa-śarîra, lingaś., and sthûlaś.

[3] In book xi. Darśayâm âsa paramam rûpam aiśvaram. He showed his supreme form as Lord. Cf. Viśvamûrti, viśvarûpa, anantarûpa.

[4] Bhag. Gîtâ, x, 27; ix, 19; xv, 17; x, 20.

[5] Lotus, xiv, verse 44.

[6] The world is not real as ordinary men suppose. Lotus, chap. xv, Dṛishtam hi Tathâgatena traidhâtukam yathâbhûtam. Na jâyate na mriyate, etc. The doctrine of the Void, or Śûnyatâ, is frequently commended. See chap. v, verses 41, 52, 75, 80, and chaps. viii, xi, and xiii. The Lotus several times calls the

nor it would seem, in most respects the Ruler of the world. But his constant purpose is to help and save mankind by bringing them to Enlightenment: like Kṛishṇa, from time to time he manifests himself when ignorance and vice prevail,[1] and he causes all beings to reach nirvâna by means of his own complete nirvâna: all his disciples, even Devadatta, will become Buddhas.[2] Though the language of the Lotus is most authoritative and dogmatic, it is not always precise. In particular, the relations of Śâkyamuni to other Buddhas are not entirely clear. Often (for instance, in the second chapter) the Buddhas who have won Enlightenment and who save the world are spoken of as many. But other passages seem to make Śâkyamuni something above ordinary Buddhas and speak as if he were the universal essence and spirit from which they all derive their being. They are said to be his emanations and to be made (nirmita) by him[3]: from the very beginning (âdita eva) he has developed them and by him alone have they all been brought to maturity. A somewhat similar obscurity occurs in later forms of Buddhism. Philosophy seems to require the Dharmakâya to be above plurality and personality. Yet sometimes a particular Buddha is said to have a Dharmakâya.

The more purely philosophical views about the Dharmakâya, such as are found for instance in the Mâdhyamika Kârikâs of Nâgârjuna, are a not illogical amplification of the statements found in the Nikâyas about the impossibility of making any assertion about a Buddha after his death and even (as the dialogue with Yamaka shows) during his life.[4] This is expanded to mean that the true Buddha nature is the absolute. Since it is in no sense relative, no ordinary words apply to it. It is beyond definition and characterization: it can be understood only by intuition. But still it is the one without a second, it is truly real, whereas nothing

Budda Father, or Father of the world, and his disciples are his sons. See iii, verse 97; iv, verse 36, and specially xv, verse 21. Lokapitâ syayambhûḥ. But apparently the word Father is always used in the sense of one who cherishes and protects, not one who begets or creates. For the sentiment cf. Asokâvadâna, chap. iv, trans. Przyluski, p. 291, " Mon père est le roi Asoka . . . et j'ai aussi un autre père, le grand roi de la Loi qu'on appelle le Bouddha."

[1] Lotus, xv, 22. Cf. Bhag. Gîtâ, iv, 7.

[2] Lotus, iii (*S.B.E.*, xxi, p. 81) and v, verse 44, and xi, after verse 46.

[3] Lotus, xi (*S.B.E.*, xxi, 231 and 235); xiv (ib., p. 295) and xiv, verses 38 and 43. The language is often perplexing. Thus, in chap. viii, verse 14, it is stated that Pûraṇa shall *become* a self-existent (svayambhû) Buddha in the world. But how can one *become* self-existent? The quality seems to be original and essential.

[4] See above, Chaps. II, p. 50, and III, p. 81.

which is manifold and relative can be real in the same sense. The obvious criticism on such doctrines is that they are metaphysics and not religion. In making it we must remember that even in the Far East, which is not metaphysical in temperament, portions of the Prajñâpâramitâ,[1] if not exactly popular, are constantly read by the devout.

## 3

Though only about four of all the millions of Buddhas extolled in the Mahayanist scriptures are known to popular Buddhism, the images seen in Chinese and Japanese temples suggest a much larger pantheon and recall the passages in the Nikâyas[2] which tell how throngs of Devas and spirits came to do homage to the Blessed One. Triads of large figures surrounded by smaller attendants are common and other supernatural personages guard the vestibules or receive homage in separate shrines. The more important of them are Bodhisattvas, but many can only be described as deities, generally Indian in origin, whose worship is sanctioned by Buddhism, at least by the older sects, though it is really not Buddhist. The inquirer is warned that whatever title, Bodhisattva or other, may be given to these personages, it is often difficult to ascertain what are their real names and attributes. Not only the laity but even the clergy are generally hazy about such matters unless they have some special interest. In the same way in Europe many excellent Christians might be perplexed if they were asked to give the names of the three Magi or of the Archangels.

The distinction between a Buddha and a Bodhisattva[3] is easy to define in technical language. A Buddha is one who has obtained enlightenment and has entered into nirvâna: a Bodhisattva, on the other hand, is in the older sense an aspirant to Buddhahood, like Gotama before his enlightenment: in the later sense he is such an aspirant who deliberately renounces nirvâna in order that he may help and instruct mankind. But it will be noticed that Śâkyamuni in the Lotus and Amitâbha in the Sûtras which treat of his paradise are indubitably Buddhas, yet their very essence is benevolent activity and they seem to belong to the same class as Avalokiteśvara, who indeed is Amitâbha's assistant. One dogmatic

[1] Especially the Prajñâpâramitâ-hridaya-sûtra. See above, p. 83.

[2] e.g. Dîg. Nik., xx and xxxii.

[3] 佛 Butsu; 菩薩 Bosatsu.

explanation is that, though a Buddha may have passed beyond all things mundane and human so far as his Dharmakâya is concerned, yet his Sambhogakâya remains as an immaterial but still radiant and beneficent presence for the help and instruction of mankind. The reader must remember that there is in the Mahâyâna no one authoritative statement of these mysteries analogous to the Athanasian Creed. Every important sûtra uses formulæ of its own. Thus it is asserted that for those who have true intuition there is no difference between saṃsâra and nirvâna, which is equivalent to saying none between Bodhisattvas and Buddhas. But though in many Far Eastern sects the great Bodhisattvas are for devotional purposes as important as the Buddhas, yet the distinction of nomenclature is, so far as I know, always observed. Some late Tantric works seem to neglect it and to speak, for instance, of Mañjuśrî as a Buddha.[1]

The scriptures of the Mahâyâna constantly describe the Bodhisattvas, like the Buddhas, as hosts of incalculable millions in this and other worlds, but the numbers of those who have any sort of personality are far more modest. The Dharma-sangraha gives a group of eight, obviously those who have been selected for devotional purposes.[2] The Śikshâsamuccaya mentions about twenty, some well known, others merely ancient names though generally connected with some edifying anecdote. In the Far East of the present day the most important figures are (to call them by their Indian names) Maitreya, Avalokiteśvara, Mañjuśrî, and Kshitigarbha. Less popular but still often represented by imposing images are Samantabhadra and Mahâsthâmaprâpta. A group of twenty-five Bodhisattvas (Ni-jū-go Bosatsu) is sometimes depicted in Japanese art, but many of the members have little individuality.

Maitreya[3] is of special importance for the history of doctrine, for he connects the older and newer conceptions of the nature of a Bodhisattva. He is mentioned in the Pali Canon but with few details. All that is said, however, suggests that his career was

[1] A work is quoted called the Jñâna-sattva-manjuśri Âdi-Buddha-sâdhana. What is the meaning of the Tathâgata-guhya sûtra quoted in Śikshâsamuccaya, p. 159, which says that when a Bodhisattva has the Dharmakâya, all beings who touch him are cured of their passions and distress (Tasya dharmakâya-prabhâvitasya Bodhisattvasya)?

[2] Dharmasan., § 12. Maitreya, Gaganagañja, Sammatabhadra, Vajrapâṇi, Mañjuśrî, Sarvanivaraṇavishkambhi, Kshitigarbha, Khagarbha.

[3] Sanskrit Maitreya, Pali Metteyya. 彌勒 pronounced Mi-Li in Chinese, Miroku in Japanese. He is also called Ajita, the unconquered one.

supposed to be closely parallel to Śâkyamuni's own, and to consist of a long series of births in which he followed the arduous ideals of Buddhahood. All branches of Buddhism recognize him, and he is mentioned frequently in the later Pali literature and in such Sanskrit Buddhist texts as the Lalita-vistara and Mahâvastu. Nor is he neglected in the Lotus. He is prominent there as a future Buddha, but receives instruction as befits his position and appeals to Mañjuśrî as one of greater experience.[1] He appears to be represented in the oldest Gandharan sculptures, and about A.D. 400 Fa-hsien saw a celebrated statue of him in Udyana which was considered to be very ancient. There are still temples dedicated to him in Ceylon, but probably his worship was favoured by the Sarvâstivâdins more than by the Theravâdins. It appears to have been prevalent in northern India in the centuries following and probably in those preceding our era and perhaps owed something to Iranian influence, for he is distinctly the Messiah, the Buddha of the future who will restore true religion and virtue. This idea, though not absent in India, never had much life there, whether the destined saviour was regarded as a Buddha or a coming incarnation of Vishṇu, but among Iranians, as among the Jews, an expected liberator and regenerator does seem to have fired the popular imagination. The Chinese pilgrims not only mention statues and sites connected with Maitreya but seem to feel a personal devotion for him and to think of him as occupied in protecting the faith while waiting his own time to appear on earth. He makes revelations, and saints like Kaśyapa, hidden in mountains and absorbed in trance, await his advent.[2] I-Ching speaks and even sings of the joy of meeting him, much as devout Christians look forward to the second coming of Christ, and a temple dedicated to him as an active and benevolent spirit manifesting himself in many forms has been found at Turfan. The prince to whose memory the temple was erected seems to be regarded as one of the manifestations. The Chinese Tripiṭaka contains several works dealing specially with Maitreya,[3] most of which deal with his advent on earth and exhort believers to make themselves worthy of joining the glorious band who will surround him. But one (Nan. 204) treats of him as at present lord of the Tusita heaven where the faithful will be welcomed and

[1] Lotus, chap. i.

[2] Watters's *Yüan Chwang*, i, p. 355 ff.; ii, p. 144.

[3] See Nanjio's Catalogue, Nos. 204 to 208. The earliest translator is Dharmaraksha, A.D. 265–316; the latest I-Ching, A.D. 701.

attended by beautiful nymphs. In Japanese records of the seventh and eighth centuries his images are mentioned and we also hear of the Miroku-ye, a festival celebrated in his honour. But in more recent times his influence seems to have waned. His statues in the Far East are numerous and sometimes gigantic, though less conspicuous in Japan than in neighbouring countries. His position as the Buddha to come is not challenged and some secret societies in China are said to regard him as their patron. Also, as mentioned below, he has undergone a strange transformation as Hotei, one of the gods of luck. But Avalokiteśvara, Mañjuśrî, and Kshitigarbha —or, to call them by their Japanese names, Kwannon, Monju, and Jizō—play a far larger part in popular religion. All three have certain characteristics which they share to some extent with Amitâbha. The Pali scriptures contain no hint of their existence, and, though they are frequently spoken of in Sanskrit Buddhist literature, they appear irregularly and are not always mentioned when we should expect it. Their origin is most obscure : even the meaning of their names is not clear. It is plausible to suppose that they come from Persia or Central Asia, but positive proof is lacking. They are not connected with history or mythology and most of the anecdotes which have gathered about them are obviously later accretions. Though they are represented with the dress and attributes of Indian deities, they are more like the Amesha Spentas of Zoroastrianism or the Angels of Jewish tradition ; they are not personifications of natural forces but pure and benevolent spirits, devoid of passion and ambition and desirous only of doing good.

Avalokiteśvara [1] is undoubtedly the personification of divine mercy and as such is called Mahâkaruṇa, the Great Compassionate One. He is also known as Lokanâtha or Lokeśvara, Lord of the World, and Padmapâṇi, or Lotus-handed. The earlier images represent him as a young prince wearing a jewelled head-dress, usually surmounted by a small image of Amitâbha,[2] and carrying in his left hand a red lotus, while his right is extended in the gesture known as charity (varamudra). The name Avalokiteśvara is not easy to explain. One traditional rendering is the Lord who looks down (from heaven), but in form avalokita is clearly a passive participle meaning "looked at or observed". Hence the title has

[1] 觀音 Chinese Kuan-Yin. Japanese Kwannon or Kannon.

[2] The Amitâyurdhyâna S., 19, says that he bears on his head a crown in which there is a transformed Buddha standing 25 yojanas high, but the name is not mentioned.

been explained as referring to the small image in the diadem, which looks down on the figure wearing it. But the image is not specially characteristic of Avalokiteśvara and no particular importance seems to attach to it.[1] The common Chinese translations Kuan-Shih-Yin or Kuan-Yin, the deity who looks upon the region of voices, or simply voices, make one suspect that the translator found in the latter part of Avalokiteśvara not the word *îśvara*, Lord, but *svara*, sound,[2] and it has been suggested [3] that the original title, invented not in India but in Central Asia, was Avalokita-svara—supposed to mean one aware of imploring voices. This does not seem to be a very classical form, but they may have used queer Sanskrit in Central Asia. It is noticeable that the Lotus [4] sometimes uses the form Mañjuśvâra instead of Mañjuśrî and consecrates a whole chapter to a Bodhisattva called Gadgadasvara. But if the name is to be regarded as a genuine Indian word, I would suggest that it means Lord of the World and is parallel to the titles Lokeśvara and Lokanâtha, *avalokita* meaning that which is looked at, hence the visible universe.[5] If this is so, the well-known names Kwan-Yin and Kwannon will be simply mistranslations and the scholarly Hsüan-Tsang may have purposely used another rendering. The Lotus in chap. xxiv actually raises the question why Avalokiteśvara is so called, but unfortunately the explanation is not very lucid, being to the effect that it is because he saves from danger all who think of him. Possibly the author interpreted Avalokita as meaning he who is beheld or looked to by those in trouble, but as emphasis is laid on his wonderful power to save everywhere, Lord of the whole world would be equally appropriate.

The worship of Avalokiteśvara is mentioned by the three Chinese pilgrims, but his name seems not to occur in the Lalita-vistara, Divyâvadâna, Jâtakamâla, or in any of the works attributed to Aśvaghosha. He is mentioned once in the Śikshâsamuccaya, which also quotes a work called Avalokiteśvara-Vimoksha, but he has not the prominence which we might expect. In the larger Sukhâvatî-

[1] Also Sanskrit Dictionaries indicate that the base of avalokita and similar words means to look at or observe, rather than to look down.

[2] But Hsüan-Tsang's rendering is Kwan-Tzŭ-Tsai, meaning apparently the Seeing and Self-existent One, but containing no reference to sound. The Tibetan rendering is Spyan-ras-gzigs, meaning he who sees with bright eyes.

[3] Mironov, in *J.R.A.S.*, 1927, p. 241 ff.

[4] Chap. i, verses 50 and 56. Chap. xxiii.

[5] It is noticeable that the shorter form, Avalokita, though used by Europeans, is rare in Sanskrit. The Bodhicaryâvatâra, ii, 51, has Avalokitan nâtham.

vyûha[1] he is called son of the Buddha and is mentioned in connection with Mahâsthâmaprâpta. It is the light of these two beings which causes Paradise to shine with glory. In the Amitâyurdhyâna-sûtra, as mentioned above, this idea is greatly developed and Paradise is represented as ruled by a Triad, the Buddha Amitâyus and the two Bodhisattvas.

In the first chapter of the Lotus Avalokiteśvara is mentioned after Mañjuśrî as second in the list of Bodhisattvas, but chapter xxiv, which is probably a later addition, is specially devoted to his praises under the name of Samantamukha, he who looks every way or is omnipresent. This chapter is often printed separately and is one of the most popular books of devotion in China and Japan. Three features may be specially noted in this remarkable eulogy. First, Avalokiteśvara is the great saviour of the world. Śâkyamuni solemnly declares that one invocation of his name is as efficacious as invoking a number of Buddhas equal in number to sixty-two thousand times the sands of the river Ganges. He saves those who call upon him from physical danger, from shipwreck, execution, robbers and violence, and also from moral evils such as passion, hatred, and folly. Secondly, he can assume any form[2] for his benevolent purposes, and in order to appeal to different classes of hearers he will preach the law in the guise of a Buddha, a disciple, a Brahman, or any shape human or divine. Thirdly, he grants children to women who worship him. This boon i generally granted by female deities and is interesting as being the first hint of his becoming a goddess. In the long list of his transformations a female shape is not mentioned, though perhaps the invocation[3] to his beautiful eyes, full of pity and kindness, has a somewhat feminine ring about it. Also the Śikshâsamuccaya[4] states that another Bodhisattva, Âkâśagarbha, appears in the form of a maiden. But against such hints one must set the dogmatic statements that

[1] Sukhâv.-vyûha, § 31 and § 34. The latter passage is not very plain, but the meaning apparently is that they were both inhabitants of this world and then were reborn in Sukhâvatî.

[2] Even in Indian iconography and without counting Far Eastern forms Avalokiteśvara is extremely polymorphic. Benoytosh Bhattacharyya (*Indian Buddhist Iconography*) gives fifteen main types of his images and illustrates 108 more from a Vihara in Nepal.

[3] Lotus, xxiv, verse 20.

[4] Śikshâsam., chap. iv, page 64 of text, quoting the Âkâśagarbha-sûtra. The Karaṇḍa-vyûha says that in order to impart true knowledge he assumes all forms, including those of father and mother. Mâtâpitṛivaineyânâm sattvânam mâtṛipitṛirûpena dharmam deśayati.

there are no women in paradise,[1] and no clear proof has been adduced that Avalokiteśvara was regarded as feminine in either India or Tibet.[2] It is therefore remarkable to find that in China, Japan, Korea, and Annam the female nature is unquestioned, and that it is only in ancient images and pictures that the Bodhisattva is represented as a young man. Still, in whatever shape he is represented, Avalokiteśvara or Kwannon is not a sexual deity like Kṛishṇa or Durgâ: there is nothing erotic about the figure, be it male or female: the gracious face is inspired solely by compassion and benevolence: it is not even interested in human love.

The precise time and circumstances in which Avalokiteśvara became a goddess are unknown.[3] The artists of the early T'ang dynasty seem to have generally represented him as a young man, and female figures of him are not common until the Sung period. It was under this dynasty that a monk called Pu-Ming published in 1102 the story of Kuan-Yin's earthly life, which did much to popularize her worship. It is a religious romance and a product of Chinese fancy which owes nothing to Indian tradition. There was a tendency in both China and Annam to identify Kuan-Yin with ancient native heroines, for Faery Queens and magic maidens had always appealed to the popular taste. There was also probably some confusion between Kuan-Yin and Hâritî and also Târâ. The latter is an Indian goddess with obvious analogies to the Śâktis of Śiva. Tantric Buddhism, which assigned female counterparts to the various Buddhas and Bodhisattvas, associated her with Avalokiteśvara and, like him, she assumes many forms. She is mentioned by Hsüan-Tsang,[4] but except in Lamaist temples is not an object of popular worship in China. It is possible, however, that the association of Avalokiteśvara with a goddess in Tantric literature may have facilitated his own change of sex. But Kuan-Yin is not an adaptation of Târâ. She is undoubtedly the Bodhisattva who has a share in Amitâbha's paradise and who is

[1] It was one of Amitâbha's vows that women calling upon him should be born in his Paradise, but as men. See Sukhâv.-vyûha, § 8, 34. Even the Lotus in the chapter quoted (xxiv, verse 31) says: "There (i.e. in the Paradise ruled by Amitâbha and Avalokiteśvara) no women are to be found." See, too, Lotus, xxii, towards the end, for women being reborn in Paradise as men.

[2] I confess that the explanation which regards the words mani-padme in the celebrated formula as a feminine vocative seems to me very plausible.

[3] See for some further observations my *Hinduism and Buddhism*, vol. ii, p. 17.

[4] See Watters, *Yüan Chwang*, vol. ii, pp. 105, 107, 171.

extolled in chapter xxiv of the Lotus—that is, Avalokiteśvara himself.[1]

Everything connected with this great being is multiform and protean. Even while listening to a prayer he seems to turn into something else. Kuan-Yin, or in the Japanese form of the name, Kwannon, is like his other aspects, polymorphic, and gives rise to a whole gallery of wonderful shapes which naturally become for the ignorant different personalities, like the many Madonnas worshipped by the peasantry in Russia. I shall deal with them later, for in the main they are products of Japanese imagination rather than of Indian tradition.

Mention should perhaps be made of Potala or Potalaka,[2] a sacred mountain where Avalokiteśvara is supposed to dwell. The name occurs in the most various localities: it was borne by two mountains in India, one in the south and one near the mouth of the Indus: in later times it was given to the palace of the Grand Lama in Lhasa and to another Lamaist building at Jehol in North China, and it reappears in the sacred island of P'u-t'o near Ningpo. But it is sad to have to confess that, like so many things connected with this subject, its origin is most obscure.[3] The Japanese have legends which relate how images of Kwannon were miraculously wafted to their shores from Potala "in the southern seas", and the temple at Nachi in Kishū, which is the first of the thirty-three places sacred to Kwannon, is called Fudaraku-ji.

Mañjuśrī,[4] the second great Bodhisattva, offers many resemblances to Avalokiteśvara, but benevolent as he is (and benevolence is the essential nature of a Bodhisattva) he is the personification of wisdom and intellect rather than of compassion. It is for this that he has in his hands the sword of knowledge and a book, and a figure from Java (now in the British Museum) which represents him as bearing these emblems is one of the most beautiful products of Eastern art. Even Tantric Buddhism is chary of associating him

[1] The Japanese show a certain inclination to think of the Divine Nature as feminine. Shintō recognizes the Sun-goddess and many others. In a very different order of ideas Hōnen says that Amida has "all the deep sympathy of a compassionate mother" (Coates and Ishizuka, p. 437).

[2] 補陀落 Potalaka. Japanese, Fudaraku.

[3] Hsüan-Tsang locates it in Malakuta but apparently did not visit it. See Watters, *Yüan Chwang*, vol. ii, pp. 228–232. It is mentioned in one version of the Kegon-sûtra (Nanjio, No. 88, chap. 68), but the earlier version (Nanjio, No. 87) calls it Kōmei (Kuang-Ming).

[4] 文殊.

with female companions, but the representations of Prajñâ-pâramitâ, that is, the scripture of that name personified as a goddess, are practically replicas of his images.

He has much the same history in literature as Avalokiteśvara, being unknown to the Pali scriptures and such Sanskrit works as the Lalita-vistara. But even in the earlier Mahayanist sûtras he assumes great prominence, and the Chinese pilgrims mention his worship. In the Lotus he is introduced at the head of the Bodhisattvas and is styled the Prince Royal (Kumârabhûta), a title which he also receives in the Lesser Sukhâvatî-vyûha, apparently because it is his duty to see to the preservation of the true Faith in the interval between two Buddhas. The Lotus also recounts how he gives instruction to Maitreya and how he once visited the depths of the sea and converted the daughter of the king of the Nâgas. He is the principal interlocutor in many important sûtras, for instance, the Yuima-kyō or Instruction to Vimalakîrti,[1] which is very popular in Japan, and the Chinese Tripiṭaka contains several works composed in his honour, some of which must be of respectable antiquity.[2] He is mentioned more frequently than any other Bodhisattva in the Śikshâsamuccaya, which concludes with a remarkable prayer to him as " sorrow's physician, the giver of the feast of happiness, by whom in every way we live ".[3]

The name Mañjuśrî is somewhat strange, but even in Vedic Sanskrit there are forms like Agniśrî and Kshatraśrî. The variants Mañjunâtha, Mañjuśvara, and Mañjughosha are also found. But the use of the word Mañju, sweet or charming, as applied to the spirit of transcendental wisdom, does not seem very appropriate and one is tempted to seek for some other derivation of the name in the languages of Central Asia. The Hindus themselves were disposed to connect him with China, but traditions to this effect must be used with caution, for they are all late. I-Ching[4] is the first to tell us that the Indians believed that Mañjuśrî came from China, but the earlier pilgrims Hsüan-Tsang and Fa-Hsien, though they speak of his worship, do not mention any such belief, and since it is a point which would have interested Chinese authors and readers,

[1] Vimalakîrttinirdeśa. Nanjio, Nos. 144–7, 149, 181.

[2] e.g. the Ratnakaraṇḍa-vyûha (N., 168, 169) translated in A.D. 270 and the Mañjuśrî-vikrîdita sûtra in A.D. 313.

[3] He is also mentioned several times in the Bodhicaryâvatâra, especially in Book X.

[4] See Takakusu's translation, p. 136.

their silence is remarkable. Clearly when I-Ching made his pilgrimage (671–695) the idea that Mañjuśrî came from China had become familiar,[1] but by that time China had become celebrated as a Buddhist centre and the visits of distinguished Chinese Buddhists may have created the impression that it was a haunt of Bodhisattvas and Tantric adepts. One form of the goddess Târâ is called Mahâcînatârâ,[2] but it has no Chinese characteristics and the name seems to have been used simply to give a spice of exotic romance. But though the traditions about the connection of Mañjuśrî with China seem to be late and imaginative, they may possibly be based on the forgotten knowledge that he was originally introduced into India by the Kushans or some other invading tribe. On the one hand, when he first appears, for instance in the Lotus, his position is assured and there is no hint that he is a newcomer whose presence needs any explanation: on the other he has, like most Bodhisattvas, a certain pure and abstract quality, an aloofness from sex and mythology, which seem to dissociate him from native Indian deities like Kṛishṇa and recall the Amesha-Spentas of Persia.

The later stories [3] connect him definitely with the mountain of Wu-T'ai-Shan in the province of Shansi, rendered in Sanskrit as Pancaśirsha, or Pancaśikha, and still covered with temples erected in his honour, the oldest of which dates from the end of the fifth century. The Svayambhû Purâṇa relates that when residing there he became aware that the Âdi-Buddha, the original essence of all Buddhas, had manifested itself in the form of a flame rising from a lotus on the waters of a lake which then filled the valley of Nepal. Accompanied by his disciples and by the King of China who was called Dharmâkara, he set out to adore the miraculous flame and, finding that the water rendered approach difficult, cleft the mountain barrier to the south with his sword and drained the valley. He then erected several buildings, made Dharmâkara King of Nepal and returned home, where he obtained the divine form of a Bodhisattva. Some have treated this legend as a reminiscence of the introduction of Chinese culture into Nepal, but the story is late, for the Svayambhû Purâṇa in its present form is not earlier than the sixteenth

[1] Japanese tradition says that the Indian Bodhisena who arrived at Nara in 735 began his pilgrimage by going to China to find Mañjuśrî.

[2] Benoytosh Bhattacaryya, *Indian Buddhist Iconography*, p. 77.

[3] Found in the Svayambhû Purâṇa and supported by the text appended to various miniatures.

century. Earlier accounts do not suggest that there is any connection between Mañjuśrî and Nepal or that he is a recently deified hero, for in the Lotus he is accepted as the chief of the Bodhisattvas and is appealed to as one who has long experience of the teaching of many Buddhas in the past. Still, it cannot be denied that in later times there was a widespread impression that he had been active in China and the lands to the west of it. He was said to have been incarnate in the monk Vairocana who introduced Buddhism into Khotan [1] and in the Tibetan reformer Atîśa. In A.D. 824 a Tibetan envoy was sent to ask the Chinese Court for an image of Mañjuśrî and the Grand Lamas recognized that he was incarnate in the Emperor, being influenced perhaps in later times by the name Manchu.

Kshitigarbha [2] makes his appearance in Sanskrit literature later than the other great Bodhisattvas and does not seem to have attained much importance on Indian soil at any period. In China and Japan, however, under the names of Ti-Tsang and Jizō [3] he became a most popular deity. He is not mentioned in the Lotus nor, so far as I know, in any of the great Mahayanist sûtras. But the Dharma-sangraha includes him among the eight great Bodhisattvas, he is invoked in the Bodhicaryâvatâra, and a work called the Kshitigarbha-sûtra is several times quoted in the Śikshâsamuccaya. The Chinese Tripiṭaka [4] contains books composed in his honour, but the earliest translation of them was made between A.D. 397 and 439.

The name seems to mean Earth-womb or Earth-storehouse and he is often coupled with a more shadowy double called Âkâśagarbha or Kha-garbha.[5] The original meaning of the title is not very plain, but it was interpreted to mean that he is Lord of the nether world. In China especially he plays a great part in ceremonies for

[1] See Watters, *Yüan Chwang*, 12, 296, 300.

[2] In *Ost-Asiat. Ztsft.*, 1913–15, Visser has published a most interesting monograph on this Bodhisattva and on the strange transformations which he has undergone in various countries.

[3] Ti-Tsáng 地藏 is a literal Chinese translation of Kshitigarbha. The same characters are read in Japanese pronunciation as Jizō.

[4] Nanjio, Nos. 64, 65, and 1003.

[5] Though Âkâśagarbha, or Kokūzō 虛空藏, has not become a popular deity like his counterpart, several works in the Tripiṭaka are written in his honour (Nanjio, 67–70) and his statue may be sometimes seen in Japan at the right hand of Śâkyamuni or Vairocana. Kōbō Daishi is said to have regarded him as his personal protector. In some forms of Ryōbu-Shintō he is identified with the deity of Mt. Asama. See Anesaki, *History of Japanese Religion*, plate ix, fig. C.

the welfare of the dead, and large temples often contain special halls dedicated to him. He has vowed to deliver all creatures from hell: he visits them in their places of suffering and endeavours to procure their release. He is even said to suffer in their stead. In Japan he is the special protector of dead children. But his benevolent activities have many sides. The earth was often thought of as a goddess and Kshitigarbha has some feminine traits. In previous births he is said to have been twice a woman: in Japan he was identified with a mountain goddess and he helps women in labour. He is also a guardian of roads and is sometimes represented as a militant priest on horseback. But the commonest images are those which show him as a monk, with staff in hand and shaven head. Frequently he is represented by six images signifying that he multiplies his benevolent personality and helps beings in all the six states of existence.

Samantabhadra, or Fugen,[1] is mentioned in the Dharma-sangraha and is the hero of chapter xxvi of the Lotus, where he vows to undertake the special duty of protecting those who follow the doctrine there expounded. He describes himself as riding on a white elephant with six tusks and he imparts a talismanic formula which averts all danger. He is the patron saint of Mount Ōmei in China,[2] with which he is associated much as Mañjuśrî is with Wu-t'ai-shan. In Japan his image is not unfrequently to be seen on the right hand of Śâkyamuni's and he has an honourable place in Buddhist tradition, though at present he may not have many worshippers. For instance, he appeared to Hōnen at the beginning of his career. A Japanese priest told me that Fugen and Jizō are considered to be the same, but I have found no evidence of such an identity in India.

As mentioned above, Mahâsthâmaprâpta[3] is described in both the Larger Sukhâvatî-vyûha and the Amitâyurdhyâna-sûtra as one of the spirits who administer Amitâbha's paradise. The latter work instructs its readers to meditate on him and asserts that in appearance he is as glorious as Avalokiteśvara. The two, no doubt,

[1] 普賢 Chinese P'u-Hsien, Japanese Fugen.

[2] For an interesting account of this sacred mountain, see Johnston, *From Peking to Mandalay*.

[3] 大勢至. Chinese Ta-Shi-Chih, Japanese Dai-sei-shi. He is said to be the Arhat Maudgalyâyana deified. For mention of him in the Amida-sûtras see Sukhâv.-vyûha, § 34, and Amit.-Dhyâna S., § 19. The Lotus mentions him and Avalokiteśvara together in chap. i, but says nothing about Sukhâvatî.

are not equal in popular esteem, but Seishi, as he is commonly called in Japan, is constantly represented in art as attending on Amitâbha with Kwannon, one on either hand, and with them he visits the deathbeds of the faithful and welcomes the dying to paradise. The great temple of Zenkōji at Nagano is dedicated to Amida, Kwannon, and Daiseishi. His name alludes to strength and he gives strength, but his special attributes are not very clear, and though a chapter of the Lotus (xix) is addressed to him, it does not tell us much about his personality. According to Japanese tradition he was incarnate in Hōnen.

The great beings of whom we have been treating are often spoken of as celestial or superhuman Bodhisattvas, and rightly, for, as they appear in most Mahayanist sûtras, they seem to be inhabitants of another world, or in the language of Christian theology, angels. If their Iranian origin can be proved, this conception of their nature may be the oldest. But it must be remembered that, according to Buddhist theory, whether ancient or modern, Hina- or Mahayanist, Bodhisattvas and Buddhas are merely the perfection and full development of humanity. Even Śâkyamuni and Amitâbha, if considered not as the Dharmakâya but as individual existences having relations with this world, attained their present position by the good resolutions which they formed as human beings and maintained through a long series of births. In the principal Sanskrit sûtras there is little disposition to dwell on the previous existences of Avalokiteśvara, Mañjuśrî, and the other great Bodhisattvas, but occasional references show that they were believed to have taken vows and dedicated themselves through incalculable ages to the salvation of the human race. The Far East was naturally inclined to euhemerism, to turn great men into deities, and if there was no ancient legend about the human origin of a god, to invent some edifying romance. In this way arose many stories which have no precise prototypes in India about the kindness and unselfishness shown by Kwannon and Jizō in other existences. But neither Chinese nor Japanese seem to have had much taste for a class of literature which was very popular in India and Ceylon, the Jâtaka stories which tell of the Buddha's previous births as an animal.

## 4

As already mentioned, the Mahâyâna brought together the human and divine.[1] It dilates on the numbers, power, and splendour of the heavenly host in language which goes far beyond anything which can be found in the Pali Nikâyas, but at the same time it not only assures the faithful that they *can* become Bodhisattvas and Buddhas but bids them try to do so and to begin here and now.[2]

The ideal of the Bodhisattva takes the place of the older ideal of the Arhat and the moral point of view undergoes a corresponding change: the goal is not personal and individual salvation, but the salvation and happiness of all living beings. Nor does this career, though strenuous, involve a monastic life. The Ratnakaraṇḍa-sûtra [3] says expressly that even a man of the world may become a Bodhisattva, that is, a devout person who tries to perform to the full the duties which religion prescribes. The manual of Śântideva describes the rules of life and faith which he who desires to become a Bodhisattva should follow. The neophyte, when first conceiving the thought of obtaining Bodhi or supreme enlightenment, offers adoration to the Buddhas and Bodhisattvas, surrenders himself to them unreservedly and takes refuge in them.[4] He confesses his sins and feels a sympathetic joy in the good actions of all living beings: he makes over to others whatever merits he may possess, he gives himself and all his possessions as an offering for the salvation of the

[1] Eckhart is quoted as having said, "Our Lord says to every living soul: I became man for you. If you do not become God for me you do me wrong."

[2] The idea of becoming a Buddha is not entirely unknown in Ceylon, where the following prayer is in use: Sîla-nekhamma-paññâdin pûretva sabbapâramin Pârami-sikharam-patva, Buddho hessam anuttaro.

A devout Sinhalese Buddhist told me that it is usual to close all prayers with a mental aspiration to become (1) an Arhat, (2) a Pratyeka Buddha, (3) or a Buddha, but that the first aspiration is the commonest. It will be noticed that the word Bodhisattva does not occur.

[3] Quoted in the Śikshâsamuccaya, p. 6. Ratnakaraṇḍaṣûtrâcca prithagjano'pi Bodhisattva iti jñâyate. Cf., too, the same work's quotation from the Ugraparipricchâ given above, p. 96.

[4] The old formula of the Hînayâna is preserved. Bodhicaryâvatâra, ii, 48. Adyaiva śaraṇam yâmi jagannâthân. The formula of self-surrender is found, ibid., ii, 8. Dadâmi câtmânam jinebhyaḥ, sarvena sarvam ca tadâtmajebhyaḥ: Parigraham me kurutâgrasattvâḥ: yushmâsu dâsatvam upaimi bhaktyâ. "I give myself to the Jinas and their sons entirely and without reserve. Take possession of me, Great Beings. In devotion I make myself your slave."

whole world [1] and makes a vow (praṇidhâna) to win enlightenment for the good of all. He has now become a " son of Buddha ", and the manual proceeds to describe the virtues (pâramitâ) which he must practise—self-sacrifice, morality, patience, energy, meditation, and knowledge [2] or intuition.

Indians love systematic classification, and the career of a Bodhisattva was divided into ten stages catalogued with great elaboration in several works which describe the aspirant's progress from ordinary humanity through a long series of births until he attains complete enlightenment. In reading a work like Asanga's account of this wonderful spiritual development, the student of the Pali scriptures will feel that he has wandered into unfamiliar regions, yet in many respects it is clear that this new theory has grown out of the old rules and promises dealing with the religious life and its happy culmination. The real change is the emphatic substitution of an unselfish and altruistic ideal—the salvation of the world—for the old aim of personal peace and happiness.[3] But the Pâramitâs, or virtues, appear already in the later Pali literature. The Cariyâpiṭaka, which is practically a small collection of Jâtakas, is divided into three sections illustrating three of them, and the Nidânakathâ makes the future Buddha declare, when making his vow, that he will practise no less than ten.[4] Surrender of oneself to the Buddha is mentioned in the Pali commentaries,[5] and even the division of the Bodhisattva's career into numbered stages has a parallel in the Hînayâna. Progress in the holy life is there measured in terms of the obstacles overcome or, in technical language, of the fetters broken. The aspirant who has broken three is called

[1] Bodhicaryâvatâra, iii, 10. Âtmabhâvâṃs tathâ bhogân sarva-try-adva-gatam śubham Nirapekshas tyajâmy esha sarva sattvârtha-siddhaye.

[2] Dâna, śîla, kshânti, vîrya, dhyâna, and prajñâ. Dâna, though meaning liberality, is used like câga in the sense of readiness to give life and everything else for others, and hence is equivalent to self-sacrifice. Special chapters are devoted to the other five paramitas but not to dâna, apparently because it is assumed from the beginning and is the impulse which prompts the original vow.

[3] Even in the Pali Piṭakas the altruistic ideal seems to be implied though it is not clearly enunciated, for a Sammâsambuddha like Gotama is invariably represented as superior to a Paccekabuddha who has the same knowledge but keeps it to himself and does not preach.

[4] Dâna, sîla, nekkhamma, viriya, khânti, paññâ, adhitthâna, sacca, mettâ, upekkhâ.

[5] For Âtmabhâvaniyatana, surrender of oneself to the Buddha, compare Sumangalavilasini, i, 231 (on the Samaññaphala S.). Ajjâdim katvâ aham attânam Buddhassa niyatemi, Dhammassa, sanghassati evam Buddhâdînam attapariccajanam, etc.

Sota-âpanna, he who has entered the current, that is the stream of salvation which will bear him to nirvâna in not more than seven births. The Sakadâgâmin will be born only once more in this world and the Anâgâmin, or he who does not return, also once only but in a Brahmâ world, while the Arhat, or he who has broken all the bonds, attains nirvâna here and is not subject to rebirth.[1]

It is not clear to what extent the stages in a Bodhisattva's career were regarded as practical realities. Though Śântideva sets up a high ideal, he distinctly writes for ordinary human beings, but in Asanga we seem to leave this world and to soar among Buddhas in other spheres. Was it usual or possible to say that a living person had reached a particular stage? There seems to be no evidence on which we can decide, but at any rate in Japan the ten stages are not a part of practical religion, though in the Zen sect the Kō-an, or problems which students have to solve, are divided into classes according to their proficiency. The title of Bodhisattva (Bosatsu) is freely bestowed on eminent churchmen of the past and may be used colloquially of a generous person, just as we say he is a perfect saint or an angel. But the aspiration to become a Buddha has lost most of its meaning owing to the politeness of the Japanese language. The dead are habitually spoken of as Buddhas (hotoke)[2] and to become a Buddha (jōbutsu) is merely a pious expression for dying, much like the inscription "entered into his rest" on a tombstone, and has no dogmatic significance.

But the aspiration to become a Bodhisattva implies aims and ideals which are still living and influence religion. One is the duty of treating others as we would wish to be treated ourselves, which is common as a theory (though not as a practice) in many creeds. To make no difference between oneself and others is a well-known Indian precept among both Brahmans and Buddhists.[3] Śântideva says[4] with beautiful simplicity: "I ought to alleviate others' suffering, because it is suffering like my own. I ought to show kindness to others because they are beings like myself." This

[1] Compare, too, the list of six happy destinies enumerated at the end of Maj. Nik., xxii.

[2] The expression is probably due to the analogy of Shintō in which the dead are said to become Kami, an extremely vague word.

[3] See e.g. Mahâbhârata, xiii, 5571, where the proper rule of action is said to be to look on one's neighbour as oneself (âtmaupamyena). Cf. the Sigâlovâda-sutta, 31—a man should minister to his friends (samânattatâya) by treating them as he treats himself.

[4] Bodhicary., viii, 94.

motive, the pursuit of others' happiness at the risk of sacrificing one's own, is the moral side of the doctrine of anattâ and is insisted on throughout the ethical literature of the Mahâyâna. But side by side with it we find held up another motive which is new and not common in Indian theology. Since Buddhas and Bodhisattvas are animated by love for all and by the desire to help all, they rejoice when living creatures are happy and grieve when they suffer. Hence unkindness and want of consideration for others is an offence against these merciful beings, nay, it causes them actual pain. On the other hand, unselfishness and particularly the transfer of one's own merits to others gives them pleasure. Śântideva discourses eloquently on the duty of pleasing our Masters (svâminaḥ) and the sin of making them feel distress.[1]

Beautiful as the moral ideals of the Mahâyâna often are, they are sometimes threatened by a danger which is common in Indian religious systems and which seems to us to arise from a certain want of common sense and proportion, a tendency to exaggeration and extravagance which does not shrink from immorality, extreme asceticism, and even suicide, if such consequences seem to follow from exclusive attention to any one principle. Though the Buddha himself protested against this fault,[2] his followers have not always escaped it. The doctrine that a Bodhisattva will go to hell and suffer there instead of the unhappy inhabitants is perhaps justified by the theory of the transfer of merit. If we can make over our good deeds to others, parity of reasoning suggests that we can accept the responsibility for their sins. But there is something shocking in the idea of powerful and benevolent beings suffering the torments of the damned, and we read with pleasure other passages which state that they descend even into Avîci as gaily as wild geese into a lotus pond.[3] But what is to be said of the proposition that a Bodhisattva may commit sins if he thereby increases the happiness of others ? This astounding doctrine is clearly enunciated in the Bodhicaryâvatâra and illustrated in the Śikshâsamuccaya.[4] The latter work quotes a story from the Upaya-Kauśalya-sûtra

[1] See especially Bodhicary., vi, 119–124.

[2] In formulating the Path he recommended the middle way and the avoidance of extremes. Both self-indulgence and self-torture are ignoble. Cf. Maj. Nik., lvii, about the fakirs who imitated the ways of dogs and oxen.

[3] Bodhicary., viii, 107, and Śikshâsam., p. 360.

[4] Bodhicary., v, 84. Evam buddhvâ parârtheshu bhavet satatam utthitaḥ : Nishiddham apy anujñâtam kṛipâlor arthadarśinaḥ. The explanations and quotations will be found in pages 167–8 of the Śikshâsam. (Bendall's edition).

which relates how a young man who had kept a vow of chastity through many births broke it to make a certain lady happy, and it emphatically asserts that if a Bodhisattva sees that he can cause a single being to acquire merit at the cost of himself committing a sin which will make him burn in hell for long ages, it is his duty to commit that sin. The Ratnamegha is cited as saying that it is permissible to kill a man who is intending to commit a deadly sin and thus to prevent him. "And so," is the conclusion, "when there is an opportunity of doing good to others, a sin arising from passion is declared to be no sin."

Somewhat dangerous, too, is the efficacy ascribed to confession, that is, not a public avowal made before a congregation as contemplated by the older discipline, but merely an acknowledgment of one's sins made in the course of private devotions before the Buddhas. These merciful saviours desire nothing better than to forgive and grant peace of mind. Confession made before them secures pardon of even deadly sins, including parricide.[1]

It is sad to find that one of the supplementary chapters of the Lotus[2] countenances religious suicide and self-inflicted tortures which, though condemned by Gotama, are only too common in Hinduism. It relates how in ancient times the Bodhisattva Bhaishajya-râja burnt his own body in honour of the Buddha. Such self-immolation is commended as the highest form of worship, and we are told that to burn a toe, or finger, or a limb at the shrine of the Tathâgata is more meritorious than to give up a kingdom. Subsequently cauterizing the head became part of the ordination ceremony and still is so in China.[3] I-Ching discusses at considerable length and reprobates the practice of burning the body and limbs. He comments on such Hindu customs as drowning oneself in the Ganges, but justly observes that the Buddha condemned them and that we are "disregarding his noble teaching" if we burn our bodies.[4] The good sense of the Japanese seems to have made them incline to the same opinion, but it is said that attractive nuns sometimes brand their faces in order to spoil their beauty.

[1] See Śikshâsam., p. 169, where the formula of confession (deśanâ) is given and the names of thirty-five Buddhas, beginning with Śâkyamuni, who are sometimes called the Buddhas of confession.

[2] Lotus, chap. xxii.

[3] See, too, De Groot, *Code du Mahayana en Chine*, p. 228, and the article of MacGowan (*Chinese Recorder*, 1888) there cited for cases of self-cremation in China.

[4] I-Ching, *A Record of Buddhist Practices*, trans. Takakusu, chaps. xxxviii–xl.

## 5

In addition to Buddhas and Bodhisattvas a multitude of images may be found in the temples of the older Japanese sects, especially in the neighbourhood of Kyōto and Nara. Many of them have a definite connection with Buddhist tradition. They are guardians of the faith or attendants on higher powers, or disciples, or spiritual beings with which the Mantrayâna, or Shingon sect, peopled the spheres. But some are simply Indian deities unknown to the Piṭakas, whose worship is conducted under Buddhist auspices, though in the strict sense it can hardly be said to be Buddhist.[1] With very few exceptions all these deities and personages are of Indian origin, though Japanese attributes and legends have collected round some of them. For a long period Buddhist priests were in charge of Shintō temples, but the reformers of 1868 put an end to this arrangement, and while it lasted it meant that Buddhist emblems were introduced into Shintō shrines rather than vice versa. Shintō used no images: its deities were identified with Buddhas and Bodhisattvas but did not as a rule take their places beside them in the same company.

Of guardian deities the principal are the Two Kings and the Four Deva Kings.[2] The former are represented by two gigantic figures of ferocious aspect which are to be found at the outer gate of most Japanese temples. They are sometimes described as Brahmâ and Indra, but their more correct designations are Kongō-Rikishi and Misshaku-Rikishi.[3] Perhaps they were originally two figures of Vajrapâṇi. The Four Kings are generally placed in an inner court and are somewhat similar figures who hold weapons in their hands and trample demons underfoot. They are the regents of the four quarters and in the Nikâyas are represented as paying homage to the Buddha.[4] It is said that Amoghavajra, who was

[1] It is not, however, contrary to Buddhism to honour such deities. See above, Chap. II, pp. 57–8.

[2] 仁王 Ni-ō: 四天王 Shi-tennō. The names of the two Kings are 金剛力士 Kongō-Rikishi and 密跡力士 Mishaku-Rikishi. The four Kings presiding over the points of the compass are 持國 Jikoku or Dhṛitarâshtra, the East: 廣目 Kōmoku or Virûpâksha, the South: 增上 Zōjō or Virûdhaka, the West: 多聞 Tamon or Vaiśravana, the North.

[3] See Nanjio, 23, Ratnakûta section, No. 3, which is called in Japanese pronunciation 密跡金剛力士會 Misshaku-Kongō-Rikishi-E.

[4] Dīg. Nik., xx and xxxii, where they are styled Cattaro Mahâraja.

in China between 719 and 774, first introduced the practice of placing their images in temples. But the Nihongi mentions them (though without special reference to their being guardians of temples) in its entries for the year 642 and also records the erection of the temple of Shitennōji in 593. Vaiśravana or Bishamon, the regent of the North, who is often identified with Kuvera, the god of wealth and is likewise regarded as the god of war, is also worshipped independently and has temples of his own. The Hachi-bu-shū,[1] or genii of eight classes, are the Nagas, Yakshas, Kinnaras, Asuras, etc., who are also represented in the Nikâyas as doing homage to the Buddha, either independently or as forming the retinue of the Four Kings. A more special group are the so-called Twelve Generals [2] who are the retainers of the Healing Buddha and correspond to the twelve vows which he made.[3]

More difficult to define are the Myō-ō, a class of deities which originated in the mysteries of the Tantric school, though some of them have a much wider popularity. The name appears to correspond to the Sanskrit Vidyârâja [4] and, like the Two Kings, they are terrible in appearance, but this awful aspect is assumed merely to frighten evildoers and guard the Buddhas and their servants. The best known of the Myō-ō is Fudō,[5] whose name is a translation of Acala, the immovable, a form of Śiva. The great temple of Narita is dedicated to him and burnt offerings form part of his worship.[6] Another is Aizen,[7] also a deity of terrible appearance, though popularly regarded as the god of Love. He appears to be a personification of the Divine Love which embraces the whole Universe and destroys all vulgar passions.

These beings are the product of a special type of religious fancy prevalent in India in the period when late Tantric Buddhism

[1] 八部衆 Hachi-bu-shū.

[2] 十二神將. The story of the twelve vows is related in the 藥師如來本願經 Yao-shih-ju-lai-pên-yuan-ching, Nanjio, 170. See also Nanjio, 171–3.

[3] Near the entrance of Chinese temples there is generally an image of the guardian deity Wei-To, whose name has passed into Japanese as Ita-ten and has become a proverbial expression for a swift runner. But statues of him are not common.

[4] See Przyluski, "Les Vidyârâja: Contribution à l'histoire de la Magic dans les Sectes Mahâyânistes," *B.E.F.E.O.*, 1923, pp. 301–318. He points out that in its oldest use Vidyârâja means the personification of a magic formula.

[5] 不動明王.

[6] They are called Goma, which is the Sanskrit word homa.

[7] 愛染明王 Aizen Myō-ō.

became amalgamated with the worship of Śiva and his consort. Śiva is not said to become incarnate like Vishṇu, but from time to time he shows himself in forms which are generally terrible and is surrounded by fierce attendants with many heads and limbs. In Tibet an excessive love for these strange and horrible shapes often makes a Buddhist temple look like a pandemonium, but the good sense and artistic feeling of the Japanese kept this tendency within bounds and, as a rule when they represent the sterner side of the divine nature, the figures are awe-inspiring rather than monstrous.

As a counterpoise to these well-meaning but alarming guardians of the faith, Japanese temples often contain images of human saints or Rakan (arhats). A group of Śâkyamuni's ten principal disciples may often be seen. It includes, besides the well-known Apostles such as Sâriputta, others such as Furuna (Puṇṇa), Rakora, that is Râhula, the Buddha's son, and Subhûti, who figures in the Diamond Cutter and other Mahayanist sûtras. Statues of the pious layman Yuima, or Vimalakîrti, are also frequent. Groups of sixteen or eighteen may also be found, though not so often as in China. In a few temples, such as the Dairyūji at Nagoya, are images of no less than five hundred Rakan.[1]

The respect paid to Binzuru,[2] or Piṇḍola, seems peculiar to Japan, though the practice of making offerings to him and inviting him to visit a particular temple was known in China and even in India. His image is usually found seated outside temples, for legends tell how he somehow offended against the rules of the order and was banished from the sacred precincts. But according to another story his entry into nirvâna was indefinitely delayed and meanwhile he was charged with the protection of the Church. In Japan he underwent another transformation and somehow came to be regarded as the God of Medicine, and even to be styled a Buddha. Suppliants afflicted with disease rub the corresponding part of his image so that the limbs and features of his statues are often worn away.

In Binzuru, as in Jizō, we seem to find a mixture of an Indian original with native legends, and a similar combination is still more striking in the mysterious deity Kompira,[3] though it is by no means clear that the Indian part of his composite character is the oldest.

[1] This number is also not uncommon in large Chinese temples.

[2] 賓頭盧.

[3] 金比羅.

A great temple dedicated to him stands above the town of the same name in Shikoku and is said to have been built by Kōbō Daishi. It was formerly served by Buddhist priests but has now been transferred to Shintō control. Possibly Kompira, who is specially worshipped by sailors, was an ancien local deity of the sea, but in Buddhist times he was identified with Kumbhîra, who in the Dîgha Nikâya [1] is the presiding deity of Râjagaha and comes to do homage to the Buddha. Later Buddhism made him a spirit in the retinue of Bhaishajyaguru and Shintoists identified him with Susano-ō and other Shintō gods.

Kishi-Mojin [2] is another Indian figure with a curious history. She is the Indian Hâritî, an ogress whom the Buddha converted and cured of her wicked habit of eating children, as is related in the Sarvâstivâdin version of the Vinaya. In one of the later chapters of the Lotus [3] she is represented as appearing before him with other female monsters (Râkshasî), and offering to teach a charm which will protect his disciples against devils, goblins, sorcerers, and other plagues. I-Ching describes how offerings were made to her in Indian monasteries,[4] and Nichiren established the same usage in the institutions of his sect, doubtless on account of the passage in the Lotus. In Japan she has come to be regarded as the special guardian and protectress of children and has perhaps been to some extent confounded with Kwannon.

It is remarkable that Japanese Buddhism has preserved so many Indian figures which are lost or unknown in China. This is illustrated by Kishi-Mojin and also by several Indian deities of whom we hear nothing or very little in Pali literature but who are still worshipped in Japan. Foremost among them is Ganeśa, called Shōten Sama or Kangi-ten,[5] to whom several temples are dedicated, notably one at Ikoma, between Nara and Ōsaka. His images generally consist of two human figures with elephant's heads, wearing long robes and standing face to face with their trunks

[1] Dîg. Nik., xx, 8. Kumbhîro Râjagahıko Vepullassa nivesanam Bhiyyo nam sata-sahassam Yakkhânam payirûpâsati Kumbhîro Râjagahiko so p'âga samitim vanam. The word seems to mean a crocodile.

[2] 鬼子母神. Sometimes called Kishi-Bojin. See Péri's monograph on her in *B.E.F.E.O.*, 1917, pp. 1–101, where the literature about her is collected and translated. The most important works are the Sarvâstivâdin Vinaya, N. 1121, and the Mahâmâyâ-sûtra, N. 380.

[3] Lotus, xxi, near the end.

[4] I-Ching (trans. Takakusu), *Records of Buddhist Practices*, p. 37.

[5] 聖天 or 歓喜天.

on each other's shoulders. They are kept in brass cases, remarkably like the lingakośas which are occasionally found in India and were extensively used in medieval Cambodja. Offerings of food, including saké or alcohol, are spread out before the case and an image of Kwannon is generally worshipped in the same shrine. Ganeśa seems to be unknown in China at the present day except in Lamaist temples, but the Chinese Tripiṭaka contains several sûtras [1] which describe the ritual of his worship. The translations are ascribed to Bodhiruchi, Amoghavajra, and others of about the same period, so that this deity must have been familiar to the Chinese of the eighth century. But it is stated [2] that in A.D. 1017 the Emperor Chên-Tsung issued an edict prohibiting the inclusion in the Tripiṭaka of the sûtra about him in four volumes and the translation of similar works, so that probably his cult was suppressed after this time.

Ganeśa is sometimes called a Bodhisattva,[3] but sometimes under the name of Binayaka seens to be regarded as a power to be dreaded and propitiated. The word (Vinayaka in Sanskrit) really means the remover of obstacles, but in some Buddhist works was understood as meaning a spirit who creates them, though he can also remove them if appeased.[4]

Another Indian deity who has several temples in Japan is Benten or Benzaiten,[5] that is Sarasvatî, the goddess of eloquence and riches, who is also connected with islands as is testified by her shrines at the Shinobazu Pond at Ueno and at Enoshima. A chapter of the Suvarṇaprabhâsottamarâja-sûtra [6] is consecrated to her. Kichijō-ten or Lakshmî, Katen or Agini, that is Agni the God of fire, regarded as a purifier, Suiten or Varuna now become the god of luck, and Kōjin or Rudra [7] all still have worshippers;

[1] The new edition of the Chinese Tripiṭaka published by Takakusu ("Taishō Issaikyō") contains ten of them, Nos. 1266–1275, in vol. xxi, pp. 286–293. Most of them are quite short, but No. 1272 is in four books.

[2] In the Fo-tsu-t'ung-chi of Chih-Pan (Nanjio, No. 1661), pp. 405–6. The sûtra in four volumes, Takakusu, vol. 21, serial No. 1271, authorizes the use of all kinds of flesh (including human flesh) for ritual purposes.

[3] e.g. in Takakusu's Trip., vol. 21, No. 1271.

[4] A work called the Vinayaka-sûtra (Takakusu, vol. 21, No. 1270) says that Maheśvara had 3,000 children, of whom 1,500 on the right hand were benevolent and under the command of Senayaka, an incarnation of Kwannon, whereas 1,500 on the left under Vinayaka were the reverse. But these are late Tantric fancies.

[5] 辯天 or 辯財天.

[6] Nanjio, No. 126.

[7] So according to Takakusu in *The Young East*, 1925, p. 147. But others say that he is Seimen-Kongō, described as a messenger of Indra. He is popularly regarded as the God of the Kitchen.

and in the older temples statues such as Marishi (Marîcî), Light; Nikkō and Gakkō, the Sun and Moon, may sometimes be seen.

Indra, or Taishaku,[1] and Brahmâ, or Bonten,[2] who are constantly mentioned in the Piṭakas as the protectors and respectful assistants of the Buddha and his disciples, are represented by statues, but, so far as I know, temples are not dedicated to them. This honour is, however, accorded to Emma-ō[3] or Yama-raja, the ruler of the Underworld and Judge of the dead. By him stand two attendants who write down and read out the sins of mankind. He, too, is fully recognized in the Nikâyas, for instance, in the celebrated sûtra called the Messengers of the Gods,[4] in which before punishing the sinner who is led before him he asks why he did not attend to the warnings sent to him by Heaven.

The Seven Gods of Luck are a most miscellaneous group of ambiguous position, for though everyone would wish to conciliate them, they hardly belong to serious religion. Daikoku[5] is apparently Mahâkâla, Benten and Bishamon[6] are the deities already mentioned, all three being Indian. Jurōjin and Fukurokuju[7] seem to be of Chinese origin, both genii of Long Life. Ebisu[8] is native Japanese. He carries a fishing rod and a tai fish, and his festival is widely celebrated on the tenth of January. Hotei[9] is a strange transformation of the Bodhisattva Maitreya. He is represented as an enormously fat and hilarious cleric, the tradition being that in China under the Liang Dynasty there was a monk called Pu-Tai whose benevolence caused him to be regarded as an incarnation of the Bodhisattva, though his prosperous appearance made him a subject of popular caricature.[10]

Sometimes a Buddhist and a Hindu deity seem to be combined. Thus we have Batōkwannon,[11] an image of Kwannon with a horse's head set above or even replacing the human head and revered in

[1] 帝釋. [2] 梵天. [3] 閻魔王.

[4] Devadûta-sutta, Maj. Nik., cxxx. For a medieval account of a visit to Emma-ō's Court see the adventures of the priest Jishin Bo Sonei as related in the Heike Monogatari (Sadler's translation, p. 110 ff.).

[5] 大黑.

[6] 辨天 and 毘沙門.

[7] 壽老人 and 福祿壽.

[8] 惠比須. [9] 布袋.

[10] He is the "Laughing Buddha" commonly seen in Chinese temples. Finot says that in Cambodja a similar figure is called Kaccayana, for unknown reasons.

[11] 馬頭觀音.

Japan as the protectress of horses. Hayagrîva is a similar figure of Vishṇu in Brahmanic mythology. But it must be remembered that in India the same myth sometimes reappears in both Buddhist and Brahmanic forms. In the Jâtaka book we read [1] how shipwrecked traders in Ceylon were saved from the attacks of goblins by the Bodhisattva in the form of a flying horse uttering "human speech full of mercy".

The object of the above remarks is merely to show how numerous Indian deities have been introduced into Japan, and I have not attempted to give a guide to the iconography of Japanese Buddhism, a vast and intricate domain, or to describe the various shapes which fancy, learned or popular, has invented for these personages. Something more will be said on this subject in subsequent chapters as occasion offers.

[1] Jâtaka, No. 196. Karuṇâya paribhâvitam mânusibhâsam bhâsati.

# CHAPTER V

## BUDDHISM IN CHINA

### 1

BUDDHISM came to Japan from China, at first through Korea and afterwards by direct intercourse. But even in the earliest period Korea was simply a transmitter. Buddhism there has some slight individuality in art and architecture: in literature and doctrine it has none at all. The Koreans seem to have taken no interest in such matters. What had come from China passed on to Japan practically unchanged. But the temperament of the Chinese was different. Their Buddhism represents a sincere attempt to understand the true doctrine and practice as prevalent in India, but so numerous, intelligent, and artistic a people with ancient ideals and customs of their own were not likely to accept unchanged and without modification a new philosophy and moral system, especially when the country from which the novelties came was distant and not easily accessible. There was continual contact, but it was contact of individuals, not of the masses. The imported religion underwent little change in essentials, but it somehow acquired a foreign dress and manners and, so far as we can distinguish between Indian and Chinese Buddhism, it is definitely the latter which reached Japan. The scriptures carried there had been selected and translated in China: Chinese became the ecclesiastical language, like Latin in Catholic Europe, and sects like the Zen and Tendai which have no exact equivalents in India made themselves at home and flourished. It will therefore be well to notice briefly the chief phases of religious history in China in order to understand clearly what the Japanese imported at different epochs.

According to the common story, Buddhism was introduced into China in A.D. 67 in consequence of the dream of the Emperor Ming-Ti.[1] It is not necessary for our purpose to discuss the details of this and other legends, but the statements that even before this date there were Buddhist communities in Western China are not

[1] See Maspéro, "Le Songe et l'Ambassade de l'Empereur Ming-ti," *B.E.F.E.O.*, 1910, and also Pelliot in *B.E.F.E.O.*, 1906, p. 393 ff.

improbable, for before the Christian era Buddhism had spread among the tribes living to the north of India and about 138 B.C. the Han Emperor Wu-Ti sent to Central Asia the first of several expeditions which made the Chinese familiar with those regions. But even in the first century of our era Buddhism in China can have been represented only by a few scattered settlements. Our evidence for its existence and progress during the second century is chiefly literary. About ten persons are mentioned as having translated various sûtras, and other translations are ascribed to unknown authors. The most sceptical criticism must admit that this list implies considerable missionary activity.[1] The translators were all foreigners and most of them came from Central Asia, including the celebrated An Shih-Kao, a prince of An-hsi or Parthia. Only a few were Indians. But about the same time a native Chinese, Mou-Tzu,[2] wrote a work of questions and answers about Buddhism which resembles the Questions of Milinda, though full of Taoist ideas. Still, it is not until the third century that Buddhism becomes prominent as a force among the masses of the people and also at Court. Its progress was no doubt connected with the divisions which threatened to break up the Empire and with the rise of Tartar states within the limits of what was supposed to be China.

Confucianism, which was dominant at the Imperial Court, had always been somewhat contemptuous of Buddhism and Taoism as popular superstitions, and up to the present day the Buddhist priesthood have never been able to establish themselves in popular esteem as the guardians of learning and the proper supervisors of education, that position being successfully monopolized by the Confucian literati. But the Tartar states, among which the most important was Wei, had no such prejudices. They were not pro-Buddhist and anti-Confucian, for they were anxious to acquire Chinese civilization of every kind, but the zealous Buddhist missionaries, many of whom were themselves of Tartar extraction, made converts among them more readily than did the somewhat supercilious Confucian philosophers. In the fourth century the spread of the new faith—for it was only now beginning to be accepted as a natural part of Chinese life—was even more remarkable. In 335 the Prince of Chao, a Tartar state which included

[1] According to the various catalogues cited by Nanjio there flourished under the Latter Han Dynasty (A.D. 25–220) twelve translators who produced 292 or 359 works of which 96 are reputed to be among those extant.

[2] See Pelliot in *T'oung Pao*, xix, 1920.

Shansi, issued a decree allowing the population to become monks freely, a permission which is interesting as already indicating a theory often put into practice in later times that a subject had no right to abandon family life without his master's leave. In 372 Buddhism was introduced into Korea and apparently accepted as the flower of Chinese civilization. In 381 we are told that in north-western China nine-tenths of the inhabitants were Buddhists. Nor was the movement confined to the Tartar states. The Eastern Tsin dynasty (317–420), which ruled at Nanking and, according to Chinese ideas, represented the legitimate Empire, was also favourable to it and Hsiao Wu-ti of this line was the first Emperor of China to embrace the faith.

Meanwhile the output of Buddhist literature was considerable. Up to A.D. 400, if we can trust the old Chinese catalogues, something like thirteen hundred works had been translated, of which about four hundred are still extant. About that time there arrived the celebrated Kumârajiva.[1] He was the child of Indian parents but born at Kucha in Central Asia. Like Vasubandhu, who, though of uncertain date, perhaps lived about the same period, he originally followed the Hînayâna but subsequently became an enthusiastic Mahayanist. In 383 Kucha was captured by the troops of the Former Ts'in Dynasty, a line of Tartar Princes who reigned at Ch'ang-An, Kumarâjiva was carried off and after some adventures settled at their capital. He was appointed Kuo-shih, or Director of Religion and Public Instruction, and is said to have had three thousand students to whom he lectured in a hall specially built for him. From about 402–412 he made numerous translations from the Sanskrit, of which fifty are still extant, and was one of the most important foreign scholars who influenced Chinese Buddhism in its early days. About the same time (A.D. 399) Fa-Hsien, the first Chinese pilgrim, started on his journey to India and began the long procession of travellers and inquirers who visited the sacred places of Buddhism and its centres of learning with the object of collecting books and ascertaining by their own researches what was the true doctrine and correct monastic discipline.

In the fifth century Buddhism was on the whole in a flourishing condition both under the legitimate dynasty of Liu-Sung which reigned at Nanking and under the Tartar Princes of Wei. But it is not surprising if this progress caused a certain opposition and

[1] 鳩摩羅什.

reaction. In both states we hear of protests against the multiplication of monasteries and the expenditure of public money on costly ceremonies, of accusations of conspiracy brought against the monks, and finally of restrictive edicts and persecution. But in both the time of trial was short and the current of popular opinion set definitely in favour of toleration. The Princes of Wei became again defenders of the Faith: the sculptured grottoes of Yün-Kang in Shansi were executed in the latter half of the century and there are said to have been thirteen thousand temples in Wei. Hu, the Dowager Empress, was a fervent devotee (though like many such an indifferent example in matters of secular morality), and in 578 sent Sung-Yün and Hui-Shêng to Northern India in search of sûtras. At Nanking, Wu-Ti, the first Emperor of the Liang dynasty, rivalled Asoka in piety but not in prudence or prosperity, for though he had a long reign (502–549) he ultimately lost his kingdom and his life owing to his intrigues with disaffected factions in Wei, which appear to have been neither skilful nor scrupulous. He was originally a Confucianist, but about 510 he became a most zealous Buddhist. He forbade the slaughter of animals, was reluctant to inflict capital punishment, expounded the scriptures in public, and three times became a monk for short periods. Under his auspices was produced the first edition of the Chinese Tripiṭaka, which is said to have contained 2,213 works, including the travels of Fa-Hsien.[1] It was in his reign, too, that Bodhidharma, of whom more anon, came to China from India; but according to the common though perhaps apocryphal story his views did not agree with those of the pious Emperor and he left Nanking for the north. Wu-Ti also sent a mission to Magadha to obtain Sanskrit texts, and it brought back not only many valuable manuscripts but also the learned scholar and translator Paramârtha.

It was about this time (A.D. 552) that Buddhism was first introduced into Japan from Korea. Wu-Ti's death was followed by a slight reaction. A Prince of Northern Chou, who bore the same name, defined the precedence of the three religions as Confucianism, Taoism, and Buddhism, and in 575 ordered temples to be destroyed and monastic bodies to be dissolved. But the persecution as usual was short, his son revoked the edict, and a few years afterwards the founder of the Sui dynasty gave permission to all who desired it to take monastic vows. He seems indeed to have used Buddhism

[1] See Nanjio's Catalogue, Introduction, pp. xvii and xxvii.

as a means for unifying the Empire, and during the period 594–616 no less than three new collections [1] of the Tripiṭaka were made.[2]

With the seventh century began the great T'ang dynasty under which intercourse with India continued. Shortly after its advent Hsüan-Tsang made his celebrated journey (629–645) and on his return was received by the Emperor with great honour. A little later I-Ching won almost equal fame by his travels (671–697). In 751 Wu-K'ung accompanied a political mission to the King of Kipin. He remained some time in India, became a monk, and returned to China with numerous books and relics. The first half of this dynasty and the period immediately preceding it, that is, the two centuries from A.D. 550 to 750, was clearly the age when the creative force of Chinese Buddhism was most vigorous, when the greatest teachers flourished, and the most important sects took shape, even though their origin may be referred to earlier saints. Only slightly later, say 615–815, is the period when most Chinese sects were introduced into Japan.[3]

Remarkable as was the progress of Buddhism it could never pretend to be the only religion of China and only occasionally and locally could it be called paramount. Though there were long spells of truce, the triangular conflict between Confucianism, Buddhism, and Taoism was only dormant, not ended, and any one of the three which could bring influence to bear on the Court often secured a striking though transitory triumph, at least in the neighbourhood of the capital. In many ways it is wonderful that Buddhism should have met with so large a measure of success. Its ideals of asceticism and celibacy were repugnant to popular Chinese views, which regarded the perpetuation of the family as a sacred duty. It set no store on loyalty and the political virtues

[1] The word collection is perhaps more accurate than edition, for they were not mere editions in the sense in which we speak of a new edition of the Bible or of the works of Virgil, but the actual material published on each occasion varied considerably. Thus we are told (Nanjio, p. xvii) that the oldest catalogue mentions 2,218 works of which only 276 can be identified with those now existing. Many of the collections were published in more than one edition.

[2] About this time (540–594) lived Hsin-Hsing, the founder of the San-Chieh sect which lasted till about 845, though often denounced as heretical. The writings of this sect have been preserved in Tun-huang and some in Japan, but I cannot discover that it ever had any practical importance there. See for an extensive monograph Yabuki Keiki's work entitled *Sankai-kyō no Kenkyū*, published at Tokyo, 1927.

[3] One might indeed say all sects for, though Zen propaganda was not successful till the thirteenth century, the sect was first introduced in 736, or according to some traditions even in 654, but died out.

which are so dear to the ethics of the Far East, and its monasteries and ecclesiastical organization were dangerously capable of becoming political associations and creating an *imperium in imperio*. But the prudence and suppleness of the clergy removed these objections. By taking charge of funeral and memorial ceremonies, to which national sentiment attached the greatest importance, they played a part in family life and, though they could not be said to keep aloof from politics, they usually tried to compass their ends by loyal if not lofty methods, that is, by exercising influence at Court. But still it must be confessed that from the days of the White Lotus to the Triad Society of recent times it was generally possible to accuse them plausibly of inspiring secret political societies.

Yet the Emperor Wan-Li made a true epigram when he said that Confucianism and Buddhism were like the two wings of a bird: each required the help of the other. Buddhism was strong because it offered a better combination of moral, philosophic, and emotional teaching than either of its rivals. They were native growths and doubtless the Chinese feel their deficiencies less than foreigners, but still it is clear that Confucianism can be considered to be a religion only if we exclude both emotion and speculation from that term. No doubt it was a natural craving for them that brought Taoism into existence. It has two sides. As a philosophy it deserves all respect and exercised a considerable influence on some Buddhist schools. As a popular creed it was less admirable. It encouraged grosser superstition than did Buddhism at its worst—for instance, the elixir of immortality of which many Emperors died—and its deities, such as the Jade Emperor and the Eight Genii, seem fanciful and unsatisfactory creations, denizens of fairyland rather than heaven, who do not appeal to the heart like Amitâbha or the merciful Kwan-Yin.

Not only were the periods of restrictive legislation short, but it is clear that the return to religious liberty was a national relief. The policy of most Emperors was statesmanlike rather than consistent. Not a few of them after issuing repressive edicts performed some devout and complimentary act which seemed to indicate that they merely desired to curb extravagance and not to interfere with religion and learning. Thus Hsüan-Tsung (A.D. 713–756) forbade the building of monasteries and the copying of sûtras, but subsequently the seventh collection of the Tripiṭaka was made and published by his orders. So, too, nearly a thousand years later K'ang-Hsi issued the well-known Sacred Edict forbidding heterodoxy (i tuan), in which the official explanation clearly includes Buddhism, but later he issued a gracious rescript to the monks of P'u-T'u in which (though admitting that he had not had time to study Buddhism properly) he used most polite and devout language about their deities.

But the T'ang dynasty was a period of genius and extravagance and many of its sovereigns expressed their religious convictions with vehemence and publicity. The Empress Wu, who dominated the second half of the seventh century, was an example of lavish but not humble piety, for she assumed divine honours and caused herself to be styled Maitreya or Kuan-Yin. The Emperor Su-Tsung (756–762) was conspicuous for his devotion, as was also his successor Tai-Tsung, who expounded the scriptures himself and attracted even more attention by the magnificent ceremonies which he caused to be performed for the repose of his mother's soul. In 819 the Emperor Hsien-Tsung provoked a celebrated incident by installing in the palace a bone alleged to be a relic of the Buddha and to possess miraculous powers. Han Yu, one of the best known scholars and statesmen of the time, presented to His Majesty a written protest, celebrated in China as a literary masterpiece, but achieved no result except exile for himself. On the other hand, the Emperor Wu-Tsung was a zealous Taoist and in 845 issued a most trenchant edict ordering Buddhist temples to be destroyed, ecclesiastical property to be confiscated, and monks and nuns to return to the world. Indeed, he would either have crippled Buddhism or have provoked a rebellion but for his sudden end, which is a warning to make sure that your own superstitions are beneficent before you persecute other people. On the recommendation of his Taoist advisers he began to take the Elixir of Immortality and soon died of the treatment. His successor revoked the edict, executed the Taoist priests who had instigated it, and things went on much as before.

Both Manichæism and Nestorian Christianity were known in China under the T'ang. The former, called Ming-chiao, or the religion of light, was at first discouraged, but when the Uigur princes, who were formidable neighbours of China, adopted it in 763 as the state religion, it was thought prudent to tolerate it (though reluctantly) and Manichæan places of worship were opened at Lo-Yang and Ch'ang-An. But as soon as the power of the Uigurs was broken by the Kirghiz in 840, Manichæism in China was promptly suppressed (843).

Nestorianism, known as Ching-chiao or the radiant religion, appeared in 635 and received favourable treatment under the early T'ang Emperors, though that zealous Buddhist the Empress Wu persecuted it. Her successors, however, even when they shared Buddhist convictions as did Su-Tsung and Tai-Tsung, gave it toleration and even patronage. The celebrated inscription in Chinese and Syriac discovered at Si-Ngan-fu [1] and commonly known as the Nestorian Stone, which dates from 781, gives a long account of the doctrines and history of the Nestorian Church. It has led several authors to maintain that the development of Buddhism in China was materially influenced by Nestorian Christianity, but without sufficient warrant in my opinion. It is clear that Christians and Buddhists consorted together amicably and also that their doctrines and ceremonies had certain obvious though often superficial resemblances. But there is no proof, for instance, that Buddhist services for the dead were in any way imitations of Christian funeral masses as has been contended. The details of the two rites and the methods by which they propose to help the departed are entirely different, and Indian and Chinese usages fully explain the origin of the Buddhist ceremonial. So, too, though the image of Kuan-Yin with a child may look like the Madonna and the infant Christ, it does not represent divine motherhood but a benevolent power ready to hear the prayers of women who wish for children. It is not clear that the Manichæans exercised much influence on Buddhism, but they certainly felt its influence, for they borrowed its phraseology, symbols, and doctrines.[2] And it looks as if Nestorian Christianity to some extent did the same. The Nestorian Stone uses many Buddhist terms (such as Sêng and Ssŭ for Christian priests and monasteries), and, what is far more remarkable, though it describes at some length the life of Christ and its results, it omits all mention of the crucifixion and merely says in speaking of the creation that God arranged the cardinal points in the shape of a cross. The reason must be that the doctrine of the atonement was felt to be unacceptable and was suppressed under Buddhist influence.[3] And when we hear that the Emperor Hsüan-Tsung presented to Nestorian churches portraits of his

[1] Hsi-an-fu.

[2] See the three articles by Chavannes and Pelliot in *J.A.*, 1911, 1913, entitled "Un traité Manichéen retrouvé en Chine". A Chinese edict of 739 accuses the Manichæans of falsely taking the name of Buddhists and deceiving the people.

[3] See Havret, "La Stèle Chrétienne de Si-ngan-fu" in *Variétés Sinologues*, p. 54.

ancestors and inscriptions written in his own handwriting, we cannot help suspecting that the buildings thus honoured did not look much like Christian places of worship.

Like the Emperors of the T'ang dynasty, its authors and artists had various convictions of their own, but such great names as the painter Wu Tao-Tzŭ and the poet Liu Tsung-Yüan are instances of Buddhist inspiration. And in the Sung dynasty, justly famous for culture, learning, and art, especially landscape painting, the same inspiration is often obvious. The school of Buddhism which had the greatest influence on art and literature was the Ch'an (better known in its Japanese form Zen),[1] which, though said to have been founded by Bodhidharma, had at first a somewhat variable and uncertain position and did not definitely win the sympathy and esteem of the cultured classes until long after his death. The earlier Emperors of the Northern Sung dynasty on the whole encouraged Buddhism. Though T'ai-Tsu, the founder, published some restrictive edicts, yet a new collection of the Tripiṭaka was made by his orders in A.D. 971 and furnished with a preface of his own. This was the first printed edition, previous collections having been in manuscript only, and the labour and expense involved in this gigantic undertaking are a proof of the esteem which the literary world must have felt for Buddhism. Under T'ai-Tsu's successors, it continued to flourish, religious intercourse with India was active, and the Emperor Jen-Tsung encouraged the study of Sanskrit. Hui-Tsung, the last Emperor of the Northern Sung, a patron of the arts and a painter himself, fell under the influence of a Taoist priest named Lin Ling-Su and at first endeavoured to suppress Buddhism, not by ordinary persecution but by amalgamation. The Buddhas and Bodhisattvas were enrolled as members of the Taoist pantheon, and temples and monasteries were allowed to exist only on condition of describing themselves as Taoist. But, as on previous occasions, the reaction was rapid. Lin Ling-Su fell owing to pride and insolence : the Emperor reversed his edict and his convictions and proceeded to legislate against Taoism. But grave events interfered with His Majesty's religious and artistic interests. In 1126 the Kin Tartars conquered his kingdom and carried him off captive, in which unhappy state he died.

An interesting feature of this period is the attempt of Wang An-shih to introduce a sort of State Socialism (1021–1086) into

China, which met with considerable, though intermittent, imperial patronage. It does not appear that there was anything definitely Buddhist in his theories, but one of his proposals, which his opponents violently attacked, was to introduce Buddhist and Taoist subjects into the public examinations. Had this reform been successful it would have meant a change in the intellectual and social life of the governing classes which it is difficult for Europeans to understand, but in the crash which brought about the fall of Hui-Tsung no more was heard of Wang An-shih.

The Chinese Government, unable to face the Tartars in the north, retired to the south of the Yangtse and the Empire was reconstituted at Hangchow under the Southern Sung dynasty, which perhaps witnessed the perfection of Chinese culture, though not of genius. Buddhism was not persecuted : indeed, the Zen school remained fashionable, but clearly the interest in religion was not very lively. This was the only great dynasty which did not publish its own edition of the Tripiṭaka, and not a single translation or Buddhist treatise is recorded as having been made under its auspices.[1] The system which was influential and characteristic of the period was the new Confucianism of Chu-Hsi (1130–1200), a restatement of the Master's teaching which has received the approval of succeeding ages. Though Chu-Hsi was anti-Buddhist, yet he evidently felt that the old philosophy which treated exclusively of social and political ethics had neglected large departments of knowledge of which other religions took account. He devotes much space to cosmology and the doctrine of world periods in which growth and decay alternate : he teaches the transformation of matter into various forms of life and also something very like Karma or the retribution of good and evil actions. There is nothing necessarily Buddhist in such ideas, but one can hardly doubt that they assumed prominence at this time because Buddhism had posed the perplexing questions to which they seek to find an answer. Chu-Hsi's contemporary, Lu Chiu-Yüan, though one of the worthies whose names are inscribed in Confucian temples, taught that learning is not indispensable and that the mind can by meditation attain to a perception of absolute truth. There is clearly more of Bodhidharma and of Lao-tzŭ than of Confucius in this doctrine.

Religious conditions in China entirely changed with the advent of the Mongol dynasty known as Yüan (1280–1368). The Mongols

[1] Observe the blank in Nanjio's Catalogue.

were tolerant, they had no religious prejudices, and were ready to consider impartially which creed suited them best. But when Khubilai had once decided in favour of Buddhism, it became the State Church and so remained while his house ruled. This was something entirely new, for in previous ages the devotion of the most pious Emperors, such as Wu-Ti, had been purely personal. They had never been able to make the Empire a Buddhist institution. But now the Church was recognized as a department of the Government, and huge sums of public money were expended on ceremonies and subventions to monasteries. Naturally a new edition of the Tripiṭaka was printed and many other religious books. Still, the change did not promote the welfare of Buddhism in China so much as might have been expected, for the sect which practically became the established Church was Lamaism, the peculiar form of the faith developed in Tibet, and a Lamaist ecclesiastic was recognized as the hierarchical head of all Buddhists, other religions receiving toleration and being placed under the supervision of a special board. It does not appear that under the Yüan dynasty any distinction was drawn between Lamaism and other sects. Nevertheless, the difference both in ritual and doctrine was real and made itself felt with time: a Chinese of the present day regards a Lama as quite different from a Buddhist monk. The subject has only a negative interest for our present inquiry, since Japanese religion was not influenced by Lamaism. Khubilai Khan made two attempts to conquer Japan. They were successfully repulsed, but naturally the Yüan dynasty was an object of popular detestation, and when intercourse with China was renewed the Japanese turned to the old art and literature which they already knew and admired, not to importations from Tibet and Mongolia. The Ming dynasty, too (1368–1644), which drove out the Mongols and claimed to restore Chinese civilization after the havoc wrought by a foreign invasion, were not disposed to regard the religious institutions of their predecessors with favour, but political reasons induced them to treat the Lamaist hierarchy with great consideration. Until the eighteenth century the Chinese Court could not rid themselves of the apprehension that the Mongol tribes might unite in an attack on the Empire, and obviously one of the best means of restraining them was to use the good offices of the Lamas, for whom they had an extraordinary respect.

The establishment of the Ming dynasty was an act of national self-assertion and an escape from foreign bondage, but it was not accompanied by any striking revival or development in thought, art, and literature. Authors, painters, and sculptors were indeed numerous, but they showed distinction rather than genius, and perhaps it is only in porcelain that art reached the highest standard. In philosophy the most remarkable figure is Wang Yang-ming (1472–1528), called Ō Yō Mei in Japan, where he had some influence.[1] His teaching shows affinity to that of Lu Chin-yüan, already mentioned, but was even more clearly influenced by Buddhism, though he professed to base it on the Chinese Classics. He held that truth can be obtained by meditation, and used the expression Liang-chih,[2] taken from Mencius, to designate intuitive knowledge which is present in all human minds but in different degrees, since it can be developed or allowed to atrophy. To develop it should be our constant object, and in its light when pure all things are understood and peace is obtained. The influence of Zen is here obvious.

Buddhism was no longer the State Church as under the Yüan dynasty, and reverted to the position which it had held under the T'ang and which is so difficult to define in European formulæ, though perfectly natural to the Chinese. Education and administration were in the hands of the Confucian literati, who regarded both Buddhism and Taoism as unscholarly superstitions. The Emperor was, however, free to patronize them, though he might receive memorials and protests if he went too far. The earlier Ming Emperors were on the whole favourable to Buddhism, though from policy more than devotion. The founder had been a novice in his youth and seems to have left his monastery with a grateful regard for the Church which had sheltered him, together with a knowledge of its weaknesses. He treated the clergy with courtesy, but issued edicts restricting their numbers and raising the standard of learning necessary for candidates. He caused a new collection of the Tripiṭaka to be made, and in 1377 he published an edict ordering that the priests of the Ch'an (Zen) sect should compose commentaries on the Lankâvatâra, Vajracchedikâ, and Prajñâpâramitâhridaya sûtras and that all the clergy should study them.[3] Though this was a century before Wang Yang-Ming, the choice of works is interesting as showing the direction which the thought

[1] 王陽明.

[2] 良知. In Japanese pronunciation Ryōchi.

[3] See Nanjio's catalogue, Nos. 1613–15.

of the age tended to take. Similarly, the third Emperor Ch'eng-Tsu was educated by a Buddhist priest whom he greatly respected. Yet he was so drastic in limiting the number of priests that on one occasion he ordered 1,800 candidates for ordination to be enrolled in the army instead. On the other hand, he not only published yet another collection of the Tripiṭaka [1] but wrote prefaces and laudatory verses which were included in it, and even compiled the memoirs of 209 remarkable monks with an introduction.[2] His Empress went so far as to imagine that a sûtra was revealed to her in a vision, and it is duly registered.[3]

It is about this time, too, that we begin to hear of the secular clergy. Edicts against them were issued in 1394 and 1412, but they continued to increase. Apparently when restrictions were placed on the number of monks many persons acted as priests, though they married and did not live in monasteries.[4] In 1458 an edict ordered that ordination should be held only once a year, but in 1507 in the reign of Wu-Tsung we hear that no less than 40,000 persons became monks, either Buddhist or Taoist. Wu-Tsung was a learned and pious Emperor, but he was in the hands of a band of eunuchs who were known as the Eight Tigers, and it must be confessed that at this period Buddhism often prospered through this not very creditable form of Court influence, especially in the reigns of Ying-Tsung and Ching-Ti (1436–1464). But its power among the masses also seems clear, and the early Catholic missionaries evidently regarded it as their most formidable rival. Thus Ricci, who arrived in China in 1582, and his pupils disputed with the Buddhist clergy both in public controversies and in written polemics. As late as 1655 the Ōbaku sect was introduced into Japan.

The Ming dynasty succumbed in 1644 before another invasion of Tartars, the Manchus, and since thought, art, and literature had shown little brilliancy in the last days of native rule, they were not likely to revive under foreign invasion. The beautiful porcelain which was produced in the reigns of the earlier Manchu Emperors makes Europeans think of the period too favourably. There was

[1] Called the Northern Collection because it was printed at Peking.

[2] Nanjio, 1616. A small volume containing ten imperial compositions in prose and verse, and Nanjio, 1620.

[3] Nanjio, No. 1657.

[4] Their status was long a troublesome problem to the Chinese Government. In 1735 Ch'ien tried to make them either enter monasteries or become ordinary laymen, but he abandoned the attempt and ultimately they were allowed to continue and have one pupil each.

no religious or intellectual movement of any importance until the influx of Western ideas, political and other, in the last century. It is generally agreed that in quite recent times the interest in Buddhism, particularly in Buddhist philosophy, has also increased. But it owes nothing to official patronage. Unlike the Mongols, the Manchus as a race had little taste for Buddhism, and not one of their Emperors showed signs of being a convinced believer. But they were also not persecutors, although they limited the number of monks from time to time as other dynasties had done. K'ang-Hsi's attitude, which I have already described, was characteristic of his successors. They were courteous to the Buddhist clergy, especially the Lamas and Tibetan Church, for political reasons, and this courtesy often took a form which seems to imply more belief than it really did. Thus K'ang-Hsi published the Tibetan scriptures, the Kanjur, with a preface of his own. His son and grandson issued the last collection of the Tripitaka (1735–7), and the latter, the Emperor Ch'ien-Lung, wrote a complimentary preface to a sûtra for producing rain.[1] He is also said to have printed the Tripiṭaka in Tibetan, Mongol, and Manchu as well as in Chinese.[2]

## 2

In early times Chinese Buddhism already existed in the form of sects, or rather schools, some imported direct from India, some the result of native reflection on the new foreign doctrines. There was little hostility or even aggressive rivalry between them, and with time their differences tended to disappear. But when the Japanese first sought instruction of their neighbours these schools were still fresh and vigorous. The Chinese teachers who came to Japan taught the special doctrine of one or other of them, and the Japanese students and inquirers who went to China usually resided in a monastery and brought back with them its special system. It will, therefore, be well to see what they were likely to find there at various epochs.

Two early schools, the Chêng-shih-tsung and San-lun-tsung,[3]

[1] Nanjio, Nos. 187–8 and 970. See, too, Beal, *Catena of Buddhist Scriptures*, pp. 417–19.

[2] See Möllendorf in China Branch of *J.A.S.*, xxiv, 1890, p. 28.

[3] 成實宗 and 三論宗.

have only a historical interest since they have ceased to exist, and when they flourished were philosophical rather than popular. They had, however, sufficient vitality to reach Japan in 625, though there also they have now no temples or adherents. The former, called Jōjitsu in Japanese pronunciation, apparently represented the ancient Indian school called Sautrântikas which was in some ways a bridge between the Hîna- and Mahâyâna. Their chief text-book was the Satyasiddhi of Harivarman, which is not extant in Sanskrit but was translated into Chinese by Kumârajiva, probably about A.D. 408.[1] The San-lun or Sanron, that is, the school of three treatises,[2] was so called because it accepted as its authorities three works of Nâgârjuna and Âryadeva and taught their negative dialectic.

Another early school which taught the worship of Amitâbha is far more important, for even at the present day it continues to be one of the most potent influences in Far Eastern Buddhism. Its name is Ching-t'u [3] or the pure land, perhaps better known in its Japanese pronunciation as Jōdo. Chinese tradition credits the Parthian Prince An-Shih-Kao with having preached this doctrine and translated the Sukhâvatî-vyûha about A.D. 148, and, however much such statements may be criticized, it is clear that the Chinese themselves considered that the worship of Amitâbha was introduced at a very early date.

Hui-Yüan, who lived from 333 to 418, is generally regarded as the founder of the school, that is to say, he made it in some sense a brotherhood or corporation. He was originally a Taoist, and after he was converted to Buddhism is said to have still used the writings of Chuang-Tzŭ to explain his new faith. He settled finally in the Lu-Fêng monastery in Hupeh, which was famous for its ponds covered with white lotus. The school was hence known for some time as the Pai-lien-chiao, or white lotus creed, but in later times a similar name was used by a powerful and persistent secret society and it was hence dropped as a religious designation. Nor did the Lu-Fêng monastery continue to be the centre of the school, which was for some time a definite sect and produced a series of eminent teachers, very well known in Japan, where they are called the five

[1] Nanjio, No. 1274.

[2] The three treatises are the Mâdhyamaka śâstra, N. 1179, the Dvâdaśanikâya śâstra, N. 1186, both attributed to Nâgârjuna, and the Śata śâstra of Âryadeva, N. 1188. All three were translated by Kumârajiva.

[3] 淨土.

patriarchs.[1] They did not follow one another in immediate succession, and though the school soon spread all over China the provinces of Shansi and Shenši were the chief scene of their labours. Tan-Luan (called Donran in Japanese)[2] was a native of the former province and lived from 476 to 542. He was an ardent student of the Sanron school and set about writing a commentary on the Mahâsannipâta-sûtra, which had recently been translated into Chinese. But he fell ill and the difficulties of his task made him feel that a scholar could accomplish nothing without long life, so he went to consult a celebrated hermit at Nanking who was apparently a Taoist, and asked him how to obtain it. On his way back he met the Indian monk Bodhiruchi, who said that the hermit's advice was useless and, handing him a copy of the Amitâyurdhyâna-sûtra, told him that he would find eternal life there. Donran accepted the doctrine, and devoted the rest of his life to preaching the power of Amida and the efficacy of invoking his name. He resided at Fên-Chou in Shansi[3] and wrote a commentary on Vasubandhu's treatise on Paradise.[4]

The second Patriarch, Tao-Ch'o or Dōshaku[5] (562–645), was born near T'ai-Yüan-fu and at first studied the Nirvâna-sûtra, but when about forty-five abandoned it and made a vow before the memorial to Donran erected in his monastery at Fên-Chou that he would preach nothing but the doctrine of salvation by faith in Amida. He made a celebrated collection of scriptural passages respecting the Happy Land,[6] in which he emphasized the doctrine that common mortals can be born there if they simply utter the holy name, which he himself is said to have repeated 70,000 times a day. He appears to have been the first to use the terms Holy Path and the Pure Land[7] (which are practically equivalent to salvation by works and salvation by faith) to designate the two methods of leading the religious life. According to the legend he never turned his

[1] 五祖. Their biographies are contained in the second and third parts of the series called the Lives of Eminent Priests, Nanjio, Nos. 1493 and 1495. They appear to be credible in the main, though they include legends.

[2] 曇鸞.

[3] In the temple called Hsüan-chung-ssŭ, or in Japanese pronunciation, Genchūji.

[4] Nanjio, 1204.

[5] 道綽.

[6] 安樂集 Anrakushū.

[7] 聖道 Shōdō and 淨土 Jōdo. The passage is quoted by Hōnen. See his Life, translated by Coates and Ishizuka, p. 340.

back to the west or spat westwards.[1] He died in the Genchūji temple.

The most celebrated of the Patriarchs was the third called Shan-Tao, or Zendō[2] (613–681). He was considered as an incarnation of Amida and his works were accepted as equivalent to scripture. Hōnen, the founder of the Jōdo sect in Japan, says of him, "Zendō was an incarnation of Amida and so, though we have had many teachers of the Pure Land sect, we should depend solely upon Zendō," and again, speaking of his own book the Senchakushū, "The most important passages give you the heart and soul of Zendō, the founder of the Pure Land sect."[3]

Zendō (613–681) was born in Shantung and, like his predecessors, was at first a student of the Sanron school, but accidentally discovering the Amitâyurdhyâna-sûtra in a temple library, thought it much better suited to his spiritual needs. He therefore studied under Dōshaku and subsequently settled at Ch'ang-An, where he devoted himself to preaching the doctrines of his new sect. He is said to have made ten thousand copies of the Lesser Sukhâvatî-vyûha and to have painted three hundred pictures of Paradise. His most important work was his commentary on the Amitâyurdhyâna-sûtra, in which he insists that meditation on Amida and invocation of his name are all important, though it is only just to add that he also dwells on the need of combining faith with good deeds. According to one story he committed suicide, but this seems improbable, as such an act was contrary to his own teaching. The dated inscriptions in the caves of Lung-mên indicate that the worship of Amida was specially prevalent from A.D. 647 to 715, and it seems very probable that this was due to the preaching of Zendō.

The date of the fourth Patriarch, Huai-Kan or Ekan,[4] is not known accurately, but we are told that he was a priest of Ch'ang-An who had doubts as to whether admittance to Paradise could be obtained by the mere invocation of Amida's name. He accordingly

[1] But he was beaten at this particular form of piety by Rensei, a companion of Hōnen's, who whenever he used to travel from Kyōto to the Kwantō would always put the saddle on the horse backwards and ride facing west. *Hōnen, the Buddhist Saint*, trans. by Coates and Ishizuka, p. 494.

[2] 善導.

[3] Ibid., pp. 467 and 718. In 1930 it was announced that the 1250th anniversary of the death of Zendō would be celebrated in China, and nineteen priests were sent from Japan to represent the Jōdo sect at Tientsin, Mukden, and Peking, where memorial services were held.

[4] 懷感.

laid his difficulties before Zendō and by his advice practised meditation [1] for three years. His mind was then at ease and he wrote a book called Gungiron in which he discussed and solved various difficult points of doctrine.[2] The date of the eminent priest Fa-Chao (Japanese Hosshō) is also uncertain, but he appears to have been alive in 770. He visited Wu-T'ai-Shan and there received a revelation from Mañjuśrî extolling the worship of Amida as the best of all rites. He wrote both hymns and musical services described as consisting of "five intonations", which were studied by Jikaku Daishi when he was in China about 840 and introduced by him in the temples of Hieizan. Fa-Chao's special teaching is said to have been derived from T'zŭ-Min (680–748), who went to India in 702 and spent eighteen years there.[3]

Shao-K'ang or Shōkō,[4] the last of the Patriarchs, was separated from the others by a considerable interval, for he died in 805 and his sphere of activity was also somewhat different. He was born and laboured in Chêkiang, but having heard of Zendō's doctrine went to Ch'ang-An and prayed at his tomb. There he heard a voice bidding him preach to the world faith in the Pure Land, and he executed this commission by returning to his native province and building a temple on Mount Wu-Lung near Yen-Chou, where he taught for many years. Like Fa-Chao he was celebrated as a musician and composer of hymns.

Though the doctrine of the Pure Land continued to be and still is very popular in China, yet after the ninth century the sect seems to have had a less definite existence as a corporation than others. Nanjio's Catalogue of the Tripiṭaka describes many authors as belonging to the T'ien-tai, Avataṃsaka, or Dhyâna schools but none as belonging to the Pure Land, and though the Tripiṭaka contains numerous writings dedicated to the praises of Amida, the authors appear to belong to all schools and not, as we should expect, to the one which preached his worship as the only way to salvation. The explanation seems to be that the doctrine of salvation by faith

[1] That is, Nembutsu-Zammai 念佛三昧, the special form of meditation practised by the Pure Land Sect.

[2] 群疑論 Gungiron. For instance, Hōnen quotes his decision that if a man has recited the Nembutsu when he is in good health and his mind is clear and so laid up a store of merit, he will be born in Paradise even if at the hour of death his mind is confused and he is not able to pray.

[3] See Gemmyō Ono in *Proc. Imp. Acad. of Tokyo*, 1926, vol. ii, No. 8, pp. 361–3.

[4] 少康.

was so easy and popular that no section of Buddhists could afford to neglect it, and it became not so much the creed of a special sect as an aspect of all sects. Something of the kind had already happened in India. For instance, the Friendly Letter (attributed to Nâgârjuna) and the Awakening of Faith distinctly countenance the worship of Amitâbha, though it is not their main teaching. It is noticeable, too, that the introduction and dissemination of Amidism in Japan is not like the history of the other sects. The Tendai, Shingon, and Zen all arrived in the same way. Japanese studied in Chinese monasteries, and finally (sometimes after unsuccessful attempts) a man of talent mastered the doctrine and practice of the sect which appealed to him and on returning established a similar organization in his own country. But in the case of Amidism things went differently. The worship of Amida and the scriptures concerning his paradise were known very early, at least as early as 640, and the knowledge was spread by other sects, for instance, the Tendai, which approved of that worship. Later various priests, such as Kūya, Genshin, and Ryōnin, gave it special prominence, and finally in the twelfth and thirteenth centuries Hōnen and Shinran founded the two great sects which still flourish. But though they express profound veneration for Zendō and other Chinese Patriarchs, neither of them visited China.

Bodhidharma,[1] the reputed founder of the school called Ch'an or Zen which has played so large a part not only in the religion and philosophy but also in the art and even in the social life of the Far East, arrived in Canton from India about A.D. 520. The common account says that he was the son of a king in southern India and also the twenty-eighth Patriarch [2] of a school whose teaching is summed up in four well-known lines—

> A special tradition outside the scriptures :
> Not to depend on books or letters :
> To point direct to the heart of man :
> To see (one's own) nature and become Buddha.[3]

Study of the scriptures, prayer, and even good works are all equally vain. All that man need do is to turn his gaze inward and see the Buddha in his own heart. The pious Emperor, Wu-Ti, was then

[1] 達磨.
[2] See above, III, 5 (p. 89).
[3] 教外別傳.不立文字.直指人心.見性成佛. Though often attributed to Bodhidharma, the lines are probably much later.

reigning at Nanking, and on hearing that a distinguished Buddhist teacher had arrived from India summoned him to the capital. But the interview was not a success. Wu-Ti did not relish being told bluntly that he had acquired no merit by causing temples to be built and the scriptures to be translated into Chinese, and Bodhidharma considered that His Majesty had no eye for the essentials of religion. So he left Nanking, crossed the Yangtse, and betook himself to Lo-Yang, where he lived in a country temple avoiding the company of princes and high ecclesiastics and, according to one popular legend, spent nine years sitting and gazing at a wall until at last his legs dropped off. The expression wall-gazing was probably in its original sense metaphorical. The legend is perpetuated in a kind of legless doll which is a popular plaything among Japanese children and is still called Daruma.

It is not easy to ascertain how much real history there is in this narrative. Bodhidharma's visit to China seems to be a fact.[1] His personality and even his features, which, as represented in numerous paintings, are not at all Chinese and show remarkable individuality, struck the popular imagination; but in seeking for facts one must be cautious in admitting the evidence of art, for some of the best known portraits represent his miraculous passage across the Yangtse standing on a reed. It is most remarkable that no reference to him has been discovered in Indian or Tibetan writings and the Chinese statements about his career in India are neither detailed nor lucid. He is generally described as having

[1] Pelliot in *T'oung Pao*, 1923, p. 253, observes: "Non seulement Bodhidharma n'a pas de notice dans les Annales des Wei ou dans les Annales des Leong, mais je ne crois pas qu'il soit nommé," but, as evidences for his existence, he cites *first* Yang Hsüan-chih, author of the Lo-Yang-Ch'ie-lan-chi, written about 547, who says that at a date which is calculated to be between 516 and 534, but nearer the latter, Bodhidharma who was a prince of Po-ssŭ (Persia) was at Lo-Yang, and *secondly* "l'ancienne histoire des T'ang dont l'auteur a dû mourir en 946". This last contains most of the elements of the legendary biography. The Lo-Yang-Ch'ie-lan-chi, which is printed in vol. 51 of Takakusu's Tripiṭaka, is a description of forty-five Buddhist temples at Lo-Yang and mentions under the first temple (Ei-nei-ji) that when the author visited it an Indian priest called Bodhidharma, a foreigner from the Po-ssŭ country, was stopping there (p. 1000, col. 2). He is also mentioned under Shūbonji, the 8th temple on the list. Now other Chinese accounts (e.g. the transmission of the Lamp, N. 1524) say that Bodhidharma was a Prince of Kan-Chi (香至) or Conjeevaram. As the Pallava dynasty was connected with this city and was likewise supposed to have come from Persia, it seems possible that the author is alluding to Bodhidharma's Pallava lineage, real or imaginary. The reality of the connection of the Pallavas with Persia does not affect the question.

been a prince of southern India but, in the earliest mention of him, as of Persia; and his title of twenty-eighth Patriarch offers difficulties. As I have already mentioned, more importance was attached to the Patriarchs in the Far East than in India, and according to most sects there were only twenty-three or four, of whom the last was put to death by the Huns and left no successor. The reckoning which makes Bodhidharma the twenty-eighth must represent the tradition of some school about which we have no information from Indian sources and which had special views about the succession. Ch'ie-Sung, who wrote a history of the Zen school [1] and died in 1071, criticizes the account of the Patriarchs [2] accepted by other sects and says that when Simha was in danger of death he transmitted his office to Basiasita, a native of Kashmir, who proceeded to travel in Central and South India and appointed Punyamitra (the name is doubtful) as his successor. Punyamitra went to the east and designated Prajnâtara, who thereupon removed to the south where he travelled for some time and finally passed his dignity on to a prince called Bodhitara, who on becoming patriarch changed this name to Bodhidharma. It is quite probable that during the persecution of the Huns eminent Buddhists left the north and wandered about in the central and southern districts, but if Bodhidharma arrived at Canton in 520 the chronology offers great difficulties. In Chinese ecclesiastical histories we find the Patriarchs dated in terms of the reigns of Chinese Emperors who are supposed to have been their contemporaries. But this apparent accuracy hides an entire ignorance of Indian history. Also the works treating of the Zen Patriarchs are relatively late. Thus Tao-Yüan's Transmission of the Lamp [3] was composed in 1004 and Nien-Chang's History of Buddhism,[4] which comments on it and sometimes corrects it, in 1333. These two books date the appointment of the first Patriarch Kâśyapa at 905 B.C., Aśvaghosha (the twelfth) about 332 B.C., Nâgârjuna (the fourteenth) at about 212 B.C., Simha at about A.D. 258, and Bodhidharma at A.D. 495. This strange chronology is clearly due to antedating the death of the Buddha by about 400 years and, if allowance is made for this, Aśvaghosha and Nâgârjuna fall into approximately their right periods. But the dates to be assigned to Simha and the later Patriarchs on the same principle are impossible and the last four of them up to the death of Bodhidharma are made to cover nearly

[1] Nanjio, 1528.
[2] As given in Nanjio, 1340.
[3] Nanjio, 1524.
[4] Nanjio, 1637.

300 years. Nor are earlier works more satisfactory. Chi Chia-ye's [1] history of the Patriarchs which ends with Simha says that he was beheaded by Mirakutsu in Keihin. Nanjio states that this work was translated—more probably compiled—in A.D. 472, but the Hun chieftain Mihirakula, who is apparently meant, is usually believed to have ruled about A.D. 530.

The accounts of Bodhidharma's doings in China have also aroused much scepticism. The most trustworthy is perhaps the biography in the Su-kao-seng-chuan [2] composed by Tao-Hsüan between A.D. 645 and 667, but it does not mention his interview with Wu-Ti. Later is the work called Records of the Transmission of the Lamp,[3] a collection of notes respecting prominent Zen teachers compiled by Tao-Yüan about 1004. It contains an account of the imperial interview and obviously regards Zen as a recognized branch of Buddhism with definite doctrines of its own, which the earlier work can hardly be said to do. There are also four treatises in Chinese attributed to Bodhidharma himself but probably spurious,[4] though they may contain some of his sayings. The second of them describes his reception by the Emperor and the sermon which he preached on the occasion. In it he insists that religion means nothing but the vision of the Buddha nature in one's own heart. It is a simple natural experience like a physical act and to those to whom it comes it gives light and deliverance: it is inevitable and convincing. If we substitute âtman in passages like this for Buddha nature the doctrine ascribed to Bodhidharma closely resembles certain well-known passages of the Upanishads.[5] It is generally admitted that there was much interchange of ideas between Brahmanic and Mahayanist philosophy and that the main conceptions found in the Vedanta as expounded by Śankara, though Brahmanic in their origin, had been elaborated by Buddhists before him, for he was accused by his opponents of being "a Buddhist in disguise". It may be that Bodhidharma belonged

[1] Nanjio, 1340. See vol. vi.

[2] Nanjio, 1493.

[3] Nanjio, 1524, 景德傳燈錄 Ching-tê-chuan-têng-lu. It is said to have been presented to the Emperor by the author in A.D. 1006.

[4] Such different authors as Pelliot (*T'oung Pao*, 1923, p. 253 ff.) and Suzuki (*Essays in Zen Buddhism*, p. 218) agree in thinking them late compositions made when the school had become flourishing. They are in the supplement to the Tripiṭaka, B. 15, 5.

[5] There are noticeable verbal coincidences. Thus it is said that the Buddha nature reveals itself in dreams: that it embraces the whole Universe and yet is so small that a needle cannot prick it.

to some such school intermediate between Buddhism and Vedantism and that he left India because his special teaching did not win many adherents there. It is clear, however, that in China students of Taoist philosophy were in sympathy with it and the difficulty is to find out what was imported from India and what was due to native influences. Great as was the prestige of Confucius's ethical system, it was not satisfying to all minds, and another current of thought which was old and strong bade men abstain from action and look for light within. The ideal of the amiable hermit was at least as old as Chuang-Tzŭ and in spite of disputes there was much similarity in thought and language between Buddhism and Taoism. In later times Chinese Buddhists studied Taoist books.[1]

Tradition is unanimous in reporting that Bodhidharma attached little importance to the scriptures and held that knowledge of the truth is obtained by sudden enlightenment, well-known by its Japanese name of Satori. This disdain of scripture is very un-Indian, and a well-known legend which is often cited to justify it appears to be a Chinese invention and cannot be traced to any Sanskrit or Pali source. It relates that Śâkyamuni, wishing to explain to his disciples the essence of his doctrine, said nothing but held up before them a bunch of flowers. None of them understood what he meant except Kâśyapa who looked at him and smiled, also in silence.[2] This story is considered typical of the right way to impart instruction, not by explanation or reference to books but by a sort of telepathy, and the biographies of Zen saints contain countless instances of how some trivial and apparently irrelevant action of a master brought sudden illumination and peace to his pupil. Nevertheless, the Zen school, though it disparaged the scriptures, did not neglect letters, and both in China and Japan produced a long succession of ecclesiastical authors. More than twenty of their treatises are included in the Chinese Tripiṭaka and it is said that two hundred and

[1] I-Ching in his Memoirs of Eminent Monks mentions three pilgrims who had studied the works of Chuang-tzŭ and his own writings show an acquaintance with this author. Kumârajiva is said to have written a commentary on the Tao-tê-ching. I do not know if it is extant but it is frequently quoted in the work called 老子翼 Rōshiyoku of the Chinese scholar 焦竑 Shōkō who collected sixty-four commentaries on Lao-tzŭ (A.D. 1573–1619). The Yüan-jên-lun (N. 1594), written by the fifth Patriarch of the Avatamsaka school who died in 841, criticizes Taoism and the Hînayâna as imperfect rather than erroneous systems.

[2] The story is found in the chapter called 拈華品 nengehon of the apocryphal sûtra called 大梵天王問佛決疑經 Dai-bon-tenō-monbutsu ketsugi-kyō, which was apparently composed in Chinese and has no Sanskrit original or counterpart.

thirty works on Zen were published under the Manchu dynasty.[1] It is stated, but also denied,[2] that Bodhidharma regarded the Lankâvatâra-sûtra as the best exposition of his teaching and handed a copy of it to his disciple Hui-K'o for his own guidance and the salvation of the world. One may doubt if Bodhidharma gave his approval to the sûtra, but in China it had a certain connection with the Zen school and it was one of the three works on which the first Ming Emperor ordered the doctors of that school to write commentaries.[3] Though studied by modern scholars in Japan, it does not seem to be commonly regarded as a specially sacred book.

Bodhidharma is credited with a fabulous age but there are various accounts of his death, all legendary. Tradition, however, is agreed in asserting that he transmitted his teaching to a line of five Chinese Patriarchs, making six including himself.[4] He handed the insignia of office, a robe and bowl, to Hui-K'o (Eka), the most eminent of his pupils. Hui-K'o had studied Taoism till his thirty-third year, but, hearing of Bodhidharma, desired to be instructed in his doctrine. In spite of his eagerness to learn he met with a cold reception, and, according to the legend, at last cut off his own arm and handed it to the master in order to attract his attention. The story goes on to relate that when he had become Patriarch he associated freely with butchers, debauchees, and the lowest of the people, avoiding the company of Buddhist priests, though he was a learned man. His preaching was most popular and the hierarchy at last induced the authorities to put him to death.

The third Patriarch, Sêng-Ts'an (Sōsan), wrote a celebrated poem called the Hsin-hsin-mei [5] but lived a retired life, as did also his successor, but the fifth Patriarch, Hung-Jên (Kōnin), was well-known as a teacher and his residence, the Yellow Plum monastery

[1] Wieger, *Bouddhisme Chinois*, p. 108.

[2] See Suzuki, *Studies in the Lankâvatâra-sûtra* (1930), p. 44 ff., where the question is discussed. The statement is made by both Tao-Hsüan (Nanjio, 1493) and Tao-Yüan (Nanjio, 1524) but criticized and denied by Ta-kuan T'an-ying (A.D. 985–1061).

[3] Another of the three works, the Vajracchedikâ, is also reported to have had an early connection with Zen and to have influenced the sixth Patriarch.

[4] Their names are: 2. 慧 可 Hui-K'o (Eka or Yeka), †593. 3. 僧 璨 Sêng-ts'an (Sōsan), †606. 4. 道 信 Tao-Hsin (Dōshin), †651. 5. 弘 忍 Hung-Jên (Kōnin), †675. 6. 慧 能 Hui-Nêng (Enō), †713.

[5] 信 心 銘. In Japanese pronunciation Shin-jin-mei.

in Anhui, became celebrated. Hither came a young man from Hsin-Chou in the south called Hui-Nêng (Enō), who, though illiterate, is said to have been attracted by what he heard of the teaching of the Vajracchedikâ-sûtra and was allowed to serve as a lay brother in the bakery. A well-known anecdote relates that Hung-Jên, feeling he was growing old, decided to hold a poetical competition and to nominate as his successor the composer of the best quatrain. The following lines, composed by Shen-Hsiu, his most eminent and learned disciple, called forth universal admiration :—

> The body is the Bodhi tree ;
> The mind is like the bright mirror's stand.
> Clean your mirror continually
> Lest the dust make it dim.[1]

Hui-Nêng as a lay brother was not qualified to compete and moreover could not write, but he induced another servant to inscribe the following lines on the monastery wall :—

> Bodhi is not a tree :
> The mirror has no stand.
> From the beginning nothing exists.
> How could dust cover it ? [2]

Hung-Jên was so struck by these lines that though Hui-Nêng was an illiterate lay-brother he made over to him the insignia of the Patriarchate and secretly designated him as his successor, though he himself lived four years longer. The appointment, however, was contested. Shen-Hsiu was learned and adroit. He attracted the attention of the Empress Wu and became a conspicuous figure at the capital. The doctrine which he taught is sometimes called the Northern School of Zen, or the gradual teaching, because he laid stress in the orthodox manner on study and meditation. But little is heard of this school in subsequent years and it died out. Attempts which were made to introduce it into Japan did not succeed. The illiterate Hui-Nêng, on the other hand, is universally accepted as the sixth Patriarch and as head of the Southern School

[1] 身是菩提樹
心如明鏡臺
時時勤拂拭
莫使惹塵埃

[2] 菩提本無樹
心鏡亦非臺
本來無一物
何處惹塵埃

in which was the life and future of Zen. Refusing all requests to go to the capital he taught in the country and had many pupils, the most eminent of whom was Yoka, author of the poem called Shōdōka. The Chinese Tripiṭaka contains a collection of discourses attributed to Hui-Nêng and compiled by his disciple Tsung-Pao, which is much venerated and probably contains some of his genuine utterances.[1] In opposition to the gradual teaching of the Northern School, he insisted that enlightenment is the result, not of preparation but of sudden illumination. One can see that this doctrine contains the germs of contempt for ritual, learning, and ecclesiastical institutions. Hui-Nêng refused to nominate a successor, becoming thus the last as well as the sixth of the Chinese Patriarchs.[2] This absence of hierarchy and the individualistic character of his teaching, for he was for ever bidding his pupils look into their own nature and find truth there, explain the fact that Zen split into several sects after his death. The story that the collection of his discourses was denounced and burnt is also not improbable. Nevertheless, the movement of which he was the author, or at any rate an early protagonist, was not dissipated in schisms or suppressed but contained the essence of the Zen, which became so great a religious and intellectual force not only in China but in Japan.

Hui-Nêng died in 713. Among his eminent followers, though not reckoned as a Patriarch, was Ma-Tsŭ (Baso), who is said to have trained eighty masters of Zen learning. Within about a century the Southern School became divided first into two and then into five sections, which took their names from the places where their founders lived. Two were of great importance for Japan, namely, the Lin-chi (Rinzai) and Ts'ao-T'ung (Sōtō).[3] Lin-Chi means coming to the ford, and the name was given to the school and to its founder because the latter, whose real name was I-Hsüan (†867), lived on the banks of a river in Chihli. He was the pupil of an eminent teacher named Huang-Po (Ōbaku), who was the friend of the Chancellor Hai-Kyū, but more celebrated in Zen literature for his habit of answering questions with a blow of his stick. The Zen

[1] Nanjio, 1525, 六祖大師法寶壇經 Liu-tsu-ta-shih-fa-pao-t'an-ching. Sûtra (spoken on) the platform by the sixth Patriarch, the great teacher, the treasure of the Law. The platform means the raised place on which ordinations were performed, and it is noticeable that the work is called a sûtra.

[2] This does not, however, prevent the Japanese from giving the title to much later masters. Thus Yengo (Yüan-Wu, 1063–1135) is called the Twentieth Patriarch.

[3] 臨濟, 曹洞.

teachers of this period were so unconventional and so anti-ritualistic that they seemed to be almost anti-Buddhist. A well-known anecdote relates how Tan-Hsia[1] (738–824) was once stopping in a temple where he felt chilly and calmly made a fire with one of the sacred images to warm himself. But in spite of this spirit the Rinzai sect flourished, and clearly Zen was not merely eccentric; there was also an orderly and constructive impulse. Thus Pai-Chang[2] (Hyakujō, 720–814) made regulations for Zen monasteries, especially for the discipline of the meditation hall, and laid down the very practical maxim "no work, no food". It would appear that up to this time the school had no special establishments or rule of its own but had shared cloisters with other monks.

In the eleventh century two new subdivisions arose called after their founders Yang-chi (Yogi) and Huang-Lung (Ōryū), but the name Lin-chi remained and the school became dominant to such an extent that at the present day the majority of Chinese monasteries profess to belong to it. It is consequently difficult to ascertain what were its original and distinctive tenets, but it clearly adhered to the doctrine emphasized by the Patriarch Hui-Nêng that enlightenment comes by sudden illumination and transference of thought from teacher to pupil, not by meditation, prayer, or study.

The Ts'ao-T'ung school, founded by the two teachers known as Ts'ao-Shan and Tung-Shan[3] (869), was not so influential in China as the Lin-chi but had great success in Japan, where it was known as Sōtō. It laid stress on the need for silent introspection as a preparation for enlightenment and also on ethics. The Lin-chi is not antinomian but, like the Upanishads and the Vedanta, it regards the knowledge of the Buddha nature or Brahman as an end in itself, all-satisfying and all-engrossing. When once the eye of the spirit is opened to the divine vision, nothing more is said about worship or conduct or any human ideal. But the other school held that it is necessary to have Enlightenment after Enlightenment,[4] that is to say, that the inner illumination must display itself in a good life. The Lin-chi, however, did not become the dominant school and absorb all others without assimilating their doctrines,

[1] 丹霞. [2] 百丈.

[3] Strictly speaking, these are the names of two mountains where they resided, their personal names being 良价 Ryo-kai and 本寂 Honjaku. 曹洞 Sōtō or Ts'ao-Tung is formed by combining the first syllables of the name of the mountains in Japanese or Chinese pronunciation.

[4] 悟後の悟. Pronounced in Japanese as Go go no satori.

and Zen could never have influenced Chinese philosophy, including Confucian philosophy, if it had not contained an ethical element.

The Lin-chi (Rinzai) was introduced into Japan by Eisai (1215) and the Ts'ao-T'ung (Sōtō) by Dōgen (1253), both of whom studied in China when the Sung dynasty was reigning at Hangchou.

The materials for the history of Zen consist chiefly of biographical notes. Now anecdotes are notoriously easy to invent and easy to transfer from one celebrity to another, particularly in universities and monasteries. Zen produced a well-marked type of master or professor who taught by brief paradoxical sayings varied by blows and kicks, but this eccentricity becomes so monotonous that it is difficult to follow the growth and development of doctrines and institutions which undoubtedly took place. Three stages can be traced with some certainty.

First of all a great teacher comes from India. In spite of the legends which have grown round the name of Bodhidharma in China and the absence of any record of him in the West, it seems impossible to doubt that he arrived at Canton and preached a doctrine which was called Buddhism, though in the form in which it is reported to us in Chinese literature it seems more like Vedantism expressed in Buddhist terminology. It is true that we cannot be sure that what is reported is really the preaching of Bodhidharma. It may be a later invention but, if so, it is not easy to see by what channel this Vedantist influence reached China.

The century following Bodhidharma is filled by the lives of his five successors called Patriarchs. Some of them lived in retirement. Contemporary Buddhist opinion seems to have regarded them as outside the limits permitted by orthodoxy and they even suffered some persecution. They appear to have been influenced by Taoism. Hui-K'o, the second Patriarch, was a student of Chinese philosophy and Sêng-Ts'an, the third, speaks of the Way (Tao) in exactly the same manner as Lao-Tzŭ and his followers. His poem, the Hsin-hsin-mei, opens with the words: "To attain the Way is not hard: only reject all relative ideas" (that is, ideas such as Self and others, good and evil).[1] Under the last Patriarch, about A.D. 700, we see signs of a division in doctrine and temper. Part of the school tended to follow the lines of traditional orthodoxy, but though it enjoyed the favour of the Court, it was evidently wanting in spiritual

[1] 至道無難 唯嫌揀擇

vigour which was abundantly present among the adherents of Hui-Neng. The Patriarchate came to an end: numerous schools arose: the whole tone seems protestant and anti-ecclesiastical. Then comes the third stage. In spite of divisions the sect grew and flourished as a whole: numbers and success made the need of discipline and ecclesiastical manners to be felt: special monasteries and a special rule of life were established, and the external usages of Buddhism were respected, to such an extent that the Lin-chi became the typical form of Chinese Buddhism. But it long preserved its originality and it is precisely this original element which was an inspiration for art and philosophy.

In the sixth century arose another most important school, the T'ien-t'ai or Tendai, which had also a long and eventful history in Japan. Like Zen it was truly Chinese, that is to say, it was not an importation from India but a reconstruction of Buddhism made with Indian materials, of course, but with plenty of native mortar. In other respects it was very unlike Zen. It rose from the first like some stately cathedral duly equipped with prelates, chapter, cloisters, and library, a home for theology, approved metaphysics, literature, sacred art, and music.

Hui-Wên (†550)[1] is reckoned the first patriarch of this school, but its real founder was Chih-K'ai or Chih-I (531–597).[2] He was a native of Hupeh and a pupil of Hui-Ssŭ,[3] also regarded as a Patriarch. In 575 he retired to the mountains called T'ien-t'ai, "the platform of heaven," in Chekiang, from which his school took its name. When fifty years of age he began to lecture on the Lotus-sûtra. No less then twenty-two works attributed to him are included in the Chinese Tripiṭaka, but nearly all of them are really notes of his lectures and sayings taken down by his disciple Kwang-Ting.[4] Three of them are considered of such importance that they are known as "the Three Great Works".[5] The first and second

[1] 慧文 Hui-Wên or Emon.

[2] 智顗 Chih-I, also called 智者太師 Chih-chê-tai-shih and commonly known in Japan as Tendai Daishi.

[3] 慧思 Hui-Ssŭ (†577) was a teacher of some importance in the history of the school. The Tripiṭaka contains four works attributed to him. Nanjio, Nos. 1541–2, 1547, and 1576.

[4] 灌頂. In Japanese pronunciation Kwanjō. He was also called Shōạn.

[5] 三大部. The names are: (*a*) 妙法蓮華經玄義 Miao-fa-lien-hua-ching-hsüan-i. The profound meaning of the Lotus-sûtra. Nanjio, 1534. (*b*) 妙法蓮華經玄義文句 Miao-fa-lien-hua-ching-hsüan-i-wên-chü. Commentary on the above. Nanjio, 1536. (*c*) 摩訶止觀 Ma-ha-chih-kuan. Nanjio, 1538.

are commentaries on the Lotus, one being a systematic exposition of Buddhist philosophy and the other an explanation of the text. The third is a treatise on meditation as understood by the T'ien-t'ai. These three works are usually accompanied by commentaries written on them by Chan-Jan, the ninth Patriarch of the school. Another series of similar records is called the Five Small Works [1] and consists of explanations on the Samantamukha chapter of the Lotus, the Suvarṇaprabhâsa-sûtra, and the Amitâyurdhyâna-sûtra, the first two works having each two commentaries, one comprehensive and the other textual. In all the Tripiṭaka contains about seventy works ascribed to the doctors of the T'ien-t'ai, by far the largest output which any one school has to show in the Canon.

The teaching of Chih-I is more than any other school an independent attempt of the Far East to deal with the literary and metaphysical problems which confront the student of Buddhism. It is marked by its catholic, many sided, and almost encyclopædic character. Chih-I regarded the Lotus as the quintessence of truth,[2] but fully approved of the worship of Amida and died invoking his name. He wished to find a place for every kind of religious exercise and a point of view from which all forms of thought might be seen to have some value. His method is illustrated by his classification of Buddhist doctrines under the headings the Five Times and Eight Teachings, of which I have spoken already.[3] He sees no antagonism between the Hîna- and Mahâyâna or between the various schools. All scripture is good and true if considered as a revelation made at a given time to suit the minds of particular hearers. Ordinary mankind cannot understand the absolute and complete truth all at once: they must be led up to it through relative truth which, though provisional and imperfect, is not erroneous. And though the literal division of the Buddha's life into five periods of activity as a teacher will hardly be accepted by modern criticism, there are indications that Chih-I was not merely thinking of his human existence but conceived of him (quite in the manner of the Lotus) as always preaching and always

[1] 五小部 Wu-hsiao-pu. See Nanjio, 1555–7, –48, –52, –59.

[2] Even in the choice of a sacred book his love of comprehensiveness and combination is visible. He is said to be the author of the arrangement by which the Lotus as used by the Tendai sect is combined with two other sûtras, the 無量義經 Muryōgi-kyō (Nan., 133) and the 觀普賢菩薩行法經 Kwan Fugen Bosatsu gyōhō-kyō (Nan., 394).

[3] Chapter I, p. 7.

offering to the various types of intelligence the form of truth which is best suited to their comprehension.

Since the T'ien-t'ai regards the Lotus as its principal scripture, Śâkyamuni has naturally a prominent place in its public worship. He is the Nirmâṇakâya, the Dharmakâya, and Sambhogakâya, being respectively represented by Vairocana and Locanâ.[1] But, in harmony with the general principles described above, the three bodies are regarded as one, or as three aspects of one, not as a triad in which the secondary bodies are derived from the Dharmakâya or produced by it. Further, the essential nature of the Dharmakâya is constant activity for the good of all men, and a distinction is drawn between the fundamental Buddhahood (pen) and the trace (chi) left among men by the Buddha to educate them.[2] Amitâbha, Kuan-Yin, and the other great Bodhisattvas are also worshipped and there is a special procedure for meditating on Amitâbha.

The T'ien-t'ai doctors do not like the assertion that their teaching is derived from the Zen, and indeed it is not correct to represent it as a mere amplification or development of that school. But Chinese texts certainly represent the first three Patriarchs as having started by being adherents of Zen and there is nothing uncomplimentary to the T'ien-t'ai in supposing that they found it inadequate and careless of all sides of religion except one. The ecclesiastical biographies of Tao-Hsüan[3] describe both Hui-Ssŭ and Chih-I as Ch'an-shih, teachers of Zen, and Nien Ch'ang's History of Buddhism[4] applies the same epithet to Hui-Wen. Dengyō Daishi, too, who introduced the T'ien-t'ai into Japan, traces his spiritual lineage to Bodhidharma.[5]

The monasteries, for there were several of them, in the T'ien-t'ai hills were long a centre of learning. In the eighth century flourished the ninth Patriarch Chan-Jan, who wrote important commentaries,

[1] 毘盧遮那 Pi-lu-chê-na, 盧舍那 Lu-chê-na. See above, Chap. IV, p. 107–9, for these names.

[2] 本 pen, 蹟 chi.

[3] Nanjio, 1493, 續高僧傳 Su-kao-sêng-chuan, vol. xxi, sheets 7, 11–12, and 16–17, Ōbaku edition. In the table of contents both Hui-Ssŭ and Chih-I are classed under Zen. The same title of Ch'an-shih is given by the Transmission of the Lamp (Nanjio, 1524) to Hui-Wen and Hui-Ssŭ (Ōbaku edition, vol. xxvii, sheet 6) and Chih-I (sheet 8) and also to Hui-Wen and Chih-I in Ch'ih-P'an's history of the Patriarchs, N. 1661, vol. vi, sheet 53 in the Tōkyō edition.

[4] Nanjio, 1637, 佛祖歷代通載, vol. x, sheet 70, Tōkyō edition.

[5] In his book called 內證佛法相承血脈譜 Naishō Buppō Sōshō Kechi-myaku-fu.

but in the disturbed period known as the Five Dynasties (907–960) the establishments and libraries of the school suffered severely. Fortunately it had a branch in Korea, and Ti-Kuan,[1] a learned Korean priest, came to China in 960 bringing with him copies of the principal sacred books which had been almost entirely lost. Owing to his exertions the school again became flourishing and until the fourteenth century continued to produce works which were admitted to the Tripiṭaka. But after the fourteenth century its distinctive features tended to become less conspicuous.

In the seventh and eighth centuries three sects based on Indian works flourished in China and reached Japan, where they are known as Kusha, Hossō, and Kegon. But though they testify to the lively interest in Indian philosophy then prevalent, they were somewhat literary and scholastic and had not sufficient vitality to acquire more than a restricted popularity. Hence they have either disappeared or remain only as historical survivals. The Kusha School [2] concerned itself with the study and exposition of the Abhidharmakośa, which occupies in Buddhism a position somewhat similar to that of the *Summa Theologiæ* of Thomas Aquinas in the Catholic Church. The name pronounced Fa-Hsiang [3] in Chinese and Hossō in Japanese is a translation of Dharmalakshana. The school traces its origin to Silabhadra, the Indian teacher of Hsüan-Tsang, but the great pilgrim himself was its real founder. Its textbook is the Yuishiki, of which I have already spoken and which is based on the Trimsika of Vasubandhu. The Hua-Yen or Kegon [4] School has a distinguished literary record, for about twenty-five works composed by its adherents, including four patriarchs, are contained in the Tripiṭaka; but though for a time it enjoyed the respect of ecclesiastical and learned circles, it does not seem to have had much general influence. Its doctrine is simply that of the Hua-Yen or Avataṃsaka-sûtra. It was founded by Tu Fa-Shun, who died in 640, and it appears to have declined after the tenth century. Both this school and the Hossō still nominally exist in Japan, for they are represented by ancient and learned corporations which administer very considerable ecclesiastical properties, but they do not claim to teach a special doctrine differing from that of other sects.

[1] 諦觀. He was the author of a work on the four methods of teaching. Nanjio, 1551.

[2] 俱舍. Chinese Chu-she.

[3] 法相. [4] 華嚴.

The seventh century was obviously prolific in literary and philosophical sects, but there may have been a tendency to forget that Buddhism means not merely indulgence of intellectual tastes but a life lived under a fixed rule. Such seems to have been the apprehension of Tao-Hsüan [1] (595–667), a distinguished priest who founded the Lü (Japanese Ritsu) or Vinaya School. He laid comparatively little stress on doctrine, but held that strict morality and discipline are the foundation and essence of the religious life. Eight of his works are included in the Tripiṭaka and indicate a practical mind inclined to such subjects as ecclesiastical history, biography, and Church government.[2] He also compiled a catalogue of the Tripiṭaka as it existed in his time.[3] In matters of discipline he entirely followed Indian precedents and made the Dharmagupta Vinaya, commonly known as the Code in Four Sections,[4] his chief authority; but still the idea of thus emphasizing the Vinaya seems to have originated in China and not to have been imitated from any Indian movement. He was highly respected during his life, and long after his death the Emperor Mu-Tsung (821–5) wrote a poem in his honour. The school still exists in China, and its monasteries, though not numerous, have a high reputation for learning and strict discipline. It was introduced into Japan by Kanjin in the Tempyō era and for some time played an important part in questions of ecclesiastical administration, but, though it still exists, it has only ten temples.

In the eighth century the formative period of Chinese Buddhism came to an end .Only one sect of general importance arose, and that was a direct importation from India and not a native growth or reconstruction of foreign materials. It is called Chên-yen,[5] the true word, or Mi-chiao, the secret teaching. It is simply the Mantrayâna or Tantric Buddhism which was prevalent at that time in India, especially in Bengal, and had borrowed from contemporary Hinduism many of its least admirable features, such as the use of

[1] 道宣.

[2] Thus he continued the series called Memoirs of Eminent Priests and wrote forty volumes about those who lived between 519 and 645 (Nanjio, 1493). He wrote a history of the Buddha's family and country (N., 1469–70), and compiled collections of documents respecting controversies between Buddhists and Taoists (N., 1471) and other matters.

[3] Nanjio, 1483. The fifth catalogue. It is generally known as Nei-tien-lu and was published in 664.

[4] Nanjio, 1117. It is similar to the Vinaya used in Tibet.

[5] 眞言.

spells and magic ritual. Such ceremonies were only too much to the taste of the Chinese public and in later times it is hard to see that this school was in any way a good influence. But in its earlier stages it may have been better. It attracted the attention of the great Kōbō Daishi when he studied in China and was introduced by him into his native country in 806, where it speedily became and still is one of the largest and most important sects. Its wonderful ceremonies and ample pantheon were naturally attractive, and in skilful Japanese hands its many deities lost much of the grotesqueness which mars Indian tantrism and rivalled Zen as a source of artistic inspiration. The founder and first Patriarch was Vajrabodhi, who came from Molaiye, which appears to mean the extreme south of India, in 719 and remained in China until he died in 732. He made eleven translations, many of which are connected with a tantric work called the Vajraśekhara-sûtra, but both as a translator and teacher his fame is eclipsed by his pupil and successor Amoghavajra, whose name is rendered into Chinese as Pu-K'ung.[1] Amoghavajra was apparently a native of northern India who came to China with his master in 719, and after the latter's death went again to India and Ceylon (741–6) to collect manuscripts. His return was well-timed, for he arrived in the reign of Hsüan-Tsung and remained at the capital under his successors Su-Tsung and Tai-Tsung just at the period when Buddhism enjoyed great but perhaps not very healthy favour at the T'ang court. He wished to go back to his own country but permission was refused, and in compensation he was loaded with titles and honours. He played a prominent part in the lengthy and elaborate ceremonies which were performed on behalf of the Emperor's deceased mother in 758 and subsequent years, and it seems that it was from this date that the custom of holding services for the dead according to Buddhist rites was officially recognized. Amoghavajra is also said to have introduced the practice of placing the images of the four kings at the entrance of temples. He lived till 774 and no less than one hundred and eight translations from his pen are contained in the Chinese Tripiṭaka, but they are mostly short tantric works and spells of a few pages which cannot be compared with the heroic efforts of Hsüang-Tsang and other earlier translators.[2]

[1] 不空 Pu-K'ung.

[2] A portrait of Amoghavajra by Li-Chien, who was perhaps his contemporary, is reproduced in Tajima's *Masterpieces*, vol. viii, pl. ix.

When treating of the Shingon in Japan it will be necessary to consider its special and highly complicated doctrines, but I do not propose to describe them now. Nor is its history as a sect in China eventful. Like the Pure Land school it became not so much a separate corporation as an aspect of almost every sect, and in particular it is responsible for most of the superstitious ceremonies which form a large part of Chinese funeral rites.

# BOOK II

# HISTORY OF JAPANESE BUDDHISM

# CHAPTER VI

## PREFATORY REMARKS

Japan is unique among Asiatic countries and it is not surprising to find that Japanese Buddhism, though imported from China, has a flavour of its own. The first impressions of the tourist are confirmed by the researches of the historian. Any technical definition of Japanese Buddhism as a form of Mahâyâna is inadequate. Whatever its pedigree may be, whatever the doctrines which it accepts in theory, its various phases not only to-day but in some thousand odd years of history smack of the soil. Yet having said this it may be well, at the risk of seeming inconsistent, to point out that the singularity of Japanese Buddhism is partly due to the fact that it is the only instance of Mahayanism now flourishing as a vital religion among people intellectually comparable to Siamese, Sinhalese, or Burmans. Whatever Chinese Buddhism and Lamaism may be for individuals, they are for the masses mere superstitions like the notions of the ignorant peasantry in the countries that follow the Roman or Eastern Churches. But Japanese Buddhism, in spite of national influences both political and artistic, is the lineal and recognized descendant of the creed held by Nâgârjuna, Vasubandhu, and Śântideva. Special sects treat special doctrines as the whole of religion, but this probably happened in India too. If the language of Japanese Buddhism often seems odd, this is because the writers who introduced it to the notice of Europe (such as Ryauon Fujishima, Lafcadio Hearn, and Kuroda) employed a terminology different from that used by Pali and Sanskrit scholars.

The most salient feature of Japanese Buddhism is its intimate connection with the general condition of the nation, both political and social. It has vibrated in response to many and abrupt political changes, it has registered them in its sects and expressed in its art the special note of each. This, perhaps, is only another way of saying that the history of Japan, in spite of long periods of seclusion, is unique among Asiatic peoples for variety and sensitiveness to foreign impressions, and that these characteristics appear in religion as elsewhere. But, at any rate, the result is that we have here an attitude to religion common in Europe but rare in Asia. Though Asiatic creeds are intimately connected with the life of the people, though they may flourish or decay as the favour of princes is extended or withdrawn, they still seem to be something aloof and superhuman like the forces of nature. But in Japan we have phenomena that recall Europe. Ancient churches worldly and artistic, intriguing with Emperors and ministers to establish a theocracy or endeavouring more directly to grasp temporal power by maintaining troops and turning monasteries into feudal castles: protestant sects casting aside tradition and ritual to offer the common man salvation by faith but not disdaining political power: sects preaching national or universal religion but remaining in a minority: and in the eighteenth century a comfortable Established Church, not unlike that of England at the same time, bidding people maintain their parish temples but putting no great strain on conduct or belief. For a devout Buddhist the record is not edifying, but for the student of religious evolution it is interesting to see how Buddhism could adapt itself to a new and vivacious country, fertile in fresh ideas and subject to periodic metamorphoses. To us the most conspicuous of these is the assimilation of European methods in the nineteenth century, but the earlier changes occasioned by the reforms of Shōtoku Taishi and the establishment of the Kamakura and Tokugawa Shogunates were hardly less drastic.

Buddhism is, of course, not the only religion of Japan. The position is much the same as in China. People may follow Buddhism, Shintoism, or Confucianism, any two of them or all three together. The movement called Shingaku,[1] which was active at the beginning of the nineteenth century, actually attempted such a combination. Still, the resemblance to China, if not superficial, is also not quite complete. Confucianism, though a potent influence at more than one epoch, hardly obtained the status of a separate religion. Buddhism on the other hand may be said to have been the State Church, though in no exclusive sense, during some ten centuries until in 1868 it was suddenly superseded by Shintoism.

The ancient religion of Japan was originally without a name, but after the introduction of Buddhism was called Shintō, the way of the Gods, to distinguish it from Butsudō, or the way of the Buddha. It consists in the veneration of ancestors and nature spirits and is

[1] 心學 "Heart Learning".

thus analogous to the most ancient religion of China, but differs in the total absence of any monotheistic idea corresponding to T'ien or Heaven. Some authorities, especially W. G. Aston, deny that Shintoism includes ancestor worship, and in support of this it may be urged that it considers corpses as impure and that funeral rites may not be performed in Shintō temples. But on the other hand the veneration of ancestors is undoubtedly an ancient and important part of Japanese religion : there is absolutely no indication that it was a separate creed, and the principal deity of Shintō, the Sun-goddess, is venerated less as a personification of the sun than as the ancestress of the Imperial Family.

We have little historic evidence of the nature of pre-Buddhist Shintoism except the legends contained in the Kojiki and Nihongi, but what survives to-day is so little affected by medieval or modern ideas that it may be considered the exact reproduction of the ancient creed, just as the wooden temples of Ise which are rebuilt every twenty years preserve the architecture of almost prehistoric times. If popular religion in China reminds us of the beliefs and practices prevalent in the early Roman Empire, Shintō takes us back to older forms of thought and to the archaic strata of Greek and Latin religion. It is strange that this ancient ceremonial paganism should have survived among an unusually intelligent and progressive race. It is not even artistic, for it worships no images and the strange dreamlike legends of its gods resemble the stories of the Kalewala or of Polynesian mythology. It has no moral code ; its prayers and sacrifices aim at obtaining temporal prosperity and indicate no desire for moral or spiritual blessings. Yet these strange lacunæ are somehow filled by its intensely patriotic spirit. For it Japan is the land of the Gods : the greater preside over the Empire, the lesser over towns or hamlets ; the noble or the humbler dead have their due place in the cult of the State, city, or family. So primitive is the thought of Shintō that it is hardly correct to say that natural features or individuals are deified. They are simply accepted as important facts in the continuous national life and addresses or appeals are made to them about such things as concern them. This sense of continuity in national life, though expressed in almost childlike language, is really equivalent to saying that the individual exists only as the member of a family and the family as a member of the State : that the present must sacrifice itself to the traditions of the past and the needs of the future. And thus the heroism of Japan grows naturally out of a religion which if considered unsympathetically in the light of pure reason is as foolish as a fairy tale.

It is a further testimony to the strength of Shintō that it did not collapse with the introduction and acceptance of another creed. Its survival was partly due to the tolerant temper of Buddhism so often noticed in these pages, but still it did not become a popular superstition like the worship of the Nats in Burma. After a period of hostility a compromise was arranged known as Ryōbu-Shintō, or twofold Shintō, by which the Shintō gods were recognized as incarnations of Buddhas or of Bodhisattvas and the control of their temples, except in Ise, Izumo, and some other special localities, was handed over to Buddhist priests. This arrangement acted as a preservative. Shintō, being intimately associated with a vast religious system which had infinite receipts for satisfying the emotional, speculative, and moral aspirations of a progressive people, felt no obligation to change or expand. Yet it was not smothered or embalmed: it remained the State religion for certain solemn functions, and when in the middle of the nineteenth century a wave of political feeling demanded not only a Japanese Emperor but a Japanese creed, it emerged in its pristine simplicity.

In fact, it is Buddhism that shows the influence of Shintoism rather than vice versa, for it has been obliged to sanction the veneration of ancestors as a general principle and also many local beliefs and customs. Yet the peculiarities of Japanese Buddhism cannot be explained as an imitation of Shintō. They are due rather to the bold freedom with which the Japanese made selections from the unwieldy mass of Indian and Chinese ideas presented to them. In religion as in other matters they showed a talent for combining imitation with transformation.

One obvious feature of Japanese thought, illustrated by this very compromise of Ryōbu-Shintō, is its tendency to unite religions. All creeds have met with tolerance, except those which like Catholic Christianity in the past were intolerant themselves, and all are assumed to mean much the same. Thus Bakin the novelist says: "Shintō reverences the way of the sun: the Chinese philosophers honour heaven: the teaching of the Buddha fails not to make the sun a deity. Among differences of doctrine the fundamental doctrine is the same." This is not really true as a historical statement respecting the original teaching of these religions, but it is not an incorrect description of them as professed in Japan. The Shintō Sun-goddess was identified with the Buddha Vairocana, who is perhaps a Persian Sun-god imported into Buddhism, and the assertion that these two deities are the same contains an obvious truth and it makes for peace. Even the intolerant Nichiren seems to have had no doubts about the Sun-goddess. In a letter written towards the end of his life he says: "Though Awa is far from the centre it is somewhat like the centre of Japan, because the Sun-goddess found there her first abode . . . and I, Nichiren, began the propagation of the true religion by proclaiming it first in Awa." [1]

The simple Shintō view that great men are supernatural beings is practically the same as subtle Indian theories about incarnations, and a religion which recognized the Hindu fathers of the Church as Bodhisattvas felt no difficulty in extending the same honour to the pillars of the faith in Japan. Shōtoku Taishi, Kōbō Daishi, Hōnen, Shinran, and many others receive a veneration hardly inferior to that accorded to deities. The founder of the sect is often regarded by his followers as an incarnation and the hall dedicated to him is one of the most conspicuous parts of a temple. Buddhist and Shintoist ideas thus coalesced and the title of Bodhisattva was conferred on departed Emperors and statesmen [2]—on those, for instance, who are described as Hachiman, the patron of soldiers, and Tenjin, the God of Calligraphy, and even on so recent a personage as Ieyasu.

This last step seems a parody of Buddhism, yet the view of the ordinary Japanese Buddhist is not unreasonable. He holds that it is right to be grateful to the heroes of the past and to commemorate them: that all men have in them the power to become Buddhas and that those who obtain distinction may justly bear the title of Bodhisattva as being near the final phase. This liberal appreciation of talent and learning in every form finds expression in the statement that the Buddha preached 84,000 varieties of doctrine. Similar ideas are found in India and China, and on this as on other points I ought to say that in describing a belief as characteristic of Japan I do not mean to deny its existence in China. Japanese Buddhism is at least relatively clear cut and well-ordered: its doctrines can be formulated, even if the process (as in other religions) provokes surprise from the plain man on learning what he believes. What is obscure or forgotten in China is often stated plainly in Japan.

[1] See Anesaki's *Nichiren, the Buddhist Prophet*, p. 106.

[2] Ōjin, the fifteenth Emperor of Japan, is considered to be the same as Hachiman. Sugiwara Michizane (845–903), a statesman who was exiled in life, was deified as Tenjin and has a temple in most Japanese towns.

Japanese Buddhists admit that the truth, if one in essence, need not be one in expression. The Zen holds that absolute truth is not taught in scripture and is not expressible in words. It must be discovered by intuition or learnt by telepathy. Yet *hōben*,[1] or accommodations of this absolute truth to the intelligence of the hearer, such as anthropomorphism or doctrines of heaven and hell, are not condemned. They are real and justifiable helps for some natures.

Something very like this view is held by apparently dogmatic sects though they do not emphasize it. The followers of the Jōdo schools, while advocating faith in Amida as the best means of salvation in a degenerate age, do not theoretically deny other methods and admit that Amida as a personality is merely "an accommodated[2] truth", a form of the eternal oneness but not absolute. The Tendai sect divides the life of the Buddha into five periods devoted to promulgating as many doctrines, the Tendai teaching being, of course, the last, best, and all inclusive. Even the intolerant sect of Nichiren, while claiming a monopoly of the doctrine proper to this age, admits that by the Buddha's ordinance different doctrines were preached at different times.[3] In most sects this theory of ages is coupled with the idea that the present period is Mappō, or the destruction of the Law. A new period in which the true faith will flourish again is to be inaugurated by the next Buddha Maitreya. Messianic ideas are not very prominent but are not unknown, as is shown by the legend that Kōbō Daishi is not dead but merely awaiting in his tomb the coming of a new era.

With such views as to permissible variations in belief, it is remarkable not that there should be so many sects of Buddhism in Japan but rather that they should be so clear and so well defined, not mere schools of thought but sects in the European sense of the word, self-assertive and even militant. The individualism of the faithful is as strong as the tendency to think that every one means much the same, so that the Buddhist world of Japan combines fervour with toleration. This distinction of sects is partly due to the simple fact that their teaching is distinct. The creeds of the Zen, Nichiren, and Shinshū are not really the same: they hardly have a common origin, for the Shinshū is not so much a development

[1] 方便.

[2] See e.g. "A Catechism of the Shinshū Sect," *Trans. As. Soc. Japan*, 1912, p. 268.

[3] This is a legitimate deduction from the Lotus-sûtra.

of Buddhism as a set of new ideas ingeniously fitted on to it. Sectarian differences have also been strengthened by social and political circumstances. Some sects are old and aristocratic, embodied in great monastic foundations, whose vitality as corporations outlasted the importance of their special tenets. Others are popular and protestant, striving when they were founded and still striving now to bring religion up to date. Among these popular sects some are reactions against others. Almost all have at some time or another fought as corporate bodies and in defence of their temporal possessions. Hence side by side with the sentiment that a respectable family should follow the rites of its parish temple there is not wanting religious enthusiasm. The former sentiment is a legacy of the Tokugawa régime. In the troubled period which preceded it there were philosophers, but the average religious man was a partisan and combative.

In Japan as in all Far Eastern countries Buddhism is closely connected with the veneration paid to the dead. Until the Meiji era all funerals were performed by Buddhist priests, and even now many Japanese who have little to do with Buddhism during their lives are buried according to its rites. Some of the older sects seem to be literally religions of the dead. For instance, it seemed to me when I was visiting the great temple of Tennōji at Osaka that the priests and the numerous worshippers were all engaged in intercessory or commemorative ceremonies on behalf of the departed. In Buddhist families the mortuary tablets are placed before the household shrine which occupies a shelf in one of the inner apartments and the dead are commonly spoken of as Buddhas (hotoke-sama). This bold language is, so far as I know, peculiar to Japan and is an imitation of Shintō. The Shintō dead become (it is not explained how) Kami or superhuman beings, for the translation "gods" is an exaggeration: it could hardly be allowed that the Buddhist dead had an inferior status and they were therefore termed Buddhas, Buddha and Kami being, according to popular ideas, much the same.

Further, the notion that every one, nay even every grain of dust, can become a Buddha, though not unknown to Indian Buddhism, is more popular in Japan than elsewhere,[1] and to Japanese politeness it does not seem an exaggeration to speak of the commonplace dead as having achieved the highest destiny. This close connection with

[1] A common saying is "Grass, trees, land and earth will become Buddha".

family and national sentiment has preserved Buddhism from many dangers, particularly during its lethargy under the Tokugawa régime. It is remarkable how in the various religions of the world sentiment and practice vary with regard to intercessory and commemorative services on behalf of the dead. Such rites are not countenanced in the Old or New Testaments nor in the Koran, and apparently did not appeal to Semites. On the other hand, they formed the greater part of religion among the Chinese, Japanese, and ancient Egyptians and a considerable, though less conspicuous part among Hindus, Slavs, and Roman Catholics of all nations. Protestants of all races seem to eschew them. The desire to perform such ceremonies seems to depend partly on race and partly on religion.

The externals of Japanese Buddhism are its own and increase the feeling that we are dealing with something native and individual, though such a sect as the Shingon is hardly separable in theory from the theology of China or Tibet. There is little that is grotesque or monstrous, perhaps little that is majestic. But everything is marked by reticence, grace, and kindliness : pathos and humour are not absent. There are colossi and pictured demons for those who want them, but in most temples the worshipper is welcomed by compassionate angels and gods of healing : the images are natural and benevolent and are often set behind screens or in cabinets, thus suggesting the worship of some half-seen presence rather than idolatry.

The pantheon offers some peculiarities. Dogmatic, though perhaps not popular, theology recognizes the existence of a Universal Buddha mind manifested in various forms. According to the older sects these are theoretically five, but in practice one is selected for adoration. Thus the Shingon sect reveres Dainichi (Vairocana): the Shinshū worships Amida (Amitâbha) only, rejecting all other Buddhas and Bodhisattvas. The Nichiren sect declares (with considerable historical truth) that Dainichi, Amida, etc., are mere inventions and regards Shaka, that is Gotama the historical Buddha, as the one manifestation of the Eternal Buddhahood suitable for veneration in modern times. It admits, however, the worship of Bodhisattvas. All sects except the Shinshū pay reverence to a great number of these, the distinction between a Buddha and Bodhisattva being often ignored in practice. As in China, Kwannon (Kuan-Yin) is much worshipped and corresponds to the Madonna or Goddess of Mercy. Ancient masculine images of this deity occur, but in modern times she is universally regarded as feminine, though perhaps it would be truer to say that the figure is sexless like a Christian angel. Though the images of the great Bodhisattvas Monju and Fugen often stand by the side of Shaka, they do not receive much attention, but Jizō (Kshitigarbha), a deity inconspicuous outside China and Japan, is, so to speak, a male Kwannon. He is regarded as the helper of all in trouble and in particular as the protector of dead children.

It is somewhat remarkable that several Indian deities who are little known or forgotten in China should still be well known in Japan. Such as Shōden or Kwangiten (Ganeśa): Kishi Mojin or Hâritî, another protector of dead children and, like Jizō, honoured by many touching offerings: Benten or Sarasvatî, and Fudō, commonly, though perhaps erroneously, regarded as the god of fire. Etymologically his name is equivalent to the Sanskrit Acala and he appears to be a form of Śiva. Binzuru (or Piṇḍola) is another figure at present apparently known only to the Buddhism of Japan, though he has Indian antecedents. He is regarded as the god of medicine and his image may often be found outside temples representing him in a sitting position. I find it somewhat difficult to explain the presence of these Indian deities in Japan when they are unknown or neglected in China. The absence of Ganeśa in that country [1] may perhaps be due to a prohibition of his worship, and in Binzuru, Kompira, and perhaps other figures there may be a mixture of a Buddhist original with something native. But how are we to account for Benten, Fudō, and others? The Indian and Cambodjan priests who settled at Nara in early days do not seem to have been sufficiently numerous to explain the wide diffusion of these cults.

Apart from sects and doctrines, there are at least three types of Japanese Buddhism. One may be called the old parochial form. Japanese when born are registered in a certain temple: when they die, their funeral rites are performed there or in another of the same sect. During their life they are mostly not regular worshippers but from time to time subscribe money for pious objects and go on pilgrimages which are half picnics. The second form, exhibited by the Shinshū and Nichiren sects, is an active and popular religion. Its temples are beautiful: it has created many excellent institutions, both educational and philanthropic: among its leaders are men of

[1] See Chapter IV, p. 139.

learning, intelligence, and ability. Yet neither sect can be said to represent educated public opinion. A large class of people in England, important both socially and intellectually, would be astonished if asked whether they attended the services of the Salvation Army and revivalist meetings. A similar class in Japan would be equally astonished at the idea of attending Buddhist services.

A third form of Buddhism may be studied by English readers in the writings of educated Japanese such as Sōyen Shaku and M. G. Mori,[1] who endeavour to combine Buddhism with European science and philosophy. Their writings remind one of those western apologists who attempt the same task for Christianity. In reading these Japanese works we feel that the words remain, but that the sense given to them is not that which they bore in Sanskrit or even in Chinese. The expositors are less anxious to let the Buddha or Nâgârjuna speak for themselves than to prove that their sayings are agreeable to the latest European theories in science and philosophy. Yet though the reader feels that these reinterpretations give him neither what the ancients meant nor what ordinary modern Buddhists believe, they are not unreasonable, for the fundamental principles of Buddhism are more in harmony with the results of scientific research than are the postulates of Christian theism. A considerable amount of valuable learned literature dealing with Buddhism—such as dictionaries of Buddhism in general and of special sects, biographies, critical editions, and historical studies—is being published in Japanese. The principal works are noticed in the bibliographies which appear from time to time in the *Bulletin de l'École Française d'Extrême Orient*. Archæological expeditions also have been sent from Japan to China and Central Asia.

It may seem that I do not credit Buddhism with much influence in Japan. That assuredly is not my intention, but it would be misleading to speak of it as having the same position as Islam used to have in Turkey or Hinduism still has in large parts of India. It has often been asked whether the Japanese are a religious people or not and the question has received diametrically opposite answers.[2] The affirmative is, I think, the truer, if religion is taken in the wide sense of devotion to something beyond individual existence, of

[1] Sōyen Shaku, *Sermons of a Buddhist Abbot*. Mori, *Buddhism and Faith*.
[2] e.g. from Lafcadio Hearn and B. H. Chamberlain.

readiness to sacrifice to it earthly welfare and life itself, nay, even a passion for such sacrifice as the true end of man. This temper is probably commoner in Japan than in any other country. But the daily external signs of piety do not assume the serious forms common elsewhere, such as frequent religious services attended by the laity. In Japan there has survived the old pagan spirit (pagan for want of a better word and in no sense a reproach) which identifies religion with Government, with law, with family duties and festivities. They are identified in the strictest sense : religion does not regulate them : they are religion.

But it may be urged that whether this sentiment is religion or not, it certainly is not Buddhism, for Buddhism is concerned with the salvation of individuals. It is true that the Buddha, like Christ, took little heed of states or families but concentrated his attention on suffering human personality, and the peculiar conditions of life in ancient India caused the non-social, ascetic, individual side of religion to be emphasized in most sects. Yet the morality of the Sigâlovâda-sûtra and of Asoka's edicts is practically the same as the morality of the Far East, and though Buddhism may not hold up the state or family as realities or ideals, yet it persistently inculcates self-sacrifice, and if it bids the individual work out his own salvation, he must do so by learning that he does not really exist as an individual. And though the monastic law is anti-social, it has much that fits in with the national spirit. Self-control and self-conquest are the ideal of the Samurai as much as of the priest. The archaic, heroic temper of Japan finds a simple and direct expression in Shintō, but that expression is hardly adequate, and those who require an intellectual complement find it in Buddhism.

As already mentioned, the connection between Buddhism and the political history of Japan for both good and evil is very close. The change wrought by its introduction is clear, for native documents admit that pre-Buddhist Japan was barbarous and, though it may be difficult to discriminate between the results of Chinese civilization and of Buddhism, yet the increase in humanity and sympathy seems immediately traceable to religion. A little later an attempt was made by Dōkyō to establish direct ecclesiastical control over the state.[1] This was frustrated, but during the long Fujiwara epoch the connection between the Court and the Church was close and took special forms. Thus it became the custom for the Emperor to

[1] See Chapter VIII.

abdicate early and become a monk, retaining the real power while a minor occupied the throne.[1]

On the other hand, Church and State often came into collision owing to the growth of great monasteries which kept armies of their own and used them to get their own way in secular as well as ecclesiastical affairs. But in spite of such differences the Fujiwara régime was essentially religious and its religious character was one cause of its long duration. In the struggle between the houses of Taira and Minamoto the collapse of the former was largely due to the hostility of the clergy. In the Kamakura period when Japanese institutions underwent a thorough change, Buddhism showed that it was in sympathy with the pulse of the people by assuming new forms, all permanent and influential, and again under the Ashikaga Shogunate it supplied what was wanted not only in art and culture but in political advice. In the troubled period of Nobunaga and Hideyoshi, it is clear that the Buddhist monasteries were one of the strongest powers in the land and that those leaders feared the establishment of some form of ecclesiastical rule.

It is perhaps useless to speculate what position the priesthood might have achieved had vigorous measures not been taken against them, but two points may be mentioned. First, the Church never showed an approximately united front. It is difficult to imagine the forces of Hieizan, Kōfukuji, and Kōyasan combining to support any serious political question: it is almost impossible to think of them making common cause with the more modern sects. Secondly, the great monasteries and even the newer warlike sects seem to have kept their clerical and military activities distinct. They were great corporations which insisted on receiving the same respect and having the same influence as feudal lords, but, with the exception of the Nichiren sect, they did not unite politics and religion or maintain that the State ought to be ruled by those who have seen the vision of truth and know the will of higher powers. The Nichiren sect did dream of uniting all Japan in the kingdom of the Buddha, but they were so intolerant and quarrelsome, so apt to split into factions themselves, that they had less chance than any other body of making this dream a reality and of founding a Church which could direct the policy of the State. They received a few sharp raps over the knuckles but otherwise did not attract

[1] The same practice has survived to the present day in humbler spheres under the name of *inkyō*. That is to say, elderly persons hand over the cares of their household and business to the younger generation and take their ease.

much attention, whereas the fate of the great monasteries shows in which direction the fears of the Government lay. The ruthless destruction of Hieizan and Negoro shook the political power of Buddhism, and that power might have collapsed but for the struggle against Christianity. The opponents of Christianity were actuated by political motives, and since they needed something native to set against the foreign creed, they reaffirmed, not without occasionally contradicting themselves, that Buddhism was the national religion.

The debt of art to Buddhism is even greater in Japan than in China, for on the whole the gift of Buddhism to China was ideas rather than technique, whereas in ancient Japan there was no art worth mentioning. Painting, sculpture, and architecture, as well as engraving, printing, and even writing, were all introduced in connection with Buddhism. It might be urged that art came to Japan as a part of Chinese civilization and was brought not by Buddhism but together with it. But the first manifestations of Japanese art, whether in pictures, statues, or buildings, are all definitely religious, and had Chinese civilization brought only Confucianism, it is clear that Japanese art would have been entirely different.

The revolution wrought by Buddhism was moral as well as literary and artistic. It was the wish of Shōtoku Taishi, who may be regarded as the real founder of Japanese Buddhism, to give his people a better moral code. Although in later ages the austere principles of Shintō may have had a salutary and tonic effect, yet it was clear that in the sixth and seventh centuries there was a lack of humanity. Modern as well as ancient history testifies that the Japanese character has a severe as well as a kindly side, and if this kindly side has become the more usual and conspicuous that is mainly due to Buddhist influence. Reluctance to kill animals and the general use of a diet restricted to fish and vegetables are direct results of Buddhist teaching. In 675 the Emperor Temmu forbade the people to eat the flesh of kine, horses, dogs, monkeys, or barndoor fowls.[1] Although the rebirth of a human being as an animal does not seem to be a common idea in modern Japan and the Jâtakas are not popular as religious literature, yet animals are believed to have future lives. Now that eating meat has become the fashion under European influence, butcher's guilds have masses said regularly on behalf of the souls of slaughtered cattle. Thus the

[1] Aston, Nihongi, vol. ii, p. 328.

newspapers[1] report how on 7th November, 1930, "a simple but impressive service—the eighth annual one—was held at the Kobe municipal slaughter house for the thousands of animals killed for human consumption during the past year." Prayers were offered that their souls might be blessed in Paradise and reincarnated in a higher form, and "brief elegies" were read from the Governor, the Mayor, and the head of the Health Office. After the earthquake of 1923 special services were held in several Buddhist temples for the souls of the animals which had perished in the disaster.

The magnitude of the revolution wrought in moral conceptions becomes plain if we consider that though literature, folklore, and daily language are full of the idea of Karma or the inevitable result of actions, good or bad, for the doer of them, this idea is not indigenous and is entirely due to Buddhism. Shintō, too, like Confucianism, had nothing to say about the state of the dead. The doctrines of future reward and punishment, golden paradises and blazing hells, of successive existences wherein new bodies and destinies are built out of the good and evil deeds of previous lives, the custom of performing good deeds on behalf of the dead, so that the merit may accrue to them and help them on their way to higher realms, all this is purely Buddhist. Shintō had no educational side: its priests did not teach or preach. But the Buddhists took in hand the education of almost all ranks of society except the military class, and even the military class often supplemented its special instruction by studying under them. The parish temple gradually became the parish school where children received for a very small cost an excellent education, not purely religious but permeated with religion. The parish priest, besides being a teacher, acted as Government registrar and kept a record of births and deaths. The very different positions of Buddhism in Japan and China are closely connected with this question of education: the literary knowledge so much esteemed in China was the special property of Confucianists, and Buddhist priests were not regarded as repositories of sound learning or as the natural instructors of youth.

The mighty influence of Buddhism not only in the strictly religious sphere but in politics, education, and art makes it seem that little room was left for Shintō. Yet Shintō, though encrusted with Buddhism, remained a living force ready to work openly so soon as it received official sanction, and was also recognized by the rulers

[1] e.g. *Osaka Mainichi* of 8th November, 1930.

of Japan during the period when it seemed to be most ignored. Thus Chikafusa used it about 1340 to prove the divine right of the Emperor, and the Yui-itsu, or Unitarian Shintō, was founded towards the end of the fifteenth century. It was nominally a protest against the Ryōbu or double Shintō, but really a mixture of Shintō with Buddhist and Chinese ideas. Somewhat later Hideyoshi, in two remarkable letters [1] which he wrote to the Portuguese Viceroy of the Indies and the Governor of the Philippines in 1591, expressly states that Shintō is the religion of Japan and says not a word about Buddhism. Even more remarkable is the testimony of Ieyasu. He was a member of the Jōdo sect and his policy indicates that he was a sincere patron of Buddhism (patron, perhaps, rather than follower). Yet the fifty-second section of his Legacy—a work which though spurious probably gives a not incorrect exposition of the Tokugawa policy—is as follows :—" My body and the body of others being born in the Empire of the Gods, to accept unreservedly the teachings of other countries—such as Confucian, Buddhist, or Taoist doctrines—and to apply one's whole and undivided attention to them, would be in short to desert one's own master and transfer one's loyalty to another. Is not this to forget the origin of one's being ? " These words may seem strange in the mouth of a Buddhist, but the explanation, I think, is that Buddhism is an influence : it has affected and altered every department of life in Japan. Shintō is not an influence : it is the expression of fundamental ideas about family and national life. Hence come both its strength and its limitations. It gave nothing to Japan but expressed the most private and vital ideas of the Japanese people. Buddhism, on the contrary, gave much : it educated, refined, and humanized the national character but it did not express the national ideals, though it accommodated itself to them. The frank statement that a Japanese should not give his whole attention to Buddhism means little more than that a man's religion must not interfere with the interests of his country. India is perhaps the only land where the contrary opinion has been not only held but put into practice. There under native rule religion has constantly overridden law and political considerations, but in Europe and America it is assumed that religion must be useful to the State and, if it is not, that the State may interfere in such ways as breaking up

[1] See Murdoch, *History of Japan*, ii, 37, for a translation. Hideyoshi's description of Japan is far from correct, for he does not mention the Emperor and implies that he himself was the real sovereign of Japan.

monasteries or forbidding polygamy. Ieyasu's attitude should be intelligible to a western statesman: a Japanese may believe anything he likes provided that his beliefs are not hostile to the institutions of Japan.

In the following chapters I propose to trace the part played by Buddhism in the history of Japan. Though most educated Europeans have now some knowledge of that history, it may be well to recall its general outlines and also to mention two curious features which it presents. The first is the constant tendency to separate titular and real power or rather to preserve a venerable hereditary office which had ceased to be the head of the State and to set up beside it a recognized and efficient ruler. Not only was the Government administered during long periods by Shōguns who rendered merely ceremonial homage to the Emperor, but the authority of the Shōgun sometimes passed into the hands of a deputy and at other times the real power was in the hands of an ex-Emperor who had nominally abdicated. The other feature is the remarkable attitude towards foreigners. Japan appears throughout the ages to have been the most assimilative of all nations and the most anxious to borrow from others, and yet the most deliberately self-secluded and anxious to avoid contact with all without. The wholesale adoption of Buddhism and of Chinese culture in the sixth century was the work of individuals rather than the result of international intercourse, and after about 850 such intercourse altogether ceased. The attempted invasions of Khubilai Khan were not likely to renew it, but relations were more friendly with the Ming dynasty. When Christianity arrived from the west, the Japanese were at first perfectly friendly and imitation of Christian customs was for a moment fashionable, but as soon as political consequences were suspected, Europeans, with the exception of a few Dutch, were expelled and Christianity was forbidden. One remarkable result of this seclusion was that the Japanese, though a military nation, had no one to fight with except themselves. It is not needful to dilate on the evils of civil war and they are amply illustrated in the annals of Japan. But for all that, perpetual contests between men of the same race do tend to eliminate the more barbarous forms of massacre and devastation and to encourage a chivalrous spirit, for the simple reason that if you are fighting for the lordship of certain lands and their inhabitants your object is to acquire rather than destroy.

The phases through which Japan has passed may be summarized

as follows. Before the middle of the sixth century A.D. we have to do with archæology rather than history, and authentic records begin with the entry of Buddhism and Chinese civilization. Korea served as the intermediary and was of primary importance to Japan both for foreign politics and internal culture. In 645 the growth of Chinese influence culminated in a sudden and complete administrative revolution, the whole government being remodelled on the plan of the Chinese bureaucracy. In 793 the capital which had previously been at Nara was established in Kyōto. The Emperors retired more and more from active life and from 826 to 1050 the real political power was held by the Fujiwara family. This long predominance broke up in the eleventh century, when the houses of Taira and Minamoto came to the front and struggled for supremacy. The conflict resulted in the overthrow of the former, and Yoritomo, the head of the Minamoto, received from the Emperor the title of Shōgun or Generalissimo.

For the greater part of the period from 1190 to 1867 Japan was not only practically but avowedly governed by Shōguns of the Minamoto family,[1] although the line of Emperors, known to Europeans as Mikados and reputed to be the descendants of the Sun-goddess, continued and the theoretical right of this family to rule was not disputed. The seat of the Shōgunate was at first Kamakura, but for more than a century (1205–1333) the real power was held by Regents of the Hōjō family, and thus the government was exercised by the deputy of a deputy. This singular arrangement proved successful in practice, for while it lasted Japan repelled a foreign invasion and enjoyed a century of internal peace which was broken in 1332 by a dispute as to the succession not of the Shōguns, or Regents, but of the Emperors. The powerful Ashikaga family took sides in the struggle. Its candidate was established as Emperor in Kyōto and the Ashikagas ruled as Shōguns until 1573. But the dynasty became effete and the last thirty years of its rule were troubled and eventful. In 1542 arrived the Portuguese and with them Christianity. At this critical period, the real power was successively in the hands of two soldiers of fortune, Nobunaga and Hideyoshi. The latter invaded Korea and dreamed of conquering China, but both died without attaining the position of Shōgun. This was seized by another favourite of fortune, more a statesman than a soldier, namely, Ieyasu. He founded the Tokugawa dynasty of Shōguns who ruled at Yedo from 1603–1868.

[1] The Ashikaga and Tokugawa are both branches of the Minamoto family.

In 1624 Japan was closed to foreigners, Christianity was prohibited, and for two and a half centuries the country was completely isolated. This isolation was broken by the United States, who in 1853 demanded the establishment of international relations. The Tokugawa Government was already tottering from internal weakness and there was a strong party in favour of purely Japanese institutions as opposed to institutions borrowed from China. European and American interference coincided with this movement. The result was one of the most sudden changes known to history. Feudalism and the Shogunate were abolished : the Emperor was recognized as the real as well as theoretical head of the State : Japan was not only thrown open to the world but entered on that phase of development which has made her the equal of European states.

# CHAPTER VII

## INTRODUCTION OF BUDDHISM

### 1

THE official date for the introduction of Buddhism into Japan from Korea is A.D. 552, but it is probable that the Court were not wholly ignorant of it at that time, for it is recorded that in the reign of the Emperor Ōjin a learned man called Wang-In instructed the Heir Apparent in Chinese writing and literature.[1] But Wang-In, if Chinese, came from Korea and not direct. Buddhism had reached the Koreans in A.D. 372 and they were in close communication with China, for they had relations by land with the northern kingdoms and by sea with the Yang-tse valley. On the other side they were in touch with Japan and sent thither at various times weavers, masons, carpenters, Chinese scholars, physicians, diviners, and persons skilled in the mysteries of the calendar. But though Korea was the intermediary it is clear that it was Chinese culture which the Japanese wished to acquire.

In the sixth century Korea was divided into several states, of which the principal were Kōkuli or Kokuryö[2] in the north, Pekche[3] or Kudara in the south-west, and Silla or Shiragi in the south-east. Between the southern extremities of the two latter lay a territory called Imna or Mimana, in which the Japanese had certain rights. There was a considerable Japanese population and a Japanese Resident-General. Both Japan and Pekche had constant difficulties with the kingdom of Silla and hence an alliance arose between them, the King of Pekche sending many missions to the Emperor to offer presents and request the dispatch of troops. Buddhism had been accepted by Kokuryö in 372 and by Pekche in 384, but it was not predominant in Silla until considerably later. The chief authority for the events which follow is the Japanese chronicle called the Nihon-shoki or Nihongi which was presented to the Empress Genshō

[1] Aston, Nihongi, i, p. 262, thinks that this was probably in A.D. 405, but the chronology of the period is somewhat uncertain.

[2] The name is spelt in various ways, Kōkuli being that used in the official publications of the Government-General of Chosen. Koguryū and Koryö are also found in some writers.

[3] Also spelt Pakche and Paikchoi.

in 720 and brings the history of Japan down to 697.[1] It is apparently a collection of extracts from older sources arranged in chronological order but forming a somewhat disjointed narrative. In the earlier period the chronology appears to be seriously inaccurate, but as it becomes correct after about A.D. 500, it may be accepted for our purposes.

In 545 Syöng-Myöng, the King of Pekche, found himself in a very difficult position because the local Japanese authorities at Imna were inclined to conspire with Silla. He made representations to the Emperor and the chronicle adds[2] that in the ninth month he "made an image of the Buddha sixteen feet high (the traditional dimensions) and drew up a written prayer saying . . . By the merit which I have acquired in reverently constructing this image I pray that the Emperor may attain great virtue and that all the land of the Miyake (Japanese possessions in Korea) may receive blessings. I also pray for the final emancipation of all living creatures under Heaven". It is not plain whether the image and prayer were sent to any Japanese authority, but the entries for the year 552 are more explicit. The King of Pekche sent a mission to Kimmei, the Emperor of Japan, to inform him that the two kingdoms of Kokuryö and Silla were contemplating a joint attack on Pekche and Imna and to ask for the dispatch of an auxiliary force. The Emperor's reply was gracious, though not very clear, and in the tenth month the King of Pekche sent another mission with presents consisting of "an image of Shaka Butsu in gold and copper, several flags and umbrellas and a number of sûtras", the names of which are not mentioned. He also presented a memorial in which he spoke of the merit of diffusing religion, saying, "This is the most excellent among all doctrines but it is hard to explain and hard to understand. Even the Duke of Chou and Confucius had not attained to a knowledge of it. It can give merit and reward without measure and without bounds and so lead to a grasp of the highest wisdom. Imagine a man possessing treasures to his heart's content and able to satisfy all his wishes. So it is with this wonderful doctrine. Every prayer is fulfilled and naught is wanting. Moreover, it has spread from distant India to the three Han (Korea) where all receive

[1] It was translated by Aston and originally published by the Japan Society. But my references are to the reissue (two volumes in one) published by Kegan Paul in 1924, though I have occasionally altered the wording. I have not always referred to the pages because the date is given in the margin, and the mention of the year when an event is recorded is therefore sufficient.

[2] Nihongi, ii, p. 59.

it with reverence. Your servant therefore has humbly dispatched his retainer to transmit it to the Imperial Court and to spread it throughout the home provinces,[1] in order to fulfil the words of the Buddha, My Law shall spread to the East."

The political consequences of the King of Pekche's piety were not what he hoped, for he was killed and his country conquered. In 562 Silla destroyed Imna and massacred the population. It was a long time before Japan regained any foothold in Korea.[2] But though the introduction of Buddhism into Japan naturally met with some opposition, it does not appear that these disasters impeded its progress or were regarded as a bad omen.

The presents and letters received from Pekche engaged the serious attention of the Japanese Court. The Emperor, we are told,[3] leaped for joy but thought it prudent to consult his ministers. Opinion was divided. On the one hand it was argued that Japan ought to follow the example of other civilized countries, on the other that the native gods might be offended by the respect shown to a foreign deity. The cleavage of opinion was indicated at the first council held to discuss the matter: the Soga family was for Buddhism, the Mononobe and Nakatomi were against it. They had old grounds of difference with the Soga and held important charges connected with Shintoism which seemed threatened by these religious innovations. It was finally decided that the Soga should take the image and worship it as an experiment. But the experiment was not a success. When Soga no Iname turned his house at Mukuhara [4] into a temple and installed the image there a pestilence broke out. His rivals demonstrated that this was due to the foreign cult and obtained imperial permission to burn the temple and throw the image into the Naniwa canal.[5]

[1] The name of home provinces or Go-kinai was commonly given to the five provinces nearest to the old capital, Yamashiro, Yamato, Kawachi, Settsu, and Izumi.

[2] The influence of the Japanese in Korea appears to have really come to an end in 562, but they continued to send expeditions and to receive missions from Silla, described as bearing "tribute" for some years. But in 661 Silla with the aid of the Chinese annexed Pekche and decisively defeated the Japanese.

[3] See Nihongi, ii, p. 66 ff., for the narrative. Soga's full title is given as Soga no Oho-Omi Iname no Sukune.

[4] A magnificent temple called Mukuhara-dera was subsequently built on the site and the present Kōgenji temple in the village of Toyura in Yamato is said to be a portion of it.

[5] The place is still known as Hori-e Machi in Ōsaka. According to tradition the image is still preserved in the Zenkōji temple at Nagano.

But the gradual infiltration of Buddhism continued. In 577 another mission arrived from Pekche with three priests, a nun, a temple architect, and a maker of images. Two years afterwards Silla sent "tribute" and a Budhist image. According to the Nihongi, the successor of Kimmei, the Emperor Bidatsu (572–585), "was not a believer in Buddhism but was fond of literature" and seems to have been fairly tolerant. In 584 [1] Umako Soga (the son of Iname), with the assistance of a person called Shiba Tattō, began to seek for Buddhists. He erected a temple in which he enshrined a stone image of Miroku (Maitreya) and maintained three nuns. He also built another temple at Ishikawa. "From this," says the Nihongi, "arose the beginning of Buddhism", but the events of 552 above related are generally considered to mark its introduction. The narrative goes on to say that next year Umako was taken ill and was told by a diviner that this was a curse sent by the Buddha who had been worshipped in his father's time but now, apparently, was neglected. One would have expected this incident to occur earlier in the story before the construction of the temples was mentioned and perhaps something is wrong with the text. At any rate, the Soga were allowed to resume Buddhist worship, on which the pestilence reappeared. The other party found no difficulty in having the permission revoked, for the connection between the reintroduction of the new worship and the recrudescence of the epidemic seemed clear. Mononobe went in person to the Soga's estate, burnt the temple and images, again threw the ashes into the canal, and beat and imprisoned the unfortunate nuns. But the anti-Buddhist arguments became less convincing when in spite of these summary measures the pestilence grew worse, "old and young said privately to one another: Is this a punishment for burning the image of the Buddha?" The Soga were then permitted to practise Buddhism as a family cult, but not with too great publicity, and the three nuns were released. The Emperor died but Umako apparently recovered, for he had an unseemly quarrel with Mononobe at the imperial funeral.

[1] Nihongi, ii, p. 101 ff. On p. 104 the Nihongi notices that there are slight variations in the story and that according to "one book" Soga would not allow the temples to be burnt. The name Shiba Tattō has not been satisfactorily explained. His son became a monk for the sake of the Emperor Yōmei (see below), and in 606 his grandson successfully accomplished the difficult business of erecting a sixteen foot statue of the Buddha at Gangōji. On this the Empress Suiko conferred on him various honours and addressed to him a most gracious rescript enumerating the services which his family had rendered to religion.

Of the next sovereign, Yōmei, the Chronicle says that "he believed in the law of the Buddha and reverenced the way of the gods". He reigned less than two years and the most remarkable thing about him was his death. When taken ill he expressed a wish to accept the three Treasures—that is, to become a Buddhist—but asked his ministers' advice. The old dispute broke out at once, Mononobe and Nakatome taking sides against Soga. While a violent altercation was proceeding an Imperial Prince (perhaps Shōtoku Taishi himself) introduced a Buddhist priest into the Imperial Palace.[1] As the Emperor's end approached, we are told that the son of Shiba Tattō above mentioned came forward and said that he would renounce the world on His Majesty's behalf and make an image of the Buddha and a temple. The dying monarch was deeply moved. Though this narrative is not very lucid, it implies that Buddhism was already well-known at Court. The Emperor, when taken ill, thinks of embracing it, doubtless as a means of recovery, not of going to heaven: priests are about who can be introduced into the Palace and Imperial Princes are ready to introduce them.

On the death of Yōmei there was a fierce dispute as to the succession, in which the two bitter enemies, Soga and Mononobe, were naturally on different sides. The latter was defeated and slain, and the Nihongi[2] relates how Soga and Prince Umayado, the future Shōtoku Taishi, who fought with him both made Buddhist vows before entering battle and severally promised to build temples to the Four Heavenly Kings if they were successful. Soga also swore to spread the worship of the three Treasures. In fulfilment of these promises the Prince erected the temple of Tennōji at Ōsaka, to which part of Mononobe's estate and slaves were dedicated, and Soga the temple of Hōkōji, near Nara. Sujun was proclaimed Emperor and during his short reign (587–592) we hear that another mission arrived from Pekche with priests and relics, that many temples were built, and that the nuns whom Mononobe had flogged were sent to Korea for a course of study and returned safely. Unfortunately for himself, the Emperor disliked Soga and gave him cause for alarm. Soga on this had him assassinated and proclaimed his own niece as

[1] The narrative is very abrupt and obscure. It is not clear who the Imperial Prince was nor why the son of Shiba Tattō was there.

[2] Nihongi, ii, 114. The Prince made wooden images of the Four Kings and bound them in his hair, which (as he was only a boy) was tied over his temples. Soga also invoked Daijinnō, the great Spirit King, said to be Mahâkâla.

Empress with the title of Suiko.[1] She reigned for twenty-five years, but the really important figure in this period, although he never became Emperor, was Umayado who became Prince Imperial and Regent and is known to history as Shōtoku Taishi.[2] He was the son of the Emperor Yōmei and had Soga blood in his veins. He was the real founder of Japanese Buddhism and worthy of the task at which he laboured.

The *début* of the faith had not been glorious, but though it was judged by the crude standard of its power to stop plague and though it triumphed as part of the principles of a noble house, these accidents must not blind us to the fact that it came as the epitome of Indian and Chinese civilization and wrought a moral as well as an intellectual revolution. The Sogas had clearly not attained a high standard in either learning or political morality. But Shōtoku Taishi was of a different stamp. He was perfectly sincere in his convictions. He was the greatest scholar of his time, a student of the Chinese classics as well as of the Buddhist scriptures and a lover of art: his life was above reproach and as a ruler he won the hearts of his people. When he died in 621 at the early age of forty-nine, the whole nation wept for him, the young as if they had lost a father, the old as if they had lost a child.[3]

Naturally Buddhism spread and flourished. The direct and public instructions of the Empress encouraged the zeal of the Regent and ministers. Officials "vied with one another in erecting temples".[4] In 605 orders were issued for the construction of representations of the Buddha in copper and embroidery, sixteen feet high, and in 607 the great monastery of Hōryūji was founded, which became not only a cathedral but a national museum. Two Korean priests named Hye-cha and Hye-chhong were energetic in propaganda and the former became the Regent's tutor.[5] Several missions from Korea presented images and were accompanied by priests. In 608

[1] Her father was the Emperor Kimmei and her mother the sister of Soga no Umako.

[2] His various names are perplexing, for the Nihongi also calls him 上宮 Kamitsumiya or Jōgū. The name Umayado—Prince Stable-door—is explained by a story that he was born unexpectedly while his mother was inspecting the offices of the Palace and had just arrived at the stables. See Nihongi, ii, p. 121. It adds that he was able to speak as soon as he was born.

[3] Nihongi, ii, p. 148.

[4] Nihongi, ii, p. 123.

[5] He is apparently the same person who is called Eji or Weji.

embassies were exchanged with China,[1] whither a Japanese envoy had been sent in the previous year. The Emperor of China stated in his letter that he wished to diffuse civilization, but it is not mentioned that he sent Buddhist books or emblems like the Korean potentates. When, however, the return mission was dispatched by the Japanese Government, persons described as students and student priests were sent with it in order to complete their education in China and remained there until 622. The Nihongi states[2] that in 623 there were in Japan 46 temples, 816 priests, and 569 nuns. As one priest struck his grandfather with an axe, the question of discipline arose. Superintendents were appointed with the titles of Sōjō, Sōdzu, and Hōtō, and a list of priests and nuns recording the dates and circumstances of their ordination was compiled. An important step was taken in 616 when the oracle of Miwa declared that Buddhist priests were the proper persons to perform funeral rites.

In 604 Shōtoku Taishi published a celebrated edict known as the Jū-shichijō no kempō, consisting of seventeen clauses, but not as the name seems to imply, a constitution or a code of laws. It is a series of ethical maxims in Chinese style and containing no illusion to Shintō. The first, quoting Confucius, dwells on the need of harmony. The second runs as follows: "Sincerely reverence the Three Treasures. These three—the Buddha, the Law, and the Order—are the refuge of the four classes of living things[3] and are in all countries the supreme object of faith. What man in what age can fail to reverence this Law? Few men are utterly bad. They may be taught to follow it. But if they do not betake themselves to the Three Treasures, how shall their crookedness be made straight?" This seems to make Buddhism almost the Established or at least the Approved Church, and so indeed it was for the Court and upper classes, but this did not mean such a break with other religious ideas as would be implied by the conversion of a country to Christianity or Islam. In 607 the Empress issued an edict ordering that there

[1] The Nihongi calls China T'ang, but the word must be used retrospectively for the T'ang dynasty did not begin till 618 and in 608 Yang-Ti of the Sui dynasty was on the throne.

[2] The numbers do not seem large, for it is stated that on one occasion—when Soga fell ill in 614—a thousand persons entered the order. But perhaps there is some mistake in the figures.

[3] Living things are divided into four classes according to their supposed method of birth. (1) From a womb, (2) from eggs, (3) from moisture, as insects, (4) from no apparent cause, as Bodhisattvas.

should be no remissness in the worship of the gods of Earth and Heaven. It says not a word about Buddhism but speaks in Chinese phraseology about the Imperial Ancestors, temples dedicated to mountains and rivers, and the male and female principles in nature (the Yang and Yin). A few years previously she had ordered that sacrifices should be offered to the God of Earthquakes in all districts. Yet her devotion to Buddhism is not to be doubted.

Like Asoka, Shōtoku Taishi was naturally kind and humane and perhaps was a greater constructive statesman. He was not made good by Buddhism but was attracted by the humanity which it inculcates. His maxims seem to us trite moral commonplaces, but there is no doubt that ancient Japan was terribly barbarous and that the simplest injunctions to avoid cruelty were almost a revelation. The Nihongi [1] relates how Shōtoku Taishi fed and clothed with his own raiment a starving man whom he found lying by the road as he was travelling, but it evidently does not regard such deaths by the wayside as remarkable, and speaking of the year 562 it observes " now at this time between father and child, husband and wife there was no commiseration ".[2] Compare the edict issued by the Emperor Kōtoku in 646 in which he complains that a younger brother will not help his elder brother if he dies by the way or is drowned, and the edict of 691 about younger brothers being sold as slaves by elder brothers and children by parents. To such people the admonitions to behave with friendliness and decorum (the Confucian *Li*) and avoid gluttony, covetousness, and envy were not superfluous. And sometimes the maxims refer pointedly to the special abuses of the period. Forced labour is to be required only at seasonable times and in moderation. Provincial authorities are not to levy exactions. For " in a country there are not two lords. The Sovereign is the master of the people of the whole country ". But this does not mean arbitrary despotism. " Decisions on important matters should not be made by one person alone. They should be discussed with many."

Quite apart from his position in the history of religion, Shōtoku Taishi was one of the best and most benevolent—perhaps the very best and most benevolent—of all the rulers of Japan. His literary activity was considerable. He was well acquainted with the Chinese classics as the style of his edict shows, and in conjunction

[1] Nihongi, ii, 144–5.

[2] Nihongi, ii, p. 84. It is perhaps only just to observe that the remark is made respecting the manners of Japanese in Korea.

with Soga no Umako he compiled various historical works on Japan,[1] most of which unfortunately perished in the conflagration which accompanied the downfall of the Sogas a few years later. But his most serious studies were no doubt devoted to the Buddhist scriptures. At the request of the Empress he lectured during three days on the Shōman-kyō and also on the Lotus.[2] Though the Nihongi does not mention the fact, it appears to be true that he wrote seven volumes of commentaries called Jōgū go Seisho which are often referred to and cited in temple archives, such as the Hōryūji Engi. Four volumes deal with the Lotus, one with the Shōman-kyō, and two with the Yuima-kyō. A copy of the commentary on the Lotus believed to be in his own handwriting is preserved in the Imperial Palace at Tōkyō. He had independent judgment as a commentator and was not bound by tradition : for instance, he sometimes criticizes standard Chinese explanations making remarks such as " my own view differs slightly " or " this view is no longer accepted ".

The Lotus and the Shōman-kyō are the only sûtras mentioned in the Nihongi during this reign, but later authors agree in stating that the Yuima-kyō also was popular.[3]

In the Shōsōin at Nara are preserved manuscripts of the following works which are said to date from Shōtoku Taishi's time :—

(1) The Mahâsannipâta-sûtra. Nanjio, No. 61.
(2) An extract of the same. Nanjio, No. 80.
(3) Part of the Kegon-sûtra. Nanjio, No. 90.
(4) The Aksharamatî-sûtra. Nanjio, No. 74.
(5) The Suvarṇaprabhâsa-sûtra. Nanjio, No. 126.

Shōtoku Taishi and Soga no Umako had been good friends but these amicable relations did not continue between their descendants. The Sogas were obviously dreaming of supplanting the Imperial family, and as Yamashiro, the son of Shōtoku, was popular he was attacked by their orders. He died like a martyr, amid celestial portents as we are told,[4] and worthily of his father. " If," he said, " I had raised an army and attacked Soga I should certainly have conquered. But for the sake of one person, I was unwilling to

[1] This was in the year before his death. See Nihongi, ii, p. 148.

[2] Nihongi, ii, 135. The Shōman-kyō is Nanjio, No. 59. Śrîmâlâdevîsimharada, translated by Gunabhadra about A.D. 440.

[3] See *Hōnen, the Buddhist Saint*, trans. by Coates and Ishizuka, pp. 286 and 306.

[4] Nihongi, ii, 182.

destroy the people." So he and his family strangled themselves. But the arrogance and ambition of the Sogas provoked a conspiracy in the reign of the Empress Kōgyoku in which the heads of the house were killed and its power and pretensions brought to an end. One of the chief conspirators was Kamatari, a man of great ability and known by many names, for he received subsequently the appellation of Fujiwara and became the head of that celebrated family. But he was also by birth a Nakatomi, descended from the Minister who had originally opposed the introduction of Buddhism in 552. He was possibly influenced by hereditary enmity against the Sogas, but he does not appear to have had any religious animus, for when the Empress, after seeing Soga killed in her presence, thought it prudent to abdicate he selected as her successor the Emperor Kōtoku, of whom the Nihongi says more decidedly than of any previous sovereign that "he honoured the way of the Buddha and despised Shintō". It is noticeable that Prince Furubito, a possible candidate for the throne, avoided the dangerous honour by shaving his head and becoming a monk, but only temporarily, for he subsequently rebelled and was killed. This practice of princes entering, or being made to enter, a monastery in troubled times afterwards became very common.

The reign of Kōtoku is memorable in history on account of the reforms of Taikwa enacted in 645 by which the Japanese of the seventh century adopted as much of Chinese civilization as suited them, just as they made use of European civilization some twelve hundred years later. The title is significant, for Taikwa is a name given according to Chinese custom to a certain series of years. This became the regular method of calculating time in Japan and is still in use. But at present one nengō (such as Meiji or Taishō) covers the whole of the Emperor's reign, whereas in earlier ages the interval thus designated was often quite short and arbitrary, any event regarded as a good or bad omen being a sufficient reason for instituting a new nengō.

The object and result of these reforms, supplemented in 702 by the code of Taihō, was to organize and centralize the administration, the Emperor becoming a sovereign analogous to the Son of Heaven in China, instead of being merely the head of the principal clan. The arrangement of details and the organization of "the eight departments of State and hundred bureaus" now created was entrusted to two commissioners, both of whom had studied in China and one of whom was a Buddhist priest called Bin or Min.

It does not appear, however, that any formal change was made in the State religion, and the board called Jingikwan attended to the due performance of Shintō ceremonies. Nevertheless the introduction of Chinese institutions was favourable to Buddhist interests, for the best authorities on such subjects—for instance, the Calendar —were generally priests, either immigrants or Japanese who had been sent to study abroad. And in one respect the progress of Buddhism was easier and quicker than in China: there was no organized non-Buddhist literary class corresponding to the Confucianists. On the contrary, it was the Buddhists who could pose, especially in early times, as scholars and the guardians of learning.

An edict of 546 restricting the size of funeral monuments and forbidding cruel ceremonies like the sacrifice of men and horses at burials was doubtless due to Buddhist influence. The expense of these monuments and the hardships entailed by levying forced labour for their construction were a burden of which the nation was grateful to be relieved. It is true that under the new régime enormous sums were spent on building temples and erecting gilded images, but Buddhism, as observed by Murdoch who was by no means prejudiced in its favour, at least encouraged art, whereas "from the mausolea the nation had got no return whatsoever".[1] The edict also condemned the rule which required those who have been in contact with the dead to undergo rigorous purification, because it led to cruel consequences. If people died by the roadside or were drowned, those who had been with them had to be purified (which was apparently an arduous ceremony), and hence even brothers would not help one another in such disasters.

When the Emperor Kōtoku died the Crown Prince Naka-no-Oye refused to ascend the throne and reinstated his mother, the late Empress, who reigned a second time with the new name of Saimei from A.D. 655 to 661. The Nihongi[2] not only mentions the performance of several Buddhist ceremonies by imperial order during this period but suggests that Shintō was treated with scant courtesy, for the Empress provoked the wrath of the gods by cutting down trees belonging to the Asakura shrine in order to clear the ground for a new palace. Many courtiers died and she herself expired in the offending building two months later. The

[1] Murdoch, *History of Japan*, i, p. 176. It should be remembered, however, that many of the objects found in them are of fine workmanship.

[2] See Nihongi, ii, pp. 257, 259, 263, 265, and for Asakura, 271.

Crown Prince at last became Emperor under the name of Tenchi, though he did not assume the title and dignity for some years.

A slight change in religious sentiment seems observable at this period. Possibly his mother's rash act and its apparent punishment were taken as a warning: at any rate, both he and his successor Temmu paid more attention to Shintō than had been usual of late. Tenchi "laid out Shintō places of worship" with appropriate offerings and litanies, but still when his last illness came upon him he felt the claims of the rival creed.[1] A hundred Buddhist images were consecrated in the palace and rich presents sent to the temple of Hōkōji. Temmu was most assiduous in showing his regard for the native cult. The Nihongi records his veneration for the Sun-goddess, the numerous offerings made to the gods of Tatsuta and others, the worship of the imperial ancestors, and the repeated performance of the Shintō rite of national purification.[2] When we remember the dangerous power subsequently acquired by the Buddhist clergy we are inclined to suspect that even at this early period the Court may have thought it well not to let them have everything their own way, but the rest of Temmu's legislation was in no respect anti-Buddhist or restrictive and his motive was probably merely to keep the Shintō deities and their priests in a good temper.

It was in this reign that a most remarkable step was taken to popularize the new creed, which had hitherto flourished mainly in the immediate vicinity of the Court. "Orders were sent to all the provinces," says the Nihongi,[3] "that in every house a Buddhist shrine should be provided and an image of Buddha with Buddhist scriptures placed there. Worship was to be paid and offerings of food made at these shrines." "Every house" doubtless means every official house, but in time the practice spread to private dwellings, and this edict is probably the origin of the Butsudan, or family oratory, still to be found in Japanese households. The chronicle adds no explanation or comment, but does not appear to regard the enactment as directed against Shintō, and the next entry (also without comment) is that "worship was paid to the deities of Hirose and Tatsuta". Religions in the Far East are not mutually exclusive.

[1] Nihongi, pp. 293 and 297.

[2] Nihongi, ii, pp. 307, 322; 332 and often, also 334–5 and 378. For the Purification see pp. 333, 338, 352, and 378.

[3] Nihongi, ii, p. 369, speaking of A.D. 685.

Many other instances of imperial favour to Buddhism are recorded, such as gifts and vegetarian banquets offered to priests and nuns, ordinations in the Palace, temple and regulations (in no wise restrictive) about the management of temples and the status of the clergy. A copy of the Issai-kyō[1] or entire Buddhist canon was made and recited, and during the Emperor's last illness both Buddhist[2] and Shintō ceremonies were performed on his behalf.

His successor the Empress Jitō (A.D. 686–697) showed a similarly impartial piety, for though she already was inclined to Buddhism there is a long list of the Shintō ceremonies which she had performed and of the gifts which she gave to Shintō shrines. As for Buddhism, besides the usual gifts and banquets the following items of interest are noted. The clergy grew in numbers: as many as 3,363 belonging to seven temples being present on a single occasion. It is three times recorded that a "public great congregation" was held in the Palace. Priests came from Korea and students who had completed their studies returned from China. In 689, images of Amida,[3] Kwannon, and Daiseshi were brought from Silla. The killing of animals was prohibited in certain places. In 693 the Ninnō-kyō[4] was expounded "in the hundred provinces" and in the previous year the Viceroy of Tsukushi (Kyūshū) was ordered "to propagate the Buddhist religion".[5] Most remarkable of all, when the Empress died she was cremated, which must have seemed a strange and almost terrible innovation in imperial ceremonial.[6]

In 710 Nara was made the imperial residence and remained so for more than seventy years. Hitherto it had been the custom for the Court to move at the beginning of every new reign and its migrations are generally described as a change of capital. As a matter of fact the various sites were nearly always in the same district and the change meant little more than removal to a new palace, the reason

[1] 一切經. Nihongi, ii, p. 322. Five collections of the Tripiṭaka had already been made in China between A.D. 518 and 616.

[2] Three sûtras were read to cure him: the Yakushi-kyō or sûtra of the Buddha of healing (see Nanjio, 170, 172, 173), the Kon-kwō-myō or Suvarṇaprabhâsa, and the Kwannon-kyō or chap. xxiv of the Lotus. Also 180 persons took the vows and a hundred images of Bodhisattvas were set up in the Palace.

[3] This is the earliest mention which I have found of images of Amida, but the Sukhâvatî-vyûha was recited in 640, and see Nihongi, ii, p. 408.

[4] Nanjio, No. 16. A portion of the Prajñâpâramitâ.

[5] Nihongi, ii, p. 408. He was ordered to send priests to propagate it in Ohosumi and Ata, that is the southern part of the modern provinces of Osumi and Satsuma.

[6] This was 701. The first instance of cremation was the priest Dōshō in the previous year.

being that a house was supposed to be defiled by death. Buddhist influence had no doubt something to do with the decay of this superstition, and the selection first of Nara and then of Kyōto as the permanent residence of successive Emperors did mean the creation of a new capital. It also meant the opening of new chapters in the history of Japanese Buddhism, and it will be well at this point to look back for a moment at the first chapter or preface, that is to say, the century and a half which had elapsed since A.D. 552.

The introduction of Buddhism into Japan was not due to missionary enterprise or comparable to the efforts of Asoka to spread the Good Law. The King of Pekche no doubt thought that his action was meritorious, but still his main object was clearly political. He wished to make an alliance with the Emperor of Japan, and therefore to please him and knowing the desire of the Japanese to acquire Chinese civilization, he thought he could not do better than make them acquainted with Buddhist literature and ritual. It may seem strange that he did not think of Confucianism as representing Chinese culture. Possibly his own knowledge of it was slight. At any rate, Buddhism was much easier to transplant and acclimatize, for it had already made its way from India to China and from China to Korea. Evidently it was considered that the King of Pekche's presents had made a good impression, for during many years the various Korean states continued to send images, sûtras, and priests whenever they thought it expedient to humour the Japanese. Yet it does not seem that these priests were exactly what we should call missionaries. They were sure of a good reception and were ready to instruct and advise. Somewhat later, when the condition of Korea was disturbed, the influx was considerable. Thus in 666 the Nihongi records that 2,000 people of Pekche were settled in the east country and maintained by the Japanese Government for three years without any distinction being made between priests and laymen. Still less did the Chinese act as evangelists in this early period, that is before A.D. 700. The missions recorded seem to have been entirely political and not to have brought religious presents like the envoys of Korea.[1]

On the other hand, there can be no doubt of the desire of the Japanese to learn. When once they had made up their minds that Buddhism was a good thing, they were not evangelized by self-denying foreigners: it was they who encouraged and besought

[1] Still, the Nihongi, ii, p. 408, mentions the "image of Amida, made by the T'ang Envoy Kuo Wu-Ts'ung" and apparently left in Kyūshū.

foreign priests to settle in Japan with as much eagerness as modern Orientals show in importing guns and military instructors. They also sent numerous batches of young men to study in China. A peculiarly interesting example of this is the dispatch in 658 of two priests who received instruction from the great Hsüan-Tsang.[1] Naturally there was some hostility between the imported faith and native religious institutions which had hitherto had neither competitors nor special designation, but were now styled Shintō, the way of the Gods, in opposition to Butsudō, the way of the Buddha.[2] At first the quarrel was acute and followed the lines of rivalry between certain noble houses. Then when Buddhism had established its position, Shintō seemed to have fallen somewhat into neglect, but it soon recovered and in the last half of the seventh century the Emperors, though clearly encouraging Buddhism, were careful to honour both creeds. Their attitude was dictated by statesmanship and superstition alike: they could see that the Shintō priesthood must be reckoned with as a political force and they probably believed that the Shintō deities were capable of sending pestilence or earthquake if annoyed.

This impartial piety led to the religious compromise called Ryōbu-Shintō [3] or twofold Shintō, which lasted until 1868 and more or less fused the two religions, though not so completely as to cause any difficulty when there was a desire to separate them. This arrangement has been attributed to both Gyōgi Bosatsu (670–749) and Kōbō Daishi (774–835). Both of them helped to formulate it, but it represents a natural tendency of the Japanese mind and not the work of one man. Perhaps Dōshō (c. 655) was one of the earliest priests to approve and propagate the idea. Both in China and Japan it has always been considered quite natural to follow the observances of more than one religion and Buddhism raised no objection to the practice. As mentioned in previous chapters, the earliest texts fully recognize the existence of Hindu Devas. The Buddha himself is represented as recommending the laity to honour them. They are not guides to salvation but they are defenders of the true faith, they protect from evil and they can give the good things of this life. It was precisely in this spirit that early Japanese Buddhism raised no objection to the performance of Shintō

[1] Nihongi, ii, p. 254.

[2] 神道. The word appears to occur for the first time in the Nihongi, book xxi, in speaking of the year 585.

[3] 両部神道.

ceremonies. Theories identifying the native deities with Buddhas and Bodhisattvas came a little later.

It is said that four sects were introduced into Japan before A.D. 700, namely, the Jōjitsu and Sanron both in 625, the Hossō in 654, and the Kusha in 658. But they were not sects in the later sense, that is corporations pledged to support particular doctrines, but simply philosophical schools which expounded certain textbooks. How little rivalry there was between them is shown by the statement that the Korean priest Ekwan, who resided at the Genkōji temple, introduced both the Sanron and Jōjitsu and that the two Chinese priests Chitsu and Chitatsu propagated both the Hossō and Kusha.[1] Also some sects are said to have been introduced more than once. This probably means little more than that learned persons from time to time lectured on their doctrines, which concerned philosophy rather than practical questions such as what deity one ought to worship. Little is heard of Amida before the Nara period, but the Nihongi mentions that in 640 and again in 652 the priest Eon who had studied in China for thirty-one years was invited to the Palace to expound the Muryōju-kyō, that is, the Greater Sukhâvatî-vyûha. On the second occasion it is said that a thousand priests were present. But there is no hint that Eon represented any special school.

I have said something about the tenets of these four sects in speaking of China in the last chapter. They have all disappeared in both countries except the Hossō, which still exists because it owns the temples of Hōryūji, Yakushiji, and Kōfukuji in or near Nara, ancient and interesting sites which are protected by the Government. The Hossō is said to have been introduced no less than four times. First in 654 by Dōshō,[2] who was one of a large body of priests sent to study in China in the previous year and who received instruction from Hsüan-Tsang himself: then in 658 by Chitsu and Chitatsu, who are said to have also propagated the Kusha: later in 703 by three priests called Chihō, Chiran, and Chiyu, and finally in 735 by Genbō, the adversary of Fujiwara

[1] Péri (*B.E.F.E.O.*, 1917, p. 17) maintains that the Kusha never had an independent existence in Japan and that its special textbook was merely studied in the Hossō sect. This may be true, but all lists which I have seen, Japanese as well as foreign, reckon it as one of the Hasshu or eight ancient sects.

[2] Statements vary as to the exact date. Some give 653 or 657. Dōshō was not one of the priests mentioned in Nihongi, ii, 254. Like Gyōgi and Kōbō Daishi he is credited with many useful practical enterprises such as making bridges, wells, and roads.

Hirotsugu. It had two branches known as Northern and Southern and thus illustrates, even at this early date, the tendency of Japanese sects to split into subdivisions. In the eighth century the Hossō sect was influential in politics and produced many ambitious priests such as Genbō and the more celebrated Dōkyō.

An interesting figure is En-no-Gyōja (634–701),[1] a hermit and mystic who lived on Mount Katsuragi in solitary communion with the winds and forests. He was credited with miraculous powers, which brought upon him an accusation of sorcery, and he was banished to the islands of Izu but subsequently pardoned. He is said to have remembered that in previous births he had been a disciple of Gotama and also an Emperor of Japan. This type of recluse became frequent in later times, but in the earliest records we hear little of the mystic and ascetic side of Buddhism.[2] Our information, which comes mostly from the Nihongi, is perhaps incomplete, for it is only natural that an official publication should deal chiefly with matters affecting the material prosperity of the country, but still the utilitarian and *quid pro quo* view of religion implied by this record is very noticeable. Ceremonies which seem to have an educational or devotional value are constantly interpreted as if they were magical rites performed for the public good. Thus when we read that "men were sent to all parts to expound the Kon-kwō-myō (Suvarṇaprabhâsa) and Ninnō sûtras"[3] we are inclined to suppose that propaganda and popular instruction were the object, but numerous passages show that sûtras were thus "expounded" as a measure of public security, to give peace and prosperity to the Empire, to bring rain, to stop pestilence, or to avert the consequences of evil omens such as eclipses. The Ninnō-kyō[4] was considered especially efficacious for such purposes. It is a portion of the great Prajñâpâramitâ and relates how sixteen

[1] 役行者. Also known as En-no-Shōkaku and En-no-Otsunu.

[2] There are also interesting legends about the monk Hōdō, who is said to have come from India riding on a purple cloud and to have lived on Hokkesan in Satsuma sunk in meditation. He had friendly relations with the Emperor Kōtoku whom he cured of a disease in 649. See Visser, *Ancient Buddhism in Japan*, p. 195, and for other instances Takakusu's article "What Japan owes to India" in *The Young East*, Sept., 1925, pp. 106–7.

[3] Nihongi, ii, p. 335, speaking of the Emperor Temmu. Cf. p. 413 for similar orders of the Empress Jitō. The best authority for ancient Buddhist ceremonies is Visser's *Ancient Buddhism in Japan* in the series called *Buddhica*. It deals mainly with the seventh and eighth centuries, but also contains much interesting information about later Japanese ritual and parallel usages in China.

[4] 仁王經. Nanjio 17, translated by Kumârajîva.

kings headed by Prasenajit of Śrâvastî waited on the Buddha, who explained to them in eight chapters the best way of protecting their countries. In the eighth century Ninnō-e or assemblies for reading the Ninnō are frequently recorded,[1] and ultimately they seem to have become a regular spring and autumn festival. They formed part of the Court ceremonial at Kyōto until the troubles of the Ōnin era (1467–9).

Even more remarkable is the practice of entering the Buddhist order not for one's own salvation but as a species of self-sacrifice on behalf of another person.[2] We have already seen this illustrated in the account of the last illness of the Emperor Yōmei when the son of Shiba Tattō became a monk for the sake of his dying sovereign,[3] and many other examples are recorded in the Nihongi. Thus in 614 one of the principal Ministers fell ill and a thousand persons, men and women, entered the Order for his sake. In 665 three hundred and thirty did the same on account of the sickness of the Empress Dowager, and in 682 one hundred and forty for the Crown Princess. Shortly afterwards three men became monks in the vain hope of saving the life of a comparatively small official.[4] So completely had the practice become recognized as a method of propitiating the higher powers that in 696 the Empress Jitō ordered that on the last day of every year ten persons of pure life should be made to enter the Order, apparently as an expiation for the sins of the past and a good omen for the future.

In the chronicle of the three months preceding the death of the Emperor Temmu there is a long catalogue of the pious measures taken for his welfare and Shintō rites were also performed. (1) Fiefs of several hundred houses were granted to various temples; (2) images and lanterns were presented; (3) the clergy were entertained at vegetarian banquets; (4) the nengō was changed; (5) taxes and forced labour were remitted, debts were cancelled, and a general amnesty proclaimed; (6) sûtras were read; (7) finally, "seventy persons of pure conduct were selected to retire from the world." First eighty and then a hundred others followed their example. It is clear that loyalty and filial piety, the principal

[1] 仁王會 Ninnō-e. See Visser, loc. cit., 117–18, for dates.

[2] Even in modern China it is popularly believed that if a man becomes a monk his ancestors will go to heaven. Cf. Paraphrase of the Sacred Edict, vii.

[3] Nihongi, ii, p. 111. The Empress Suikō subsequently praised his conduct in a rescript.

[4] Nihongi, ii, p. 375.

virtues of old Japan, had much to do with promoting devout practices. In 594 the Nihongi tells us that all provincial officials "vied with each other in erecting Buddhist shrines *for the benefit of their lords and parents*", and images of Amida and Kwannon dating from this period have been discovered which bear inscriptions showing that they were votive offerings made on behalf of father and mother.

The list of ceremonies performed for the Emperor Temmu, as described above, comprises most of the rites recorded at this period. Vegetarian banquets offered to the clergy (sai-e) [1] were a specially frequent form of piety and can be traced back to the ancient custom often spoken of in the Piṭakas of inviting the Buddha and his disciples to partake of a meal. The Nihongi mentions them first in 584 under the Emperor Bidatsu and innumerable times in subsequent reigns. We soon detect a tendency to regard them as a sort of mass performed annually for the repose of departed souls seven days after death, and in 735 the Emperor Shōmu made it a rule that after the decease of an Imperial Prince a hundred priests should be entertained on the seventh day during seven years.[2] Any act of clemency and kindness, such as sparing life and preventing suffering, is a means of acquiring merit and this merit may legitimately hope for its reward. Therefore in times of danger it was the custom to proclaim amnesties, remit or reduce sentences, and lighten the burden of forced labour, also to refrain from killing animals for a certain time or in certain places. In 676, when there had been a drought and an ominous comet, the Emperor Temmu mitigated punishments by one degree and twice ordered "living things to be let loose". In 691 there was dangerously heavy rain and an eclipse of the sun. The Empress Jitō accordingly prohibited the use of strong drink and animal food and subsequently "long-life places (that is places where animals might not be killed) each of 1,000 paces were instituted in the Home provinces and others". In a decree published the same year she mentions that former Emperors had observed six fasting days in each month and it is probable that animals were not killed on these days. The formal prohibition to take animal life was known as hōjō-e, a meeting for liberating living creatures.[3] Nearly all the ceremonies mentioned are described by the word E or meeting, Ninnō-e, Hōjō-e, Musha-dai-e, and

[1] 齋會.

[2] 七七齋 Shichi-shichi-sai.

[3] 放生會.

so on.[1] Buddhism in ancient Japan was evidently very sociable. The more numerous the priests and the larger the congregation, the greater seemed the chances that success would follow.

In 606 we are told that the 15th day of the seventh month was observed for the first time. The nature of the ceremony is not further defined, but in 657 and 659 we are told that the Empress Saimei celebrated the Urabon-e on this day on behalf of her ancestors for seven generations. She also caused a model of Mount Sumi—that is, Meru—to be constructed.[2] The word Urabon apparently corresponds to the Sanskrit avalambana and Pali olamba, and a learned discussion of the origin and history of the festival will be found in Visser.[3] It appears not to correspond to any one Indian rite but to be a mixture of several with Chinese additions. In China it is first recorded in the reign of Wu-Ti A.D. 538, but its character was considerably modified by Amoghavajra (A.D. 746–774), who introduced the idea of making offerings of food not on behalf of but *to* the spirits of the dead. The Bon, as it is now called, is still celebrated in Japan in July or August, the old calendar being used for religious purposes in country districts.

It will be noticed that most of the observances mentioned have a direct reference to human troubles and are concerned with averting disasters like drought, sickness, and death. The anniversary of the Buddha's birth has, however, a different character. The chronicles lay little stress on it, precisely because it was a recurring festival and not connected with special public events, but it is doubtless the eighth day of the fourth month mentioned in A.D. 606 and 647. On the former occasion a copper image of the Buddha sixteen feet high was enshrined in the Golden Hall of the Temple of Gangōji and a great vegetarian banquet was held. The festival is still observed on 4th April, when it is the custom to pour sweet tea over the head of an image of the youthful Buddha, this liquid having replaced the original water. Fa-Hsien and I-Ching both mention bathing images as a common religious rite in India.

The principal scriptures read in public have been noticed in the

[1] For the Musha-dai-e see Visser, loc. cit., chap. vi, A. They were equivalent to the Indian Pancavarshika or Mahâmoksha-prasâd. Musha means limitless, i.e. anyone could attend the meetings; but was probably also a corruption of Moksha.

[2] The Nihongi also mentions the construction of such a model in 612, 659, and 660.

[3] Visser, loc. cit., chap. iv.

above remarks.[1] The Lotus (particularly the chapter about Kwannon), the Sukhâvatî-vyûha, the Ninnō, and the Suvarṇaprabhâsa seem to have been held in special esteem. Doubtless the professors of the Sanron, Hossō, and other schools expounded the texts on which they based their teaching, but we do not hear of these works being recited on official occasions and probably there was felt to be a distinction between philosophic works and scriptures which could be used to acquire merit. Still, any one who had mastered the Lotus and Suvarṇaprabhâsa must have had a good knowledge of Mahayanist doctrine, and some no doubt like Shōtoku Taishi were serious students, though we have no means of judging how many. But the usual method of reciting the scriptures was the process called *tendoku*,[2] that is, intoning a few lines at the beginning, middle, and end of a sûtra, turning over the pages and taking the rest as read. The *tendoku* was specially used when the whole canon (Issaikyō) was recited, as is recorded in 651 when the Emperor was about to change his residence and in 677 when there had been a great earthquake. There was some excuse for speed in these ceremonies, for the collection of scriptures read, if, as is probable, it was that made under the Sui dynasty, consisted of 5,058 volumes.

[1] They are conveniently tabulated in Vissor, loc. cit., chap. i.

[2] 轉讀 "turning and reading".

# CHAPTER VIII

## NARA PERIOD: THE OLDER SECTS

In 710, in the reign of the Empress Gemmyō, the capital was fixed at Nara. The step was a natural consequence of the Reforms of Taikwa, for a centralized administration requires a centre and the example of China doubtless weighed with educated Japanese. It was also popular, for the frequent construction of new palaces under the old system had meant onerous demands for forced labour and the clergy were favourable. It seemed most suitable to surround the sovereign and ministers with temples and monasteries which could bring religious influence to bear on their decisions, and the powerful Hossō sect lost no time in establishing itself. The new city was constructed at the western extremity of the modern Nara, and in the same year the temple of Kōfukuji was moved to the site where its remains still stand. The great Kamatari had originally built it at Yamashina, but in those days temples were transferred as easily as palaces: it was shifted in 672 to Unasaki, and in 710 Kamatari's son, Fujiwara Fuhito, removed it to the capital, where it became the cathedral of the northern branch of the sect and the residence of the ambitious priest Genbō. The still more eminent Gyōgi belonged to the southern branch which had its headquarters at Gangōji.[1] Shintō, however, was not neglected, for in the same year, 710, Fuhito also dedicated the celebrated Kasuga shrine, which still exists, to the tutelary deities of the Fujiwara family.

The Empresses Gemmyō and Genshō (whose reigns cover the period 707–723) both patronized literature, and by the orders of the first were compiled the Fūdoki, or provincial gazetteers, and the Kojiki, which is almost a sacred book for Shintō. In Genshō's reign the code was revised, and this amended version, known as Yōrō-ryōritsu, remained nominally in force, though with considerable modifications in practice, until 1868. But unlike most Empresses neither of them performed any special acts of Buddhist piety. This was

[1] The seven great temples of Nara are often mentioned, namely, Tōdaiji, Gangōji, Yakushiji, Hōryūji, Kōfukuji, Daianji, Saidaiji. Many of them are outside the present town.

left for their successor Shōmu (724–748), perhaps the most religious of all the Emperors of Japan. The name of the nengō which practically coincides with his reign—Tempyō—is often used to designate the whole period when art and Buddhism were flourishing at Nara. His Empress also, Kōmyō, the daughter of Fujiwara Fuhito, was most devout and the heroine of many edifying legends. For instance, a well-known story relates how she washed and tended a leprous beggar covered with loathsome sores who suddenly revealed himself as the Buddha Akshobhya.

Shōmu has so often been described as priest-ridden and fanatical that it may be well to remember that he also had an eye for the material welfare of his country. He opened a public establishment for dispensing medicines, he caused a survey of the various provinces to be made, he prescribed examinations for candidates desiring official appointments, and caused roads, bridges, and dykes to be constructed in the provinces. In these enterprises he was greatly helped by the eminent priest Gyōgi Bosatsu,[1] who, like Dōshō, one of his predecessors in the Hossō sect, divided his time between theology, art, and civil engineering. Gyōgi (670–749) was, according to some accounts, of Korean origin, according to others a native of the province of Izumi. At any rate, he is said to have been ordained at Yakushiji in 685 at the age of fifteen and to have studied the Hossō doctrine under the best scholars of the time. He travelled extensively in Japan, occupied in propagating Buddhism and improving irrigation and communications. Tradition says that he was a remarkable sculptor and invented a new kind of earthenware. He is also credited, but no doubt erroneously, with the introduction of the potter's wheel. It is likewise not accurate to speak of him as the author of Ryōbu-Shintō, though many authors do so, but still he pursued a consistent policy of preaching that there was no antagonism between the two creeds and of promoting harmony between them. His many talents won the confidence of the Emperor, who conferred on him in 745 the rank of Daisōjō, equivalent to Archbishop, this being the first time that the Crown assumed the right to nominate to that office, and ultimately bestowed on him the posthumous title of Bosatsu or Bodhisattva.

It may be mentioned that, great as the political power of Buddhism became in Japan, the Church was always regarded in theory as a department of the State. The office called Jingikwan supervised

[1] His life is contained in the Honchō Kōsōden, vol. 65.

all matters relating to Shintō, while Buddhism was dealt with by the Jibushō,[1] one of the Eight Departments which exercised control over priests and temples just as other departments did over the Army and the administration of justice. Its somewhat miscellaneous functions included the charge, not only of priests and nuns, but also of music, the Imperial mausolea, State funerals, and the reception of foreigners. It is true that in later times the priests of Hieizan were sometimes in rebellion and refused to accept the nominee of the Government as Abbot, but this was regarded as an act of insubordination analogous to the rebellion of a feudal chief which it might be prudent to condone, because punishment would involve awkward consequences. In principle the right of the Emperor to appoint to ecclesiastical posts and to grant titles, posthumous and other, was not disputed and the various priestly ranks were tabulated so as to correspond with the Court ranks.

Shōmu had another influential counsellor in Rōben (689–773), of the newly introduced Kegon sect, who was eminent as a writer and an artist, as well as in ecclesiastical matters. He is reckoned as one of the founders of the Tōdaiji monastery. Less edifying is the career of Genbō, head of the Northern Hossō and the first of those ambitious priests who rendered little service to religion and ended by making the Court afraid of the Church. He studied for nineteen years in China and on returning was well received at the Palace, but is said to have been both scheming and immoral. According to the common story he attempted to seduce the wife of Fujiwara Hirotsugu, the viceroy of Kyūshū, who was absent from the capital. Hearing what had occurred Hirotsugu demanded Genbō's removal and, being unsuccessful, rebelled and lost his life in 741. Genbō himself died in Kyūshū five years later and does not figure in the most celebrated of the Emperor's pious achievements, the construction of the Daibutsu.

In the earlier part of Shōmu's reign no special acts of Buddhist piety are recorded, and though on his accession he presented gifts to the priests and nuns of the capital, he uses in his edicts the ordinary official language about the gods who dwell in heaven and on earth deigning to bless the Empire.[2] But his religious inclinations were apparently stimulated by a terrible epidemic of smallpox which ravaged the country in 735–7 and did not spare the aristocracy,

[1] 治部省.

[2] Shoku-Nihongi Edicts 5 and 6. For these documents see Sansom, "The Imperial Edicts in the Shoku Nihongi," *Trans. Asiatic Society of Japan*, 1924.

especially the Fujiwara family. According to an edict of 737 every province was provided with an image of the Buddha sixteen feet high and a copy of the Prajñâpâramitâ, and further edicts issued in 741 ordered that in every province monasteries and convents (Kokubunji), each for twenty priests and ten nuns, should be established and seven-storied pagodas built. The monasteries were placed under the supervision of the Tōdaiji temple and the convents under the Hokkeji.

The Emperor also conceived the project of erecting a colossal image of the Buddha Roshana.[1] This idea was probably inspired by Rōben, for Roshana is the central figure of the Kegon sûtra of which he was an enthusiastic student, and he appears to have been in charge of the operations at Nara while Gyōgi travelled about the country collecting money. It was, however, thought prudent to consult the Sun-goddess before commencing the work and to ask if she approved. All versions of the story say that her answer was favourable, but they do not agree as to the exact wording and other details. The Genkō Shakusho,[2] which is perhaps the best authority, states that the priest Gyōgi mentioned above was sent to Ise bearing a Buddhist relic as a present. The oracle which he received began, "The sun of truth and reality shines over the long night of life and death: the moon of the eternal and everlasting dispels the heavy clouds of passion and ignorance," and accepted the relic with grateful thanks, but otherwise was not explicit. Tachibana no Moroe, the compiler of the Manyōshū, was then sent. The text of the reply which he brought back is not given, but the next night the Emperor had a dream in which the Sun-goddess appeared to him and said, "The sun is Birushana. Understand this and execute your enterprise."[3] This was unequivocal and satisfactory, but the revolt in Kyūshū already mentioned interfered with the imperial plans and for two years the capital was shifted.

Shōmu first planned to erect his colossus at Shigaraki, but the effort was unsuccessful, then at Sōnogami,[4] and finally in 747 in the

[1] For the name see above, Chap. IV, pp. 108–10.

[2] Written by Kōkan Shiren in 1322. This is rather a late date and the silence of the Shoku-Nihongi makes the whole episode suspicious. Also according to the Shoku-Nihongi, in the reign of Kōnin the goddess Amaterasu forbade a temple to be built near her shrine at Ise. On the other hand, one must remember that to consult the oracle at Ise was entirely in keeping with the customs of the age.

[3] The Miryū-Shintō-Kuketsu, attributed to the Emperor Saga, says (vol. ii): "Amaterasu is the true body of the Buddha, all pervading, without beginning or end."

[4] Or Sockami. Some authorities think that it was a part of Nara.

Tōdaiji at Nara. The work lasted three years and the Emperor himself took part, carrying earth in his sleeves in order to help raise a platform necessary for the operations. The artists made no less than eight unsuccessful attempts to construct the image, which was formed of a number of metal plates, only the head and neck being cast in one piece. 986,180 Japanese pounds of copper are said to have been used in the construction besides gold, lead, and other metals. The image at present to be seen at Nara and known as the Daibutsu or Great Buddha is a figure over 53 feet high sitting cross-legged on a lotus throne which is 68 feet in diameter and formed of 56 petals. These are probably the original dimensions, but the temple was twice burnt down in 1180 and 1567. The Daibutsu itself suffered severely and underwent serious repairs, the head and upper part having been restored after the last conflagration. The brush with which the pupils were painted at the original ceremony of opening the image's eyes is still preserved in that wonderful treasure house of antiquities, the Shōsōin at Nara.

It was regarded as a special sign of divine approval that early in 749 gold, which had hitherto been known only as an import, was discovered in the province of Mutsu. Accordingly a service of thanksgiving was held. The Emperor, attended by the imperial family and the Court, proceeded to Tōdaiji and took his place before the image, facing north, that is in the position of a subject before his sovereign, while Tachibana no Moroe stepped forward and read the following edict [1]: " This is the word of the sovereign who is the servant of the Three Treasures that he humbly speaks before the image of Roshana." The discovery of gold is then announced and the Emperor continues: " Hearing this we were astonished and rejoiced, and feeling that this is a gift bestowed upon us by the love and blessing of Roshana Buddha we have received it with reverence and humbly accepted it and have brought with us all our officials to worship and give thanks. This we say reverently, reverently, in the great presence of the Three Treasures whose name is to be spoken with awe."

If one compares the language of this address with the usual phraseology of imperial edicts the difference is astounding and must have seemed to old-fashioned Japanese an ominous innovation. In previous pronouncements the Emperors (including Shōmu

[1] Shoku Nihongi Edict 12, Sansom's translation.

himself) described themselves as "manifest Gods"[1] and used such expressions as "we divinely think": now the Sovereign not only avoids such majestic phrases but he calls himself the servant (Yakko) of the Three Treasures and uses humble language (e.g. the verb mōsu, to speak) which implies that he is addressing a superior. In another edict, apparently issued about the same time but addressed to his subjects, he reverts to the ordinary Court language in informing them of the discovery of gold.[2] This document is not very clearly worded, but apparently its object is to prove that there is complete harmony between Buddhism and Shintoism. People seem to have regarded the scarcity of gold and the difficulty of completing the image as a sign of divine disapproval, "yet now the Three Treasures have vouchsafed this excellent and divine great sign of the word and we think that this is a thing manifested by the guidance and grace of the gods that dwell in heaven and on earth and likewise by the love and kindness of the august sovereign spirits" (i.e. the imperial ancestors). Whereas in the previous edict there is no reference to Shintō deities, in this one they are repeatedly mentioned with respect and gifts are promised to their shrines and priests.

The relations of Buddhism and Shintō are further illustrated by an exceedingly curious incident which forms the theme of another edict.[3] We gather from it that Hachiman, described as the god of Yahata (eight banners), had delivered an oracle promising that he would assist the construction of the Daibutsu and urge the other gods to do the same: he further expressed a wish to visit Nara. As a token of his gratitude the Emperor bestowed on the deity a cap of honour (the usual sign of rank in those days) and sent high officials with an escort of soldiers to his shrine at Usa near Beppu to conduct him to the capital. As images are not used in Shintō the god was probably represented by some emblem conveyed in a sacred car. He was then installed in a special shrine in the compound of the Tōdaiji where forty Buddhist priests recited prayers during seven days and a priestess of Yahata, who was also a Buddhist nun, likewise figured in the proceedings. The relations between the two cults were thus perfectly peaceful. Hachiman is treated as a compeer of the Four Kings, of Indra and

[1] Akitsukami. The gods in heaven are invisible. The Emperor is a visible god manifest on earth.

[2] Shoku Nihongi Edict 13. See Sansom's notes.

[3] Shoku Nihongi Edict 15.

Brahmâ. But he is not of the same class as Kwannon or Miroku.[1] Like an Indian Deva he is regarded as a protector of the faith; he is not so much worshipped as given a chance of listening to edifying services and he receives a decoration. The term Bosatsu is used of Hachiman in an order to the Government of Kyūshū which was issued in 793. It concerns the property of the Usa shrine and refers to events which occurred in 783. But though this term is significant, it would probably be a mistake to attach much doctrinal importance to its use here, for it had many shades of meaning. Even in Indian works it had come to be little more than a name for a pious person, and the title of Bosatsu had been officially bestowed on the deceased Gyōgi. The Yakushiji near Nara possesses an image of Hachiman said to date from the Kōnin period (810–823) which represents him as a Buddhist priest.

The views of the age, at any rate of enlightened persons, are clearly explained in an edict of 765 [2] published on the occasion of the Shintō ceremony of offering first-fruits. The Empress who issues it was a fervent Buddhist and states that she considers her duties are first to serve the Three Treasures, next to worship the Shintō gods, and finally to cherish the people. Some think, Her Majesty continues, that the gods should be kept distinct from the Three Treasures, but if they examine the scriptures they will find it there stated that the gods ought to revere and protect the teaching of the Buddha. Since there is no reason why Buddhists and others should not mix together on religious occasions, she considers that there is no objection to the participation of priests and nuns in this Shintō festival, though it has hitherto been considered wrong. In a similar spirit Fujiwara no Muchimaro constructed a building called Jingūji or Miya-tera in which the rites of both religions were performed, and such edifices became common.

After taking part in the ceremonies described, Shōmu abdicated towards the end of 749 in favour of the lady just mentioned, his daughter Kōken, and became a monk, being the first Emperor to do so, though the practice subsequently became frequent. Kōken, like her father, was most devout and left the administration in the hands of her minister Emi no Oshikatsu,[3] but was probably

[1] In the eleventh and twelfth centuries he was identified first with the spirit of the ancient Emperor Ōjin and also spoken of as a Bodhisattva or even a Buddha. It is still more strange to find that the Buddhist reformer, Hōnen, was identified with him. See Coates and Ishizuka, *Hōnen, the Buddhist Saint*, p. 644.

[2] Shoku Nihongi Edict 38.

[3] His family name was Fujiwara no Nakamaro.

personally responsible for many ordinances concerning religion, such as a prohibition to take animal life. But Chinese learning was not neglected, for another edict ordered every household to provide itself with a copy of the Classic of Filial Piety.

Though the Daibutsu had been installed in 749, it was not solemnly dedicated until 752, and in connection with both ceremonies we hear of the presence of interesting foreigners who had arrived some time previously. It is probable that at this period there were not a few learned strangers at Nara, natives of India and Central Asia as well as Chinese. Prominent among them was Bodhisena, sometimes known as Baramon Sōjō or the Brahman Bishop, whose life is an instance of the adventurous odysseys not infrequent in those days. He was by birth a Brahman of South India and according to tradition went to China in the hope of finding Mañjuśrī. Instead of this, however, he made the acquaintance of the Japanese Ambassador and was persuaded to visit Japan. On the same ship with him were the notorious Genbō and several other interesting passengers, including Dōsen, who introduced the Kegon sect into Japan, and Kibi-no-Makibi, who is said to have brought back with him the arts of embroidery, of playing the lyre, and the game of Go (a kind of draughts). Kibi is also said to have invented the Kata-kana syllabary, and, if this is true, he may have learned something of the Sanskrit alphabet from Bodhisena and made use of the knowledge. The party arrived at Naniwa (the modern Ōsaka) in 736 and were met by Gyōgi, who conducted Bodhisena to Nara and presented him to the Emperor. He was treated with great honour and lodged in the temple called Daianji, where he taught Sanskrit. He died in Japan in 760.[1]

With Bodhisena came also a Cambodjan priest and musician called in Chinese Fo-t'ieh,[2] who likewise resided at Daianji and wrote a work on the Sanskrit alphabet. He also composed religious dances representing subjects taken fron Indian mythology and called Rin-yu or Champa dances.[3] These have survived, and I had

[1] For some interesting information about Bodhisena see Takakusu's article, "Le Voyage de Kanshin," in *B.E.F.E.O.*, 1928 and 1929, p. 24 ff. He mentions that the Manyōshū compiled by Bodhisena's fellow-passenger Kibi contains a poem about a crow that fed on rice grown by a Brahman.

[2] 佛哲. Also pronounced as Buttetsu and Fat-triet.

[3] Eight kinds are enumerated. See Takakusu, loc. cit., in *B.E.F.E.O.*, 1928 and 1929, pp. 27, 28, and Demiéville, *La Musique Čame au Japon*. Music and dancing were highly esteemed in ancient Japan. Religious dances formed part of Shintō worship, and Edict 9 of the Shoku Nihongi refers to a dance composed

the pleasure of seeing some of them performed at Horyūji in April, 1928, in honour of the anniversary of the Empress Suiko. A dais was erected in the courtyard of the temple: the dancers and the numerous clergy present were dressed in ancient costumes taken from the temple stores and the whole scene was probably a lifelike reproduction of the pageants of Nara in the eighth century.

The Empress had apparently taken little interest in secular matters, and in the years following the dedication of the Daibutsu was troubled by conspiracies and plots against the throne. It did not, therefore, seem surprising that she should abdicate in favour of a grandson of Temmu, the Emperor Junnin,[1] and become a nun. But, as often happened in later history when the practice of abdication became frequent, she felt the attraction of mundane pleasures and interests more strongly after renouncing the world than when she was in it, so much so that she played a not very dignified part in an astounding clerical romance which has few parallels in the political and ecclesiastical history of any country. She fell under the influence of a handsome and ambitious priest called Dōkyo and at his instigation continually intervened in public matters. Hence there quickly arose a serious rivalry and quarrel between Dōkyo and her former Minister Oshikatsu, who aspired to rule in the name of the young Emperor. Oshikatsu began the attack, which was perhaps unwise, for the high rank and many favours conferred on him had made even his kinsmen jealous, and he further put himself in the wrong by stealing the imperial seal, which was in the custody of the ex-Empress, and by using it for the issue of commissions to raise troops against Dōkyo. He was defeated and killed. The Emperor was exiled to the island of Awaji on the ground that he was privy to his minister's misdeeds, and was subsequently made away with. The Empress reascended the throne with the new title of Shōtoku (765–9) and all authority was in the hands of Dōkyo, who was appointed first Daijin-Zenji,[2]

by the Emperor Temmu and performed by the Princess Imperial in 743. It observes (quoting the Chinese classics) that for good government it is necessary to have everywhere and always two things—namely, ceremony and music. Four kinds of music were in use at the Court—Chinese (T'ang), Korean (Kan), that of Champa, and that of Tamra or the Quelpaert Islands.

[1] Strange to say, this title was not conferred on him till 1871. History had till then known him simply as Awaji-no-haitei, the deposed Emperor of Awaji.

[2] 大臣禪師, 大政大臣, 法皇. Hō-ō is the modern Japanese translation of Pope, but in that sense it is written with slightly different characters (法王).

which may be rendered as Minister Priest, then Dajō-daijin, or Chancellor, and finally Hō-ō, the two latter titles having hitherto been reserved for members of the Imperial Family.

And it was in that direction that Dōkyo's overweening ambition now turned. He caused to be circulated stories that the God Hachiman of Usa [1] had appeared in dreams and recommended that he be appointed Emperor. The situation was most grave, and it is to be noted that at this moment and also in the sixteenth century when the great monasteries were dangerously strong, it seemed by no means impossible that Japan might be ruled by an ecclesiastical Government like Tibet. The attitude of the Empress is not very clear. Perhaps she had sufficient dynastic and family sentiment to raise objections. At any rate, she insisted on specially consulting the oracle of Hachiman and dispatched a trusted official named Wake no Kiyomaro to Usa with instructions to put the question directly and return with the reply. Dōkyo interviewed him before his departure and endeavoured to win him over by promises and threats, but he proved worthy of the trust reposed in him and reported that the answer was unequivocal: Hachiman declared that only persons of the Imperial Family which is descended from the gods were eligible as Emperor. Dōkyo was furious, and strange to say had still sufficient influence over the Empress, who was probably in bad health, to have an edict [2] issued degrading and banishing Kiyomaro, who was also punished by having the sinews of his legs cut, and would probably have been killed on his way to exile had he not been protected by the Fujiwaras. The Empress died next year and Dōkyo's power was at an end. He was at once exiled to the province of Shimotsuke in northern Japan, where he died three years afterwards. Kiyomaro was recalled and made Udaijin, or Minister of the Right Hand, the third highest office in the State.

Kōnin, who succeeded to the throne, was elderly and easy-going and nothing remarkable is reported of his twelve years' reign, but doubtless the memory of Dōkyo's audacious attempt was one of the chief reasons which induced the next Emperor, Kwammu, to move

[1] The relations of the Hachiman shrine with the monarchy were perhaps unsatisfactory, though we do not know enough to form any definite opinion. In 749, when Hachiman was brought to Nara as related above, a Shintō priest and priestess arrived in his train and were lodged in the Tōdaiji. In 755 they were found to be involved in a conspiracy and punished.

[2] Shoku Nihongi Edict No. 44.

the capital from Nara in 784. Another result was that for a long time there were no more reigning Empresses. In the last two centuries there had been six, two of whom had reigned twice, but there were only two more in all Japanese history and the next did not come to the throne till A.D. 1630. In the twelfth century the ex-Emperor Toba had promised his favourite wife that in the event of their son dying one of their daughters should ascend the throne, but when the death actually occurred in 1155, he found that the national sentiment against a female sovereign was so strong that he had to break his pledge. It was evidently felt that ladies were too susceptible to ecclesiastical and other personal influences to be safely trusted with the supreme power.

The seventy-five years or so during which the Court resided at Nara (710–784) form a well-marked epoch in the history of Buddhism and are often spoken of as the period when it was most prosperous. And prosperous it was in a certain sense. The monasteries were well endowed with estates and treasure and their property tended to increase, for it paid no taxes and hence the peasants were ready to surrender their lands to the Church and then hold them as tenants in return for a rent less than the imposts exacted by the Government. Never were the clergy more wealthy or more powerful: they enjoyed and sometimes dispensed the imperial favour and rarely met with any serious obstacle. The extravagant ambition of Dōkyo alarmed the civil administration, but merely because it was extravagant and took no account of the venerable traditions on which the Empire, the imperial house, and the whole system of government as then understood were founded. Otherwise public opinion seemed to regard it as perfectly natural that the Church should be the principal part of the State: that prelates should be as powerful or more powerful than officials or soldiers, and that more money should be spent on temples and ceremonies than on all the other needs of the country. Even the old native religion and its priesthood joined in the general acquiescence.

Yet it may be doubted whether the really great influence of Buddhism in Japan dates from this epoch, except in matters relating to art, and did not rather begin a little later when new conditions gave a new impetus to all human activities, including religion. Clearly it would be absurd to deny that Buddhism left its mark on Nara and the neighbourhood in art. Many Buddhist priests were themselves artists, whereas Shintō had no images and little in the way of architecture. But now there arrived from China a new religion offering a copious series of sacred subjects, mostly Indian or Central-Asiatic in their ultimate origin, and specimens showing how they could be represented in painting and sculpture. At this period statuary in wood or bronze seems to have appealed to the Japanese more than painting, and they cultivated the new art with signal success, sometimes transforming by the charm of their own genius what they had borrowed, as for instance the Kwannon in the Chūgūji nunnery.[1]

In literature the debt was less remarkable. A special department attached to the Court under the Presidency of an Imperial Prince was charged with the duty of making copies of the Tripiṭaka, one of which was supplied to every monastery, but the literature of the period does not show so many signs of Buddhist influence as we might expect. The chronicles called Nihongi and Shoku Nihongi (the latter not completed till 797) record impartially events of interest for Buddhism and Shintoism. The former opens with the origin of the world and the Age of the Gods. It accepts the Chinese doctrine of the two principles called Yin and Yang and quotes without naming them ancient "writings". But it does not allude to Buddhist theories. It duly records the advent of Buddhism but does not celebrate it with pious fervour as do, for instance, the chronicles of Ceylon. The Manyōshū is an ample anthology of ancient and contemporary poems [2] and the desire to preserve them does credit to the nascent literary spirit of the age, as do also the compositions of Akahito and Hitomaro. But the religious inspiration of this poetry, so far as there is any, seems to be Shintoist rather than Buddhist. Buddhist sentiments may be found in it, but they are mostly concerned with such obvious themes as the brevity and uncertainty of life. Nor is it clear how far the influence of Buddhism extended beyond the capital and the Home Provinces. In 685 and again in 737 orders were sent for the erection of temples and monasteries in all provinces, but we have no information as to

[1] Close to the Hōryūji monastery. Shōtoku's mother is said to have resided there. Examples of painting are rarer. The best known are the mural paintings in the Golden Hall at Hōryūji, which are singularly like the frescoes of Ajanta and were probably executed by a Korean. The painting of Shōtoku Taishi and his two sons is now generally considered to be a copy of an original painted during his life.

[2] It contains more than 4,000 poems, and I have no pretension to have read them all. But I have seen few quotations which contain any definite reference to Buddhist doctrines. One poem, however, speaks of its being a rare chance to be born as a human being.

the practical results of the measure at this period. Still, it is only just to remember that the sovereigns and ecclesiastics of Nara did not limit their interests to the capital. They obviously wished to spread religion throughout the empire.

It is certainly remarkable that of the older sects of Japanese Buddhism the two which became and still are most numerous and important, the Tendai and Shingon, did not originate in Nara but fixed their centres at Hieizan and Kōyasan shortly after the Court had moved to Kyōto. I have already mentioned the four sects which were introduced before the capital was fixed. To these must be added the Kegon and Ritsu, which were brought from China to Nara and as compared with the older four show a certain advance, for the one is a more definite type of religion than any previous school and the other more practical. Still, if they are to be judged by their success as appeals to the religious consciousness of the nation, they clearly cannot be placed in the same class as the great sects of the next century.

The Kegon is said to have been introduced into Japan by the Chinese priest Dōsen, who arrived in 736 on the same ship as Bodhisena and others, and its success also owed much to the efforts of Rōben. I have already said something [1] about the Buddha whom it specially honours, about its sacred book the Kegon or Avataṃsaka sûtra, and about its fortunes in China. The monastic code called Bommō-kyō [2] describes how Roshana is seated on a lotus throne of a thousand petals, each of which is a universe with a presiding Shaka, but each containing millions of worlds like ours with smaller Buddhas of their own. Just as the Japanese Court paid special attention to the portions of the Ninnō-kyō which deal with good administration, so they saw an edifying political analogy in this vision. Roshana, the great Shakas, and the smaller Shakas seemed to their bureaucratic eyes to correspond to the Emperor, his officials, and the people. Yet, exactly as in China, the sect though wealthy and not without learning did not show real vitality. The imposing colossus at Nara attracted and still attracts crowds of devout admirers, but Roshana or Birushana was never a popular figure like Shaka or Amida, for he was cosmic rather than human. If for a large body of the intelligent clergy he became a great world force whose manifestations in nature they strove to understand

[1] Chap. IV, pp. 108–10; Chap. V, p. 173.

[2] The Brahmajâla-sûtra, Nanjio, 1087. Dōsen is said to have composed a commentary on it.

and depict in symbolic art, this was the work of the Tendai and Shingon rather than of the Kegon school. Yet for many centuries it produced men of erudition, energy, and holy life such as Shōsen, Keiga, and their pupil Kōben or Myōe (1173–1232) of Takao-Zan. The last named was the friend and adviser of Hōjō Yasutoki and may be responsible for some of the vigorous measures taken against the clergy, for he is said to have declared that " if Buddhism were such a religion as is represented by the monks of the present day, it would be the worst in the world ". Another story relates how he successfully stopped military violence within the precincts of his temple, saying that not even animals might be killed there, much less men. He was a strong opponent of Hōnen, the founder of the Jōdo sect at the end of the twelfth century, holding that for salvation it was essential that every man should form for himself the aspiration to become a Buddha, and that trust in another, like Amida, was not sufficient.

The Risshū or Ritsu [1] sect was the Lü-tsung founded in China by Tao-hsüan, its main principles being the importance of strict monastic discipline and, above all, of the correct transmission of holy orders. It was introduced by a celebrated priest of Yang-chou called Kanjin,[2] who was invited to Japan as early as 738, though his journey was delayed by an extraordinary series of misadventures, due to pirates, storms, and the unwillingness of the Chinese Government to let him depart, for the Emperor Hsüan-Tsung who was then on the throne was in favour of Taoism rather than Buddhism and did not approve of a Buddhist priest being officially invited to Japan. On his fifth attempt to leave, Kanjin was shipwrecked and lost his sight, but in spite of this disaster he tried once more and at the age of sixty-six arrived in 753 at Nara, where he was lodged in the Tōdaiji and treated with great honour. A Kaidan or platform for performing the ceremony of admission to the Order was erected, and 400 persons, including the Empress Dowager, received ordination at his hands. Others whose previous

[1] 律宗. Ritsu is also the name of a branch of the Shingon sect, and is likewise sometimes used to designate the Shinzei division of the Tendai sect.

[2] 鑑眞. Chien-Chen in Chinese pronunciation. In Japanese it is indifferently Kanjin or Kanshin or Ganjin. The authorities of the Tōdaiji temple at Nara use the last pronunciation. For more about him see Takakusu's articles already referred to in *B.E.F.E.O.*, 1928 and 1929 ff., entitled " Le Voyage de Kanshin en Orient ". The work in question was composed in 779 by Genkai, a pupil of Kanshin and grandson of the Emperor Kōbun.

admission as monks or nuns was considered to be invalid for any reason were reordained.

Although according to strict doctrine (though perhaps popular beliefs may not always agree with it) the Buddhist clergy have no special power of administering sacraments, not only in the Far East but in Hinayanist countries such as Burma, the greatest importance is attached to what the Christian Church calls Apostolic succession. Ordination is regulated by stringent rules which no doubt had their origin in very early times when the community of monks enjoyed many privileges and for the sake of its good name had to keep a sharp look out for unworthy candidates. According to the Ritsu sect holy orders could be conferred only by a properly selected chapter and only in a specially delimitated area, the aforesaid Kaidan. Previous to Kanjin's arrival the Japanese had probably been somewhat lax in such matters and his regulations had serious consequences for the ecclesiastical polity.

At first there was only one Kaidan where ordinations could be performed, that at Nara, but in 761 for the convenience of the more distant provinces the Empress Kōken ordered two more to be constructed, one for Kyūshū at the Kwannonji temple in Chikuzen and one for the northern districts at the Yakushiji in Shimotsuke. But difficulties arose when new and vigorous sects sprang up at Kyōto. In 819 Dengyō Daishi, the founder of the Tendai, wished to have a Kaidan of his own at Hieizan, but though there was nothing irregular in this ambition, the opposition of the Nara priesthood was so strong that for some years the Emperor, who had come to be regarded as the arbiter in such matters, withheld his sanction and did not grant it till 827, after Dengyō's death.

After the establishment of this new Kaidan, the Risshū seems to have declined, though it somewhat revived in the twelfth century under the leadership of Shōshō Shōnin, who wrote a treatise called Kaidan Shiki on the ceremonial to be observed at ordinations. Its principles were excellent, but everyone admitted them in theory and it had no authority to enforce them in practice. But it still exists, though it has only ten temples, of which the Tōshōdaiji near Nara is the principal. Ordinations are now held in any large temple which has the necessary accommodation.

# CHAPTER IX

## HEIAN PERIOD: TENDAI AND SHINGON

In 784 the Emperor Kwammu removed his Court from Nara to Nagaoka, but as the new site shortly became distasteful to him he decided to transport the capital again in 793 and selected another locality in the neighbourhood to which he gave the name of Heiankyō, or the capital of peace and tranquillity, though it became more commonly known as Kyōto, that is simply the capital. This time the change was permanent: a new city was constructed on the model of Chang-An, the imperial residence of the T'ang dynasty in China, and continued to be the official metropolis of Japan until 1868. From the end of the eighth to the end of the twelfth century—that is, until the rise of Kamakura—it was also the centre of Japanese Buddhism, though Nara occasionally endeavoured to assert its claims.

There is little doubt that this resolution to leave Nara was mainly due to the fear that ecclesiastical influence was growing unduly strong and that so long as the Imperial Family was overshadowed by the great fanes and their priestly occupants it had little chance of being independent and its own master. Yet the change implied no hostility to Buddhism and, as if to show that all was well, the Church actually forestalled the imperial movements. In 788 a young priest called Saichō built on the mountain of Hieizan a monastery afterwards called Enryakuji, which was destined to be regarded as the guardian of the Emperor and Court and their protection against the noxious influences which, according to the Chinese science of geomancy, came from the north-east. Enryaku was the name of the period (782–805) in which the reign of Kwammu commenced and in which the two transferences of the capital to Nagaoka and Kyōto took place, but the temple was not so called until the reign of the Emperor Saga, who rightly bestowed the designation on it as being the most remarkable monument of a great epoch. Kwammu himself recognized it as being in some sense the metropolitan cathedral, for in 793 Saichō was requested to hold in it a ceremony for the purification of the site of this new capital, and again on visiting it in 797 the Emperor is said to have saluted it as the true guardian of the Empire.

It can hardly have been mere chance but rather something in the spirit of the time, some new ardour and freedom, which caused two young men, Saichō above mentioned (767–822) and Kūkai (774–835), who were nearly contemporaries, to have careers so similar in their incidents and their consequences. They are better known by their posthumous names of Dengyō Daishi and Kōbō Daishi, Daishi or great teacher being a title of honour first bestowed upon Saichō. Each of them studied for a short time in China, and each of them returned master of the doctrines of a great Chinese school which he popularized so successfully that Tendai (T'ien-t'ai) and Shingon (Chên-yen) became the dominant types of Japanese Buddhism until the rise of new sects, which may be termed protestant, in the twelfth century, and even in spite of these formidable rivals are strong in numbers and influence at the present day. And though according to the standards of later times their doctrines seem complicated and their ceremonies elaborate to excess, yet they offered residence in some paradise to every one who tried to obtain it, whereas the older Nara sects denied the possibility of such high destinies to the "common man".[1]

Saichō was born in Shiga,[2] a town of the province of Ōmi, and became a priest at the age of fourteen. After building the monastery on Hieizan when still quite a young man he attracted the notice of the Emperor Kwammu and was sent to pursue his studies in China in 802. He investigated there the doctrines of the Chên-yen school and likewise of the Zen, but seems to have given the preference to the T'ien-t'ai. It is noticeable, however, that the connection between these three sects is closer in Japan than in China and that there has been considerable interchange of ideas between them. On Mount T'ien-t'ai he resided at the Kuo-ch'ing temple and there received instruction from the priest Tao-Sui. In 805 he returned home and resumed his position as abbot of the Enryaku-ji, but soon found himself embarrassed by the hostility of the older sects of Nara, who did not at all relish the importation of what seemed to them to be impertinent novelties. The Tendai was indeed recognized as a sect, that is to say, the higher clergy registered as belonging to it received funds from official sources, but it was not allowed to conduct ordinations of its own, the right of performing that ceremony being reserved to Nara and the two supplementary Kaidans founded by the Empress Kōken. Saichō had been

[1] See *Hōnen, the Buddhist Saint*, pp. 188 and 197 ff.

[2] Said to be the modern Ōtsu on Lake Biwa.

reordained at T'ien-t'ai according to what was considered the correct ritual there, and he considered himself entitled to continue the succession and to make arrangements for the ordination of others at his own monastery. He appears to have held one such ordination in the last month of 807, which is described as being the first ichijō-tai-kai held in Japan, this being the name given by the Tendai sect to the precepts laid down in the Bommō-sûtra and held by them to represent what is universally binding (the one vehicle) as opposed to the regulations of the Sarvâstivâda and other schools of the Vinaya. But permission to hold further ordinations was long refused in spite of the efforts made to obtain it, and it was only in 827, after Saichō's death, that his disciples Kōjō and Jikaku succeeded in obtaining the imperial sanction. When once established the Kaidan on Hieizan became the centre at which most of the celebrated priests of Japan were consecrated, and the monastery grounds grew into an immense enclosure containing a multitude of magnificent buildings, destined, alas, to destruction in the sixteenth century. It is said there were no less than 3,000 temples and halls arranged in three sections to the east, west, and north called Tōdō, which which lay in the middle, with Saidō and Yokawa more or less surrounding it. The whole sacred mountain was sometimes styled Miyako-Fuji, and its superior was an Imperial Prince who lived in the temple called Seirenji.[1] But at the time of which we are speaking Hieizan had not yet attained the material prosperity and power which ultimately proved its ruin.

There can be no question of the magnitude of Saichō's achievements: the institution which he founded beccame a great school of art, and all the later sects, whether they were Japanese creations or adaptations of Chinese originals, arose from within the Tendai. But he himself had only a moderate success after his return from China. He wrote several books, of which his commentary on the Lotus and a work called the Defence of the Country[2] are the best known: he was respected and duly honoured at Court but apparently was neither a favourite nor very influential. Perhaps he was over zealous and too much disposed to religious controversy. Shortly before his death the title of Dengyō Hōshi was conferred on him, which was changed by the Emperor Seiwa in 866 to Dengyō Daishi.

Kūkai, who was his junior by only a few years, was born at

[1] Originally on Hieizan but afterwards removed into Kyōto.

[2] 守護國界章 Shugo Kokkai-shō.

Zentsūji, where an interesting temple erected in his honour still stands, not far from the town of Kotohiro in Shikoku. He studied Chinese literature under the guidance of his uncle and at first followed the Sanron sect, but when he was twenty-one years of age was ordained at the Tōdaiji at Nara. Three years later he is said to have written a book called Sankyō-shiki,[1] in which he endeavoured to harmonize the teachings of Buddhism, Confucianism, and Taoism. This is interesting, if true, as showing the same tendency which led him later to advocate the doctrine known as Ryōbu-Shintō. In 804 he went to China and landed at Fu-chou, whence he proceeded to the capital Ch'ang-An, and studied under Hui-Kuo the mysteries of the Chên-yen or, in Japanese pronunciation, Shingon sect which was still very influential and popular although its great exponent Amoghavajra had been dead some twenty-seven years. It is also recorded that he studied Sanskrit under Prajña, an Indian who is said to have collaborated with Adam, the Nestorian priest who is celebrated on account of his connection with the monument known as the Nestorian stone. After spending about three years in China he returned to Japan and his life was one long series of triumphs. He was a *persona gratissima* at the Court and, though he cannot be accused of flattery or subservience, was evidently of a gentle and conciliatory disposition, anxious to be on good terms with Buddhists of all sects and also with Shintoists. But besides this he impressed the popular imagination more than any teacher had done, nor has he been ousted from his position by later figures like Shinran and Nichiren. He is still the most celebrated of Japanese saints, the hero of countless legends, the reputed author of a hundred books and more works of art than any one man could have executed, and in the estimation of his followers an incarnation of Vairocana not yet dead but awaiting within his tomb the coming of the future Buddha.

On arriving in Kyōto he introduced[2] the rite known as Kwanjō[3] (Abhisheka) or sprinkling with water, which offers many analogies to baptism. It is not, however, regarded as a sign that the recipient has entered the Buddhist religion but rather that he is on the way

[1] 三敎指歸. The same tolerance finds expression in the saying attributed to him that Buddhism, Confucianism, and Taoism (Shintō) are the three legs of a tripod on which the welfare of Japan rests.

[2] According to some accounts it was Saichō who first brought the rite to Japan.

[3] 灌頂. As at present performed the ceremony occupies several days and includes at least six sprinklings.

to the highest spiritual enlightenment and has taken the first step in the road which leads to Buddhahood. At the present time it is practised chiefly by the Shingon sect, but Kūkai is said to have administered it to many priests, including Saichō, and even to the Emperor Heijō, the son of Kwammu. He was appointed abbot of the Tōji in the south of Kyōto and organized there a popular school, in which connection it may be mentioned that one of the many inventions ascribed to him is the Hiragana syllabary. He also induced the Emperor Nimmyō to build the temple of Shingon-in within the precincts of the Palace, in which Buddhist rites were performed on the occasion of the principal festivals. But the architectural enterprise dearest to his heart was the foundation of the great monastery of Kōyasan, of which the first temple called Kongōbuji was built under his own supervision. Kōya was then a lonely mountain in the province of Kii and even now is not much frequented except by pilgrims. But perhaps Kūkai had a better instinct than Saichō in the choice of sites. Kōyasan has suffered severely from accidental fires, like many ancient buildings in Japan, but it escaped the political notoriety and the consequent destruction with which Hieizan was visited. Kūkai died there peacefully in the spring of 835, after exhorting his disciples to follow the precepts of the Buddha, and an enormous cemetery containing the corpses or cenotaphs of many celebrities has grown up near the tomb in which he is supposed to be merely reposing, for it became the fashion to be buried near the saint in the hope of sharing his resurrection. In 921 the Emperor Daigo conferred on him the title of Kōbō Daishi by which he is commonly known.

In origin the Tendai and Shingon are different. The first was a Chinese attempt to found a great eclectic school recognizing all known forms of Buddhism as phases of true doctrine but accepting the Lotus-sûtra as its crown and quintessence. The Shingon is really the Mantrayâna, a late form of Indian Buddhism which was successfully transported not only to China but to Tibet and Java. How similar some of its ideas are to those of Lamaism may be seen by looking at the plates in the publication called *Art Treasures of Kōyasan*,[1] which depict terrible spirits quite in the manner of Tibetan

[1] Published by the Kokka Company, Tokyo. See, for instance, plates Nos. 46, 61, 73. Compare also plate 5 (sacred objects possessed by Kōbō Daishi) with the figure in Waddell's *Buddhism of Tibet* (p. 341) representing a Dorje, or short sceptre held by Lamas during religious rites, or the eleven-headed statue of Avalokiteśvara reproduced in Kokka No. 20 with the similar figures in Waddell (p. 15) and Grünwedel's *Mythologie* (p. 65). See also the figures from Bali represented in Pleyte's *Indonesian Art*, plates ii and xvi.

paintings. Its doctrinal system is extremely intricate and is complicated by the fact that a distinction is drawn between the esoteric or secret and the ordinary teaching. I shall attempt to elucidate this obscure subject in a subsequent chapter when considering the special tenets of the various sects, and here will simply give a brief epitome which may be sufficient to explain the important part played by Shingon in Japanese history and art.

Its fundamental doctrine is that the whole universe is a manifestation of the Buddha Vairocana, but the manifestation is twofold and is divided into the categories called Diamond or indestructible and Womb or material and perishable,[1] in Japanese Kongō-kai and Taizō-kai. These two principles may also be contrasted as spiritual and material or as static and dynamic, and their precise meaning is explained only in the secret doctrine communicated to adepts but not set forth in literature. But the manifestations of Vairocana's body to himself, that is the various Buddhas and Bodhisattvas, are represented symbolically by diagrams called Mandara. Maṇḍala in Sanskrit means a circle, but its equivalent in Japanese usually signifies a rectangular arrangement of figures or of mystic Sanskrit letters which stand for the figures of Buddhas and Bodhisattvas, each set within a square or circle. These Mandara are often of high artistic merit and reproductions of two of them representing the Material and the Diamond cycles of existence, which may be seen in Anesaki's work on Buddhist Art,[2] will give the reader a better idea of this intricate symbolism than any attempt at description could do. But though the elegant shapes of the Devanagari letters in a slightly modified form play a considerable part in this symbolism, yet it also revels in human or superhuman figures representing various Buddhas, Bodhisattvas, and spirits. In some ways the Shingon could give better inspiration to painters than other schools. The fault of most Buddhist art in Japan is a monotony of kindliness, an infinite repetition of benevolent deities and bland clerics. But the Shingon with its doctrine that the whole cosmos is the expression of the Buddha nature did not hesitate to represent the terrible and even the grotesque as aspects of the divine.

As already mentioned, the Chên-yen sect from which the Shingon

[1] Sanskrit Vajradhâtu, Garbhadhâtu; Japanese 金剛界 Kongō-kai and 胎藏界 Taizō-kai.

[2] Anesaki, *Buddhist Art*, plate xvi, A and B.

is derived does not hold a high position in China. It probably had more vigour when it attracted the attention of Kōbō Daishi, but for several centuries it would seem that it has been occupied rather with magic and incantations than with the idea that the whole universe is an expression of the Buddha nature. And certainly that same charge of confusing prayer with spells and magical formulæ or ceremonies can be brought against the Japanese branch of the sect. But still Shingon is entitled to the credit of emphasizing the main idea which seems in danger of being forgotten in China and of giving it adequate expression in art. The merit of this is no doubt partly due to Kōbō Daishi himself. He was attracted by the good elements in the school which commended itself to him: his learning was a process of selection not of mere absorption. But some credit must also be allowed to the artistic nature of the Japanese people which seized upon the nobler and not the more superstitious side of the new religious system presented to it. In tracing the history of religious ideas one has too often to follow a process of degeneration, and such a process is painfully evident in the history of later Indian Buddhism, especially in Bengal, where the teaching of the founder gradually decayed away and disappeared. But in China, as also in Tibet and Java, it was for a time, at any rate, revivified. In China it purged itself of the evils commonly known as Śâktism: in Japan it took on a new lease of life: it eliminated numerous dangerous abuses which were growing up, it taught noble and profound ideas and gave them worthy expression in art. On the other hand, this profundity and copious use of symbolism was its greatest danger. Its adherents, except those rare spirits who could fathom its deep mysteries, mistook the symbol for the reality and lapsed into polytheism and superstition. Unlike Amidism it had no message for plain men who want simple definite teaching and not mysteries and beautiful allegories.

In Japan the Shingon and Tendai sects are closely connected and represent a type of Buddhism which was prevalent during the Heian or Fujiwara period, say from A.D. 800 to 1100. They were imported from China almost simultaneously and it does not seem that there was any hostility between them in that country. The Tendai was obviously and professedly eclectic and was able to agree with the Shingon on many points of doctrine. Thus while holding the Lotus-sûtra and the person of Śâkyamuni in the utmost reverence, it did not hesitate to recognize Vairocana as representing the Dharmakâya. And the Shingon tended to become equally tolerant and comprehensive in practice. Its fundamental doctrine of a great cosmic force which displays itself in many manifestations was not likely to raise objections to the inclusion of any personage in its already numerous pantheon or to make difficulties about any rites which might be considered specially appropriate in his worship. Jikaku (the posthumous name of the priest Ennin), who was appointed abbot of the Tendai in 854, had a special sympathy for the Shingon, from which he borrowed much, thus obliterating many of the differences between the two sects. Also, although the Tendai and Shingon both became no inconsiderable forces in politics as well as in religion, their secular aspirations do not seem to have brought them into direct collision. This was largely the result of Kōbō Daishi's wisdom in locating the headquarters of his sect at Kōyasan at some distance from the metropolis. The quarrels of Hieizan were rather with the monasteries of Nara and with its own offshoot and rival, the great temple of Onjōji or Miidera near Ōtsu, than with the Shingon.

This conciliatory and comprehensive spirit had important results in another sphere, namely, the relations between Buddhism and the national cult or Shintō. I have already traced the beginnings of this tendency to identify the two religions, or rather the two pantheons, in the Nara period and even earlier, and found that though it is clearly laid down that the Shintō deities respect and protect Buddhism, the idea that they are simply another form of the Buddhas and Bodhisattvas had hardly yet obtained general acceptance, though the current of popular opinion was evidently setting in that direction. It can scarcely be said to have become the popular belief before the Kamakura period and the twelfth century, but still the whole influence of Dengyō Daishi and Kōbō Daishi was favourable to some system of amalgamation. The former when he first selected the site of the future Enryakuji was careful to enter into good relations with the Shintō deity who was regarded as lord of the place, and showed him all honour under the name of Sannō, or the King of the Mountain. There is some uncertainty, however, as to whether he was one or many, for we also hear of the seven Sannō gods as being the guardians of the monastery.[1] A couple of centuries later Gyōen, a priest of Miidera, saw a profound meaning

[1] There were seven Sannō shrines situated in the province of Ōmi, one of which was dedicated to a deity of healing considered to be an incarnation of Yakushi Nyorai. One legend, possibly late, states that Sannō appeared to Dengyō in the form of the three Buddhas—Amida, Shaka, and Yakushi.

in the two Chinese characters 山 王 Sannō, used to write the deity's name. He considered that the three strokes, perpendicular in the first character and horizontal in the second, signify affirmation, negation, and that which is neither the one nor the other but yet is both, while the single stroke horizontal in the first character and perpendicular in the second shows the mysterious union of this trinity in a unity expressed by the Tendai formula Isshin Sandai. This ultimately developed into what was called Sannō ichijitsu Shintō or the One truth Shintō of the mountain god, according to which a Shintō deity, like the Buddha of the Tendai philosophy, represents the affirmations and negations of the phenomenal world and their synthesis in a higher unity. Even more remarkable is a legend related of Keimyō (965–1038), who was head of the Tendai sect. He prayed to Ōmiya, one of the seven Sannō deities, and besought him to reveal his true nature, on which the deity replied that he had for ages been striving to save all living beings. This reminded Keimyō of a passage in the Lotus [1] in which it is said that in all the Universe there is not a spot as small as a mustard seed in which Shaka has not sacrificed his body for the sake of living creatures, and he felt convinced that Ōmiya was only another name for the Buddha Shaka himself.

It is said that the name of Ryōbu-Shintō was given to the doctrines of Kōbō Daishi by his admirer the Emperor Saga (810–823). It is clear that the teaching of the Shingon sect was particularly well adapted to theories of amalgamation, for it began by stating that the whole Universe is a manifestation of the Buddha, and starting from such a premise it was easy with a little good will to identify deities who represent natural features and forces (as most Shintō deities undoubtedly do) with roughly similar manifestations of the Buddha. The process was further facilitated by the singular vagueness of Shintō deities and the legends concerning them. Any tendency towards monotheism, to imagine a being resembling Jehovah or Allah, was conspicuously absent. The gods were not represented by statues or pictures or by any form, and few of the stories told about them give them any definite characteristics. There was no objection to identifying them with anything which was majestic and benevolent.

Nevertheless, the process of identification was gradual: it was complete in the Kamakura period when we find, for instance, that

[1] Chapter xi, after verse 48.

the Shintō deity Hachiman is accepted as a Buddha—sometimes as being the same as Amida—or as a Bodhisattva, the use of both terms being a significant reminder that we are not in the realm of strict Buddhist orthodoxy. Yet it would seem that in their undoubted works Dengyō Daishi and Kōbō Daishi use the older language which describes Shintō deities as guardians or protectors of the faith. When the complete fusion of Buddhas and Shintō deities is spoken of in later times the phrase Honji Suijaku [1] meaning "home land and footprints" is often used. It appears to have been originally employed of the Lotus-sûtra, which is regarded as composed of two parts, that which deals with the nature of the Buddha as it exists in eternity, that is in its true home, and that which describes his appearance in this world as Śâkyamuni, that is the traces which he has left of his passage across the world of phenomena. But subsequently it was used in a much more extended sense to signify the true nature of any Buddha and his appearance in Japan as incarnate or manifested in a Shintō deity.

The process of amalgamation was probably favoured by the rise of a hermit section in both the Shingon and Tendai, known as Yama-bushi, those who sleep on mountains, or Shugenja,[2] those who practise austerities, for they frequented the sacred places of Shintō and made them sacred also to Buddhists. The ascetic and mystic who dwells alone in the forest is of course a well-known figure in India among Brahmans as well as Buddhists: the type was sympathetic to a large section of Chinese, as is shown by the example of the Taoist sages, and it appealed to the Japanese love of nature and of wild scenery. An early example of this spirit is offered in the seventh century by En no Gyōja already mentioned, and later it received the recognition of orthodoxy in both the Shingon and Tendai sects. In the former the celebrated priest named Shōbō (or Rigen Daishi), who flourished 832-909, founded associations called Shugendō, and his example was followed in the Tendai by Zōyo about a century later (1090). The members of these confraternities frequented the wild mountains and peaks of Yamato, especially Mount Ōmine or Kimbu in the county of Yoshino, where the two branches held an annual meeting and performed religious exercises in union. Yamato was one of the holy lands of Shintō: its high places and forests were all under the protection

[1] 本地垂迹. [2] 山伏: 修験者.

of Shintō deities and now Buddhist pilgrims and hermits made them their haunt, not in any spirit of aggression but honouring and respecting their guardians, as Saichō had honoured Sannō when he founded his establishment at Hieizan. Mount Ōmine came to be regarded as the very body of the Buddha Vairocana and the smaller peaks were similarly identified with other Buddhas and Bodhisattvas. The three temples of Kumano in Kii are a striking example of Ryōbu-Shintō in its fully developed form. They were originally dedicated to various Shintō deities, one of whom was afterwards known as Shōjō Gongen, Gongen [1] being a word used to express the incarnation or manifestation of a Buddhist deity. The Life of Hōnen states that this deity was really Amida and relates how he advised a certain Yamabushi to apply to Hōnen and learn the way of salvation. He is also said to have revealed to Ippen the special views about Amida professed by the Ji sect. Shirakawa and several other Emperors made numerous pilgrimages to Kumano after abdicating.

Nor did the movement towards assimilation and amalgamation come only from the Buddhist side. The Shintō priests were not in the habit of defining their dogmas, or the nature of their gods, but the number of applications made for permission to build Buddhist temples within the precincts of Shintō shrines is in itself a proof that they considered such union as desirable. In the great majority of cases a request for the foundation of such a Buddhist temple was based on an oracle said to have been delivered by the Shintō deity of the shrine and promulgated by his ministers. Indeed, if an amicable arrangement had not been made, if Buddhism had struggled with Shintoism as Christianity and Islam struggled with paganism in Europe and Africa, it is probable that the victory would have remained with Buddhism. It is true that Shintō could count on the conservative instinct of the peasantry and agricultural classes, but since in the Nara and Heian periods the whole weight of the official and educated world, including the Emperor and Court, was on the Buddhist side and Buddhism was long considered as another name for civilization and progress, it was pretty clear that Shintō had all to gain and very little to lose in responding to the advances made by antagonists who would have been powerful and probably irresistible if things had been allowed to come to an open rupture.

[1] 權現.

But the union between Buddhism and Shintō was not so complete as isolated quotations from Buddhist doctors or others might lead one to suppose. When we try to explain it, it is not to be defined in terms of European logic. At the end of the last century, when the two religions were declared separate, there was no difficulty in disentangling them. The ownership of ecclesiastical property may have given rise to disputes, but neither system showed any signs of being encumbered with the doctrines of the other. And this distinction of creed seems to have existed even in the days when Ryōbu-Shintō was most flourishing. Hōnen, for instance, was regarded by some as an incarnation of Hachiman,[1] but his works do not contain any mixture of Shintō and Buddhism. He writes as a Buddhist and appeals to Buddhist scriptures. Neither did Shintō entirely lose the sense of its own separate existence. Though almost all its temples except those of Ise and Izumo were managed by Buddhist priests and showed signs of Buddhist influence in their images and architecture, yet in a limited sphere it asserted itself. The goddess Amaterasu in the reign of the Emperor Kōnin is said to have forbidden the construction of a Buddhist temple near her shrine at Ise.[2] At the same shrine the name of the Buddha might not be pronounced.[3] He was spoken of as "the child of the centre" and many Buddhist terms were also tabooed.[4] Curious rules are mentioned which seem to indicate that Buddhism was regarded as a distinct, not to say hostile, creed. Thus a Buddhist priest who wished to make a pilgrimage to the shrines had to hide his shaven head by wearing a wig, and in the Middle Ages such wigs could be purchased in special shops in the outskirts of the town.

Again, though it is obviously true that the Japanese had a strong tendency to unite and amalgamate religions, they had an equally strong proclivity to create sects and multiply divisions. This is perhaps partly due to the fact that local sentiment was specially strong. A sect was generally connected with the foundation of a particular temple such as Tōdaiji or Enryakuji. When another temple was built, if the priests who managed it were active and zealous, it was apt to appear not merely as another cathedral of the

[1] *Hōnen, the Buddhist Saint*, trans. by Coates and Ishizuka, p. 644.

[2] Shoku-Nihongi, xxxvi.

[3] See Waley, *Genji Monogatari*, vol. iv, p. 207, chapter called Wakana.

[4] e.g. Buddhist temples, sûtras, sthûpas, monks, laymen, etc. See Genchi Kato, *A Study of Shintō*, p. 94, quoting the Kotaijingū Gishikichō or Records of the Shintō rites at the inner shrine of Ise.

same sect, but as an institution having certain usages and peculiarities of its own of which it was justly proud, and in fact of possessing and preaching a more exact version of the truth. These claims to doctrinal superiority, especially if combined with questions of territorial jurisdiction, led to violent quarrels between the various establishments and branches of the same sect, and it is often difficult to ascertain whether any real distinction of doctrine and ideas was involved or whether the whole difference was not analogous to the quarrels which divided noble houses. The Shingon sect had a comparatively peaceful history, but at an early date its great temples in or near Kyōto, such as the Tōji (816), Daigoji (874), and Ninnaji (885), became the centres of various branches which, while avoiding public disputes, had peculiarities of their own. Thus the last-named is the headquarters of the Omuro branch which specially studies certain scriptures [1] in addition to those accepted by the rest of the sect. But about three centuries after the death of Kōbō Daishi, a priest named Kakuhan or Kōkyō Daishi founded the great monastery of Negoro in Kii and with it a new division of the sect called Shingi [2] or the reformed Shingon, from which again sprang two divisions known by the names of Chizan and Buzan. Negoro brought upon itself a disaster which most Shingon sects managed to escape, though it was only too common in the history of medieval Japanese Buddhism. The huge estates which it owned, its wealth and prosperity, and the army of mercenaries which it maintained made it a great feudal power and it was destroyed by Hideyoshi in 1585. Nobunaga had dealt out the same treatment to Enryakuji a few years previously in 1571, and it is the Tendai sect which must bear the blame of having originated a system which deprived the great monasteries of much of the moral force they ought to have exercised and which ultimately brought upon them the most terrible vengeance.

There was an eminent priest of Hieizan who bore the name of Enchin and the posthumous title of Chishō Daishi.[3] He studied in China from 853 till 858, visited the temples of T'ien-t'ai, and returned with numerous copies of the scriptures and also certain new views. On his return he founded a temple called Sannōji, where

[1] Nanjio, Nos. 1024 and 1025.

[2] 新義眞言 Shingi Shingon.

[3] These names are somewhat confusing, as the eminent head of Hieizan, who was to some extent his opponent, was called Ennin and received the posthumous title of Jikaku Daishi.

he preached the doctrine as he learned it in a form somewhat irritating to the disciples of Jikaku, the chief abbot of Hieizan, who had himself studied in China and had become the successor of Dengyō Daishi. In 873 Enchin was appointed head of the temple called Onjōji, or Miidera, at Ōtsu, and the two branches of the sect became known as the Sammon and Jimon or Mii.[1] He does not appear to have abandoned his connection with Hieizan, which lasted until his death in 891, but when one of his followers named Yokyō (919–991) became head of Hieizan the quarrel grew acute. Yokyō was strongly opposed by the section which followed the older teaching of Jikaku and he and his adherents had to retire to Miidera leaving Hieizan in the possession of their opponents.

Henceforward there was bitter enmity between the two divisions of the Tendai. About 960 a dispute broke out between Ryōgen (also called Jie Daishi) and the Gion temple in Kyōto. Ryōgen, who enjoyed the esteem of the Court, used force to get the better of his adversaries and then for the protection of his rights proceeded to organize a body of mercenaries known as Sōhei[2] commanded by priests. This example was followed by other monasteries such as Miidera and at Nara by Kōfukuji and Tōdaiji. In 968 these latter had a dispute about the possession of certain ricefields and the matter was settled by an appeal to arms. In 989 Hieizan started a disastrous precedent by using similar methods against the Government. They refused to accept the Emperor's nominee as their abbot and resisted with violence. Nor were they satisfied with asserting their independence: they also had recourse to arms to enforce their pretensions. In the eleventh century it became the custom for a monastery which claimed some privilege or considered itself wronged to send into Kyōto armed bands together with a sacred emblem. They were thus able to use force themselves and to complain of sacrilege if any one showed disrespect towards the holy object.[3] After 1080 these demonstrations grew frequent and mobs of many thousand monks or their mercenaries were wont to blockade the houses of the ministers and even imperial palaces, so that the Emperor Shirakawa (1073–1086), who was a most fervent Buddhist, once remarked that there were three things which he could not control: the inundations of the river Kamo, which flows through

[1] After careful inquiry I have been unable to find that there was any difference of doctrine between them.

[2] 僧兵. Chinese Sêng-ping or monk soldiers.

[3] See the Heike Monogatari, I, xli–xv, for a description of one of these affrays.

Kyōto, the hazards of gambling, and the monks of Hieizan.[1] Purely ecclesiastical quarrels became equally violent. It is said that during a little more than two centuries beginning from 1081 Miidera was nine times burned down by the priests of Hieizan.[2] The prestige and wealth of the successful monasteries increased but their moral and intellectual life was in danger of decay, for they became garrisons of armed adventurers and, apart from this decadence, their continual squabbles occasioned much loss of property.

Such a state of things was obviously unhealthy, and indeed the whole condition of Japan during the Nara and Heian periods presents so many singular and abnormal features that one cannot be surprised if the religious situation was unsatisfactory. Japan had absorbed Chinese culture and organization with extraordinary rapidity, from the written characters and a copious Chinese vocabulary to the system of political administration and religion, which latter naturally included much that had reached China from India and Central Asia. But how far this enormous mass of imported materials had been really assimilated may be doubted. In the Nara period history tells us of little except the affairs of the capital and the province in which it was situated: we hear of the doings and bickerings of courtiers, officials, and ecclesiastics: ecclesiastical influence threatens to control the whole machinery of government. But we have little information as to whether such questions interested the bulk of the population or how they affected it.

In the Heian period the horizon becomes wider: there is a national movement and there is a certain freedom and development. Yet the stage is small and there is extraordinary uniformity in the characters who play their parts on it. It is not merely that we have not escaped from the world of courtiers, officials, and ecclesiastical dignitaries but that this world is isolated in a manner unparalleled in history.

Japan as an island adjacent to a great continent has often been compared with England, but the greater breadth of the separating Straits produced a marvellous difference. The acquisitiveness of

[1] A similar phenomenon is noticeable in Egypt in the fourth century. "The monks appear as hordes of turbulent fanatics who could be summoned from their desert monasteries to riot and slay in the streets of Alexandria. In this way they wielded enormous power." Scott Moncrieff, *Paganism and Christianity in Egypt*, p. 214.

[2] The present temple dates from only 1690.

the Japanese and their extraordinary desire to learn from their neighbours overcame these natural barriers. Considering the difficulties of communication they showed surprising eagerness to study abroad and they even induced learned foreigners to visit their shores. But they could not be expected to take voluntary lessons in the hard school of foreign invasions in which all the great nations of Europe and Asia have had to graduate. With the exception of the unsuccessful Armadas dispatched by the orders of Khubilai Khan in the thirteenth century, Japanese history does not contain any record of attempted incursions by foreigners, and when Europeans arrived in the sixteenth century the only result was that after a short trial of foreign intercourse the Japanese again deliberately and successfully isolated themselves from all outside influences until the middle of the nineteenth century. The people were brave and warlike, yet after the easy subjugation of the non-Japanese aborigines their military instinct found an outlet only in internal struggles and feudal quarrels. The Korean expedition of Hideyoshi merely showed how little such enterprises were to the taste of the nation of that time. There was no cosmopolitan life such as resulted in Greece, Rome, Alexandria, and even Persia and northern India either from the clash of arms or from more peaceful intercourse. Perhaps the history of southern India offers some resemblances, though even there the presence of a land frontier in addition to a coast line renders the analogy far from complete.

The Emperors who succeeded Kwammu were devoted to literature and had little taste for active life. With the exception of expeditions against the Ainus there were no wars and for the moment no pressing questions of domestic policy. The Emperor Saga, for instance, was prouder of his poetry and of his handwriting than of his administrative achievements, which were considerable, and with Kōbō Daishi and Tachibana Hayanari formed the triad known as the Sampitsu or three pens of the age. Chinese learning was all the fashion, yet relations with China were not intimate and in 894 the practice of sending periodical embassies to the Chinese Court was discontinued. The introduction of Buddhism had brought with it not merely the Buddhist scriptures but the Confucian Classics and Chinese poetry. Extraordinary importance was attached to good calligraphy and the power of composing elegant Chinese prose or, still better, well-turned verses was the surest passport to official promotion, nay, it was almost indispensable for success. Most of those who rose to high posts in the Heian administration, if not members of great families, were distinguished Confucian scholars like Shigeno Sadanushi (785–852), the Minister of the Emperors Junna and Nimmyō, who took a leading part in composing an anthology of Chinese prose in one thousand volumes. This style of composition, or rather compilation, was exactly suited to the talents and taste of the age. The number of anthologies and commentaries published during the ninth century was astonishing, particularly if one considers how restricted was the public that could make any use of them. In this century were also written the Shoku-Nihongi (continuation of the Nihongi) and four other chronicles which give a pretty complete record of the events of the period and are mostly the work of members of the Fujiwara family.[1]

This great house has justly given its name to the whole epoch, which is often known as the Fujiwara period. They became the principal power in Japan at the expense of the Imperial family, and until the time of Go-Sanjō (1068–1072), who in a short reign of only four years succeeded in asserting the sovereign's right to personally superintend the government, their power was unchecked. They did not use the later title of Shōgun, but the most influential male of the family acted as regent and so many of the daughters became Empresses that one Fujiwara was the father-in-law of four Emperors and the grandfather of four more. It became the custom to put on the throne a child who retired into a monastery at a comparatively early age with the title of Hō-Ō. But this arrangement led to a further complication, for the Hō-Ō did not always retire. Although the affairs of the country were nominally in the hands of a child Emperor under the supervision of a regent, the ex-Emperor in his monastery retained much real power and often used it to the advantage of the Church, which was thus brought into even closer connection with the government and worldly affairs. This system by which the administration passed into the hands of an Emperor who had abdicated was called Insei and, paradoxical as it may seem, abdication became the Sovereign's best chance of ruling. Princes who became priests were known as Nyūdō-Shinnō or Hō-Shinnō. A Court official of the third rank or higher who had nominally

[1] They are—
(*a*) The Shoku-Nihongi (covering the period A.D. 700–791) in 40 volumes.
(*b*) The Nihon-Kōki (792–833).
(*c*) The Shoku-Nihon-Kōki (833–850).
(*d*) The Montoku Jitsuroku (850–858).
(*e*) The Sandai Jitsuroku (858–887).

retired from the world was described as Nyūdō, a title often given to Kiyomori, the head of the Taira clan.

Even in the time of the Emperor Saga the imitation of Chinese luxury had caused the cost of living to rise so much among princes and Court officials that it became the practice to grant them domains or Shōen which were exempt from taxes and not subject to the provincial authorities. This led to grave economic evils, and the situation was complicated when there was not merely one Court to support but several. As early as 986 there were three Emperors living and in 1300 there were as many as five, each with his own establishment, and long before this the expense of maintaining ex-Emperors, which included many items strictly speaking ecclesiastical, became a serious fiscal burden. Thus Shirakawa (1063–1129) came to the throne at the age of ten, abdicated at thirty-three, and became a priest but continued to have a Court, ministers, and guards of his own. He expended immense sums on temples, images, and religious ceremonies, and in order to obtain funds extended the practice of selling provincial governorships and of alienating large tracts of land as quasi-independent manors. His grandson Toba became Emperor at the age of five and abdicated at twenty-one. When Shirakawa died Toba stepped into his place and ruled in the same manner and by much the same means for twenty-five years.

We have two remarkable pictures of this period in the Genji Monogatari or Tale of the Genji, by Murasaki Shikibu, and the Makura no Sōshi or Pillow Book, by Sei Shōnagon, both of whom were ladies in waiting about A.D. 1000 at the Court of Akiko, consort of the Emperor Ichijō, for the subordination and seclusion of women did not begin until the Ashikaga period some centuries later. They represent Japanese life at Kyōto as an æsthetic coterie, intensely interested in art and literature and, after a fashion, in the things of the mind, but so preoccupied with style and culture as to be intelligent rather than intellectual. Calligraphy and prosody are as important or more important than vigour or originality. There is little that deserves the name of philosophy or science. The art of blending the fragrance of various brands of incense demands as much attention as the selection of sûtras to be read or of doctrines to be accepted. In its way the age was not irreligious. Retired but still powerful Emperors were dignitaries of the Church: the lands owned by ecclesiastical foundations and the troops with which they protected themselves placed them on a level with the greatest territorial magnates, and in less material ways Tendai and Shingon

Buddhism was the main inspiration of the age, for instance, in art and to some extent in literature, for the recitation of sacred texts was an important branch of a gentleman's education and the standard of correctness required was exacting. Also then, as now, there was a national taste for uniting ritual with the enjoyment of natural beauty, for combining a pilgrimage with a picnic in one excursion to view the cherry blossoms at some holy place.

Yet though the chief note of the age may be found in this æsthetic culture, so simple in its naïve enjoyment and so artificial in its limitations, there were other currents of religious feeling destined to burst forth with a mighty rush in the twelfth century and meanwhile preparing their strength. The most noticeable of them was the worship of Amida. As I have already mentioned in treating of China, it came to be regarded less as a separate sect than as an aspect of most sects, and we find it so accepted in the Heian period. It was not unknown to the Buddhism of Nara and later we find it countenanced by the Tendai and Shingon. We have seen that these two sects were somewhat weak as popular forms of religion. They addressed themselves to the educated classes, and the Tendai, in particular, strove to be wide and catholic in its intellectual and artistic appeal. But they were in danger of either holding up ideals which seemed difficult to practise or even to understand or of offering superstition and magic to those who desired an easier way. The invocation of Amida's name which purges of sin and leads to rebirth in his paradise was a happy middle course : it was not too difficult and it seemed to be a prayer addressed to a merciful and intelligent being rather than an arbitrary magical formula. At this period the repetition of the Nembutsu,[1] as prayer to Amida was ordinarily called, was not made, as later by Hōnen and Shinran, the one and universal method of salvation. It was simply held that to fix one's mind on a Buddha was the easiest way to secure forgiveness of sin and the certainty of heaven and that Amida was the best, though by no means the only one, for the purpose. In this spirit

[1] 念佛, pronounced Nembutsu in Japanese, is the name of the well-known formula Namu Amida Butsu, equivalent to the Sanskrit Namo 'mitabhâya Buddhâya. It appears to have originally meant thinking of the Buddha, and the Tendai and older sects understood it as implying meditation. But the later Amidist sects expressly deny this and hold that it means simply calling on the name of Amida. Thus Hōnen (*Hōnen, the Buddhist Saint*, chap. xxv, § 9) says categorically, " The Nembutsu does not mean calling to mind the Buddha's being or meditating on his signs of eminence but calling with all one's heart upon the sacred name of Amida."

Dengyō Daishi is said to have built the hall called Jōgyōdō on Hieizan for reciting the praises of Amida, and his successor Jikaku to have introduced there the musical services invented by Fa-Chao which he had heard during his stay in China. We are also told that there were special halls for reciting the Nembutsu at the Tōdaiji at Nara and at Kōyasan, the latter called the Shinbessho.

In the tenth century we hear of a remarkable personage called Kūya,[1] who was, according to some accounts, a son of the Emperor Daigo and who lived from 903–972. He travelled all over Japan dancing and chanting the Nembutsu. This Nembutsu of Kūya is sometimes performed in the Tōdaiji at Nara.[2] Like many Buddhist priests he had also a taste for practical activity such as the construction of roads and bridges. He came up to the capital and was received at Hieizan in 948. A year or two later Kyōto was devastated by a pestilence which he is said to have quelled by carving a large statue of the eleven-headed Kwannon and by carrying it about the plague-stricken city until the outbreak abated.

Shortly afterwards Genshin (also known as Eshin, 942–1017), who was renowned as a painter and sculptor, did much to popularize the worship of Amida by his life and by his writings. The most celebrated of his compositions is the Ōjōyōshū [3] or a collection of the principles essential for rebirth in Amida's paradise, which is still read with approval by the followers of Hōnen and Shinran. It is remarkable for its vivid descriptions of the corrupt human life from which one should fly, of the terrors of hell and the bliss of heaven, the whole forming a popular appeal to the religious sense of the masses. We hear that in his time there were two great schools on Hiei which taught slightly different methods of reciting the Nembutsu, one called after him the Eshin-in school and the other after one of his colleagues who was head of another temple on Hiei, the Danna-in.

In 1124 was founded the first Amidist sect, known as the Yūzū Nembutsu,[4] which still exists though far inferior in numbers to the Jōdo and Shinshū. It owes its origin to Ryōnin, a priest of Hieizan, who after long study of the Tendai doctrines became convinced that

[1] 空也上人 Kūya Shōnin.

[2] I witnessed a performance of it which was part of the ceremony performed on 2nd May in honour of the Emperor Shōmu.

[3] 往生要集.

[4] 融通念佛 Yūzū Nembutsu, 良仁 Ryōnin.

they were not suited to the needs of the age. He therefore retired to a temple in Ōhara where he is said to have recited the Nembutsu 60,000 times a day. Once while he was thus engaged he had a vision in which Amida appeared to him and warned him that the Nembutsu was infinitely more meritorious if repeated on behalf of others than for one's own selfish ends. It brings salvation not only to him who utters it but to the whole human race, and if a man teaches others to repeat it, their merit will become his own. It is said that he was inspired by the deity Bishamon to found a new sect and to travel throughout the country bearing with him a book in which were inscribed the names of all who became his followers and recited the Nembutsu according to his directions. He enjoyed the favour of the ex-Emperor Shirakawa and does not appear to have encountered any opposition. It is noticeable that he based his teaching chiefly on the Lotus and the Kegon-kyō and not primarily on the Amida sûtras. The criticism of later schools on his doctrine was that it would do very well for divine beings but not for ordinary men.[1]

About the same time as Ryōnin lived two other distinguished priests, Yōkwan (1032–1111) and Chingai[2] (1091–1152), who advocated the invocation of Amida's name by their teaching and writings. The former was Abbot of the Zenrinji monastery at Kyōto and wrote a work called Ōjō-jū-in,[3] or the ten conditions for attaining rebirth in paradise, among which he emphasizes not only the protection of Amida but also meditation and good works. Chingai was a learned priest of the Tōdaiji temple at Nara who practised the recitation of the Nembutsu and wrote a well-known treatise called Ketsujō Ōjō shū,[4] or a collection of passages on the certainty of rebirth in paradise.

Kakuhan, or Kōkyō Daishi, who founded the great monastery of Negoro in 1130 and also a new branch of the Shingon, completely accepted the doctrine of salvation by calling on Amida but accommodated it to the principles of his sect. Amida, he taught, is the same as the Buddha Vairocana, of whom the whole world is a manifestation. Hence we are already in Amida's paradise: we have only to realize it in order to know that we are saved.

[1] *Hōnen, the Buddhist Saint*, trans. by Coates and Ishizuka, p. 626.

[2] 永觀 and 珍海.

[3] 往生十因 Ōjō-jū-in.

[4] 決定往生集.

# CHAPTER X

## RISE OF NEW SECTS: JŌDO AND SHINSHŪ

By the middle of the twelfth century it is clear that the condition of Japan, both political and ecclesiastical, as described in the last chapter, had reached a point when collapse or revolution had become inevitable and, as might be expected from so virile a nation, it was a revolution which occurred in both spheres. That a thoroughgoing political revolution was accomplished with comparatively little violence was largely due to the ingrained Japanese habit of not abolishing ancient hereditary offices but of leaving their titles and to a great extent their privileges intact while their duties were performed by a deputy or even, as the period to which we are coming illustrates, by the deputy of a deputy. The religious revolution, too, was mild, if compared with similar struggles in Europe. The armed contests of the great monasteries are certainly not edifying reading: they occasioned much bloodshed while they lasted and ultimately brought on many of the offending institutions a bloodstained revenge. But this was the result of the priesthood interfering in secular matters. On the other hand, in the twelfth and thirteenth centuries there arose four new sects which entirely changed the character of Japanese Buddhism. One of them, founded by Shinran, was subversive of most conventional Buddhist institutions: another, founded by Nichiren, was most provocative and pugnacious. Yet there was comparatively little persecution. We hear of reformers being banished, of temples being burnt, and of restrictions being imposed, but martyrdom was rare and most martyrs were accused of some political crime.

By the middle of the twelfth century the long predominance of the Fujiwara came to an end. The race became luxurious and effeminate and the power passed from their hands into those of the great military houses whose prestige and influence steadily increased owing to the system of granting manors which were tax free and which tended to become veritable *imperia in imperio*, not subject to the jurisdiction of the local officials. The sovereignty of the country was bound to belong to the feudal lord who could acquire the most extensive manors, and by partitioning them judiciously among his retainers secure the services of the largest number of troops ready to assist his enterprises in time of need. The Heian period closes with a struggle for supremacy of this kind between the great families of Taira and Minamoto, both of them descended from the younger sons of former Emperors. In the end the Minamoto were victorious and established themselves as Shōguns at Kamakura, but about 1160 the Taira had the upper hand and the reversal of this position was partly due to the animosity of the clergy. The quarrel between the Taira and the Church went back to as early as 1039, when the monks of Hieizan, who were dissatisfied with the ecclesiastical appointments made by the Regent Fujiwara Yorimichi, entered Kyōto and besieged him in his palace. The Regent asked assistance of Taira Naokata, who dispersed the priests not without slaughter and imprisoned their leader.

Taira Kiyomori, the famous protagonist of his clan in the final contest with the Minamotos, was a man of much the same metal. His father had enjoyed the confidence of the Emperor Shirakawa and the son found an influential position ready made for him. After the civil wars of the Hōgen (1156) and Heiji (1159) eras he was master of Japan, for the strength of the Minamoto seemed broken, although Kiyomori with a clemency which did more credit to his heart than his head spared the life of Minamoto Yoritomo, then thirteen years old. He showed a similar mildness in dealing with Yoshitsune, Yoritomo's younger brother, being moved by the charms of the youths' mother whom he made his concubine, and the two young men lived to bring the house of Taira to ruin. In 1160 Kiyomori had a serious illness and took the tonsure according to the custom of the times in such circumstances, whence in the Heike Monogatari [1] he is commonly spoken of as the Nyūdō, a title given to those who had taken Buddhist orders. As soon as he had recovered, however, his clerical duties sat very lightly on him. Not only did he live in splendour and luxury but he showed continual enmity to the Buddhist priesthood. Thus he executed the priest Saikō (a Fujiwara who had become a monk) and his sons for conspiracy against the Tairas, but raised far more indignation by his conduct respecting the ceremonies attending the abdication of the Emperor Takakura who had married his daughter.

[1] A Court official down to the third rank on taking the tonsure was known as Nyūdō 入道, one who has entered on the path. Those of lower grade were known as Shimpotchi 新發意. Hō-ō and Nyūdō clearly observed as many of the rules of clerical life as they chose and no more.

It was usual for the ex-Emperor, immediately after renouncing his position as reigning sovereign, to make a solemn pilgrimage to one or more temples belonging to the monasteries of Hieizan, Miidera, or Kōfukuji, and great importance was attached to the visit owing to the prestige which it conferred and also owing to the largesse incidentally distributed. But the young ex-Emperor—he was only twenty—in order to please his father-in-law decided to make his pilgrimage to the island of Miyajima, where were the shrines of Kiyomori's tutelary deities. The troops of Hieizan and the other great temples prepared to detain him by force, but Kiyomori succeeded in dispersing them without violence and in escorting the imperial cortège to Miyajima and back with a great train of Taira retainers. But this apparent success was really a formidable danger, for it united the monasteries by giving them a common grievance. Their considerable military strength was usually dissipated in quarrels between different temples, but if they once made common cause, they were perhaps equal to any one of the aristocratic houses.

Minamoto Yorimasa, who though he apparently enjoyed the confidence of the Taira was secretly their enemy, took advantage of this to revolt against them, relying on the support of the monasteries. The rising was unsuccessful, partly because Kiyomori was able to detach Hieizan by bribes, and Yorimasa committed suicide, though supported by 30,000 troops from Kōfukuji. For the moment the influence of the monasteries was strong enough to prevent them from being punished, but shortly afterwards Kiyomori's sons burnt Miidera and at Nara Kōfukuji and Tōdaiji shared the same fate. It must be admitted that the priests of the latter town invited misfortune, for they not only maltreated the messengers sent to them but, according to the Heike Monogatari,[1] they made a great wooden head which they struck and kicked about calling it the head of Kiyomori. But the punishment which he meted out to them brought him no luck. There followed a pestilence and famine interpreted as the wrath of the Buddha, and the Taira had to struggle not only against the hostility of the Court, the Minamoto, and the Fujiwara, but against the hatred of the Buddhist hierarchy and the resentful feelings of all respectable and superstitious persons. Kiyomori in his desire to escape from his priestly enemies removed the Emperor, who was an infant,

[1] Heike Monogatari, v, chap. xv.

to his estate at Fukuhara near the modern Kobe and attempted to make it the capital, but the plan raised such a storm of indignation that it had to be abandoned after a few months, and to crown all, shortly afterwards in 1181, Kiyomori himself died of an awful disease, but not before he had heard that Yoritomo was preparing a rising in the East. His body is said to have become so hot that it was difficult to approach him and cold water poured over him to relieve his agony began to bubble and boil. His wife had a terrible dream in which she saw a flaming chariot come to take him to the lowest hell for his crime in burning the great bronze image at Tōdaiji. His son Shigehira, who had actually perpetrated the crime, also did not escape the vengeance of Heaven, or at any rate of the priesthood. He was subsequently taken alive and handed over to the monks of Nara. It was proposed, we are told,[1] that he should be executed with ignominy and torture, but the older monks objected that a religious body ought not to pass so severe a sentence and he was simply beheaded, worshipping in his last moments an image of Amida which was brought to him by a former retainer.

The end of his father Kiyomori was less edifying. When dying in torments he summoned up his failing strength to review briefly the glories of his career, and added, "The only thing I have to regret is that I cannot see the head of Yoritomo. When I am dead do not perform any Buddhist ceremonies or make offerings for me: do not build temples or pagodas. Only make haste to slay Yoritomo and cut off his head and lay it before my tomb. That will be the best offering you can make to me either in this world or the next." So deep was his guilt, adds the Chronicle. But the ceremony proved impracticable. The Minamoto advanced on Kyōto: Kiyomori's son fled with the child Emperor and after a series of defeats the power of the Taira was finally annihilated by Yoshitsune at the sea fight of Dan-no-ura in 1185.

Yoritomo after many quarrels with his relatives, whom he put out of the way with unnatural severity, assumed undisputed sway. He obtained for himself the title of Sei-i-tai-Shōgun (usually shortened to Shōgun) or generalissimo against the barbarians, a rank which previous Emperors had conferred on their subjects from time to time but which now became permanent and even hereditary, with the result that the throne lost control of the troops and in all but name the sovereignty of Japan. The administration of Yoritomo

[1] Heike Monogatari, xii, chap. i.

was called Bakufu or tent government, the simple soldier's rule as opposed to the learned and luxurious Court of Kyōto, and a difference becomes perceptible between the life and ideals of the capital and of the districts east of Hakone known collectively as the Kwantō. Though Yoritomo inaugurated this military system with intelligence and vigour, his descendants proved incapable of filling the position he had created for them and the power passed away from them just as it had passed from the Emperor to the Shōgun. From 1200 to 1333 the Hōjōs acted as regents (Shikken) or prime ministers in the name of a nominal Shōgun who was often a minor, and by a strange irony of fate these Hōjōs were a provincial branch of the Taira, rather looked down upon by their kinsmen of Kyōto in the days of Kiyomori. They were absolute masters of Japan for about a century. In 1219 the death of Sanetomo left the Minamoto family without an heir to the Shōgunate and a child of Fujiwara stock was appointed to the post. Immediately afterwards the Court at Kyōto attempted to upset the Government of Kamakura but failed entirely, the Emperor and the ex-Emperor Go Toba, who was the prime mover in the plot, being both banished. When this conspiracy was disposed of, the supremacy of the Hōjōs was undisputed.

The change inaugurated by Yoritomo and continued by the Hōjōs was sudden and prodigious. It meant a new capital, a new system of government, new social conditions, a new style in art, and it is not surprising if religion also found new modes of expression. It was certainly at this period that Japanese Buddhism showed most originality and creative power. Japan was cut off from China and did not feel the influence which had moulded her intellectual and political youth. The feudalism of the Hōjōs was a native and insular institution. A revolution is visible in architecture and there was a revulsion against scholarship, etiquette, and ritualism. The life of the nobility was simple and austere. Rough justice was administered impartially under a collection of maxims and rules [1] which embodied the principles of the Samurai or warrior class. In the century from about 1160 to 1260 religion was transformed by the rise of four new sects, the Jōdo, Zen, Shin, and Nichiren, which throw into the shade the eight older divisions. Whereas these had been mere importations, the new sects, especially the two last named, had a distinctly national character. Though the

[1] Called Jōei Shikimoku from the Jōei era (1232) in which it was introduced.

founders of all came from Hieizan, their doctrines were perhaps more influential in the Kwantō than in Kyōto. There the great monasteries maintained their ascendancy and the Emperor Go-Toba, whose object was to get rid of the Hōjō domination, was careful to humour them and countenanced the repression of novel doctrines. But they were chiefly occupied with their own quarrels. In the thirteenth century Miidera at least once burned Hieizan and several times suffered the same violence at its hands. In 1235 the monks of Nara rose in arms on account of some dispute about property and the Court of Kyōto requested the Hōjō regent to bring them to reason. Hōjō Yasutoki did so and confiscated their manors until they asked for terms. But as a rule the administration of the Bakufu kept clear of the old monasteries and while respecting all forms of Buddhism showed more sympathy with the newer sects. Thus Masako, the wife of Yoritomo, who after his death in 1199 ruled in the name of her sons until 1225 and having taken orders was known as Ama Shōgun (the Nun Shōgun), was a devout follower of Hōnen and a letter from him to her is preserved.[1]

The most glorious achievement of the Hōjō Regents and of all the thirteenth century was the repulse of the two Armadas sent by Khubilai in 1274 and 1281 to subdue Japan. In this the Japanese were aided by the powers of Nature which sent two tempests against the invaders, and though European scepticism may hesitate to regard the prayers of the Church as the sole cause of these storms, yet it is beyond doubt that in this critical period Buddhism came to the front as a national and patriotic faith—a part which it has seldom played elsewhere. Many of the warriors were already disciplined by the austere principles of Zen. Nichiren, the new prophet, not only preached the need of national religion but in a singularly acute prophecy predicted a foreign invasion as a punishment for the sins of the age: and though the older monasteries had no very stimulating message to deliver, they were at least indefatigable in public prayer. It is curious that the Shintō temples do not seem to have taken an ostentatious part in the work of intercession. The triumphant result was claimed by the Buddhist priests as a testimony to the efficacy of their ritual and they received their reward in the liberal treatment accorded to ecclesiastical property. Many new grants of land were made to monasteries, and estates which had been mortgaged or forfeited were restored. On the whole, Buddhism,

[1] *Hōnen, the Buddhist Saint*, chap. xxv.

apart from internal dissensions, had never been more prosperous than under Yoritomo and the Hōjō Regents, at least three of whom became monks in their later years, and though this period is poor in art and literature compared with those which succeeded and followed, it witnessed the erection at Kamakura of the temple of Hachiman, formerly a magnificent structure though now somewhat defaced by the ravages of time, and of the more celebrated Daibutsu, a gigantic image of Amida which is now exposed to the elements, the temple which formerly sheltered it having been destroyed by tidal waves. Yoritomo was most careful to conciliate the clergy and to avoid the mistake made by Kiyomori in antagonizing them. In 1195 with the aid of national subscriptions he rebuilt the Tōdaiji at Nara [1] which had been burnt by the Taira, and during the dedication he conceived the idea of setting up a similar colossus at his new capital but died before he could execute the project. The present figure is said to have been set up in 1252.

Learning was not the strong point of Kamakura ; in fact, a very large proportion of its stout warriors were illiterate, and whatever literature has been preserved was mainly the work of the clergy. The Heike Monogatari, a romantic chronicle of the fall of the Taira, was composed near the beginning of the thirteenth century. Its authorship is not certain but it is attributed to a certain Yukinaga, a layman who had taken orders, and it was chanted by itinerant priests. It is strongly tinged with Buddhist sentiment and relates how the evil Karma which the Taira had accumulated by their impiety brought about their ruin.

But I must proceed to recount the rise of the four sects which render this period remarkable in the annals of Buddhism. The first name that claims attention is that of Hōnen,[2] the founder of the Jōdo or Pure Land School. He lived from 1133 to 1212 and thus witnessed the struggle between the Minamoto and Taira, the victory of Yoritomo, and the establishment of the Hōjō Regency at Kama-

[1] On the Japanese stage Yoshitsune and Benkei are represented as wandering in the guise of mendicant priests who are collecting subscriptions for rebuilding Tōdaiji.

[2] This is the title by which he is most commonly known, but, like most Japanese, he had an embarrassing number of designations. He is frequently called Genkū and also Enkō-Daishi, the latter a posthumous title. As a child his name was Seishimaru but as a priest he called himself Genkū, compounded of the names of his two teachers, Genkō and Eikū. He was also nicknamed by his teacher Hōnenbō (Nature's own priest), and when he was banished and treated as a layman he received the secular name of Motohiko Fujii.

kura. Ample materials for the study of his career are provided by his biography written by Shunjō and translated with most valuable notes and introductory chapters by Coates and Ishizuka.[1] He was the son of an official in the province of Mimasaka, who was killed by an enemy and died bidding his son to take no revenge and become a priest. The boy showed such talents that a local priest persuaded his mother to allow him to be sent to study at Hieizan. In the letter commending him to the attention of the authorities of the Sacred Mountain he was called an image of Mañjuśrî (Monju) and quickly justified the description by his extraordinary ability. After being ordained a priest he retired to Kurodani on the outskirts of Kyōto resolving to seek no preferment and to devote himself to prayer and study, entirely renouncing the world. He is said to have read through the whole of the Tripiṭaka five times but, though the fame of his wisdom and learning spread widely, he did not find any doctrine which satisfied him. This was the period of the civil wars of Hōgen and Heiji and the rise of Kiyomori, and naturally a religious and gentle soul like Hōnen felt that the great need of mankind amidst such troubles was religious peace. In spite of the anti-Buddhist conduct of the Taira, the age was not in its way irreligious, but it tended either to superstition which sought merely to avoid temporal misfortunes or to the difficult doctrines of the Kegon, Tendai, and Shingon schools. These agreed that all men have in themselves the Buddha nature but that it must be realized and developed by exercises in which meditation as a rule played a prominent part. It was a difficult road for the ordinary man, and besides how amid riots and rebellions, in which the clergy played a prominent part, was one to believe statements such as that Saṃsâra is really nirvâna and that this troubled life is really identical with peace and enlightenment?

As mentioned in the previous chapter, the worship of Amida had already been growing as an alternative to this form of religion and had found several exponents such as Kūya, Genshin, and Ryōnin. They had none of them succeeded in inspiring many followers or of leaving after them any body of believers. Nevertheless, according to tradition, it was Genshin's work, the Ōjōyōshū, that led Hōnen to the light and inspiration which he needed. It is based on a commentary on the Amitâyurdhyâna-sûtra written by Zendō, the

[1] *Hōnen, the Buddhist Saint: His Life and Teaching.* Printed at the Chion-in in Kyoto, 1925. An account of Shunjō's work and of other Japanese biographies of Hōnen is contained in chapter viii, pp. 77–83.

third Patriarch of the Amidist sect in China. Zendō's works are not included in the Tripiṭaka, which perhaps accounts for a man of Hōnen's erudition not having read them earlier, but now the following passage [1] deeply impressed him: "Only repeat the name of Amida with all your heart—whether walking or standing still, whether sitting or lying never cease this practice for even a moment. This is the practice which brings salvation without fail, for it is in accordance with the original vow of the Buddha." [2] In these words he thought he had at last found what he was seeking for: he had become convinced that in this turbulent and degenerate age mental and moral discipline is of small avail and that peace can only be found in self surrender and in reliance on a higher power—in Tariki or the strength of another, that is Amida, not in Jiriki, or one's own strength. Zendō showed him how this was to be done, so he abandoned all other religious practices and devoted himself to the recitation of the Nembutsu only.

It was in the spring of 1175, when he was forty-three years of age and had spent some twenty-five years in seeking after the truth, that he reached this conviction and began to teach it to others, and this year is commonly reckoned as the date of the foundation of the Jōdo sect, but as a matter of fact it was not legally recognized as a distinct corporation until the time of Ieyasu. Hōnen, however, conceived that he had a message for his age and his influence became considerable. He removed to Yoshimizu near the present Chion-in but frequently changed his residence. He was credited with miraculous powers and with seeing visions. He enjoyed the confidence of the Emperors Go-Shirakawa, Takakura, and for a time of Go-Toba, assisting them in the performance of their religious duties and attending at the death-bed of Go-Shirakawa, who died repeating the Nembutsu with his last breath. Many courtiers and members of the aristocracy were among his friends and adherents, especially Kanezane the Regent, who was the founder of the Kujō branch of the Fujiwara family. Many Samurai also followed him. Nor was he less successful among the clergy. As he said himself, his teachers became his disciples and his biography enumerates a number of distinguished priests such as the famous Tendai scholars,

[1] It occurs in the fourth volume of the Commentary, which treats of good works other than meditation.

[2] 本願 Hon-gwan or pûrva-praṇidhâna means the 48 vows of Amida, the substance of which is that all who call on his name should be saved. The vows are sometimes reckoned as 46. See Nanjio's note in *S.B.E.*, vol. xlix, p. 73.

Kenshin and Jichin, and Myōhen of Mount Kōya. In 1198 Hōnen wrote a work called the Senchakushū,[1] consisting of sixteen chapters containing selected passages from the Amida sûtras and of Zendō's commentary together with his own explanations. He sent a copy of it to Kanezane, but forbade his disciples to publish it during his lifetime and it was not made known to the world till a few months after his death. He also wrote a work called Ōjō Taiyōshō[2] (an outline of birth into the Pure Land) and many letters, but his retiring disposition made him avoid publicity as either a writer or teacher.

I have already spoken of the original literature about Amida. Hōnen follows Zendō's interpretations of these works and says boldly[3] that Zendō was an incarnation of Amida and that we should therefore depend solely upon him. He draws a sharp distinction between the Shōdō, the holy path, consisting of good works and religious exercises as recommended by other sects, and Jōdo or the Pure Land; and his cardinal doctrine is that the best, if not, the only way to obtain salvation in these evil days is to strive to be reborn in the western paradise. This result is secured by simple faith in Amida and by repetition of the formula Namu Amida Butsu. If a man, no matter who, how wicked or how unlettered, repeat these words with a believing heart, Amida will appear to him in the hour of death and conduct him to the happy land. The Jōdo sect approves of ordinary monastic discipline and religious ceremonial but, as the special ritual for salvation, it prescribes the repetition of the Nembutsu. Hōnen and other eminent doctors are said to have recited it not less than 60,000 times daily. Still he was not an unreasoning fanatic. While believing that even the greatest sinner if he has faith in Amida may be born in the Pure Land, "So far as you are concerned," he says, "be not guilty of even the smallest sin."[4] "If you have any time to spare after saying the Nembutsu, then you may use it to do good works."[5] This is no doubt well meant, but it is a little suggestive of the undergraduate's definition of the Church of England's view of good works as laid down in the Thirty-Nine Articles that "a few of them will do no harm". But still Hōnen was quite alive to the danger of antinomianism, the

[1] The full title is Senchaku Hongwan Nembusshū 選擇本願念佛集.

[2] 往生大要鈔.

[3] *Hōnen, the Buddhist Saint*, p. 467.

[4] Ibid., p. 403.

[5] Ibid., p. 495.

doctrine that one may do what one likes because Amida loves to save sinners, which actually threatened to bring the Nembutsu into discredit in later times. "Those who say that the effort to avoid sin and improve oneself is making light of Amida's vow . . . are nothing less than a company of devils and their work is heathenish."[1] Also, unlike Shinran, he was careful not to deprecate the worship of other Buddhas: "You should not think lightly of, in the least despising those excellent sûtras the Lotus and the Prajñâparamitâ. Though you may believe in Amida your faith is one-sided if you despise the many Buddhas or doubt Shaka's holy teaching. . . . It is no obstacle in the way of the sole practice to pray for worldly good not only by reciting the Nembutsu but by praying to the other Buddhas or deities, by reading or copying the sûtras or by making images of the Buddhas."[2]

It is not surprising, however, if in spite of these reasonable and tolerant views and in spite of Hōnen's not posing as a popular preacher, his doctrines were exceedingly distasteful to the clergy of the great monasteries, for whatever courteous explanations he might make,[3] they amounted to an assertion that the recitation of the Nembutsu, and of that only, was the best way to salvation. In 1204 the priests of Mount Hiei held a great meeting to petition Shinshō, their Chief, to condemn this thesis. Hōnen replied by an open letter addressed to his disciples in which he forbade religious disputes and disparagement of the Shingon and Tendai and of other Buddhas and Bodhisattvas besides Amida. He also expressly condemned the teaching that those who recited the Nembutsu might indulge in eating meat and in immoral practices on the ground that the formula cleanses from all sin. This declaration and a letter addressed to Shinshō by Hōnen's protector, the Regent Kanezane, had apparently the result of calming opinion at Hieizan, but next year the priests of Kōfukuji presented a memorial to the Government asking for Hōnen's punishment. But only some of his disciples were punished and no penalty was inflicted on himself. He issued, however, another declaration in which he insisted on the comprehensiveness of Shaka's teaching and on the incompatibility of the

[1] *Hōnen, the Buddhist Saint*, p. 405.

[2] Ibid., pp. 404 and 460. See also p. 422.

[3] See for an instance the end of the letter quoted in *Hōnen, the Buddhist Saint*, p. 422. "If anyone has been learning the scriptures and finds it difficult to believe in the Nembutsu, let him bear in mind that everything else which he does according to other forms of religious discipline is all right, provided that he makes it an occasion for directing his thought and prayer to Amida and to Paradise."

Nembutsu with a life of immorality. The frequency with which he returns to this point suggests that the charge of teaching that everything was permissible to true believers because everything would be pardoned was the main accusation brought against him and that he felt it sufficiently formidable to require careful refutation.

The ex-Emperor Go-Toba had been friendly to Hōnen, but doubtless received many bad reports respecting him and his followers from the priests of Hieizan. At the end of 1206 these were aggravated by a misunderstanding. During the absence of the ex-Emperor on a pilgrimage to Kumano, Jūrin, Anraku, and other disciples of Hōnen held special services for the recitation of the Nembutsu which were attended by two maids of honour. They became nuns, and it was suggested to the ex-Emperor on his return that improper affection for the priests was their real motive and they were severely punished. Anraku, hearing of it, quoted a passage from Zendō in which he speaks of "infidels, blind to the truth, who hate to see others acting religiously". This utterance was reported to the ex-Emperor, who was furious. Jūrin, Anraku, and a few more were beheaded and others were banished, and in the second month of 1207 Hōnen was exiled to Tosa. Kanezane, who had recently lost his son and had devoted himself almost entirely to religion, was determined to do all in his power to have the sentence altered, but thought the moment inopportune. He was able, however, to have the place of exile changed to Sanuki, the north-eastern district of Shikoku, which was not so distant as Tosa in the south, and thither Hōnen repaired after exchanging farewell poems with his patron. On his way he is said to have met some old fisherfolk who were in trouble because they had heard that those who take life must suffer for their sins in hell. But Hōnen assured them that if they repeated the Nembutsu they would be born in Paradise. So to their great joy they continued to catch fish by day and to pray by night.

In Sanuki he spent his time in visiting the sacred spots of the province, such as Zentsūji founded by Kōbō Daishi, but his sojourn was not prolonged. Though Kanezane died, he obtained a pledge from an influential friend, Fujiwara Mitsuchika, to look after Hōnen's interests, and as there was fortunately an amnesty to commemorate the erection of a temple by the ex-Emperor, Hōnen was allowed to leave Shikoku in the last month of 1207, but not to return to the capital. He resided for four years in the Kachiodera temple near Ōsaka, at the end of which time Mitsuchika, making use of a dream which troubled the ex-Emperor, secured for him permission to return to Kyōto, where he was received by glad crowds at the end of 1211. But his health had suffered and in March, 1212, he was taken seriously ill. When asked where a memorial temple should be built for him, he replied, "My memorial shall fill the land. Wherever among high or low the Nembutsu is recited, there is my memorial temple, be it but the thatched cottage of a humble fisherman." Another anecdote of his deathbed is that, according to custom, his disciples brought an image of Amida and fastening a five-coloured cord to its hands bade Hōnen take hold of the other end. But he gently replied, "This is the ceremony for most, but hardly necessary for me." He told them that as a result of repeating the Nembutsu he had for the last ten years or more been gazing continually on the Pure Land and the Buddhas and Bodhisattvas which inhabit it, though until his last hours he had refrained from speaking of these experiences. He died in his eightieth year, at the same age as Śâkyamuni. He was buried at Ōtani, but the Sammon priests attempted to destroy the tomb and after several removals the bones are said to have been deposited in the compound of the Nison-in temple.[1]

Many of the qualities commonly possessed by the founders of new religions or sects were wanting in Hōnen. He was not apparently a remarkable preacher, organizer, or writer, his best compositions being the private letters which he addressed to his friends. Though he most sincerely believed in the truth and importance of what he taught, he was not self-assertive. He was, on the contrary, the least combative and aggressive of men and most anxious to avoid giving offence, to make allowance for the prejudices of others and their habits of thought, to smooth over difficulties, and to explain away or not insist on doctrinal subtleties. His great personal influence was due to his singularly amiable character, which made him beloved of all his friends and acquaintances. They flocked to him and "converted his residence into a sort of popular market".[2] He offered in the gentlest and most persuasive form a simple and attractive teaching, and this in a violent age when the strife of factions was mingled with pestilence and famine, when the Church

[1] See *Hōnen, the Buddhist Saint*, chap. xlii. The fate of Hōnen's bones is, however, far from clear.

[2] From Kakunyo Shōnin's *Life of Shinran*, i, 6. It says that there were generally about 380 persons with him.

was not only worldly but turbulent and when at its best its doctrines were difficult for the unlearned to follow. In such disturbed and comfortless times he preached a simple creed which offered salvation to those who could justify themselves neither by learning nor by good works and he gave a decisive impetus to one of the greatest religious movements which Japan has witnessed, for it is not clear that without him any previously existing forms of Amidism would have become important, or that Shinran's mind would have developed as it did.

Shortly before his death he is said to have written with his own hand at the request of one of his disciples called Seikwambō the following statement of his belief and teaching called the Ichimai Kishōmon, or the document on one sheet of paper.[1] "What I teach is neither a sort of meditation such as has been talked of by many priests both in China and in our own country nor is it an invocation such as is possible only to those who have grasped by thought its real meaning. No, all that is needed to secure birth in the Paradise of perfect bliss is merely to repeat the words Namu Amida Butsu without a doubt that one will certainly arrive there. Such details as the three states of mind and the fourfold practice [2] are all included in the repetition of the words Namu Amida Butsu with perfect faith. Had I any other profound doctrine besides this, I should miss the mercy of the two Holy Ones [3] and have no share in the vow of Amida. But those who believe in the power of calling on the Buddha's name, though they may have thoroughly studied all the doctrines which Shaka taught in the course of his whole life, should behave like a simple man of the people who cannot read a word or like an ignorant nun and without giving themselves airs of wisdom should simply fervently call on the name of the Buddha."

[1] 一枚起請文. The original will be found in Hōnen Shōnin Zenshū by Kuroda and Mochizuki, pp. 422–3, where two slightly different versions are given.

[2] The three states of mind are: (1) a most sincere heart, (2) a deep-believing heart, and (3) a longing heart which offers in the hope of attaining paradise any merits it may have acquired, the point being not that Ōjō or birth in paradise can be obtained merely by personal merit and without faith in Amida, but that any merit one may have obtained should not be devoted to any other object. The fourfold practice, as prescribed by Zendō, is (1) to treat images and other sacred objects with profound reverence, (2) to practise the repetition of the Nembutsu only, (3) to practise it continually and, if any sin has been committed, at once to purify the heart by uttering it, (4) to observe the above three rules continuously throughout one's life.

[3] i.e. Shaka and Amida. It is noticeable that in this summary of his faith Hōnen alludes to both powers.

Though Hōnen's statement of his own faith seems remarkably simple and to brush aside all technical subtleties as of no importance, yet the innate Japanese propensity to subdivide sects on minute points of doctrine may be seen as clearly in the Jōdo as in any other community. He had six prominent disciples, Shōkōbō (or Benchō), Zennebō (or Shōkū), Ryūkan, Chōsai, Kōsai, and Shinran, every one of whom had his own method of formulating the master's teaching and some of whom founded permanent sects. The first two founded the Chinzei and Seizan, which are the principal divisions recognized in the Jōdo.

The Chinzei represents the main body of the sect and is called simply Jōdo, for Shōkōbō merely elaborated the doctrine of Hōnen. He held that the Nembutsu is an act of adoration addressed to Amida as a special personal being: that it should be repeated as earnestly as if one were going to die the next moment; but he also held, with a liberality which as we have seen was shared by Hōnen himself, that man could obtain birth in paradise by other practices than the Nembutsu.

The school of Zennebō, known as Jōdo-Seizan, held that salvation is only possible to those who repeat the Nembutsu and is not a result of meditation or other good works, while not denying the value of these if accompanied by the Nembutsu. The following are extracts from the works of the founder: "Even if we do good works all our lives and wish to attain the Land of Purity, we cannot achieve that end." "The belief in Buddha . . . is to know for certain and believe firmly that we are saved by the original vow of Amida: that the doctrine of Shaka teaches this and that all Buddhas testify uniformly to its truth." "Further, Buddha means enlightenment or profound wisdom. When this wisdom is realized in our hearts we are enlightened. Shaka and all other Buddhas are thus one in the attainment of Namu Amida Butsu. As they are all one and possess the same enlightenment, so we who pass into this state also share Amida's own enlightenment." [1]

It will be observed that Hōnen had not succeeded in banishing subtle and difficult doctrines so completely as he had wished. Ryūkwan advocated the practice of "many callings"; Kōsai that of "one calling", in which the devotee is united to the Buddha in faith; while Chōsai went even further than Shōkōbō in holding

[1] See "The Pure Land Doctrine as Interpreted by Shōkū, founder of the Seizan sect", by Shizutoshi Sugihira. *Eastern Buddhist*, v, No. 1.

that Amida definitely prescribed other practices as being of equal efficacy with the Nembutsu.

These three disciples have left no enduring school, but the sixth and last, named Shinran, rivals and perhaps eclipses his master in success and celebrity. He was born in Kyōto in 1173 as the son of a Court noble named Hino Arinorî, and the blood of both the Fujiwara and Minamoto flowed in his veins. This much seems sure, but the same cannot be said of his biography as a whole. A Japanese scholar once told me that Sasaki Gasshō,[1] the eminent writer on Shintō, had confessed to him that the more he studied Shinran's life the more uncertainty he felt about the incidents commonly accepted as authentic. The various accounts of his marriage illustrate this. It is usually asserted that his wife was the daughter of the Regent Kanezane who had discussed the matter with Hōnen and obtained his approval. But the earliest biography, written by Kakunyo Shōnin about 1296, makes no mention of this marriage, though it records a vision in which Kwannon authorized the marriage of the clergy in general terms.[2] Another early biography written by Songaku in 1352 [3] relates the conversations between Hōnen and Kanezane and the marriage of Shinran with the latter's daughter when she was eighteen. It says nothing about a second marriage. But a third account, written by Ryōkū in 1715 and preserved in the temple at Takata,[4] relates the marriage with Kanezane's daughter as described above, but adds that she died at the age of twenty-six leaving one son and that Shinran subsequently married the daughter of Miyoshi Tamenori in the Kwantō, by whom he had four sons and one daughter. When he returned to Kyōto his second wife and his children remained behind and Zenran, the eldest son, became hostile to his father.

In the following pages I shall give the account of Shinran's life as ordinarily accepted by his followers, warning the reader that its accuracy has been called in question.

[1] Author of *The Life of Shinran Shōnin*, Tokyo, 1910 (Japanese); *A Study of Shin Buddhism*, Kyōto, 1925 (English).

[2] It contains the phrase (i, 3) 行者宿報設女犯我成玉女身被犯 in which the words 玉女 have been interpreted as referring to Kanezane's daughter.

[3] Shinran Shōnin Shōmyōden 親鸞上人正明傳 by 存覺.

[4] Takata Shinran Shōnin Shōtōden 高田親鸞上人正統傳 by 良空.

His original name was Zenshin, which he changed first to Shakku and then to Shinran. Being left an orphan, he entered Hieizan when only nine years old. As a young man he received rapid preferment but was dissatisfied with the Tendai teaching. He also visited Nara but returned to Hieizan. Still, he found no rest until Kwannon appeared to him in a dream and bade him study under Hōnen.[1] He did so in 1201 and became his teacher's favourite pupil. In the Tannishō [2] he says, "As far as I am concerned my sole reason for repeating the Nembutsu lies in the teaching of the good man who made me understand that the only condition of salvation is to say the Nembutsu. . . . I should never regret even if I were to go to Hell by being deceived by Hōnen Shōnin." One day Fujiwara Kanezane the Regent, who according to this account must have been the originator of many of Shinran's views, told Hōnen that he wished his daughter to marry a priest who would thus become a householder and combine religion with a layman's life. Hōnen was not shocked at the suggestion and suggested Shinran as a suitable candidate. Shinran hesitated for a year and then became Kanezane's son-in-law. His wife was known as Tamahi no Miya (Princess Burning Crystal) and they had six children. It is remarkable, however, that Shunjō's Life of Hōnen does not mention Shinran's marriage nor indeed anything else about him, which perhaps indicates that at the time it was composed (the beginning of the fourteenth century) the Jōdo sect did not approve of him. If the story is correct, the Shinshū have some reason to call themselves the true Jōdo sect (Jōdo Shinshū), for it implies that Hōnen approved of Shinran's innovations and countenanced monasticism merely from a reluctance to break too violently with tradition. It appears that Hōnen and Shinran were in complete harmony. They both enjoyed the favour of Kanezane and were both banished from Kyōto in 1207, Shinran's place of exile being Echigo, and both allowed to return in 1211. Shinran, however, started on a missionary journey to the north-eastern provinces and Hōnen died the next year. It was not till after this, it would seem, that the two sects regarded themselves as separate bodies, the one following the practice of Hōnen who had lived like an ordinary priest and the other accepting the innovations of Shinran which

[1] But Kakunyo Shōnin's biography says that he first became Hōnen's disciple and then had a vision of Kwannon which merely authorized marriage in general terms.

[2] Tannishō 歎異鈔, § 2.

Hōnen is said to have sanctioned but not imitated. The Shinshū was also inclined to the doctrine of "once calling" to which Hōnen had objected.[1] Shinran was far from objecting to the repetition of the Nembutsu, but he held that the essential thing was to say that prayer with full faith and confidence in the Buddha; that one such believing utterance is sufficient to secure birth in the Pure Land, and that all subsequent repetitions are to be regarded as simply expressions of joy and gratitude. He is also reported in the Tannishō[2] to have said that even a good man is reborn in the Pure Land, much more a wicked man. People generally put this the other way, he added, and say that even a wicked man is so reborn, much more a good man, but the first statement is really more correct. For a good man who trusts to his own merits and not to the strength of another is not the object of Amida's vow: but one who does not rely at all on himself but entirely on Amida's strength is the person contemplated by the vow and in virtue of it will be born in the Pure Land.

Shinran lived with his wife in the province of Hitachi and preached his doctrines among the inhabitants, whom he probably found less prejudiced than the population of the capital. In this way he spent more than twenty-five years and settled for part of the time at Inada, where he appears to have first founded a new sect called Jōdo Shinshū or the True Sect of the Pure Land and also Montoshū or Ikkōshū,[3] and in 1224 to have published an exposition of his teaching in six volumes called Kyōgyōshinshō,[4] or Doctrine, Practice, Faith, and Realization. It is a collection of 143 passages from various works such as the Avataṃsaka and Nirvâna sûtras which, in Shinran's opinion, justified his views, and is regarded as the fundamental textbook of the Shinshū sect. He was not any more than Hōnen a great writer, for the work just mentioned is largely an anthology, but there are also ascribed to him Wasan, or hymns to Amida, and a longer poetical composition called the Shōshinge,[5] describing the history of the faith and praising the seven Fathers

[1] *Hōnen, the Buddhist Saint*, chap. xxix.

[2] Tannishō, § 3.

[3] 門徒宗, 一向宗.

[4] 敎行信證.

[5] Or 正信念佛偈 Shōshin-nenbutsu-ge. It is translated in Lloyd's work *Shinran and his Work* and Haas' *Amida Buddha*, 116. Some of the Wasan were published with an English translation by the Western Hongwanji in 1922. The complete edition (Sanjō-Wasan) consists of three volumes.

or Patriarchs—two Indians, Nâgârjuna [1] and Vasubandhu; three Chinese, Donran, Dōshaku, and Zendō; and two Japanese, Genshin and Genkū (Hōnen). This work is frequently recited at Shinshū services. Some time after his death Yui Embō, who was one of his immediate disciples, wrote a collection of his sayings entitled Tannishō [2] in order to put an end to misunderstandings of his teaching. The Shōshinge and the Kyōgyōshinshō are written, as was the custom, in Chinese, but the Wasan are in Japanese, and Shinran seems to have favoured the use of the Kana script and of the national language as being more intelligible to the uneducated.[3] The clergy of the sect disclaimed all learning and a common Japanese proverb says Monto mono shirazu—the Monto know nothing—which was certainly untrue of Hōnen and Shinran and many of their followers, who were learned theologians.

Finding that he was growing old, Shinran returned to Kyōto about 1230, but stopped at Kamakura and other places on the way. In the capital he apparently spent his time quietly. At any rate, few incidents are recorded of his last years, but he lived to the advanced age of nearly ninety and apparently he composed hymns after he was eighty. The first two volumes of the Sanjō Wasan contain references to the year 1248, when he was over seventy, and the last to 1258, ten years later. When asked where he should be buried he is said to have replied: "Throw my body into the Kamogawa and let the fish feed on it." But he was cremated and his ashes buried partly at Higashi Ōtani and partly at Takata.

Though the Jōdo-Shinshū seems to have been speedily recognized by popular opinion as a distinct sect and is indeed rendered conspicuous by some differences of discipline, for instance, the marriage of the clergy, it is not easy to separate the doctrines of Hōnen and Shinran. They lived together as teacher and pupil, each approving the life of the other. The Jōdo does not differ conspicuously in discipline and ritual from the older sects; it honours other Buddhas and Bodhisattvas besides Amida, but it teaches that salvation is best obtained by invoking his name. The

[1] On the statement (L. 49) that Shaka foretold Nâgârjuna's advent in the Lankâvatâra-sûtras see Suzuki, *Studies in the Lankâvatâra-sutra*, p. 24, whence it appears that the Sanskrit text does not support the assertion.

[2] 歎異鈔. It has also been attributed to Nyoshin Shōnin, the grandson of Shinran; but the name of Yui Embō occurs in the text (§ 9 and § 13) in a way which suggests that he was the writer.

[3] Kōa Shōnin (1264–1330), an eminent priest of the Jōdo, wrote a work called Sambu-kana-shō. Three volumes in Kana.

Shinshū has abolished monasticism and its temples are easily distinguishable from others: worship is offered to Amida only: salvation is obtained by faith which is the gift of Amida and it begins in this world as soon as faith begins in the believer. But most of these distinctions, though valid as a rough statement, are not absolute. Shaka and other Buddhas are invoked in the funeral ceremonies of the Shinshū.[1] The doctrine of salvation by faith is old—it is found in the Jōdo as clearly as in the Shinshū—and the Shinshū is emphatic in extolling the efficacy of the sacred name.[2] The doctrine of immediate salvation, too, was not an invention of Shinran, for Hōnen said, "How happy the thought that though we are still here in the body we are numbered among the holy ones of Paradise."

Both the Jōdo and the Jōdo Shinshū spread rapidly. Zennebō, one of Hōnen's six disciples mentioned above, with his pupils laboured at Kyōto: Ryūkan when banished to the north-eastern provinces was assiduous in propaganda: Konkōbō was sent by Hōnen himself to evangelize Mutsu, while Ryōchō, who is reckoned as the third Patriarch of the Jōdo sect, was the apostle of the Kwantō and converted the Hōjō Regent Tsunetoki, whom he induced to build a temple at Kamakura. The Jōdo Shinshū were also active. In 1212 Shinran himself founded the Bukkōji, or temple of Buddha's Light, at Yamashina near Kyōto, originally called the Kōshōji or restoration of right, in allusion to his return from exile,[3] and in 1235 the Kinshokuji in Ōmi. His grandson Nyoshin built the Hongwanji temple at Ōtani, which became a sort of imperial chapel. Shinran is also credited with having founded during his wanderings the Senshuji at Takata in Shimotsuke and other temples. Although the older sects persuaded the Government to prohibit the Nembutsu, it is clear that the new creed was too strong for them. In 1235 we are told that the capital and country alike swarmed with people who wore black priestly robes and who recited the Nembutsu.[4]

A small sect which still exists as a corporation was founded in 1276 by Ippen (1239–1289). He was originally a priest of the

[1] See Lloyd, *Shinran and his Work*, p. 136, and also the interesting account in *The Times* of 11th August, 1910, of a memorial service held by the Shinshū in honour of King Edward VII.

[2] It is remarkable that modern Japanese Amidists constantly speak of the whole formula Namu Amida Butsu as *the name*, though they are clearly aware that it is an invocation like Ave Maria.

[3] 興正寺.

[4] So the Azuma Kagami, a history of Japan from 1180 to 1266, written near the end of the thirteenth century by an unknown author.

Tendai, but not being satisfied with its teaching took lessons of Shōtatsu, a pupil of Zennebō already mentioned as the founder of the Seizan sect. He then went and prayed for a hundred days to the deity of Kumano, who was believed to be Amida himself,[1] and received from him a direct revelation communicating certain special doctrines. These are somewhat extravagant: the mere sound of Amida's name, even when uttered by an unbeliever, is declared to be efficacious and by reciting it all living beings can become Buddhas. Another tenet of Ippen's was that faith is useless and powerless to effect salvation, because it is an activity of the corrupt human mind. One must simply repeat the sacred name, without relying upon anything that comes from oneself. Ippen's theories were probably influenced by Zen, which was affecting Japanese thought at this time. He said, for instance, "When I repeat the Nembutsu, there is neither myself nor the Buddha but simply the invocation." And again: "Single-mindedness is when one discards all thought of the body and is absolutely one with the Nembutsu." Dancing formed part of the worship of this sect which was called Ji,[2] or the Time, because its founder maintained that it was the proper religion for the times in which he lived. He spent his time in travelling and preaching, whence he was popularly known as Yūgyō Shōnin, or the wandering priest. In 1886 he was given the posthumous title of Enshō Shōnin.

It will be observed that the story of the foundation of the Ji sect illustrates the extreme development of Ryōbu-Shintō. Shōjō, the Shintō deity of Kumano, is not only regarded as a form of Amida, but his explanations of the niceties of Amidist theology are accepted as authoritative, just as if they were passages from some recognized sûtra. Hachiman also was regarded as an incarnation (if indeed that is the right word) of Amida, and Tadachika Nakayama, who died in 1195, is quoted as saying[3] that the Emperor Ōjin, who was identified with Hachiman, "was called Hachiman Dai Bosatsu because at his birth eight banners came down from heaven. This showed that he was an incarnation of the Amida of the Eightfold Path." Ippen was at least anxious that the Shintō deities, if accepted as Buddhas, should behave as such, for he is said to have persuaded the priests of the Mishima shrine to abstain from making offerings of fishes and birds.

[1] See for a direct statement to this effect the story of Sabutsubō in *Hōnen, the Buddhist Saint*, pp. 389–390.

[2] 時宗.

[3] *Hōnen, the Buddhist Saint*, p. 107.

# CHAPTER XI

## RISE OF NEW SECTS: NICHIREN AND ZEN

NATURALLY such a simplification of religion as that described in the last chapter could not become current without exciting protests. They took shape, not only in the jealousy of the older sects but in the preaching of Nichiren, whose followers are still, with the Shinshū, the most active and influential, though not the most numerous, among the Buddhists of Japan. Both put unusual animus into their doctrines, for while the Shinshū assert that Amida and none other should be worshipped, the other side retort that a single invocation of his name requires long expiation in purgatory. A well-known anecdote relates Nicheren's indignation when on one of his missionary journeys he found some children playing with the image of Shaka, which had been cast out of a village temple to make room for an image of Amida. His anger was typical of his doctrine and manners: he reinstated the original Buddha, or at any rate the Shaka of the Lotus-sûtra—whom the Shinshū had entirely dethroned—but his real importance in Japanese thought is that he held religion to be something national and not merely individual. Again and again, with a vehemence which recalls the Hebrew prophets, he summoned the Government to suppress all sects except his own, with the result that he was twice banished and narrowly escaped with his life. His numerous writings contain so many personal touches that we are able to form an unusually vivid picture of his eventful career, which is a contrast to the monotony of most Buddhist Acta Sanctorum even when they include travel and exile.[1]

Nichiren was born in 1222 in Kominato, a little fishing town on the east coast of the province of Awa or Bōshū, where the place of his birth is still commemorated by a celebrated temple. According to local tradition, however, the site of the house where he first saw light is now covered by the encroaching sea and is marked by the shoals of *tai*-fish which frequent it and are carefully

[1] For Nichiren's life and teaching see in English (*a*) A. Lloyd, *The Creed of Half Japan*, 1911, chaps. xxiv and xxv, which includes a partial translation of the Risshō Ankoku Ron, (*b*) M. Anesaki, *Nichiren, the Buddhist Prophet*, 1916.

respected by the local fishermen. His father was a fisherman himself, but is said to have been of good lineage and to have been exiled for some political offence to this distant spot. Nichiren was originally named Zennichimaru, and when eleven years old was sent to a neighbouring monastery on a hill called Kiyozumi, where he was ordained at the age of fifteen and received the name of Renchō. He had apparently been instructed to recite the Nembutsu, but began to have doubts and passed through a violent crisis which affected his health. His active and precocious mind formed the idea of purifying and unifying Japanese Buddhism, and with that object he resolved to study it in all its varieties. He visited Kamakura and other places, and spent ten years (1243–1253) at Hieizan. The conclusion at which he arrived was that the Truth is to be found in reviving the Tendai doctrine—that is, the Tendai as preached by Dengyō Daishi—in a form suitable to the needs of the age and, if he did not approve of Hieizan as he knew it, he still had a double portion of its combative spirit. He returned to his old monastery on Kiyozumi, and on 17th May, 1253, proclaimed his new doctrine, the watchword of which was Namu Myōhō Renge kyō or Homage to the Sûtra of the Lotus of the Good Law,[1] that is, the sûtra called Saddharmapuṇḍarîka, which he declared to be the final and perfect revelation of the truth. He evidently felt the need of a formula to set against the hated Nembutsu.

He expressed his views with so much violence and so much vituperation of all who differed from him that no monastery would shelter him and the most that his former instructors would do was to aid him to escape the attacks which threatened him from both clergy and laity. After wandering about for some time he built himself a hermitage near Kamakura and rapidly made a reputation as an itinerant outdoor preacher. But the times were troubled: earthquakes, pestilence, and famine were mingled with political disorder. There were plots against the Hōjōs, who succeeded in defeating them, and no one knew what was going to happen next. As Nichiren himself says, "Many minds were turning to religion,"[2] but turning in perplexity. So he determined to give them a clear and definite answer. He retired to the monastery of Iwamoto and

[1] 妙法蓮華經. It is difficult to say how myō in this formula should be translated. It means in Japanese wondrous rather than good. On the other hand, it is the accepted translation of Sat in Saddharma and is also used to render the Sanskrit Su. See Sumati in the title of Nanjio, No. 23 (30).

[2] Opening passage of the Risshō Ankoku Ron.

there composed a tract called Risshō Ankoku Ron,[1] or A Treatise on the Establishment of Righteousness and the Peace of the Country, which he presented to the Hōjō Regent in 1260. It is in the form of a dialogue between the master of the house—no doubt meant to be Nichiren studying in his hermitage—and a visitor who comes to talk about the signs of the times.

This striking work shows the characteristics which mark Nichiren and his sect. One of its remarkable features is the identification of religion with national life. This was to some extent a fact in the Fujiwara times but it was not formulated as a principle, whereas the theme which gives life to his tract is that religious and national life are one, whether in health or disease. Equally remarkable is the intolerance of its tone. It is definitely laid down that to kill heretics is not murder and that it is the duty of the Government to extirpate heresy with the sword. Hōnen and his works receive special censure, which shows incidentally what progress his teaching had made by this time. It is also remarkable that Shinran is not mentioned, possibly because he did not preach in the same districts as Nichiren and possibly because his doctrines were not yet sufficiently distinguished from those of Hōnen. Of the latter Nichiren says that he was worse than Zendō and the ancient Chinese whom he imitated, for he bade men reject the scriptures of the Mahâyâna and the hosts of Buddhas and Bodhisattvas of whom they speak. " In this he preaches not Buddhism at all but his own perverse opinions. His words are false and wicked beyond comparison and no blame is too great for him. People all believe his false words and all admire his Senchaku.[2] So they prize the three Sûtras of the Pure Land and reject the rest. They depend upon the one Buddha of the Western Paradise and forget all other Buddhas. In truth he (Hōnen) is the enemy of all Buddhas and all Scriptures, the foe alike of saints and common people. This wicked doctrine has spread widely and penetrated in all directions."

A third feature of the tract is the apocalyptic character of Nicheren's speculations, which was also prominent in his sermons. He divided the history of Buddhism into three millenniums, starting from the Buddha's death, which is dated 947 after the Chinese fashion. The first of these is the period of Shōbō or the Hînayâna. The second is the period of Image-law or Zōbō, beginning about the time of the Christian era, that is to say, the period of the Mahâyâna

[1] 立正安國論.

[2] Hōnen's book, Senchakushū. See last Chapter, p. 263.

as revealed by Avalokiteśvara and other Bodhisattvas. It is apparently admitted that this doctrine, though contemplated by Śâkyamuni as a revelation to be made in his name, was not taught by him in his human life.[1] The third period is called Mappō[2] or the destruction of the law, and began according to Nichiren about A.D. 1050.

The Lotus-sûtra, especially in chapters xii and xiii called Energy and The Peaceful Life, contains the germs of Nichiren's apocalyptic theories, and it relates how a Bodhisattva called Viśishṭacâritra[3] was commissioned to preach the truth after the Buddha had passed away. Nichiren considered that he was Viśishṭacâritra appearing in a new birth to fulfil the command. In the Risshō Ankoku Ron and in his sermons Nichiren clearly warned his countrymen that an invasion was imminent, and he lived to see his prediction fulfilled by Khubilai Khan. As an inquirer he may have been in touch with Chinese priests and have learnt from them something about Chinese politics which accounts for his prescience.

The doctrine which is to be the light and guide of the Mappō period, which is to unify Buddhism and to give the nations peace and prosperity is the teaching of the Lotus concentrated in the invocation Namu myō-hō renge-kyō. The essence of this teaching is that Śâkyamuni, not as the man Gotama but as the eternal omnipresent Buddha mind, is one with all reason and with all nature. Neither realism nor idealism as generally taught is the whole truth. Phenomena are real inasmuch as they exist in the Buddha mind and share its essence. Every grain of dust can become a Buddha. There is little in the substance of these doctrines which is new, though it is unusual in Mahayanist works to find the personality of Śâkyamuni thus emphatically connected with the Dharmakâya. What was new and what aroused attention and anger was Nichiren's uncompromising denunciation of other sects and other Buddhas. In the Risshō Ankoku Ron the Jōdo sect are chiefly attacked, but in other of his writings of this same period the Zen fare no better, and in later works he wrote with equal violence against the Shingon and Risshū. Hardly one of the most venerated

[1] See Lloyd's quotations in *The Creed of Half Japan* from the Seigoroku (a collection of extracts from Nichiren's works), p. 645.

[2] The characters for the names of the three periods are: 正法 Shōbō, 像法 Zōbō, 末法 Mappō.

[3] Lotus, chap. xx, near beginning. Viśishṭacâritra is rendered as 上行 Jōgyō.

names is spared. He bluntly said that Amida and Birushana were figments; that every repetition of the Nembutsu cost those who uttered it ages in hell: that Kōbō Daishi was the biggest liar in Japan (Nihon no dai mōgo), and the Zen a doctrine of demons and fiends. It is said that at the beginning of the Meiji era a conference of representative Buddhists was held with the object of drawing up an account of the doctrines of the twelve sects, but when it came to formulating the views of the Nichirenites the meeting found it impossible to proceed and ended in a lawsuit. Nichiren's opinion of other religious bodies is often quoted in the concise form of "The Nembutsu is hell: the Zen are devils: Shingon is national ruin and the Risshū are traitors to the country".[1]

The Hōjō Government were shocked on receiving a memorial couched in such language as the Risshō Ankoku Ron, and Nichiren's ecclesiastical opponents incited a mob to attack his hermitage. He escaped for the moment, but on returning to Kamakura was arrested and banished to what was then the desolate coast of the peninsula of Izu (1261). Here he formulated the five fundamental principles of his preaching.

The banishment in Izu did not last long. It is not known why Nichiren was released, but he returned to Kamakura and was well received by his adherents, who, however, requested him to moderate his attacks on other forms of faith. But he refused to compromise or to admit that salvation is to be found outside his own creed, and a work which he composed about this time called the Ji Myō-Hokke Mondō-shō,[2] or Questions and Answers as to how one should hold the Lotus of Truth, is even more violent than his earlier writings. In 1264 he was recalled to his native place by the serious illness of his mother, who, however, recovered in answer to his prayers, as he believed. He subsequently set out on a four years' missionary journey in the Eastern provinces. Soon after leaving home he was attacked by a band of his enemies but had a wonderful escape. Nichiren, who often writes of the incident as the Peril in the Pine Forest, regarded it as a miracle and a manifestation of the Buddha's power to protect his servants and the faith entrusted to them. In 1268 he returned after making many converts, and, though there is some uncertainty as to his movements in the next four years, at

[1] 念佛無間 Nembutsu Muken. 禪天魔 Zen Temma.
眞言亡國 Shingon Bōkoku. 律國賊 Ritsu Kokuzoku.

[2] 持妙法華問答鈔.

first his vigorous attitude was not without success, for the troubles of the time lent colour to his diatribes against the Church and State. But he would not learn moderation and is said to have introduced into sermons personalities unusual even in militant theology, such as that the late Hōjō Regent, Tokiyori, was already in hell and that his young son and successor, Tokimune, was on his way there. The arrival of the Mongol envoys, who came at the end of 1268 to demand tribute, stirred him to action. He addressed letters to the principal officials and ecclesiastical dignitaries recalling the warnings of a foreign invasion which he had issued eight years before and insisting that the only way to save the country was to adopt as the national religion the faith which he preached. He also sent a circular to his followers telling them what he had done with the purpose of awakening Japan from its torpor: he awaited exile or death with composure, he said, and urged them to do likewise and not to fear the authorities.

Nevertheless, he was not interfered with till 1271, when he reappeared at Kamakura. He was arrested, tried, and apparently sentenced to banishment, but, according to the custom of the times, his custodians had the right to dispose of his life and prepared to execute him at midnight on 17th October. On the way to the execution ground where the temple of Ryūkōji at Katase now stands, he passed before the temple of Hachiman and upbraided him and the Sun-goddess for not keeping their oath to guard those who work for the truth. There are different stories as to how he was saved at the last moment. According to the more sober version a messenger from the Government arrived just in time to stop the execution and to order that the prophet should be merely banished. But Nichiren himself relates [1] that just as his head was about to be struck off something bright like a ball of fire flew across the sky from the south-east to the north-west. The sword fell from the executioner's hand and all was panic and confusion. At any rate, it is certain that the execution did not take place: Nichiren was detained for a month and then removed in December, 1271, to the island of Sado, which lies in the Sea of Japan off the coast of Echigo. Here he spent about two years suffering considerable hardships but absorbed in meditation and the composition of various treatises, especially one celebrated work entitled the Eye-opener,[2] in which he

[1] Nichiren's works, Tōkyō, 1904, p. 1394.

[2] 開目鈔 Kaimokushō.

vehemently reiterates his intention of continuing to work for the establishment of the Truth and says, in words which are often called Nichiren's three vows, "I will be the pillar of Japan; I will be the eyes of Japan; I will be the great vessel of Japan."[1] He also designed a Mandara or graphic representation of the universe and the Buddhas and Bodhisattvas mentioned in the Lotus. It was apparently at this period that he first definitely enunciated the conviction that he was Viśishtacâritra or Jōgyō, the Bodhisattva whom Shaka had charged with the defence and propagation of the faith.[2]

But this exile, like the first, was comparatively short. Nichiren had friends, especially among the officers of the Bakufu army, and the Hōjōs were evidently not entirely hostile to him. In 1274 he was released and allowed to return to Kamakura. The Government again endeavoured to come to an arrangement with the troublesome prophet and induce him to accept recognition on a par with other sects. But in vain: he would hear of nothing but the union of Japan under Buddhism as he understood it. He left Kamakura and settled with a few disciples at Minobu on the western side of Mount Fuji. His prestige was greatly increased by the occurrence of the Mongol invasions which he had predicted, and the remainder of his life was spent in peace. He founded the temples of Minobu and Ikegami which are still the chief sanctuaries of his sect, and he dreamed of establishing a Kaidan which should be a central cathedral for the Universal Church and the Kingdom of Buddha on earth. He died at Ikegami in 1282, repeating with his last breath stanzas from the Lotus.[3] On the first anniversary of his death his disciples met together and collected his writings. It was not until 12th October, 1922, that the posthumous title of Risshō Daishi was conferred on him.

Nichiren left a vigorous sect behind him. His six chief disciples were sturdy propagandists, and one of them, Nichiji, is believed to have started on a missionary journey to Siberia in 1295. But there is little to be said about the history of the sect. Its temples are

[1] Great vessel apparently means the giver of life.

[2] He is mentioned first in chap. xiv as one of the four chiefs of the hosts of Bodhisattvas who issue from the earth and are declared to be all sons of the Tathâgata: in chap. xx he accepts the commission to preach the Truth after the nirvâna of the Tathâgata: after being mentioned once or twice incidentally his name reappears in the last sentence as the leader of the host of newly appeared Bodhisattvas.

[3] The passage which he is said to have recited is the verses at the end of chap. xv.

beautiful and spacious, but it had not much obvious influence on art, and strange to say, though pugnacious and self-assertive, it never cut the same figure in politics as the older sects of the Shinshū.

There are many records of the violent attacks made by the Nichirenites on other religious bodies by which they alienated the sympathies of the Government and probably of the respectable public, and naturally they received hard blows in return. In 1532 they had a prolonged conflict with the Tendai known as the Tembun no Hōran, or the religious war of the Tembun period, in which they suffered severely. A little later Hideyoshi sent to Korea two regiments, one of Nichirenites and one of Christians, and probably felt that Japan was the better for getting rid of both.

The sub-sects, of which nine still exist, could not refrain from fighting with one another and weakened the power of the body as a whole. Though they were bitter opponents of Christianity and thus helped the Tokugawa Government, it is remarkable that Iemitsu, when prohibiting Christianity, also prohibited the most extreme section of the Nichiren known as the Fuju-fuze,[1] "No give or take" branch. The edict of 1614 makes the nature of their offences clear and is an interesting statement of the Japanese official view respecting differences of religion. Christians and Fujufuzes were alike in insisting on having their own priests and temples and in refusing to support the worship of the parishes where they might reside. The Government's reply is that people might have their own preferences in doctrine and add to every day religion special observances, but that those who ostentatiously reject the form of Buddhism prevalent in their neighbourhood are antisocial, "enemies of the Empire and the object of the people's hostility."

It remains to speak of one other very important sect which was introduced into Japan in this same eventful period and which still attracts attention, for its adherents are not only numerous at the present day but an unusually large proportion of them belong to the aristocratic and literary classes. It is the Dhyâna sect which claims Bodhidharma as a founder and which we have already met

[1] 不受不施. It was founded in 1595 by Nichi-Ō, a priest of the Myōza-kuji temple in Bizen. It was suppressed in 1624 and reauthorized in 1868. According to the statistics published in the *Bulletin de la Maison Franco-Japonaise* (1927, i) there are at present two sections recognized: one, the Nichiren-Shū-fu-ju-ze-ha, with three temples and one abbot: the other, the Nichiren-shū-fuju-fuze-kōmon-ha, with only one temple and one abbot.

with in China under the name of Ch'an.[1] In Japan this name was pronounced as Zen and, though the success of the teaching was tardy, it was remarkable when it once began. It is said to have been first introduced in 654, but the notices about it are obscure and at any rate it died out, probably because it did not satisfy the need which was then felt for a simple and definite faith capable of becoming a national religion. About 815 a Chinese priest called Gikū[2] is said to have preached the doctrines of Zen at Kyōto. He was well received by the Emperor Saga and his Empress, but appears to have returned to China without making much impression. Again, we hear that a certain Japanese monk called Egaku visited China about 858, and after studying Zen there made an attempt to import it into his own country without success.[3]

But the real founder in Japan was Eisai[4] (1141–1215), a native of the province of Bitchū in the west, but educated at Hieizan. In 1168 he went to China and visited the temples of T'ien T'ai but soon returned. In 1187 he started on a second voyage, intending to proceed to India, but was detained by bad weather at Chekiang and studied again at T'ien T'ai until 1191, when he went back to his native country. His visit to China coincided with the rule of the Southern Sung dynasty at Hangchou, when the philosophy of Chu Hsi and Zen were all the fashion, and it is not surprising to find that he brought back the latter to Japan and preached it there.

He is sometimes said to have also introduced tea, but it appears that this honour really belongs to Kōbō Daishi. Tea, however (like the Zen itself), was not appreciated in the ninth century, and Eisai can at least claim the credit of making it fashionable and of inventing the tea ceremonies. These had originally a religious object. Tea kept the mind wakeful and alert for midnight devotion and was therefore drunk as an accompaniment to Buddhist services. In time the ceremonial became more secular, and during many centuries had a singular fascination for the upper classes, who regarded its complicated etiquette as a test of the manners, tastes, and temper of a gentleman. Eisai wrote a book about tea and is said to have cured an indisposition of the young Shōgun Sanetomo by inducing him to drink it instead of wine.

His return coincided with the advent of Yoritomo to power and his relations with the Kamakura Shōguns were extremely good.

[1] 禪.

[2] 義空.

[3] See Johnston, *Buddhist China*, p. 320.

[4] 榮西.

On first arriving from China he founded a temple at Hakata in Kyūshū, but in 1202 he was appointed by the Shōgun Yoriie as head of the new monastery of Kenninji and as Dai-Sōjō, the highest ecclesiastical title, in the following year. Subsequently he was summoned to Kamakura to superintend the erection of the Jūfukuji shortly before his death at the age of seventy-five.

The sect introduced by Eisai was the Rinzai, the Lin-chi of the Chinese, of whose origin and principles I have already spoken.[1] The other chief branch, known as Ts'ao-T'ung in Chinese and as Sōtō or Sōdō in Japanese, was brought over to Japan by his pupil Dōgen (1200–1253), often called Shōyō Daishi,[2] a title conferred on him in 1880. He was of aristocratic birth, being the son of Kuga Michichika who held the post of Naidaijin. After studying Zen under Eisai he followed his example by going in 1223 to China, where he remained for five years. On his return he taught first at the Kenninji, but subsequently built the Eiheiji near Fukui in Echizen, which is still the headquarters of the sub-sect and perhaps the finest monastery in Japan. In 1250 the retired Emperor, Go Saga, conferred on him the title of Buppō-Zenji and at the same time sent him a robe of honour. But Dōgen, while too polite to return the imperial rescript and present, replied in a well-known quatrain in which he said that he would be laughed at by the monkeys and cranes among whom he lived as the old man in the purple robe.[3]

Another figure in the early period of Japanese Zen is the Chinese monk Dōryū[4] who arrived in 1247. He attracted the attention of Tokiyori, the fifth Hōjō Regent, and in 1253 was made abbot of the newly-erected Kenchōji temple. He was subsequently transferred to the Saimyōji, to which Tokiyori himself retired when he took the tonsure in 1256.

The Rinzai and Sōtō (as well as the much later Ōbaku introduced in 1655) are often reckoned as separate sects (shū) and not merely branches (ha) of one sect. The Sōtō is by far the most numerous and has the distinction of being a united body without subdivisions, whereas the Rinzai is split into at least ten. The Sōtō is also, as I have mentioned in speaking about China, less open to any charge of extravagance and lays greater stress on the need of good conduct and morality in the spiritual life, whereas the Rinzai, without being

[1] Chapter V. [2] 道元：承陽大師.

[3] The lines in Japanese are: 永平雖谷淺. 勅命重重重. 却被猿鶴笑. 紫衣一老翁. [4] 道隆.

in the least open to the charge of immorality, emphasizes the importance of sudden spiritual enlightenment without insisting so strongly that a good life is the best training for such an enlightenment and the sure result of it.

In many Japanese sects there is a small but extravagant subsection. In Zen this is the Fukeshū,[1] started as early as 1254 by the priest Kakushin. He visited China and learnt there not only theology but music. On his return he wandered about Japan preaching and playing the flute. The sect thus formed is often called Komusō, from the name of one of his successors, and the custom grew up for wandering Samurai and outlaws to join it. It became so much a method of evading justice that Ieyasu subjected it to strict regulations and it was entirely suppressed in 1871. But in springtime strolling flute-players may still be seen in various country districts (for instance, at Nara) wearing large hats shaped like beehives which entirely cover the upper part of the face and are part of the traditional costume of the Fukeshū. But I believe that these modern minstrels claim no connection with Buddhism.

Zen, so far as our knowledge of its history goes, is a Far Eastern religion and it is not easy to say anything definite about its connection with India. Even if the Lankâvatâra-sûtra [2] expresses its main doctrines, it expresses them in a thoroughly Indian way and the idea of "not depending on books and letters" is not at all Indian. Though Bodhidharma is stated to have brought Zen from India to China, no reference to it in Sanskrit is known and the influence exercised on it by Taoism is clear. At times certain sections of it at any rate rejected not only the study of the scriptures but all the conventionalities of Buddhism. It was thus exceedingly pliant and appealed to classes who had little taste for dogma or ceremony.

It was not a suitable religion for Japan in the seventh or eighth centuries because what was needed then was a clear and decided creed which could school and civilize a people among whom the masses were in a rudimentary stage of culture. But things were very different about 1200, when men's minds were weary of the old religious forms, and new sects, national and Japanese, were coming into being. Zen did not spring up like the systems of Shinran and Nichiren: it was introduced by the time-honoured process of Japanese going to China and bringing back the instruction which

[1] 普化宗.

[2] See on this point *Studies in the Lankâvatâra Sûtra*, by D. T. Suzuki, p. 89 ff.

they had received there. Still, the instruction was so flexible and contained so little that was in any way suggestive of Chinese nationality and usages that Zen has become as decidedly Japanese as tea ceremonies or Nō plays.

The future which awaited it was not what might have been expected. It might have been supposed that in a troubled period this contemplative and mystic doctrine, which finds truth not in scripture but in the immediate experience of the human mind, would have flourished in monastic harbours of refuge among those who had left the storms of the world, but not that it would have been accepted as the favourite rule of life for the military class. Yet such it became and the cause of the transformation is clear. Soldiers were not repelled by a doctrine which held that book learning is useless, and Zen is essentially discipline. The mind in which it trusts is not the wayward impulsive mind but the mind which is in training to win the race for truth, the mind which is receptive but under control, which remains calm and collected though threatened by physical danger from without or assailed by passion from within. Such a mind makes a soldier as well as an abbot. A well-known story relates that when Nobunaga was fighting against Takeda in the province of Kai his troops surrounded and set fire to a temple. The priest Kwaisen Shōki with his companions perished in the flames as he recited an impromptu poem which he had composed saying that even fire is cold to the mind that thinks it is. This shows how the military, priestly, and poetic ideals can sometimes unite.

At the present time soldiers in Japan do not perhaps study Zen, but fencers do so and are not considered perfect unless in addition to acquiring manual skill they have also mastered a secret treatise which is confided by teachers to their pupils. The main idea is that the mind should be kept "empty", that is, clear, unprejudiced, and ready to follow any inspiration.

Another instance will perhaps explain what is to Europeans an unusual view of the function of religion and of the advantages which come from studying it.[1] A Japanese school-girl applied to a well-known missionary in Tōkyō and stated that she wished to become a Christian. When questioned as to her reasons she replied that her great desire was to go up in an aeroplane. "On being invited to explain the connection between aeroplanes and

[1] The story is taken from the *Kobe Chronicle* of 3rd May, 1927, which quotes it as being told by Miss Susan Ballard in *The East and West*.

Christianity, she replied that she had been told that before she went up in an aeroplane she must have a very calm and well-regulated mind and that this kind of mind was only acquired by religious training. She thought that among the religions Christianity was probably the best and so she came to ask for teaching."

The warriors of the Bakufu reasoned very like this school-girl, and it is not surprising if Zen, which laid so little stress upon scriptures and ceremonies and so much upon mental discipline, became popular among them. But its transformation into a military creed is for all that most remarkable: it makes Zen as essentially Japanese as is the teaching of Nichiren, for the development of the school in China gives no indication of the future which awaited it on the other side of the Straits. Zen priests in China may perhaps have been more ready than others to consort with all sorts and conditions of men, but probably, like most literary Chinese, they held soldiers in scant esteem. At Kamakura Zen was not the only new form of Buddhism which was popular: the Daibutsu is a proof of that. But Eisai received marks of high favour from the Government when the young Yoriie (son of Yoritomo) was nominal Shōgun under the direction of his mother, Masako, the daughter of the first Hōjō Regent, who herself became a nun, but of the Jōdo school. Eisai himself did not live long enough to see the Hōjō power completely established, but his successors continued to be influential. The fifth Hōjō Regent Tokiyori became a monk in 1256 and resided in the Saimyōji monastery, but is said to have made frequent journeys incognito in order to learn the real feelings and needs of the people. Though he had received full initiation into Zen, we also hear that he confessed his belief in the efficacy of Amida's vow.[1]

Under the Hōjō there were five great Zen temples known as the Go-zan,[2] of which three were at Kamakura, namely, the Enkakuji, Kenchōji, and Jūfukuji, while two were in Kyōto, the Kenninji, the earliest Zen monastery, built by the Shōgun Yoriie in 1202, and the splendid Tōfukuji which it took the founder of the Kujō family nearly twenty years (1236–1255) to construct. Subsequently (1336) there were five chief temples in Kyōto and as many in Kamakura. In the former, in addition to those already mentioned, were the Tenryūji, an imperial villa which was turned into a temple and had the distinguished Soseki as its first abbot, the Shōkokuji or Sōkokuji,

[1] See *Hōnen, the Buddhist Saint*, p. 467.

[2] 五山.

and the Manjūji: in Kamakura were the Jōchiji and the Ikkenji. Above them all was the Nanzenji, which had also been originally an imperial residence, but the celebrated priest Mukwan was allowed to convert it into a temple in 1290. The five temples at Kyōto were also a centre of Chinese studies and produced somewhat later several historical works, which were not mere annals and records of events. Nor was popular education neglected. The establishment called Terakoya, or little temple, schools, which were mostly in the hands of Zen priests, taught the young people of the villages religion and morality as well as reading and writing.

# CHAPTER XII

## THE DARK AGES

THOUGH the administration of the Kamakura Bakufu had won for it general confidence and credit, and though the successful repulse of the two Mongol invasions in 1274 and 1281 had crowned it with glory, yet in the next century it began to show signs of weakness and suddenly collapsed. The earlier Hōjō Regents were men of exceptionally high character, but after the abdication of Sadatoki, the seventh, the real power was wielded by Ministers of doubtful probity, and the ninth and last Regent, Takatoki, is generally described by historians as a youth of weak intelligence and vicious habits.

In addition to this the administration of the country and the political position was incredibly complicated. There was an Emperor at Kyōto, often a child, and at least one, and sometimes several, retired Emperors who exercised in his name what imperial authority was left. Then there was a Shōgun, who was at this time an imperial Prince [1] but officially the successor of Yoritomo, and, thirdly, there was the Hōjō Regent, nominally the Deputy of the Shōgun who was the Deputy of the Emperor. But the Regent himself might be a minor, as was Takatoki, and be in the hands of regents. But this is only the beginning of the intricacies. The Emperor Go-Saga (1242–6) had two sons and made a will directing that the future sovereigns should be chosen from the descendants of these two alternately, a rule which seemed bound to produce trouble. The Regent Hōjō Sadatoki further complicated matters by ordering in 1288 not only that the Emperors should be chosen alternately from the two branches but that each Emperor should hold office for only ten years. One wonders that this complex machinery of government could have lasted even for a short time. It is also a remarkable proof of the permanence of the monarchical principle in Japan that the result of it should have been

[1] When the last Minamoto Shōgun died in 1219, the Hōjō appointed a child of the Fujiwara family named Yoritsune as Shōgun. He abdicated and was succeeded in 1244 by his son, who, however, was deposed in 1252 because Yoritsune was implicated in a plot against the Hōjōs. The remaining four nominal Shōguns till 1332 were Imperial Princes nominated by the Hōjōs.

not abolition of the Empire but the collapse of the Hōjō Regents and the rise of a new dynasty of Shōguns, the Ashikagas.

The Court of Kyōto had on several occasions participated in plots against the Hōjōs whom they naturally disliked, and the Emperor Go-Daigo, taking advantage of the unpopularity of Hōjō Takatoki, made an attempt on a large scale. Only the merest outline of a most complicated story can be given here, but it is interesting to note that one of Go-Daigo's preparations was to make two of his sons enter the priesthood in order to win the great monasteries to his side. In brief, he failed and was banished but escaped in 1332: the sudden defection of Ashikaga Takauji, the commander of the Bakufu army, completely changed the position: the Hōjō Regent committed suicide and Go-Daigo, entering Kyōto as Emperor in 1333, attempted to restore civilian government, as it had been, without Shōgun or Regent. But Takauji, when his request to be made Shōgun was refused, proclaimed himself as such and was master of the situation. Go-Daigo took refuge in Hieizan which underwent a blockade, but he ultimately escaped and set up an independent Court at Yoshino which was known as the Southern Court, while Takauji recognized the other branch of the imperial family as Emperors and established the Northern Court at Kyōto. For fifty-six years there was a double succession of Emperors and constant war, and the real power tended to be in the hands of the Shugo or constables, a relic of the institutions of Yoritomo. Unity was restored only in 1392 under the third Ashikaga Shōgun, Yoshimitsu, who was the virtual ruler of Japan with the Emperors of the Northern Court as nominal sovereigns.

It is hardly necessary to observe that this troubled period, which at best can be called romantic, was far from favourable to the interests of Buddhism. A war between the branches of the imperial family appealed strongly to the worst instincts of the old monasteries, to their love of political intrigue and of military adventures. We hear little of religious movements in Kyōto and the neighbourhood at this period, and in temporal matters, in wealth and power, Hieizan and other holy places suffered severely. The Zen, perhaps, came out of the conflict best. The eminent priest Soseki was first of all patronized by Go-Daigo, but subsequently enjoyed great influence as the confidential adviser of Takauji, who appears to have had pious scruples and regrets about many incidents in his adventurous career and to have done his best to make amends by vows and temple building. Also Kusunoki Masashige, the celebrated champion of Go-Daigo, is said to have been encouraged to sacrifice his life for his imperial master against overwhelming odds by a Zen priest called Soshun, who told him that life and death are not more real than the empty space which a sword divides.

The Shinshū sect also flourished, but at this period its record is eventful rather than edifying. The marriage of the clergy had as one important consequence the institution of hereditary abbots and, though the founder had felt Hieizan too worldly for the peace of his soul, his successors showed no aversion to war or politics. The fact that ecclesiastical office was transmitted by descent within the family made a Shinshū religious establishment very like a barony, as one of them actually became, and though the sect had no monasteries, it very soon began to construct fortified temples. It also soon split into ten sub-sects which did not differ in doctrine but recognized the jurisdiction of different temples whose abbots were descended from Shinran or his disciples.[1] They were, in fact, analogous to bishoprics, but the authority of a Christian see is local, whereas in the Shinshū the succession of the abbots was hereditary and sees were moved from one place to another, particularly in disturbed periods. One often reads in Japanese records of temples being transferred, as if they were portable objects.

In 1272 the daughter and the grandson of Shinran erected the Hongwanji temple at Kyōto to which the Emperor Kameyama accorded the status of an imperial chapel. It subsequently suffered much violence, the temple being burned and the see frequently transferred. The direct descendants of Shinran continued to hold it, however, and in spite of minor differences received general recognition as primates of the whole sect. Another important temple was the Bukkōji, or Temple of Buddha's Light, which was founded by Shinran himself in Yamashina, one of the suburbs of Kyōto, and was his residence for fifteen years. It was subsequently handed over to his younger brother Shimbutsu and his descendants. The seventh abbot called Ryōgen[2] removed it to Higashiyama in 1320 and also acquired some celebrity by his contest with a faction within the sect who called themselves Akunin Shōki,[3] Evil doers whose faith is right. As already mentioned, antinomianism, though expressly repudiated by the founders, from time to time made its appearance in the Amidist sects, and in the troubled times of the

[1] The division into the Eastern and Western Hongwanji is later and dates from the time of Ieyasu.

[2] 了源.

[3] 惡人正機.

Emperor Go-Daigo it was very convenient to interpret justification by faith as meaning that deeds do not matter provided that the belief is correct. This creed was openly preached, and when Ryōgen equally openly opposed it he was waylaid and assassinated by his adversarics. The monstrous doctrine does not appear, however, to have been publicly advocated after this period.

Shinran is also said to have founded in 1225 and 1235 respectively the Senshūji at Takata and the Kinshokuji at Kibe in Ōmi. The former was transferred to Isshinden near Tsu where there is now a celebrated temple. The latter had as its first abbots Shinran's son Zenran and his great-grandson Kakunyo. Kakunyo was appointed abbot of the Hongwanji, and the administration of the Kinshokuji passed into the hands of Kōgen who claimed to be of Fujiwara lineage. His descendants, who bear the title of Baron Kibe, are still the heads of this section. The Shinshū had also temples in Echizen, Echigo, and Kaga which played an important part in local politics, but their activity began a little later.

The Jōdo sect was less prominent and enterprising than the Shinshū. It worked quietly and steadily increased its influence, but it had to suffer a good deal of minor persecution and hardships. Jōdo temples were often burned and the priests of Hieizan attempted to confiscate or destroy all Jōdo books. Six editions of Hōnen's work, the Senchakushū, are said to have been publicly burnt and his biography had to be published under another name. The Jōdo was not even recognized as a separate body until Tokugawa times, and in 1322 Shiren, a Zen priest who wrote a Biographical History of Buddhism, calls it a parasite because it had no independent domicile of its own.[1] It is interesting to find that in this period of confusion it was the only sect which produced important novelties in theology. Ryōyo Shōgei (1341–1420),[2] the author of a work called Jugi[3] and reckoned as the seventh patriarch of the Jōdo, enunciated a new doctrine which materially modified the teaching of Hōnen. He taught that birth in the Pure Land does not mean rebirth in another region. All language about being born again is purely metaphorical. The Pure Land is everywhere and to go there is a change of mind and condition, not of place. This idea has had considerable influence in recent times. Shōsō or Yuyō Shōnin was a celebrated disciple of Ryōyo Shōgei and built the

[1] See *Hōnen, the Buddhist Saint*, p. 60. I am indebted to the same work for the account of Ryōyo Shōgei and his doctrines.

[2] 良譽聖冏. [3] 頌義.

Zōjōji temple which now stands in Shiba park at Tōkyō, though that is not its original site and the present building is a reconstruction due to Ieyasu.

Ashikaga Takauji had established a new Shogunate which bears his family name and which lasted for more than two centuries (1338–1573), but the first fifty years or so, when there were two rival Courts, naturally had special characteristics and it is only after the year 1392, when the double line of Emperors was abolished by the recognition of the Northern Court, that the Ashikaga period can be said to begin.[1] It was in many ways a remarkable contrast to the Kamakura period. During the greater part of the Hōjō's rule there was internal peace, few dealings with China except one successful war, little productivity in art and literature, but a disciplined and chivalrous military spirit as well as religious movements of force and originality. The Ashikaga rule was marked by chronic internal dissension, onerous taxation and economic distress, intercourse with China and an influx of Sung culture, some graceful literature and many brilliant works of art, by luxury and corruption in social life, and in the monasteries by turbulence or artistic indolence.[2]

The most remarkable of the Ashikaga rulers was the third, the Yoshimitsu (1358–1408) already mentioned. He succeeded as a minor and for many years his rule was troubled. He had time, however, to cultivate the arts of peace and maintained friendly relations with the Ming dynasty. He was a fervent follower of the Zen and built the monastery of Sōkokuji. At the age of thirty-six he nominally abdicated and became a monk, following the example set by Emperors and the Hōjōs. In reality he continued to rule until his death and built for his residence the Kinkaku or Golden Pavilion which is still one of the sights of Kyōto. In his reign flourished the painters Chō Densu, Shūbun, and Josetsu, who were all priests, the last two from Sōkokuji. Josetsu had among his pupils the celebrated Sesshū and Masanobu, the founder of the Kanō school and father of the more celebrated Motonobu. Most of the great artists were priests, for monasteries, though they often took part in the prevailing turbulence, were on the whole a welcome refuge in troublous times and this is specially true of Zen

[1] The Ashikaga period is often called Muromachi 室町 from the name of the quarter of Kyōto in which the Ashikaga Shōguns lived. The period 1336 to 1392 is known as Nambokuchō 南北朝.

[2] But see Binyon's works for a more favourable estimate.

monasteries. As might be expected, the work of these painter-monks often deals with religious subjects. Even when it does not, the inspiration seems to come mainly from Zen philosophy which had a special influence on landscape painting. An anecdote relates that a Zen teacher when asked what was the essence of Buddhism replied " the oak tree in my garden ". It is not wise as a rule to paraphrase Zen apophthegms, but this utterance at least indicates that a love and understanding of nature were regarded as an aspect of religion, just as much as introspection.

Literature was almost entirely in the hands of ecclesiastics, but their writings breathe an eclectic and easy-going spirit. Thus the Taiheiki, a romantic and poetic chronicle like the Heike Monogatari, is ascribed to a monk of Hieizan, but the author attempts to reconcile Buddhism not only with Shintō but with Chinese philosophy. The Ashikaga Gakkō, or College, in the town of the same name in the province of Shimotsuke, patronized by the Uesugi family, became a great centre of Chinese culture under the priest Kwaigen, and Chinese learning also flourished in the five Zen monasteries of Kyōto. Yoshida Kenkō, the author of the Essays and Anecdotes called Tsure-Dzure Gusa [1] and master of an admirably light and easy style, was a Zen monk but spoke sympathetically of Shintō, Taoism, and Confucius as also of gallantry. The Nō [2] or older and more solemn form of drama, which arose in this period and apparently had its origin, in part at least, in the recitations of itinerant monks, shows the same mixture, but the predominant line of thought is Buddhist, and priests and temples play a large part in the dramatis personæ and scenery.

The most prominent and flourishing sect during the earlier Ashikaga period was the Zen. I have already said something about its rise and influence at Kamakura and about the ten great monasteries which it possessed, five at Kamakura and five at Kyōto, all subordinate to the head monastery of Nanzenji in the latter. Especially celebrated was the Sōkokuji, built by the Shōgun Yoshimitsu to be a mortuary temple of his family. It became exceedingly wealthy and was the home of many celebrated artists and also gained notoriety in another way, as two of the fiercest battles of the Ōnin war (1467–1477)—a complicated contest arising out of the succession to the Shōgun Yoshimasa—were fought for its possession

[1] Translation published by Sansom in *Trans. As. Soc. Japan*, 1911.

[2] 能

and recapture. For the credit of Zen, however, let it be said that its monks are not recorded to have maintained troops or fought like Hieizan and the other older monasteries. Indeed, it sometimes gave way, as in 1344 when the violent opposition of Hieizan prevented the Emperor from attending the dedication of the Tenryūji, and in 1368 Hieizan was made to listen to reason by the intervention of the Shogunate, not by direct military resistance on the part of the Zen. Its great influence was exercised by diplomacy rather than by force of arms. Its abbots were powerful in the Council Chamber of the Shōguns. Soseki (or to call him by his posthumous title Musō Kokushi) and, later, Manzai were both of them influential and capable advisers.

The clergy, too, were strong in the lower branches of the Civil Service, for monks were employed as clerks in the Government secretariat, and also a department which is not usually considered as ecclesiastical, namely, shipping and commerce, was in the hands of the Zen hierarchy. When Takauji was turning an old palace into the Temple of Tenryūji, he sent Soseki, who was then the abbot, to China on the ship called Tenryūji to buy appropriate decorations and ornaments. This was in 1342, but the voyage was so successful that Tenryūji-bune became the regular name for a ship trading with China. In 1452 there was a fleet of ten such ships which, though managed by the Zen clergy, engaged in ordinary commerce. Books and pictures, however, formed a considerable part of the cargo imported to Japan. The Myōshinji temple of Kyōto, which is charged with the supervision of 3,800 others, was celebrated for its businesslike activity, its management of clerical finance, and its accurate accounts.

Meanwhile the political situation in Kyōto had undergone material changes. Though the Ashikaga Shōguns had paid no attention to an agreement made in 1392 that the Emperor should be chosen alternately from the northern and southern branches of the imperial family, the southern branch made several attempts and the various military houses were continually fighting among themselves. It became almost impossible to collect dues from the imperial estates in the provinces and the Court and nobility fell into great poverty.

One result of this was that the custom of abdication and of maintaining separate establishments for ex-Emperors, who generally entered the Church, fell into abeyance for want of the necessary funds. Whereas in 1300 there were five Emperors living, each with his own Court, in the whole period from 1400 to 1500 there were but four reigns and two ex-Emperors, and the funeral of the last Emperor of this century was delayed for forty-four days because no money could be found to defray the expenses. Nearly all the princes except the Crown Prince had to become priests, whereas previously only certain temples had been allowed the privilege of having a princely Abbot (Miya Monzeki). This does not, however, imply a close connection between the Court and the Church. The imperial power and prestige suffered considerably, whereas the magnificence of the Shōguns increased, and even a single door in one of their palaces is said to have cost twenty thousand gold pieces.

Hieizan and the older monasteries indeed suffered from financial straits like their imperial patrons, but the Zen accommodated itself to the new regime. At the instigation of Soseki, Takauji had ordered that in addition to the imposing array of temples at Kyōto and Kamakura, a Zen monastery and pagoda to be styled Ankokuji should be built in every province, so that Zen came near to being the State Church. This, no doubt, was one of the motives which prompted Takauji and Soseki, but the former also desired to show his regret for the many deaths and misfortunes which he caused. Similarly he established the Tenryūji already mentioned as a propitiation to the wounded spirit of Go-Daigo.

The Shōguns, however, did not neglect the interests of other religious bodies. Temples and Shintō shrines were relieved of the burdens of taxation, and in many cases a tax called Dansen, a somewhat miscellaneous impost, hitherto levied for special ceremonies such as coronations, was collected in order to repair monasteries. It had become the custom to erect barriers for the collection of transit dues on all important roads and the proceeds of a particular barrier were often assigned to the upkeep of some religious foundation. Thus Kōfukuji was given the right to the customs of the port of Hyōgo. But monasteries were not allowed to erect toll-barriers or to collect dues themselves, though they showed some desire to do so. They were practically the only non-military manors which survived through this period and many of them can hardly be called non-military, though the Zen have a better right to the title than others. The monks of Hieizan were under arms in 1435, but were suppressed and suffered the same fate in 1499, when they took part in the quarrels between the Shogunate and the Hosokawa family.

Besides the military monks attached to various monasteries there were "wandering swash-buckling priests" called Komusō or Boro.

The Tsure-Dzure Gusa says that they were dissolute and cruel in appearance but praises their bravery and relates how one challenged another in the middle of a religious service. It was objected that they would pollute the temple if they crossed swords in it, so they went outside and fought till both were killed.

An example of another kind of eccentric itinerant priest is furnished by Ikkyū [1] (1394–1481), said to have been a son of the Emperor Go-Komatsu. In his youth he entered the Zen monastery of Daitoku-ji in Kyōto, of which he became Superior, and won renown as a poet and painter. He is more celebrated, however, as the hero of innumerable anecdotes which represent him as a wandering monk, eccentric and apparently contemptuous of holy things, but really a profound philosopher. He is said to have died advising his disciples to eat fish and live long enjoying themselves.

The fifteenth century was also important for the history of the Shinshū. I have already mentioned the trouble occasioned by the section called Akunin Shōki or Evil doers whose faith is right. The disappearance of such abuses was probably due in great measure to Rennyo Shōnin [2] (1415–1499), whose influence on his sect was so great that he was styled its second founder. He was the son of the head of the Hongwanji temple in Kyōto, and on the death of his father succeeded him as eighth hereditary abbot in 1457 and rendered himself conspicuous by his reforming energy and his literary work. He was favoured by the Emperor Go Hanazono who restored his temple. But this aroused the jealousy of the monks of Hieizan, who in 1465 made a sudden attack on his residence and burnt the building to the ground, he himself barely escaping with his life and carrying with him the image of Shinran. He spent many years as an itinerant preacher and at last settled in 1471 at Yoshizaki in Echizen, where crowds flocked to hear his eloquence in the temple which he built for himself. It was here that he began to write his Ofumi or Epistles. But again he was the victim of jealousy and this time at the hands of a subdivision of his own sect. The priests of the Senshūji, belonging to what was called the Takada-ha, attacked and burnt his temple in 1474 and he again took to a wandering life. In 1480 he obtained permission to rebuild the Hongwanji, which had been burnt by the priests of Hieizan, and transferred the site to Yamashina. But a wandering life had become part of his nature. He handed over the management of the new temple to his

[1] 一休. [2] 蓮如上人.

successor and began another missionary tour, which was only ended by his death at Ōsaka at the age of eighty-four.

In spite of the attacks made upon him by the priests of Senshūji, Rennyo's preaching greatly contributed to strengthen the cause of the Shinshū in Echizen and the neighbouring provinces, where it became not only a spiritual but a political force of considerable importance. The end of the fifteenth and beginning of the sixteenth century in these regions is known by the name of Ikkōto no ran,[1] or the wars of the Ikkō sect, in which the priests made war on the Daimyōs and seized a great number of estates. Kaga was distracted by a quarrel between two branches of the Togashi family, the hereditary chiefs of the province, each supported by a branch of the Shinshū. Finally, Togashi Masachika was besieged by his priestly enemies and escaped to Etchū, where he committed suicide and the power of his family collapsed. The clergy came out best in the quarrel and remained as practical rulers of Kaga until they were driven out by Nobunaga in 1576.

Though the history of the Shinshū often reads like the annals of a fighting clan or feudal house, yet religious activity and development were not lacking. Rennyo wrote a number of Ofumi[2] or letters, arranged after his death in five parts, which are venerated like the Epistles of St. Paul and still read in the services of the sect. He also wrote about 1460 a sort of Creed called Ryōgemon.[3] The weakness of Shinran's teaching lay in its ethical side. It seemed to say that all that is necessary is to invoke the mercy of Amida, and although Shinran protested against the interpretation which made his words mean that moral conduct is a matter of indifference, the existence of the Akunin Shōki was a sufficient proof that there was a real danger of such an inference being drawn. Rennyo accordingly, who had practical experience of such extremists, laid great stress on the necessity of discharging one's moral duties and of living as a good citizen. The last article of his creed deals with this obligation, and he appears to have been effectual in putting a stop to all theories within the sect which were tantamount to a repudiation of the moral law. He insisted that unless the thought and mind were sound, no lip-service was of any avail. It was

[1] 一向徒亂. Ikkō means single-minded.

[2] 御文.

[3] Translated in Haas's book *Amida Buddha unsere Zuflucht*, p. 142. It is now called Ryoge-mon by the Western and Kaige-mon by the Eastern Hongwanji. See also Anesaki, *History of Japanese Religion*, p. 231.

essential to put one's whole faith and trust in Amida and that implies a pure heart and an absence of selfish striving.

Rennyo's teaching about Ryōbu-Shintō was also important.[1] He held that since the Shintō deities are really Buddhas and since all Buddhas are comprised in Amida, therefore the worship of Amida is sufficient and includes in itself the worship of all other deities. Although the members of the Shinshū declare that in worshipping Amida they honour the national deities, it is clear that absorption of this kind amounts to ignoring and even rejecting all other cults, and the practical result of Rennyo's arguments has been that the Shinshū have for their family worship only an altar to Amida and reject all other images and symbols.

At this same period Shinzei (1443–1495) founded a new sect which still bears his name and is justly reckoned as a subdivision of the Tendai rather than of the Jōdo or Shinshū. He enjoined the repetition of the Nembutsu, but taught that it should be combined with the observance of all the ordinary Buddhist Code.

About this time, or somewhat later, there arose among the Shinshū a secret sect called Hiji Monto, apparently organized as a protest against the autocratic administration of the Hongwanji at Kyōto. From Jesuit records quoted by Léon Pagès it seems that they had some influence in the sixteenth century, but I have been unable to find out anything about their origin, their tenets, or their practices, except that they still exist and keep their secret.[2]

After Yoshimitsu the Ashikagas quickly deteriorated, though they did not collapse for some time. The Shōguns became feeble and dissolute, often minors and mere puppets in the hands of their Chief Minister or Kwanryō, a post for which the powerful families of Hosokawa and Ōuchi fought and struggled. The confusion was incredible. At one time there were five rival Shōguns living, most of them minors and tools in the hands of contending factions. Of the last six Shōguns five died in exile and one committed suicide. Anarchy prevailed, the only effective power being in the hands of the great Barons who were constantly at war with one another. Social conditions became changed. The old feudalism had been based on the service owed to a chief by those who held land from him: now chiefs began to take into their service landless men and to maintain private armies of mercenaries, debtors, and adventurers.

[1] It is said to have been anticipated by Zonkaku (1290–1373), but Rennyo appears to have made it popular.

[2] Anesaki, *History of Japanese Religion*, pp. 232 and 305.

The oppressed and degraded populace constantly broke out into riots. Owing to internal dissensions and land troubles the ancient noble houses had lost their pre-eminence, and upstart families led by some capable chief became lords of large territories.

This explains one feature of the eventful interval between the Ashikaga and the Tokugawa periods, namely, the almost simultaneous rise of three great men, Nobunaga (1534–1582), Hideyoshi (1536–1598), and Ieyasu (1542–1616), who, starting with little except their talents, became one after another masters of their country. The other feature is the arrival of the Portuguese and of Christianity. This event would have been momentous at any time, but both its immediate effect and the subsequent reaction were unusually violent because hereditary authority and tradition were at their weakest and the *de facto* rulers of the country had the power and energy to do whatever their varying interests and policies dictated.

I have not space to discuss here the political parties of this period nor the fortunes of Christianity in Japan, and must be content to say that politically Nobunaga and Hideyoshi prepared the way for Ieyasu. A well-known caricature represents them as grinding flour and baking whereas he eats the cake. Equally apt as an illustration of their methods is the story which tells how they tried to make a nightingale sing. Nobunaga said "If you don't sing, I'll wring your neck"; Hideyoshi, "If you don't sing, I'll make you"; but Ieyasu, "If you don't sing, I'll wait till you do." Nobunaga, though he had little constructive genius, brought a considerable extent of territory under his sway and thus left to his successor the possibility of a united Japan. Hideyoshi made this possibility a fact, but instead of consolidating the state thus formed he dreamed of conquering China and died in the midst of his preparations. It was left for Ieyasu to create a dynasty and institutions which lasted more than two centuries and a half.

Nobunaga was an enemy of Buddhism: he feared the power of the great monasteries and in his early days they sided with his enemies. He therefore from purely political motives favoured Christianity. Hideyoshi at first followed the same policy, but subsequently believing that the Catholic missionaries had political designs suppressed them and their creed. The first persecution was followed by a lull, but Ieyasu and his successor Iemitsu renewed it in an effective form and Christianity was practically exterminated in Japan, though it is said that in 1858, when the country was thrown open again to foreign intercourse, Roman Catholic priests found Christians in considerable numbers in Kyūshū and even in Sado who had maintained their worship in secret.

The story of Christianity in Japan at this period is interesting, but I cannot discuss it here, for the most striking point about it is for our purpose purely negative. Whatever influence Christianity may have had in the Meiji era, it appears that the Catholicism which the Portuguese attempted to introduce in the sixteenth century had not the smallest effect on the doctrines or ideals of any Buddhist sect. The ardour of controversy may perhaps have stimulated the interest in purely religious issues and awakened certain sects which had become too engrossed in politics, but no instance is quoted of Buddhism being affected by Catholic dogma. Many writers have shown great ingenuity in attempting to discover analogies (often imaginary) between certain aspects of Buddhism and Christianity and to find traces of Manichæan, Nestorian, and Gnostic influence, but no one, so far as I am aware, has even attempted to produce a particle of evidence indicating that the contact of the two religions in the sixteenth century, though undoubted, occasioned the least change in Buddhism. This should surely make one cautious in assuming that the association of Buddhist priests with a few Nestorian priests in China can have seriously modified Buddhist beliefs.

During all the latter half of the sixteenth century Buddhism was an important force in Japan, but, strange to say, more conspicuous as a military and political force than in its proper sphere. The principal monasteries appear on the scene from time to time in exactly the same way as the great military houses with armies and forts of their own, with territorial ambitions and designs to crush or annex their rivals. But the same period witnessed the end of this system and the definite defeat of the Church Militant. There was evidently a danger that the country might be ruled by priests like Tibet. The leaders of Japan forestalled this danger, but were careful to avoid anything like a war against religion as such, which, indeed, was not difficult since the whole trouble arose from the great temples behaving not as if they were religious centres but as if they were military or feudal institutions.

Hieizan was the first to suffer. It paid dearly for its participation in politics, for it joined the enemies of Nobunaga and was almost annihilated by him in revenge. The enmity between Nobunaga and the Buddhists is no credit to the latter, for at bottom its origin was that the great monasteries could terrorize the feeble governments of the Emperor and Shōgun but were kept in order by a vigorous military despotism. In 1570 Nobunaga's rule in Kyōto was exposed to a double danger. The Miyoshi family in conjunction with the Shinshū priests of Ōsaka threatened the city, and while Nobunaga was dealing with them his old enemies the nobles of Echizeṇ and Ōmi planned another attack on him with the help of Hieizan. Nobunaga forced his lay enemies to surrender and next year dealt out retribution to the ecclesiastics. It was said that there were then 3,000 monasteries on the holy mountain: all were destroyed and most of their inmates, who must have numbered many thousands, were massacred, the remainder being banished. Ieyasu rebuilt some of the temples, but the number was limited to 125 and the monasteries never regained their political power.

Another of the older sects, the Shingon, also brought vengeance on itself at the hands not of Nobunaga but of Hideyoshi, thus making it clear that the severity shown to these turbulent monks was not the result of religious animosity. The original Shingon monastery of Koyasan had an offshoot—or rival—founded by Kakuhan in 1130 in the province of Kii which became extremely powerful. It owned 2,700 temples and a large army of mercenaries: it was partly responsible for the introduction of firearms into Japan, and the Jesuit Vilela compared its constitution with that of the Knights of Rhodes. In 1561–2 it offered formidable opposition to the forces of the Shōgun. In 1584, when Hideyoshi was beginning the construction of his great castle at Ōsaka, no less than 15,000 monks from Negoro are said to have marched against the town. They were routed by his generals who killed 4,000, and the peasantry clubbed large numbers of the fugitives—a proof that these military abbeys were not popular. Hideyoshi completed the reduction of Negoro in person next year. He abstained from wholesale carnage, but it is significant that by capturing the monastery he obtained the whole of the rich province of Kii.

In the latter part of the sixteenth century the Shinshū becomes conspicuous. As I have already mentioned, its protestant and popular theology did not include any objection to the temporal power of the Church, and since it did not require celibacy its hereditary abbots were even more like feudal barons than those of other sects. In 1532 the Nichiren drove the Shinshū out of their headquarters at Yamashina, near Kyōto, and burnt their edifices. Though their influence in the capital temporarily waned, they had a brilliant career in the provinces. They acquired extensive estates in Echizen, Kwantō, and elsewhere and became feudal lords of Kaga. As early as 1475 they built a fortified temple at Kanazawa, the capital of this province, and held it till they were ejected by Nobunaga one hundred years later. In 1532, after being driven out of Kyōto, they built at Ōsaka a great castle or fortress which enclosed their principal temple. Nobunaga had been able to drive them out of Kaga, but in this stronghold Kennyo Shōnin,[1] the eleventh abbot and a most competent soldier, was able to defy him for about ten years. At last Nobunaga besieged the castle with 60,000 men. Kennyo escaped in 1580 and, as both besiegers and besieged were coming to the end of their strength, they accepted the intervention of the Emperor, who evidently considered this prolonged war with a religious body to be a public scandal. It was agreed that the priests should surrender the fortress in return for estates elsewhere, but before they left they burned all the buildings, leaving nothing for the besiegers. The temple, or rather the see, was transferred to Nakajima in Settsu and subsequently to Kyōto in 1601. Kennyo had to surrender his title in favour of his son, but remained a personage of political importance. In 1587 he was utilized by Hideyoshi, who found it difficult to obtain information about what was going on among the Christians in Satsuma. Kennyo visited the district, nominally for the purpose of inspecting Buddhist establishments, but really as Hideyoshi's emissary, and by facilitating the subsequent campaign materially contributed to the extirpation of Christianity. Subsequently the population took vengeance on the Shinshū monks for what they considered their treachery and the local authorities endeavoured to suppress the sect. It may be that it was in return for these services of Kennyo that in 1591 the Shinshū were allowed to build a great temple in Kyōto where their influence had been small since their expulsion by the Nichirenites sixty years before.

The persecutions of Christianity form an interesting chapter in the religious history of Japan. The first began in 1587, the second and more rigorous in 1616. After what has been said about the turbulent spirit of the Buddhist monasteries the reader will not expect to hear that they imitated the tolerance of Gotama in dealing with error. In fact they were not much more humane than the contemporary

[1] 顯如上人. See Murdoch (*History of Japan*, ii, p. 23 and elsewhere), who thinks that the Buddhist priesthood was the greatest political power in Japan at this period and that Kennyo aspired to be a Pope or Grand Lama.

Christian sects of Europe. My knowledge of the doings of these latter does not permit me to make a comparison of the inquisitions established by Japanese Shōguns and by European princes, but the following points may be mentioned. First, the reasons for the persecution of Christianity were entirely political. The rulers of Japan wished to be tolerant in matters of belief and had always shown themselves so in the past, but they thought, and with justice, that Christianity as introduced was not merely a belief but political intrigue in disguise. Secondly, the Christians had themselves set the example of violence. They attacked with intolerable presumption the Buddhist religion and spared no pains to vilify its doctrines and the character of its priests. When the nobles of Kyūshū took a fancy to Christianity, it was propagated there with the same violence afterwards used to suppress it. Thirdly, the Government made use of Buddhist priests to detect Christianity and certify to orthodoxy. The priests would have been superhuman in gentleness had they not given a helping hand to the measures directed against their wanton aggressors, but I have not found any proof that they instigated and superintended the work of inquisition and execution in the same direct way as the Catholic Church in Europe.

# CHAPTER XIII

## TOKUGAWA PERIOD: CRYSTALLIZATION OF THE CHURCH

In 1603 Ieyasu founded the Tokugawa Shogunate which lasted until 1868. The isolation of Japan during this period (though not until Ieyasu had ceased to rule) is well-known. Japanese were forbidden to leave the country and foreigners to enter it, and these rigorous proscriptions were surprisingly well observed. Isolation was nothing new to the Japanese and this long period of peace and seclusion was of value, for without it they would hardly have been able to preserve their individuality when subsequently invaded by the horrors of European and American civilization. At first it was also a healthy change for Buddhism after the irreligious militarism of the previous century. We hear no more of monastic and priestly troops. The strongholds of Hieizan, Ōsaka, and Negoro had been destroyed. The monasteries of the first mentioned were restored by Ieyasu but as comparatively modest and unfortified buildings. So, too, the Hongwanji temple erected by the Shinshū at Kyōto after their castle at Ōsaka had been burned, though magnificent, was a purely ecclesiastical foundation. But subsequently in the eighteenth and nineteenth centuries Buddhism sank into a torpid condition, from which it was only awakened by the somewhat active measures taken against it in 1868.

Ieyasu came of a family which belonged to the Jōdo sect, and several anecdotes relate that he was influenced by its doctrines. When defeated and pursued by Nobunaga in 1560, he retreated to the Daijuji temple in his native province of Mikawa. The abbot consoled and exhorted him: "How can one like you, brought up in a Jōdo family, behave like a coward?" said he, "Who can resist you, if you have the spirit of Amida with you? If a man is afraid of losing anything, he will certainly lose it, but if he is willing to give it up, he will gain it. So be willing to give up your life for the sake of your followers." Ieyasu took the abbot's blessing, followed his advice, attacked the pursuing army and utterly routed them. This shows that the Jōdo as well as Zen could inspire soldiers, but it must be admitted that it did not usually preach martial ardour, though the closely allied Shinshū produced an abundance of military heroes.

Another story relates that in his old age, when he was living in retirement near Shizuoka, Ieyasu was visited by the abbot of the Zōjōji temple at Yedo and confided to him his ambition to become a god and protect his country. The abbot replied that the way to attain his desire was to recite the Nembutsu and by the power of Amida become born as a Buddha in the Pure Land. Then he would be able to assume any form he might wish and bestow blessings on his descendants and the Japanese race. Ieyasu is said to have gladly accepted this advice and to have repeated the Nembutsu regularly till he died. Officially he was assumed to have attained his ambition, for the year after his decease the Emperor Go-Mizuno-O granted him the posthumous title of Tōshō Dai Gongen,[1] or the Great Manifestation of Divine Light from the East, Gongen being the name for a temporary manifestation of the Buddha, such as the abbot had described. Ieyasu is still spoken of as Gongen sama. He and his grandson Iemitsu are both buried in the magnificent mausolea at Nikkō which were originally Buddhist foundations, though now under Shintō management. Iemitsu's death was marked by the most unbuddhist ceremony of ten of his faithful retainers committing suicide in order to accompany him to the next world.

Ieyasu consistently favoured the Jōdo sect. Its official existence was duly recognized and many large temples were erected for its use. The Zōjōji temple at Yedo (Tōkyō) was transferred to its present position in Shiba Park and magnificently rebuilt. The Chion-in temple in Kyōto, which had formerly been a dependency of the Seiren-in, was also rebuilt with great splendour and was constituted the headquarters of the Jōdo sect, as the Nanzenji had previously been for the Zen. Further, in Yedo and the surrounding district eighteen Jōdo temples were constructed which under the direction of the Zōjōji paid especial attention to educating candidates for the priesthood. The learned priests Tenkai and Taku-an,[2] both of the Miura family, enjoyed Ieyasu's confidence and were frequently consulted on questions of policy. When Ieyasu erected the temples of Ueno, known as Tō-ei-zan [3] (or Hieizan of the East, suggesting

[1] 東照大權現.

[2] He is also celebrated in another way as having invented the Takuanzuke, a method of seasoning daikon or large radishes which is still called after him.

[3] 東叡山.

that they were the counterpart of the once powerful sacred mountain at Kyōto), Tenkai was named as Abbot and at the same time Superior of the great temples at Nikkō, thus holding an almost archiepiscopal position. Ieyasu also ordered him to superintend the reprinting of the Tripiṭaka, which took eighteen years (1633–1651) to complete. Another clerical intimate of Ieyasu was his secretary, Denchōrō, a Zen priest who was head of the Nanzenji and Konchi-in. He not only accompanied his master on all his campaigns but occasionally rendered military as well as secretarial services. After the battle of Mikata-ga-hara he presented three heads as trophies, and the Konchi-ji was consequently allowed to use three black stars as its armorial bearings. He was subsequently made superintendent of all the religious establishments of the Empire, Shintō as well as Buddhist.

But neither Ieyasu nor Iemitsu was single-minded in his piety and both used Buddhism as an instrument to assist them in working out their general policy. For instance, the abbots of the great monasteries in Yedo were often relatives of the Emperor and most of the imperial princes and princesses were obliged to become priests or nuns until the Shōgun Ienobu (1709–1712) relaxed the rule which practically forbade them to marry and found houses. They served as hostages for the good behaviour of the Imperial Court [1] and their celibacy reduced the numbers of the imperial family, which was thus drawn into the Buddhist fold, though later it was made the representative of Shintō and became almost anti-Buddhist. Again, Ieyasu was insistent in advising Hideyori, the young son of Hideyoshi and a possible rival, to spend on rebuilding the temple of Hōkōji money which might otherwise have been used for military purposes. Many disasters overtook this edifice and finally Ieyasu picked a quarrel with Hideyori about the inscription which he had placed on a colossal bell destined to be its chief ornament. This pretext led to the conflict in which Hideyori perished, but the real cause of the quarrel was clearly political.

Ieyasu also seized an opportunity which presented itself of dividing the strength of the Shinshū. It is clear that at the end of the sixteenth century the rulers of Japan, however anxious they might

[1] The idea was that a Prince Abbot might be proclaimed Emperor if necessary. Thus in 1868 the last supporters of the Shogunate carried off to the north Prince Kitashirakawa, head of the temples of Ueno and Nikkō, with the design of setting him up as Emperor. He subsequently gave up his orders.

be to utilize Buddhism against Christianity, feared its political power. Though Nobunaga had destroyed the military and political importance of Hieizan and Hideyoshi had crushed Negoro, the Shinshū remained very strong and the net result of Kennyo's complicated dealings with several Governments was that a magnificent Hongwanji temple was re-erected in Tōkyō in 1591 to replace the edifice burnt by the Nichirenites nearly sixty years before. Kennyo had three sons of whom the eldest, Kōjū, became abbot of the new temple. He had to retire in three years in favour of his youngest brother Kōchō but did not abandon his pretensions. Ieyasu seized this opportunity to divide the sect by promoting the building of a second or Eastern Hongwanji (in contradistinction to the older or Western establishment) and Kōjū was made abbot of it. The sect was thus divided for financial and administrative purposes and the division restrained its political activity. But in other respects it did not suffer.[1]

The legacy of Ieyasu, although a spurious document and considerably later than the Shōgun whose name it bears, probably gives a fairly correct picture of his ideas and principles. It contains several references to Buddhism besides that which I have quoted above.[2] It deprecates religious disputes and promises toleration to all except Christians, described as the "false and corrupt school" (chap. 31). It alludes to the title to be borne by temples and to the Tōeizan at Ueno [3] (chap. 29), and contains an interesting expression of gratitude (chap. 28) in which Ieyasu is made to speak of the many dangers that he has undergone in war and the eighteen escapes that he has had from death. "On this account," he continues, "I have founded eighteen temples [4] at Yedo as a thank-offering. Let my posterity ever belong to the honoured sect of Jōdo."

Iemitsu, the third Tokugawa Shōgun, was perhaps the most effective champion who ever supported the Buddhist cause, for it was mainly to him that the proscription of Christianity was due and he was also a builder of temples. On the other hand, being (apart from Christianity) of liberal views, he gave effective

[1] The temples of the two divisions are distinguished by their architecture. Those of the Western branch have one roof only, those of the Eastern two, one above the other.

[2] Chap. VI, p. 193.

[3] This is one of the passages which prove that the legacy, as we have it, is spurious, for Tōeizan was not built until sixteen years after the death of Ieyasu.

[4] Danrin, literally sandal groves, a metaphorical expression for temples.

encouragement to Confucianism and also proscribed the extreme militant division of the Nichiren sect known as Fuju-fuze.

Tsunayoshi, the fifth Tokugawa Shōgun, was the only one of the family who could be called a fanatical Buddhist. His devotion was due to the loss of his son and his inability to obtain another heir. The most elaborate and costly ceremonies were performed in the hope of bringing him male offspring, but in vain. In order to explain this want of result, Ryūkō, a priest who enjoyed the Shōgun's confidence, hit upon the idea that in previous births he had been guilty of bloodshed, which might, however, be expiated by special regard for animal life, in particular the life of dogs, His Highness having been born in the year of the dog.[1] The taking of life was accordingly made punishable with extreme rigour, and not only dogs but all animals were protected, for a Court page was beheaded for killing a bird. His many laws for the protection of birds and beasts made the populace call him the Shōgun of Dogs[2] and his successors took warning by his unpopularity, for we hear no more of extreme religious legislation. Nevertheless, Tsunayoshi was not in other respects a bigot. He was a patron of Confucianism, and it was on his initiative that the Shintō festivals called Daijō-e and Kamo-sai, which had long fallen into neglect, were revived.

The position of Buddhism under the Tokugawa regime was defined by the decree of 1614. The preamble of this strongly anti-Christian document[3] is in other respects remarkably tolerant, for it identifies Shintoism with Buddhism. "Japan is called the land of Buddha," it says, "and not without reason. . . . God and Buddha differ in name but their meaning is the same. . . . Japan is the country of gods and of Buddha. It honours God and reveres Buddha." It also quotes with approval Chinese speculations about the positive and negative principles and bestows a high encomium on the Lotus-sûtra. But when it proceeds to lay down rules for conduct—that is, for avoiding punishment—orthodoxy is defined as attending the Buddhist temple of the parish where a person resides, to whatever sect that temple may belong.[4] Every one is to receive a certificate from the parish temple and to be entered in its register: every one

[1] The eleventh year in the old cyclical system.

[2] 犬公方.

[3] See *T.A.S.J.*, VI, i, 1878, p. 47.

[4] The decree is expressly directed against Christians, the Fujufuze branch of the Nichiren sect, and the Hiden, who are said to be three branches of the same sect. For conjectures as to the meaning of Hiden see *Tr. As. Soc. Jap.*, VI, i, 47.

is to be buried according to its rites. Should any desire be expressed to perform funeral or ancestral ceremonies according to the ritual of another sect, the officials concerned are charged to make strict inquiry. Parishioners are to attend the parish temple on the anniversary of the Buddha's death, certain other days, and the days of their ancestors' deaths on pain of forfeiting their certificates. On the last-named days they are also to receive the visit of the parish Buddhist priest. It will be seen that the result of this decree was to crystallize the Buddhist Church as it was in 1614 and render any new development in religion a political misdemeanour. The legal status thus accorded to all Buddhist temples preserved in name sects which might otherwise have disappeared, but this apparently favourable legislation was really dangerous, for though an excellent preservative, it was not vivifying.

Buddhism was also favoured by the prosperity of the merchant class, whose solid and generous piety often helped it. There was an old connection between religion and trade guilds, which often held their festivals in temple grounds. The prohibition of foreign trade did not greatly affect existing commercial interests. It stopped the growth of new wants and the creation of new industries, but internal commerce offered steady profits and the merchants did not feel the loss of ventures which they had scarcely tried. On the other hand, the temper of the Samurai, who in this period come forward as the characteristic national type, was not Buddhist. They might be duly registered in their parish temples but many of their principles, such as the disregard of human life, the obligation of revenge and, in some cases, of suicide, the extreme but not rare form of filial piety which held that it might be a daughter's duty to support her parents by prostitution, all this was against the letter and the spirit of the Buddha's law.

Thus during the Tokugawa period Buddhism was in most respects the established Church, but it had had some hard and salutary lessons. There were no more fortified monasteries and military monks: the clergy had to learn that their business was religion and not politics or fighting. They did produce a certain number of scholars and anchorites, but it must be confessed that the majority, being well provided for, lived in ease and inoffensive idleness to which the Government did not at all object, for who can tell what trouble may come out of a religious movement?

The Zen sect showed some vitality during this period in a discreet fashion. The priest Hakuin had so great a reputation that he was considered by the Rinzai school as its second founder and was also master of a vigorous and popular style which caused his sermons to be widely read. Bashō, too, the poet who brought into fashion the little poems of seventeen syllables called Hokku or Haikai, owed much to Zen. He was an official in the Waterworks Department of Yedo, but threw up his appointment and became a Zen monk, though he was no bigot but mingled Zen freely with Tendai and Taoist philosophy. Though the brevity and lightness of these tiny poems made them a fashionable craze, Bashō regarded his art quite seriously (which is the chief reason no doubt why his compositions were so much better than other people's) and as the expression of a spiritual mood. He warned his disciples that verse-making was not an amusement but almost a religious exercise, based on sympathy with nature.[1]

The only new sect which was founded in Tokugawa times was the Ōbaku branch [2] of the Zen introduced by the Chinese priest Ingen, who was invited to Japan in 1655. The ex-Emperor Go-Mizuno-o and the Shōgun Ietsuma received him most favourably and accepted his teaching. He was granted a piece of ground at Uji near Kyōto, where he erected a temple called Mampukuji or Ōbaku-san. The chief peculiarity of this sect is its markedly Chinese character. Ingen and the first thirteen of his successors were Chinese by race, and though the abbots are now Japanese, the architecture and all the appointments of the temple are still thoroughly Chinese in appearance. The monks wear Chinese caps and shoes and in reciting prayers they use the Ming pronunciation of Chinese, which differs from the ordinary Sino-Japanese of other sects. In 1681 a learned priest of the Mampukuji named Tetsugen published a reprint of the Ming edition of the Tripiṭaka, which is still remarkable for its admirably large and clear type and is perhaps the only edition of the Tripiṭaka which can be used without injury to the eyes.

One may suspect that the favour shown to the Ōbaku school in high quarters was due as much to its being intensely Chinese as to its being Buddhist. From the seventeenth century onwards two strong currents of opinion, important for religion and politics and neither of them friendly to Buddhism, make their appearance, namely, the Confucian current and the Shintō.

[1] Another clerical poet of some distinction in the Tokugawa period was Bengyoku of the Jōdo sect (1818–1880).

[2] 黃 檗, Chinese pronunciation Hwang-po. 萬 福 寺 Mampukuji. 隱 元 Ingen.

Admiration of Chinese learning was nothing new, but rarely had Confucianism received so much popular favour and so much patronage from Emperors and Shōguns. Ieyasu, though determined to banish Christianity as a danger to the nation, had no desire to stint the intellectual nourishment of his subjects. The exordium of the decree of 1614 indulges in Chinese philosophical speculations in a way which must have seemed unnecessary to a good Buddhist. Chinese culture had long been esteemed in Japan as a necessary part of the education of a gentleman: Confucianism had a great literature, sound ethics, and for ages had been in China the support and servant of a most durable empire. It therefore seemed an eminently suitable study for the educated classes in Japan; but perhaps in one way the subjects of the Tokugawa Shōguns learned more than their masters intended, for the Chinese doctrine that the people are the principal part of the State and that unsatisfactory rulers should be changed had undoubtedly something to do with the revolution which ended the Shogunate.[1]

The form of Confucianism most approved by the Government and consequently most studied was called Tei-shu,[2] which is a combination of the names of the brothers Ch'êng (in Japanese pronunciation Tei) and the celebrated philosopher Chu-Hsi (or Shushi, 1130–1200). The more modern school of Ō-Yō-Mei (Chinese Wang Yang Ming, 1472–1528) was looked at askance by the authorities, and such teachers as Nakae Tōju and Kumazawa got into trouble for advocating its principles. In Japan as in China Confucianism was somewhat contemptuous of Buddhism, although the Zen favoured Chinese learning.

Fujiwara Seikwa (1561–1619), the founder of the Teishu-gaku-ha, had become a Buddhist priest in order to study philosophy, but deliberately separated himself from Buddhism and was assisted by Ieyasu to found a school in which he taught Chinese philosophy. He had a celebrated pupil named Hayashi Dōshun or Razan who won the favour of Ieyasu and was appointed principal secretary and recorder of the actions of the Government. In this position he used all his influence against Buddhism and endeavoured to persuade Ieyasu to deprive priests of all power and prevent them from holding official positions. But that astute prince, who wished to preserve

[1] The school of Anzai is said to have had considerable influence on those who brought about the change of government. See Dening, "Confucian Philosophy" in *T.A.S.J.*, 1908, vol. XXXVI, ii, p. 140.

[2] 程朱.

both Buddhism and Confucianism, arranged that he should have a public dispute with Tenkai, the ablest Buddhist priest of his time, in which he did not get the best of it.

The Shōgun Tsunayoshi (1680–1709), who, in his insistence on the sanctity of animal life, seemed to be a fanatical Buddhist, was yet a most fervent admirer and patron of Confucianism. His Court had to listen to Confucian lectures and Chinese scholarship was made independent of the Buddhist hierarchy. Scholars were no longer required to shave their heads like priests, as had been the rule, but were allowed to let their hair grow long and to wear the swords of the Samurai. In 1795, during the minority of the Shōgun Ienari, Hayashi Jussai, an adopted grandson of the Razan mentioned above, persuaded the Government to issue an edict which required all candidates for government posts to subscribe to the principles of the Teishu school, the followers of Ō-Yō-Mei being excluded, and this edict had an important political effect in contributing to the unpopularity of the Shōgun's government.

Yet, in spite of all this official patronage, Confucianism never became a religion in Japan. Even in China, where its influence and authority are enormous, its neglect of emotional and speculative questions prevents it from covering the same ground as the European word religion, and in Japan of the Tokugawa period it had the further disadvantage of being foreign and imported. It hence came into collision with the other strong religious current of these times, namely, the revival of Shintō. Buddhism, it is true, was also a foreign religion, but it was an ancient importation and had undergone so many changes and developments that it might reasonably be called more Japanese than Chinese, whereas Confucianism of all schools meant simply the introduction of relatively modern Chinese ideas in their native dress.

The establishment of Shintō as the State religion in 1868 is an extraordinary phenomenon, but its causes were at least as much political as religious. The Tokugawa Shogunate met with less opposition than might have been expected, but its unpopularity with a certain section of its more intelligent subjects, those, for instance, who desired to make acquaintance with foreign learning, needs no explanation, and this unpopularity found comparatively safe expression in extolling native ideals at the expense of Buddhism and Confucianism. It was not easy to blame admiration for purely Japanese literature, history, and religion, particularly as the Tokugawa professed and to a great extent practised toleration of all beliefs except Christianity. Still, Confucianism and Buddhism received such strong official support that to blame them was little less than to blame the Government, and enthusiasm for Shintō was parlously near to enthusiasm for the Emperor, whom the Tokugawas wished to keep as a faint but venerable shadow. Yet the Shintō movement began in the Mito branch of the Tokugawa family. Mitsukuni (1628–1700), the head of this line, devoted himself to literary pursuits and founded a school of historians. His great work on the history of Japan in 243 volumes was not completed until 1715, after his death, but a considerable portion of it was published in 1697. Mitsukuni had no prejudice against Confucianism, for he gave a home to the exiled Chinese scholar Shu-Shunsui who collaborated with him in composing his history, but in literature and everything else he gave the preference to native Japanese products. The practical bearings of his studies on religion are shown by the fact that he destroyed a thousand Buddhist temples on his estates and that his literary assistants called themselves Samurai and let their hair grow long. This was before Tsunayoshi had given the permission mentioned above and in days when a shaven head and a clerical demeanour were still considered a mark of a man of letters.

The Shintō movement, which included an ultra-patriotic admiration of everything Japanese, became more conspicuous and more political in the eighteenth and nineteenth centuries. In Kyōto, Kada Azumamaru (1668–1736) opened a national school in opposition to fashionable Confucian ideas and appears to have enjoyed the favour of the Shōgun Yoshimune. His pupil was the celebrated Kamo Mabuchi (1697–1769), who was followed by the still more famous Motoori (1730–1801). Motoori published an edition of the Kojiki with an elaborate commentary, in which he advocated pure Shintō uncontaminated by either Buddhist or Confucian ideas. The work had considerable influence in turning popular opinion against both Buddhism and the Government of the Shōgun, yet it does not appear that any of the authors mentioned incurred official displeasure. But the works of their successor, Hirata, attracted the attention of the cautious or somnolent Shogunate. To praise Japan as the country of the Gods, superior to all other regions of the earth, was all very well, but things looked different when it was made clear that Japan's greatness came solely from the Emperor and not from the Shōgun. In 1836 the latter suppressed a book of Hirata's which had been warmly praised by the Emperor, and four years later the author was requested to cease writing and retire to his native town.

It will be noticed that during more than two centuries of anti-Buddhist attacks, no Buddhist champion came forward to defend the faith. Even politically the position of the Buddhists was not indefensible, for the many varieties of Ryōbu-Shintō offered them a whole arsenal of arguments, and in any comparison of the two systems as religions one would have imagined that Buddhism must win. But to the best of my belief no such refutation of the Shintoists was ever published, at any rate, none which had a tithe of the importance and influence of the works of Motoori or Hirata. In the early days of the Tokugawa period (1655) one new sect, the Ōbaku, which was practically Chinese, was founded: two editions of the Tripiṭaka were printed or rather reprinted by Tenkai (1651) and the Ōbaku monastery (1681). In the eighteenth and nineteenth centuries the level of scholarship seems to have been respectable. Books dealing with history, biography, and dogma were published, or more often ancient works were re-edited, but the annals of Buddhism contain no mention of movement, remarkable personalities, or of stirring events. In fact, the only incident mentioned by ordinary histories in which Buddhist priests played a part was a quarrel between sects in the regency of Ienari (1793–1841). The house of Tokugawa followed by tradition the Jōdo, but in this Shōgun's time one of his favourite concubines was a devout adherent of the Nichiren sect. Its priests were admitted to the palace and received numerous favours. After Ienari's death there was a reaction and the Nichiren priests not only lost their influence but were severely punished. But as a rule the phlegmatic apathy of the Buddhist clergy was not even disturbed by sectarian quarrels. They had comfortable emoluments, they supervised the registers of their various temples in which all the inhabitants of the parishes attached to them had to be entered, they performed religious services, and more especially they buried the dead, a form of public service which may be remunerative but is hardly likely to be enlivening or stimulating.

Thus at the time when the Shogunate collapsed and the Meiji era commenced Buddhism was at its weakest. It was identified with the regime that was passing away and had little more connection with the Court of the Emperor than with Western civilization. But it was at last awakened by the attacks directed against it. In 1855 it was proposed that all monastery bells should be converted into cannon. The decree was actually published, but the abbots of the Chion-in and the temples at Ueno, who were Imperial Princes, had sufficient power to cause it to be withdrawn. The reformers of 1868, however, were not to be stopped by any such clerical objections. They declared Shintō to be the State religion: Buddhism was disestablished and to a great extent disendowed: its emblems and ceremonies were no longer seen in the palace: Buddhist images and Buddhist clergy were removed from the Ryōbu-Shintō temples, which were handed over to Shintō priests: Buddhist priests were forbidden to ask for alms and were ordered to call themselves by their family names. If we are astonished at the torpor of Buddhism during the two preceding centuries, it must be admitted that it is a great testimony to its real strength that it did not decay after such a catastrophe and has to-day more vitality than Shintō. A little rough handling and persecution are an excellent tonic for religions.

From 1868 until 1875 the Government was openly hostile to Buddhism and endeavoured to inculcate a patriotic but otherwise colourless creed. Officials were appointed to propagate this system and a Ministry of Public Worship, which changed its name and powers several times, was created. In 1872 a commission of priests belonging to the Shinshū sect started to study the ecclesiastical organization of European States, and its return in 1875 seems to mark the turn of the tide. The Government conferred on Shinran the posthumous title of Kenshin Daishi (1876), or the Seer of Truth, and private interest in Buddhism was shown by the dispatch of missionaries to Shanghai and by the publication of the Tripitaka with accessory treatises in 1880–1884. This edition, which consisted of 8 534 volumes, was known as the Shukusatsu Zōkyō [1] and was due to the enterprise of a learned Buddhist called Bankan Shimada. A society called the Buddhist Patriotic Union was formed to oppose the progress of Christianity and was joined by many Conservatives who were Confucianists or Shintoists. Later, however, the opposite tendency asserted itself and Buddhists combined with Christians to oppose the secularists who wished to exclude religion from education and the national life.

In 1884 what remained of the Ministry of Public Worship was abolished, the administration of Buddhism and Shintō was entrusted to the heads of the various sects, and the direct control

[1] 縮刷藏經.

of the State over the Church thus ceased. The Constitution of 1889 granted liberty of religion to all and the restrictions placed on Buddhism were removed, but Shintō was made equally independent and the arrangement by which Buddhist priests controlled Shintō temples was not renewed. Though the subject does not concern us, it may be mentioned that many Japanese maintain that Shintō is not a religion in the ordinary sense but a system of national ethics in whose ceremonies persons of all creeds can properly take part.[1]

[1] See for a full discussion of modern Shintō the elaborate paper by Dr. Holtom called "The political philosophy of modern Shinto" in *Trans. As. Soc. Japan*, vol. xlix, part ii, 1922. See also, for a short statement of the recent official attitude towards religions, *Hōnen, the Buddhist Saint*, pp. 75, 76.

# BOOK III

# THE SECTS AND THEIR DOCTRINES

# CHAPTER XIV

## TENDAI

THE Tendai has a great record in both China and Japan, but its history in the two countries is somewhat different. In the first place, its connection with the Shingon was much closer in Japan than in the land of its birth, where the two sects were felt to be different in origin and not to be united by any special relationship. In Japan, on the contrary, they were both officially introduced at the same period, the first years of the ninth century, both under imperial patronage and both in the same district, Kyōto and its neighbourhood. They formed a natural body of religious opinion opposed in early times to the older sects of Nara and later to the new schools which arose about the twelfth century. But, in the second place, the Tendai achieved a position as a political and even as a military power such as never fell to the lot of any Buddhist denomination in China, for even Lamaism under the Yüan dynasty, though it became the Established Church, was strictly under imperial control, though it was not so in Tibet. But in Japan the Tendai, and to some extent the Shingon, were semi-independent organizations maintaining friendly relations with the Court, though fighting with one another and with other religious bodies—a fact by no means inconsistent with the close connection just mentioned, for one of the bitterest quarrels was between Enryakuji and Miidera, both temples of the Tendai sect. And just as a certain period in Japanese history is commonly known as the Fujiwara period, so for ecclesiastical purposes it may be appropriately designated as the Tendai period. We are inclined, and not wholly unjustly, to think of the Tendai as primarily a political power actuated by worldly motives and to forget that it was, especially in the beginning, a great Church inspired by lofty spiritual and philosophical ideals which seemed to the priesthood of Nara dangerously liberal.

Its introduction into Japan was closely connected with the removal of the capital from Nara to Kyōto in 793. One of the principal motives for this transference was the apprehension caused by the ambitious designs of the priesthood, which reached a climax in the attempt of Dōkyō to usurp the imperial power. A somewhat similar mistrust of the worldliness of the Church as established in Nara seems to have worked strongly on the mind of a young man called Saichō, the future Dengyō Daishi. He was of Chinese origin, and after entering a monastery at an early age was ordained when eighteen in 785. But the clerical life of Nara was uncongenial to him. He left the city and lived at first in solitude on Mount Hiei, near which he had been born, but gradually collected a band of companions and built a small monastery. But he was by no means an unpractical recluse and, though he had found the atmosphere of Nara unspiritual, he had no objection to mixing with Courts and Princes. Somehow or other the humble cloister on Mount Hiei became identified even during his lifetime with the new capital and was recognized as the new religious centre just as Kyōto was the new political centre of Japan. In 804 he was sent by the Emperor to China to inquire what was the best form of Buddhism, and studied the school of T'ien-T'ai [1] at its headquarters and also both the Shingon under Shun-Hsiao at Yüeh-Chou and the Zen at T'ang-Hsing. It is noticeable that these were the three important sects which had not taken root at Nara. He gave the palm to the Tendai which was then at the zenith of its power and fame, but evidently retained much sympathy for the other sects. He returned next year laden with books and knowledge. I have already given some account of the Tendai sect as it existed in China and have related in the historical section the striking growth of the humble shrine on Hieizan into a priestly city of some three thousand temples and its eventual tragic destruction by Nobunaga in 1571, and will now proceed to inquire what were the religious ideas which Saichō brought back with him and which dominated Japan for about five centuries. Though based on what he had learnt and seen in China, the doctrines and practices which he taught somehow acquired a distinctly Japanese flavour and, as in many other cases, hardly seem to be foreign importations.

The Tendai sect is based on the Hokke-kyō or Lotus-sûtra, and is perhaps the most notable instance among many others of the enormous influence which that work has exercised in the Far East. Conformably to this, it teaches that all men can become Buddhas and urges them to try to do so. Aspirants are exhorted in the often quoted words of the sacred text [2] to " enter the abode of the

[1] 天台, Japanese pronunciation Tendai.

[2] Lotus, chap. x, shortly before verse 16 (*S.B.E.*, xxi, p. 222).

Tathâgata, put on the robe of the Tathâgata and sit in the seat of the Tathâgata. And what is the abode of the Tathâgata? It is to abide in charity to all beings. And what is his robe? It is sublime forbearance. And what is his seat? It is to enter into the emptiness of all things". The Mahayanist Nirvâna-sûtra (Nanjio, 113, 114), as containing the last and complete instructions of the Buddha, and the Prajñâpâramitâ [1] are also much respected. But though it is based on the Lotus-sûtra, the most remarkable characteristic of the Tendai is its comprehensive and encyclopædic character. It finds a place for all scriptures, regarding them as a progressive revelation gradually disclosed by the Buddha during his life as he found that the intelligence of his auditors ripened, and though one may hesitate to accept the scheme as chronologically exact, one cannot but admire the wide knowledge and liberal spirit which inspired it. If it is sometimes difficult to define what were the special doctrines which it taught in Japan, this is because it was always eclectic and disposed to adopt rather than to combat new views unless they seemed to threaten the organization of the Church. The later sects, whether they were Japanese creations or adaptations of Chinese originals, all arose within the Tendai. Hōnen, Shinran, Eisai, Dōgen, Nichiren, and many lesser reformers were all students who had graduated in the same University, and their special doctrines mostly consisted in emphasizing some views which they had found in the spacious store. The religion taught in Hieizan was not a stagnant orthodoxy to which all must conform or be excommunicated. Its three thousand temples contained several schools which differed not indeed in essentials but in their method of presenting doctrines, and it was perfectly correct to study in more than one school. Thus Shōshien, who was considered a paragon of learning, was proficient in the doctrines of both the Eshin-in and the Danna-in and was also deeply read in esoteric works. The first two mentioned were the principal schools of Hieizan, founded by Eshin (942–1017) at the temple which bore his name in Yokaba and by Kaku-un (953–1007), abbot of the Danna-in temple in the Eastern section. There were also thirteen schools of the Yuga sammitsu, generally rendered as esoteric doctrine.

If Hieizan was a school of arms it was none the less a school of thought and also of art, and the ideal which inspired its abbots,

[1] The Tendai philosophy seems to be chiefly based not on this work itself but on Nâgârjuna's Śâstra or Commentary. Nanjio, 1169, called in Japanese Dai-Chi-Do-Ron 大智度論.

though perhaps dangerously ambitious, was not ignoble. They wished to found a national Church including all forms of religion, whether Buddhist or Shintō, and closely connected with the Emperor, who was regarded as the patron of all possible gods and sects. To further this end they for a long time identified themselves with the interests of the Fujiwara family, who were the Emperor's guardians. Secondly, Hieizan was a great school of art. From the tenth to the twelfth centuries, before the rise of the Zen sect, the religious painting and sculpture of Japan was inspired by the Tendai and Shingon. Perhaps the major part of the artistic impulse came from the latter and its cosmotheistic doctrines, its tendency to regard every natural phenomenon as a divine manifestation which could be appropriately represented by the image of a deity. But the spaciousness, the power, and the wealth of Hieizan made it unrivalled as a museum in which the works of either sect could be displayed to the nation.

The introduction of Shingon mysticism into the Tendai is generally attributed to Ennin, better known by his posthumous title of Jikaku Daishi,[1] who lived from 794 to 864. When about forty he became seriously ill, but an angel appeared to him in a dream and gave him a miraculous drug which completely cured him. He then made a copy of the Lotus-sûtra, and his rules for such transcription, which became a regular practice among the pious, were considered classical. In 838 he accompanied Fujiwara Tsunetsugu on an embassy to China, where he spent nine years. Like Saichō he studied the doctrines of the Tendai, Shingon, and Zen sects and also suffered much hardship during the persecution of Buddhism under the Emperor Wu-Tsung. On his return he wrote a voluminous account of his studies and was made head of the Tendai. The introduction of Shingon mysticism into the sect, which was continued by Annen (c. A.D. 890), was no doubt greatly facilitated by the fact that the Tendai already recognized Vairocana, the chief Buddha of the Shingon, as the Dharmakâya, Śâkyamuni as represented in the Lotus being the Nirmâṇakâya, or Buddha as seen by human eyes. Also the temporal interests of the Shingon did not collide much with those of the Tendai, its headquarters being at Kōyasan, some distance from the capital. For it is sad to confess that though the Tendai seemed so catholic and comprehensive, so ready to include in its large and liberal creed any doctrine which could be called Buddhist,

[1] 慈覺大師.

it was, when matters of organization and temple property were concerned, extremely apt to pick a quarrel, and that not only in the twelfth and thirteenth centuries but in the middle of the ninth. In 858 a priest called Enchin (posthumous title Chishō Daishi) returned from China and began to preach certain novelties which were not to the taste of the disciples of Jikaku. He was appointed head of the celebrated temple called Onjōji or Miidera [1] on the shores of Lake Biwa, and appears to have maintained a connection with Hieizan as long as he lived. But under his successors disputes became acute and resulted in the maintenance of troops and of literal warfare between the two establishments. In spite of many statements that the Sammon and Jimon, as the two parties were called, were divided by doctrinal differences, I have been unable to ascertain that any such distinctions are known at the present day.[2]

The Tendai was wide and comprehensive in another sense. It taught that all men ought to strive to become Buddhas and that it was in the power of all to succeed in so doing. This was contrary to the teaching of the Hossō, the ancient and then very powerful sect which possessed the great monasteries of Kōfukuji and Hōryūji at Nara. The Hossō held that human nature is not one and the same in all, but that mankind are divided into five classes.

1. The Mushō-ujō,[3] or those who have no Buddha nature at all, who cannot attain nirvâna but must wander for ever in the world of transmigration.

2. The Shōmonjō-jōshō, those who have the śrâvaka (Hînayâna) nature.

3. The Engakujō-jōshō, or those who have the Pratyeka-Buddha nature. Both of these classes are destined to attain nirvâna by meditation but not to become Buddhas.

4. The Bosatsujō-jōshō, or those who have the Bodhisattva nature and may become perfectly enlightened Buddhas.

5. The Fujō-Shūjō, or indeterminate natures, who still have the power of becoming Buddhas.

[1] 圓城寺 or 三井寺.

[2] The *Bulletin de la Maison Franco-Japonaise*, i, 1927, says that the Jimon recognizes as one of its fundamental texts the Shikikōen-Hokkegi Juketsushū 指歸講演法華儀授決集 of Enshin, which is apparently not accepted by the Sammon.

[3] The characters for the five classes are: (1) 無性有情. (2) 聲聞乘定性. (3) 緣覺乘定性. (4) 菩薩乘定性. (5) 不定種性.

It will be seen that not only the lowest natures but higher ones, Śrâvakas and Pratyeka-Buddhas, for whom religion consists chiefly in solitary meditation, are excluded from the possibility of becoming Buddhas, but Saichō would have none of this and gave practical expression to his views by establishing a Kaidan, or place of ordination, at Hieizan which somewhat modified the old ceremonial as practised at Nara. Candidates were supposed to take their vows not merely in the presence of their ecclesiastical superiors but before the Buddha himself, and thereby to awaken the higher part of their nature, which would develop and bear fruit in a long series of future lives. This theory was apparently most distasteful to the prelates of the older school: they protested against the establishment of the new Kaidan and it did not receive the imperial sanction until after Saichō's death.

But though the Tendai deserves all credit for introducing new, fruitful, and more spiritual ideas into Japanese Buddhism, I doubt if its disputes with Nara should be regarded as a contest between the democratic and aristocratic sides of religion. For the Hossō was not the only sect in the old capital, and the Kegon, which owned the great temple of Tōdaiji, holds and apparently then held the thesis that all men can aspire to Buddhahood as strongly as the Tendai did. And, again, Hōnen was not satisfied with the Tendai's view of human destinies any more than with the Hossō's. It is true that he wrote in the latter part of the twelfth century and had many other complaints which made him separate from the Tendai. He says,[1] "According to the Tendai sect the ordinary man may be born into the so-called Pure Land, but that land is conceived of as a very inferior place. Although the Hossō conceived of it as a very superior place, they did not allow that the common man could be born there at all." In Hōnen's time, at any rate, the Tendai conceived that there were four lands of the blessed, the lowest of which, or the Bonjō-zōgodo,[2] corresponded to Hōnen's Pure Land, while the Hossō reckoned three and made the Pure Land correspond to the middle one.

The Tendai is both a religion and philosophy. One can imagine that the latter aspect—its ontology or theory of being—though well worthy of attention, was somewhat in the background among the politicians and military men who formed so large a proportion of the sect during a long period of its history. But it is not easy

[1] *Hōnen, the Buddhist Saint*, pp. 188 and 198.

[2] 凡聖雜居土.

to describe what are its doctrines as a popular religion, which it undoubtedly was. Even now its numbers are not inconsiderable, for it is reckoned to possess nearly 5,000 temples and a little under two million members. Owing to its comprehensive character already alluded to, the difficulty is to say what Buddhist beliefs it does not countenance. It had, for instance, no objection to the worship of Amida. Chih-K'ai, the founder of the sect in China, died repeating his name, and in Japan Dengyō Daishi himself, Jikaku, Genshin, Ryōnin, and other eminent names can be cited as his worshippers. If Hieizan persecuted Hōnen and Shinran, the only objection to the doctrine of these two was that it held that the invocation of Amida's name was all sufficient and that other observances were superfluous, which threw into confusion all ecclesiastical organization.

The Tendai held the ordinary Mahâyâna doctrine that the Buddha nature is present in every human being and that it can and ought to be stimulated and developed until each one becomes a Bodhisattva and ultimately a Buddha. Theoretically fifty-two stages had to be passed through before perfect enlightenment could be obtained, namely, ten stages of faith, ten of knowledge, twenty of religious practice, and ten of understanding ultimate truth. The two further stages were called tō-gaku and myō-kaku,[1] meaning similar and wonderful enlightenment, that is to say, the last is the supreme conclusion and the proceeding stage almost equal to it. Persons of great eminence might be considered to have already merited the title of Bodhisattva or to be incarnate Bodhisattvas who have deigned to take flesh for the salvation of mankind. But as a rule such attainments were postponed indefinitely to future lives, though perhaps the politeness of the Japanese made them somewhat free of speaking of the living as Bodhisattvas and the dead as Buddhas. It would seem that Dengyō Daishi gave up the 250 precepts of the Hînayâna, and that the initiation performed at the Kaidan of Hieizan and the vows duly taken in the presence of the Buddha were regarded as constituting not merely ordination in the simple ecclesiastical sense but an awakening of the dormant Buddha nature, a bracing of the spirit to a nobler moral life, a planting of the feet on the first rung of the lofty ladder which leads to higher existences.

With this ceremony and its object was perhaps connected another

[1] 等覺, 妙覺.

called Kwanchō [1] (or Kwanjō), a translation of the Sanskrit Abhiśekha, or sprinkling,[2] sometimes rendered in English by the most misleading expression baptism. It is true that part of the ceremony generally consists in the religious aspersion by water, but it is not at all a rite performed on children or others when they first become members of the sect, but a form of initiation into the higher mysteries granted only as an exceptional privilege. It might also be doubted whether Kwanjō should not be classed among the mysteries of the Shingon sect which were accepted by the Tendai soon after its introduction into Japan, but it is expressly stated that Saichō was instructed in it by Shun-Hsiao and administered it for the first time in Japan in the temple of Seiryūji at Takao in 805 to various distinguished priests selected by imperial order. Kōbō Daishi, on the other hand, received it from Hui-Kuo, a disciple of the celebrated Pu-K'ung (Amogha), and administered it first in 822 to the ex-Emperor Heijō.[3] At present it is performed by both sects, more frequently perhaps by the Shingon, and also by the Kegon in the Tōdaiji temple at Nara. The original object of the rite is succinctly defined by Kōbō Daishi,[4] who says, "By Kwanjō is meant the bestowal of the Buddha's great mercy upon sentient beings to enable them to obtain the highest perfect enlightenment." As a matter of fact, the sprinkling with water does not appear to be the most prominent part of the ceremony as at present performed. The candidates are arranged in order and as a preliminary ceremony their heads are sprinkled with water. They are then consecrated by the use of various formulæ and, their faces being covered with red veils, are led blindfolded to a *mandara*, or sacred picture containing representations of numerous Buddhas and Bodhisattvas which is set on a raised dais against a wall or spread on the floor. Each candidate receives a flower which he throws or drops on the mandara in the presence of eight priests, who declare the name of the figure

[1] 灌頂. A full account of this ceremony as it used to be performed will be found illustrated with plates in the first volume of the Asoba-jō, composed by Shōchō, a contemporary of Nichiren. It is reprinted in the Dai Nippon Bukkyō Zensho.

[2] For the metaphorical use of the word see Dīg. Nik., xvi, 5, 30: "Fortunate are ye who have been sprinkled with the sprinkling of discipleship in the presence of the master."

[3] Bunyiu Nanjio, *Short History of the Twelve Japanese Buddhist Sects*, p. 75. *Hōnen, the Buddhist Saint*, p. 175.

[4] Hizōki, cap. lix.

which he has struck, and a name corresponding to this figure is then bestowed on him. The most auspicious result is for the flower to strike the figure of the Buddha Vairocana. The fortunate candidate is congratulated by the priests and receives special honours, being made to sit on a Lotus seat that is, a cushion on which a lotus is embroidered. This form of Kwanjō is sometimes required as a sort of initiation, for instance, at Miidera, before persons are allowed to see a specially sacred image, and I am informed that in such cases there is no sprinkling, though a person who had undergone the ceremony told me that as he was blindfolded he was not quite sure. Another form of initiation without sprinkling is called Hako-Kan and consists in receiving reverently by placing it on one's head a box containing a copy of the precepts.

Since the Tendai is based on the Lotus-sûtra, it naturally specially reverences Śâkyamuni and in fact regards all other Buddhas as aspects of him. But since it also endeavoured to be an all-embracing State church, which included even Shintō deities, it is not surprising to find that it accorded full recognition to Vairocana,[1] Amida, Yakushi, and in fact all Buddhas[2] and Bodhisattvas. No doubt the tendency towards a friendly amalgamation with the Shingon did much to make the worship of Vairocana popular, but independently of this he was recognized as the Dharmakâya. As the Dharmakâya is the highest form of Buddhahood, so is Vairocana, in so far as he is a personification of it, superior to Shaka, but it must be understood that he is not regarded as a separate being but merely as a higher aspect. Shaka, inasmuch as he is the Nirmâṇakâya, is a condescension and concession to the weakness of the human intellect which is often unable to understand the Dharmakâya. Four paradises are recognized which are conditioned by the character of their inhabitants, that is to say, that where beings of a certain character are found, there is *ipso facto* the paradise of which they are worthy. These four paradises are :—

[1] I confess that Nanjio's account in his Twelve Sects of the "Action of Vairocana" is completely unintelligible to me.

[2] Besides the Buddhas ordinarily known, the Tendai has also six peculiar to itself (called Roku Soku Butsu 六即佛) who correspond to and preside over six stages of enlightenment. They are merely aspects of the one Buddha and are called Risoku, Myōjisoku, Kangyōsoku, Sōjisoku, Bunshinsoku, and Kugyōsoku Buddhas. 理即, 名字即, 觀行即, 相似即, 分眞即, 究竟即.

1. The Bonjōzōgodo,[1] or the land in which ordinary men and saints live together. The Pure Land of Amida is such a paradise.

2. The Hōben-uyodo, a region of compromise inhabited by those who have become free from saṃsâra and have attained nirvâna in the sense of the Hînayâna but not in the higher senses of the Mahâyâna.

3. Jippōdo, or paradise in which are the Sambhogakâya and Bodhisattvas who have become partly free from ignorance concerning the nature of Being.

4. Jōjakkōdo, or the Land of Eternal Peace and Light, inhabited by Vairocana and those Bodhisattvas who have entirely got rid of ignorance.

Naturally, so important and popular a deity as Amida was not neglected, and the growth of the Jōdo and Jōdo-Shinshū shows how a whole series of doctors prepared the way for Hōnen and Shinran. The Jōgyōdō hall on Mount Hiei, though there are differences in the account of its original construction, was used after the time of Jikaku for services which he had introduced from China and in which the Nembutsu was sung with a musical intonation. I have not found any explanation of the exact position assigned to Amida among the Buddhas of the Tendai, but such problems appear to have offered no difficulties to the Japanese. For instance, Kakuhan (1095–1143), the founder of a new division in the Shingon, simply declared that Amida was the same as Vairocana.

It is noticeable, however, that the Tendai seem to have considered meditation on the mystery of existence which leads to enlightenment as a necessary part of worship, and to have regarded the Nembutsu as a means of clearing the mind and enabling it to concentrate itself in the presence of Amida. Four kinds of such meditation are prescribed: (1) Jōza Zammai,[2] or Ichigyō Zammai: the devotee sits cross-legged, facing west for ninety days and nights consecutively, concentrating his thoughts solely upon Amida and calling on his name. (2) Jōgyō-Zammai: he walks

[1] The Japanese characters for the four paradises are as follows:— (1) 凡聖雜居土. (2) 方便有餘土. (3) 實報土. (4) 常寂光土.

[2] The Japanese characters for the four names are: (1) 常坐三昧. (2) 常行三昧. (3) 半行半坐三昧. (4) 非行非坐三昧.

round Amida's image for the same period, invoking and meditating on him in the same way. (3) Hangyōhanza-Zammai: he alternately recites some sacred text, for instance, the Lotus, and sits down to meditate on it. If the practice is continued for three weeks, the Bodhisattva Samantabhadra will appear before him. (4) In the last form of meditation called Higyōhiza more freedom is allowed. The devotee concentrates all his mental efforts on realizing the truth, but follows his inclinations as to sitting or walking.

Little importance seems to have been attached to mortification of the flesh apart from meditation. Twenty-five kinds of austerities are catalogued which may be useful in the lower stages of spiritual progress "to polish the heart", but they are not prescribed in the higher stages. I have already mentioned in treating of Buddhism in China [1] that the Chinese saw a connection—not much relished perhaps by the T'ien-t'ai itself—between that sect and the Zen and called some of the earlier T'ien-t'ai teachers Ch'an-shih. The Japanese had no hesitation in admitting the connection. The Tendai authorities quoted by Nanjio,[2] who give the views of the modern sect, represent it as having received a special transmission of the Law of Bodhidharma. Saichō was commissioned to find out the best form of Buddhism. He studied Zen among other varieties and, true to the eclectic principles of Tendai, he accepted it in so far as he approved it. Tradition states that even before he went to China he studied Zen under Gyōhyō, the pupil of Dōsen, a Chinese priest of the northern school of Zen, and that subsequently after reaching China he received instruction from Shōnen, who represented the line of Hui-Nêng. On returning to Japan he imparted the instruction which he had received to Jikaku. Without criticizing these statements, which are probable enough, it seems clear that the study of Zen was never a popular or important part of the curriculum of Hieizan. It was not in the least like Shingon, which did exercise a continual influence on Tendai doctrine and ritual. So far as I know, there is no record of Zen even forming a subject of discussion, and when in the twelfth and thirteenth centuries Eisai and Dōgen preached it to the Japanese public, they were to all intents and purposes introducing a new school.

Though the Tendai attached much importance to meditation,

[1] p. 172.

[2] Nanjio, *Twelve Buddhist Sects*, pp. vi, 72, 77.

it must not be supposed that it was an inactive or merely contemplative sect. Indeed, the reader who has followed however cursorily its political and military fortunes is not likely to fall into this mistake but rather to think of it as devoted to secular ambition. But this, at least in its early days, had a good side. Dengyō Daishi's ideal was a Church which so far as the things of this world were concerned should be devoted to the public service and be the moral and religious agent of the Government. He himself wrote a book called *The Defence of the Country*.[1] The careers of the monastic students were mapped out with this view. After studying for twelve years, they were divided into various categories according to their qualifications for service. Some were kept at Hieizan and took part in the general direction of affairs: others were appointed to act in the city temples or to serve for a fixed period in the Government provincial temples (Kokubunji) and were officially styled dempō.[2] In 806 the Emperor Kwammu ordered the priests of fifteen large temples at Nara, Kyōto, and of the Kokubunji to observe the ceremony of Ango,[3] corresponding to the Indian vassa or retreat during the rainy season. In Japan it consisted originally in reciting such sûtras as the Ninnō and in offering prayers for the peace of the country and a good harvest and in preaching to the laity. The latter were expected to make offerings, but Dengyō Daishi left careful instructions that all contributions should be used for the public welfare.[4] In the beginning of the Meiji period the Ango was abolished. It has since been revived in several large temples but I believe is now a purely spiritual ceremony.

But the Tendai is a philosophy as well as a religion. When speaking of the views prevalent in the Far East about the date and authenticity of the Buddhist scriptures I have already discussed the Tendai theory of gradual revelation commonly known as the Five Periods.[5] Much more difficult to understand is the series known as the Eight Teachings described by eight Chinese expressions which are not easy to translate.[6] They may perhaps be rendered as sudden, gradual, secret, undetermined, collection, progress, distinction, completion. Though these are commonly regarded

[1] 守護國界章 Shugo Kokkai-shō.
[2] 傳法, transmitters of the Law.
[3] 安居.
[4] Abuses crept in, however, in this matter. See *Hōnen, the Buddhist Saint*, p. 717.
[5] See above, Chap. I, pp. 6–7.
[6] 頓, 漸, 秘密, 不定, 藏, 通, 別, 圓.

as one group of eight, they seem to be really two groups of four, of which the second is a consecutive and ascending series, though the first is not. Sudden means teaching without preparation and is useful only to the highest intelligences such as Bodhisattvas who can grasp the truth the moment they hear it, while gradual is the method suitable for ordinary men which leads them from the Âgamas to the Vaipulya sûtras, thence to the Prajñâpâramitâ, and finally to the ultimate truth as set forth in the Lotus. The expressions secret and undetermined refer primarily to the narratives which represent the Buddha as preaching to mixed audiences. If he preaches to mortals and deities at the same time the teaching is said to be secret, for the hearers do not see one another and their impressions differ according to their capacities. Or again the hearers may be aware of one another's presence but, as in the former case, understand the teaching in very different ways. This is the undetermined method. But since the Buddha is really a cosmic force, not limited by the span of human life or human geography, he is regarded as continually appealing to the spirit, for instance by the scriptures or by instructive incidents. Men are sure to interpret such an appeal in various ways and they may or may not know that it is addressed to others as well as themselves. The remaining four methods form an ascending series. Zō (Tsang), meaning collection or store, refers to the Âgama or Hinayanist portion of the scriptures. Progress or transition is the gradual passage from this to Mahayanist doctrine. Distinction is the teaching distinctive of Bodhisattvas. It is occupied with the idea of totality. It sees that parts depend on one another and all depend on the whole. The complete or perfect teaching goes beyond this. It sees that the whole and the parts are identical. The whole cosmos and all the Buddhas are present in a grain of sand or on the point of a hair. A celebrated maxim says: One thought is the three thousand (that is, the whole universe) and the three thousand are one thought.[1] That is to say, the relations involved in the simplest thought are so numerous that they imply the existence of the whole universe, our perceptions and thoughts being identical with absolute reality. This leads on to the doctrine of ontology. There are three forms of existence, the void, the temporary, and the middle.[2] The meaning of these somewhat

[1] The expression 3,000 is the result of an elaborate calculation of the attributes of the dharmas and the variations they may present in various forms of existence.

[2] 空 K'ung; 假 Chia; 中 Chung.

mysterious words is that all the elements of existence (dharmâḥ), as we know them, depend on their relations. If you try to isolate them and to conceive of them as entering into no relations, they become unthinkable and in fact non-existent. But as temporary formative parts of the whole they do exist and the whole could not realize its true nature if it did not manifest itself in particulars. The term middle or middle path is borrowed from Nâgârjuna and is equivalent to Tathatâ or Dharmakâya in Sanskrit.[1] The elements exist or do not exist according to our view of their relations to it, but the middle exists absolutely. The example given by Chih-I in his work called Chih-kuan[2] is a mirror. Its brightness is k'ung, for it has no existence apart from the mirror: the objects reflected are chia, and the mirror itself is chung. The brightness and the reflections both depend on it in various ways, but still it would not be a mirror if it was not bright and did not reflect. This view of the nature of Being is known in Japan as Isshin Sandai, One thought, three truths. It is interesting as being apparently a genuinely Chinese piece of philosophy. The Chinese have not much inclination to metaphysics, but Chih-I seems worthy to rank with Nâgârjuna[3] or even with Hegel, to whom he shows some resemblance. It may be noticed that whereas Indian metaphysics (in spite of qualifying explanations) leave a disconcerting feeling that the Universe, as known to our senses, is non-existent or at best an illusion very different from the reality, the practical Chinese comes to the comfortable conclusion that phenomena and the one absolute truth are, if rightly regarded, synonymous. The greatest importance is attached to a form of meditation on the three truths which is called Isshin Sangwan[4] and when the three are seen as perfectly amalgamated, that is enlightenment as obtained by the Buddha himself. Meditation is described in a well-known phrase which is

[1] Or 眞如 Chên-ju in Chinese and Shinnyo in Japanese.

[2] Chih-Kuan, vol. i, 2nd part, sheet 40 (Tokyo edition). "A bright mirror may be taken as an illustration. The brightness is like k'ung: the reflections are like chia: the mirror is chung. Not joined, not separate: combination and separation just as they are."

[3] Hui-Wen, the first Patriarch, is said to have been first inspired by reading a well-known verse of Nâgârjuna's Chung Lun (Nanjio, 1179), vol. iv, chap. 24. 衆因緣生法、我說卽是無、亦爲是假名、亦是中道義 "Various causes and conditions produce the dharmas: I (Nâgârjuna) state that they are void. But that (void) may also be regarded as Chia and this knowledge (to deny existence and non-existence) is the principle of the middle way."

[4] 一心三觀.

almost the motto of the school, as Chih-Kuan,[1] which seems to be the equivalent of the Sanskrit words Samatha and Vipassanâ, calm and insight. The truth does not come by sudden intuition as the Zen teaches. It needs preparation, training, and concentration. The Pali Piṭaka, too, regards Samatha and Vipassanâ as a compendium of the higher life, as they are respectively the results of two sets of religious exercises called adhicitta and adhipanna.[2]

The above brief statement is all that I venture to write about the Tendai philosophy, for I must confess that I cannot understand the rest and I do not think that it has much influence on the majority of the members of the sect in Japan. Those who feel further curiosity about it can consult the works mentioned in the note [3] and I hope they will be more successful in grasping their meaning than I have been.

[1] 止觀, Japanese Shi-kwan.

[2] Ang. Nik., iii, 88.

[3] (*a*) Maeda, *An Outline of the Tendai Sect* (Japanese); (*b*) Armstrong, *Doctrine of the Tendai Sect*, *Eastern Buddhist*, iii, 1924, p. 32 ff.; (*c*) Petzold, *The Chinese Tendai Teaching*, ib., iv, 1928, p. 299 ff.; (*d*) McGovern, *Introduction to Mahayana Buddhism*.

# CHAPTER XV

## SHINGON

The Shingon and Tendai sects go naturally together and form a pair. They were introduced into Japan at the same time: they borrowed from one another: they both enjoyed the favour of the Court and combined to form the new religion of the new capital, with the establishment of which their introduction coincided. The Tendai from the very beginning claimed to be the State religion, or rather the State in a religious form. Its political and military pretensions drew upon it later the vengeance of Nobunaga. Shingon was more modest but not wholly dissimilar in its aspirations. Its centre was fixed at Kōyasan at some distance from Kyōto and removed from the tumults and intrigues of the capital. This was, no doubt, a wise precaution and a source of religious as opposed to political strength. Yet it did not avoid entirely the dangers which brought ruin to Hieizan. Its great branch monastery of Negoro in the same region as Kōyasan became so wealthy and powerful, and with the aid of its army of Sōhei [1] was so successful in asserting its independent jurisdiction over the surrounding territory, that Hideyoshi thought it prudent to destroy it in 1585. Yet this blow by no means destroyed the religious influence of the Shingon sect. It still is the third largest religious corporation in Japan, coming after the Shinshū and the Sōtō [2] and owning about twelve thousand temples. It possesses many qualities which are valuable to a religious sect and are not often found united. No one can accuse it of being wanting in mysticism, philosophy, or whatever name we give to the deeper side of religion, and these profundities are illustrated by a lavish and on the whole successful use of art. But it also appealed to the common man, especially in the Heian period. Its elaborate ritual was not only pleasing as a spectacle and added an attraction to pilgrimages but also provided magical methods of obtaining one's desires. If any one wanted power or fame, children or wealth, to help his friends or to injure his enemies,

[1] 僧兵 armed mercenaries.

[2] That is, counting the Sōtō as a sect by itself.

an appropriate ceremony could be found with special deities, gestures, ornaments, and formulæ warranted to bring about the wished for results. The reformers of the twelfth and thirteenth centuries naturally denounced such things as low superstitions and not true religion, but they appeal to a side of human nature and are also connected with a practice to which Shingon owes much of its influence, that is, that it takes under its protection the shrines of popular deities. A Shingon temple is very often not an edifice built for the performance of a particular kind of religious service like a Hongwanji or Nichiren temple (or for the matter of that churches or mosques), but a shrine dedicated to the worship of some special deity who has perhaps selected that spot to manifest himself or show his power, and the deity is often not well known except locally and from the point of view of strict Buddhism may be of doubtful antecedents. Another advantage enjoyed by the Shingon sect is the personality of its founder Kūkai, or to call him by the posthumous name by which he is best known, Kōbō Daishi. In all the annals and legends of Japanese Buddhism there is no more celebrated name than this, and whether as saint, miracle-worker, writer, painter, or sculptor he is familiar alike to the most learned and the most ignorant of his countrymen. The equivalent of our phrase "Homer sometimes nods" is in Japanese "Kōbō mo fude no ayamari; Even Kōbō sometimes makes a slip of the pen". His exploits are celebrated in a popular religious ballad called *Namudaishi* which has been translated by Lloyd.[1]

It would appear that Shingon doctrine, or at least Shingon literature, was not unknown at Nara even before Kūkai's mission to China. The foundation of the Shingon-Ritsu sect, whose centre is the temple of Saidaiji near Nara, is sometimes attributed to Kanjin, but it is more probable that he was responsible only for the Ritsu doctrine and that the admixture of Shingon is a later addition. Tradition is undoubtedly correct in crediting Kūkai with being the first to make Shingon well known in Japan. He spent two years (804–6) in studying it under Hui-Kuo, the celebrated abbot of the Ch'ing-Lung temple at Ch'ang-An. He is also said to have applied himself to Sanskrit under the guidance of an Indian monk called Prajña, and is believed to have introduced into Japan the slightly altered form of the Devanagari letters called Shittan which is written in vertical columns and much used in

[1] *The Creed of Half Japan*, chap. xxi.

Shingon books. Prajña is believed to have co-operated with Nestorian priests in making translations. Kūkai in this way may have come into contact with Christians, and this and other facts have been cited as arguments to show that many ideas in his system were borrowed from Nestorianism, Gnosticism, or Manichæism. As there were many foreign religions in China in the ninth century, it is well not to be too dogmatic, but it may be observed that Gnosticism is not the same as Nestorianism or Manichæism, that there is (so far as I am aware) no proof of Gnosticism having penetrated to Central Asia or China, and that the attempts to identify certain mysterious terms used in Alexandrine Gnosticism, such as Abraxas and Kaulaukau,[1] with the terminology of Shingon, have not met with general acceptance. Also, although there is an evident similarity between the form of Manichæism known in Central Asia and Buddhism, this similarity is due to Manichæism having in those countries borrowed extensively from Buddhism and not vice versa. The origin of the doctrine learnt by Kūkai in China and imported by him to Japan seems to be perfectly clear. It is, making due allowance for the alterations made by his own genius and the genius of his countrymen, the late Indian form of Buddhism known as Mantrayâna, rendered in Chinese as Chên-yen (in Japanese pronunciation Shingon), meaning true word, that is, sacred spell or mantra. About the time of Kūkai's visit this doctrine was exceedingly popular in China. It was first introduced in 719 by Vajrabodhi, a Brahman of Southern India, and further popularized by his disciple Amoghavajra, whose Chinese name was Pu-K'ung. He revisited India in order to collect sacred books and before his death in 774 had translated no less than 108 of them (mostly, however, very short) into Chinese. It was his disciple Hui-Kuo who instructed Kūkai during his stay at Ch'ang-An. In India the sect claimed Nagabodhi, Nâgârjuna, and Vajrasattva as its principal authorities, the last named, who was apparently a supernatural personage, having received the doctrine from Vairocana himself. Its sacred books are the Mahâvairocana-sûtra or Dainichi-kyō, the Susiddhikâra-sûtra or Soshitsuji-kyō, and the Vajraśekhara-sûtra or Kongōchō-kyō.[2] All are quite late Tantric works and were not translated into Chinese until about A.D. 725. It is true that about

[1] e.g. by Lloyd in *The Creed of Half Japan, Shinran and his Work*, etc.

[2] Nanjio, Nos. 530, 533, and 534. The Chinese titles are: 大毗盧遮那成佛神變加持經. 蘇悉地羯羅經. 金剛頂瑜伽中略出念誦經.

A.D. 700 Indian Buddhism had become a very mixed creed and may have incorporated many Iranian and Central Asiatic elements, but no one can study Shingon without being impressed by its strongly marked Indian character. It worships incidentally many deities which are Hindu and not strictly speaking Buddhist, such as Ka-Ten (Agni) and Sui-Ten (Varuna), and its temples and sacred pictures are profusely ornamented with the peculiar form of the Sanskrit alphabet mentioned above.

Kōbō Daishi, then known as Kūkai, returned to Japan in 806 and was well received by the Emperor. During the lifetime of Saichō, the founder of the Tendai, however, he evidently thought it well to avoid competition and busied himself with the construction of the great monastery at Kōyasan in the province of Kii. Saichō died in 822 and the year after Kūkai was summoned to Kyōto and appointed abbot of the Tōji monastery. He made it the head temple of the Shingon, which it still is, and the form of esoteric doctrine taught there was called Tōmitsu,[1] whereas another form which was in vogue among the Tendai at Hieizan was known as Taimitsu.[1] He was subsequently named Presiding Priest of the Nai-dōjō, or shrine within the Palace where the Emperor attended Buddhist ceremonies, and he died at Kōyasan in 835. He left ten chief disciples, of whom the most celebrated was Shinga who stood high in the favour of the Emperor Seiwa, and in the second generation from him were the two eminent prelates Yakushin (827–906) and Shōbō (832–909). Yakushin was head of the Ninnaji temple to which the Emperor Uda retired and received the sacrament of Kwanjō at his hands. He was also the founder of the Hirosawa school of Shingon, school meaning merely a branch which prescribes a special method of study, not which has new doctrines of its own on any important point. Similarly, Shōbō founded the Ōno school and sometimes seven of these schools are enumerated: Kōya, Tōji, Ōno, Hirosawa or Ōmuro, which have been mentioned above, Daigo, Yamashina, and Senyūji. The last is said to have been a place of study for the four sects Shingon, Tendai, Ritsu, and Zen, but in 1872 was recognized as belonging to the Shingon.

More important than these divisions is the branch called Shingishingon,[2] founded in 1130 by Kakuhan at the new monastery of

[1] 東密 Tōmitsu; 台密 Taimitsu.

[2] It is usual to speak of the two branches of the Shingon, namely, the Kogi 古義 founded by Kūkai and the Shingi 新義 founded by Kakuhan. It is said that Negoro was really built by Raiyu in 1280, but that as Kakuhan's tomb is there, he is considered the founder.

Negoro. He made meditation on Amida an important part of his teaching, Amida being practically identified with the Sun-Buddha Vairocana, of whom he is a special manifestation or faculty. Jōdo, the Pure Land of Amida, is really everywhere, and he who meditates on Amida in the way agreeable to the rules of Shingon is really already in the Pure Land and can become a Buddha here and now. The Shingi branch has two subdivisions called Chizan and Buzan: the chief temple of the latter is the celebrated Hasedera near Nara.

It is doubtful how far Shingon as we see it in Japan is the system which Kōbō Daishi learnt in China and how far it is a reconstruction due to himself or to the well-known Japanese habit of borrowing but at the same time changing. Obviously a copious pantheon and multitudinous rites can easily have degenerated into a magical ritual, which is the principal contribution of the Ch'en-yen to Chinese Buddhism. Later Buddhism in India also does not seem to have had many admirable sides, and even in the new forms which it assumed when imported into Tibet and Java its chief merit lies less in thought than in art, which is vigorous at the risk of being often grotesque. But the Shingon of Kōbō Daishi, though it does not altogether escape the danger of becoming mere magic, has the merit of being a well-thought-out system illustrated by an art which if it sometimes becomes conventional and tiresome, the inevitable result of a symbolism which consistently endeavours to represent ideas by fixed devices, is capable of being sometimes awe-inspiring and sometimes of evoking visions of peace, calm, and benevolence.

The main idea of Shingon is cosmotheism, which is not quite the same as pantheism. The whole Universe is regarded as the body of the Supreme Buddha Vairocana, being composed of the six elements earth, water, fire, air, ether, and consciousness. These elements play a prominent part in Shingon symbolism and are represented not only by various letters and colours but by a peculiar form of monument often found in cemeteries and called Sotoba. It is, as the name indicates, a modified form of the Stupa and consists of a ball, crescent, pyramid, sphere, and cube, placed one on the top of the other, standing for ether, air, fire, water, and earth, while the surrounding space typifies consciousness. All thoughts, words, and actions, called the three mysteries,[1] are the thoughts, words, and actions of Vairocana: he is present in

[1] 三密.

a grain of dust or in a word, and the object of the elaborate mystic ritual is to make us feel that our thoughts, words, and actions derive all their meaning and force from the fact that they are his. It will be noted that thoughts, words, and actions are described as the three mysteries. Shingon has two doctrines, the apparent or Ken-gyō and the secret or Mitsu-kyō : the former can be studied in literature, the latter is taught only orally and to the initiated : the former is the teaching of Shaka (who counts for very little in the Shingon system), the latter is the hidden doctrine communicated secretly by the Dharmakâya or Hosshin. The former is compared to formal conversation with a guest, the latter to intimate family talk between relatives. Thus the hopes of the outsider who attempts to fathom the mystery of Shingon do not receive much encouragement. The position is not, however, quite so desperate as in Zen, where even the nature of enlightenment is incommunicable and every one must find out for himself what it means. In Shingon there are definite secret doctrines which can be communicated orally, and though he who is uninitiated cannot claim to understand the explanations, he can guess on what points they throw light.

Two of the most important doctrines of Shingon are the theory of the development of spiritual life, rising from blind animal instincts to the realization of complete enlightenment, and what may be succinctly described as the theory of the two Mandaras. As the former is much easier to understand, we will take it first. Shingon, like other sects of this period, taught that mankind has the Buddha nature and that by proper ritual processes we can come to feel that the Buddha nature in ourselves is identical with the great cosmic Buddha Vairocana. The doctrine of the Ten Stages is expounded in a book written by Kōbō Daishi in 822 called the Jūjūshinron [1] and is said to be founded on a chapter of the Dainichi-kyō which also bears the title of Ten Stages.

(1) The first stage [2] is that of simple animal existence : the only desire is for the satisfaction of appetite and there is no consciousness of the distinction between good and evil.

(2) The succeeding states are not only described by epithets but the meaning is made plainer by comparing them to the doctrines

[1] 十住心論.

[2] 異生羝羊心 I-shō-tei-yō-shin. Explained as meaning the heart of utterly ignorant people who are different in birth from the wise and are like sheep.

of certain sects. Thus the second [1] is called the heart of a foolish boy who practises fasting. It is the state of ordinary mankind in which sufficient moral precepts are observed to prevent society from falling into disorder. Among religious systems it corresponds to Confucianism, which sees the importance of morality and insists on respecting the five relationships and so on but has no spiritual motive power.

(3) Somewhat better than this is the state of those who have religious aspirations but who merely desire to attain supernatural powers without having any true idea of why they are valuable or how they should be obtained.[2] It is illustrated by Taoism. Shingon is not sceptical as to Taoist claims to grant long life and teach magic arts but simply thinks them useless.

(4) and (5) are two stages of progress which are represented by the beliefs of the Hînayâna leading up to the superior illumination of the greater vehicle. The first [3] realizes that there is no self and that what is called the ego is merely a collection of Skandhas but it falls into the error of nihilism. The second [4] consists in discovering and entirely uprooting the evil karma until all passion and trouble ceases. This is the doctrine of Pratyeka-Buddhas who are enlightened but only for themselves and do not help others.

(6) With the sixth [5] stage we rise to the realm of the Mahâyâna as shown in the Hossō sect. Those who have reached this stage are convinced that nothing exists but thought and feel an infinite compassion for all beings and a desire to save them.

(7), (8), and (9) The next three stages correspond to various views taught by the Mahâyâna in its different phases. The seventh [6] stage is that of the Sanron, which establishes the doctrine of the mean by eight denials of apparently obvious truths, such as there is no birth and no destruction, no identity and no diversity. The

[1] 愚童持齋心 Gudōjisaishin.

[2] 嬰童無畏心 Yōdōmuishin, the heart of a young boy without fear.

[3] 唯蘊無我心 Yuiunmugashin, only collection, no self heart.

[4] 拔業因種心 Batsugoinshūshin, the heart which extracts action causing seed.

[5] 他緣大乘心 Taendaijōshin, the Mahayanist thought about relation to others.

[6] 覺心不生心 Kakushin fushōshin, enlightened thought without production. Fushō (short for "there is no birth and no destruction") is cited as typical of the eight denials.

eighth is the Tendai [1] defined by the phrase "One way without action", a dark saying which means that ultimate reality is identical with our experience of the phenomenal world, and the ninth [2] is the Kegon or Avataṃsaka sûtra which is given the highest rank among exoteric doctrines.[3] It is said to state that absolute truth transcends the nature of self but is realized in the ceaseless activity of the Universe.

(10) But it is inferior to the tenth [4] and highest stage, which is naturally Shingon itself. The nine previous stages are really nothing but the elimination of passion and error. The doors of truth are now open and by the performance of the mystic rites of Shingon the adept learns to feel that Man and the Universe are Vairocana himself.

Hōnen [5] severely criticized Kōbō Daishi for having arranged the various Buddhist sects in an ascending scale of truth. His periphrasis of the last five stages is appreciative, for he defines them as "(6) the heart which makes the welfare of others its aim; (7) the illuminated heart which has transcended all illusions such as birth and death; (8) the heart which has entered on the middle way, having transcended the states of relative being and the absolute; (9) the heart which realizes that nothing has an independent nature of its own but that everything exists in virtue of its relations to other things as well as to the absolute; and (10) the heart which rising completely above exoteric doctrine, or what is taught by a Buddha in human form, enters into the very heart of the Absolute Buddha". But he objects to the graded classification of sects and the sûtras on which they are founded as likely to produce only ill-will. The Buddha revealed various doctrines, each amplifying one point, some likely to appeal to one class of intellect and some to another, but to make them like the rungs of a ladder, each one higher than the last, is most objectionable.[6] Indeed, it is clear that the order of ascending merit laid down by Kōbō Daishi is open to much argument.

[1] 一道無爲心 Ichidōmuishin.

[2] 極無自性心 Gokumujishōshin. Literally, extreme without self-nature thought.

[3] Kengyō 顯教.

[4] 秘密莊嚴心 Himitsushōgonshin, thought ornamented by mystery.

[5] *Hōnen, the Buddhist Saint*, p. 158 ff.

[6] Hōnen also accuses Kōbō Daishi of misunderstanding his sources, which are said to be the Gishaku, a collection of lectures by Śubhakara, the Indian translator of the Dainichi-Kyō, transcribed by the Chinese Ichigyō.

But the most remarkable feature in Kōbō Daishi's scheme of spiritual development, though Hōnen does not criticize it, is that whereas in the first nine stages we are concerned only with the evolution of thought which is assumed in most systems of philosophy, both Eastern and Western, to be the only means of discovering or attempting to discover the mystery of the Universe, in the tenth and highest stage this principle is suddenly supplemented or perhaps superseded by another which is called respectfully the esoteric or secret doctrine and disrespectfully magical ritual. It is closely connected with the use of the two Mandaras, of which it is exceedingly difficult to give any coherent explanation. A Mandara, the Sanskrit word Maṇḍala,[1] means a circle or assemblage of persons in a limited space and thence a picture, round or more often quadrangular, divided into several compartments in which are arranged a number, often very considerable, of deities for whom are sometimes substituted the Japanese forms of Sanskrit letters known as Shūji [2] or seed, a translation of bîja, the Sanskrit name given to letters which are mystically used to express the name of a deity. A Mandara in this restricted sense appears to be a Japanese invention and is usually formed of a silk kakemono with figures painted in colours, though apparently some of the oldest Mandaras are woven. But evidently it is only the technical details of construction which are Japanese, the whole idea of the Mandara, the name itself, the use of Sanskrit letters, and the figures of deities which are simply Hindu and not specifically Buddhist, are all obvious indications of an Indian origin. In Benoytosh Bhattacaryya's *Indian Buddhist Iconography* there are many descriptions of Maṇḍalas,[3] that name being used, and it is said [4] that in the Nishpannayogambara Tantra, Kriyâsamuccaya, and Vajravalinâma-maṇḍalopâyikâ there are descriptions of twenty maṇḍalas each containing a number of deities. Most of the plates do not much resemble Far Eastern mandaras, but plate xliii, 1 from Nepal representing Hayagrîva Lokeśvara as the central figure enclosed in a circle with six figures similarly enclosed set round it, all the seven small circles being surrounded by a large circular border, is distinctly suggestive of Japanese designs. So, too, we hear that

[1] See on the subject of Maṇḍalas or Mandaras Toga no O's works (in Japanese) Mandara no Kenkyū, 1927, and Rishu Kyō no Kenkyū, 1930.

[2] 種子.

[3] See pp. 39, 40, 64, 67, 71.

[4] p. 194.

Lokanâtha sits on a lotus on the eight petals of which are Maitreya and other deities; that Buddhakapala is surrounded by twenty-four goddesses arranged in eight circles, and we are given numerous details as to the mudrâs (positions of the hands) of these deities and the Vajras, lotus flowers, and other objects which they carry. Picture Mandaras are also forthcoming from Tibet,[1] whither they were introduced from Northern India. In China there is the Hokke Mandara [2] ascribed to the middle of the ninth century, and there are several instances of the interior of caves being decorated with designs strikingly similar to those found on Japanese mandaras. See, for example, Pelliot's plates of the mural designs at Touen-houng (V. ccciii and V. cccxviii).

There are two mandaras which are supposed to represent the two aspects of cosmic life. They are called respectively the Diamond element (in Sanskrit Vajradhâtu and in Japanese Kongōkai) and the Womb element (in Sanskrit garbha-dhâtu and in Japanese Taizōkai).[3] Diamond is explained as having the two qualities of hardness and utility. As being hard, it represents eternal and indestructible truth, which nothing can alter. Its usefulness is seen in the way which wisdom spreads light and destroys all the obstacles raised by the passions. It represents the eternal and fundamental ideas which have their seat in the soul of Vairocana and which are always active in every part of the Universe. The other Mandara is called the Womb because Shingon regards all the many deities and powers acting in the cosmos as being contained in it as children are contained in their mothers' wombs and as ready to issue and take their part in eternally creating a universe, not of lifeless matter but perpetually living and growing. It is to be noted that with this statement of the two categories—Kongōkai and Taizōkai—of the Universe, the written or open teaching of Shingon ends. Further explanation, which is obviously necessary, is part of the secret teaching which is only communicated by word of mouth to the initiated. Such teaching is said to enable one to understand the origin of one's own thought and the constituents of one's own body. It does not appear to me that much light is thrown on the two mandaras by describing one as static and the other dynamic or by the orthodox conception that the Kongōkai represents the action of wisdom and the Taizōkai the action of reason.

[1] See, for instance, G. Roerich, Tibetan Paintings, No. 14.

[2] It is reproduced in Anesaki's *Buddhist Art*, plate vi.

[3] The Japanese characters are 金剛界 and 胎藏界.

The prevailing colour of the Kongōkai is pure white. The field is divided into nine squares and the whole is surrounded by two borders. In the centre is Vairocana, white and absorbed in contemplation. He is surrounded by the four Buddhas Ashuku, Hōshō, Muryōju, and Fukujōjū.[1] The whole number of figures represented in this mandara is said to be 437, but it is often abbreviated to 37 and generally letters are substituted for the numerous deities. The details of these figures, their attitudes, headdresses, and, above all, the position of their hands and what they carry in them are all of the deepest symbolic importance. A lotus, for instance, is the emblem of mercy, a coloured ball, supposed to represent a jewel, of wealth and generosity, while vigour and determination are shown by the divine thunderbolt or vajra.[2]

The prevailing colour of the other mandara, the Taizōkai, is red. The middle portion consists of a red lotus flower and is surrounded by four enclosing borders. In the central capsule of the lotus flower is seated Vairocana and on each of the eight petals surrounding him is one of the four Buddhas already mentioned above or one of the great Bodhisattvas, and round these are set numerous other figures of which there are said to be 428 altogether. Apparently it is believed that by intense meditation on one's own heart as being a lotus like the centre of the mandara, the petals will open and the five Buddhas and four Bodhisattvas will take up their abode within the happy being thus illuminated.[3] It is noticeable that this is exactly parallel to the procedure recommended in Indian Buddhist Tantras. The adept is bidden to meditate on himself as being such and such a Buddha, when the desired consequences will follow.

It is most difficult to give an account of the doctrines and deities of the Shingon sect. To begin with, the most important teaching is admittedly secret, but even apart from this, the inquirer is bewildered by the number of deities, ceremonies, mandaras, and symbols which confront him. Some idea of the extent of the subject matter may be derived from perusing a list of only a few of the handbooks which have been published as guides to this complicated

[1] That is, Akshobhya, Ratnasambhava, Amitâbha, and Amoghasiddhi. The same Buddhas have a rather different appearance and bear different names in the Taizōkai, viz. Hōdō, Kaifuke Ō, Amida, and Rai-in.

[2] Called Go-kō (or Go-kō-shō) if it has five points, San-kō if three, and Tokkōshō if only one.

[3] Nanjio, *Twelve Japanese Buddhist Sects*, pp. 97–9.

creed.[1] One obviously cannot describe all the objects of worship, but yet one cannot dismiss them in a general phrase, for some, such as Fudō who has a great temple at Narita, are important for both religion and art, though they may be little known outside the Shingon and sects which have borrowed from it. I shall, therefore, say a few words about the more conspicuous members of this multitudinous heavenly host.

The Myō-ō are a group of gods (the expression is hardly inaccurate) peculiar to Shingon, except in so far as the Tendai has imitated Shingon in practising their worship. M. Przyluski [2] considers that the name is equivalent to the Sanskrit Vidyârâja and that the Myō-ō were originally personifications of magic formulæ. At any rate, they are a class of deities imported from late Indian Tantric Buddhism in which the corresponding beings are called Bhairava or Krodharâja. Though of awful appearance, their terrors are really benevolent, for they are designed to protect their worshippers by frightening away evil spirits or to destroy passion and ignorance. They correspond to the manifestations of Śiva in Brahmanism, as is indicated by the fact that they are represented as having a third eye in the centre of the forehead. They perhaps correspond even more closely to the emanations of Akshobhya as described in Benoytosh Bhattacaryya's *Buddhist Iconography*, chapter v. He points out that more emanations are ascribed to this Buddha than to any other, that they are of a blue colour (as are often the Myō-ō) and of a terrible appearance, being sometimes surrounded with flames. They also have three eyes. As many as twenty-three Myō-ō are sometimes reckoned, but a group of five is frequently found which consists of Fudō, who is placed in the centre, with Go Sansei to the east, Dai Itoku to the west, Gundari Yasha to the north, and Kongō Yasha to the south. Fudō is undoubtedly the most important and is represented as a terrible figure, livid blue in colour and of a ferocious expression. He is surrounded by flames and carries a sword and a rope to smite and bind evil. He is generally explained as typifying the fierce aspect assumed by

[1] (*a*) Asoba-jō, written by Shōchō, a contemporary of Nichiren, and published in the collection called Dai Nippon Bukkyō Zensho. 7 volumes.

(*b*) Jikkanshō (also called Sonyō shō), by Eiju'. Kamakura period. 10 volumes.

(*c*) Shoson Zu-zō-sho. 11 volumes.

(*d*) Kaku-Zen-shō. 111 volumes. Published in the Juei era (1182–3).

(*e*) Butsu-zō-zukan. Prepared under the supervision of Gonda Raifu. First volume appeared in 1930.

[2] See above, Chap. IV, p. 136.

Vairocana when resenting wrong doing. The name Fudō, however, means immovable and is equivalent to the Sanskrit Acala, which is one of the names of Caṇḍaroshana, an emanation of Akshobhya.[1] This personage is represented by a figure which closely resembles those of Fudō. He is surrounded by flames and carries a sword and rope, so that the two deities are probably historically identical. There is, however, an important difference. Acala, like most late Indian Buddhist deities, is represented as holding his Śâkti, or female counterpart, on his lap, but as I have already pointed out, Saktist practices and symbolism were alien to the spirit of the Far East.[2] Fudō is represented as waited on by two attendants who stand beside him, Kongara, a youth, and Seitaka, an old man. He is specially worshipped at the great temple of Shinshōji at Narita in the province of Shimosa. According to the legend, the image there enshrined was brought by Kōbō Daishi to Japan, having already come to China from India, and the deity having signified in a dream his desire to make this further voyage. It was deposited in the temple of Takaozan where it remained until the rebellion of Taira Masakado, who established in his native province of Shimosa a Court in imitation of Kyōto. The Emperor Shujaku was informed that no deity had such power as Fudō to suppress evil doers and accordingly the abbot Kwanchō, himself an imperial Prince, was dispatched with his image to the scene of rebellion and set it up in a shrine near the insurgent's capital where the ceremony of Goma was performed before it for three weeks. Thanks to Fudō's puissant help Masakado was defeated and killed, but when the victors attempted to escort him back to Kyōto it proved impossible to remove the image, and the god, appearing in a dream, declared that he wished to remain in that district and to civilize Eastern Japan. The grateful Emperor accordingly decided to build a sumptuous temple. Lots were cast as to which of thirty-three villages should have the honour of being the site and Narita won. The exact position of the temple was, however, altered several times and the buildings which now stand on a hill in the town were erected only in 1704. Probably the growth of Yedo increased the popularity of the shrine, which came to be specially frequented by actors. In the temple Treasury is said to be kept a sword presented by the Emperor Shujaku, the mere

[1] Benoytosh Bhattacaryya, op. cit., pp. 60–1, and pl. xxv a.

[2] I have been informed that about 1400 the priest Kōshi endeavoured to introduce Saktist practices into Japan.

touch of which cures insanity and all the evils that come from being possessed by foxes. Another celebrated Myō-ō is Dai Itoku, who is also a personification of death in the sense of being the destroyer of evil. Typically he is represented with six faces and six arms, but the number varies. Like Fudō he is usually of a livid blue and no effort is spared to make his appearance horrible. He is closely connected with Monju (Mañjuśrî) and hence has been identified with the Indian Yamântaka.[1] That deity is generally represented as having a buffalo's head, a form which, so far as I know, is not given to Dai Itoku, though he is represented as riding on a white ox.[2] In this, as in many other cases, Japanese art shrinks from the violent combinations of human and animal anatomy so dear to India.

Another well-known Myō-ō is Aizen, who is often spoken of as the God of Love and whose name appears to correspond to the Sanskrit Râga Râjâ. At first sight his appearance seems to be most unsuitable to such a title: he is represented as a terrific being, in a sitting posture, of a dark red colour, with one head but six arms which carry various weapons.[3] But the passion which he represents is not love in any ordinary sense. Like other deities of this class he is formidable in order to be benevolent: he is the destroyer of all the vulgar passions in order to replace them by a purer universal love which aims at nothing but the salvation of all beings.

The Myō-ō are almost peculiar to the Shingon, but it also adores many Bodhisattvas recognized by other sects. Bodhisattvas are among the most popular objects of worship in Japan and this may be a good place to mention some of the more important of them, if it be remembered that their various forms and the legends about them often repose on doubtful scriptural authority and do not form part of the serious doctrine of any sect.

Kwannon is undoubtedly one of the deities most widely honoured in Japan, though not worshipped by the important Shinshū sect. I have endeavoured in a previous chapter[4] to trace the early history of this Bodhisattva who has the singular peculiarity of

[1] For the connection of Yamântaka and Mañjuśrî see Benoytosh Bhattacaryya, loc. cit., p. 69.

[2] In the Asobajō, vol. v. Anesaki's *Buddhist Art*, plate xvii, gives a good reproduction of a statue of Dai Itoku.

[3] See Anesaki, loc. cit., plate xviii, and Hōbōgirin, illustrations to article Aizemmyō-ō.

[4] Vol. I, Book II, p. 120 ff.

having changed his sex in his wanderings across Asia. In India he is invariably a male deity : in the Far East he is generally female, though the older statues and pictures sometimes represent him as a young man.[1] Some authors say that Kwannon is not so much female as sexless, and it is true that he or she has none of the attributes of Venus and is a deity not of love but of mercy and pity, but I fancy that the ordinary Japanese thinks of her as female just as we think of the angels as male without attributing to them any particular masculine qualities. Kwannon is also sometimes represented with a child, which has caused some foreigners to see a resemblance to the Madonna. But this is a mistake. The child is not her own but one which she is ready to give to women who pray to her for offspring, and it is remarkable that in India the male deity, Avalokiteśvara, also grants children.[2]

The worship of Kwannon is probably coeval with the introduction of Buddhism into Japan, and the statue of her in the Yume-dono or Hall of Dreams at Hōryūji where Shōtoku Taishi used to meditate is said by tradition to have been made, or at least ordered to be made, by the Prince himself, who was later held to be an incarnation of the Bodhisattva. Even at the present day a pilgrimage to the thirty-three shrines of Kwannon in Kyōto and the neighbouring provinces [3] is still a most popular form of religion. They are sometimes called Fudasho, or ticket-places, because they each issue to every pilgrim a stamped ticket attesting his visit. The pilgrimage is said to have been first made by the Abbot Tokudo in the eighth century. He apparently died and was led before the judgment seat of Yama, who explained to him the merits of the thirty-three places, gave him a list and assured him that no one who completed the itinerary should ever fall into Hell. His attendants then conducted Tokudo back to the world of the living where he made the pilgrimage with his disciples. The practice, however, fell into disuse but was revived and the present order of stations was established by the Emperor Kwazan, who, overcome with grief at the death of his Empress, abdicated in 986 at the age of eighteen and devoted the remainder of his life to religious observances. The list and order of

[1] See for a clear instance the Amida triad traditionally ascribed to Eshin and reproduced in pl. i of Anesaki's *Buddhist Art*.

[2] See Lotus, chap. xxv.

[3] These are the original shrines, but in imitation of them another set of thirty-three has been established in Eastern Japan and also in the district of Chichibu. Kwannon is said to have assumed thirty-three forms, adapted to save the various types of beings.

the temples as fixed by him and still observed is as follows. The places marked with an asterisk are specially celebrated :—

In Kishū :

1. Fudaraku-ji at Nachi which derives its name from Potalaka, the mythical Indian residence of Kwannon.
2. Kimiidera, said to have been founded in 770 by a Chinese missionary.
3. Kokawadera.

In Izumi :

4. Sefukuji.

In Kawachi :

5. Fujiidera.

In Yamato :

6. Tsubasakadera.
7. Okadera.
*8. Hasedera.
9. Nan-endo at Nara.

At Uji in Yamashiro :

10. Mimurotodera.
11. Kami Daigo-dera.

In Ōmi :

12. Iwamadera.
*13. Ishiyamadera.
*14. Miidera.

At Kyōto :

15. Imagumano.
*16. Kiyomizudera.
17. Rokuharadera.
18. Rokkaku-dō.
19. Kodo.
20. Yoshiminedera.

In Tamba :

21. Anoji.

In Settsu :

22. Sōjiji.
23. Katsuodera.
24. Nakayadera.

In Harima :

25. Shinkiyomizudera.
26. Hokkeji.
27. Shoshasan.

In Tango :

28. Nare-ai-ji.

In Wakasa :

29. Matsuodera.

In Ōmi :

30. Chikubu-shima.
31. Chōmeiji.
32. Kwannonji.

And in Mino :

33. Tanigumi-dera, where the weary pilgrims at last deposit their pilgrim shirts or *oizuru*. Each of the stations has a special hymn or *eika* of thirty-one syllables which is chanted by the pilgrims many hundred times.

One of the most marked characteristics of Kwannon is that, like Avalokiteśvara, he or she is polymorphic. Besides the change of sex the merciful Bodhisattva is ready to adopt any form which may be useful to suffering humanity. Japanese iconography is inclined to restrain the exuberance of Indian art in creating monstrous shapes, but still it cannot wholly get rid of the tendency to represent Kwannon as a being with many heads and arms, many eyes looking in mercy on the unhappiness of the world, and many hands stretched out in help. The simplest form is that known as Shō-Kwannon, representing a seated female or, less frequently, male figure with the usual number of heads and arms, wearing a crown in which is set an image of Amida. The left hand holds a lotus while the right is raised in a gesture which is interpreted as encouraging the flower to bloom more fully, the whole meaning that she strives to help human souls struggling towards enlightenment. Another variety of the simple form is the white-robed (Byaku-e) Kwannon, a female figure of a pale gold colour holding a casket in which lie the scriptures and a cord to restrain the disasters which she is prayed to avert. It should be mentioned that Kwannon in all her forms is frequently accompanied by attendants. When there are only two they are the Myō-ō, Fudō and Aizen. But sometimes they are twenty-eight and then represent as many constellations.

Figures with eleven faces (Jū-ichi-men) or a thousand hands (sen-ju) are also not infrequent and are found in India, China and Tibet as well as in Japan. The monstrosity of such representations is generally softened by reducing the thousand hands to forty, which carry various emblems, and by making the extra faces appear like plates in the crown which the image wears. In Kyōto there is a singular temple called San-jū-san-gen-dō,[1] founded by the ex-Emperor Toba but rebuilt by the Emperor Kameyama in 1266 and subsequently restored by the Shōgun Ietsuna in 1662. It is commonly called the temple of the 33,333 Kwannons and consists of a very long hall in which are arranged, tier above tier, rows of gilded images of the thousand-handed Kwannon, each 5 feet high. Two hundred of them are said to be the work of the celebrated sculptor Unkei. Though the general impression is that the number of these gilded statues is almost incalculable, there are only a thousand of them and the higher number, though not inaccurate, is formed by adding the numerous small images which are set on the heads of the larger ones or elsewhere. A curious tradition

[1] The name has nothing to do with the number of images, but refers to the long building being cut into thirty-three divisions by the row of pillars which traverses its entire length.

attaches to the large seated figure in this assemblage. The ex-Emperor Go-Shirakawa suffered from severe headaches and was informed by a celebrated Indian physician whom the oracles advised him to consult, that in a previous state of existence he had been a monk of Kumano and as a reward for his merits had been reborn as an Emperor. His skull as a monk, however, was lying at the bottom of a river and a willow tree had grown out of it, which trembled every time that the wind blew through its boughs and this caused the imperial headaches. On this the ex-Emperor caused a search to be made for the skull and when found had it enclosed in the head of the large Kwannon mentioned and, we will hope, suffered no more.

The type known as Batōkwannon,[1] or Kwannon with the horse's head, is also considerably modified, for the Japanese evidently felt that there was something barbarous in such mixtures of the human and animal form. A human body terminating in a horse's head is the rarest way of representing Batōkwannon. She is usually represented with one or more human faces (sometimes of terrible aspect, a device rarely employed in representing the goddess of mercy) surmounted by a small horse's head, which has more the appearance of an ornament than of an integral part of the figure. The temple of Matsuodera (No. 29 of the thirty-three stations) is dedicated to this form, which has also its place in the Mandara and is chiefly invoked in such ceremonies as prayer for the destruction of enemies. Batōkwannon is also a popular deity worshipped as the protectress of horses. There is a celebrated temple dedicated to her in this capacity at Entsūji near Gotemba which, strange to say, belongs to the Zen sect. Here prayers are offered for sick horses, thank-offerings made if they recover, and should they die, funeral rites are performed near one of the many stones dedicated to Batōkwannon in this part of the country.

Another favourite form is the Nyoirin Kwannon, which represents the goddess as holding a wheel which like the jewel called in Sanskrit Cintamani can grant all desires. Sometimes this form has six arms, in which case each hand holds some object, such as a rosary or lotus, emblematic of the goddess's desire tc save all the six classes of sentient beings.

Other forms are: Jintei Kwannon with eighteen arms; Fuku-Kensaku, or Amoghapaśa, Kwannon, represented by two celebrated

[1] See above, Chap. IV, and Hōbōgirin, s.v., where several figures are given.

statues at Nara; Koyasu Kwannon, holding a child; Gyoran Kwannon with a fishbasket.

Often some local legend attaches to the temples of Kwannon (and of other deities, too, for that matter) which is given an air of sanctity by being made to inculcate some Buddhist virtue. For instance, the following story is told of Kanimanji, a small temple near Tanimura in the Nara district. A very pious farmer once rescued a frog which was being eaten by a snake, by promising his daughter in marriage to the snake on condition that he would desist. The girl was horrified at the idea, spent her time in praying to Kwannon in the temple shrine, and when on the third day the snake appeared in the guise of a young man, refused to marry him. The snake was furious, turned into a dragon and began to destroy all around him. But an army of crabs appeared, drove him away, and the maiden was free. This was because she was very kind to animals and had once bought a basket of crabs from a fisherman and saved their lives.

Next to Kwannon the most popular Bodhisattva is undoubtedly Jizō,[1] the Indian Kshitigarbha who, obscure in origin, has remained obscure in India, which is the furthest point to which we can trace him, but has become extremely popular in China and Japan, in the latter of which his stone images are frequently to be seen by the wayside. Like Kwannon, he is an essentially benevolent deity but, being connected with the earth (Kshiti), he is thought of as helping the suffering dead and by a pathetic turn of popular fancy is believed to take a special interest in the souls of dead children. Piles of pebbles are often found heaped round his images in allusion to a superstition that dead children are tormented by demons on the banks of the Sai-in, an imaginary river corresponding to the Styx, and forced to engage in the endless task of piling up stones. Jizō is generally represented as a shaven priest, with a large halo and often clad in rich vestments. He carries in his right hand the shakujō [2] or clerical staff and in his left a jewel, signifying that he is ready to give anything out of compassion. His counterpart, Kokūzō, is not much worshipped, though revered in the Shingon sect as having been the patron saint of Kōbō Daishi. The name is equivalent to the Sanskrit Âkâśagarbha, which is said to indicate

[1] See Chap. IV, pp. 127, 128.

[2] Sanskrit Khakkara, said to have been originally used to strike on the ground and frighten away small animals who might otherwise be trodden on. There is a Japanese poem of nine verses called Shakujō gatha describing the duties of a priest.

that his wisdom and benevolence are as wide and indestructible as the sky.

Miroku or Maitreya receives little attention in modern Japan, but Monju (Mañjuśrî), Fugen (Samantabhadra), and Seishi (Mahâsthâmaprâpta) are all fairly popular. The first two are both deities of wisdom: Monju can generally be known by his lion and sword and also by his youthful appearance.[1] Dai Itoku is said to be a manifestation of him in a severe mood. Fugen rides on an elephant which is often white and often has three heads. Seishi is with Kwannon one of the two Bodhisattvas who attend on Amida and with him visit the deathbeds of the pious and welcome them to Paradise.

But perhaps the most remarkable feature of the Shingon pantheon and the clearest proof of its close connection with India is the presence in it of a number of deities many of whom have no connection originally with Buddhism but are simply Hindu gods. Such are Shōten Sama (Ganeśa), Kishi-Mojin (Hâritî), Bishamon (Kubera or Vaiśravara), Marishi, Taishaku (Indra), Katen (Agni, Ten being equivalent to Deva), Emma-ō (Yama) with his attendants, Benzaiten or Benten (Sarasvatî), sometimes called Uga,[2] Suiten (Varuna), Futen (Vâyu), Ishana, Bonten (Brahmâ), Jiten (Prithvi, the Earth), Nitten and Gatten (Suvya and Candra), and many others. Though most of these deities are venerated only as forming part of a Mandara, some of them, such as Shōten Sama, Kishi-Mojin, Emma-ō, Suiten, and Benten are popular objects of worship and have temples dedicated to them. In particular the worship of Ganeśa[3] as the Lord and giver of wealth appears to have been popular both during the Heian period and later in Tokugawa times, and even now its prevalence is attested by several temples in Tōkyō and in the districts near Kyōto. In the former they are said to exist and be well frequented in Mukōjima, Asakusa (Matsuchiyama no Shōden), and on an island in the lake of Shinobazu near Ueno Park. In the latter district I have myself seen several, such as a chapel in the Sambōin at Daigoji close to Kyōto, a temple near the Uguisu no Taki, about three miles from Nara,[4] and the considerable fane of

[1] But sometimes these characteristics are wanting in his pictures. See, for instance, Anesaki, *Buddhist Art*, plates xxv and xxxv.

[2] See Hōbōgirin, s.v. Benzaiten, p. 63.

[3] See for other details Chap. IV, pp. 138, 139.

[4] Strange to say, it is not under the superintendence of the Shingon but of the Kōfukuji, the head temple of the Hossō sect. Shintō influence is also visible in most of these shrines.

Hōzanji at Ikoma between Nara and Ōsaka. The worship in all these places is similar and has peculiar features of its own. The deity is called Shōten Sama (sage) or Kangi-ten (joy) and is apparently identical with the Binayaka (Vinayaka) of some sûtras, though that title appears to be deprecatory and to mean the God who creates obstacles but can remove them if appeased. Shōten Sama is usually worshipped in conjunction with Kwannon, but his image is rarely seen,[1] being enclosed in a cylindrical brass case remarkably like the Lingakośas, or cases used to cover Lingas, which are occasionally still to be found in India and which received a special worship in medieval Cambodja, apart from the symbol they contained. I have, however, seen one of the images in the house of a priest at Nara and also several photographs. They are generally double and consist of two human figures with elephants' heads, a form which is remarkable, for Japanese art generally modifies the common Indian device of representing a divine person as man and animal combined. Otherwise the two figures are not in the least like the ordinary Indian images of Gaṇeśa. They wear long robes and stand facing one another with their heads and trunks on each other's shoulders. One of the photographs shows two bronze figures in similar drapery, but standing back to back, not face to face.

In the shrines dedicated to Gaṇeśa an elaborate offering of food is generally spread out on plates and I am told that saké (alcohol) is used in the ritual, and at Uguisu no Taki a strange ceremony is performed from 1st January to 16th March (the first and sixteenth of the month being the two days sacred to the deity), when the image is bathed in boiling oil. Oil is also poured over it from a long spoon 108 times, repeated seven times. This ceremony is apparently due to the fact that Shōten Sama was formerly specially worshipped by oil merchants. Another rite is in use at Hōzanji at Ikoma which is much frequented by those who desire luck in any enterprise. Suppliants write their names and wishes on a piece of paper, which is then pasted on a stick about 10 inches long and the stick is planted in the ground. If a thousand such sticks are planted, it is believed that success is certain. Along the

[1] The reason why the images are not shown is that they are considered indecent. This is not true of any of the photographs in my possession, but it may be true of other figures. See G. Katō, *A Study of Shintō*, p. 172. In India Gaṇeśa is generally represented by a single seated figure, but standing figures are also found. See Gopinatha Rao, *Elements of Indian Iconography*, vol. i, part i, plate xv, and for a standing figure ib., plate xii.

sides of the tramway leading up to the temple may be seen many white patches which are plantations of these prayer sticks.

Bishamon has also an independent cult. He is Vaiśravana, the Regent of the north, and even in India was identified with Kuvera, the god of riches. In the Far East he became the god of war and in medieval Japan was regarded as the patron deity of warriors. Children whose parents desired for them a military career were sometimes consecrated to him. Near Ōji in Yamato is the temple city of Shigi which is dedicated to him. Here Shōtoku Taishi is said to have defeated Mononobe-no-Moriya, one of the enemies of Buddhism, in 587 and the victory was attributed to Bishamon's assistance. In later times Shigi was the scene of other warlike exploits.

Suiten or Varuna is said to be much worshipped in Tōkyō as a god of luck, but it must be remembered that there is a tendency to confound Indian marine deities and native Shintō deities which have some connection with the sea. The gods of the temple of Suminoe (or Sumiyoshi) in Settsu, for instance, belong to this latter class. But Kōbō Daishi and his sect after him had a strong inclination to see in such cases merely two forms of the same deity, one in Japanese and one in Indian dress. Anesaki (*Buddhist Art*, plate xxviii) gives a copy of a Mandara in which all the Shintō deities of Kasuga are represented in Buddhist form.

It is only natural that a sect which recognizes such a multitude of deities as the Shingon should also have many ceremonies and ritual observances. Two of these are specially remarkable, Kwanjō and Goma. I have spoken of Kwanjō already in treating of the Tendai, for it seems to have been first practised in Japan by that sect, although it has now come to be regarded as a special observance of the Shingon. Kwanjō is a translation of the Sanskrit *abhisheka*, which is commonly used in ancient and modern times to describe the ceremony corresponding to coronation, which in India was performed by sprinkling the king with water. At an early period, in the Dîgha Nikâya,[1] for instance, it is used in Buddhist works in a metaphorical sense. Later, when the career of a Bodhisattva is divided into stages or bhumis, the last or supreme stage is often called abhisheka. The term occurs first in the Mahâvastu and afterwards in the Śatasahasrikâ, Lankâvatâra, Dasabhûmika, and other works as a synonym of Dharmamegha, the idea apparently

[1] Dîg. Nik., xvi, 5–30.

being that the Bodhisattva, now at the end of his successful career, is sprinkled by the other Buddhas with their own hands and formally accepted by them. Kōbō Daishi, it will be remembered, defined [1] Kwanjō as "the bestowal of the Buddha's great mercy upon sentient beings in order to enable them to attain the highest perfect enlightenment".

In the Yung-Chia period A.D. 307–312 we hear that a monk of the Western country named Srimitra came to China, administered this rite of Kwanjō, and translated the Mahâbhishekârddhi-dhârani.[2] It would thus be possible for the Tendai sect, which was founded about A.D. 550, to have learnt about the ceremony not from the Chên-yen (Shingon), which was founded about two centuries later, but from some earlier source.

As mentioned already under the Tendai sect, the ritual for performing Kwanjō varies greatly and so do the objects for which it is performed. It may be a species of ordination and serve as a certificate that one has reached the highest grade of esoteric lore and is competent to instruct others. It may, on the other hand, fulfil some quite trivial purpose, such as a necessary formality before some specially holy object can be seen, or it may be used simply as an adjunct to prayer for health and wealth and any other private end.

Another remarkable ceremony is the Goma (Sanskrit Homa) or burnt offering, remarkable because one would as soon expect to find such oblations forming a part of Christian as of Buddhist worship. Nevertheless they were used by late Indian Buddhism and adopted by the Chinese, who passed them on to Japan, where they are used by most of the older sects, especially the Shingon, the Tendai, Kegon, Hossō, and Risshū. The Goma is also said to form part of the ritual of the Nichiren. In all sects the ceremony is said to be performed for some special object, either private or public, such as peace or victory. I am told that in cases of illness offerings with this rite are frequently made to Yakushi, the healing Buddha. For its performance a stage or table is erected before an image or mandara and a metal basin is let into it to receive the burnt offerings. These consist of fragrant wood, poppy seeds, oil, incense, perfumes, and similar substances. Cakes and flowers are placed upon the table and offered but are not burnt. The

[1] See Chap. XIV, p. 328.

[2] Nanjio, No. 167, wherein it is stated that the work is a collection of twelve sûtras. See also Nanjio, ii, 36.

officiant sits in front of the table and all his actions, especially the position of his hands (the mudrâ), are of great moment. In all Shingon ceremonies the greatest weight is attached to such gestures.[1] Like the Indian Tantric mudrâs, from which they are borrowed, they are considered to be the essence and manifestation of the various deities, and it is most important that the officiant should imitate the gesture appropriate to the particular deity whom he is worshipping in order that he may be as like that deity as possible.

[1] The subject is treated fully with numerous diagrams in the work called Si-do-in-dzou, published in 1899 by the Musée Guimet, text by Horiou Toki, notes by L. de Milloue.

# CHAPTER XVI

## AMIDISM

THOUGH Amida, or Amitâbha, is well known as a benevolent deity in China, Tibet, and other countries of the Far East, it is above all in Japan that his worship has developed into distinct, well organized, popular, and progressive sects which claim attention if only for the numbers and wealth of their adherents. In the earlier sections of this work I have already spoken several times at length of the history of this worship which is summed up in the names of its seven Patriarchs: two Indian, Nâgârjuna and Vasubandhu; three Chinese, Donran, Dōshaku, and Zendō; and two Japanese, Genshin and Hōnen.[1]

The cult of Amida seems to have begun in India about the time of the Christian era, or possibly a little earlier, and perhaps was not originally Indian but introduced from the Iranian districts lying to the north, but in saying this it must be remembered that the earliest Amidist scriptures, the two Sukhâvatî-vyûhas, are entirely Indian in tone and outlook. Though remarkable analogies, verbal and other, may be found with the Avesta, there are only two points which suggest that the worship is really not Buddhist in origin. They are, it must be confessed, sufficiently important. The first is that the chief figure, Amitâbha or Amitâyus, Measureless Light or Life, as he is indifferently called, is totally unknown in the oldest Buddhist literature, whether Pali or Sanskrit, and when he first appears is far from having the same pre-eminent position which he acquired in later times. Although numerous works of respectable antiquity recommend his worship and represent it as prevalent in India, his adorers do not seem to have formed a corporation as they did later in Japan or as did the Bhâgavatas at an early period in India itself. Secondly, the essential doctrine of the sect, the transfer of merit or of being saved by the exertions of another, is repudiated by early Buddhism. The Buddha shows men how they can save themselves, but he is not a saviour except in the sense that a teacher is one. Our future is determined by our

[1] This is the list given in Shinran's Shōshinge. Other versions give Hōnen and Shinran.

own good or bad actions. Still, even in Indian religions the idea of a saviour, though less common than in other countries, is not unknown. It is an easy and comfortable doctrine and appeals in all countries to both sinners and good men who shrink from the labour of elaborate ritual or arduous thought. The special form of saviour which appealed to the Far East was a Buddha who has obtained enlightenment by his exertions continued through long ages and on the express condition that he does not need Buddhahood unless he can admit to his paradise all who call on his name. It is to be noted that the Buddha to be is not praying to or making vows to any Supreme Being. By refusing Buddhahood except on conditions he is instituting a new kind of Karma which enables him to share with other men his marvellous merit, which is more than is needed to make one man a Buddha. According to the Mahayanist sûtras, Amida is only one of many Buddhas who have performed this feat, though for practical purposes his name has eclipsed all others.

The worship of Amitâbha was introduced into China at an early date and seems to have been made a definite sect or school by Hui-Yüan (333–418). The school was most successful and produced several renowned doctors of whom Zendō [1] was the most celebrated, being regarded in Japan as an incarnation of Amida himself. He is the author of the celebrated parable of the White Path which is regarded as an epitome of religion. It tells how a traveller proceeding westwards across a vast plain found himself confronted by two rivers or rather sheets of water, for they were unfathomable and so wide that no one could see the further shore. The only way across them was a narrow white path a few inches wide, continually washed by the waves and flames which came upon it from the two sides. Wondering what he should do, he looked backwards and saw a band of brigands and a pack of wild beasts following his track. In desperation he decided to advance along the white path at any risk. As soon as he had taken this decision, he heard a voice calling to him, "With right thought and singleness of heart walk on without fear. I will protect thee." It was the voice of Amida, and stepping resolutely along the narrow way, the traveller was soon welcomed by him in his paradise of the West.

But after some centuries the popularity of Amida's worship prevented it from being appropriated by any one sect. It became

[1] 善導.

not the special tenet of a particular Church but an aspect of all, because none could afford to neglect so attractive a doctrine. This partly accounts for the manner of its introduction into Japan. It was not brought back like the Tendai, Shingon, and Zen by priests who had gone to study in China, but after Amida had become a familiar figure, the idea that he was to be regarded not only as a saviour but as the only Saviour was preached by Hōnen, Shinran, and others and became a great religious movement which seemed thoroughly national and to owe nothing to China.

It is recorded that the Sukhâvatî-vyûha was publicly recited at the Japanese Court as early as A.D. 640. In the Nara period Gyōgi Bosatsu and other famous priests are said to have preached the doctrine of Jōdo, the Pure Land, though I have not found any detailed account of their activities in this respect. When after the removal of the capital to Kyōto Dengyō Daishi and Kōbō Daishi had established the Tendai and Shingon sects on a firm basis, the worship of Amida became increasingly popular, but it differed from the later teaching of Hōnen in two respects. In the first place, it nearly always involved meditation on Amida: mere invocation or the repetition of his name was not sufficient. Secondly, though concentration of the mind on a particular Buddha and especially on Amida (since tradition and literature rendered him eminently suitable for the purpose) was recognized as a method of attaining paradise, still it was only one method. The Tendai and Shingon had numerous other receipts for salvation and the chief recommendation of this procedure was its easiness. There was no notion that it was the one and only form of religion practicable in the present decadent age. Still it was undoubtedly popular. Dengyō Daishi and his successor Jikaku (794–864) are said to have repeated the Nembutsu: the ex-Emperors Uda (866–931) and Go-Shirakawa (1125–1192) died invoking Amida with their faces turned to the west: Kūya, the itinerant preacher and dancer, spread the use of the Nembutsu: Kakuhan, the founder of a new branch of the Shingon, accommodated it to the principles of his sect: Yōkwan and Chingai also recommended its use with various slight modifications of their own. More important for the history of dogma is Genshin [1] (942–1017), who is often recognized as the first Japanese patriarch of the Amidist school, because he came near to preaching

[1] Often called Eshin Sōzu 惠心僧都. He was Abbot of the Eshin-in in Yokawa on Mount Hiei.

the same doctrine as Hōnen in holding that the mere repetition of the Nembutsu without the practice of meditation is sufficient to cleanse from sin and to secure rebirth in paradise. He was also the spiritual ancestor of Hōnen in another sense, for he wrote a book called Ōjōyōshū,[1] in which he explained the views of Zendō, and it was the perusal of the Ōjōyōshū which turned Hōnen's attention to Zendō, whom he came to consider an infallible authority in matters of doctrine. The work of Genshin is remarkable for its vivid descriptions of paradise and also of the terrible destinies which await the wicked. He has been compared to Dante, but was a painter and sculptor as well as a writer. Perhaps he was really most remarkable and influential as a painter, for the pictures attributed to him, if genuine, show a freedom both in colour and outline which marks a change in the conventional Buddhist art of that date. He seems indeed to have been an artist rather than a preacher or philosopher and he left no sect behind him. The first to do this was Ryōnin [2] (1072–1132), a younger contemporary of Genshin's who founded a sect called the Yūzū Nembutsu, which still exists though small in numbers.[3] The formation of a sect, however, having as its cardinal principle the worship of Amida was an event of some importance since he had hitherto been adored as one of the many Buddhas recognized by the older religious bodies. In this respect Ryōnin paved the way for Hōnen's teaching, but in others his doctrine shows considerable differences. First, he did not appeal to the three Amidist sûtras as his authorities but to the Lotus and the Kegon-sûtra, thus maintaining a sort of connection with the Tendai. Secondly, he claimed to have received personal inspiration from Amida and the god Bishamon. Thirdly, he held, as a part of Amida's special revelation, that the recitation of the Nembutsu, which he recognized as the principal act of devotion, should be made on behalf of others as well as for oneself, and that if made with this larger application it was a thousand million times more meritorious than if uttered as a merely selfish prayer. It is strange that this idea does not seem to have been taken up by any of the later Amidist schools.

In 1133, a year after Ryōnin's death, was born Hōnen [4] (or Genkū), the real founder of Japanese Amidism. It is true that his followers were not officially recognized as a sect until the time of

[1] 往生要集.

[2] 良忍.

[3] It has about 350 temples.

[4] 法然, 源空.

Ieyasu, though in practice they formed a religious body from Hōnen's lifetime onwards, and also that Shinran developed certain points of doctrine with greater precision. Yet Genshin, the only previous doctor who enunciated almost the same doctrine, was not a teacher and had practically no followers, while it is not clear that apart from Hōnen, Shinran's convictions would have taken the form which they did. He always professed to be Hōnen's disciple and Hōnen is therefore rightly considered as the founder of Jōdo,[1] or religion of the Pure Land, in Japan. This name is perhaps the designation most widely used and is simply the Japanese pronunciation of Ch'ing-tu, the title given to Amida's Paradise by the Chinese. Shinshū, or more correctly Jōdo Shinshū,[2] means simply the true form of Jōdo, that is, the Jōdo faith as more clearly defined and, in the opinion of his followers, improved by Shinran.

I have already given some accounts of Hōnen's life and it remains to examine his doctrines in more detail. His personal character influenced his teaching. His was a peculiarly amiable and gentle nature, always anxious not to offend, to see things from other's points of view and to formulate his own so as to raise as few objections as possible. Indeed, some passages in his writings have been much criticized by later Jōdo doctors for their too great liberality, for instance, one [3] in which he seems to say that other forms of worship are as good as the Nembutsu provided that the thought and prayer be directed towards Amida and the Pure Land. In another passage,[4] too, he says that it is allowable to pray for worldly goods, not only by practising the Nembutsu but by invoking the other Buddhas or gods, by reading or writing the sûtras, or by making images of the Buddhas. It is clear that the school which he inaugurated was part of the larger religious movement which was everywhere evident in this period and which found expression in the informality of Zen and in the polemics of Nichiren. The universal effort was to find some intelligible and easy form of religion [5] which would bring light and comfort to souls which had sought them in vain in the ritual and philosophy of the older systems. Hōnen says this frequently in his own way, and he once stated [6] that the reason why he founded

[1] 淨土.

[2] 淨土眞宗.

[3] *Hōnen, the Buddhist Saint*, p. 422.

[4] Ibid., p. 460.

[5] It may seem strange to speak of Zen as easy, but it had become a system of training which was intelligible to the military classes in a way in which ceremonies and metaphysics were not.

[6] *Hōnen, the Buddhist Saint*, p. 138.

the Jōdo sect was to show ordinary man how to be born into the Buddha's own country. He was also under the influence of the idea that the world had entered on its last and worst phase, or the Age of Mappō, in which the true Law and virtue were decaying. In spite of his profound learning, his teaching is emotional rather than reasoned and addressed to the ignorant and simple-minded. He defines it himself in the "One Sheet of Paper", the last thing which he wrote, as being "nothing but the mere repetition of the Namu Amida Butsu without a doubt of his mercy whereby one may be born into Paradise".

As an exponent of these views Hōnen was perhaps at his best in conversation and in intimate letters, but he wrote several books, the best known of which is the Senchakushū,[1] consisting of sixteen chapters quoting many passages from the three Amidist-sûtras as well as from the Chinese Patriarch Zendō, of whom he says that he was an incarnation of Amida and that though we have had many teachers of the Pure Land sect we should depend solely on Zendō.[2] As Hōnen is said to have read the whole Tripiṭaka several times, he had probably perused the Âgamas (equivalent to the Pali Nikâyas), but so far as I know he never quotes them or attaches the smallest importance to the fact that though they are the most ancient and authoritative accounts of Shaka's preaching they contain no mention of Amida. With his usual charity he says[3] that no one should speak of the Lotus or of the Prajñâpâramitâ with the least disparagement, but evidently the three Amidist-sûtras are for him the ultimate source of truth and Shaka's mission was to make them known to the world. I have already given some account of these books[4] and of the little we know of the origin of the doctrines they contain. Hōnen seems to attach especial importance to the Amitâyurdhyâna-sûtra, Shinran to the larger Sukhâvatî-vyûha.

The Senchaku opens by dividing religious practices into the Shōdō, or holy path, and the Jōdo, or pure land, which are equivalent to the distinction (first drawn by the Chinese Patriarch Donran) between Jiriki, or reliance on one's own strength, and Tariki, or

[1] Or in full 選擇本願念佛集 Senchaku Hongwan Nembutsushū, "A collection of passages bearing on the Nembutsu of the original vow." Other books of Hōnen also quoted are the Ōjō Taiyōshū and a commentary on the larger Sukhâvatî-vyûha. See *Hōnen, the Buddhist Saint*, pp. 348, 351.

[2] *Hōnen, the Buddhist Saint*, p. 467. Cf. pp. 347 and 87.

[3] Ibid., p. 404.

[4] Chapter IV, p. 105 ff.

reliance on the strength of another. The Mahâsannipâta-sûtra [1] is quoted as making Shaka himself say that in these latter days of the Law the Shōdō, or path which he himself preached, has become impracticable. Not one of the many who have attempted to walk in it have obtained salvation. The only hope for mankind is to endeavour to reach the Paradise called the Pure Land and to do so not by accumulating merit but by trusting simply and solely to the benevolence of Amida, that is, the Buddha Amitâbha or Amitâyus, for the shorter form answers to both of the original longer names. The sûtras relate how this great Being became a Buddha in the same way that others have done. Incalculably long ages ago he was a Bhikshu called Dharmâkara, rendered in Japanese as Hōzō, in the time of the Buddha called Lokeśvara-râja (in Japanese Sejizaiō Butsu), and made a vow (pranidhâna),[2] or rather series of vows, to save the human race, the gist of them being that he would not accept Buddhahood, which was his due in virtue of the merits acquired by his unselfish exertions continued through innumerable births, except on certain conditions. "For whose sake was it," asks Hōnen, "that Amida went through austerities for such long kalpas of time? He was transferring the merit of his discipline to all the sentient beings of all coming time. What was the reason for that transcendent vow which he made? It was indeed for our sakes who live in these latter days." [3] Of these conditions there are no less than forty-eight,[4] though of varying importance. The principal is number eighteen, which stipulates that "any being who calls on my name at least ten times shall be born into my land", that is, the Paradise which he will own as a Buddha.[5] Rebirth in the Paradise is commonly called Ōjō.[6] He further vowed that all the inhabitants of this wondrous land

[1] Nanjio, No. 63.

[2] The figure of a Buddha making such vows is a peculiarly frequent subject in the frescoes discovered in Central Asia.

[3] *Hōnen, the Buddhist Saint*, p. 587.

[4] The numbering is somewhat different in the Sanskrit text, which makes forty-six vows in all, and in the Chinese translations, which makes forty-eight. See Nanjio's note on p. 73 of Sukhâvatî-vyûha. *S.B.E.*, vol. xlix.

[5] The Greater Sukhâvatî-vyûha, *S.B.E.*, xlix, p. 15, § 19, seems to require ten repetitions and to exclude those who commit the five deadly sins, whereas Hōnen seems to hold that even such sinners can be saved (*Hōnen, the Buddhist Saint*, p. 395). "While believing that one guilty of the ten evil deeds and the five deadly sins may be born into the Pure Land . . . let us not commit the smallest sins." Cf. ib., pp. 402, 403, and p. 330.

[6] 往生.

should be certain of obtaining nirvâna (a stipulation which is often forgotten by those who speak of it as a permanent heaven) and be eligible as a candidate for Buddhahood. All women who pray for rebirth in Paradise shall be changed into men.

If we ask why we should put our trust in Amida rather than in any other Buddha, the answer must be that he vowed to become a Buddha and save mankind, that he succeeded in becoming a Buddha, that Shaka came into the world to explain this vow, and that innumerable Buddhas testified that there was no doubt as to the correctness of his explanation. Yet Hōnen's belief and trust in Amida, though deep and intense, was not in the least polemical. " You should not say as some do that because you trust in Amida and the Nembutsu it is right to have nothing to do with the merciful vows of the many Buddhas and Bodhisattvas. . . . Your faith is quite one sided if you despise the many Buddhas or doubt Shaka's holy teachings." Similarly, in the " One Sheet of Paper " he is careful to allude to " the mercy of the two Holy Ones ", that is, Shaka and Amida. Hence the Jōdo sect is sometimes known as the Ni-son Ikkyō, or one religion with two deities. Similarly, various Bodhisattvas such as Kwannon and Seishi are adored in Jōdo temples (which is only natural considering the position given to them in the Amitâyurdhyâna-sûtra), and Hōnen himself was believed to be an incarnation of Seishi. He speaks incidentally of the protection of Brahmâ and Śakra (Indra).[1]

The salvation offered by Amida consists of rebirth in his Paradise, which all ancient accounts agree is situated in the West and where all shall enjoy wonderful powers of body and mind. Later accounts tend to regard it as a permanent residence for all eternity, but the sûtras speak of it as being rather a blissful and peaceful sojourn where one can obtain nirvâna or even become a Buddha. The idea that one who has obtained Ōjō or birth in paradise can return to the world and work for the salvation of others is countenanced by Hōnen,[2] but he explains that such a one is not returning to the round of births and deaths but voluntarily and for the sake of helping others revisits temporarily this sinful world. In the Buddhist periodical called the *Young East* [3] will be found an interesting article by Professor Takakusu in which he relates the death in 1928

[1] *Hōnen, the Buddhist Saint*, p. 754. [2] Ibid., p. 425.

[3] *Young East*, 8th April, 1928. The title of the article is " Ōsō Ekō and Gensō Ekō ", which are technical terms, the first for receiving the blessing of being born in paradise and the second for returning to this world in the manner described.

of Baroness Kujō, a lady of great piety, and describes how at the entreaty of her friends she promised to return to this earth. There is also an annex to the Pure Land called Keman-Kai, literally the realm of laziness, in which the spirits of doubters have to spend a certain time. Hōnen does not appear to mention it, though a similar idea is to be found in the Greater Sukhâvatî-vyûha,[1] according to which those who are filled with faith are born miraculously in the Pure Land sitting cross-legged on the petals of a lotus, while doubters have to spend five hundred years in the interior of the flower without seeing the Buddha until they are freed of their doubts. In the works of Kōa Shōnin (1269–1330), one of the early lights of the Chinzei division of the Jōdo, may be found clear descriptions of Keman-Kai as a place of probation outside Paradise and nearer to this earth.[2]

Shinran also in his work Kyōgyō Shinshō [3] cites passages from various sûtras about Keman-Kai, and the Tannishō mentions "the outskirts (邊 地 henji) of the Pure Land" as a sort of purgatory for doubters but condemning the view that its inmates can ultimately go to hell.

To obtain admission to this paradise it is only necessary to recite the Nembutsu—that is, the formula Namu Amida Butsu, or reverence to Amida Butsu—and according to the eighteenth vow, ten repetitions of the sacred words are sufficient. It is important to observe that, according to Hōnen, nothing is required except repetition of the formula with faith. He is emphatic in declaring that meditation on Amida, which was considered a necessary part of the Nembutsu according to the older sects and which is certainly prescribed in the Amitâyurdhyâna-sûtra, is superfluous. The system is primarily one for the ordinary man: no one can complain that he does not understand it. But though it is certainly no tax upon the intellect, the repetition of the Nembutsu as enjoined by Hōnen makes severe inroads on one's time. "Even if you are doing something else, do it while you go on with the main work of life, which is the practice of the Nembutsu, and do not let the Nembutsu be a sort of side work to anything else."[4] Hōnen and many other saints are said

[1] §§ 40 and 41.

[2] In his Sai-yō-shō, translated by Haas in *Amida Buddha unsere Zuflucht*. Haas also says that Hōnen's predecessor Yōkwan (1032–1111) gives a detailed account of Keman-Kai in his book Ōjō-jū-in.

[3] 敎行信證, vol. vi. Tannishō, xvii, and postscript.

[4] *Hōnen, the Buddhist Saint*, p. 395.

to have repeated it sixty thousand times a day. Services were even held for repeating it a million times. A number of men sat together with an immense rosary about 10 feet in diameter and repeated the Nembutsu about 150,000 times in twenty-four hours.

It is even stated in Hōnen's Life [1] that the Emperor Go Shirakawa during his last illness repeated it a million times two hundred times over, and was rewarded with a peaceful end.

It is strange that a man of Hōnen's intelligence and real piety should have approved and enjoined what seems a monstrous number of repetitions of one prayer. He did not deny that in certain cases to say the Nembutsu ten times, or even once, was enough to secure Ōjō, but he held that when once the wish to be born in the Pure Land had arisen one should make that wish one's chief occupation and, so far as possible, think of nothing else. In the "One Sheet of Paper" he deprecates all technicalities and says that "the mere repetition with firm faith includes all details such as the three states of mind", but this is because he wants to emphasize the simplicity of his essential teaching. In another letter [2] he expounds the said states with great eloquence and makes it plain that the recitation of the Nembutsu, as he contemplated it, was not merely mechanical. The definition of the three states of mind originated with Zendō, who laid it down that prayer should be offered with a sincere heart, a deep-believing heart, and a longing heart. A sincere heart is one in which every thought is true and full of genuine devotion. A believing heart explains itself. "If a man thinks there is any uncertainty about his birth in the Pure Land, it is uncertain, whereas if he thinks it certain, it is certain." By a longing heart [3] is meant one which wishes all the merits which it may have acquired in this or previous existences to be presented and dedicated to the Buddha with the one object of attaining birth in the Pure Land. This sounds like a contradiction of the fundamental principles of the Jōdo creed, and to make one's entry into Paradise depend on one's own merits and exertions and not solely and entirely on Amida. Hōnen's explanation is that the object is to avoid having any desires except for birth in the Pure Land. The believer presumably acquires some good karma by his actions and he should not dream of making any use of it except to offer it humbly to Amida.

[1] *Hōnen, the Buddhist Saint*, p. 235.

[2] Ibid., p. 414.

[3] Ekōhotsugwanjin 回向發願心, literally a heart which turns and vows.

The real importance of these psychological arguments respecting the proper state of mind in which to pray lies in their bearing on the forgiveness of sins. Amida is all-merciful. He will come to the deathbed of a criminal who calls on him and conduct him to Paradise. Then why not sin as much as one likes, say the Nembutsu when suitable with perfect faith and go in good time to heaven? The Jōdo and the Shinshū were continually accused of preaching this immoral doctrine, and throughout Hōnen's active life we find him continually arguing against such a perversion of his teaching. Yet it is a mistake which it is very easy to make and even Hōnen himself wrote passages which he might have done well to word differently. "If you have any time to spare after saying the Nembutsu," he wrote to Rensei,[1] "then you may apply it to doing good works. . . . If you say the Nembutsu thirty or fifty thousand times, even if you should break a few of the commandments, that cannot affect your attainment of Ōjō at all." But generally, as one might expect, he vigorously affirms the need of good conduct. "While believing that even a man guilty of the ten evil deeds and the five deadly sins may be born into the Pure Land, let us for our part not be guilty of even the smallest sins."[2] And again, "If your faith is not right, it is not in harmony with the mind of Amida and it is certain that his merciful vow has nothing to do with you. . . . Some say that the effort to avoid sin and improve oneself is making light of Amida's vow. . . . Do not be for a moment misled by such false ideas. Is there any place in any of the sûtras where Amida encourages men to sin? Certainly not. Such things come from those who make no effort to get away from their own evil deeds and who go on in their former sinful life. . . . Such persons are nothing less than a company of devils, their work is heathenish and you should think of them as enemies to your attaining birth in the Pure Land." In other words, the idea that it is possible to continue sinning deliberately and to do away with the sin by reciting the Nembutsu has the appearance of logic but it is an entire misunderstanding of the Nembutsu. Amida is full of compassion for sinners, but he hates sin for he knows it is the cause of misery, and any device to increase sin must be hateful to him. The recitation of the Nembutsu with faith implies repentance for sin in the past and the desire to avoid it in the future. Doubtless, too, the repetition of the Nembutsu was regarded as a preventative

[1] *Hōnen, the Buddhist Saint*, p. 495.
[2] Ibid., p. 395, and in almost identical words, p. 403.

of sinful desires: according to Hōnen prayer is not merely a help to life, it should be the whole of life and the object of life. One should not have any desire except to be reborn in the Pure Land, and consequently there will not be room in one's mind for passion or ambition.

Nevertheless, the Pure Land sects were long troubled with the heresy that since Amida's object is to save and help sinners who call on him, he may be said in a certain sense to love sinners and to enjoy sin, since it gives a larger scope for the display of his grace. The same theory is found among some Vishnuist schools in Southern India, where it is called Doshabhogya (enjoying sin), and, lest it should be supposed that Orientals have a monopoly of these queer ideas, it also crops up in the works of Oscar Wilde, who says in De Profundis: "Christ through some divine instinct in Him seems to have always loved the sinner as being the nearest approach to perfection in man. . . . In a manner not yet understood of the world He regarded sin and suffering as being in themselves beautiful holy things and modes of perfection. . . . Christ, had He been asked, would have said—I feel quite certain about this—that the moment the Prodigal Son fell on his knees and wept, he made his having wasted his substance with harlots, his swine-herding and his hungering for the husks they ate beautiful and holy moments in his life."

Hōnen's amiable and undogmatic temper led him to formulate his views in simple and untechnical language and so far as possible to avoid contradicting other sects. But after his death his successors were inclined to be more precise and to define and develop doctrines which he had perhaps purposely left somewhat vague. Six of his disciples, Shōkōbō, Zennebō (also called Shōkū), Shinran, Ryūkan, Chōsai, and Kōsai, founded sects or sub-sects of which the first three survive, while the others have become extinct. Shōkōbō's school, which is called Chinzei,[1] is the ordinary Jōdo sect as it exists at present and appears to represent correctly Hōnen's views. It emphasizes the need of frequently reciting the Nembutsu with as deep earnestness as if each repetition was made with one's last breath. But it also gives due importance to Amida's twentieth vow, which is that those who acquire merit by practices other than the Nembutsu shall be born in the Pure Land at the end of the third rebirth after the present at the latest.

[1] 鎮西.

Zennebō founded the Seizan[1] school, which is still recognized as an orthodox branch of the Jōdo and has the Zenrinji temple at Kyōto as its headquarters. I find it exceedingly difficult to state what are its special views, although Hōnen's Life contains a long chapter on the teachings of Zennebō (No. xxvii).[2] The Japanese as a nation have perhaps not much talent for metaphysics and probably most of what they have to say on such questions is borrowed. But the religious public (like the Protestant denominations of Europe) seems to have a taste for discussing such matters as faith, freewill, grace, and the relations of the Buddha or God to the human soul. It is the last question—the intimate union existing between Amida and his devotees—which seems to have preoccupied Zennebō. He is quoted as saying that "rebirth is attained when Amida enters into our hearts and when this happens our works are his and his are ours: in the unity of Amida and ourselves Amida realizes his Buddhahood and on our side rebirth is attained". He also appears to have attached little importance to the twentieth vow and to have maintained that the Nembutsu was essential to salvation, which could not be obtained by merit arising from meditation or other good works. Chōsai, on the other hand, considered that this vow definitely authorized such meritorious practices as means of salvation equivalent to the Nembutsu. He founded a school which is now extinct called Kuhonji, from a temple of the same name in the suburbs of Kyōto.

Another point on which the opinion of Hōnen's disciples was strongly divided was the question of "one calling" or "many callings",[3] that is, one or many recitations of the Nembutsu. Hōnen's practice was certainly in favour of "many callings", and another strong advocate of the principle was his disciple Ryūkan,[4] who held that a devout man should continue calling on the Buddha's name all his life until the day of his death. The partisans of "one calling" raised no objection to repeated invocations but insisted on the absolute sufficiency of one. This one invocation must be a solemn act of faith by which the devotee is made one with Amida in spiritual union, and without such faith mere recitation is of no avail. Kōsai, one of Hōnen's disciples, is said to have held this

[1] 西山.

[2] There is also a study of Shōkū's (Zennebō's) teaching by Shizutoshi Sugihira in the *Eastern Buddhist*, vol. v, No. 1 of March, 1929. But I confess that very little of it is intelligible to me.

[3] In Japanese — 一念義 and 多念義.

[4] For an account of him see *Hōnen, the Buddhist Saint*, chap. xliv.

view.[1] He had been brought up in the Tendai sect and held that Amida had two personalities, the original (hommon) and the incarnate (shakumon).[2] The latter is the Amida who ages ago appeared in the world as Hōzō and ultimately attained Buddhahood, but the original personality is without beginning and is identical with the Buddha nature which is in all of us. It is sufficient for salvation to realize this truth and in its light to recite the Nembutsu once only. Kōsai [3] also appears to have held that there was no objection to Jōdo priests marrying.

Hōnen strongly objected to the "one calling" principle and contended that it was contrary to Zendō's views, in which he was no doubt right. But Kōsai insisted in maintaining his errors "until Hōnen could no longer have him for his disciple" and so expelled him from the sect. Hōnen also "issued a written instruction" denouncing the once-calling doctrine in strong language, which was very unusual to his gentle temper. He seems to have been particularly irritated by the statement that it was the doctrine which he really held and that the many thousand daily repetitions of the Nembutsu which he was said to make were an empty pretence. He also seems to connect the once-calling principle with the doctrine that immorality is permissible.

Kōsai and his sect have for all practical purposes been long forgotten, but his interest lies in the fact that the Life of Hōnen represents him as holding, and as being condemned by the master for holding, the same views—once-calling and the marriage of the clergy—as were undoubtedly approved by far the most important of Hōnen's disciples, namely, Shinran. The sect founded by Shinran is known as the Jōdo Shinshū, or True sect of the Pure Land, that is, the correct doctrine about the Pure Land. It is the largest Buddhist denomination in Japan and numbers at the present day above thirteen million adherents against about three million belonging to the Jōdo of Hōnen. I have given above some account of the life of the founder and of the history of the sect, which differed considerably from that of Hōnen's school. Shinran founded during his life many temples in provinces distant from Kyōto, such as Echizen and Shimotsuke, and these developed into a formidable military power like the old monasteries, though their manner of conducting operations was somewhat different. The permission given to the priests to marry made the hereditary Shinshū abbots

[1] *Hōnen, the Buddhist Saint*, chap. xxix. [2] 本門 and 迹門.
[3] Ibid., p. 524.

almost exact counterparts of secular nobles, and they transferred their temples, or fortified residences, from one place to another as pleased them. The Shinshū is divided into ten sub-sects, but they present no differences of doctrine and in constitution resemble bishoprics.

According to the Shinshū Catechism[1] the name of the sect is taken from the Chinese Patriarch Zendō, who uses the expression "Shinshū, or the true sect, is hard to find". It is most remarkable to find that Shinran himself uses it of the teaching of Hōnen, of whom he says in one of his hymns, "Out of the might of the light of wisdom appeared the great founder Genkū. He founded the Jōdo Shinshū and preached the vows of Amida." It is not quite clear when a distinction was first drawn between the Jōdo and the Jōdo Shinshū and when Shinran's followers separated themselves from those of Hōnen, particularly as for a long time the latter were not reckoned as a distinct and officially recognized sect. It is claimed by the Shinshū sect that Hōnen countenanced all Shinran's innovations and merely tolerated the old monastic discipline for fear of doing more harm than good if he broke too violently with ancient usage. As I have mentioned elsewhere, the incidents of Shinran's life are extremely doubtful. It seems, however, certain that he was not only a devoted follower of Hōnen but his favourite disciple. The Tannishō records his emphatic assertion that he would not mind going to hell if he had been deceived by Hōnen. They appear to have lived together in perfect harmony until they were banished, Hōnen to Shikoku and Shinran to Echigo. Shinran made use of his banishment for missionary propaganda, and on being pardoned prepared to return to Kyōto in 1226, but hearing on his way that Hōnen was dead, returned voluntarily to Echigo to continue his missionary labours. He then spent several years in Hitachi, made a long tour in which he not only preached and made converts but also built temples, and finally settled down in Kyōto after an absence of twenty-eight years. These circumstances

[1] I shall often have occasion to quote this work, which seems to be a concise and authoritative statement of modern Shinshū doctrine, by R. Nishimoto. Its Japanese title is Shinshū Hyakuwa and it was published in Tōkyō about 1910. It is translated by A. K. Reischauer in vol. xxxviii, part v, of the *Trans. of the As. Soc. of Japan*, 1912. The passage here referred to is § 23. See also *Synopsis of the Jōdo Shinshū Creed*, compiled (in English) by the Educational Department of the West Hongwanji, Kyōto, 1920. This body has also published *Hymns of the Pure Land* (Japanese text and translation), which is one of the three volumes of Shinran's hymns.

make the Shinshū account of the division seem highly probable. Hōnen was most conciliatory and anxious not to offend: he was even open to the charge of occasional inconsistency and we know that there were varieties of opinion among his disciples. He may have raised no objections to Shinran's views while not thinking it wise to give them his public approval. Then comes the period of exile and Shinran's absence from Kyōto during twenty-eight years. One can well imagine that those of Hōnen's disciples who remained in the capital would feel the pressure of ecclesiastical opinion and, though they were regarded as heretics, shrink from incurring the charge of being immoral antidisciplinarians. Shinran, on the contrary, moving as a missionary among rural populations who probably knew little of Buddhism, would not feel the same restraints or find any inconvenience in preaching new doctrines and practices. When he at last returned to Kyōto the breach between himself and those of Hōnen's followers who remained in the capital had probably perceptibly widened, and we can imagine that the habit of instructing comparatively ignorant audiences had made him somewhat dogmatic, so it is not wonderful if he and his followers declined to unite with the others and claimed to be the "True sect of Jōdo".

It is noticeable that Hōnen's biographer Shunjō, though he relates the anecdotes about Kōsai mentioned above, says nothing about Shinran and passes him over in silence, though he devotes special chapters to the other eminent disciples. This is perhaps merely the result of sectarian disapproval, but it is also most remarkable that neither he nor Kakunyo, the earliest biographer of Shinran, mention Shinran's marriage to Kanezane's daughter, whereas the accepted story is that Hōnen approved of and even arranged the said marriage. It may be taken as certain that Shinran approved of the marriage of the clergy and was married himself, but still it may be doubted if the above story is true. If it were, it is strange that we hear nothing about the matter in Shunjō's life, for considering the high social position of the bride the scandal in Kyōto would have been considerable, and on the other hand no reason can be assigned for Kakunyo's silence, for the followers of the Shinshū evidently consider the marriage as a credit to their communion. But the course of events seems to me easier to understand if we suppose that Hōnen and Shinran discussed many subjects together, including the marriage of the clergy and the question of "once-calling", but that Shinran did not actually marry and mature his views on various doctrinal points until after Hōnen's death. Ryōkū's biography of Shinran states that Kanezane's daughter died and that Shinran married again in the Kwantō and had five children, four boys (Zenran, etc.) and one girl. But I do not venture to express any decided opinion on the question, for the documents have not been examined critically and religious prejudice may have affected the accuracy of the statements made by both sides.

It is not easy to separate the doctrines of Hōnen and Shinran. The Jōdo does not differ conspicuously from the older sects in discipline, ritual, and the appearance of its temples : it honours other Buddhas and Bodhisattvas besides Amida, but teaches that salvation is best and most easily obtained by invoking his name. The Shinshū, on the other hand, has abolished monasticism and its temples are easily distinguishable from others : worship is offered to Amida only : salvation is obtained by faith, which is the gift of Amida, and it begins in this world as soon as faith begins in the believer. But most of these differences, though valid as a rough statement, are not absolute. Shaka and other Buddhas are invoked in the funeral ceremonies of the Shinshū. The doctrine of faith is old : it is found in the Jōdo as clearly as in the Shinshū, and the Shinshū is emphatic in extolling the efficacy of the Nembutsu, though not for quite the same reasons. The doctrine of immediate salvation, too, was not an invention of Shinran, for Hōnen said, "How happy the thought that though we are still here in the flesh we are numbered among the holy ones of Paradise." But though there is this community of doctrine, the distinctness and prominence of the Shinshū cannot be ignored. It has no endowments and relics or voluntary subscriptions, yet its temples are the largest and most conspicuous in Japan and are built within cities so as to be immediately accessible to the ordinary population, whereas those of other sects were originally built outside cities or on their edges, though they may have become surrounded by the growth of suburbs. The magnificent temple called Higashi Hongwanji in Kyōto was rebuilt in 1895 entirely by popular enterprise. The inhabitants of the surrounding provinces, who were largely peasants, presented subscriptions amounting to a million yen, besides building materials offered in kind. Coils of gigantic hawsers made of human hair with which the pillars and timbers were hoisted into their places are still shown. Yet though the sect appeals so strongly to the people, its connection with the aristocracy and even the Imperial Family is equally remarkable. Count Otani Kōchō, the abbot of this temple, married the Princess Satoko, daughter of Prince Kuni, and sister of the present Empress of Japan.

The teaching of Shinshū is frequently summed up in the phrase Shinzoku Nitai, or in full, Shintai and Zokutai.[1] The phrase is in common use in other sects as well and describes the two great divisions of religion, faith and morality. Shintai refers mainly to the next world, the salvation offered by Amida and how to obtain it. Zokutai is a man's duty as a member of society, but duty in the sense of conduct arising from faith. It is the peculiar merit of Shinshū, says the Catechism, that it alone of all Buddhist sects shows how the religious faith of a believer and his daily conduct as a citizen of the world may be made to harmonize. The Ryōgemon of Rennyo, a sort of creed, is perhaps the simplest and most authoritative statement respecting Shintai and Zokutai.

"Rejecting all other religious practices and works and all idea that I can help myself, I pray wholeheartedly to Amida for my salvation in the life to come which is the most important of all things. I believe that the moment I have faith in him my entry into the life of paradise is certain and I exult in the thought that henceforth invocation of his name is an expression of thankfulness. Moreover, I remember with thankfulness that I have learnt this doctrine by the grace of the founder and of the righteous and wise men who succeeded him. Further, I will observe all my life the commandments as appointed."

The Catechism states that the doctrines of Shinshū are based on the Daimuryōjukyō, or the Greater Sukhâvatî-vyûha, the first portion of which teaches Shintai and the second Zokutai. It is remarkable that the Lesser Sukhâvatî-vyûha and the Meditation-sûtra are not mentioned here, though they are duly recognized as canonical in § 27 with the proviso that the Greater sûtra is the most important. Shinran's own writings are also much studied and regarded as quasi-scripture. The best known of them is the poem or hymn called Shōshinge,[2] which is constantly used in religious services and forms part of the daily devotions of the devout. In a hundred and twenty verses it comprises a brief statement of the Shinshū belief and also a brief history of the faith and of the

[1] 眞諦 and 俗諦, literally spiritual truths and worldly truths.
[2] 正信偈.

seven patriarchs. He also wrote when about fifty-two years of age and while staying at the village of Inada in Hitachi a work in six volumes which is said to have laid the foundations of the Jōdo Shinshū.[1] It is called the Kyōgyō Shinshō,[2] that is, Doctrine, Practice, Faith, and Attainment, and the six volumes deal with Real Truth, Right Practice, True Faith, True Understanding, Real Paradise, and This World. These themes are illustrated by a collection of passages selected from twenty-three sûtras, not merely the three Amidist books mentioned but such works as the Avataṃsaka and Nirvâna Sûtras.

When well advanced in years Shinran also wrote a number of hymns which are now sung at morning and evening services. They are in three volumes, and it appears from references in the first two that he wrote them at the age of seventy-six, while the third was composed when he was ten years older. Considering his age, they show extraordinary vigour. The whole collection is called Sanjō Wasan and consists of the following sections: The Jōdo Wasan or hymns of the Pure Land, the San-Amida-ge, based on the poems of the Chinese Patriarch Donran, the Kōsō-Wasan in praise of the seven Patriarchs, and the Shō-zō-matsu Wasan describing the changes which will come upon the True Law in the lapse of centuries. The Ofumi or Epistles of Rennyo[3] are also read at services.

The doctrines expounded in these various works are not exactly those of the Jōdo sect, which claims with apparent justice to represent the teachings of Hōnen, but it must not be supposed that he is the object of any criticism or polemic. The attitude of Shinran and the Shinshū is rather that they preserve the true meaning and intention of Hōnen, who is always spoken of with the utmost veneration as a Patriarch of the sect and is commemorated in a special festival held on 25th January. The most important differences are practical and concern the organization of the Church. The principal of them, of course, is the abolition of the monastic system and the permission given to the clergy to marry and eat meat, which in Shinran's time probably meant fish. Then, as now, it was the custom for many of the clergy in all sects to be privately married and no doubt the open recognition of wedlock did away with many abuses. The order of nuns was abolished and religiously disposed women were instructed to live as devout wives. Shinran's

[1] Catechism, § 19. [2] 教行信證.

[3] See Troup, "Ofumi or Gobunsho of Rennyo Shōnin," *T.A.S.J.*, xvii, part 1.

object was avowedly to break down the division between the clergy and laity. There were to be no masters or disciples: all were to be friends and brothers before the Buddha. Yet this did not mean at all that he belittled the clerical calling. In no branch of Buddhist literature with which I am acquainted do we hear so much of patriarchs and saintly priests, even in the daily prayers, of the benevolence they have shown in enlightening and instructing the world and of the thanks that we owe them. In Shinshū temples Shinran himself, the successive high priests of each sub-sect and the seven Patriarchs, including Hōnen, all receive worship, and the respect shown to living abbots extends to their sons.[1]

The Catechism enumerates five classes of venerable beings[2] who receive worship in Shinshū temples, namely, the three categories mentioned above, Shōtoku Taishi as having introduced Buddhism into Japan, and Amida himself. Of course, the worship (matsuri) offered to these saints is of a lower degree than the adoration due to Amida (like the *latreia* and *douleia* of Catholic theology), but still the Catechism, while stating that Amida is the principal object of worship, also says that the Gosonsama (i.e. Amida and the four categories of saints) are worshipped in temples, although in private family shrines Amida only is adored. In Shinshū temples the main building is generally the founder's hall and the image enclosed in a cabinet behind the high altar is that of Shinran. The image of Amida is enshrined in a side building called Amida-dō. These temples, which are often called Hongwanji, have a special style of architecture and ornament which is very effective. All the buildings are constructed of black wood and the main edifice consists of a great hall supported by enormous pillars. The only colour is supplied by a few inscriptions in golden letters and by the decoration of the high altar, which is a blaze of gold in striking contrast with its sombre surroundings. There are no images of Buddhas except Amida or of Bodhisattvas, and Shaka is neither represented nor worshipped. In explanation of this remarkable omission, the Catechism offers the following explanations: "In Shinshū there are two ways in which the relation between Amida and Shaka is conceived. One way regards the two as one and the same being; the other as distinct. When the two are regarded as one and the

[1] Thus at the Shinshū anniversary in 1922 at Kyōto certain solemn ceremonies were performed by the Abbot of the Hongwanji and others by his son, as if he were a prince imperial.

[2] Gosonsama. Catechism, § 29.

same being, the teacher Shaka is looked upon as the incarnation of Amida Nyorai. He is regarded as coming temporarily into this world. When the two are conceived of as distinct beings, Shaka is looked upon as the Teacher of the world and Amida as the Saviour of the world. The reason then why Shaka is not worshipped specially is because he and Amida are regarded as one and the same." This is not very lucid, but the author evidently took the view that the two are the same. That indeed is the only explanation which can be offered of the strange way in which Shaka is ignored, for how comes it that Shōtoku Taishi, who introduced Buddhism to Japan, and Zendō and Shinran, who are said to have been incarnations of Amida, receive honour in temples whereas none is rendered to Shaka who introduced it to the world? Moreover, the three Amidist sûtras contain no hint that Shaka was an incarnation of Amida. Shinran's own poem, the Shōshinge, says (v. 21): "The reason why the Tathâgata Śâkyamuni was revealed to the world was solely that he might proclaim the boundless ocean of Amida's original vow." Apparently[1] it is only in funeral ceremonies that Shaka is invoked. In this service a fourfold invitation is solemnly addressed to the following to be present: (1) The Buddhas of the ten directions; (2) Shaka; (3) Amida; (4) Kwannon Seishi (Mahâsthâma-prâpta) and the other Bodhisattvas. Otherwise no worship is offered to Bodhisattvas nor are their statues placed in temples, although the two mentioned are particularly prominent in the description of Amida's paradise given in the Meditation-sûtra and although tradition represents a vision of Kwannon as having been the turning point of Shinran's own career. Bodhisattvas are also praised in the Wasan.

The Catechism says (§ 86): "the gods, Buddhas and Bodhisattvas are numberless but since all these are branch bodies of Amida they are ultimately contained in the six characters Namu Amida Butsu. For this reason it is sufficient to worship the one Buddha Amida and not necessary to worship these many deities separately." Rennyo says: "As the body called Namu Amida Butsu includes all Gods, Buddhas and Bodhisattvas and everything good and every good work, what need is there to worry your mind about various works and things good? The name Namu Amida Butsu is itself the complete body of all good and of every good work." It is remarkable that here, as often (see Catechism, § 53 ff.), Namu

[1] Lloyd, *Shinran and His Work*, pp. 156–7.

Amida Butsu[1] is treated not as an ejaculation or invocation (Reverence to Amida Buddha) but as the name of the Buddha. It is stated still more definitely (§ 39 and § 40): "Amida Butsu is the Buddha whose name is Namu Amida Butsu. This is Sanskrit and when translated means The Glorious One who has boundless Life and Truth. . . . The Buddha essence and the Buddha name are one and the same thing."

It is not easy to imagine what can have been the cause or motive of this extreme simplification of religion. So far as I am aware, Buddhism in all its other branches has always shown a tendency to increase its pantheon not only by adding Buddhas and Bodhisattvas but by according some status to non-Buddhist deities. And, if Shintō can be taken as showing the natural bent of the Japanese mind in religious matters, it certainly indicates no inclination towards monotheism. Shinran presumably felt that the heavenly host whose statues adorn the temples of the Tendai and Shingon were part of the system of elaborate ritual and magic which the common man could not understand and from which he was anxious to deliver him. At any rate, he seems to have judged popular feeling correctly, for no tendency to restore the old pantheon is visible. But the Shinshuist is especially instructed to be respectful to the deities worshipped by others: "Every God and Buddha worshipped by man deserves reverence and worship . . . only as a matter of faith one cannot believe everything."

Moreover, the worship offered to Amida does not consist of prayers for health, temporal welfare, or any such petitions. After a man has once obtained faith in Amida he commits all to his power (mina Butsuriki ni makaseru), and his worship, though frequent, consists of nothing but thanksgiving. The Shinshū sect have more than once got into trouble by raising difficulties about offering definite supplications for some event connected with the Imperial Family, though all other sects have obeyed the order without hesitation. The form of prayer in use in temples and private houses varies considerably, but as a rule the Shōshinge is recited, together with verses of the Wasan or hymns interspersed with repetitions of the Nembutsu.

This brings us to the question of "one-calling" or "many-callings", which was the subject of grave controversy in Hōnen's

[1] The Sanskrit word Namaḥ, meaning bending or obeisance, is constantly used with the names of deities, the formula being very similar to the English "Glory be to the Father," etc.

lifetime, as related above. Shinran appears to have taken the opposite point of view to that accepted by his master, according to Shunjō's Life, which does not, however, indicate that there was any difference of opinion between them. The one all-important thing, according to Shinshū, is faith in Amida: "When we hear what is the meaning of Namu Amida Butsu we recognize that we are deeply involved in sin and evil from which we cannot extricate ourselves through our own efforts. . . . But when we listen to the voice of salvation we are saved from our sinful condition, being taken into the eternal light of Buddha and so we are able to share his merit and receive his favour. Thus we feel as if we had escaped from the jaws of the tiger and entered the life boat. Relying on this Amida Nyorai [1] we utter the Nembutsu with gratitude and reverence, with exultation and devotion. Our heart is filled with a great peace and a great joy." [2] This faith is not due to our own efforts. It is the gift of Amida. It enters into our depraved hearts, which cannot wash and cleanse themselves but are made pure when the heart of Amida enters into them and is united with them. Shinran says that faith is heart-union. Rennyo says: "To rely on Amida is to appropriate Namu Amida Butsu.[3] To appropriate Namu Amida Butsu is to have faith." When he has this faith the believer has obtained the Buddha nature and is certain to become a Buddha, though he cannot be said to be one yet. "How happy the thought," said Hōnen, "that though we are still here in the flesh we are numbered among the holy ones of paradise."

When faith has been obtained the believer should continue to utter the Nembutsu out of gratitude. "It being the doctrine of Shinshū that faith is the true cause of salvation and that the Nembutsu is uttered out of gratitude, the believer should utter the Nembutsu in order to make his faith and election sure and thus give thanks for the grace of the Tathâgata." The author of the Catechism adds that the Nembutsu is regarded as an act of thanksgiving, because if heard by an unbeliever it may awaken faith in his heart or at least dispose him in the right direction and thus become the means of helping Amida's work of grace. Further, in answer to the question how we can best nourish our faith, the answer is: (1) The best way is to repeat the Nembutsu, and it is said elsewhere that not to utter the Nembutsu is to stray farthest from divine protection;

[1] Nyorai = Tathâgata. [2] Catechism, § 59.

[3] To understand this strange language one must remember that Namu Amida Butsu is regarded as a name.

(2) Read the scriptures; (3) Dwell in imagination on the joys of Paradise; (4) Adore the images of Amida; (5) Talk about religion with other believers. Though there is nothing in these passages in the least derogatory to the Nembutsu, which is assigned a very important position, one cannot help feeling that the tone is not exactly that of Hōnen, who said that the Nembutsu ought to be treated as the main occupation of life and not as a sort of side work, and wrote in the "One Sheet of Paper" that all that is needed to secure birth in Paradise is to repeat the words Namu Amida Butsu with the certainty that one will arrive there. In fact it would seem that for Hōnen the essential part of religion is to repeat the Nembutsu, only it must be said with faith and conviction and not become a merely mechanical recitation: for Shinran faith is the essential: it finds expression in the Nembutsu, and subsequent utterances of the Nembutsu are signs of gratitude.

The Catechism proceeds to explain that though to utter the Nembutsu is the chief work of gratitude, our whole life must be one long expression of gratitude: we must regard life as being a service which Amida demands of us. "When the believer regards all his activities as expressions of gratitude, he is set free from the spirit of selfishness. He does not mind hardships nor is his heart filled with pride, but he thinks of his work as service rendered in return for great mercy. All his actions become true and straight and help Buddha's Law." "But," inquires the Catechism with great candour, "in worldly affairs lies and sharp practices seem inevitable. Are we to regard these things also as expressions of gratitude?" "Lies and sharp practices," is the reply, "are not in themselves expressions of gratitude. When we pursue our daily duties and work cheerfully and assiduously, even though we indulge in lies and sharp practices, we help to spread the way of the Buddha and so even our lies and sharp practices become expressions of gratitude." Though the Shinshū is, so far as I am aware, a most respectable sect in practice, it seems to have a dangerous tendency to excuse lapses from morality.

The principle that all worship should consist of giving thanks rather than of making petitions is also applied to festivals which thus have not the same meaning as in other sects. The Hizan, for instance, is a period of seven days at the spring and autumn equinox[1] devoted by most sects to making prayers and offerings on behalf

[1] The equinox is a sacred season in India, too. See Vishnu Purâna, 2, 8.

of the dead. In Shinshū the occasion is observed but is used for offering thanks to Amida on behalf of the dead, who are believed to be safe in his keeping and for whose welfare it would be wrong to pray. Sermons are also preached at this season, not in the temple but in an adjoining building. The usual method is for a succession of preachers to give short discourses, each lasting about a quarter of an hour, between ten and four o'clock. The congregation drop in and leave as they like. The various anniversaries of deaths in a family, the ceremonies of saying masses for the departed and offering intercession for them are all observed in a similar spirit, as is also the festival called Bon held in the seventh month, when the spirits of the dead are supposed to revisit their homes. It is known in the Shinshū as Kangi-e, or the festival of Joy, that is, rejoicing at the happy lot of the dead in paradise. The days dedicated to Shinran and Hōnen are natural occasions for thanksgiving. The commemoration of Shinran lasts a week, closing with the day of his death, 28th November. On the night of the middle day his biography as written by Kakunyo is read with great solemnity and is said to inspire the liveliest emotions in the congregation.

I have spoken in earlier chapters [1] of the history of the two sects, Jōdo and Shinshū. The former was relatively peaceful and obscure until Tokugawa times, while the latter during the same period has a political and military record which, though eventful, is hardly edifying from a religious point of view. After Ieyasu the positions become reversed and the Jōdo, owing to its connection with the Shōgun's family, is accepted as almost the established Church, but remaining, as beseems such a body, placid and dignified and exercising its great influence through the recognized authorities. In the mass of political and military details which smothers the annals of the Amidists in Japan, two names stand out as important for doctrine, namely, Ryōyo Shōgei (1341–1420) and Rennyo (1415–1499).

The former was the seventh patriarch of the Jōdo and indefatigable as a writer and researcher. After a prolonged investigation of the doctrine of all schools, he demonstrated to his own satisfaction that the name of Tongyō,[2] or quick Enlightenment, used by the Tendai and other older sects is really more applicable to the teaching of the Jōdo than to that of any other. Secondly, he taught

[1] X, XI, and XII.

[2] 頓教.

that the idea of the Western Paradise and of Amida welcoming the souls of the faithful there is purely metaphorical. Amida is omnipresent and his paradise is simply absolute reality. If we can change our point of view and see things as they really are, we can be in the Pure Land here and now. This doctrine seems due to Zen influences and has become of considerable importance in the modern developments of Amidism.

Rennyo Shōnin was the eighth patriarch of the Shinshū and, after Shinran, was certainly the most striking personality that it has produced. I have spoken elsewhere of his missionary efforts, his wanderings and struggles, his Ofumi or Epistles, and his Ryōgemon or creed; also of his views as to the relation of Buddhism to Shintō. But his most important service to Shinshū was his insistence on the necessity of observing moral precepts, whereas there was a tendency often appearing at various times and in various surroundings to maintain that faith or prayer were the only things necessary and to neglect conduct. But Rennyo insisted that one cannot leave oneself in Amida's hands with complete faith and trust unless one has abandoned selfish desires and fleshly lusts. Therefore he held the observance of all the Confucian virtues and obedience to the law of the land and the will of the Sovereign to be necessary parts of the believer's daily conduct. It is strange to find a devout Buddhist appealing to the works of Confucius when he wishes to cite a canon and standard of moral conduct. It shows how strong was the literary and philosophic influence of China in Japan at this period and also how completely Amidism had become a religion of the other world. It does not seem to have occurred to Rennyo or even to Shinran that Shaka had provided a code of every-day morality quite as good as that of Confucius, though perhaps according to Far Eastern standards he did not lay sufficient stress on political ethics.

The names of Ippen (1239–1289) and Shinzei (1443–1495) also deserve mention, for though the bodies which they founded were not important, they are interesting as showing the strength of the Amidist movement, which found expression in sects which were unable to accept all the principles of the Jōdo or Shinshū. I have described Ippen's doctrines in the historical section above.[1] They are somewhat extravagant but have vitality, for the sect which he founded still exists though its adherents are not numerous and are

[1] Chapter X, ad fin.

mostly members of the lower classes. The curious thing is that the special teaching of the sect is represented as a revelation made by the deity of Kumano who is boldly identified with Amida, the fusion of Buddhism with Shintō being thus complete. Shinzei represents a quite different tendency, namely, an attempt to combine the recitation of the Nembutsu, which he himself repeated 60,000 times a day, with ordinary Buddhist observances and ritual. This was directly contrary to the principles of Hōnen and Shinran, and it is not surprising if the religious body founded by Shinzei and called the Ritsu is counted as a sub-sect of the Tendai rather than of either of the Jōdo schools. Nevertheless it may be doubted if Shinzei does not represent the teaching of the three ancient sûtras on which Amidism claims to be based more correctly than they do. There is no sign that the Sukhâvatî-vyûha would have approved of ignoring the whole of the practical and theoretical instruction imparted by Gotama, together with many of the ideas and personalities added to it by the later Mahâyâna.

During the Tokugawa regime the Shinshū, like most Buddhist sects, did not show much life or activity. The condition of the times favoured chiefly quiet studies; the editing of texts, the making of commentaries, and the systematic exposition of doctrinal systems were considered safe and suitable occupations for the learned. Two erudite priests, Eku (1644–1721) and Jinrei, did a good deal of work of this sort for the Shinshū and had a large following. There were elaborate discussions with the object of securing uniformity and extirpating heresy and also discussions as to the right of using the title of Shinshū or True Sect.

But the attack on Buddhism which marked the beginning of the Meiji era and the attempt to replace it by Shintō as the national State religion awakened the old pugnacious instincts which had been so strong in the fifteenth and sixteenth centuries, and the Shinshū were among those who fought most strenuously and successfully for Buddhism. In 1872 they sent abroad a commission to investigate how European States dealt with ecclesiastical problems, and the celebrated priest Mokurai (†1911) who accompanied it visited not only India but also Palestine. The return of this mission in 1875 marked a reaction in the attitude of the Japanese Government. Shinran was given by Imperial decree the posthumous title of Kenshin Daishi[1] and finally the attempt

[1] 見眞大師.

at State control of religion was abandoned, the heads of the various Buddhist sects being charged with their administration.

The original teaching of Shinran was the most complete transformation of Buddhism ever witnessed, and it is perhaps not surprising if in an age when Japan was imitating European institutions wholesale, his spiritual descendants showed no hesitation in borrowing both from Christianity and from European philosophy. The former tendency is illustrated by Tada Kanai, a noted Shinshū preacher of Chiba who was alive in 1910. He published a volume of sermons called Shūdo Kōwa [1] which are deeply impregnated by foreign ideas. One, for instance, contains an analysis of Tolstoy's *Resurrection* and another refers to an American novel and to *Les Misérables*. He is said to have held services on Sunday and many such imitations of European customs are common.[2] Songs are composed (some, it is said, even in English) and are sung so as to resemble Christian hymns. Even organs are used. I have myself seen a Shinshū place of worship (a missionary chapel, it is true), the floor of which was covered with seats of a European pattern while at the end was an erection which superficially resembled a Christian altar. Yet though Western usages are copied in such a glaring and often most unpicturesque fashion, what is borrowed is nearly always external observances only. Even Lloyd, who was always on the look out for resemblances to Christianity, says of Tada's doctrine that for him "Amida is not the Father in the sense of being the creator". And this, I fancy, is true generally. In English renderings of the Wasan, the phrase "Eternal Father" may be found, but I have been assured at the Ōtani University that the translation is illegitimate. In older works such as the Lotus, though the Buddha is often called a father, I think that the idea is always that he helps or protects like a father, not that he has created the world or its inhabitants.

In this connection the last question and answer of the Catechism from which I have already made so many quotations are worth citing. Why, it is asked, do unbelievers and sinners abound and

[1] 修道講話. Three of them are translated by Haas (*Amida Buddha Unsere Zuflucht*) and seven by Lloyd (*The Praises of Amida*, Tokyo, 1907). The sermons referred to are Numbers 6 and 4 in Lloyd.

[2] Anesaki (*History of Japanese Religion*, p. 356) quotes the following opinion expressed by Tōyama, who was apparently not a Christian: "In the following three respects the influence of Christianity on the improvement of society is very great: (1) the gathering of men and women in a church once every week; (2) the church music; (3) the marriage and funeral service."

even increase? Cannot Amida of his grace compel them to believe? The significant answer is that even a Buddha cannot act with perfect freedom and thus defy Heaven's laws.[1] There are three things which a Buddha cannot do: (1) He cannot change or stop the effect of works when once fixed; (2) He cannot save beings who are not destined to be saved; (3) He cannot exhaust the world of sentient beings. It will be seen that Amidism has not discarded the older ideas of Buddhahood so completely as might be supposed. The phrase "Heaven's laws" may sound Chinese, but the thought is the same as that contained in the ancient words attributed to Gotama after his enlightenment, in which he resolves to honour and respect the Dhamma which he had come to know.[2]

The imitation of Christianity is apt to affect chiefly the externals of worship: it is widespread but somewhat superficial. The influence of European philosophy is just the opposite: it naturally appeals only to a select few, who are scholars and mostly recluses, but it affects not temples and the details of ritual but the fundamental conceptions of religion. As an example may be cited Kiyozawa (1863–1903), who came of a Shinshū family and devoted himself to the study of Hegel under Fenellosa. Hegel has puzzled many Europeans and I am not prepared to say how much of his works Kiyozawa may have understood. The bent of his mind was apparently religious and pietistic rather than metaphysical and this imparts a Christian tone to much of what he wrote, but he dwells continually on such themes as the infinity of the Buddha nature, the elimination of the finite self, and absolute dependence on the grace of the Infinite Light (Amitâbha). The important point is not his precise theories but the emphasis which he and those who think like him lay on the infinite nature of the Buddha. Amitâbha is no longer the Buddha of the Sukhâvatî-vyûha, that is to say, the monk Dharmâkara, who by a surprising course of austerities has won for himself the position of a Buddha and a paradise in the west in which he can receive those who trust in him. He is for these writers a being without beginning, end, or limits, and rebirth in his paradise may be attained anywhere in this world by the awakening of love and faith in him. These ideas are not wholly alien to earlier Japanese thought, but their popularity in modern times seems to be largely due to the works of those who like Kiyozawa have come under the influence of Western philosophy.

[1] v. *T.A.S.J.*, 1912, p. 394.

[2] See above, Chap. II, p. 38.

The sensitiveness of Shinshū to European influence is shown in yet another way, namely, the publication of plays and novels in the last two decades representing Shinran in very human moods and disinclined to deal severely with social errors which are generally reprobated by the religious. Such are the plays *The Priest and his Disciple* by Kurata Hyakuzō [1] and *The Human Shinran* by Ishimaru Baigwai. Though these works, especially *The Priest and his Disciple*, had a very good reception from the general public, they were strongly criticized by religious persons, who not unnaturally objected to what they correctly considered as misrepresentation of Shinran's character and teaching. It is the old story of the tendency to condone immorality. Amida saves sinners in the midst of their sin: he demands an appeal for his help and faith that he will give it: he does not demand repentance or purification. It is easy to imagine how this doctrine is treated by "naturalistic" writers. The characters indulge in vice, and when it brings them unhappiness they are forgiven by the all-merciful Buddha. An account of this literature, giving the names of many authors and magazines, will be found in an article entitled "The Shinran Revival of the Last Year" contained in the *Eastern Buddhist* of 1923,[2] which gives an idea of the extent of the movement. The title refers to the impressive celebration at Kyōto of the seven hundredth anniversary of Shinran's work, the Kyōgyō Shinshō. A week was spent in gorgeous and impressive ceremonies in which it is said that 550,000 laymen and about 1,500 priests took part.

Another side of the varied activities of modern Shinshū is illustrated by the society called Ittō-en, or the Confraternity of the Lantern.[3] The name is derived from a legend which tells how at a great festival thousands of costly lanterns were offered by rich devotees and dedicated to the Buddha, but that the light of one offered by a poor woman—a sort of widow's mite—outshone all the others. The members of the Confraternity must give up all their wealth and possessions and be ready to serve humanity without demanding any return.

The worshippers of Amida in Japan are numerous, prosperous, and progressive, but should this worship be called Buddhism? It has grown out of Buddhism, no doubt: all the stages except the

[1] Translated into English by G. W. Shaw, Tokyo, 1922.
[2] *Eastern Buddhist*, vol. ii, No. 5, 1923, p. 285 ff.
[3] Some authorities are inclined to class the Ittō-en as belonging rather to Zen.

very earliest are perfectly clear, but has not the process of development resulted in such a complete transformation that one can no longer apply the same name to the teaching of Gotama and the teaching of Shinran ? The phenomenon has, so far as I know, no precise parallel in the history of religions. It is usual enough to alter the doctrines taught by the founder of a creed, but most unusual to cease treating him with the outward signs of respect while still making use of the designation generally given to the original teaching. Yet this is what Shinshū has done. There are no images of Shaka in Hongwanji temples, with the rare exceptions mentioned above he is never invoked : at most he is mentioned as the messenger who came to tell the world about Amida. It is as if there were a denomination calling themselves Christians who worshipped exclusively the Third Person of the Trinity and respected Christ only because he spoke of the coming of the Comforter.

There is something, however, to be said on the other side. No Japanese, I believe, has even argued that the Amidists are not Buddhists, though Nichiren came very near to saying it. Whenever there has been common action in which all the Buddhist sects have joined, for instance in defending Buddhism at the beginning of the Meiji era, the Jōdo and Shinshū have played a prominent part. Further, although Shaka is ignored, the word Butsu or Buddha is sufficiently prominent : the phrases Nembutsu and Namu-Amida-Butsu seem to be used with superfluous frequency. And Buddhism is a religion which more than others tolerates divergent views about the correct conduct of life, the best means of obtaining salvation, and the best kind of salvation to be obtained. In the very earliest period we find two classes recognized : members of the order, or monks, and laymen. The former are the true disciples of the master and they only can be said to attempt to follow exactly the law which he taught. But the position of the laity is also perfectly well defined. They cannot make the same efforts as the monks and their spiritual ambitions are different and humbler : they do well, for instance, to strive for temporary rebirth in some paradise. Indeed, these paradises of early Buddhism bear some resemblance to the Pure Land and the anâgâmin, or man who will not come back to earth but will attain arhatship in some one of them, is not unlike its inhabitants. For it must be remembered that according to strict doctrine (though perhaps not according to popular ideas) the Pure Land is not a place where one simply lives in bliss for ever, but a sojourn where one can obtain nirvâna or become a Buddha and return to help the world. The difference between the old idea and the new lies in the methods prescribed for gaining entrance to paradise. According to all Amidist sects, permission to enter is granted solely by the grace of Amida and all that is necessary to obtain that grace is to invoke his name with faith. In the older Buddhism, on the other hand, paradise is won as the reward of special efforts, not the greatest efforts but those of which laymen are capable. The Brahmavihâras,[1] for instance, consist in the cultivation of kind thoughts and corresponding deeds which results in rebirth in Brahmâ's heaven. Brahmâ himself being free from all anger and malice, it is natural that those who have made themselves like him should reside in his paradise, but it is never said that his benevolence will lead him to let in sinners who ask for admission. The motive which led the Buddha to devote his life to laborious teaching and preaching is generally described as compassion for mankind. He teaches them the only road to happiness. They must be their own light and refuge and not seek for another refuge, as the well-known precept says. Shinshū scholars [2] have attempted to show that there is no real gap between the teachings of Shaka and Shinran : that the former if interpreted in an emotional and not too intellectual a sense are equivalent to salvation by faith. I confess that I cannot follow their arguments nor can I see that the interview between the Buddha and King Ajâtaśatru, even as recorded in the Chinese Mahâparinirvâna-sûtra,[3] is an instance of the simple faith in Amida which Shinran required, for the King's faith is established by an elaborate metaphysical discourse of the dying master. I would rather say that three ideas grew up which tended to make men take a different view of the Buddha's compassion, to think of him as actively helping men not as merely teaching them how to help themselves. The first is the idea of the benevolent Bodhisattva who vows to devote himself to helping all mankind. The germs of this idea may be found even in Hinayanist literature. Thus in the Nidânakathâ Sumedha's resolution to become a Buddha has a resemblance

[1] See Chap. II, pp. 58, 59.

[2] e.g. Sasaki in his book *A Study of Shin Buddhism*, Kyōto, 1925, and Shūgaku Yamabe in his article "The Buddha and Shinran" in the *Eastern Buddhist*, vol. ii, No. 5, 1923.

[3] This work, which is not the same as the Pali-suttanta of the same name (D.N., xvi), represents Ajâtaśatru, tortured by illness and remorse for his sins, as visiting the dying Buddha.

to Amida's vow. He resolved to attain the truth, to enable mankind to cross the sea of the world and only then to enter nirvâna. There is, however, no hint that he will save those who call on his name, though this train of thought, too, appears to have its roots in India. In the Bhagavad Gîtâ we have the deathbed prayer and a deity who will take his servants to himself. Secondly comes the idea of the transfer of merit. It is not to be found in the Piṭakas but appears plainly in the works of Śântideva.[1] He bids the neophyte who aspires to become a Bodhisattva make over to others whatever merit he may now have or may acquire in future and offer himself and all his possessions as a sacrifice for the salvation of all beings: further, he is to make a vow to acquire enlightenment for the good of all beings. Thirdly, we have the idea that the world is degenerating: the weaklings of modern times are no longer capable of the efforts made by the heroic saints of old to obtain salvation. This idea is also Indian. It is constantly stated that the Vedic sacrifices cannot be performed at present and therefore an easier ritual is prescribed by merciful deities.

The anaology between the Shinshū and modern Indian sects is close and is an interesting example of parallel development. The worshippers of Śiva and Vishṇu at the present day theoretically accept the authority of the Vedas, but in practice their sacred books are the Tiruvaçagam or Nalayiram or some volume selected out of a whole library of comparatively recent literature. Modern Hinduism is mostly emotional: the worshipper approaches the deity, who as a rule is only one, with bhakti (faith and love) and receives in return a promise of grace and of admission to paradise or even of union with the deity. The form of prayer is often the repetition of the divine name, for instance, Hari, Hari among the worshippers of Vishṇu, and all that is necessary is devotion and absolute reliance on the deity. Even in the Bhagavad Gîtâ it is declared to be too hard for flesh and blood to find their way by meditation or ritual to the Supreme Spirit, whereas Kṛishṇa comes straight to those who make him their sole desire. "Set thy heart on me and worship thou me. Then shalt thou come to me. Leave all other deities and come to me alone for refuge. I will deliver thee from thy sins. Sorrow not."[2]

The date of the Bhagavad Gîtâ is uncertain, but it was probably

[1] Bodhicaryâvatâra, iii, 10.

[2] Bhag. Gîtâ, xviii, 65, 66.

composed shortly before or after the Christian era and represents the same current of thought which in other surroundings produced Amidism. In both systems we have a loving deity who offers salvation in return for faith and devotion: in both the deities, Kṛishṇa and Amida, are new and so is the form of worship which they demand. The chief difference is that Amida supersedes a well-known figure, Gotama the Buddha, whereas Kṛishṇa does not appear to do this to the same extent, but this is simply because there is no deity in the ancient Vedic pantheon who was sufficiently prominent to make us feel that he is being ignored. In reality Kṛishṇa and the religion of bhakti (loving faith) displace all the old gods and their worship. The transformation of Buddhism seems surprising, but it has only obeyed the same law as other Indian religions. Shinshū does not differ from the original faith more than does the later Tantric Buddhism found in India itself, and the changes which it has shown are due not merely to the lapse of centuries but to long travel and to transplantation among alien races, of whom one, the Japanese, are noted for borrowing but also for adapting what they borrow and leaving on it the mark of their own genius.

Another question which has often been discussed is, does Amidism owe anything to Christianity? I am not referring to recent imitations such as I have discussed above, but to the original ideas on which the sect is founded. They certainly contain an element additional and even contrary to the teaching of Gotama, namely, a saviour who offers to deliver from death and hell all who will but believe in him and call on his name. No such figure is to be found in the Piṭakas or in Vedic mythology, and hence many have supposed that it is due to early Christian influence in India and perhaps was reinvigorated by later contact between Nestorians and Buddhists in China. But plausible as the hypothesis may seem at first sight, if examined more carefully it presents difficulties which are in my opinion insuperable. In the first place, though the precise dates of the Pure Land-sûtras are uncertain, it is highly probable that they were composed in the first century of our era, at which time it is hardly possible that Christianity had reached India; and a parallel development of ideas which are in many respects similar is to be found in the Bhagavad Gîtâ.[1] And secondly, though

[1] The Bhâgavata sect is certainly pre-Christian, for there are allusions to it in Panini and the Besnagar inscriptions which are ascribed to the earlier part of the second century B.C. The coins of Kanishka bear images of the Buddha and of Persian deities, but not Christian emblems.

the resemblances between Amidism and Christianity are obvious, the differences are profound. Both Amida and Christ are saviours, but Christ is the Second Person of the Trinity, and he saves mankind by his death, by offering himself as an atonement for the sins of the whole world. But the position of Amida is entirely different and his method of salvation is different too. In the oldest documents he is a man who becomes a Buddha in the traditional manner. The fundamental idea is not that God is Love but rather that Love is God: lovingkindness raised Amida to a place which may be called divine, though exception might be taken to the epithet if it is held to imply the attributes ascribed to God in Christianity. For Amida is not the creator of the world: the Universe is without beginning or end and the evil from which he saves is the interminable round of births and deaths. He seems Godlike because he is given the same quasi-divine attributes as Śâkya in the Lotus and the other Buddhas of the Mahâyâna. Like them he comes to be regarded as having three bodies and as being identical with the Bhûtatathatâ. Further, Amida is not offered as an atoning sacrifice in the sense that Christ was offered according to Christian theology. It is true that he deserves gratitude because he has laboured and suffered for mankind, but the reason is quite different. As the Synopsis says, "To be responsible for all our sins, Amitâbha must acquire all virtues by which our sins are to be effaced. For this purpose he went through unutterable sufferings during numberless æons to find out the means of salvation."[1] And, as we have seen, the modern exponents of Shinshū state that there are things which Amida cannot do, whereas all ordinary Christian conceptions make God omnipotent.

I have already touched[2] on the contact between certain forms of Christianity and Buddhism in China. Statements may be found in various writers as to the influence of Gnosticism on Shingon or on other Buddhist sects. But what evidence is there that Gnosticism ever penetrated to China, Central Asia, or even India? There is none whatever, so far as I know. The two religions which did have some influence in Central Asia and China and some relations with Buddhism are Manichæism and Nestorianism. The former was strangely composite and assimilative, always ready to borrow something from the other creeds professed in the various countries into which it found an entrance. As it travelled westwards it

[1] Synopsis, p. 26.

[2] Chap. V, p. 149.

adopted so many Christian ideas that it achieved the distinction of being considered the worst of heresies. As it spread into Central Asia and China, it received a large admixture of Buddhism. We find Mani called Ju-lai or Tathâgata and Manichæan deities represented as sitting in the attitude of Bodhisattvas cross-legged on lotus flowers.[1] In such cases there can be no question of which side exerted and which received influence, and even if we hold that the influence was reciprocal there is no proof that Manichæism *as known in China and Central Asia* contained any Christian elements which it could impart. It borrowed them itself in its western expansions.

The most interesting information about the history of Nestorianism in China is afforded by the monument discovered at Si-Ngan-fu, which dates from 781 and is commonly called the Nestorian Stone. It has often been cited as evidence of the debt of Buddhism to Christianity, for it bears a long inscription partly in Chinese and partly in Syriac composed by a foreign priest called Adam, or in Chinese King-Tsing, giving an account of the history and doctrines of the Christian Church as he understood them. It shows that Buddhist and Christian priests associated together on friendly terms and we also know that King-Tsing set about translating a sûtra from the Hu language. But the inscription really proves that Nestorianism in China, like Manichæism, was strongly influenced by Buddhism and not vice versa. Not only does it contain many Buddhist words, such as Sêng and Ssŭ for Christian priests and monasteries, but though it treats of Christ's life in some detail, it omits all mention of the Crucifixion. The motive of the omission can hardly be anything but the feeling that redemption by his death was not an acceptable idea,[2] and it is hardly likely that a form of Christianity which could make such an astounding concession would be strong enough to exert any powerful influence on Buddhism.

[1] See for Manichæism in China and Central Asia the series of three articles by Chavannes and Pelliot entitled "Un traité manichéen retrouvé en Chine" in *J.A.*, 1911, 1913. A Chinese edict of A.D. 739 accuses Manichæism of deceiving the people by falsely taking the name of Buddhism.

[2] See especially Haviet, "La Stèle Chrétienne de Si-ngan-fu" in *Variétés Sinologiques*, pp. 7, 12, and 20. He has some interesting remarks about the unwillingness of the Nestorians and also of the Jesuits to give publicity to the Crucifixion. (See l.c., iii, p. 54.)

# CHAPTER XVII

## ZEN

In previous chapters I have already touched on the history of Zen in both China and Japan, but perhaps it may not be amiss to point out once more how great a power it has been in the artistic, intellectual, and even the political life of the Far East. To a certain extent it has moulded the Japanese character, but it is also the expression of that character. No other form of Buddhism is so thoroughly Japanese.

No clear Indian origin for Zen can be discovered. The scepticism which doubts the existence of Bodhidharma and his visit to China is perhaps excessive, but it must be confessed that though he has a considerable position in the popular imagination, his place in history, whether we look backwards or forwards, is very hard to define. His name is unknown to Sanskrit and Tibetan tradition: he is connected with no known sect, and the doctrine of an inward revelation apart from scripture, which is attributed to him, is very un-Indian. Somewhat in contradiction with this is the tradition, approved by Tao-Hsüan but discredited by Tao-Yüan, that he handed the Lankâvatâra-sûtra to his first disciple to be his guide. But the said sûtra may be described as a miscellaneous collection of notes on philosophical subjects, and Suzuki,[1] the most recent authority on the question, is no doubt right when he says, "The teaching of Zen is not derived from the Lankâvatâra but only confirmed by it. Zen stands on its own footing, on its own facts, but as all religious experience requires its intellectual interpretation, Zen, too, must have its philosophical background which is found in the Lankâvatâra." That is the most that can be said about the relationship of the Indian sûtra to Zen, and it must be remembered that subsequently the Vajracchedikâ superseded it as being the best explanation of the Zen point of view to be found in Buddhist works written in Sanskrit. There is also some resemblance, especially in manner, between Zen and the more paradoxical parts of Nâgârjuna's teaching. But no doubt the closest Indian analogy to Bodhidharma's doctrine is offered, not by any variety of Indian

[1] D. T. Suzuki, *Studies in the Lankâvatâra Sûtra*, p. 50.

Buddhism, but by some utterances of the Upanishads—" To see into one's nature and become Buddha " is really the same idea which declares that Brahman the eternal and universal spirit is identical with the soul in every man. It is also true that there is a striking likeness between the thought of Zen and such passages (e.g. Kena Upan., § 5) as those which say " You cannot think it with thought, hear it with the ear, see it with the sight, breathe it with the breath, etc.", but here the resemblance to Lao-Tzŭ and Taoist mysticism is equally obvious. Nor is it easy to connect Bodhidharma with the later development of Zen in China. He was succeeded by five Chinese Patriarchs who appear to have been regarded as Buddhists of doubtful orthodoxy by other sects and whose teaching shows the strongest traces of Taoism. Subsequently, as the school became large and powerful, the need of discipline and hierarchy was felt. Zen assumed the respectable externals of other Buddhist sects and was even able strongly to influence Confucianism, but I fancy that its most important characteristics grew up in the century following Bodhidharma's death and were derived from the mystic and romantic element in Chinese culture which is commonly called Taoism. How close was the connection, even in external mannerisms, may be seen in the conversations attributed to the Taoist philosopher Lieh-Tzŭ.[1]

Zen became fashionable in China under the Sung dynasty of Hangchou and undoubtedly influenced the new form of Confucianism made popular by Chu-Hsi (1130–1200); about the same time it was successfully introduced into Japan by Eisai (1141–1215) and Dōgen (1200–1253), both of whom studied in China. This was not the first time that it had been brought to the notice of the Japanese, but previous attempts to naturalize it had proved unsuccessful. It had not been in harmony with the genius of the age and now it was only by a rather surprising metamorphosis that it adapted itself to the vigorous but rough spirit prevailing under the Hōjōs at Kamakura. It became, as I have described in the historical section, the religion of the military class. In China, where soldiers are not much respected and often not distinguished accurately from brigands, such a transformation was unthinkable, but in Japan, though strange, it is explicable, for Zen as a system demands above all things individual discipline. It makes light of learning (in spite of having produced an enormous literature)

[1] See Suzuki, *Essays in Zen Buddhism* (1st series), pp. 330 and 351 ff.

and of all attempts to found a spiritual life on scriptural knowledge, and bids those who would become adepts cultivate such virtues as courage, perseverance, and clear insight, all of which are as useful to a soldier as to a priest. Nor in spite of taking on this new character did it sever its connection with Chinese thought and literature. Its later progress in Japan was closely connected with Confucian studies. Under the Hōjō Government Zen received definite, though not exclusive, patronage and favour. It had its five great temples at Kamakura and Kyōto and, what is perhaps more important still, popular education was in its hands, for the Terakoya or village temple schools had mostly Zen priests for masters. But it was in the immediately succeeding period, that of the Ashikagas, that the power and influence of Zen were most conspicuous. Ecclesiastical statesmen played a part in politics like the French Cardinals of the seventeenth century, and the lower branches of the civil services were largely recruited from the inmates of Zen monasteries. Even shipping and trade with China were in the hands of these versatile clerics. Nor did the practical things of life such as statesmanship and commerce blind them to the beauty and importance of art and literature. Their influence on painting is admitted by all critics of Far Eastern art. They hardly had time to show this side of their genius among the warriors of Kamakura, but the great Zen temples of Kyōto were all schools of painting and the long list of artists who were directly connected with them includes such names as Chō Densu, Josetsu, Sesshū, and Kanō Masanobu. And though Zen rejected scripture as a medium for communicating truth, it encouraged literature as a help and ornament of the religious life, and many secular works, such as the Tsure-Dzure Gusa and later the poems of Bashō, came from the pen of Zen monks. Naturally more strictly religious forms of activity were not neglected. The eminent prelate Soseki (1271-1346) saw to it that a Zen monastery and temple were erected in every province and established the whole hierarchy in a most businesslike fashion on a sound financial basis. All this great system was inaugurated and maintained by comparatively peaceful methods. Zen taught soldiers and perhaps its priests occasionally showed that they could practise the military virtues as well as preach about them. But they did not build fortified monasteries or wage campaigns. Judged by ecclesiastical standards their annals will compare very favourably with those of the Shinshū or of Hieizan.

In the time of the Sung Zen may have been the full flower and expression of Chinese culture, but in later periods it is characteristically Japanese and challenges us to define what this characteristic but elusive teaching is. When a sect boldly states that its doctrine must be felt and not read and that every attempt to state it in speech or writing must be *ipso facto* a failure, the expositor need say no more. Yet the rash pen longs to formulate the ineffable and is apt to suggest that the mysteries which cannot be expressed in words are really non-existent and that the literary history of Zen, though copious, is not a heap of philosophic jewels buried in a little dust but a farrago of anecdotes reporting grotesque and irrelevant sayings and still more grotesque and often brutal actions. I confess that I am not quite in sympathy with the Zen view of things, and that is why I wish to emphasize the great practical achievements of the sect and to point out that a creed which has produced such remarkable results must be based on something more than eccentricity.

Also, though the importance of the mystical, paradoxical, and eccentric element in Zen is not to be minimized, there are other elements. An ordinary visitor would notice nothing remarkable in the arrangements of a Zen temple except perhaps that it is exceptionally neat and clean. Shaka and the Bodhisattvas such as Kwannon and Jizō are represented by images which are honoured with the usual marks of respect, although Amida is absent. Nor is there anything unusual about the teaching given to the laity. I have at present a little manual called *The Buddhist Way of Practice according to the Sōtō Sect*,[1] which sums up its doctrine by saying that the most important things are to understand the nature of life and death and to realize that our own hearts are the Buddha himself. This is not the language of the Pali Piṭakas, it is true, but it is commonly used by most Mahayanist sects. The Manual is an extract of a much larger work called Shōbō Genzō written by Dōgen,[2] who founded the Sōtō in Japan and built the magnificent monastery of Eiheiji near Fukui in Echizen.

Before going further I may remind the reader that Zen in Japan has three divisions often reckoned as separate sects, the Rinzai, Sōtō, and Ōbaku. The Sōtō is the largest Buddhist denomination in the country except the Shinshū and is remarkable for not having

[1] Sōtō Kyōkwai Shushōgi 曹洞教會修證義.

[2] Often called Jōyōdaishi or Shōyōdaishi 承陽大師, a posthumous title conferred on him in 1880.

any subdivisions. It was introduced from China immediately after the Rinzai at the beginning of the thirteenth century, and clearly the two schools form part of the same movement. The Ōbaku [1] is much later, having been founded in 1659, and has preserved a great number of Chinese usages. All three sects are similar in their doctrines, though they have each their own hierarchy and line of patriarchs. There is, however, a slight difference of method and teaching between the Sōtō and Rinzai. The former emphasizes the importance of moral training and gradual development for obtaining enlightenment; the latter insists that enlightenment is rather a sudden revelation which cannot be caused or accelerated by study: the former hold that a good life is alike the cause and result of enlightenment; the latter are accused by their opponents (though I am far from even hinting that the charge is true) of believing in secret something very like the Indian doctrine that the acts of a Yogi "are neither white nor black".

The use of this word Enlightenment brings us to the main conception and theme of Zen, all the other activities described being merely preparatory and external. It must not be supposed that other sects do not claim to show the way to enlightenment. A common saying among Buddhists compares enlightenment to a mountain peak approached from all sides by paths and each sect maintains that its own road is the best and shortest. Also enlightenment is only for the few: the little Sōtō manual already quoted only alludes to it as a counsel of perfection. But there is no doubt that all Zen literature deals with it, though in a special manner not readily intelligible to outsiders. No one can aspire to be a serious student of Zen unless he at least strives to obtain Enlightenment, and the great difficulty of treating the whole subject is that no one who has not obtained Enlightenment can know what it is and not even those who have obtained it can tell others what it is. "This incommunicableness of the transport is the keynote of all mysticism," as William James observes.[2] The word Enlightenment is a rendering of satori in Japanese, which in its turn is a translation of the Chinese Wu,[3] and the rendering

[1] See above, Chapter XIII.

[2] *Varieties of Religious Experience*, p. 405.

[3] Giles's Dictionary gives 悟 as meaning to become conscious of the truth of a doctrine. Japanese dictionaries give satori and its derivatives as meaning understanding or apprehension and quote idiomatic phrases in which they are used like: to open a person's eyes; he will not take a hint; when I perceived it, it was too late.

seems suitable, for enlightenment is the word commonly used to describe the Buddha's own experience under the Bo-tree which (I believe) Zen adepts consider to have been similar to their own satori. One gathers that satori is not a mystery or secret or anything intellectual which can be imparted. It is a new view of life and of the Universe which must be felt. It will prove satisfying and be "the purifier and liberator of life", breaking down the prison walls in which the intellect is said to confine us. But no definition of it is intelligible, coherent, or consistent with other explanations. When Unmon [1] was asked what is Zen, his answer on one occasion was "not a word can be predicated". On another he was more hopeful and replied simply "that's it". Probably the personality of the two questioners had something to do with the difference in the answers which they received.

Out of a mass of utterances about Zen and satori, two seem to me to offer some light to the uninitiated. The one is that saṃsâra and nirvâna are the same,[2] which is equivalent to the statement which I have already quoted from the Sōtō manual. I presume it means that they are not locally different as states or abodes, but depend on feeling: he who has satori is already in nirvâna, although to others he is apparently immersed in the troubles of this world. The other is a statement that enlightenment is somehow a unification of the inner man (I deliberately use this popular phrase because I do not know what in the present instance is the scientific equivalent) which has somehow become divided. I will quote from the works of that distinguished Japanese writer on Zen, Dr. D. T. Suzuki.[3] "In the beginning which is really no beginning and which has no spiritual meaning except in our finite life, the will wants to know itself and consciousness is awakened; and with the awakening of consciousness the will is split into two. The one will, whole and complete in itself, is now at once actor and observer. Conflict is inevitable: for the actor now wants to be free from the limitations under which he has been obliged

[1] Or Yun-Men, a well-known Chinese monk who lived at the end of the T'ang dynasty and was reckoned as twelfth in spiritual descent from Bodhidharma and as the founder of the Unmon school. He is celebrated on account of the painful means by which he obtained Enlightenment. He went to seek instruction of his master Bokujo, who seized hold of him, vociferating "Speak, speak". Unmon hesitated, on which the master abused him, turned him out and shut the gate so violently that he broke his unfortunate scholar's leg. But in the same moment Unmon was enlightened and counted the pain as nothing in comparison with the reward.

[2] 生死涅槃平等.

[3] *Essays in Zen Buddhism*, p. 119.

to put himself in his desire for consciousness. . . . Ignorance prevails as long as the will remains cheated by its own offspring or its own image, consciousness, in which the knower always stands distinguished from the known. The cheating, however, cannot last: the will wishes to be enlightened, to be free, to be by itself. Ignorance always presupposes the existence of something outside and unknown. The unknown outsider is generally termed ego or soul, which is in reality the will in the state of ignorance. Therefore when the Buddha experienced enlightenment he at once realized that there was no Âtman, no soul entity as an unknown or unknowable quantity." I do not quote this passage as pretending to understand its dark sayings but because it seems to me to give some indication of the ideas and aspirations of a Zen adept. But the author would no doubt remind us that all attempts to describe satori in words are predestined to failure. They are, in Zen phraseology, pointing at the moon with the finger and mistaking the finger for the moon.

Satori is obtained by gradual training but culminates in sudden illumination. The relative importance of the two parts of the process are, as I have mentioned, a subject of dispute between the Rinzai and Sōtō sects, but normally both take place. After a long period of anxious and even despairing search, illumination comes suddenly, generally as the result of some trivial, often grotesque act or remark, difficulties vanish, everything becomes clear, and the happy *illuminatus* wonders why he has so long been making such a fuss about what is so obvious. Novices are generally trained by asking them to solve problems called Kō-an,[1] and a selection of a hundred such problems is contained in the celebrated collection called Hekiganshū, which was introduced into Japan in the thirteenth century and has ever since been excessively popular, especially in the Rinzai sect.

Hakuin has left an interesting account of his experiences as a novice in dealing with one of these formidable Kō-an. He lived from 1683 to 1768 and may be called the second founder of the Rinzai sect, since all the Rinzai masters of the present day are proud to trace back their spiritual lineage to him. He was master of a vigorous colloquial style and did not disdain to quote popular songs. He also wrote a celebrated poem on meditation which is

[1] 公案, Chinese Kung-an, literally a public document but used since the early days of Zen in the sense of a theme or question given to a student to solve as a test of whether he has really obtained enlightenment.

still sung in temples. When he was stopping in a monastery of Echizen at the age of twenty-four a celebrated problem was given him to solve called Jōshu's Mu.[1] Jōshu was an early Chinese master of Zen under the T'ang dynasty, and the problem which the novice has to explain relates how when he was asked by a monk whether the Buddha nature was in a dog, he replied Mu, the Japanese pronunciation of the word Wu, meaning "Not". I can only tell the reader that if he took this simple dialogue in its obvious sense, a Zen master would call him a fool and probably box his ears. Mu must be understood as meaning that neither affirmation nor negation is possible and that the true answer, which touches on the nature of the Absolute, must be felt, not expressed in words.[2] Bukkō, the founder of the Engakuji monastery near Kamakura, tells us that this Mu obsessed him for more than six years before he understood its meaning. In Hakuin's case the period of waiting was not so long and this is how he describes his experiences.[3] "Jōshu's Mu being the theme given to me I assiduously applied myself to it, I did not sleep for days and nights and forgot to eat or lie down, when suddenly a great concentration took place in my mind. I felt as if I were freezing in an icefield extending thousands of miles and in myself there was a sense of complete transparency. There was no going forward or backwards. I felt like an idiot and there was nothing in the world but Jōshu's Mu. I attended lectures but they sounded like a discussion in some distant hall and sometimes I felt as if I were flying in the air. Several days passed in this way when one evening the sound of a temple bell upset everything. It was like smashing an ice basin, or pulling down a house made of jade. When I suddenly awoke I found I was Ganto the old master and that through all the changes of time nothing of my personality had been lost. My doubts and indecisions were dissolved like melting ice. I called out loudly 'Wonderful, wonderful!'

[1] It is contained in the collection of problems compiled by Mu-mon (or Wu-Wen, a Chinese Zen master) in 1228 and called Mumon Kwan, or The Barrier that has No Gate.

[2] Jōshu is said on another occasion to have given an affirmative answer to the same question because the Buddha nature is present in all beings.

[3] In his book called *Orategama* and also other writings. I am indebted to Professor Suzuki's translation in *Essays in Zen*, pp. 238–9. The strange word *Orategama* is unintelligible to modern Japanese and is explained as an ancient colloquialism meaning "My own kettle", and compounded of *Ora*, the first personal pronoun, *te*, hand, and *kama*, kettle or brew. Though this explanation offers difficulties it appears to be accepted in the sect. The book called *Orategama* is a collection of letters.

There is no birth and death from which one has to escape! There is no supreme knowledge after which one has to strive. All the thousand and seven hundred problems [1] are not worth the trouble of describing them."

Ganto was a Zen master in the T'ang period (828–887) who was murdered. His untimely end had much troubled Hakuin, who could not understand how if Zen was a religion of salvation, one of its great exponents should perish in this way. Satori is commonly described as a convulsion which upsets and destroys all one's old ideas, but the comparison of the antecedent state to a frozen expanse is, so far as my very limited knowledge of Zen literature goes, unusual. Hakuin was fond of metaphors from ice. His celebrated hymn on meditation begins :—

"All living beings are in their original nature Buddhas :
It is like ice and water :
Without water there can be no ice."

and perhaps the last lines of the same poem give a hint as to his interpretation of the "Mu" :—

"This very earth is the Lotus Land
And this body is the Buddha."

But Hakuin's troubles did not end with the solution of the Mu question. In Zen monasteries there is an institution called Sanzen,[2] which means that the pupils have an interview with their master and submit for his criticism their views on some of the many Kō-ans or problems. Hakuin, who by this time was well satisfied with the progress he was making, came to call on his old master Shōju one day and submitted his view, probably with some self-complacency. Shōju, who was sitting in the verandah cooling himself, simply observed "Rubbish". "Rubbish, is it?" said Hakuin, rather angrily. Shōju's only reply was to seize his pupil, give him several sound slaps and push him off the verandah whence he fell into the mud, for it was rainy weather. When he came to himself he reflected that he had behaved indecorously to his master, so he returned to the balcony and bowed respectfully, but was rewarded by being called a devil out of the black pit. Hakuin determined to have it out with Shōju, and after due preparation paid him another visit in which he vehemently pressed his own point

[1] There are said to be 1,700 Kō-an or problems.
[2] 參禪. Literally the study of Zen.

of view against his master, with the result that Shōju again slapped him, pushed him off the verandah, and laughed heartily at his struggles as he lay wriggling on his back. Hakuin was furious and thought of leaving the monastery, when suddenly a perfectly irrelevant incident brought him complete enlightenment. One day when begging, according to custom, in the village he stopped in front of the house of an old woman who refused to give him any rice. Hakuin, however, being immersed in meditation, remained immovable while the old woman continued sweeping the front of the house. Irritated at his apparent importunity she at last gave him a severe blow with her broom, which knocked him down, the sort of treatment to which he must have been accustomed by now. But this time it had a magical effect. He picked himself up fully enlightened as to the whole truth of Zen and his first act was to run to the house of his old master to whom he now felt most grateful. Shōju saw him coming and called out " What is the good news that you are bringing ? Come in quick ". When he heard the story he said " There, you have it now ", patted him on the back and treated him with the utmost affection ever afterwards. This behaviour is characteristic of Zen teachers. They abuse and even illtreat their pupils when an outsider would expect them to help and encourage, but when once the pupil obtains enlightenment, the master immediately knows it and the two become fast friends. It is also to be noticed that in this, as I think in most cases, the immediate occasion of enlightenment is some trivial circumstance totally unconnected with philosophy or mental discipline but which startles and upsets the brooding mind and thus serves to bring to an end an uncomfortable state of tension. In the Pitakas enlightenment is rarely represented as coming suddenly in this fashion. The nearest parallel is Ânanda, who according to the Cullavagga, xi, 1, 6, became an Arhat in the act of lying down to sleep : " before his head had touched the pillow and his feet were still far from the ground," in the interval he became emancipated. But as a rule Enlightenment is represented as the result of instruction and is quick or slow according to the learner's capacity.

It must not be supposed, however, that the training of Zen monks is left to chance. The Chinese teacher Hyakujō (720–814) first drew up the rules of the order, which are unusually strict. He became celebrated on account of his maxim " No work, no food ".[1]

[1] 一日不作一日不食.

It is not the custom of Buddhist monastic societies to dwell on the duty or sanctity of manual labour, but Zen is an exception in insisting on its monks rising early and doing their share of farm labour or such-like active work, as a counterpoise, no doubt, to excess in so-called meditation which is apt to degenerate into stupor. Zen is also the only sect in which monks beg for food regularly in the early morning. I believe that in all other sects the observance is only occasional. The marriage of Zen priests is discouraged though not absolutely forbidden.

Monasteries consist as a rule of seven buildings, a gateway with a sort of tower, the Buddha hall or temple, the lecture hall, the meditation hall, the abbot's quarters, the dining-room, and the bath house. The meditation hall, which also serves as a dormitory, is provided with a series of raised floors on either side, with a path down the middle extending the whole length of the building and used for devout promenades.[1] Each monk is allowed a space of one mat in Japanese measurement, that is, about 3 feet by 6, for meditation by day and sleep by night, and one quilt for sitting or sleeping. It is here that monks practise Zazen,[2] that is, sitting cross-legged and meditating while regulating the inhalation and expulsion of the breath. Lectures are delivered in the lecture hall especially in the periods called Sesshin,[3] during which only absolutely necessary manual labour is performed and the whole time of the monks is devoted so far as possible to meditation and study. The Sesshin are said to be an institution peculiar to Japanese Zen and the exact period differs in various sub-sects. A common arrangement is to have one week in every month in the summer sessions from April to August and the same in the winter session from October to February. The lecture, though not given in the monastery temple, is almost as formal as the services which are daily performed there. Its commencement is announced by the ringing of a bell. The master or lecturer enters and while he burns incense in honour of the Buddha and of his own master the monks chant a dhâraṇî,[4] the rhythm being marked by blows struck very audibly on a wooden fish (mokugyo). It is also usual to recite in chorus at this point of the proceedings some well-known short sermon or the hymn by Hakuin called Zazen. Then follows the lecture. I believe that it is not usual to employ either explanations

[1] 經行 Kin-hin. [2] 坐禪. [3] 攝 or 接心.

[4] A formula recited in the original Sanskrit and often corrupt and unintelligible. Many of them are found in Nanjio's catalogue of the Sûtra Piṭaka, part iii.

or arguments, for which, as we have seen, Zen has a singular dislike. The lecturer is not expected to do more than paraphrase in his own language some well-known textbook. When the lecture is over what are known as the Four Great Vows are chanted three times:

Sentient beings are innumerable: I vow to save them all.
Our evil passions are inexhaustible: I vow to extinguish them all.
The holy doctrines cannot be measured: I vow to study them.
The path of the Buddhas is hard to reach: I vow to attain it.

In modern days I fancy that the lectures are conventional, stereotyped gatherings, but in older times the unconventional, eccentric spirit was visible there as well as in more intimate conversations between masters and pupils. One day, for instance, Ōbaku mounted the platform as if he were going to lecture, waited till all the monks had collected, and when all were assembled took up his staff and drove them out. When he had cleared the room, he called them back and observed that "the moon looks like a bow: less rain and more wind". The reader must draw what instruction he can from this dark saying. At any rate, it seems to be accepted that the master had the best of his pupils, which apparently was not the case in the following instance. Baso [1] was one day walking with his pupil Hyakujō when a flock of wild geese flew over their heads. He asked, "Whither are they flying?" and Hyakujō replied, "They have flown away, sir." Baso on this abruptly seized his pupil's nose and gave it such a violent twist as to make him cry with pain. "You say they have flown away," he said, "but all the same they have been here since the very beginning." Strange to say, Hyakujō received sudden and complete enlightenment. The next day Baso was about to deliver a lecture when Hyakujō stepped forward in front of the congregation and began to roll up the matting, which was equivalent to declaring that the ceremony was over. Baso did not protest but came down from his seat and retired to his own apartments. He sent, however, for Hyakujō and asked him to explain his extraordinary conduct. "Yesterday," said Hyakujō, "you pulled my nose and it hurt very much." "And where was your thought wandering then?" said Baso. "It does not hurt any more" was the reply, and that is the end of the story.

[1] 馬祖 or Ma-Tsŭ. A Chinese Zen master who died in A.D. 788.

Another peculiarity of Zen masters is the use of loud exclamations such as Kwan or Kwats which convey nothing to the ordinary hearer. The Kwan of Unmon and the Kwats of Rinzai are specially celebrated. Sometimes these ejaculations were used in the lecture hall: sometimes an unfortunate student who thought he had asked a particularly pointed question received no reply but a thunderous shout of Kwats, which, according to the narrator, left him deaf for three days.

All these apparently meaningless anecdotes merely show what has already been often stated that the enlightenment which Zen can give is nothing that can be reasoned about, explained, or described in words. It is rather a new adjustment of oneself to the Universe, a new feeling of one's place and use in the order of things. When Unmon was asked to explain what is the Tao, that is, the way or the truth, his reply was simply "Walk on". I do not pretend to understand Zen, but I would again point out how distinguished has been the part which its adherents have played in the history of Japan. It certainly does not claim that any secret is to be learnt by mere meditation, by becoming absorbed in contemplation and forgetting the affairs of ordinary life, as the following anecdote about the youth of Baso, mentioned above, will show. He used to sit cross-legged all day meditating. His master once found him thus engaged and asked what he was trying to do. "I wish to become a Buddha." The master said nothing but picked up a piece of brick and began to polish it with a stone. Baso asked him what he was doing. "I am trying to polish this brick into a mirror." "But no amount of polishing will ever make a mirror of the brick." "And no amount of sitting cross-legged will ever make a Buddha of you." "What am I to do then?" "It is like driving a cart. When it won't move, will you whip up the cart or the ox? Are you sitting cross-legged in order to practise meditation [1] or to become a Buddha? If it is meditation, that does not consist of sitting or lying down. If it is to become a Buddha, the Buddha has no fixed form. You cannot take hold of him or let him go. To think you can obtain Buddhahood by sitting is simply to kill the Buddha and until you give up the idea that you can so obtain it, you won't come near the truth."

A Zen priest once informed me that in Zen schools the manual used for teaching children is the anthology of easy passages from Dōgen's works already alluded to.[2] They are taught that it is

[1] Zen in the original.

[2] 布施, 愛語, 利行, 同事, 報恩.

most important to confess their sins to the Buddhas (not of course to priests), which is called *Zange suru*, to strive for emancipation (Kaihō wo ukeru), and to practise good conduct, which has five branches. (1) Fuse or almsgiving, (2) Ai-go or kind language, (3) Ri-gyō or benevolent conduct, (4) Dōji or putting oneself in other people's places, (5) Hō-on or gratitude. The title Buddha refers to Śâkyamuni [1] and not to Vairocana or Amida, but the expression "all Buddhas" is often used and at the end of the Shushōgi we are told that they are all the same as Śâkyamuni, though it is not plain how far he is regarded as a historical person or how far as a spirit universally present. The priest was emphatic on the necessity of teaching that the Buddha's Enlightenment consisted in seeing that all beings "men, animals, plants and trees" can become Buddhas (Jō-Butsu). He said that the four truths are known in the sect but only to well-educated persons. He was himself a student of the Âgamas, but admittedly as a branch of learning introduced by foreign scholars.

Japanese Zen refuses to base itself on any sûtras. Such works as the Lankâvatâra and Vajracchedikâ are studied by a few of the learned as compendiums of philosophy, but have not a position in any way comparable to that accorded to the three Amida-sûtras by the Jōdo and Shinshū sects. Tokusan [2] was a profound student of the Vajracchedikâ, but when he obtained enlightenment in Zen he burned all his precious notes and commentaries, exclaiming that all philosophy was only like a hair floating in measureless space. It would seem that the attitude of many Zen masters was not only antiscriptural but what the uninitiated can only call antireligious. The anecdote of Tanka [3] warming himself when he felt chilly by burning a wooden statue of the Buddha is well known, and there is not much respect in the saying attributed to Rinzai, "The Buddha is just like other bald-headed monks. Woe unto those who seek enlightenment through him. Seek for your Buddha and he is lost to you: seek for your way and it is lost to you: seek for your Patriarch and he is lost to you." Still more extraordinary is a sermon by Rinzai which I do not quote fully because I do not understand it. The curious will, however, find a longer extract in the Zen Essays of Suzuki,[4] who cites in illustration

[1] Shakamunibutsu in the original.

[2] Tê-Shan 德山, also called Hsüan Chien 宣鑑, 779–865.

[3] See above, Chap. V, p. 158.

[4] *Essays in Zen Buddhism* (first series), D. T. Suzuki, pp. 331–3.

the saying of an unnamed Zen master, "I hate even to hear the name of the Buddha." Rinzai's object is apparently to insist that the mind of the seeker after truth must be absolutely free and untrammeled, and he expresses himself thus: "If you meet the Buddha, slay him: if you meet the Patriarch, slay him[1] . . . for this is the only way to deliverance. Do not get entangled with anything, but stand above, pass on and be free. . . . I tell you no Buddhas, no holy teachings, no discipline, no testifying." Chōkei is said to have uttered the following verses on attaining enlightenment: "What a fool I was! What a fool I was! Lift up the screen and come and see the world. If you ask 'What religion do you believe?' I raise my whisk[2] and hit you in the mouth." This is perhaps too mysterious to admit of any comment, but it does not sound very reverent.

The perverse paradoxical humour and the rough horse-play attributed to so many Zen masters are not to the taste of European saints, but parallels can be found in the West to a revelation which is perfectly satisfying to those who experience it but which cannot be communicated to those who have not had the same experience themselves. It is unfortunate that the great American authority on such abnormal religious phases of mind, William James, apparently never had his attention called to the phenomena presented by Zen, but he cites certain European instances which seem similar. For instance, he quotes a letter from the poet Tennyson which speaks of "A kind of waking trance. . . . This has come upon me through repeating my own name to myself silently till . . . individuality seemed to dissolve and fade away into boundless being and this not a confused state, but the clearest, the surest of the surest, utterly beyond words—where death was an almost laughable impossibility—the loss of personality (if so it were) seeming no extinction but the one true life. I am ashamed of my feeble description. Have I not said that the state is utterly beyond words?"[3] One may also

[1] Compare the crazy precepts of decadent Tantric Buddhism in India, though the motive does not seem quite the same. For references see Eliot, *Hinduism and Buddhism*, vol. ii, p. 123.

[2] Hossu. It was originally a whisk to drive off flies, but has come to be regarded as a symbol of authority. It consists of a long whisk of hair, such as a horse's tail, set on the end of a stick about a foot long.

[3] Tennyson to Mr. P. B. Blood quoted in W. James' *Varieties of Religious Experience*, p. 388 ff. Compare the cases of Trine, Amiel, Malwida von Meysenberg, and Trevor, all quoted by James. The curious states of consciousness under anæsthetics called "the anæsthetic Revelation" by Mr. Blood certainly sound like the paradoxes of Zen ("You could kiss your own lips"), but Zen does not countenance the use of any intoxicants.

compare the utterances of St. John of the Cross, a Spanish mystic of the sixteenth century, who said: "When you stop at one thing, you cease to open yourself to the All. For to come to the All, you must give up the All. And if you should attain to owning the All, you must own it desiring nothing."[1] Dionysius the Areopagite describes the absolute truth exclusively by negatives. "The cause of all things is neither soul nor intellect . . . nor number, nor essence, nor eternity, nor time . . . not unity, not diversity, nor goodness, nor even spirit, as we know it,"[2] and so on *ad libitum*.

In spite of Zen's refusing to be bound by scripture like other sects, it has not only had a considerable influence on secular literature but has also produced a number of treatises which are practically sacred books, though they bear such modest titles as sermons or collections of problems. To realize how vast is the collection of material one has only to look at the mass of anecdotes about Zen masters of all dates, including those of considerable antiquity, to be found in the pages of every essay on any subject connected with Zen. Many, of course, are open to considerable doubt, but, as sacred books go, the standard of authenticity does not seem to be particularly low. The treatises attributed to Bodhidharma[3] appear to be spurious, though they may possibly contain some genuine sayings, but there seems to be no reason to suspect the poem called Shin-jin-mei,[4] ascribed to Sōsan, the third Patriarch (†606). The work in the Chinese Tripiṭaka[5] entitled the Platform-sûtra on the Treasure of the Law contains portions of the sermons of Yenō, the sixth Patriarch, which appear to be in part at least genuine. One of the best known disciples of Yenō was Yoka, who is said to have obtained enlightenment after reading the Yuima-kyō (Vimalakirti-sûtra) and then to have composed a celebrated poem called Shōdōka.[6] Most influential and widely read is the Hekiganshū, a composite production consisting of one hundred cases or problems, each accompanied by an introduction and commentary followed by a hymn. These hymns are composed by Setchō (Hsüeh-Tou, 980–1052) and the commentary consists of

[1] W. James, l.c., p. 306. Cf. Yêsei's saying (Suzuki, op. cit., p. 20): "When you have a staff, I will give you one. When you have none, I will take it away from you."

[2] W. James, l.c., p. 416.

[3] See Chap. V, p. 163.

[4] See Suzuki, *Essays in Zen*, p. 381 ff. for text and p. 182 ff. for translation.

[5] Nanjio, 1525. Liu tsu ta shih fa pao t'an king. See above, Chap. V, p. 167. The platform means the place on which ordinations were performed.

[6] It is translated into German in the book called *Zen: Der lebendige Buddhismus in Japan*, by Ohasama and Faust.

the notes of Yengo's [1] lectures taken by his disciples. An authorized edition of these notes was brought out in 1125 and this was apparently the book introduced into Japan by Dōgen in 1227, but meanwhile it was suppressed and burnt by Yengo's most brilliant disciple Daiye who for some reason disapproved of it. In 1302, however, a reprint was issued and came into general circulation in China. Meanwhile the original edition was much appreciated by the newly formed school of Zen at Kamakura and new editions were subsequently published in Japan.[2]

Somewhat later (1228) was compiled another collection of forty-eight problems called the Mumon Kwan.[3] But besides such manuals compiled with a special educational object there are also numerous works, many of them contained in the Chinese Tripiṭaka, which record the sayings generally known as Yü-lu, in Japanese Goroku, of the various Zen masters. Thus about A.D. 1004 Tao-Yüan wrote the work called Records of the Transmission of the Lamp,[4] giving in thirty volumes the sermons and *obiter dicta* of Patriarchs and other eminent ecclesiastics, while under the Yüan dynasty a continuation of the same was published.[5] In its thirty-six volumes 3,118 priests of the Zen school are said to be mentioned, which will give the reader a notion of the exuberant biographical material contained in these notices, while the collection of the works of Daiye (Ta-Hui) [6] shows the amount of care and space which could be consecrated to the utterances of a single teacher. One of the chief authorities of the Rinzai school in Japan is a collection of the discourses and sermons of the founder called Rinzai-roku. It would be useless to give a further catalogue of such literature, but it is necessary to remember its existence. The books mentioned are all Chinese, but a considerable number were also produced in Japan. Hakuin, of whom I have already spoken, is the best known of these writers and Anesaki [7] says that his incisive and entertaining pamphlets are even now enjoyed by many people. The Shōbō Genzō, or The Eye of the Good Law, by Dōgen, who introduced the Sōtō school into Japan, and the Shūmon mujin-tō ron, or The Unfailing Lamp

[1] Yuan-Wu, 1063–1152.

[2] Those who are sufficiently interested are recommended to study a literal translation of one case (No. 55) in this curious work given in the *Eastern Buddhist*, vol. iii, 1924, in an article entitled "Zen Buddhism and Immortality", by D. T. Suzuki.

[3] See above, p. 143.

[4] Nanjio, 1524.

[5] Nanjio, 1658.

[6] Nanjio, 1532.

[7] Anesaki, *History of Japanese Religion*, p. 305.

of the Zen sect, by Torei, a disciple of Hakuin, are also considered important.

Zen has also a curious possession which may be called either literature or art in the set of Ox-tending pictures,[1] each supplied with an explanation in prose and a quatrain of verses. The pictures now current are said to have been drawn by Kakuan, a Chinese monk of the Rinzai school who lived about A.D. 1100 under the Sung dynasty and who states in his preface that he revised the work of a somewhat earlier artist called Seikyo. The first picture is called Looking for the Ox, that is to say, for one's own soul.[2] It represents a man exhausted and in despair, following an unending path and vainly searching while he hears nothing but the song of the evening cicadas. In the second picture he is still searching but has discovered the tracks of the Ox. This is explained as meaning that he has begun to study philosophy and various doctrines. He cannot yet distinguish truth and falsehood or good and evil: still he has found some traces of what he seeks. The third picture represents a great stride. The man sees the Ox: he begins to understand the uselessness of mere book-learning and to realize that the road to Enlightenment really lies in trifles of everyday life. Something new is working harmoniously in all his senses and all his activities, unseen and unseparable, like the salt in sea water. At last he catches the Ox, which in picture four is seen attached by a cord but not being led. The wild nature of the beast is still too unruly and refuses to be broken in: it is "the overwhelming pressure of the objective world". The Ox rushes up to a plateau and sometimes seems lost in the mountain mists. Nevertheless he is gradually broken in. In the next picture he is seen following the man, who leads him by a nose cord. "Things oppress us not because of an objective world but because of a self-deceiving mind. . . . Never let yourself be separated from the whip and tether." In No. six the struggle is over. The man is leisurely proceeding home riding on the Ox, playing as he goes simple ditties on a rustic flute. "What need to tell that he is now one of those that know?" The Ox now disappears and the man is left alone.

[1] I follow the arrangements of the pictures and text given by Suzuki in his *Essays on Zen*, pp. 349–367 and 409–411. A slightly different version has been published by Ponsonby Fane in a pamphlet called Satori-kata-no-Zu.

[2] The metaphor seems to be an old one in Zen. Hyakujō (Pai-Chang, 720–814) is reported to have said that to seek for the Buddha is like seeking for an Ox while one is riding on it.

In picture seven we see him sitting outside his house with his whip and cord lying beside him as if he were asleep and the comment is "When you know that what you need is not the snare or net, but the hare or fish that they were meant to catch, it is like gold separated from the dross or like the moon rising out of the clouds". The eighth picture is something new, not only in this series of drawings but in Buddhist art. It is merely a blank: a circular frame enclosing nothing at all. The title is simply "the Ox and the man both gone out of sight" and the following are extracts from the comments: "All confusion is set aside and serenity alone prevails; even the idea of holiness does not obtain. He does not linger where the Buddha is, and where there is no Buddha he passes on. . . .

> Who has ever surveyed the vastness of heaven?
> Over the blazing furnace not a flake of snow can fall."

The ninth picture, though not an absolute blank, shows only a few flowers and leaves of grass or some suggestion of a landscape. I will let the comment speak for itself. "Pure from the very beginning, he receives no defilement. He watches the growth and decay of things with form and abides himself secure in Wu-wei.[1] He does not identify himself with transformations: what has he to do with self-discipline? Water is blue and mountains green. He sits and watches how things change." But this life of lonely contemplation is by no means held up as the last word. The tenth picture is called "Entering the city with bliss-bestowing hands", and represents a rotund, smiling personage carrying bags full of what are no doubt good things. The comment informs us that none know his inner life but that he goes into the market place and consorts with winebibbers and butchers: he and they all become Buddhas.

These last remarks remind one of the stories told of Myōchō (also known as Daitokokushi) who in 1323 founded the Daitokuji in Kyōto. He is said to have spent a great part of his life under the Gojō bridge in the company of the meanest and most despised outcasts and begging his bread. The text does not give any general summary of the meaning of the whole series of pictures, but it is usually briefly explained by saying that the Ox is the Buddha nature in every one: you must find it but must not make too much of it. This last point is illustrated by an anecdote told of Goso

[1] The use of this well-known Taoist phrase, meaning something like absence of self-assertion, is remarkable.

(or Hōyen), a famous Chinese teacher of Zen who died in 1104 and was the master of Yengo, the compiler of the Hekiganshū already mentioned. He often indicated to his pupil that he had a slight fault but for some time could not be induced to give it a name. At last he said " Well, the fact is you have too much Zen about you ", and added, when pressed to explain what was the harm of that, " It turns one's stomach."

# CHAPTER XVIII

## NICHIREN [1]

### By G. B. Sansom

Many details of Nichiren's life have been given above in the historical section; but his doctrine was so much an expression of his unique personality that to recapitulate his biography is to summarize the development of the sect.

His life falls into three parts. In the first, after long study he reached the conviction that the true and only doctrine, the quintessence of Buddhism, was the teaching of the Lotus, and that this teaching must be followed in practice in the national as well as the individual life. When about thirty years old he publicly proclaimed his religion and attacked all other forms of Buddhism as well as hotly censuring the Government. He thus aroused such animosity that he was mobbed, possibly with the connivance of the authorities, and had to escape by night from Kamakura. Returning after some months of missionary work in the adjacent provinces, he renewed his warnings to the Government, who, inconvenienced by his criticism in a difficult period and doubtless under pressure from his ecclesiastical opponents, banished him to Izu in 1261.

Here began the second phase of his career. Alone and exiled he spent his time in intensive study of the Lotus. In a letter [2] written at this period he says that for many months he has kept at his holy task, "day and night, walking, standing, sitting, lying." Such austerities served only to deepen his conviction and to heighten his ardour. As he pored over the text, he became overwhelmingly certain that passages [3] which describe the antagonism and persecution

[1] For authorities in English see especially Anesaki, *Nichiren, the Buddhist Prophet*, Harvard, 1916; and Lloyd, *The Creed of Half Japan*, 1911, chaps. 24 and 25.

References in this chapter to the works of Nichiren give the page numbers in the Tokyo edition of 1904 known as 縮刷遺文.

[2] Known as 四恩鈔. *Works*, p. 417.

[3] Particularly in Chapters XII and XIII. He was fond of quoting such passages as "they will deride and abuse us, they will belabour us with sticks and stones", and pointing out that these predictions were confirmed by his own experience.

to be endured in a future evil age by those proclaiming the supreme Scripture were prophetic references to himself. He reached the unshakable belief that he and he alone was the predestined teacher, that his strife and suffering and the very enmity of other sects were necessary and foreordained; so that when he was released in 1263 he carried on his missionary labours with even more uncompromising zeal than before. The arrival of a Mongol envoy demanding tribute from Japan brought back to the public mind his prophecy of an invasion and increased his confidence that now at last the Government must listen to him and adopt his remedy for the evils of the day. He showered violent memorials upon officials and prelates, reminding them of his prophetic words. Finally, after many struggles and much persecution at the hands of his enemies, especially the Amidists, the stormy prophet could be tolerated no longer. He was tried for high treason, but somehow—by a miracle as he and his followers believed—escaped death at the very place of execution and was instead exiled to the inhospitable island of Sado. This was at the end of 1271.

The first two phases were militant. The third, though not lacking in activity, partook rather of a mystic character. He spent three years on Sado, where he employed his time in further developing his system. It was here that he first matured the conviction that he was the Bodhisattva Jōgyō, that he devised the graphic representation of the chief object of worship, and that he wrote some of his most important essays, including the "Eye-opener"[1] and the "Heritage of the Sole Great Thing concerning Life and Death".[2] He was released in 1274 and was recalled to Kamakura on the eve of the Mongol invasion. But though the Government endeavoured to come to terms with him he would admit no compromise. He held out for the union of Japan under his Church and the suppression of all heresies. Agreement was impossible and Nichiren retired to a mountain heritage, where he taught and studied and dreamed of a Universal Church with its Holy See in Japan. He died in 1282.

Nichiren was perhaps the most remarkable figure, as his sect was the most exceptional development, in the religious history of Japan. His life is an example of a militant reforming spirit which is hardly in keeping with the Japanese tradition of tolerance in

[1] Kaimokushō 開目鈔, written in 1272. *Works*, p. 747.

[2] Shōji Ichidaiji Kechimyaku Shō 生死一大事血脈鈔, completed just before the Kaimoku-shō. *Works*, p. 742.

doctrinal and even in ecclesiastical matters. Through it there runs a strain of aggressive individuality and stubborn belief which would brook no kind of contradiction. He said himself that he was probably "the most intractable man in Japan", and there is no doubt that the clash between his school and others is due far less to differences of creed than to incompatibility of temper. He was a master of invective, born to arouse opposition, enmity, and persecution. We have seen how he offended the Government by the violence of his language. But so addicted was he to the use of terms of abuse like "devil", "fiend", and "liar" that we find him using them in most surprising contexts, even in his less polemical writings. Thus in a letter[1] to his disciples in 1279 he says: "If Nichiren had not appeared in the period of the destruction of the Law, then Śâkyamuni would have been a great liar and all the Buddhas would have been great cheats. For in the 2,220 years since His death it is Nichiren alone who has made good His prophecy."

No single sentence could better illustrate at the same time his apocalyptic conviction and his challenging tone.

It is at first sight surprising that so exacting and quarrelsome a leader should have gained such a following as in fact he did. But he was tender to his adherents, as many warm-hearted letters show; and as to his powers of conversion the truth is that the time was ripe for the appearance of a teacher prescribing new and drastic remedies for the disorders, political and economic, from which Japan was then suffering. Moreover, by the beginning of the thirteenth century the administrative and to some extent the cultural centre of Japan had shifted from Kyōto to the eastern provinces, where men were of a bolder, rougher stamp than their gentle compatriots in the western provinces. Not only among officials and soldiers, but among all people of a vigorous habit of mind, there was a reaction against the softness of Amidist doctrine, a demand for a robuster creed. Some, as we have seen, turned to the discipline of Zen, but many were touched by the crusading spirit of Nichiren and no doubt were especially attracted by that part of his teaching which insisted that religion must not be separated from Government. Accordingly he made converts in all classes, even among men of such

[1] Known as 聖人御難事. *Works*, p. 1875. Similar language is to be found in the Eye-opener. Quoting a stanza from the chapter on Perseverance in the Lotus, Nichiren says: "If Nichiren had not been born in this country the World-Honoured One would be a great liar and the eighty million myriads of Bodhisattvas would fall into the sin of hypocrisy."

importance as Hōjō Tokimori,[1] a member of the ruling family. And since his teaching naturally attracted adherents who partook of his own bold and aggressive nature, it is not surprising that the history of the Lotus Sect, both during and after his lifetime, is a record of clashes with authority and strife with other denominations.[2]

In the first stage of his career Nichiren developed and preached his interpretations of the Lotus, and the emphasis of his teaching at this time was laid principally upon the vital need for both the Government and the people to conform to his religion. The most important of his tracts in this period have a certain political intention and an admonitory flavour, as is evident from such titles as "An Essay on the Protection of the State"[3] and "A Memorial on the Remedy for Calamities",[4] and the celebrated treatise on "The Establishment of Righteousness and the Safety of the Country". The object of these writings was to demonstrate that the dangers threatening the State could be overcome only by the adoption of Nichiren's own tenets; and they are largely devoted to an exposure of the errors of other sects, particularly the Nembutsu and Zen. Later the Shingon and Ritsu sects also became objects of his animadversion. It may thus be said that, as he developed his system, "adverse criticism of these four branches of Buddhism became an integral part of Nichirenite dogmatics."[5]

Yet the doctrine of Nichiren is remarkable not so much for its essence as for the manner in which it is set forth. In substance it is little more than a variation of the Tendai teaching, not indeed the Tendai of Nichiren's own day but as he imagined it to have been in the days of Saichō. But it was preached to the astonished Government and public with a vehemence and insistence which seemed like arrogance and were without parallel in Japan. Of course, all sects believe that they have a monopoly of truth, but the old sects of the Nara period claimed little more than to present the best and clearest

[1] He had also many women among his disciples, some of whom appear to have been of strong personality. His correspondence shows that Nichiren took special pains in the instruction of his women converts. It is interesting to observe that the closing passages of his Hokke Daimoku-shō are addressed to women. He warns them against the teachers of Nembutsu, who are "the enemies of all the women of Japan, more dangerous than tigers and wolves or brigands or pirates".

[2] The Tōkyō papers of 27th April, 1934, record a visit to a newspaper office by a member of the Nichiren sect, who, aggrieved by some disparaging reference to his religion, attacked members of the editorial staff with a sword.

[3] 守護國家論. *Works*, p. 220.

[4] 災難對治勘文. *Works*, p. 299.

[5] Anesaki, op. cit., p. 36, note.

version of what was admitted by all to be truth and to point out a few errors. The Tendai and Shingon were less disposed to contradict and condemn than to find room for all reformers who were not too refractory. But the new sects of the Kamakura period did not hesitate to upset established doctrine and to maintain their own theses in the face of it. Thus the attitude of Shinshū towards the older sects is very like that of Protestantism towards Catholicism. Nichiren took another and even more aggressive line: for him religion was something national and not merely individual. He summoned the Government to accept forthwith and enforce the truth which he taught and to suppress by force all heresy and error—that is to say, everything he himself did not teach.

Such a method of procedure was most unusual, in fact probably without parallel in any Buddhist country. To the majority of Japanese it must have seemed simply bad manners. We may admire Nichiren, the courage with which he fought for his convictions and faced martyrdom. No one can help being interested by the intensely personal note which sounds in all his sayings and writings. He is the most striking example of religious enthusiasm that Japan has to offer, yet the results that he achieved, while considerable, are not so great as might have been expected. The history of the sect makes one feel that it has suffered because it has not been able to preach the truth as a whole and to fight for it, but has been perpetually diverted into internecine squabbles about details and vituperative condemnation of other people's errors. At the present day the Nichirenites are one of the most conspicuous denominations in Japan but are only moderately numerous, being far behind the Shinshū, Zen, and Shingon in numbers. Their prominence is due partly to self-assertion and advertisement. Their services are accompanied by a clamour of drums and bells; spells and charms are freely used. But together with this there is intellectual life and a belief in a national and even universal Church.[1] If much of their history consists of petty turbulence and scandals, yet a protest such as they made in 1614 against the Government's order that every one should accept the Buddhas and the Gods of his native place, has a noble side, being in fact a violent effort to assert the sovereignty of truth. But it is

[1] The sect maintains a flourishing college, the Risshō Daigaku. In recent years there has been a revival of interest in the doctrines of Nichiren among the educated classes. It arose in the first place probably from appreciation of his literary style, but to-day his teaching seems to have a special appeal among certain exponents of nationalism in politics.

interesting to note that the Japanese Government has done tardy justice to the memory of Nichiren. On 12th October, 1922, the posthumous title of Risshō Daishi [1] was conferred upon him by Imperial Edict, exactly as that of Kenshin Daishi had been given to Shinran in 1876. According to the Tōkyō press [2] the honour was bestowed at the request of " a large number of devoted followers of the Saint ", including Admiral Tōgō, several Ministers of State, and many other distinguished persons. Further, an informal celebration of the event was at once held at the Navy Club, which must surely have delighted the spirit of one who had always insisted that the State ought to approve the truth which he preached.

The Nichiren sect, like Christianity and Islam, is the religion of a book. Few varieties of Buddhism present this feature. They have a superabundance of scriptures, mines of information which the learned can spend their lives in exploring, but which have not the same influence on the lives or beliefs of the community as the Bible or the Koran. But the scripture which Nichiren selected—the Saddharmapuṇḍarîka, often abbreviated to " the Lotus " in European translation—is such a book. It is relatively short and compact and is accepted as a guide to faith and practice. It is a book to be " read by the body ", as Nichiren said : to be worked out in the life of every true Buddhist. More than that, it has obtained a higher position than the sacred books of other creeds. The words Namu Myō-hō-renge-kyō, Reverence to the Scripture of the Lotus of the Good Law,[3] are not only a rallying cry but a prayer. The name of this book has become a synonym for all that is most holy and most divine, and it is used as an invocation precisely as the Jōdo and Jōdo-Shinshū use the name of Amida.

The work thus honoured is the Chinese translation of the Saddharma puṇḍarîka-sûtra made by Kumârajiva,[4] commonly known in Japan as the Hokke-kyō. Chapters xi and xv (Upâya Kausalya and

[1] 立正大師.

[2] See *Japan Advertiser*, 13th October, 1922.

[3] 南無妙法蓮華經.

[4] Nanjio, 134. It is noticeable that the Chinese version makes 28 chapters instead of 27, as in Sanskrit, by splitting chapter xi into two. Chapter xii begins with verse 41 of the Sanskrit xi. It sometimes appears to have a different reading from the Sanskrit text as we have it. For instance, in chapter xx (xix) Sadaparibhuta is rendered " always revering " instead of " always abused ". Nichiren attached great importance to this chapter. There are two other translations in the Chinese Tripiṭaka (Nanjio, Nos. 128 and 139), but Nichiren decidedly preferred Kumârajiva's version, which is excellent as literary Chinese.

Tathâgatâyus) are considered especially sacred. With the Hokke-kyō are usually combined the Muryōgi-kyō or Amitartha-sûtra,[1] the sûtra on the immeasurable meanings, and the Fugen-kyō,[2] or meditation on the Bodhisattva Samantabhadra, which are regarded as an introduction and conclusion to it. Nichiren's commentary on the Hokke-kyō and a work called Kuketsu,[3] or Oral Decisions, being an account of his teaching as taken down by his disciple Nichiko, are also held in great respect.

The Hokke-kyō or Lotus has often been compared to the Gospel according to St. John, and so far as both works make it their task to show the supernatural side of an apparently human teacher the comparison is just, but the setting of the scene recalls rather than the Gospel the Apocalypse, which indeed it far exceeds in exuberance, particularly in numbers and the computation of space and time. The European reader is simply bewildered when he reads how Śâkyamuni, the same who had been preaching on the Vulture Peak in human form, stretches forth his tongue until it reaches the distant Brahmâ world and continues doing so during a thousand or a hundred thousand years; or, again, how Bodhisattvas sang hymns during fifty æons though to the audience it seemed but an afternoon. Yet in matters of literary chronology [4] Nichiren follows the Tendai theory of "the five periods" and he accepts the Chinese reckoning which places the Buddha's death at 947 B.C. During the first forty years of the Buddha's life he gave instruction, as Nichiren held, by numerous sûtras which assumed that his auditors were of three classes and that there were three vehicles, or methods of instruction, differing so as to suit their different capacities. These three classes were the Śrâvakas or simple hearers; the Pratyeka-

[1] Nanjio, 133 and ii, 93. 無量義經.

[2] Nanjio, 394 and ii, 75. Its full Chinese title is 觀普賢菩薩行法經.

[3] 口決.

[4] Lloyd, however, in his *Creed of Half Japan* (p. 299) has some interesting observations about this literal acceptation of Tendai chronology. He quotes from the Seigoroku, a collection of extracts from Nichiren, a passage in which Nichiren says that in the time of the early Hînayâna patriarchs there was not a single Mahâyâna sûtra, and another which describes the astonishment of the Hinayanist doctors when they first heard the doctrines propounded by Aśvaghosha and Nâgârjuna. Both statements seem to imply that he cannot have thought that the Buddha preached the Lotus publicly in his old age. He believed that "it being a kind of Apocalypse was far too advanced for the immediate disciples of Śâkyamuni and that for this reason it lay fallow for several centuries, gradually winning recognition for itself as the spiritual intelligence of the Buddhist communities increased".

Buddhas or those who aspire to enlightenment but for themselves alone; and the Bodhisattvas, who vow to save all beings and aspire to become Buddhas ultimately. The first two classes form the Hînayâna and the third the Mahâyâna, but it is noticeable that the vehicles are always reckoned as three not two, and each vehicle has its own course of instruction suitable for attaining its own ends but not for any other. A Śrâvaka, for instance, cannot become a Bodhisattva and a Buddha.

But when we come to the last stage of the Buddha's career as a teacher, that in which the Lotus is said to have been pronounced, all this is changed. He declares that when he spoke of three classes and three vehicles it was merely an expedient—not untruth, of course, but adapted truth suited to the strong and weak points of different hearers. In reality there is but one vehicle which will lead all to one glorious destination. "Gods and men, I am the Tathâgata, the Arhat, the Perfectly Enlightened One. Having reached the shore I carry others to it; being free, I make free; being comforted, I comfort; being at rest, I lead to rest. . . . I knowing the Law which has but one essence, the essence of deliverance, do not suddenly reveal to all the knowledge of the All-Knowing, for I pay regard to the dispositions of all beings. . . . All my disciples attain to nirvâna: all my disciples shall become Buddhas. . . . It is as if a potter made different pots out of the same clay. Some are pots to hold sugar, some ghee, some curds and milk. Some are for baser purposes. There is no difference in the clay used; the difference in the pots is entirely due to what is put into them. Just so there is but one vehicle, the Buddha vehicle. There is no second, no third." Mahâ- and Hînayâna alike vanish and there remains only the one Ekayâna, the vehicle of the Buddhas.

This change in the manner and substance of the instruction given is paralleled by a change in the personality of the Buddha himself. Before the Lotus was revealed Śâkyamuni was a man who had achieved Buddhahood: who had been born and who would die. But with the new revelation we have a different view of him. The Tathâgata is not born and does not die: his birth and death are only expedients, like the three vehicles, lest men should fancy that they have always with them a master and a consoler to whom they can turn. In reality his Buddhahood is without beginning and end, and since he has prophesied that all his disciples should become Buddhas, their life, too, is not confined within the limits of birth and death, for the Buddha nature is innate in every one of them.

This emphasis on the relationship between mankind and the eternal Buddhahood is the distinguishing feature of Nichiren's religion in its metaphysical aspect. He does not deny merit to other systems, but he considers that they give only a partial or imperfect vision of the truth. It is this attitude which explains the title and the reasoning of his treatise called the Eye-opener. He argues that unless their eyes are wide open men cannot see the whole truth. Ethical systems like Confucianism are well enough but limited to practical affairs. The worship of Brahmâ or Vishṇu has its merits but it does not carry the minds of men as far as the ultimate reality. Buddhism opens men's eyes to the existence of Buddha, but many Buddhists fail to perceive his true nature and cannot fathom their relationship to eternal Buddhahood. Their failure is greater than that of those whose sight is dim, for as teachers they have wilfully distorted the image of truth.

It was for such reasons that Nicheren reserved his strongest condemnation for what he considered the heretical sects of Buddhism. At the same time he regarded the very existence of these sects as a proof that in fulfilment of the prediction of the scripture the degenerate days of the Law had come. In chapter xiii of the Lotus there occur several times expressions like " the true Law which meets with opposition and unbelief in all the world " and " the last 500 years when the true Law shall be in a state of decay ". Various Mahâyâna sûtras reckon the three periods of the Law differently, one of the commonest estimates being 500 years for the first period, 1,000 for the second, and 10,000 for the third. Nichiren seems to have divided the history of Buddhism into three millenniums, though it is not plain what will happen when the third will finish. The first period consists of the first thousand years following the Buddha's death, which after the Chinese fashion is dated 947 B.C. For historical purposes it covers the Hînayâna period and is called in Japanese Shōbō [1] or the True Law. The second is the period of Zōbō [2] or Image Law, beginning about the time of the Christian era and corresponding historically to the beginning of the Mahâyâna. The third period is called Mappō,[3]

[1] 正法. [2] 像法.

[3] 末法. The idea that a degenerate age was at hand seems to have gained ground more particularly in the eleventh century, but it had already struck the imagination of the Japanese in the days of Dengyō Daishi, who wrote a work called Mappō Tōmyōki (The Light of the Latter Days), in which he says: " There will be none to keep the Buddha's commandments in the Latter Days of the Law. If there should be such, they will be as rare as a tiger in a market place."

or Destruction of the Law, and began according to Nichiren about 1050. In this dark age there is trouble in both the political and religious world, but also hope. Nichiren was far too active and energetic a man to be a pessimist.

He had no doubt that the doctrine which was to be the light and guide of the Mappō period and to give the nations peace and prosperity was the teaching of the Lotus. He formulates this principle in simple language in the Risshō Ankoku Ron, by replying to an inquirer who deplores the evils of the day and asks what is the remedy: "If those who preach false doctrine are suppressed and those who hold the true faith are respected, then there will be tranquillity throughout the land and the country will be at peace." Here at once we see the connection between Church and State which runs through all Nichiren's writings: to believe in the only truth and to bring prosperity to one's country, which must of course be made to believe the truth.

In 1261, while suffering exile in Izu because of these political elements in his propaganda, Nichiren thought out the five fundamental principles of his teaching. The first is that the Lotus is the perfect and, as it says itself,[1] the final exposition of the truth; and the second that in a degenerate age man requires a simple, definite creed. This is also the thesis of the Amidist sects, and it may be doubted if their efforts to obtain simplicity have not been more successful than those of Nichiren, for simple is not the most obvious epithet to apply to the creed taught by the Lotus. Thirdly, this age of Mappō is the time to proclaim the doctrine, and, fourthly, Japan is the country where it should be preached and whence it should spread over the entire world. Fifthly, all other Buddhist systems have done their work and should yield to the Lotus as the one and only authority and thus unify religion.

Implicit in his statement of these five principles [2] was the corollary that he was the predestined instrument of their realization. Having enunciated them, he added: "One who would propagate the truth of Buddhism by convincing himself of the five principles

[1] Lotus, xiii, 54.

[2] The five principles, 五綱 or 五義, were summarized by Nichiren as *Kyō* 敎, the doctrine; *Ki* 機, the method; *Ji* 時, the time; *Koku* 國, the country; and *rufu no zengo* 流布の前後, the order of spread. See his Kyōkijikokushō 敎機時國鈔 and also 顯謗法鈔, both written in 1262. *Works*, pp. 424 and 430. For *rufu no zengo* is sometimes substituted *jo* 序, meaning sequence, i.e. the sequence of Buddhist systems—leading up to that of Nichiren.

is entitled to become the leader of the Japanese nation. One who knows that the Lotus of Truth is the King of all Scriptures knows the truth of religion. If there were nobody who read the Lotus of Truth there could be no leader of the nation. Without a leader the nation would simply be bewildered . . . and fall into the lowest hells in consequence of degrading the truth." [1]

This passage does not manifest the deep personal conviction, apparent in his later writings, that he himself was the chosen and predestined leader. The feeling grew as in the second phase of his career he proclaimed his gospel in the face of hardship and danger; and as he developed his system it played an increasingly important part. But it was not until the end of his second and most active phase that he began to marshal his beliefs in a schematic form. While he was on Sado he had plenty of time to think, and here he gave final shape to the main doctrine of his school.

They are generally described as the three great secret laws [2] or mysteries, which are stated to be the Honzon, the chief or original object of worship; the Daimoku, or title of the sûtra (i.e. Myōhō-renge-kyō); and the Kaidan, or place for receiving moral instruction.[3] The Nichiren sect emphasizes the somewhat startling doctrine that the original Buddha without beginning and without end—of whose body all the ten worlds, from hell up to the abode of Buddhas, are transformations—is not a mysterious nameless essence but the Buddha Śâkyamuni; and also, since we all have the Buddha nature, we ourselves are this original Buddha. Evidently this conception is too profound to be represented by any image, but when Nichiren was in exile in Sado he devised a Mandara which should symbolize these mysterious truths, and such Mandaras can still be seen in Japan in any Nichiren temple. Something has already been said about Mandaras in speaking of the Shingon sect. The Nichiren Mandara differs somewhat in appearance from others, since it contains neither figures nor Sanskrit letters. Down the middle are written vertically in bold Japanese characters the words Namu Myōhō-renge-kyō and at the sides are the names of the four Kings who rule the four quarters. Right

[1] Quoted by Anesaki, op. cit., p. 43. *Works*, p. 427.

[2] San Dai Hihō 三大秘法. The treatise known as The Perpetuation of the Three Great Mysteries, said to have been written by Nichiren in 1281, is perhaps not his work, but it may be taken as representing the doctrine of the sect. *Works*, p. 2051.

[3] 本尊 honzon; 題目 daimoku; 戒壇 kaidan.

and left above the vertical inscription are the names of Śâkyamuni and Tahō (Prabhûtaratna),[1] the mysterious "extinct" Buddha who makes his appearance in chapter xi of the Lotus; and the remaining space is filled with the names, all in Japanese characters, of the notable beings who are mentioned in the sûtra. This Mandara is considered to represent the universal power of the Buddha as all-pervading Truth. All the ten worlds, good and bad, exist in so far as they participate in his nature. The ideas which other schools strive to awaken by profound meditation and trances can, Nichiren held, be obtained by simply gazing at this Mandara, which is thus rightly considered the Honzon, the principle and primary object of worship.

The second mystery is called Daimoku, that is the title of the sûtra, Myōhō-renge-kyō, the Lotus of the good or wonderful law,[2] to which are generally prefixed the syllables Na-mu, that is the Sanskrit Namah, "Reverence be to." It is remarkable that Nichiren, who had a special hatred of the worshippers of Amida and summed up his opinion about them in the brief phrase "the Nembutsu is hell", should have recognized the utility of such a formula and should have made one so like it play the same part in his religion. And as far as the two formulas are concerned it may be doubted if the Amidists have not the best of it, for Reverence to Amida Buddha is an intelligible invocation and appeal if one believes that Amida is the source of all good, whereas Reverence to the Lotus of the Good Law, an appeal to a sacred book, is less convincing. Nichiren, however, understood it as meaning an expression of firm belief and faith in all the doctrines and mysteries taught by the sûtra. The modern explanation is that it is beyond the reach of reasoning and "is simply to be believed in and not understood at all".[3] It must be admitted that this is the conclusion one reaches upon studying Nichiren's Hokke Daimoku-shō,[4] a work which sets out to answer the question: "How is it that without knowledge of the meaning of the Lotus, without understanding of morality,

[1] 多寶.

[2] 妙 myō "wonderful" is used to translate the Sanskrit "sad" in "sad-dharma". Nichiren himself, in his Hokke Daimoku-shō, explains that 妙 is the equivalent of 具 or 圓滿, both of which represent the idea of perfection.

[3] This is the explanation, if it may be so called, of the Rev. Zejun Kobayashi of the Nichiren sect, quoted by both Nanjio and Ryauon Fujishima in their works on Japanese Buddhism.

[4] 法華題目鈔. *Works*, p. 583.

a man can avoid sins, escape the Four Evil Destinations and attain perfection by the mere utterance once a day, once a month, once a year, or even once in a lifetime of the seven syllables Na-mu-myō-hō ren-ge-kyō ? If a man cries Fire ! Fire ! he is not burned unless he touches it. If he cries Water ! Water ! his thirst is not quenched unless he drinks. How then can the utterance of a mere name . . . save him from perdition ? "

Anesaki (Nichiren, pp. 66, 67) quotes a remarkable passage from the epistle entitled " The Sole Great Thing concerning Life and Death ", written at Sado in 1272, in which Nichiren says: " To utter the sacred Title with the conviction that the three are one—the three being the Buddha Śâkyamuni who from eternity has realized Buddhahood ; the Lotus of Truth which leads all beings without exception to Buddhahood ; and we beings in all realms of existence—to utter the sacred title is the Heritage of the Sole Great Thing concerning Life and Death. . . . This is the essence of what is promulgated by Nichiren. If it should be fulfilled, the great vow of propagating the Truth over all the world would be fulfilled." [1]

The third mystery is the Kaidan, or the place for receiving the moral precepts and also the place where ordination is conferred. Observance of the moral law is the most important part of Buddhism. The law itself is comprised in the formula Namu-myō-hō-renge-kyō, and the place where we receive it, the Kaidan, is our own bodies, which partake of the Buddha nature and are further especially provided for in the Kaidan or Holy See established by Nichiren himself.

We are here of course endeavouring to make clear what Nichiren and his followers found in the Lotus and are not speculating on the real doctrine taught in that perplexing work. Should it for instance be regarded as theistic or not ? The Buddha is an existence without beginning or end and is called Devâtideva,[2] god above all gods, father of the world,[3] and is said to create Tathâgatas.[4] But, on the other hand, it may be reasonably maintained that the word Father as applied to the Buddha always means one who cares for and protects, not one who is a parent, producer, or creator. Indeed, the passage in chapter xv, beginning " The Tathâgata sees the triple world as it really is ; it is not born ; it does not die. It is not conceived ; it does not come into existence . . .", seems

[1] *Works*, p. 742.
[2] Lotus, xv, 21, and cf. iii, 97.
[3] Lotus, vii, 31, and cf. i, 89.
[4] Lotus, chapter xi, first part.

to deny all theories of creation. And what are we to understand by the expression "extinct Buddhas"? Nichiren does not appear to discuss these difficult questions. But he is penetrated by the conviction that the Buddha Śâkyamuni is an active, benevolent, governing Power, "Disposer supreme and judge of the Earth," who has a fixed plan for the improvement and enlightenment of the world, the execution of which he has entrusted to certain instruments.

It was during his exile on Sado that Nichiren, revolving in his mind these conceptions, became persuaded that he himself was Viśishṭacâritra, rendered as Jōgyō [1] in Japanese. Viśishṭacâritra is the chief of the countless host of Bodhisattvas who in the Lotus issue from the clefts of the bursting earth and are described by Śâkyamuni as having all been brought to maturity by him. To them in preference to the Bodhisattvas already present, who are somewhat curtly dismissed and put aside, is entrusted the task of promulgating this wonderful sûtra to the world. Though Viśishṭacâritra is mentioned as leader of the host and his name appears in the last sentence of the sûtra as one of the principal beings who applauded the words of the Lord, yet he is a somewhat shadowy figure for a new Messiah. Nichiren seems to have grown more and more convinced that he was this Bodhisattva come to earth again incarnate. In a letter [2] which he is said to have written towards the end of his life he boldly proclaims as follows: "These three mysteries I, Nichiren, as leader of the host that issued from the earth, did more than two thousand years ago certainly receive from the mouth of the Lord of Doctrine, the Great Enlightened One, the Revered of all the World." But he did not in any way pose as a supernatural personage or make capital out of being the Lord's special envoy predicted in the Lotus itself.

Other religious teachers have arrived at a similar conviction as their life and thought progressed; but there is no doubt that the most remarkable features of the sect are not the sacred "Title" or any other special doctrines, but firstly the apocalyptic tone which pervades all Nichiren's exposition of scripture and secondly the equally persistent manner in which he thinks of Church and State as two entities which are inseparably united. These two features are all the more remarkable because the Nichiren sect is the only Buddhist body in which they are found at all fully

[1] 上行. [2] 三大秘法鈔. *Works*, p. 2051.

developed. It is true that the germs of Nichiren's apocalyptic theories are to be found in the Lotus itself, especially in the verses at the end of chapter xii, which describe the sufferings of the religious and virtuous in the last epoch of the world. The Buddhist visions of the future rarely look forward to a "second coming", and though the advent of Maitreya seems to have been a living vision to some of the Chinese pilgrims, yet it has long ago ceased to have any influence in Japan, and is thought of, if thought of at all, as something immeasurably distant. Nichiren's whole life seems to have been built on a more sanguine prospect, though the ideas of hope and triumph do not appear to have been really strong among his disciples.

He himself, as he says in the last sentences of his treatise On Seizing the Essence of the Lotus,[1] regarded all the disorders and tribulations of his own times as preparing the way for the appearance of Viśishṭacâritra and his holy company, who were to spread and establish the truth "throughout the four quarters of the world". Here he foreshadows his ideal of a universal church; and the remainder of his life in his mountain retreat at Minobu was occupied chiefly with the development of this theme. Towards the end we find him prophesying: "When the Law of Kings shall merge with the Law of Buddha, when ruler and people alike shall hold to the Three Great Mysteries, then the Holy See shall be established in a place as excellent as the Vulture Peak. Thus the moral law will be established in actual life. In this sanctuary men of all countries in the world will receive the precepts of repentance and expiation, and thither also great gods like Brahmâ and Indra will descend."[2]

In other writings he made clear his opinion that "the place as excellent as the Vulture Peak", where the Holy See would be established, was Minobu itself. In a crowning outburst of apocalyptic fervour he says: "I live in a lonely mountain retreat. But in Nichiren's bosom, in his body of the flesh, is secretly enshrined the great mystery which the Lord Śâkyamuni transmitted to me on the Vulture Peak. Therefore it is that in my breast all Buddhas are immersed in contemplation, on my tongue they turn the wheel of the Law, in my throat they are born, and in my mouth they attain enlightenment. This place being the abode of such a man

[1] Hokke Shuyō-shō 法華取要鈔, written just after his arrival at Minobu in 1274. *Works*, p. 1035.

[2] Abridged in translation, from 三大秘法, 1281.

mysteriously realizing the Lotus of Truth, how can it be less noble than the Vulture Peak." [1]

The foregoing account of Nichiren's teaching has perhaps emphasized its mystic elements at the expense of its practical features. It should be understood that, although he arrived at his conclusions by arduous roads of philosophy and revelation, he presented them to his adherents in a very easy form. Himself erudite and profound, what he recommended to ordinary believers was by no means abstract and difficult but concrete, plain, and even matter of fact: a practical moral life, supported by the utterance of a formula, the worship of a symbol and combined with an active protest against tenets of other schools. It is these simple features rather than the deep speculations of the founder which have given to the sect its special character of sturdiness and self-assertion.

The resemblances of Amidism to Christianity have often been noticed, but the religion of Nichiren offers in other ways a parallel quite as curious and seemingly independent. His appeal to the prophetic and apocalyptic passages of scripture, his insistence on such ideas as the union of Church and State, the Kingdom of the Buddha and the love of the Buddha for mankind, which is like the love of a father [2] to be repaid by performing the tasks entrusted to us—these are among the many points which strike a European and which are rarely emphasized in Buddhism. But though he often seems to be expressing the ideas of the Catholic Church in alien language, he laid little emphasis upon hierarchy, sacerdotalism, or sacramental religion and was of the same stuff as the Protestant reformers.

[1] From a letter to Nanjō Hyōshichirō, 1281. For a fuller translation v. Anesaki op. cit., p. 129. *Works*, pp. 2069–2070.

[2] But it is to be noticed that neither the Lotus nor Nichiren speaks of the Buddha being a father in the sense of a maker or creator. He is a father because he protects, instructs, and brings to maturity.

# INDEX

## C



## D

G



H

L